PUBLIC POLICY ANALYSIS
An Introduction

Fourth Edition

William N. Dunn
Graduate School of Public and International Affairs
University of Pittsburgh

PEARSON
Prentice
Hall

Upper Saddle River, New Jersey 07458

Library of Congress Cataloging-in-Publication Data

Dunn, William N.
 Public policy analysis: an introduction/William N. Dunn.—4th ed.
  p. cm.
 ISBN 0-13-615554-5 (alk. paper)
1. Policy sciences. 2. Political planning—Evaluation. I. Title.
 H61.D882 2007
 320.6—dc22

                                                    2007021661

VP, Editorial Director: Charlyce Jones-Owen
Executive Editor: Dickson Musselwhite
Editorial Assistant: Maureen Diana
Marketing Manager: Sasha Anderson-Smith
Marketing Assistant: Jennifer Lang
Production Liaison: Joanne Riker
Creative Director: Jayne Conte
Cover Design: Bruce Kenselaar
Full-Service Project Management/
  Composition: Integra Software Services, Pvt. Ltd
Cover Printer: Phoenix Color Corporation
Printer/Binder: Courier Companies, Inc.

Credits and acknowledgments borrowed from other sources and reproduced, with permission, in this textbook appear on appropriate page within text.

Pearson Education LTD.
Pearson Education Australia PTY, Limited
Pearson Education Singapore, Pte. Ltd
Pearson Education North Asia Ltd

Pearson Education, Canada, Ltd
Pearson Educación de Mexico, S.A. de C.V.
Pearson Education–Japan
Pearson Education Malaysia, Pte. Ltd

10 9 8 7 6 5 4 3 2 1
ISBN-13: 978-0-13-615554-6
ISBN-10:   0-13-615554-5

Dedicated to the memory of
Donald T. Campbell

CONTENTS

PREFACE

This edition of *Public Policy Analysis,* like its two predecessors, is intended as a textbook and as an extended critical essay on the field of public policy. The primary audience for the book is upper-division undergraduate and graduate students completing their first course in multidisciplinary policy analysis. Because the book addresses concerns of several social science disciplines and social professions, it provides case materials and examples in policy arenas ranging from energy and environment to transportation, highway safety, and foreign policy.

This book takes a pragmatic, critical, and multidisciplinary approach. I believe that policy analysis must be distinguished from the disciplines in which policy analysis originates. Although policy analysis builds on political science, public administration, economics, and other disciplines and professions, it also transforms them into more practically useful methods, more testable theories, and more applicable findings. In this context, I define policy analysis as a process of multidisciplinary inquiry that creates, critically assesses, and communicates information that is useful for understanding and improving policies.

Special instructional devices and learning strategies are again employed throughout the book:

- *Advance organizers.* The book uses advance organizers, especially visual displays, to introduce students to the logical structure of methods and techniques covered later. The advance organizer for the book as a whole is the information-processing model of policy inquiry presented in the first chapter and throughout the book. This and other advance organizers help students grasp complex relations and critically examine the assumptions that underlie theories, methods, and techniques.

- *Learning objectives.* The objectives that students should attain by reading each chapter and completing related assignments are listed at the end of that chapter. I have tried to state these objectives in terms of the acquisition of knowledge and skills to do or perform something. For example, learning objectives refer to the acquisition of knowledge and skills needed to recognize, define, understand, compare, contrast, explain, predict, estimate, evaluate, synthesize, diagnose, plan, and apply. By stating objectives in this way, the emphasis is on active rather than passive learning, on application rather than regurgitation.

- *Key terms and concepts.* It is important to build a multidisciplinary vocabulary of policy analysis. Key terms and concepts of policy analysis are defined when first introduced in the text and listed at the end of each chapter. Because of my multidisciplinary approach, terms and concepts go beyond those used in more discipline-bound texts.

- *Review questions.* Knowledge and skills in policy analysis must be reinforced. For this reason, review questions are provided at the end of each chapter. The review questions address two kinds of skills: *higher-order* skills in conceptualizing, interpreting, explaining, synthesizing, evaluating, and applying; and *lower-order* technical skills in calculating, estimating, and computing. Review questions may be used by students for self-study and by instructors who are developing written assignments, examinations, and tests.

- *Demonstration exercises.* Knowledge and skills do not stick unless there are frequent opportunities for application to real-world problems. For this reason, each chapter contains cases that supply a basis for demonstrating the application of different kinds of knowledge and skills. By completing demonstration exercises, students are drawn away from idealized notions of "perfect" analysis ("blackboard policy analysis") and empowered by analyzing real-life problems.

- *Reference.* In addition to literature cited in footnotes, each chapter is accompanied by suggested readings keyed to the issues addressed in the chapter. In this edition, I have attempted to include literature that is representative of many of the most recent developments in public policy analysis.

- *Guidelines for written and oral communication.* Students who master methods and techniques of policy analysis often experience difficulties when they must not only obtain proper analytic and quantitative solutions but also communicate conclusions and recommendations in the form of policy memoranda, policy issue papers, and oral briefings. To overcome these difficulties, appendices present step-by-step guidelines on how to prepare policy issue papers (Appendix 1), executive summaries (Appendix 2), policy memoranda (Appendix 3), and oral briefings (Appendix 4). In addition, a new chapter (9) examines the process of policy communication and offers strategies for improving it.

- *Power Point Slides, Data Sets, and Teaching Notes.* A special Web site coordinated with this text provides Power Point slides I have used in teaching. Also supplied are data sets on key issues of public policy and, in some cases, teaching notes concerning the data sets and how to analyze them with the Statistical Package for the Social Sciences (SPSS) and other software. Additional cases in public policy and policy analysis are also provided.

In the past twenty-seven years, this book has been used, tested, and evaluated in degree programs in social science departments and in professional schools of public policy and public administration in this country and abroad. The book has been translated from English into other languages including Chinese, Indonesian, Korean, Romanian, and Spanish. I have used, tested, and evaluated parts of the book in training programs and projects in countries of the European Union, Southeastern Europe, the Middle East, North Africa, and Latin America. The revisions incorporated in this edition reflect much of what I have learned from these teaching and training experiences and from my doing policy analyses for agencies and ministries at the local, state, national, and international levels.

Over the years many students and faculty colleagues have improved this book. Although the full list is too long to present here, I will say only that my best constructive critics have been students in the MPA Program in Public Management and Policy and the Ph.D. Program in Public Policy Research and Analysis, both in the University of Pittsburgh's Graduate School of Public and International Affairs. I am also grateful to students and faculty at the Graduate Center for Public Policy and Management in Skopje, Macedonia, where I had the opportunity to work with some of the best students I have ever taught. I also thank three anonymous reviewers of this edition and reviewers of the 3rd edition, including David Nice of Washington State University, David Houston of the University of Tennessee at Knoxville, and Louise Comfort of the University of Pittsburgh. Sheila Kelly, Lien Rung-Kao, Sujatha Raman, and Eric Sevigny assisted in preparing materials for previous editions. I am grateful to Kate Freed for editorial and technical assistance with the 3rd edition, to Bojana Aceva-Andonova for assistance with this 4th edition, and to Rob DeGeorge and other Prentice Hall staff for skillfully managing the production process.

William N. Dunn
Graduate School of Public and International Affairs
University of Pittsburgh
Graduate Center for Public Policy and Management
Skopje, Republic of Macedonia

1

The Process of Policy Analysis

Policy analysis is a problem-solving discipline that draws on methodologies and substantive findings of the social sciences, social professions, and political philosophy. There are several ways to define policy analysis.[1] The definition used here is as follows: *Policy analysis* is a process of multidisciplinary inquiry designed to create, critically assess, and communicate information that is useful in understanding and improving policies.

---

[1] For a sample of alternative definitions see Harold D. Lasswell, *A Pre-view of Policy Sciences* (New York: American Elsevier Publishing, 1971); Yehezkel Dror, *Ventures in Policy Sciences: Concepts and Applications* (New York: American Elsevier Publishing, 1971); Edward S. Quade, *Analysis for Public Decisions,* 3d rev. ed., ed. Grace M. Carter (New York: North Holland Publishing, 1989); David L. Weimer and Aidan R. Vining, *Policy Analysis: Concepts and Practice,* 2d ed. (Englewood Cliffs, NJ: Prentice Hall, Inc., 1992); Duncan Mac Rae Jr., *The Social Function of Social Science* (New Haven, CT: Yale University Press, 1976).

THE PROCESS OF POLICY INQUIRY

The methodology of policy analysis is a process of inquiry leading to the discovery of solutions to practical problems. The word *inquiry* refers to a process of probing, investigating, or searching for solutions; it does not refer to solutions that have been "proved" by means of purely objective, infallible, value-free analysis that is independent of the values, interests, and beliefs of analysts and those who reward them.[2] Although policy analysis is based on scientific methods, it also rests on processes of art, craft, and persuasion.[3] Another way of saying this is that policy analysis is based on a combination of ordinary, commonsense knowing and specialized forms of inquiry practiced by the social sciences and social professions, including public administration and planning.[4] Because policy analysis involves the operations of the human understanding in solving practical problems, it is problem oriented.[5] It is this problem orientation, more than any other feature, that distinguishes policy analysis from disciplines that prize knowledge for its own sake.

Knowledge from multiple disciplines and professions is usually more effective in responding to real-world problems than is knowledge from single disciplines and professions. Real-world problems come in complex bundles that are political, social, economic, administrative, legal, ethical, and more. They do not arrive in separate packages addressed to political scientists, economists, or public administrators—to name but three policy-relevant disciplines and professions. Multidisciplinary policy analysis appears to provide the best fit with the complex and many-faceted world of public policy making.

[2] The issue here is "logical positivism," a philosophy of science and methodology abandoned by philosophers in the 1950s, but alive and well among many social scientists. Among the best critiques are Paul Diesing, *How Does Social Science Work? Reflections on Practice* (Pittsburgh, PA: University of Pittsburgh Press, 1991); Charles E. Lindblom, *Inquiry and Change: The Troubled Attempt to Understand and Shape Society* (New Haven, CT: Yale University Press, 1990); and Mary Hawkesworth, *Theoretical Issues in Policy Analysis* (Albany: State University of New York Press, 1988).

[3] Aaron Wildavsky used the terms art and craft to characterize policy analysis. See Aaron Wildavsky, *Speaking Truth to Power: The Art and Craft of Policy Analysis* (Boston, MA: Little Brown, 1979); and Iris Geva-May and Aaron Wildavsky, *An Operational Approach to Policy Analysis: The Craft, Prescriptions for Better Analysis* (Boston, MA: Kluwer, 1997). The terms policy science(s) is Harold Lasswell's. See the short methodological history in Ronald Brunner, "The Policy Movement as a Policy Problem," in *Advances in Policy Studies since 1950*, vol. 10, *Policy Studies Review Annual,* ed. W. N. Dunn and R. M. Kelly (New Brunswick, NJ: Transaction Books, 1992), pp. 155–97.

[4] On trade-offs between scientific and professional knowledge, on one hand, and ordinary, experiential knowledge on the other, see Charles E. Lindblom and David K. Cohen, *Usable Knowledge: Social Science and Social Problem Solving* (New Haven, CT: Yale University Press, 1979).

[5] On relations between policy analysis and the philosophical pragmatism of Charles Sanders Peirce and John Dewey, see Abraham Kaplan, *The Conduct of Inquiry: Methodology for Behavioral Science* (San Francisco, CA: Chandler, 1964), especially pp. 3–11 and 398–405.

MULTIDISCIPLINARY POLICY ANALYSIS

Policy analysis is partly descriptive because it relies on the social sciences to make and justify claims about the causes and consequences of policies. But it is also normative. In order to evaluate claims about the expected utility and moral worth of policies, it draws on economics and decision analysis, as well as ethics and other branches of social and political philosophy. This normative aspect of policy analysis is necessary because it involves the choice of desired consequences (ends) and preferred courses of action (means), a process that is based on ethical reasoning. The choice of ends and means requires continuing trade-offs among competing values as equity, efficiency, security, liberty, and democracy.[6] The importance of ethical reasoning in policy analysis is well stated by a former undersecretary in the Department of Housing and Urban Development: "Our problem is not to do what is right. Our problem is to know what is right."[7]

Policy-Relevant Information

Policy analysis addresses five types of questions:

- What is the problem for which a solution is sought?
- What course of action should be chosen to solve the problem?
- What are the outcomes of choosing that course of action?
- Does achieving these outcomes help solve the problem?
- What future outcomes can be expected if other courses of action are chosen?

Answers to these questions require five types of policy-relevant information, or what we may call policy-informational components. These components represent information about policy problems, policy performance, expected policy outcomes, preferred policies, and observed policy outcomes. These five types of information are shown as shaded rectangles in Figure 1.1.[8]

A *policy problem* is an unrealized value or opportunity for improvement attainable through public action.[9] Knowledge of what problem to solve requires information about a problem's antecedent conditions (e.g., school dropouts as an antecedent condition of unemployment), as well as information about valued ends (e.g., safe schools or a living wage) whose achievement may lead to the problem's

---

[6] Deborah Stone, Policy Paradox: *The Art of Political Decision Making* (New York: W. W. Norton, 1997).

[7] Robert C. Wood, "Foreword" to *The Study of Policy Formation*, p. v. Wood is quoting President Lyndon Johnson.

[8] The framework was suggested by Walter Wallace, *The Logic of Science in Sociology* (Chicago: Aldine Books, 1971). The framework has undergone several transformations since the first edition of this book.

[9] Compare Charles O. Jones, *An Introduction to the Study of Public Policy*, 2d ed. (North Scituate, MA: Duxbury Press, 1977), p. 15; and David Dery, *Problem Definition in Policy Analysis* (Lawrence: University of Kansas Press, 1984).

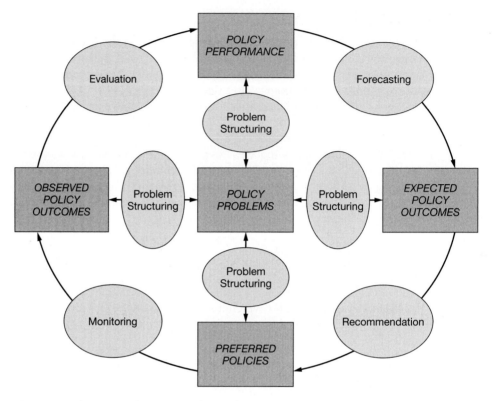

Figure 1.1   The process of integrated policy analysis.

solution. Information about policy problems plays a critical role in policy analysis, because the way a problem is defined shapes the search for available solutions. Inadequate or faulty information may result in a fatal error: solving the wrong formulation of a problem when instead one should have solved the right one.[10]

An *expected policy outcome* is a probable consequence of a policy designed to solve a problem. Information about the circumstances that gave rise to a problem is essential for producing information about expected policy outcomes. Such information is often insufficient, however, because the past does not repeat itself completely, and the values that shape behavior usually change. For this reason, analysts must be concerned with expected policy outcomes that are not "given" by the existing situation. To produce such information may require creativity, insight, and the use of tacit knowledge.[11]

---

[10] Ian I. Mitroff and Thomas R. Featheringham, "On Systematic Problem Solving and the Error of the Third Kind," *Behavioral Sciences* 19, no. 6 (1974): 383–93.

[11] Yehezkel Dror, *Venture in Policy Sciences: Concepts and Applications* (New York: American Elsevier Publishing, 1971); Sir Geoffrey Vickers, *The Art of Judgment: A Study of Policy Making* (New York: Basic Books, 1965); and C. West Churchman, *The Design of Inquiring Systems; Basic Concepts of Systems and Organization* (New York: Basic Books, 1971.

A *preferred policy* is a potential solution to a problem. To select a preferred policy, it is necessary to have information about expected policy outcomes. Information about a preferred policy also depends on judgments about the value or utility of expected outcomes. Another way to say this is that policy recommendations are based on factual as well as value premises. Facts alone—for example, the presumed fact that one policy is more efficient than another—do not justify the selection of a preferred policy.

An *observed policy outcome* is a past or present consequence of implementing a preferred policy. It is sometimes unclear whether an outcome is actually an effect of a policy, because some effects are not *policy* outcomes; many outcomes are the result of other, extra-policy factors. It is important to recognize that the consequences of action cannot be fully stated or known in advance, and many consequences are unanticipated as well as unintended. Fortunately, information about such consequences is not only produced *ex ante* (before policies are implemented); it is also produced *ex post* (after policies are implemented).

Policy performance is the degree to which an observed policy outcome contributes to the attainment of the unrealized values or opportunities for improvement that define a problem. In practice, policy performance is always incomplete, because problems are rarely "solved" they are most often resolved, reformulated, or even "unsolved."[12] To know whether a problem has been solved, resolved, reformulated, or unsolved requires information about observed policy outcomes, as well as information about the extent to which these outcomes contribute to the attainment of the unrealized values or opportunities for improvement that originally gave rise to a problem. In turn, information about policy performance provides a basis for forecasting expected policy outcomes, as can be seen in Figure 1.1.

Policy-Informational Transformations

The five types of policy-relevant information are interdependent. The arrows connecting each pair of components represent changes of one type of information into another, so that the creation of information at any point depends on information produced in an adjacent phase. Information about policy performance, for example, depends on the transformation of prior information about observed policy outcomes. The reason for this dependence is that any assessment of how well a policy achieves its objectives assumes that we already have reliable information about the outcomes of that policy. The other types of policy-relevant information are dependent in the same way.

Information about policy problems is a special case because it affects and is affected by the remaining four informational components. The reason for this interdependency is that information about policy problems already contains information about one or more of the other components. Accordingly, problems contain

---

[12] Russell L. Ackoff, "Beyond Problem Solving," *General Systems* 19 (1974): 237–39.

information about one or more of the following: preferred policies, observed and expected outcomes, and the values of these outcomes. Problems usually include some problem elements and exclude others; and what is included or excluded affects which policies are preferable, which outcomes should and should not be investigated, which values are appropriate and inappropriate as criteria of policy performance, and which potentially predictable outcomes warrant or do not warrant attention. A major and often fatal error of policy analysis is a Type III error—solving the wrong problem.[13]

Policy-Analytic Methods

The five types of information are produced and transformed by using methods of policy analysis. These methods include description, prediction, appraisal, prescription, and definition. All methods involve judgments of different kinds:[14] judgments to accept or reject an explanation, to affirm or dispute the rightness of an action, to select or not select a policy, to accept or reject a prediction, to define a problem in one way rather than another.

In policy analysis, these procedures have been given special names: monitoring, forecasting, evaluation, recommendation, and problem structuring.

- *Monitoring* (description) produces information about observed policy outcomes.
- *Forecasting* (prediction) produces information about expected policy outcomes.
- *Evaluation* (appraisal) produces information about the value of observed and expected policy outcomes.
- *Recommendation* (prescription) produces information about preferred policies.
- *Problem structuring* (definition) produces information about what problem to solve.

The last method, problem structuring, is about the other methods. For this reason, it is a metamethod ("method of methods"). In the course of structuring a problem, analysts usually experience a "troubled, perplexed, trying situation, where the difficulty is, as it were, spread throughout the entire situation, infecting it as a whole."[15] These problem situations are not problems; problems are representations of problem situations. Problems are not "out there" in the world, but stem from thought interacting with external environments. The same problem

---

[13] Type I and Type II errors—also known as false positives and false negatives—involve choosing a significance level that is too large or too small when testing the null hypothesis. On Type III errors, see A. W. Kimball, "Errors of the Third Kind in Statistical Consulting," *Journal of the American Statistical Association* 52 (1957): 133–42; Howard Raiffa, *Decision Analysis* (Reading, MA: Addison-Wesley, 1968), p. 264; and Ian I. Mitroff, *The Subjective Side of Science* (New York: Elsevier, 1974).

[14] John O'Shaughnessy, *Inquiry and Decision* (London: George Allen & Unwin, 1972).

[15] John Dewey, How *We Think* (Boston, MA: D.C. Heath and Company, 1933), p. 108.

situation can be and often is structured in different ways. For example, imagine a graph showing national defense expenditures as an increasing percentage of Gross Domestic Product over time. Analysts with different perspectives will see the graph differently, one as evidence of increasing national security (more of the budget is allocated to defense), another as an indication of declining social welfare (less of the budget is allocated to social services). Problem structuring, it should be stressed, governs the production, interpretation, and representation of information produced by the other methods. It is the "central guidance system" of policy analysis.

Policy-analytic methods are interdependent. It is not possible to use one method without first having used others. Thus, although it is possible to monitor past policies without forecasting their future consequences, it is not possible to forecast policies without first monitoring them.[16] Similarly, analysts can monitor policy outcomes without evaluating them, but it is not possible to evaluate an outcome without first establishing that it is an outcome in the first place. Finally, to select a preferred policy requires that analysts have already monitored, evaluated, and forecasted outcomes.[17] This is yet another way of recognizing that policy choices are based on factual as well as value premises.

The full set of policy-informational components (rectangles), policy-informational transformations (arrows), and policy-analytic methods (ovals) is displayed in Figure 1.1. The figure supplies a framework for integrating methods from different policy-relevant disciplines and professions. The five general methods, as already noted, are used across disciplines and professions of political science, sociology, economics, management science, operations research, public administration, program evaluation, and ethics. Attached to each general procedure are more specific techniques used solely or primarily in some disciplines and professions, and not others. Political science and program evaluation, for example, employ monitoring to investigate whether a policy is causally relevant to an observed policy outcome. Although program evaluation has made extensive use of interrupted time-series analysis, regression discontinuity analysis, causal modeling, and other techniques associated with the design and analysis of field experiments,[18] implementation research within political science has not. Instead,

---

[16] Because the explanation of a policy is not a necessary condition for predicting its future consequences, explanation and prediction are asymmetrical. Strictly speaking, a prediction is a causal inference, whereas a projection, extrapolation, or "rational forecast" is not. However, it is not necessary to understand the causal factors underlying variations in expenditure patterns to obtain a reliable projection of their future value.

[17] Causation may be assumed but not understood. Recipes claim only that a desired result is a consequence of action. Joseph L. Bower, "Descriptive Decision Theory from the 'Administrative' Viewpoint," in *The Study of Policy Formation,* ed. Raymond A. Bauer and Kenneth J. Gergen (New York: Free Press, 1968), p. 10. Physics cookbooks attempt to "correct" this "problem."

[18] William R. Shadish, Thomas D. Cook, and Donald T. Campbell, *Experimental and Quasi-Experimental Designs for Generalized Causal Inference* (Boston, MA: Houghton Mifflin, 2002).

implementation researchers have relied mainly on techniques of case study analysis.[19] Another example comes from forecasting. Although forecasting is central to both economics and systems analysis, economics has drawn almost exclusively on econometric techniques. Systems analysis has made greater use of qualitative forecasting techniques for synthesizing expert judgment, for example, qualitative techniques of policy Delphi.[20]

THREE CASES OF POLICY ANALYSIS

Three cases illustrate similarities and differences in processes of policy analysis. Case 1.1 (*Impact of Military Spending*) illustrates an analysis based on a complex economic model that estimates the relations among inputs and outputs in a regional economy. No new data were collected; data were available from existing government sources. Members of a team of analysts stated the conclusions of their analysis in a thirty-page paper, with a large technical appendix. They also participated in a public briefing. The project required about six months to complete. The report contained no policy recommendations, and it was not used to change policies. The main purpose of the report was to stimulate public debate about potential alternative uses of military spending in the post-Cold War era, that is, the so-called "Peace Dividend."

> **Case 1.1 Impact of Military Spending on Employment and Human Services.** A multidisciplinary team of faculty and graduate students is asked by the mayor of a large eastern city to prepare a report on the effects of military spending on employment and human services. The team investigates investments in the local economy by analyzing data from the Defense Procurement Data Center on the dollar value of procurement contracts awarded to businesses and universities. By using an input-output model from the U.S. Department of Labor, the team estimated the number of new jobs created, directly and indirectly, through the contracts. At the same time, personal and corporate taxes paid to the federal government exceed the dollars brought in through procurement dollars. Some of the tax dollars might have gone to support underfunded human service programs. A thirty-page report with technical appendices is presented to the mayor, who is required to make an annual report to the City Council. Although the report generated considerable public debate, and drew attention to the problem, it had no effect on military procurement, federal tax policy, or local human services.

In Case 1.2 (*Alleviating Municipal Fiscal Distress*), most of the analysis was based on newspaper reports describing the scope and severity of municipal fiscal distress in the state. In contrast to the complex modeling requirements in Case 1.1 (*Impact of Military Spending*), newspaper reports involving no significant quantification were virtually the only source of information (the reports included revenue and

---

[19] Paul A. Sabatier and Hank C. Jenkins-Smith, "The Advocacy Coalition Framework: An Assessment," in *Theories of the Policy Process,* ed. P. A. Sabatier (Boulder, CO: Westview Press, 1999), pp. 117–66.

[20] Quade, *Analysis for Public Decisions.*

expenditure data provided by municipalities). Despite the simplicity of this essentially qualitative analysis, the conclusions and recommendations were used to change existing policy. In the *Municipal Fiscal Distress* case (1.2), a long policy issue paper was made available as a "backup document." The analyst's conclusions and recommendations were communicated in a one-hour oral briefing and in a two-page policy memorandum. The short policy memo stands in contrast to the thirty-page report with technical appendices prepared in the *Impact of Military Spending* case (1.1). The oral briefing and the two-page memo led directly to the formulation of a new policy on distressed municipalities. But the policy was rarely used; it generated little public debate and fell into disuse because better economic times and increased municipal revenues made the policy unnecessary. What was originally a severe problem became a nonproblem with the passage of time and changed economic conditions.

> **Case 1.2 Alleviating Municipal Fiscal Distress.**   A policy analyst working for a nonpartisan research unit of a state legislature is asked by the chair of the Local Government Committee to examine the scope and severity of "fiscal distress" among local municipalities in the state. Using a previous policy issue paper that was based almost entirely on newspaper reports, the analyst prepared a two-page policy memorandum, which concluded that the scope and severity of fiscal distress are of such magnitude as to justify state intervention to assist municipalities. The analyst also briefed members of the committee in a one-hour session. On the basis of the memorandum and briefing, a new legislative act providing assistance to fiscally distressed municipalities was written by the committee and passed by the state's General Assembly. The provisions of the act were rarely used, or even discussed, in the ten years following its adoption.

Case 1.3 (*Benefits and Costs of the 55 mph Speed Limit*) is similar to Case 1.1 (*Impact of Military Spending*) in that both cases employed complex quantitative methods—input-output analysis, benefit–cost analysis, and time-series econometrics. However, only the military spending case required the collection of archival data prior to the analysis. In contrast to the military spending case, the speed limit case involved conclusions and recommendations that were purposefully limited to an eight-page policy memorandum, rather than a long issue paper with technical appendices. The policy memo is similar in its brevity to the even shorter two-page memo of Case 1.2 (*Municipal Fiscal Distress*). Another similarity between the municipal fiscal distress and the 55 mph speed limit cases is that both resulted more or less directly in a policy decision; the military spending case did not. Note that the 55 mph case is fundamentally different from both the other two cases. It was based heavily on moral argumentation, rather than economic or causal modeling.

> **Case 1.3 Benefits and Costs of the 55 mph Speed Limit.**   The governor of a large eastern state asks his staff to investigate the effectiveness of the 55 mph speed limit in saving lives and reducing injuries in his state. The governor needs the analysis in order to decide whether to file a request with the federal government that would permit his state to abandon the 55 mph speed limit during a "test period." The staff analysis, based primarily on a report by the National

Academy of Sciences (*55: A Decade of Experience,* Washington, DC: National Academy of Sciences, 1984), was presented in an eight-page policy issue paper. The issue paper recommended that the 55 mph speed limit be retained because it saves several hundred lives annually in the state, and several thousand nationally. The governor accepts the recommendation, joining nine other northeastern states that decide to retain the speed limit. Later, more detailed studies show that the costs of time lost by driving at the lower speed limit of 55 mph far exceed the economic benefits in lives saved, injuries averted, and fuel conserved. Other economic analyses suggest that the number of lives saved has been seriously overestimated and that most of the decline in traffic fatalities is probably the result of recessions, unemployment, and their effect on lowering the number of miles traveled (and hence the risk of fatal accidents). The governor rejects the benefit–cost and econometric analyses, defending the existing speed limit on moral rather than economic grounds.

FORMS OF POLICY ANALYSIS

Relationships among policy-informational components, policy-analytic methods, and policy-informational transformations provide a basis for contrasting different forms of policy analysis (Figure 1.2).

Retrospective and Prospective Analysis

Prospective policy analysis involves the production and transformation of information *before* policy actions are taken. This form of *ex ante* analysis, shown as the right half of Figure 1.2, typifies the operating styles of economists, systems analysts, operations researchers, and decision analysts. The prospective form of analysis is what Williams means by policy *analysis.*[21] It is "a means of synthesizing information to draw from it policy alternatives and preferences stated in comparable, predicted quantitative and qualitative terms as a basis or guide for policy decisions; conceptually it does not include the *gathering* of information." Policy *research,* by contrast, refers to "all studies using scientific methodologies to describe phenomena and/or determine relationships among them." Prospective analysis often creates wide gaps between preferred solutions and actual efforts to implement them. Allison estimates that no more than 10 percent of the work actually required to achieve a desired set of policy outcomes is carried out *before* policies are implemented. "It is not that we have too many good analytic solutions to problems. It is, rather, that we have more good solutions than we have appropriate actions."[22]

---

[21] Williams, *Social Policy Research and Analysis: The Experience in the Federal Social Agencies* (New York: American Elsevier, 1971), p. 8.

[22] Graham T. Allison, *Essence of Decision: Explaining the Cuban Missile Crisis* (Boston, MA: Little, Brown, 1971), pp. 267–68.

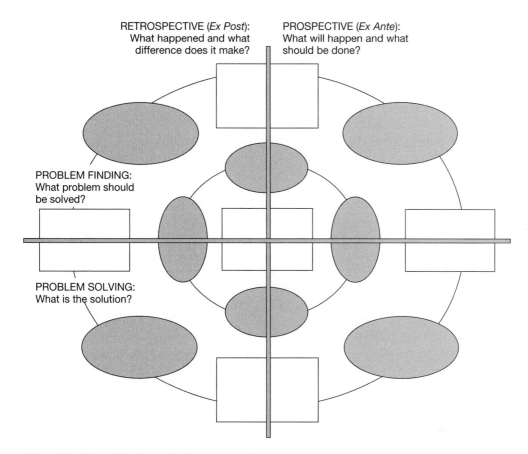

RETROSPECTIVE (*Ex Post*):
What happened and what
difference does it make?

PROSPECTIVE (*Ex Ante*):
What will happen and what
should be done?

PROBLEM FINDING:
What problem should
be solved?

PROBLEM SOLVING:
What is the solution?

Figure 1.2   Forms of policy analysis.

Retrospective policy analysis is displayed as the left half of Figure 1.2. This form of *ex post* analysis involves the production and transformation of information *after* policies have been implemented. Retrospective analysis characterizes the operating styles of three groups of analysts:

- *Discipline-oriented analysts.* This group, comprised mainly of political scientists and sociologists, seeks to develop and test discipline-based theories that describe the causes and consequences of policies. This group is not concerned with the identification of specific policy goals or with distinctions between "policy" variables that are subject to policy manipulation and those that are not.[23] For example, the analysis of the effects of party competition on

---

[23] James S. Coleman, "Problems of Conceptualization and Measurement in Studying Policy Impacts," in *Public Policy Evaluation,* ed. Kenneth M. Dolbeare (Beverly Hills and London: Sage Publications, 1975), p. 25.

government expenditures provides no information about specific policy goals; nor is party competition a variable that policy makers can manipulate to change public expenditures.

- *Problem-oriented analysts.* This group, again composed mainly of political scientists and sociologists, seeks to describe the causes and consequences of policies. Problem-oriented analysts, however, are less concerned with the development and testing of theories believed to be important in social science disciplines than with identifying variables that may explain a problem. Problem-oriented analysts are not overly concerned with specific goals and objectives, primarily because the practical problems they analyze are usually general in nature. For example, the analysis of aggregate data on the effects of gender, ethnicity, and social inequality on national achievement test scores provides information that helps explain a problem (e.g., inadequate test performance) but does not provide information about policy variables that can be manipulated.

- *Applications-oriented analysts.* A third group includes groups of applied sociologists, applied psychologists, and applied anthropologists, as well as analysts from professions such as public administration, social work, and evaluation research. This group also seeks to describe the causes and consequences of public policies and programs and is not concerned with the development and testing of discipline-based theories, unless those theories provide a guide to action. This group is concerned not only with policy variables but also with the identification of specific policy goals and objectives. Information about specific goals and objectives provides a basis for monitoring and evaluating outcomes and impacts of policies. For example, applications-oriented analysts may provide a rich account of variables that can be manipulated in order to achieve higher scores on reading tests.

The operating styles of the three groups reflect their characteristic strengths and limitations. Discipline-oriented as well as problem-oriented analysts seldom produce information that is directly useful to policy makers. Even when problem-oriented analysts investigate important problems such as educational opportunity, energy conservation, or crime control, the resultant information is often *macronegative.* Macronegative information describes the basic (or "root") causes and consequences of policies, usually by employing aggregate data to show why policies do *not* work. By contrast, *micropositive* information shows what policies and programs *do* work under specified conditions.[24] It is of little practical value to policy makers to know that the crime rate is higher in urban than rural areas, but it is practically important to know that a specific form of gun control reduces the commission of serious crimes or that intensive police patrolling is a deterrent.

---

[24] Williams, *Social Policy Research and Analysis,* p. 8.

Even when applications-oriented analysts provide micropositive information, they may find it difficult to communicate with practitioners of *ex ante* policy analysis, who in most cases are professional economists. In agency settings, *ex ante* analysts, whose job it is to find optimally efficient solutions, often have limited access to information about policy outcomes produced through retrospective analysis. For their part, practitioners of *ex ante* analysis often fail to specify in sufficient detail the kinds of policy-relevant information that will be most useful for monitoring, evaluating, and implementing their recommendations. Often, the intended outcomes of a policy are so vague that "almost any evaluation of it may be regarded as irrelevant because it missed the 'problem' toward which the policy was directed."[25] Legislators, for example, formulate problems in general or even obscure terms in order to gain acceptance, forestall opposition, or maintain neutrality.

Contrasts among the operating styles of policy analysts suggest that discipline-oriented and problem-oriented analysis is inherently less useful than applications-oriented analysis—that retrospective (*ex post*) analysis as a whole is perhaps less effective in solving problems than prospective (*ex ante*) analysis. Although this conclusion may have merit from the point of view of policy makers who want advice on what actions to take, it overlooks several important benefits of retrospective analysis. Retrospective analysis, whatever its shortcomings, places primary emphasis on the results of action and is not content with information about expected policy outcomes, as is often the case with prospective analysis. Moreover, discipline-oriented and problem-oriented analysis may offer new frameworks for understanding policy-making processes, challenging conventional formulations of problems, questioning social and economic myths, and shaping the climate of opinion in a community or society. Retrospective analysis, however, "has been most important in its impact on intellectual priorities and understandings, and not nearly so effective in offering solutions for specific political problems."[26]

Descriptive and Normative Analysis

Figure 1.2 also captures another important methodological contrast, the distinction between descriptive and normative policy analysis. *Descriptive policy analysis* parallels *descriptive decision theory,* which refers to a set of logically consistent propositions that describe action.[27] Descriptive decision theories may be tested against observations obtained through monitoring and forecasting. Descriptive theories, models, and conceptual frameworks originate for the most part in political science, sociology, social psychology, and so-called "positive economics."[28] The main function of these theories, models, and frameworks is to explain, understand, and predict

---

[25] Ibid., p. 13; and Alice Rivlin, *Systematic Thinking for Social Action* (Washington, DC: The Brookings Institution, 1971).

[26] Janet A. Weiss, "Using Social Science for Social Policy," *Policy Studies Journal* 4, no. 3 (spring 1976): 237.

[27] Bower, "Descriptive Decision Theory," p. 104.

[28] Value consensus is assumed. The task is to explain "value-neutral" dependent variables.

policies by identifying patterns of causality. The principal function of approaches to monitoring such as field experimentation and quasi-experimentation is to establish the approximate validity of causal inferences relating policies to their presumed outcomes.[29] In Figure 1.2, the descriptive form of policy analysis can be visualized as an axis moving from the lower left (monitoring) to upper right (forecasting).

Normative policy analysis parallels *normative decision theory,* which refers to a set of logically consistent propositions that evaluate or prescribe action.[30] In Figure 1.2, the normative form of policy analysis can be visualized as an axis running from the lower right (recommendation) to upper left (evaluation). Different kinds of information are required to test normative and descriptive decision theories. Methods of evaluation and recommendation provide information about policy performance and preferred policies, for example, policies that have been or will be optimally efficient because benefits outweigh costs; optimally equitable because those most in need are made better off; or optimally responsive to citizen preferences. One of the most important features of normative policy analysis is that its propositions rest on disagreements about passionately held values, including efficiency, equity, responsiveness, liberty, and security.

Problem Finding and Problem Solving

The upper and lower halves of Figure 1.2 provide another important distinction. The upper half points to methods that are designed for purposes of *finding problems,* whereas the lower designates methods for *solving problems.* Problem finding has to do with the discovery of elements that go into the definition of problems, and not to their solution. How well do we understand the problem? Who are the most important stakeholders who affect and are affected by the problem? Have the appropriate objectives been identified? Which alternatives are available to achieve objectives? Which uncertain events should be taken into account? Are we solving the "right" problem rather than the "wrong" one?

Problem-solving methods, located in the lower half of Figure 1.2, are designed to provide solutions to problems. Problem solving is primarily technical in nature, in contrast to problem finding, which is more conceptual. Problem-solving techniques, including benefit–cost analysis, decision analysis, and implementation analysis, are useful in answering questions about policy causation, statistical estimation, and optimization. How much of the variance in a policy outcome is explained by one or more independent variables? What is the probability of obtaining a correlation coefficient as large as that obtained? What are the net benefits of different policies? What is their expected utility or payoff?

---

[29] Thomas D. Cook and Donald T. Campbell, *Quasi-Experimentation: Design and Analysis Issues for Field Settings* (Boston, MA: Houghton Mifflin, 1979); Shadish, Cook, and Campbell, *Experimental and Quasi-Experimental Designs for Generalized Causal Inference.*

[30] Bower, pp. 104–05.

Segmented and Integrated Analysis

Integrated policy analysis links the several segments of Figure 1.2. Retrospective and prospective forms of analysis are joined in one continuous process. Descriptive and normative forms of analysis are linked, as are methods designed to find as well as solve problems. Practically speaking, this means that policy analysts bridge the several main pillars of multidisciplinary policy analysis, especially economics and political science. Today, this need is not being met by departments of economics and political science, which specialize in *segmented policy analysis* by producing, critiquing, and passing on intellectual knowledge. The effort to bridge these and other segmented disciplines, and convert intellectual knowledge into practical knowledge, is carried out by professions, including public administration, management, planning, policy analysis, and social work. The American Society for Public Administration, the National Association of Schools of Public Affairs and Administration, the American Planning Association, the International Association of Schools and Institutes of Administration, and the Association for Public Policy and Management represent these professions. So far, these professional associations have been more open to the discipline of economics than that discipline has been open to political and organizational analysis, notwithstanding a consensus among policy scholars and practitioners that political and organizational analysis is an essential for effective economic policy making.

The framework for integrated policy analysis presented in the first part of this chapter (Figure 1.1) helps to examine the assumptions, uses, and limitations of methods employed in segmented and largely overspecialized disciplines and professions. The framework identifies and relates major elements of policy analysis—policy-informational components, policy-analytic methods, and policy-informational transformations—enabling us to see the special functions performed by methods of problem structuring, monitoring, evaluation, forecasting, and recommendation. The second framework (Figure 1.2) points to different forms of policy analysis practiced today: prospective (*ex ante*) and retrospective (*ex post*), descriptive and normative, and problem finding and problem solving. Integrated policy analysis is a vehicle for understanding, assessing, and improving a methodology that has the ambitious mission of bridging selected aspects of the social sciences, social professions, and political philosophy.

THE PRACTICE OF POLICY ANALYSIS

Reconstructed Logic versus Logic-in-Use

The process of policy analysis illustrated in Figures 1.1 and 1.2 is a *logical reconstruction (reconstructed logic)*. The actual process of doing policy analysis may or may not conform to this or other logical reconstructions, including the so-called "scientific method," because all logical reconstructions are abstract representations of a great many observed practices.[31] The *logic-in-use* of practicing analysts, as distinguished from the logical reconstruction of their actions, always varies to one degree or another because of differences in personal characteristics of analysts, their professional socialization, and the institutional settings in which they work.

- *Cognitive styles.* The personal cognitive styles of analysts predispose them toward different modes of acquiring, interpreting, and using information.[32]

- *Analytic roles.* Policy analysts perform roles as "entrepreneurs," "politicians," and "technicians."[33]

- *Institutional incentive systems.* Policy "think tanks" encourage different orientations toward analysis, including the "humanistic-value-critical" and the "scientific."[34] Institutional rewards and punishments affect the validity of conclusions and recommendations.[35]

- *Institutional time constraints.* Government analysts subject to tight institutional time constraints (three to seven days is typical) work with much greater speed, and perhaps greater efficiency, than university researchers with few time constraints. Understandably, the former rarely collect original data; nor do they employ complex and time-consuming techniques.[36]

- *Professional socialization.* The different disciplines and professions that make up policy analysis socialize their members into different norms and values. Analyses of published papers suggest that analysts employ formal-quantitative as well as informal-narrative approaches, although sound policy recommendations sometimes require formal-quantitative procedures.[37]

- *Multidisciplinary teamwork.* Much of the analysis conducted in public agencies is carried out by multidisciplinary teams. Some members have primary responsibility for particular forms of policy analysis (Figure 1.2). For example, team members trained in economics and decision analysis are typically more

[31] On reconstructed logic and logic-in-use, see Kaplan, *Conduct of Inquiry,* pp. 3–11.

[32] Studies using the Myers-Briggs type indicator (Jungian personality types) suggest distinct cognitive styles among scientists, managers, and analysts. See Ian I. Mitroff and Ralph H. Kilmann, *Methodological Approaches to Social Science* (San Francisco: Jossey-Bass, 1978). Corporations, nonprofit organizations, and public agencies such as the U.S. Department of Corrections and the National Science Foundation use the Myers-Briggs test as a training and personnel selection diagnostic.

[33] Arnold Meltsner, Policy *Analysts in the Bureaucracy* (Berkeley: University of California Press, 1976).

[34] Pamela Doty, "Values in Policy Research," in *Values, Ethics, and the Practice of Policy Analysis,* ed. William N. Dunn (Lexington, MA: D.C. Heath, 1983).

[35] Donald T. Campbell, "Guidelines for Monitoring the Scientific Competence of Preventive Intervention Research Centers: An Exercise in the Sociology of Scientific Validity," *Knowledge: Creation, Diffusion, Utilization* 8, no. 3 (1987): 389–430.

[36] See P. J. Cook and J. W. Vaupel, "What Policy Analysts Do: Three Research Styles," *Journal of Policy Analysis and Management* 4, no. 3 (1985): 427–28.

[37] An early but representative overview of approaches is Janet A. Schneider, Nancy J. Stevens, and Louis G. Tornatzky, "Policy Research and Analysis: An Empirical Profile, 1975–1980," *Policy Sciences* 15 (1982): 99–14.

qualified to perform prospective (*ex ante*) analysis, whereas members trained in applied sociology, applied psychology, and program evaluation are usually better at retrospective (*ex post*) analysis. The effectiveness of teams depends on everyone acquiring an operational understanding of analytic methods employed throughout the process of integrated policy analysis (Figure 1.1).

Methodological Opportunity Costs

Integrated policy analysis has opportunity costs. Given limited time and resources, it is difficult to conduct thorough economic, political, and organizational analyses at the same time. On one hand, it is tempting to adopt *multiple triangulation,*[38] or what some have called critical multiplism,[39] as an umbrella for multidisciplinary analysis. *Critical multiplism* responds to some of the inadequacies of logical positivism.[40] *Logical positivism* refers to the philosophical doctrine that true statements about the world must be logically valid and empirically confirmed against an objective reality and that objective reality, rather than any subjective interpretation of it, should dictate these true statements. As a philosophy, logical positivism has almost no relation to discussions of it by social scientists, most of whom lack a rudimentary understanding of philosophy of science and epistemology. To the extent to which logical positivism refers to methods claiming to produce entirely "objective" results that do not depend on the observations and interpretations of multiple observers, "logical positivism" appears to be the dominant methodology of policy analysis and program evaluation carried out during the era of President Lyndon Johnson's War on Poverty. The advantage of multiplism over this vulgarized form of logical positivism is that it provides a better approximation of what is true by employing procedures that triangulate from a variety of perspectives on what is worth knowing and what is known about policies and their effectiveness.[41]

The disadvantages of multiplism lie in its costs. The costs of analysis vary with the number and types of methods employed. Although triangulation among several disciplinary perspectives, or the use of multiple measures, may be and often is feasible, the adoption of any method presented in this book involves

---

[38] The methodology of triangulation is analogous to practices employed in geodesic surveys, cartography, navigation, and, more recently, satellite tracking. The position or location of an object is found by means of bearings from two or more fixed points or electronic signals a known distance apart.

[39] Cook advanced critical multiplism as an alternative to logical positivism. See Thomas D. Cook, "Postpositivist Critical Multiplism," in *Social Science and Social Policy,* ed. R. Lane Shotland and Melvin M. Mark (Beverly Hills, CA: Sage Publications, 1985), pp. 21–62. The second edition of this book endorsed an unqualified form of critical multiplism.

[40] A thorough critical assessment of logical positivism is Mary E. Hawkesworth, "Epistemology and Policy Analysis," in *Advances in Policy Studies since 1950,* ed. Dunn and Kelly, pp. 293–328; and Mary E. Hawkesworth, *Theoretical Issues in Policy Analysis* (Albany: State University of New York Press, 1988).

[41] Cook, "Postpositivist Critical Multiplism," p. 57.

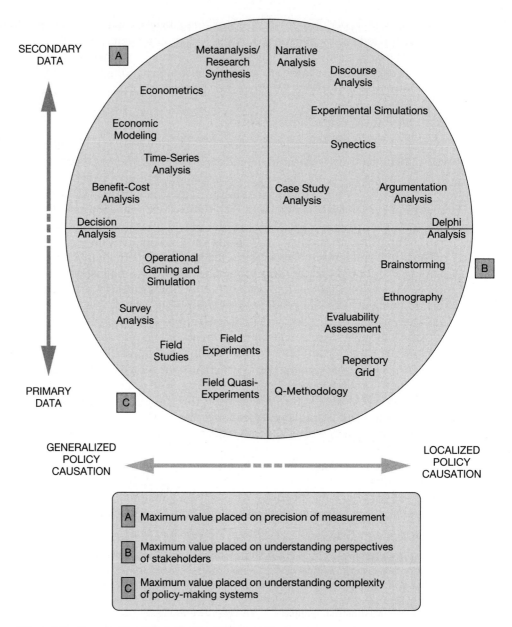

Figure 1.3 Opportunity costs of adopting different methods.

trade-offs and opportunity costs (Figure 1.3).[42] When single methods such as econometric modeling are employed to achieve *measurement precision, generalized policy causation,* and *objectivity* (in the sense that observations are partly independent of the persons making them), analysts forgo the deeper understanding of multiple stakeholder perspectives that is possible through ethnographic interviews and other qualitative methods. The latter include Q-methodology, case study analysis, and Delphi technique. On the other hand, econometric modeling and other related techniques (e.g., time-series analysis and benefit–cost analysis) involve low costs of information acquisition, because secondary data are usually available. By contrast, ethnographic interviews involve high information costs because they require substantial primary data, although they lack precision and a capacity for generalizing policy causation.

Similar trade-offs and opportunity costs apply to methods of research synthesis, or metanalysis, which purchase measurement precision and generalized policy causation at the expense of a deeper understanding of the complexity of real-life contexts of policy making. The latter can be obtained by means of field studies and field experiments, but these are expensive, especially when they are employed in conjunction with qualitative methods. To be sure, triangulation among convergent (and divergent) perspectives, methods, and measures enhances the validity of policy analysis and other applied social sciences.[43] But the time and financial constraints surrounding the practice of policy analysis make trade-offs inevitable.

CRITICAL THINKING AND PUBLIC POLICY

The world of the practicing policy analyst is complex. Analysts must sift through and evaluate a large volume of available quantitative and qualitative data, make difficult choices among methods and techniques, and meet rapid turnaround times. This practical predicament places a premium on *critical thinking*—that is, the careful analysis and evaluation of the reasons and evidence used to argue about public policies. One method available for this purpose is the analysis of policy arguments. *Policy argumentation*, which refers to the process whereby two or more stakeholders debate the merits of policies by probing the assumptions underlying policy claims, permits a critical synthesis of policy-relevant information and its role in policy analysis. The product of critical thinking is *evidence-based policy analysis*.

---

[42] See David Brinberg and Joseph E. McGrath, *Validity and the Research Process* (Beverly Hills, CA: Sage Publications, 1985). For Brinberg and McGrath and other methodological pragmatists, the choice of methods is similar to an optimization problem in decision analysis. See C. West Churchman, *Prediction and Optimal Decision: Philosophical Issues of a Science of Values* (Englewood Cliffs, NJ: Prentice Hall, 1961); and Russell Ackoff, *Scientific Method: Optimizing Applied Research Decisions* (New York: John Wiley, 1962).

[43] The case for triangulation in its many forms is Donald T. Campbell, *Methodology and Epistemology for Social Science: Selected Papers,* ed. E. Samuel Overman (Chicago: University of Chicago Press, 1988).

The Structure of Policy Arguments

Policy arguments are the main vehicle for conducting debates about public policies.[44] Social scientists too often forget, cautions Majone, that "public policy is made of language. Whether in written or oral form, argument is central to all stages of the policy process."[45] The process and structure of policy argumentation can be represented as six interrelated elements (Figure 1.4).[46]

- *Policy-relevant information.* Policy-relevant information, *I,* is the starting point of policy arguments. Policy-relevant information, as we have seen, is divided into five informational components. Figure 1.4 describes how policy-relevant information is used to make claims about public policies. An example of policy-relevant information is the following statement: "A leading expert concludes that Social Security reform is unlikely to permit employees to invest their contributions in the stock market." Not all information is relevant to a given policy issue.

- *Policy claim.* A policy claim, *C,* is the conclusion of a policy argument. The movement from policy-relevant information to claim implies "therefore." Policy claims are of different types. Some are normative: "Congress should pass the amendments to the Fair Employment Practices Act." Some are descriptive: "The use of the Internet will double in the next ten years." Normative claims typically require ethical or valuative justifications. Descriptive claims involve causal inferences that do not state what should be done; they require no ethical justification.

- *Warrant.* The warrant, *W,* of a claim answers the question *Why?* with a reason, assumption, or argument beginning with *since.* By providing one or more reasons, assumptions, or arguments, *W* attempts to justify the movement from *I* to *C.* Different types of warrants are appropriate for arguments typically made in different disciplines and professions. For example, law frequently uses case comparisons, along with other warrants, as does public administration: "Because the two countries are so much alike, the successful decriminalization of drugs in Switzerland is likely to work here." Policy makers frequently

---

[44] Frank Fischer and John Forester, ed., *The Argumentative Turn in Policy Analysis and Planning* (Durham, NC: Duke University Press, 1993). Earlier works on policy argumentation are Ian I. Mitroff and Richard O. Mason, *Creating a Dialectical Social Science* (Boston: D. Reidel, 1981); William N. Dunn, "Reforms as Arguments," *Knowledge: Creation, Diffusion, Utilization* 3 (1982): 293–326; Donald T. Campbell, "Experiments as Arguments," *Knowledge: Creation, Diffusion, Utilization* 3 (1982): 327–47; Giandomenico Majone, *Evidence, Argument, and Persuasion in the Policy Process* (New Haven, CT: Yale University Press, 1989); and Deborah Stone, *Policy Paradox and Political Reason* (Glenview, IL: Scott Foresman, 1988). See Chapter 4 of this volume for a more complete account.

[45] Majone, *Evidence, Argument, and Persuasion,* p. 1.

[46] This is the structural model of argument of Stephen Toulmin in *The Uses of Argument* (Cambridge: Cambridge University Press, 1958); and Stephen Toulmin, A. Rieke, and A. Janik, *An Introduction to Reasoning* (New York: Macmillan, 1984).

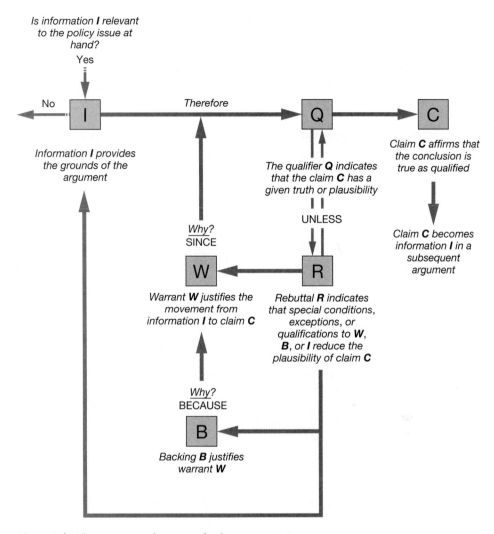

Figure 1.4   The structure and process of policy argumentation.

employ causal warrants such as "Ethnic cleansing will be deterred by air strikes that establish NATO's credibility in the region." The warrant *W* supplies a justification for accepting claims on the basis of the information supplied.

- *Backing.* The backing, *B*, of a warrant also answers the *Why?* with a more general reason, assumption, or argument that begins with *because.* Just as warrants *W* justify the move from information *I* to claim *C*, backings *B* justify the warrant *W*, when its plausibility is in question. Characteristically different kinds of backings are employed by members of different disciplines and professions and by other policy stakeholders. Backings take various forms, including scientific laws, appeals to the authority of experts, or ethical and moral principles. For example, consider the warrant illustrated above: "Ethnic cleansing will be deterred by air strikes that establish NATO's credibility in the region." Often the backing for this warrant, and similar ones involving the use of coercive force, is an informal statement of the law of diminishing utility: "The greater the cost of an alternative, the less likely it will be pursued."

Dynamics of Argumentation, Public Discourse, and Debate

The analysis of information, claims, warrants, and backings yields an essentially static analysis. The consideration of two additional elements makes the framework dynamic.

- *Rebuttal.* The rebuttal *R* is a reason, assumption, or argument put forth by another stakeholder to challenge the information *I,* warrant *W,* or backing *B* of the original argument. The rebuttal responds to *unless* by referring to special conditions, exceptions, or qualifications that diminish the plausibility of the original claim. Using the NATO air strike example again: "The NATO air strikes are unlikely to deter ethnic cleansing, because the adversary's military is composed of many competing partisan interests that make a troop withdrawal virtually impossible." All policy arguments have rebuttals, because policy making involves bargaining, negotiation, and competition among opponents and proponents of policies. Analysts who pay attention to rebuttals are more likely to take a critical perspective toward policy issues, identifying weak or hidden assumptions, anticipating unintended consequences, and questioning anticipated objections, which serves as a systematic means for criticizing their own assumptions and arguments.

- *Qualifier.* The qualifier *Q* expresses the force of the argument by stating the circumstances in which the claim *C* is true or plausible. Although social scientists may state qualifiers in the language of formal probability ($p = 0.01$ or $t = 2.74$), ordinary language is the normal mode of discourse ("probably," "usually," "barring unforeseen circumstances"). Policy claims by elected officials are typically presented as if they were unconditionally true: "The welfare reform will remove from the welfare rolls persons who do not deserve it, and maintain or increase support to those who do." It is primarily through processes of policy argumentation and debate that policy makers and other stakeholders, including policy analysts, adjust and even abandon previously unqualified or weakly qualified arguments. This process of change, when it occurs, is motivated by the consideration of rebuttals offered by those who have a real personal, professional, and moral stake in policies.

The process of argumentation (Figure 1.4) is dynamic, not only because the initial arguments and their qualifiers can and do change in response to rebuttals by other stakeholders, but also because the conclusions of one argument can serve as information in succeeding arguments, creating argument "chains" or "trees."

Multiple perspectives of problems and potential solutions are found in the warrants, backings, and rebuttals of different stakeholders. The usual effect of these multiple perspectives is that the same policy-relevant information is interpreted in distinctly different ways. For example, information about small reductions in crime rates in urban areas tends to be ignored by the urban poor, viewed with skepticism by owners of central city businesses, rejected by criminologists who attribute variations in urban crime rates to ups and downs in unemployment, wages, and homelessness, and hailed as a brilliant achievement by elected officials. Policy analysts, by critically examining such contending arguments, can uncover and critically examine reasons and evidence that otherwise go unnoticed. Policy analysts can also probe their own assumptions by examining the qualifications, exceptions, and special circumstances that affect their own conclusions and recommendations.

CHAPTER SUMMARY

In this chapter, we have defined and illustrated policy analysis, described its role in creating and transforming policy-relevant information, and distinguished its forms. No single method of policy analysis is appropriate for all or even most occasions, which means that analysts must approach the choice of methods as an optimization problem involving informational trade-offs. The actual work of policy analysts—as distinguished from logical reconstructions of the way analysts ought to work—involves difficult methodological choices among informational sources and methods. For this and other reasons, critical thinking is a valuable aspect of policy analysis. One method of critical thinking is the model of argumentation, which helps evaluate and synthesize information presented in many forms by means of many methods.

LEARNING OBJECTIVES

- define and illustrate policy analysis
- describe and illustrate elements of integrated policy analysis
- distinguish alternative forms of policy analysis
- discuss criteria for making optimal methodological choices
- contrast reconstructed logic and logic-in-use
- describe policy argumentation and its uses in critical thinking
- use argumentation analysis, scorecards, spreadsheets, influence diagrams, and decision trees to analyze a case in public policy

KEY TERMS AND CONCEPTS

Critical multiplism (17)
Critical thinking (19)
Decision tree (32)
Descriptive decision theory (13)
Evaluation (6)
Forecasting (6)
Influence diagram (31)

Logic-in-use (15)
Logical positivism (17)
Integrated analysis (15)
Metamethod (6)
Monitoring (6)
Normative decision theory (14)
Policy analysis (1)

REVIEW QUESTIONS

1. What does it mean to define policy analysis as a process of inquiry, as distinguished from a method of problem solving?
2. Distinguish and illustrate policy-informational components, policy-analytic methods, and policy-informational transformations.
3. What is integrated policy analysis? Give examples.
4. What is normative decision theory, and how is it different from descriptive decision theory?
5. List some of the key differences between problem solving and problem finding.
6. Contrast retrospective and prospective analysis. Is the difference important?
7. Discuss and illustrate methods triangulation. Why is methods triangulation important?
8. Describe and illustrate an "optimal methodological choice" in policy analysis.
9. Discuss characteristics of the "logic-in-use" of policy analysts.
10. Contrast "reconstructed logic" and "logic-in-use." Provide illustrations.
11. How can the study of policy argumentation assist analysts to become critical thinkers?
12. Discuss the usefulness of the following visual displays: spreadsheets, scorecards, influence diagrams, decision trees, and argumentation diagrams.

DEMONSTRATION EXERCISES

1. After studying Case 1: *Saving Lives and Wasting Time* (see below), consider evidence that
   a. the number of fatalities in 1974 was about 500, after taking into account that about 50 percent of fatalities occurred on roads *not* subject to the 55 mph speed limit;

Table 1.1   Scorecard Displaying Outcomes of Two Policy Alternatives

	Policy Alternatives	
Policy Outcomes	*65 mph*	*55 mph*
Annual fatalities	54.1	45.2
Annual gasoline consumed (billion gallons)	46.8	43.3
Annual hours driving (billions)	20.2	21.9
Annual vehicle miles traveled (billions)	1,313	1,281

Table 1.2 Spreadsheet Displaying Benefits and Costs of Policies

	Alternatives			
Objectives	*65 mph*	*55 mph*	*Difference*	*Value ($)*
Fatalities (thousands)	54.1	45.2	8.9	0.24
Gallons gasoline consumed (billions)	46.8	43.3	3.5	0.53
Hours driving (billions)	20.2	21.9	−1.7	5.05
Benefits				3.99
Costs ($ billions)				−8.59
Net benefits ($ billions)				−4.60

    b. only 30 percent of traffic fatalities are known to be caused by speeding rather than other factors (e.g., human error, road conditions, miles driven); and

    c. unemployment and recession resulted in a sharp decrease in the number of miles driven in 1974.

On the basis of this new evidence, revise Tables 1.1 and 1.2 and Figures 1.5 and 1.6. In Figure 1.5 (Analysis of Argument to Return to 55 mph Speed Limit), what is your new claim? How strong is the new claim? Write your answers at the bottom of your revised Figure 1.5.

2. Imagine that a consumer survey was conducted to find out how much drivers are willing to pay for an extra hour of time. The survey concluded that the value of an hour lost is $1.50, rather than the 1974 average wage of $5.05. On the basis of this new evidence, revise the spreadsheet displayed in Table 1.2. How do you interpret the revised spreadsheet? Write your answer below the new Table 1.2.

3. What quantitative evidence can you find in Tables 1.1 and 1.2 and Figures 1.5 and 1.6 to support the argument in the title of Case 1, namely, that saving lives wastes time? Write your answer on no more than one page.

REFERENCES

Campbell, Donald T. *Methodology and Epistemology for Social Science: Selected Papers.* Edited by E. Samuel Overman. Chicago: University of Chicago Press, 1988.

Diesing, Paul. *How Social Science Works: Reflections on Practice.* Pittsburgh, PA: Pittsburgh University Press, 1991.

Dunn, William N., and Rita Mae Kelly. *Advances in Policy Studies since 1950.* New Brunswick, NJ: Transactions Books, 1992.

Fischer, Frank, and John Forester. *The Argumentative Turn in Policy Analysis and Planning.* Durham, NC: Duke University Press, 1993.

Hawkesworth, Mary E. *Theoretical Issues in Policy Analysis.* Albany: State University of New York Press, 1988.

Kaplan, Abraham. *The Conduct of Inquiry: Methodology for Behavioral Science.* San Francisco, CA: Chandler, 1964.

MacRae, Duncan Jr. *The Social Function of Social Science.* New Haven, CT: Yale University Press, 1976.

Stone, Deborah. *Policy Paradox: The Art of Political Decision Making.* New York: W. W. Norton, 1997.

Toulmin, Stephen, R. Rieke, and A. Janik. *An Introduction to Reasoning.* New York: Macmillan, 1984.

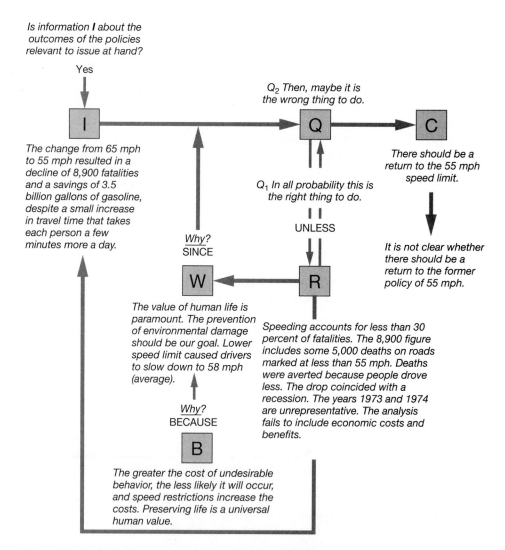

*Is information **I** about the outcomes of the policies relevant to issue at hand?*

Yes

Q_2 *Then, maybe it is the wrong thing to do.*

I → Q → C

The change from 65 mph to 55 mph resulted in a decline of 8,900 fatalities and a savings of 3.5 billion gallons of gasoline, despite a small increase in travel time that takes each person a few minutes more a day.

There should be a return to the 55 mph speed limit.

Q_1 *In all probability this is the right thing to do.*

UNLESS

Why?
SINCE

W ← R

It is not clear whether there should be a return to the former policy of 55 mph.

The value of human life is paramount. The prevention of environmental damage should be our goal. Lower speed limit caused drivers to slow down to 58 mph (average).

Speeding accounts for less than 30 percent of fatalities. The 8,900 figure includes some 5,000 deaths on roads marked at less than 55 mph. Deaths were averted because people drove less. The drop coincided with a recession. The years 1973 and 1974 are unrepresentative. The analysis fails to include economic costs and benefits.

Why?
BECAUSE

B

The greater the cost of undesirable behavior, the less likely it will occur, and speed restrictions increase the costs. Preserving life is a universal human value.

Figure 1.5   Analysis of argument to return to 55 mph speed limit.

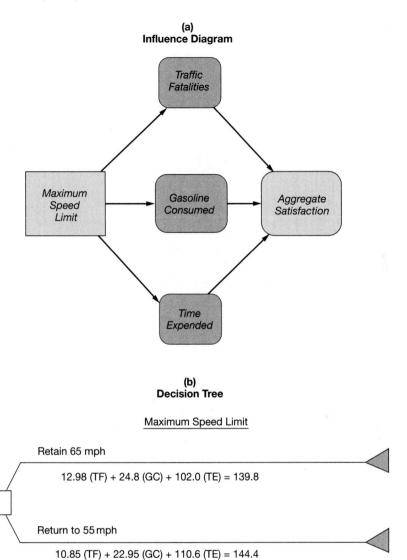

(a)
Influence Diagram

Traffic Fatalities

Maximum Speed Limit

Gasoline Consumed

Aggregate Satisfaction

Time Expended

(b)
Decision Tree

Maximum Speed Limit

Retain 65 mph

12.98 (TF) + 24.8 (GC) + 102.0 (TE) = 139.8

Return to 55 mph

10.85 (TF) + 22.95 (GC) + 110.6 (TE) = 144.4

Figure 1.6 Benefits and costs of the 55 mph speed limit displayed as an influence diagram and decision tree.

Case 1. Saving Lives and Wasting Time: Thinking Critically about Speeding and Traffic Fatalities

The structural model of argument provides a visual display or picture of how arguments move from evidence to conclusions, and how arguments change when confronted by the challenges of critics. The structural model therefore encourages what has come to be called "evidence-based" policy analysis, as well as "critical thinking" about such analysis. One use of evidence-based analysis and critical thinking is the careful examination of information, reasons, and claims presented in arguments embedded, usually implicitly, in *scorecards, spreadsheets, influence diagrams,* and *decision trees.* For example, consider the "Goeller scorecard" (Table 1.1) used to display effects of the National Maximum Speed Limit of 1974.[47] The 1974 policy, which imposed a maximum speed limit of 55 mph on interstate highways in the United States, was abandoned on an experimental basis by forty states in 1987 and 1988.[48] In 1995, Congress granted states the right to set their own speed limits, an action that was strongly opposed by the Clinton administration. Consider the following statement by President Clinton's Secretary of Transportation, Federico Pena.[49]

> Today, in response to President Clinton's directive to me to develop an action plan to help states ensure highway safety, I call on the governors and the state legislators to adjust and refashion their highway safety strategies and to work in partnership with the Department of Transportation to make our highways the safest in the world.
>
> For two decades the laws have worked. Today, our traffic fatality rate is at a record low level. In 1972, more than 55,000 Americans died on our highways. Last year, about 40,000 Americans were killed. Over the last decade, drunk driving fatalities have declined more than 17 percent and seat belt usage is now at 67 percent, up from 15 percent. I am proud of our progress on highway safety. But much more remains to be done because the fatalities have leveled off for the past two years, further emphasizing the need for us to redouble our safety efforts. We, as a nation, cannot and should not accept 40,000 fatalities and 3 million injuries a year caused by highway accidents. When a plane crashes and kills people, every news show in the country reports it. People are concerned, and that's appropriate. Last year, we lost 262 lives through seven major airline crashes. Yet on our highways, we lost 40,000 lives, and it doesn't make page one. That is the equivalent of 110 people killed in an airplane crash every day, for an entire year, 365 days of the year.

---

[47] Example based on MacRae (pp. 291–318) and Dunn (pp. 254–90) in Fischer and Forester, *The Argumentative Turn in Policy Analysis and Planning* (see note 44 above).

[48] The initial evaluation of effects is reported in National Highway Transportation Safety Administration, *The Effects of the 65 mph Speed Limit through 1988* (Washington, DC: 1989).

[49] Statement by Transportation Secretary Federico Pena on National Highway System, Press Release, November 28, 1995.

If we framed the tragedy that we see on our highways in this context, I believe most Americans and their state elected officials would be outraged at the senseless slaughter of our fellow citizens on our highways.

They are fatalities that we accept too easily. As we drive past a terrible highway crash, we seem numb to the tragedy, believing that it could not happen to us. We forget the leading cause of death for people ages 5 to 34 is transportation accidents. It does not come from crime, or domestic abuse, or disease. It comes from car crashes. And while one cannot put a price on losing a loved one or suffering an injury, motor vehicle accidents cost the public more than $137 billion a year. These costs include $45.7 billion in property losses, $39.8 billion in market productivity, $13.9 billion in medical costs, $10.8 billion in household productivity, $10 billion in insurance administration, $8.9 billion in legal and court costs and $8.4 billion in other costs. There is a possibility states may end up with the full responsibility for addressing Medicaid costs. This means that citizens in every state would be challenged to curtail the costs of Medicaid resulting from highway deaths and injuries, because these costs would be borne by taxpayers in every state.

This year, in a fundamental shift of authority from the federal government to the states, the Congress has granted the states the right to set virtually their own highway safety laws. The shift in authority brings with it much responsibility because we all pay the bill from traffic accidents.

I accept this change in legislation as an opportunity to engage in a national debate, not only with the state elected leaders, but with the American people as well, about what our true commitment is to reducing the loss of 40,000 lives.

From my travels across America, I know firsthand that governors share same the commitment the President and I share to ensuring and promoting highway safety. I hope and expect to continue to work closely with the states to save lives and prevent injuries on all our highways.

So, I am taking the following eight actions.

- Immediately urge the governors of the states where the speed limits automatically increase upon repeal of the National Maximum Speed Limit to work with their state legislatures to have public hearings to carefully consider the costs and benefits, especially in health care and Medicaid costs of increasing speed limits. There were no public hearings here in Washington on the speed limit repeal in the Congress.

- Begin a public education campaign to communicate with citizens, governors and legislative leaders, about the burdens that motor vehicle crashes currently place on their states, to provide estimates of potential cost increases due to lessening highway safety in each state.

- Immediately establish a nationwide safety team to educate state policy makers of the consequences of weakening highway safety laws. The members will include those who bear the costs, such as citizen representatives, businesses, insurance and health care providers and those who develop and implement the policies.

- Assist all states in identifying and using current data to track their state-specific costs due to motor vehicle crashes and to identify the ultimate payor of these costs. This will assist the states in fulfilling the requirements for a report on the consequences of raising the speed limits. With this data, most states, for the first time, will have the costs imposed on a state due to various accident factors. Working with the Department of Health and Human Services, the Department of Transportation will provide data to states on Medicaid costs due to highway accidents.

- Aggressively support the "zero tolerance" provision in the legislation, urging the states without such laws to promptly adopt them.
- Promote and support safety management systems. The Department will showcase "best practices" as well as provide training to ensure all states take advantage of the safety management systems. The Department is already working with 16 states on a true performance-based safety management system where the state has the lead.
- Carefully exercise discretion in the implementation of the pilot program to reduce regulations for medium-sized trucks in order to maintain safety levels.
- Carefully monitor the results of numerous statutory exemptions granted for hours-of-service requirements for different truck types.

Finally, the National Highway System represents strategic investment in not only our transportation system, but also our economy. I am pleased at its passage and would like to acknowledge the work of all the Department of Transportation employees who contributed to its fruition, particularly the men and women of the Federal Highway Administration.

The scorecard displayed in Table 1.1 has two major alternatives: the maximum speed limits of 55 mph and 65 mph. The most important outcomes of the two alternatives are gasoline consumed, time spent driving, vehicle miles traveled, and traffic fatalities. The figures are for the years 1973 (before the 55 mph speed limit) and 1974 (after the 55 mph speed limit).

In support of Secretary Pena's statement, the scorecard suggests that returning to the 55 mph speed limit may be preferable to the present 65 mph speed limit. Between 1973 and 1974, the lower speed limit produced a decline of 8,900 fatalities and reduced gasoline consumption by 3.5 billion gallons. Although the lower speed limit also had a negative side, with an additional 1.7 billion hours of travel time at the lower speed limit, this appears to be a small price to pay for saving thousands of lives and billions of gallons of gasoline. A secondary consequence of the lower speed limit was the reduction of air pollution.

The scorecard does not reveal contending arguments bearing on a possible return to the 55 mph speed limit. Although these arguments might be uncovered in other ways (e.g., through discussions with other analysts), a critical analysis of the process of argumentation surrounding the 55 mph speed limit helps identify and challenge assumptions underlying the scorecard analysis (Figure 1.5).

One of the rebuttals points to the incompleteness of the analysis, which does not take into account the economic benefits and costs of the lower speed limit. The spreadsheet (Table 1.2) is a response to these rebuttals. It is a spreadsheet, and not a scorecard, because it goes beyond a listing of outcomes. The spreadsheet places an explicit monetary value on outcomes, which are now titled objectives, because they are explicitly valued.

The spreadsheet suggests that the 65 mph speed limit should be retained, because the net benefits (benefits minus costs) are negative. On the plus side, some 8,900 fatalities were averted under the 55 mph speed limit. Multiplying this number by $240,000, which is the average value of a human life in 1974 dollars, gives $2.13 billion in benefits. To this we add 3.5 billion gallons of gasoline saved by driving at the lower speed limit. At the average cost of a gallon of gasoline in 1974 (53 cents), the additional benefits are $1.85 billion. Total benefits ($2.13 + $1.85) are $3.98 billion.

The costs of the 55 mph speed limit are primarily in time lost by driving at the lower speed limit. The loss, shown in the spreadsheet, is −1.7 billion hours. By using the average hourly wage in 1974 ($5.05) to calculate the value of each hour lost, the total costs (ignoring negligible costs of enforcement and promotion) are $8.59 billion. Subtracting costs of $8.59 from benefits of $3.98, the net loss is $4.6 billion.

Clearly, the benefit–cost calculations should be subjected to further analysis, because they conceal important assumptions that may be rebutted. Is a human life really worth $240,000? Why place a monetary value on lives, when there is no "market" for them? The cost of time provides that each hour lost is worth the average hourly wage in 1974, which was about $5.05. Are drivers willing to pay this much for an hour gained? Or is the value of an hour lost less (or more) than this? Even more important, the previous argumentation analysis (Figure 1.5) suggests that the number of fatalities reduced by the speed limit may be grossly overestimated. It seems that a more comprehensive and balanced analysis may be achieved by supplementing the scorecard and the spreadsheet with argumentation analysis.

The analysis of policy argumentation can be of equal or greater benefit when we examine influence diagrams and decision trees such as those of Figures 1.6 (a) and 1.6 (b). Both the diagram and decision tree were created with software called DPL, which stands for Decision Programming Language.[50]

The influence diagram (Figure 1.6[a]) displays the policy choice as a rectangle. A rectangle always refers to a policy choice, also known as a decision node, which in this case refers to the choice between the maximum national speed limits of 55 mph and 65 mph. To the immediate right of the decision node are three rectangles with shaved corners, which are connected to the decision node with arrows showing that the policy choice influences them. Rectangles with shaved corners always represent valued policy outcomes, or objectives. Here there are three valued outcomes: traffic fatalities, gasoline consumption, and time driving. The objectives are to avert traffic fatalities, reduce gasoline consumption, and expend minimum hours driving. To the right of the three objectives is another one, again represented as a shaved rectangle. This valued outcome refers to the aggregate (total) satisfaction attained by reaching all the objectives. Note that the slightly larger shaved

---

[50] The Decision Programming Language (DPL) is available in DPL 4.0 *Professional Decision Analysis Software-Academic Version* (Pacific Grove, CA: Duxbury Press, 1999).

rectangle to the far right is connected by arrows showing that achieving the previous three objectives affects aggregate satisfaction.

The decision tree (Figure 1.6[b]) is another representation of the influence diagram. Whereas the influence diagram is limited to showing how a decision affects valued outcomes, the decision tree displays the monetary value of these outcomes. In this simple decision tree, there are two branches that represent two alternatives: return to the 55 mph speed limit and retain the 65 mph speed limit. The tree assumes that there is no uncertainty about achieving objectives. Such a tree and the analysis it summarizes are "deterministic" rather than "probabilistic." (If we wanted to convert this into a probabilistic analysis, we might add one or more ovals to represent uncertain events, for example, the price of petroleum on the world market and its influence on gasoline prices.)

Readers should note that the decision tree compares the dollar value of *all* fatalities, gasoline consumed, and time expended, rather than the *difference* among them. The top branch (retain 65 mph) shows that the total cost of all fatalities (TF) under this option is $12.98 billion. The costs of all gasoline consumed (GC) and all time expended (TE) are $24.8 billion and $102 billion, respectively. The grand total, which places a monetary value on aggregate satisfaction, is shown at the end of the top branch: $12.98 (TF) + $24.8 (GC) + $102 (TE) = $139.8 billion. The grand total for the bottom branch (return to 55 mph) is $144.4 billion. The difference between returning to the 55 mph speed limit and retaining the 65 mph speed limit is $139.8 − $144.4 = −$4.6 billion, which is the net loss of returning to the 55 mph speed limit. Note that this is the same value obtained in the spreadsheet (Table 1.2).

The evidence assumptions, qualifications, and implicit conclusion of the influence diagram and decision tree have already been displayed as a policy argument in Figure 1.5, which states in everyday language that "it is not clear that there should be a return to the former policy of 55 mph." Of course, the plausibility of this claim rests on the soundness of the warrants, backings, and rebuttals displayed in the argumentation diagram (Figure 1.5).

2

Policy Analysis in the Policy-Making Process

As a process of multidisciplinary inquiry, policy analysis seeks to create, transform, and communicate knowledge of and in the policy-making process.[1] Because the effectiveness of policy making depends in part on the availability of policy-relevant information, the communication and use of policy analysis are essential.[2]

---

[1] Harold D. Lasswell, *A Pre-view of Policy Sciences* (New York: American Elsevier Publishing, 1971), pp. 1–2. Information *of* refers to "systematic, empirical studies of how policies are made and put into effect," while information *in* refers to understanding that "the realism of a decision depends in part on access to the stock of available information."

[2] Carol H. Weiss's *Social Science Research and Decision Making* (New York: Columbia University Press, 1980) is among the most comprehensive syntheses of research and theory on the uses of social science research by policy makers. Other syntheses include William N. Dunn and Burkart Holzner, "Knowledge in Society: Anatomy of an Emerging Field," *Knowledge in Society* (later titled *Knowledge and Policy*) 1, no. 1 (1988): 1–26; and David J. Webber, "The Distribution and Use of Policy Information in the Policy Process," in *Advances in Policy Studies since 1950,* ed. Dunn and Kelly (New Brunswick, NJ: Transaction, 1991), pp. 415–41. Journals that have focused on these problems include *Knowledge: Creation, Diffusion, Utilization* (Sage Publications—out of print) and *Knowledge and Policy: The International Journal of Information Transfer and Utilization* (Transaction Publishers).

SOME HISTORICAL BACKGROUND

In a broad sense, policy analysis is as old as civilization itself. It includes diverse forms of inquiry, from mysticism and the occult to modern science. Etymologically, the term *policy* comes to us from the Greek, Sanskrit, and Latin languages. The Greek *polis* (city-state) and Sanskrit *pur* (city) evolved into the Latin *politia* (state) and, later, into the Middle English *policie,* which referred to the conduct of public affairs or the administration of government. The etymological origins of policy are the same for two other important words: *police* and *politics.* These multiple connotations are found in Germanic and Slavic languages, which have only one word (*Politik, politika*) to refer to both policy and politics. This is among the reasons for the porous boundaries among political science, public administration, and policy analysis, all of which study politics and policy.

Early Origins

The term policy analysis need not be restricted to its contemporary meaning, where analysis refers to breaking problems into basic elements or parts, much as we disassemble a clock or machine. For example, "the decision problem can be decomposed into alternatives, outcomes, and objectives." A closely related and equally restrictive view is that policy analysis is a collection of quantitative techniques used by systems analysts, decision analysts, and economists.[3]

Understood in its widest sense, policy analysis emerged at a point in the evolution of human societies where practical knowledge was consciously cultivated, thereby prompting an explicit and self-reflective examination of links between knowledge and action. The development of specialized procedures for analyzing policies was related to the emergence of urban civilization out of scattered and largely autonomous tribal and folk societies.[4] As a specialized activity, policy analysis followed changes in social and, above all, political organization that accompanied new production technologies and stable patterns of human settlement.

One of the earliest recorded efforts to consciously cultivate policy-relevant knowledge occurred in Mesopotamia (what is now southern Iraq). In the ancient Mesopotamian city of Ur, one of the first legal codes was produced in the twenty-first century B.C., some two thousand years before Aristotle (384–322 B.C.), Confucius (551–479 B.C.), and Kautilya (ca. 300 B.C.) produced their classic treatises on government and politics. In the eighteenth century B.C., the ruler of Babylon, with the assistance of professionals whom we would now call policy analysts, created the Code of Hammurabi. The Code was designed to establish a unified and just public order in a period when Babylon was in transition from a small city-state to a large territorial state. The Hammurabian Code, a set of policies that parallel

---

[3] For example, Edith Stokey and Richard Zeckhauser, *A Primer for Policy Analysis* (New York: W. W. Norton, 1978).

[4] Lasswell, *A Pre-view of Policy Sciences,* pp. 9, 13.

Mosaic laws, reflected the economic and social requirements of stable urban settlements where rights and obligations were defined according to social position. The Code covered criminal procedures, property rights, trade and commerce, family and marital relations, physicians' fees, and what we now call public accountability.[5]

The early Mesopotamian legal codes were a response to the growing complexity of fixed urban settlements, where policies were needed to regulate the distribution of commodities and services, organize record keeping, and maintain internal security and external defense. A growing consciousness of relations between knowledge and action fostered the growth of educated strata that specialized in the production of policy-relevant information. These "symbol specialists," as Lasswell called them, were responsible for policy forecasting; for example, they were expected to foresee crop yields at the onset of the planting season, or predict the outcomes of war.[6] Because analysts used mysticism, ritual, and the occult to forecast the future, their methods were unscientific by present-day standards. Although such procedures were based in part on evidence acquired through experience, any reasonable definition of science requires that knowledge claims be assessed against observations that are independent of the hopes of analysts, or of those who hire them.[7] Then as now, policy-relevant knowledge was ultimately judged according to its success (or failure) in shaping better policies, not simply because special methods were used to produce it. Even the ancients seemed to know what some contemporary analysts forget—when methods are used to perform latent functions of ritualistic purification, political persuasion, and symbolic legitimation, analysts and their clients eventually must face the decisive test of performance.[8] Although statements such as "drug interdiction policy is based on good science" are in vogue, the invocation of "good science" in this and other contexts may represent little more than ritualistic purification.

In India, Kautilya's *Arthashastra,* written in the fourth century B.C., is a systematic guide to policy making, statecraft, and government administration. The *Arthashastra* synthesized much that had been written up to that time on material success, or what we now call economics. Kautilya, an adviser to the Mauryan Empire in northern India, has been compared to Plato (427–327 B.C.), Aristotle (384–322 B.C.), and Machiavelli (1469–1527). In addition to their work as social and political theorists, all were deeply involved in the practical aspects of policy making. Plato served as adviser to the rulers of Sicily, while Aristotle tutored Alexander of

---

[5] *The Code of Hammurabi,* trans. Robert F. Harper (Chicago: University of Chicago Press, 1904).

[6] Lasswell, *A Pre-view of Policy Sciences,* p. 11.

[7] Donald T. Campbell, "A Tribal Model of the Social System Vehicle Carrying Scientific Information," in *Methodology and Epistemology for Social Science: Selected Papers,* ed. E. Samuel Overman (Chicago, IL: University of Chicago Press, 1988), pp. 489–503.

[8] Edward A. Suchman, "Action for What? A Critique of Evaluative Research," in *Evaluating Action Programs,* ed. Carol H. Weiss (Boston, MA: Allyn and Bacon, 1972), p. 81; and Martin Rein and Sheldon H. White, "Policy Research: Belief and Doubt," *Policy Analysis* 3, no. 2 (1977): 239–71.

Macedonia from the time Alexander was fourteen years old until he ascended the throne at the age of twenty. Although Aristotle, like many social and behavioral scientists, found practical politics repugnant, he seems to have accepted the assignment because he wanted to bring knowledge to bear on policy issues of the day. In this respect, he followed his teacher Plato, who said that good government would not occur until philosophers were kings, or kings philosophers. The opportunity to influence policy by instructing the heir apparent was an offer that in good conscience he could not refuse.[9]

These are examples of preeminent individual producers of specialized knowledge, not of entire classes of educated persons who later would influence policy making in Europe and Asia. In the Middle Ages, the gradual expansion and differentiation of urban civilization brought with it an occupational structure that facilitated the development of specialized knowledge. Princes and kings recruited policy specialists to provide advice and technical assistance in areas where rulers were least able to make effective decisions: finance, war, and law. German sociologist Max Weber described the development of a class of educated policy specialists as follows:

> In Europe, expert officialdom, based on the division of labor, has emerged in a gradual development of half a thousand years. The Italian cities and seigniories were the beginning, among the monarchies, and states of the Norman conquerors. But the decisive step was taken in connection with the administration of the finances of the prince. . . . The sphere of finance could afford least of all a ruler's dilettantism—a ruler who at that time was still above all a knight. The development of war technique called forth the expert and specialized officer; the differentiation of legal procedure called forth the trained jurist. In these three areas—finance, war, and law—expert officialdom in the more advanced states was definitely triumphant during the sixteenth century.[10]

The growth of expert officialdom (what Weber called "professional politicians") assumed different forms in different parts of the world. In medieval Europe, India, China, Japan, and Mongolia, the clergy were literate and therefore technically useful. Christian, Brahmin, Buddhist, and Lamaist priests, much like some modern social and behavioral scientists, earned a reputation for impartiality and disinterestedness insofar as they stood above practical politics and temptations of political power and economic gain. Educated men of letters—whose modern counterpart is the special presidential adviser—influenced policy making until court nobles, who later came to dominate the political and diplomatic service, replaced them. In England, petty nobles and urban rentiers (investors) were recruited without compensation to manage local governments in their own interest. Jurists trained in

---

[9] J. A. K. Thompson, *The Ethics of Aristotle: The Nichomachean Ethics Translated* (Baltimore, MD: Penguin Books. 1955), p. D. 11.

[10] Max Weber, "Politics as a Vocation," in *From Max Weber: Essays in Sociology,* ed. Hans C. Gerth and C. Wright Mills (New York: Oxford University Press, 1946), p. 88.

Roman law and jurisprudence had a strong influence on policy making, particularly in Continental Europe. They were largely responsible for the transformation of the late medieval state and the movement toward modern government.

The age of the Industrial Revolution was also that of the Enlightenment, a period in which a belief in human progress through science and technology became an ever more dominant theme among policy makers and their advisers. The development and testing of scientific theories of nature and society gradually came to be seen as the only objective means for understanding and solving social problems. For the first time, policy-relevant knowledge was produced according to the canons of empiricism and the scientific method.

The Nineteenth-Century Transformation

In nineteenth-century Europe, producers of policy-relevant knowledge began to base their work on the systematic recording of empirical data. Earlier, philosophers and statesmen had offered systematic explanations of policy making and its role in society. Yet for several thousand years, there was an essential continuity in methods for investigating and solving social, economic, and political human problems. If evidence for a particular point of view was provided, it was typically based on appeals to authority, ritual, or philosophical doctrine. What was new in the nineteenth century was a basic change in the procedures used to understand society and its problems, a change reflected in the growth of empirical, quantitative, and policy-oriented research.[11]

The first censuses were conducted in the United States (1790) and England (1801). It was at this time that statistics ("state arithmetic") and demography began to develop as specialized fields. The Manchester and London Statistical Societies, established in the 1830s, helped shape a new orientation toward policy-relevant knowledge. Organized by bankers, industrialists, and scholars, the societies sought to replace traditional ways of thinking about social problems with empirical analyses of the effects of urbanization and unemployment on the lives of workers and their families. In the Manchester Society, an enthusiasm for quantification was coupled with a commitment to social reform, or "progress of social improvement in the manufacturing population."[12] The London Society, under the influence of Thomas Malthus (1766–1834) and other academics, took a more disinterested approach: "The Statistical Society will consider it to be the first and most essential rule of its conduct to exclude carefully all opinions from its transactions and publications—to confine its attention rigorously to facts—and, as far as it may be found possible, to facts which can be stated numerically and arranged in tables."[13] The London and

---

[11] Daniel Lerner, "Social Science: Whence and Whither?" in *The Human Meaning of the Social Sciences,* ed. Daniel Lerner (New York: World Publishing, 1959), pp. 13–23.

[12] Nathan Glazer, "The Rise of Social Research in Europe," in *The Human Meaning of the Social Sciences,* ed. Daniel Lerner (New York: World Publishing, 1959), p. 51.

[13] Ibid., pp. 51–52.

Manchester societies used questionnaires to carry out studies, and paid "agents" were the counterpart of today's professional interviewer. There were similar developments in France, Germany, and the Netherlands.

A preeminent contributor to the methodology of social statistics and survey research was Adolphe Quetelet (1796–1874), a Belgian mathematician and astronomer who was the major scientific adviser to the Dutch and Belgian governments.[14] Most topics in contemporary texts on survey design and analysis were addressed by Quetelet: questionnaire design; data collection, analysis, and interpretation; data organization and storage; and identification of conditions under which data are collected. In the same period, Frederic Le Play (1806–82) wrote *Les Ouvriers Europeans* [The European Workers], a detailed empirical investigation of family income and expenditures of European workers in several countries. In Germany, Ernst Engel (1821–96) sought to derive laws of "social economics" from empirical data expressed in statistical form.

In England, the work of Henry Mayhew and Charles Booth, who studied the life and employment conditions of the urban poor in natural (what we now call "field") settings, is representative of the new empirical approach to the study of social problems. Mayhew's *London Labour and the London Poor* (1851) described the lives of the laborers, peddlers, performers, and prostitutes who comprised London's urban underclass. In writing *Life and Labour of the People in London* (1891–1903), Booth employed school inspectors as key informants. Using what we now call participant observation, Booth lived among the urban poor, gaining firsthand experience of actual living conditions. A member of the Royal Commission on the Poor Law, he was an important influence on the revision of policies on old-age pensions. Booth's work also served as something of a model for policy-oriented research in the United States, including the *Hull House Maps and Papers* (1895) and W. E. B. Dubois's *The Philadelphia Negro* (1899), both of which sought to document the scope and severity of poverty in urban areas.

The nineteenth-century transformation was not the result of declarations of allegiance to canons of logical empiricism and the scientific method. Declarations to this effect did not and could not occur until the next century, when Vienna Circle philosophers engaged in the logical reconstruction of physics to propose formal principles and rules of successful scientific practice (few natural or social scientists have actually followed these principles and rules). The transformation came, rather, from the uncertainty accompanying the shift from agrarian to industrial societies, a shift that preceded the Industrial Revolution. Later, industry and industrialized science required a politically stable order to operate efficiently. Political stability was associated with profound social instability.[15]

---

[14] A significant history of statistics and statisticians is Stephen M. Stigler, *The History of Statistics: The Measurement of Uncertainty before 1900* (Cambridge, MA: Harvard University Press, 1990).

[15] J. H. Plumb, *The Growth of Political Stability in England, 1675–1725* (Baltimore, MD: Penguin Books, 1973), p. 12.

Thus, for the most part science and technology was not responsible for the growth of newly centralized systems of political control. Although science and technology contributed to problems of a newly uprooted, uneducated, and displaced class of urban workers and their families, it was politically steered policy analysis that was part of the solution. Dominant social groups valued policy-oriented research as a means to achieve political and administrative control. In the sphere of factory production, for example, the political organization of work preceded scientific and technological developments that later culminated in efficiency-enhancing machinery and the specialization of tasks.[16] In the sphere of public policy, we see a parallel development. Methods of empirical, quantitative, and policy-oriented analysis were a product of the recognition by bankers, industrialists, politicians, and the Victorian middle class that older methods for understanding the natural and social world were no longer adequate. The key questions of the day were practical and political: How much did members of the urban proletariat need to earn to maintain themselves and their families? How much did they have to earn before there was a taxable surplus? How much did they have to save from their earnings to pay for medical treatment and education? How much should capitalist owners and the state invest in day care facilities so that mothers might put in an effective day's work? How much investment in public works projects—sanitation, sewage, housing, roads—was required to maintain adequate public health standards, not only to maintain a productive workforce but also to protect the middle and upper classes from infectious diseases cultivated in urban slums?

The Twentieth Century

An important feature of the twentieth century, as compared with the nineteenth, is the institutionalization of the social and behavioral sciences and social professions. Twentieth-century producers of policy-relevant knowledge were no longer the heterogeneous group of bankers, industrialists, journalists, and university scholars who guided the early statistical societies and other institutions of policy research. They were graduates with first and advanced degrees in policy-relevant disciplines and professions who, along with professors, occupied important positions in governments or worked as consultants or researchers under grants and contracts. In background, experience, and motivation, they were members of established professions that, more or less, were guided by commonly accepted scientific and professional norms.

The new professionals played an active role in the administration of Woodrow Wilson, particularly during World War I. Later, under the Republican administration of Herbert Hoover, social scientists carried out two major social surveys, *Recent Economic Trends* and *Recent Social Trends*. The largest influx of social scientists into government came, however, with Franklin Roosevelt's New Deal. Large numbers of social scientists staffed the numerous new agencies established during the

---

[16] Stephen A. Marglin, "What Do Bosses Do? The Origins and Functions of Hierarchy in Capitalist Production," *Review of Radical Political Economy* 6, no. 2 (1974): 33–60.

Roosevelt administration (National Recovery Administration, Work Projects Administration, Public Works Administration, Securities and Exchange Commission, and Federal Housing Administration).

The primary function of social scientists in the 1930s was to investigate policy problems and broad sets of potential solutions, and not, as in later periods, to employ economic modeling, decision analysis, or policy experimentation to identify and select specific solutions to problems. The Roosevelt administration's National Planning Board (later the National Resources Planning Board), a majority of whose members were professional social scientists, provides a good illustration of the approach to policy questions characteristic of the 1930s. The board was conceived as "a general staff gathering and analyzing facts, observing the interrelation and administration of broad policies, proposing from time to time alternative lines of national procedure, based on thorough inquiry and mature consideration."[17] This same general orientation toward problems was evident among economists working for the Department of Agriculture, political scientists involved in the reorganization of the executive branch, and anthropologists conducting studies for the Bureau of Indian Affairs. Social scientists also contributed to methodological innovations; for example, the Department of Agriculture led in developing the sample survey as a new research tool and instrument of government census policy.[18]

World War II and the postwar readjustment that followed provided social scientists with opportunities to demonstrate their value in solving practical problems. Interwar achievements in the area of survey research had laid a foundation for the use of interviews by the Office of War Information, the War Production Board, and the Office of Price Administration. Military and civilian agencies relied on social scientists to investigate problems of national security, social welfare, defense, war production, pricing, and rationing. The activities of agencies such as the Office of Strategic Services were continued after the war by the Office of Naval Research, by the Department of the Air Force, and, later, by the Research and Development Board (subsequently RAND) of the Department of Defense, and the Central Intelligence Agency. Special research institutes were established by the federal government, including the Operations Research Office of The Johns Hopkins University and the Human Resources Research Office at George Washington University. Among the seminal contributions to policy research in this period was *The American Soldier* (1950), a four-volume study produced by many of the most able applied social scientists in the country. The director of the Army Morale Division commissioned this large-scale project in 1941, under the general direction of sociologist Samuel Stouffer. The project is significant, not only because of its scale but also because it was part of an emerging pattern of extensive governmental

---

[17] Gene Lyons, *The Uneasy Partnership: Social Science and the Federal Government in the Twentieth Century* (New York: Russell Sage Foundation, 1969), p. 65.

[18] Harry Alpert, "The Growth of Social Research in the United States," in *The Human Meaning of the Social Sciences,* ed. Daniel Lerner (New York: World Publishing, 1959), pp. 79–80.

support for policy research and analysis. Military policy makers turned to the social researcher, not only for facts but also for causal inferences and conclusions that would affect the lives of millions of troops.[19] This large research program contributed to the development and refinement of multivariate analysis and other quantitative techniques that are now widely used by researchers in all social science disciplines.

After World War II, the first systematic effort to develop an explicit policy orientation within the social and behavioral sciences was *The Policy Sciences: Recent Developments in Scope and Method* (1951), edited by political scientists Daniel Lerner and Harold D. Lasswell. The "policy sciences," as stated by Lasswell in the introduction, are not confined to theoretical aims of science; they also have a fundamentally practical orientation. Moreover, their purpose is not simply to provide a basis for making efficient decisions but also to provide knowledge "needed to improve the practice of democracy. In a word, the special emphasis is upon the policy sciences of democracy, in which the ultimate goal is the realization of human dignity in theory and fact."[20]

The systematic study of public policy also grew out of public administration, then a field within political science. In 1937, Harvard University established the Graduate School of Public Administration, which focused in part on public policy. In the late 1940s, an interuniversity committee was established to develop public policy curricular materials, a major product of which was Harold Stein's *Public Administration and Policy Development: A Case-Book* (1952). The interuniversity committee, composed of professors and practitioners of public administration, speaks for the close relationship between policy analysis and public administration before and after World War II.[21]

The impetus for developing methods and techniques of policy analysis—as distinguished from its theory and methodology—did not originate in political science or public administration. The technical side of policy analysis rather grew out of engineering, operations research, systems analysis, applied mathematics, and, to a lesser extent, applied economics. Most of those responsible for developing methods and techniques had received their formal training outside the social sciences. World War II had prompted the involvement of specialists whose orientation toward policy was primarily analytical, in the narrow sense of that term. The idea of "analysis" came to be associated with efforts to separate or decompose problems into their fundamental components, for example, decomposing problems of national defense into policy alternatives (nuclear warheads, manned bombers, conventional ground troops) whose consequences for the attainment of policy

---

[19] Howard E. Freeman and Clarence C. Sherwood, *Social Research and Social Policy* (Englewood Cliffs, NJ: Prentice Hall, 1970), p. 25.

[20] Harold D. Lasswell, "The Policy Orientation," in *The Policy Sciences: Recent Developments in Scope and Method,* ed. Daniel Lerner and Harold D. Lasswell (Stanford, CA: Stanford University Press, 1951), p. 15.

[21] H. George Frederickson and Charles Wise, *Public Administration and Public Policy* (Lexington, MA: D. C. Heath, 1977).

objectives could be estimated. This analycentric perspective[22] tends to preclude or restrict concerns with political, social, and administrative aspects of public policy, for example, concerns with the political feasibility of alternatives or their implications for democratic processes. Although the "analycentric turn" represents a movement away from the multidisciplinary and normative vision of Lasswell's policy sciences,[23] it has supplied more systematic procedures—from decision analysis to applied microeconomics—for selecting policy alternatives.[24]

The analycentric turn was accompanied by the growing influence of nonprofit research organizations ("think tanks") such as the Rand Corporation, which fostered the spread of systems analysis and related techniques to government agencies and the academic community.[25] The development of program-planning-budgeting systems (PPBS) was due in large measure to the efforts of operations researchers and economists working under Charles Hitch at the Rand Corporation. The RAND group wanted to find out "how the country could 'purchase' national security in the most efficient manner—how much of the national wealth should be devoted to defense, how the funds allocated to defense should be distributed among different military functions, and how to assure the most effective use of these funds."[26] Although PPBS was introduced into the Department of Defense in 1965 and was later mandated for use in all federal agencies, it was difficult to implement. After 1971 it became discretionary and soon fell into disuse. Despite mixed conclusions about its success as a tool of policy analysis, PPBS does appear to have captured the attention of government and university analysts who value systematic procedures for selecting and evaluating policy alternatives.[27]

The analycentric turn has been offset to some extent by the rapid growth of private foundations whose mission is to support traditional lines of research in the social sciences and humanities. More than three-fourths of these foundations were established after 1950.[28] In the same period, the federal government began to set aside funds for applied and policy-related research in the social sciences, although the natural sciences continued to receive the bulk of total government research support. Although in 1972 the social sciences received approximately 5 percent of all available federal research funds, funding for applied and basic research in the social

---

[22] Allen Schick, "Beyond Analysis," *Public Administration Review* 37, no. 3 (1977): 258–63.

[23] Peter de Leon, *Advice and Consent: The Development of the Policy Sciences* (New York: Russell Sage Foundation, 1988), ch. 2.

[24] Martin Greenberger, Matthew A. Crenson, and Brian L. Crissey, *Models in the Policy Process: Public Decision Making in the Computer Era* (New York: Russell Sage Foundation, 1976), pp. 23–46.

[25] Bruce L. R. Smith, *The Rand Corporation: A Case Study of a Nonprofit Advisory Corporation* (Cambridge, MA: Harvard University Press, 1966).

[26] Greenberger, Crenson, and Crissey, *Models in the Policy Process,* p. 32.

[27] For example, Alice Rivlin, *Systematic Thinking for Social Action* (Washington, DC: Brookings Institution, 1971); and Walter Williams, *Social Policy Research and Analysis: The Experience in the Federal Social Agencies* (New York: American Elsevier Publishing, 1971).

[28] Irving Louis Horowitz and James E. Katz, *Social Science and Public Policy in the United States* (New York: Praeger Publishers, 1975), p. 17.

sciences fell by approximately 40 percent in constant dollars in 1980–90.[29] At the same time, it is noteworthy that more than 95 percent of all research funded by governmental, nonprofit, and private organizations is applied research on practical problems.

By the 1970s, many social science disciplines had established institutions expressly committed to applied and policy-related research. These include the Policy Studies Organization (Political Science), the Society for the Study of Social Problems (Sociology), and the Society for the Psychological Study of Social Issues (Psychology). Each has its own journal of record. In the 1980s the process of insti-tutionalizing policy-oriented social science was carried a step further by the creation of multidisciplinary professional associations such as the Association for Public Policy and Management, which holds annual research conferences and publishes a journal of record, the *Journal of Policy Analysis and Management.* The new journal brought a more technical focus than mainstream policy journals, including *Policy Sciences,* the *Policy Studies Journal,* and *Policy Studies Review.* In addition to the mainstream journals were hundreds of others that focused on specific issues involv-ing health, welfare, education, criminal justice, education, science and technology, and other areas.[30]

In the same period, universities in the United States and Europe founded new graduate programs and degrees in policy analysis. In the United States, a number of new programs were established with the support of the Ford Foundation's Program in Public Policy and Social Organization. Most research universities in the United States have policy centers or institutes listed in the *Encyclopedia of Associations,* along with thousands of freestanding nonprofit policy research organizations and advocacy groups. Most were established after 1950. In Washington and most state capitals, and in the European Union, "policy analyst" is a formal job description. The National Governor's Association and the National League of Cities have policy analysis units. There are similar units throughout the United States government, in directorates of the European Union, and in international organizations, including the United Nations and the World Bank. Even a brief search of the World Wide Web yields scores of policy "think tanks" in all regions of the world.[31]

In the first decade of the twenty-first century, there has been increasing recog-nition that the complexity of problems faced by governments today requires the systematic use of natural and social scientists to help develop policies and assess

---

[29] National Science Foundation, *Federal Funds for Research, Development, and Other Scientific Activities* (Washington, DC: NSF, 1973); and National Science Board, *Science and Engineering Indicators—1989* (Washington, DC: NSB, 1989).

[30] Michael Marien, editor of *Future Survey* (journal of record of the World Future Society), estimates the number of policy journals to exceed four hundred. Marien, "The Scope of Policy Studies: Reclaiming Lasswell's Lost Vision," in *Advances in Policy Studies since 1950,* vol. 10, *Policy Studies Review Annual,* ed. William N. Dunn and Rita Mae Kelly (New Brunswick, NJ: Transaction, 1991), pp. 445–88.

[31] See, for example, www.nira.go.jp (World Directory of Think Tanks), a Japanese directory, and www.policy.com.

their consequences. The call for *evidence-based policy making* in the United Kingdom, the United States, and the European Union is a response to this complexity; it is also a recognition that ideological, religious, and political influences—usually hidden and lacking in transparency—have exerted a harmful effect on policy making in areas ranging from health, education, and welfare to national security and the environment. In the words of a recent British House of Commons report called *Scientific Advice, Risk, and Evidence Based Policy Making* (2006), evidence-based policy making "has its roots in Government's commitment to 'what works' over ideologically driven policy.... This Government expects more of policy makers. More new ideas, more willingness to question inherited ways of doing things, better use of evidence and research in policy making and better focus on policies that will deliver long-term goals."[32] Evidence-based policy making in the United Kingdom and the European Union takes several forms including *regulatory impact assessment* (RIA), which refers to the use of scientific analyses to examine the benefits, costs, risks, and consequences of newly introduced policies before they are adopted. In the United States, evidence-based policy has been promoted by leading program evaluators and policy analysts who founded the Coalition for Evidence-Based Policy of the Council for Excellence in Government. Some procedures of the Office of Management and Budget are based on evidence-based policy analysis, especially methods and standards of program evaluation.[33] Although some see the movement toward evidence-based policy making as a continuation of an ostensibly harmful logical positivist (scientist) approach to questions of public policy and democracy,[34] as yet it is unclear whether this negative assessment is itself based on sound reasoning and evidence.

THE POLICY-MAKING PROCESS

The development of policy analysis has been a response to practical problems and crises. Although recognition of these practical origins is important, historical awareness alone does not tell us much about the characteristics of that process and how it works.

It must always be remembered that policy analysis is an essentially *intellectual* activity embedded in a *social* process. This social process, which includes politics, psychology, and culture, is usually described as a *policy-making process,* or *policy process* for short. It is useful to visualize this process as a series of interdependent activities arrayed through time—agenda setting, policy formulation, policy adoption, policy implementation, policy assessment, policy adaptation,

---

[32] United Kingdom, House of Commons, Science and Technology Committee. *Scientific Advice, Risk and Evidence Based Policy Making.* Seventh Report of Session 2005–06, Volume I (London: HMO Printing House, 2006).

[33] Council for Evidence Based Policy. 1301 K Street, NW, Suite 450 West, Washington, DC 2005. www.excelgov.org/evidence; www.evidencebasedprograms.org.

[34] Wayne Parsons, "From Muddling Through to Muddling Up: Evidence Based Policy-Making and the Modernisation of British Government." Unpublished paper (London: University of London, 2004).

policy succession, and policy termination (Table 2.1).[35] Depending on circumstances, analysts produce information relevant to one, several, or all phases of policy making.

The policy process is composed of complex rounds or cycles (Figure 2.1). Each phase of the *policy cycle* is linked to the next, in backward and forward loops, and the process as a whole has no definite beginning or end. Individuals, interest groups, bureaus, offices, departments, and ministries are involved in policy cycles through cooperation, competition, and conflict. One form of cycle involves *policy adaptation,* where a feedback loop connects later to earlier phases. Other forms of cycles are *policy succession,* where new policies and organizations build on old ones, and *policy termination.* Policy termination may mean the end of a policy or program, although even termination affects what issues are placed on the public agenda, and in this sense represents another kind of cycle.

In some cases, a policy is adopted first, and then justified by working backward to agenda setting, where a problem is formulated or reformulated to fit or justify the policy. Parallel cycles occur, where different groups develop policies at the same time, and there may be forward ("arborescent") as well as backward ("assembly") branching from one phase to multiple successor or predecessor phases. Adjacent phases may be linked, or skipped altogether, creating "short circuits." Solutions and problems are in continuous flux, creating a degree of complexity that prompts metaphors of "garbage cans," "primeval policy soups," and "organized anarchies."[36]

MODELS OF POLICY CHANGE

Metaphors such as garbage cans, primeval policy soups, and organized anarchies are difficult to grasp, because it seems that policy making under these conditions would have no structure or organization at all.

A story should clarify these metaphors and their importance to policy making.[37]

> Some years ago, on a military base, there were reports of the possible theft of military secrets. Every day, at about the same time, a worker pushing a large wheelbarrow would attempt to leave the base by passing through the security gate.

---

[35] The policy cycle, or stages approach, is summarized by Peter de Leon, "The Stages Approach to the Policy Process: What Has It Done? Where Is It Going?" in *Theories of the Policy Process,* ed. Paul A. Sabatier (Boulder, CO: Westview Press, 1999). See also Charles O. Jones, *An Introduction to the Study of Public Policy,* 2d ed. (North Scituate, MA: Duxbury Press, 1977); James A. Anderson, *Public Policy Making* (New York: Praeger, 1975); Gary Brewer and Peter de Leon, *Foundations of Policy Analysis* (Homewood, IL: Dorsey Press, 1983). The classic work that influenced all works cited above is Harold D. Lasswell, *The Decision Process: Seven Categories of Functional Analysis* (College Park: Bureau of Governmental Research, University of Maryland, 1956).

[36] Michael Cohen, James March, and Johan Olsen, "A Garbage Can Model of Organizational Choice," *Administrative Science Quarterly* 17 (March 1972): 1–25; John W. Kingdon, *Agendas, Alternatives, and Public Policies,* 2d ed. (New York: Harper Collins, 1995).

[37] John Funari, personal communication.

Table 2.1 Phases of the Policy-Making Process

Phase	Characteristics	Illustration
Agenda Setting	Elected and appointed officials place problems on the public agenda. Many problems are not acted on at all, while others are addressed only after long delays.	A state legislator and her cosponsor prepare a bill that goes to the Health and Welfare Committee for study and approval. The bill stays in committee and is not voted on.
Policy Formulation	Officials formulate alternative policies to deal with a problem. Alternative policies assume the form of executive orders, court decisions, and legislative acts.	A state court considers prohibiting the use of standardized achievement tests such as the SAT on grounds that the tests are biased against women and minorities.
Policy Adoption	A policy is adopted with the support of a legislative majority, consensus among agency directors, or a court decision.	In *Roe v. Wade* Supreme Court justices reach a majority decision that women have the right to terminate pregnancies through abortion.
Policy Implementation	An adopted policy is carried out by administrative units that mobilize financial and human resources to comply with the policy.	The city treasurer hires additional staff to ensure compliance with a new law that imposes taxes on hospitals that no longer have taxexempt status.
Policy Assessment	Auditing and accounting units in government determine whether executive agencies, legislatures, and courts are in compliance with statutory requirements of a policy and achieving its objectives.	The General Accounting Office monitors social welfare programs such as Aid to Families with Dependent Children (AFDC) to determine the scope of welfare fraud.
Policy Adaptation	Auditing and evaluation units report to agencies responsible for formulating, adopting, and implementing policies that poorly written regulations, insufficient resources, inadequate training, etc., require the adaptation of policies.	A state Department of Labor and Industry evaluates an affirmative action training program, finding that employees wrongly believe that complaints against discrimination should be made to immediate supervisors, who seldom consider such complaints, rather than to affirmative action officers.
Policy Succession	Agencies responsible for evaluating policies, along with policy makers themselves, acknowledge that a policy is no longer needed because the problem dissolved. Rather than terminate the policy, it is maintained and redirected toward a new problem, goals, and objectives.	The National Highway Safety Administration (NHTSA) convinces Congress to maintain the 55 mph speed limit because it is achieving the new goal of reducing traffic fatalities, injuries, and property damage.
Policy Termination	Agencies responsible for evaluation and oversight determine (rightly or wrongly) that a policy or an entire agency should be terminated because it is no longer needed.	Congress terminates the Office of Technology Assessment (OTA) and its programs on grounds that other agencies and the private sector are able to assess the economic and social effects of technologies. The issue of termination is politically controversial.

On the first day, the guards at the gate asked the worker what was in the wheelbarrow. He replied "Just dirt." The guard poked into the wheelbarrow with his baton. Satisfied, he told the worker to pass through. The same procedure was repeated for the rest of the week. By the second week, the guards were growing increasingly suspicious. They made the worker empty the contents of the can on

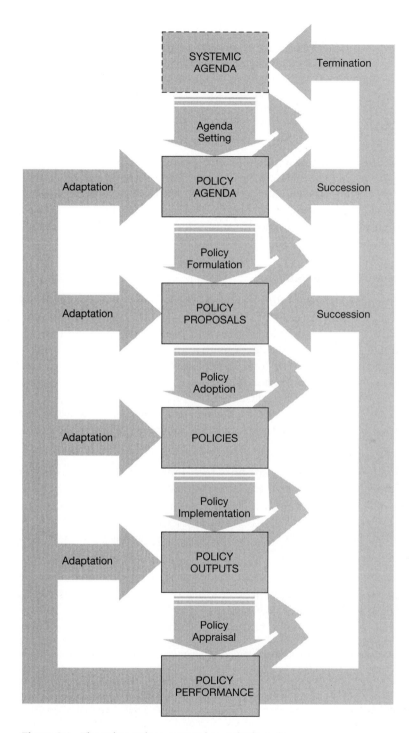

Figure 2.1 The policy-making process has multiple cycles.

the road. This time, the guards used a rake to examine the contents. Again, they found nothing but dirt. This continued for another two weeks.

In the third week, the guards called in a special investigations unit. They not only emptied the contents; they also used a special scanning device. They, too, found nothing. Subsequently, the worker was allowed to pass freely through the gate.

At the end of the month, dozens of wheelbarrows were reported missing.

Structures are just as important as their contents. Conceptual models of policy making are particular kinds of structures that help understand policy-making processes. These conceptual models are abstract representations based on metaphors such as "garbage can," "anarchy," and "primeval soup." Other metaphors are "policy observatory," "problems as infectious diseases," "policy decay," "war on poverty," and "rationality" itself.[38]

Comprehensive Rationality

The *comprehensive rationality* model portrays policy making as an exhaustive striving for efficiency. A rational economic actor is seen as *Homo economicus,* an individual or collective decision maker who weighs the costs and benefits of all available alternatives and takes actions that are motivated by a concern with the efficient use of resources. The fundamental proposition of the economic rationality model is as follows: The greater the net efficiency (perceived benefits less perceived costs) of an alternative selected from a full (comprehensive) set of potential solutions, the more likely it will be chosen as a (rational) basis for policy action and change.[39] Policy change occurs when an individual or collective decision maker:

- Identifies a policy problem on which there is sufficient consensus among relevant stakeholders that the decision maker can act on their behalf.
- Specifies and ranks consistently the goals and objectives whose attainment would constitute a resolution of the problem.
- Identifies the policy alternatives that may best contribute to the attainment of each goal and objective.
- Forecasts the consequences that will result from the selection of each alternative.
- Compares these consequences in terms of their consequences for the attainment of each goal and objective.

---

[38] Rein and Schon call them "generative metaphors" because they generate a framework for representing policy problems. See Martin Rein and Donald A. Schon, "Problem Setting in Policy Research," in *Using Social Research in Public Policymaking,* ed. Carol Weiss (Lexington, MA: D.C. Heath, 1977), pp. 240–43.

[39] Rational choice models are reviewed by Elinor Ostrom, "Institutional Rational Choice: An Assessment of the Institutional Analysis and Development Framework," in *Theories of the Policy Process,* ed. Sabatier, pp. 35–72. The classic critique of comprehensive rational choice is Charles E. Lindblom, *The Policy-Making Process* (Englewood Cliffs, NJ: Prentice Hall, 1968).

- Chooses the alternative(s) that maximizes the attainment of goals and objectives.
- Makes changes in the policy-making process by acting on the choice.

There are other versions of rational choice that involve the incorporation of institutional transaction costs into choice situations;[40] the redefinition of benefits and costs in political, social, organizational, or moral terms (e.g., *Homo politicus*);[41] and the proviso that decision makers are fallible learners with imperfect information, limited computational capabilities, and a propensity for error in institutional contexts.[42]

Second-Best Rationality

An important criticism of the rational economic model is based on and known by the name of *Arrow's impossibility theorem*. The theorem states that it is impossible for decision makers in a democratic society to meet the requirements of the economic rationality model.[43] Individual rational choices cannot be aggregated by means of majority voting procedures to create a single best choice for all parties. The impossibility of creating a collective decision that involves transitive preferences (if A is preferred to B, and B is preferred to C, then A is preferred to C) is described as the "voters paradox."

Consider a committee composed of three members: Brown, Jones, and Smith. The committee wants to decide which of three forms of energy—solar, coal, and nuclear—should be adopted to resolve the energy crisis. Brown, the leader of an energy rights organization, prefers solar to coal and coal to nuclear, reasoning that this ranking creates least risk to citizens. Because Brown's choice is transitive, it conforms to the rule: If A is preferred to B, and B is preferred to C, then A is preferred to C. Jones and Smith, who represent the coal and nuclear industries, also have transitive preferences. Jones prefers coal to nuclear, nuclear to solar, and coal to solar, reasoning that coal is most profitable, followed by nuclear and solar. In turn, Smith prefers nuclear to solar, solar to coal, and nuclear to coal, reasoning that nuclear is most profitable. Solar energy is less profitable than coal but creates fewer dangers to the environment. Smith sees coal as the least desirable of the three alternatives.

The three choices are rational and transitive from each individual's point of view. Yet, once the three members attempt through majority rule to reach a democratic decision, there is a paradox (Table 2.2). When we ask them to choose between solar and coal, we see that solar is preferred to coal by a margin of 2 to 1 (Brown

---

[40] Oliver E. Williamson, *The Economic Institutions of Capitalism* (New York: Free Press, 1985).

[41] David J. Silverman, *The Theory of Organisations* (New York: Free Press, 1972).

[42] Elinor Ostrom, *Governing the Commons: The Evolution of Institutions for Collective Action* (New York: Cambridge University Press, 1990); and Mancur Olson, *The Logic of Collective Action: Public Goods and the Theory of Groups* (Cambridge, MA: Harvard University Press, 1965).

[43] Kenneth J. Arrow, *Social Choice and Individual Values* (New York: John Wiley, 1963).

Table 2.2 The Voters' Paradox

Committee Member	Preference
Brown	A (solar) preferred to B (coal)
	B (coal) preferred to C (nuclear)
	A (solar) preferred to C (nuclear)
Jones	B (coal) preferred to C (nuclear)
	C (nuclear) preferred to A (solar)
	B (coal) preferred to A (solar)
Smith	C (nuclear) preferred to A (solar)
	A (solar) preferred to B (coal)
	C (nuclear) preferred to B (coal)
Majority	A (solar) preferred to B (coal)
	B (coal) preferred to C (nuclear)
	C (nuclear) preferred to A (solar)

and Smith versus Jones). Similarly, when we ask them to choose between coal and nuclear, we observe that coal is preferred to nuclear by a 2 to 1 margin (Brown and Jones versus Smith). However, if we now apply the transitivity rule to these *collective* preferences, we should find that if A is preferred to B (solar to coal), and B is preferred to C (coal to nuclear), then A is preferred to C (solar to nuclear). However, this is not the collective result, because two committee members (Jones and Smith) prefer C to A (nuclear to solar). Hence, individual preferences are transitive, while the collective preference is *cyclic,* which means that alternatives cannot be ranked consistently. For this reason, a rational choice is impossible.

Arrow's impossibility theorem proves by logical deduction that it is impossible to apply democratic procedures (e.g., majority rule) to reach collective decisions that are transitive. There are five "reasonable conditions" of any democratic decision procedure: (1) *nonrestriction of choices,* that is, all possible combinations of individual preferences must be taken into account; (2) *nonperversity of collective choice,* that is, collective choices must consistently reflect individual choices; (3) *independence of irrelevant alternatives,* that is, choices must be confined to a given set of alternatives that are independent of all others; (4) *citizens' sovereignty,* that is, collective choices must not be constrained by prior choices; and (5) *nondictatorship,* that is, no individual or group can determine the outcome of collective choices by imposing their preferences on others.

To avoid the dilemma of intransitive preferences, we might delegate collective choices to a few decision makers (e.g., political or technical elites) who can be expected to reach consensus and, hence, a transitive choice. Although this solves the problem of intransitive preferences, it nevertheless violates conditions of citizens' sovereignty and nondictatorship. Alternatively, we might introduce additional alternatives (e.g., wind power) in the hope that this will foster consensus. However, this violates the condition of independence of irrelevant alternatives.

In practice, political systems based on majority rule employ both procedures to reach collective choices.[44] These choices are described as *second best* decisions.

Disjointed Incrementalism

The *disjointed-incremental model* of policy change holds that policy choices seldom conform to the requirements of the economic rationality model.[45] The fundamental proposition of disjointed-incremental theory is that policy changes occur at the margin with the status quo, so that behavior at time t is marginally different from behavior at time $t + 1$. According to disjointed incrementalism, change occurs when decision makers:

- Consider only those alternatives that differ incrementally (i.e., by small amounts) from the status quo—alternatives that differ by large amounts are unlikely to result in successful policy change.
- Limit the number of consequences forecast for each alternative.
- Make mutual adjustments in goals and objectives, on one hand, and policy alternatives on the other.
- Continuously reformulate problems and alternatives in the course of acquiring new information.
- Analyze and evaluate alternatives sequentially, so that choices are continuously amended over time, rather than made at a single point prior to action.
- Continuously remedy existing problems, rather than attempt to solve problems completely at one point in time.
- Share responsibilities for analysis and evaluation with many groups in society, so that the process of making choices is fragmented or disjointed.
- Make incremental and remedial policy changes by acting on such choices.

Bounded Rationality

Another alternative to the rational economic model is *bounded rationality*. According to this model, policy makers do not attempt to be economically rational in the full, or comprehensive, sense of considering and weighing all alternatives.[46] Although choices are rational, they are bounded by the practical circumstances in

---

[44] The setting of the sequence of issues on agendas is an important example of violating conditions of citizens' sovereignty and nondictatorship. See Duncan Black, *The Theory of Committees and Elections* (Cambridge, MA: Cambridge University Press, 1958). For a review of these problems, see Norman Frohlich and Joe A. Oppenheimer, *Modem Political Economy* (Englewood Cliffs, NJ: Prentice Hall, 1978), ch. 1.

[45] Charles E. Lindblom and David Braybrooke, *A Strategy of Decision* (New York: Free Press, 1963).

[46] See Herbert A. Simon, *Administrative Behavior* (New York: Macmillan, 1945). Simon received the Nobel Prize in 1978 for his contributions to the study of decision making in economic organizations. Some of Simon's other important works are *Models of Man* (New York: Wiley, 1957) and *The Sciences of the Artificial* (New York: Wiley, 1970).

which policy makers work. The fundamental proposition of bounded rationality is that policy change occurs when policy makers use "rules of thumb" to make choices that are minimally acceptable. The originator of the bounded rationality model, multidisciplinary political scientist Herbert Simon, argues that "[i]t is impossible for the behavior of a single, isolated individual to reach *any high degree of rationality*. The number of alternatives he must explore is so great, the information he would need to evaluate them so vast that even an approximation to objective rationality is hard to conceive."[47]

This formulation recognizes the limits of comprehensive, economically rational choice when decision makers seek to maximize some valued outcome. In contrast to this type of *maximizing behavior,* Simon proposes the concept of *satisficing behavior*. Satisficing refers to acts of choice where decision makers seek to identify a course of action that is just "good enough," that is, where the combination of *satisfactory* and *suffice* produce a "satisficing" choice. In other words, decision makers do not consider all the many alternatives that, in principle, might produce the greatest possible increase in the benefits of action (i.e., maximizing behavior). Decision makers need only consider the most evident alternatives that will produce a reasonable increase in benefits (i.e., "satisfice" behavior). Bounded rationality, which is about limitations on individual rational choices, is closely related to disjointed incrementalism, which is about limitations in collective rational choices.

Satisficing behavior may be seen as an effort to maximize valued outcomes while concurrently recognizing *constraints* imposed by the costs of information. In the words of two proponents of this model of rational choice,

> It is doubtful whether any analyst of rational choice procedures would claim that a decision maker should systematically investigate and evaluate all of the alternatives available to him. Such search is both time-consuming and costly, and an optimal decision procedure should take these factors into account...the cost of decision-making should be incorporated into the maximizing model.[48]

Here, rationality is bounded by a requirement to take into account the costs and benefits of searching for and assessing new alternatives.

Mixed Scanning

Another model of change is *mixed scanning*. It is an alternative to economic rationality, disjointed incrementalism, and bounded rationality.[49] Although they accept the criticisms of the economic rationality model, Etzioni and others[50] have pointed as well

---

[47] Simon, *Administrative Behavior,* p. 79.

[48] Zeckhauser and Schaefer, "Public Policy and Normative Economic Theory," in *The Study of Policy Formation,* ed. Raymond A. Bauer (Gencoe, IL: Free Press, 1966), p. 92.

[49] See Amitai Etzioni, "Mixed-Scanning: A 'Third' Approach to Decision Making," *Public Administration Review* 27 (December 1967): 385–92.

[50] Yehezkel Dror, *Ventures in Policy Sciences* (New York: American Elsevier, 1971).

to limitations of the incremental model. Incrementalism is seen to have a conservative and status quo orientation that is difficult to reconcile with needs for creativity and innovation in policy making. In this context, incrementalism suggests (correctly) that the most powerful interests in society make many of the most important policy choices, because it is these interests that have the most to gain from policies that differ as little as possible from the status quo. Finally, incrementalism does not recognize that policy choices differ in scope, complexity, and importance. Major strategic choices, for example, are different from day-to-day operational decisions, a distinction that the incremental theory does not adequately take into account.

Mixed scanning distinguishes between the requirements of strategic choices that set basic policy directions, and operational choices that help lay the groundwork for strategic choices or contribute to their implementation. The fundamental proposition of mixed scanning is that policy change occurs when problems of choice are adapted to the nature of problems confronted by policy makers. Because what is rational in one context may not be so in another, mixed scanning selectively combines elements of comprehensive rationality and disjointed incrementalism. In Etzioni's words,

> Assume we are about to set up a worldwide weather observation system using weather satellites. The rationalistic approach [i.e., the rational-comprehensive theory] would seek an exhaustive survey of weather conditions by using cameras capable of detailed observations and by scheduling reviews of the entire sky as often as possible. This would yield an avalanche of details, costly to analyze and likely to overwhelm our action capabilities (e.g., "seeding" cloud formations that could develop into hurricanes or bring rain to arid areas). Incrementalism would focus on those areas in which similar patterns developed in the recent past and, perhaps, in a few nearby regions; it would thus ignore all formations which might deserve attention if they arose in unexpected areas.[51]

Mixed scanning, in contrast to either of the two approaches taken alone, provides for choices based both on comprehensive economic rationality and on disjointed incrementalism. The particular combination depends on the nature of the problem. The more those problems are strategic in nature, the more that the comprehensive economic rationality approach is appropriate. Conversely, the more those problems are operational in nature, the more appropriate the incremental approach. In all circumstances, some combination of the two approaches is necessary, because the problem is not to adopt one approach and reject the other, but to combine them in a prudent way.

Erotetic Rationality

A challenge to the models of policy change described earlier is *erotetic rationality*. Erotetic rationality refers to a process of questioning and answering. Erotetic rationality, although it may be unsatisfying to those who demand well-specified models in advance of analysis, lies at the core of inductive processes of many

---

[51] Etzioni, "Mixed-Scanning," p. 389.

kinds.[52] Albert has stated the major principle of erotetic rationality succinctly in his critique of the uses of benefit–cost analysis in judicial settings: "Ignorance is the sine qua non of rationality."[53] In many of the most important cases, analysts simply do not know the relationship between policies, policy outcomes, and the values in terms of which such outcomes should be assessed. Here, the frank acknowledgment of ignorance is a prerequisite of engaging in a process of questioning and answering, a process that yields rationally optimal answers to questions that "transcend accreted experience and outrun the reach of the knowledge already at our disposal."[54] Erotetic rationality is closely related to problem structuring as the central guidance system of policy analysis (Chapter 3). Erotetic rationality is at the core of recent innovations in physics, as represented by the work of Ilya Prigogine, the originator of chaos theory: "Twentieth-century physics is no longer the knowledge of certainties, it is one of interrogation. . . . And everywhere, instead of uncovering the permanence and immutability that classical science has taught us to seek out in nature, we have encountered change, instability, and evolution."[55]

Critical Convergence

Critical convergence refers to policy processes that are like a complex river delta with multiple streams converging and diverging as they cross the flood plain and meander toward the sea.[56] If we try to understand the "outcomes" of the process, by using a bucket of water to sample from the sea, we will not be able to discover the various routes by which the water reaches the sea. However, if we were able to monitor the entire process and its structure, we would find that from time to time some streams converge to form deep channels that, at least temporarily, guide the process in predictable ways.

The metaphor of the river delta and its multiple streams conveys some of the complexity of the policy-making process, but without abandoning the responsibility to identify structures that shape the process. In policy-making contexts, individuals and groups interact over time to set agendas and formulate policies. Their success, however, depends on the ability to recognize critical moments ("policy windows") when three kinds of streams—problems, policies, and politics—converge.[57]

---

[52] Nicholas Rescher, *Induction* (Pittsburgh, PA: University of Pittsburgh Press, 1980), pp. 6–7.

[53] Jeffrey M. Albert, "Some Epistemological Aspects of Cost-Benefit Analysis," *George Washington Law Review* 45, no. 5 (1977): 1030.

[54] Rescher, *Induction,* p. 6.

[55] Ilya Prigogine, "A New Model of Time, a New View of Physics," in *Models of Reality,* ed. Jacques Richardson (Mt. Airy, MD: Lomond Publications, 1984). Quoted by Rita Mae Kelly and William N. Dunn, "Some Final Thoughts," in *Advances in Policy Studies since 1950,* ed. Dunn and Kelly, p. 526.

[56] Alex Weilenman attributes the metaphor to systems theorist Stafford Beer.

[57] In contrast to Kingdon, *Agendas, Alternatives, and Public Policies* (see note 36 above), I am using "river delta" in place of "garbage can." The combination of "streams," "garbage cans," and "windows" supplies a thoroughly mixed metaphor.

The fundamental proposition of the critical convergence model is that policy change occurs at these critical moments. The recognition of these moments of convergence is part of the task of the policy analyst.

Punctuated Equilibrium

One of the difficulties of many of these models is that none satisfactorily accounts for major departures from the dominant pattern of slow, gradual change predicted by the disjointed-incremental model. The abrupt and discontinuous changes that have occurred in environmental policy under the Clean Air Act are relatively rare.[58] Recognizing that significant policy change may occur only every twenty-five years or so, Sabatier and Jenkins-Smith[59] call attention to the importance of external perturbations, or exogenous shocks, in effecting policy changes that are discontinuous and broad in scope. Such changes include relatively rapid socioeconomic changes represented by recessions, depressions, and oil crises; sudden shifts in public opinion such as those that occurred late in the Vietnam War; and the dramatic rise in nationalism and personal insecurity that occurred after the September 11, 2001, attacks on the World Trade Center and the Pentagon.

The *punctuated equilibrium model* likens the process of policy change to biological evolution.[60] Most policies are relatively stable, changing incrementally over long periods. There is a dynamic equilibrium among competing policies, much like the process of partisan mutual adjustment identified by Lindblom and Braybrooke.[61] Partisan mutual adjustment can and often does involve a competitive process among relatively autonomous bureaucracies. Bureaucratic leaders compete for recognition and resources in accordance with the institutional incentives and reward structure of their organizations ("Where you stand depends on where you sit."). Periodically, abrupt changes (punctuations) in policy occur as a consequence of new political images, which, in turn, are products of "policy earthquakes" and other external shocks. The fundamental proposition of the punctuated equilibrium model is that external shocks are a necessary but not sufficient condition of major policy change. The sufficient condition is that new political images and understandings of the political world suddenly arise in response to these shocks. However, when new political

---

[58] See Charles O. Jones, *Clean Air* (Pittsburgh, PA: University of Pittsburgh Press, 1975). Jones calls his model of discontinuous change "speculative augmentation."

[59] Paul A. Sabatier and Hank C. Jenkins-Smith, "The Advocacy Coalition Framework: An Assessment," in *Theories of the Policy Process,* ed. Sabatier, pp. 117–66. Two causally relevant conditions affecting policy change are external shocks and core values. Their "advocacy coalition framework" parallels theories of population dynamics in biology.

[60] See James L. True, Frank R. Baumgartner, and Bryan D. Jones, "Punctuated-Equilibrium Theory: Explaining Stability and Change in American Policymaking," in *Theories of the Policy Process,* ed. Sabatier, pp. 97–116; and Frank R. Baumgartner and Bryan D. Jones, *Agendas and Instability in American Politics* (Chicago: University of Chicago Press, 1993).

[61] Charles E. Lindblom and David Braybrooke, *A Strategy of Decision* (New York: Free Press, 1963).

images, beliefs, and values develop gradually, over long periods of time, the process is not "punctuated."[62]

POLICY ANALYSIS IN THE POLICY PROCESS

The main purpose of policy analysis is to improve policy making. This is no simple task when we consider that many of the most important policy changes are gradual, disjointed, and incremental. Large, discontinuous changes are relatively rare; and they stem from shocks that are exogenous to the policy-making process, not from the relatively marginal influence of analyses conducted within the process. Nevertheless, multidisciplinary policy analysis is important because of the potential uses of policy-relevant information to improve policy making (see Figure 2.2).

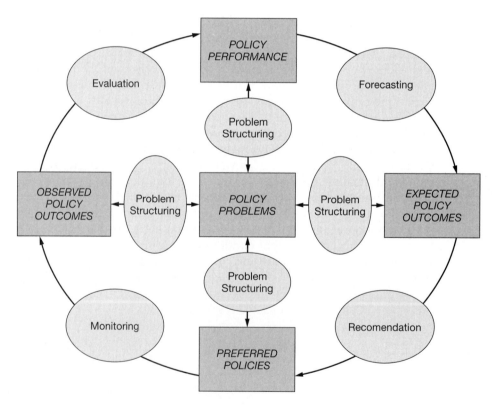

Figure 2.2 The process of policy analysis.

---

[62] See Sabatier and Jenkins-Smith, "The Advocacy Coalition Framework."

Potential Uses of Analysis

Among policy analysts, it is an unspoken article of faith that good analysis potentially yields better policies. The reasons for this potential are evident in the purposes of policy-analytic methods.

Problem Structuring. Problem structuring methods supply policy-relevant information that can be used to challenge the assumptions underlying the definition of problems at the *agenda-setting* phase of policy making (see Table 2.1). Problem structuring assists in discovering hidden assumptions, diagnosing causes, mapping possible objectives, synthesizing conflicting views, and visualizing, discovering, and designing new policy options. For example, the problem of race and sex bias in the some 20 million standardized tests administered annually in the United States was placed on the legislative agendas of several states throughout the late 1980s. In Pennsylvania, analysts challenged the assumption that test bias is a problem requiring legislative action—for example, the outright prohibition of standardized tests—after synthesizing and evaluating research on test bias recommended by different stakeholders. The large observed discrepancies in minority and white achievement test scores were not viewed as a problem of test bias, but as an indicator, or gauge, of inequality of educational opportunity. Analysts recommended the continued use of standardized tests to monitor and mitigate these inequalities.[63]

Forecasting. Methods for forecasting expected policy outcomes provide policy-relevant information about consequences that are likely to follow the adoption of preferred policies (including doing nothing) at the phase of *policy formulation*. Forecasting helps examine plausible, potential, and normatively valued futures; estimate the consequences of existing and proposed policies; specify probable future constraints on the achievement of objectives; and estimate the political feasibility (support and opposition) of different options. Analysts in the Health Care Finance Administration, for example, employ forecasting methods to estimate the effects of revenue shortfalls on the Medicare trust fund, which could be exhausted in the next decade. In the absence of new health care policy initiatives, future benefits under Medicare might be reduced by $40–50 billion, creating a program reduction of 50 percent. In the meantime, the some 40 million persons who have no health insurance are likely to increase in number.[64]

Recommendation. Methods for selecting preferred policy alternatives yield policy-relevant information about the benefits and costs—and more generally the value or utility—of expected policy outcomes estimated through forecasting, thus aiding policy makers in the *policy adoption* phase. Through the process of recommending

---

[63] William N. Dunn and Gary Roberts, *The Role of Standardized Tests in Minority-Oriented Curricular Reform,* policy paper prepared for the Legislative Office for Research Liaison, Pennsylvania House of Representatives, February 1987.

[64] Sally T. Sonnefeld, Daniel R. Waldo, Jeffrey A. Lemieux, and David R. McKusick, "Projections of National Health Expenditures through the Year 2000." *Health Care Financing Review* 13, no. 1 (fall 1991): 1–27.

preferred policies, analysts may estimate levels of risk and uncertainty, identify externalities and spillovers, specify criteria for making choices, and assign administrative responsibility for implementing policies. For example, the debate over maximum speed limits in the United States has focused on the costs per fatality averted under the 55 and 65 mph options. In the 1980s, one recommendation, based on the conclusion that the 55 mph speed limit will continue to account for no more than 2–3 percent of fatalities averted, was to shift expenditures for maintaining the speed limit to the purchase of smoke detectors, which would save many more lives.[65] By 1987, some forty states were experimenting with higher speed limits. In 1995, the 55 mph speed limit was abandoned altogether.

Monitoring. Methods for monitoring observed policy outcomes provide information about the consequences of adopting policies, thus assisting in the *policy implementation* phase. Many agencies regularly monitor policy outcomes and impacts by employing policy indicators in areas of health, education, housing, welfare, crime, and science and technology.[66] Monitoring helps assess degrees of compliance, discover unintended consequences of policies and programs, identify implementation obstacles and constraints, and locate sources of responsibility for departures from policies. For example, economic and social welfare policies in the United States are monitored by analysts in several agencies, including the Bureau of the Census and the Bureau of Labor Statistics. A 1991 analysis concluded that real median household income in the United States grew by merely 2 percent between 1969 and 1989. In the same period, the share of national income by the top fifth of households grew from 43 to 46.7 percent, with all other income groups experiencing a decline. In this case, policy monitoring revealed a marked increase in income inequality, an erosion of the middle class, and a decline in the standard of living between 1969 and 1989.[67] The situation in the period 1989–2000 has been marked by greater income inequality.

Evaluation. Methods for evaluating observed policy outcomes yield policy-relevant information about discrepancies between expected and actual policy performance, thus assisting in the *policy assessment, policy adaptation, policy succession,* and *policy termination* phases. Evaluation not only results in conclusions about the extent to which problems have been alleviated, but it also may contribute to the clarification and critique of values driving a policy, aid in the adjustment or reformulation of policies, and establish a basis for restructuring problems. A good example of evaluation is

---

[65] See, for example, Charles A. Lave and Lester B. Lave, "Barriers to Increasing Highway Safety," in *Challenging the Old Order: Towards New Directions in Traffic Safety Theory,* ed. J. Peter Rothe (New Brunswick, NJ: Transaction Books, 1990), pp. 77–94.

[66] A thorough and insightful source on the use of policy indicators is Duncan MacRae Jr., *Policy Indicators: Links between Social Science and Public Debate* (Chapel Hill: University of North Carolina Press, 1985).

[67] Gordon Green, Paul Ryscavage, and Edward Welniak, "Factors Affecting Growing Income Inequality: A Decomposition," paper presented at the 66th Annual Conference of the Western Economic Association International, Seattle, Washington, July 2, 1991.

the type of analysis that contributes to the clarification, critique, and debate of values by proposing that ethical and moral reasoning augment the now dominant mode of technical reasoning driving environmental policies in the European Community and other parts of the world.[68]

Uses of Analysis in Practice

In principle, policy analysis has the potential for creating better policies. In practice, however, policy analysis and other fields within the social (and natural) sciences have some or all of the following limitations.[69]

- *Use is indirect, delayed, and general.* Policy analysis is seldom used directly and immediately as a basis for improving specific decisions involving the allocation of human and material resources. The use of analysis is typically indirect and general, and single analyses are rarely important unless they are part of a larger body of information on an issue. The indirect and general character of use is understandable when we recognize that policy making is a complex process composed of numerous cycles, ranging from termination and succession to adaptation and short-circuiting.

- *Improvement is ethically controversial.* When policy analysis is used, the question of what constitutes an improvement depends on the political, ideological, or ethical stance of observers. Those who believe that the public interest is served by assisting those who are worst off by taxing those who are best off view "improvements" differently from those who believe that the public interest is served when individuals solve their problems without government intervention. Although the goal of "efficiency improvement" is sometimes seen as something everyone supports, it too is an ideological or ethical matter, because it involves the selection of some values and norms over others.

- *Being useful reflects personal, professional, and institutional interests.* As social scientists and as persons, policy analysts seek to enhance their personal status and professional rewards and those of their institutions or agencies. Opportunities for involvement with persons of political power, privilege, or economic standing—as their advisers, consultants, expert witnesses, or staff—are part of the motivation for being an analyst.

A good deal of the difficulty surrounding questions of the practical uses of policy analysis stems from a failure to recognize that the process of using policy

---

[68] See, for example, Silvio O. Funtowicz and Jerome R. Ravetz, "Global Environmental Issues and the Emergence of Second Order Science" (Luxembourg: Commission of the European Communities, Directorate-General for Telecommunications, Information Industries, and Innovation, 1990). See also Funtowicz and Ravetz, "A New Scientific Methodology for Global Environmental Issues," in *Ecological Economics,* ed. Robert Costanza (New York: Columbia University Press, 1991), pp. 137–52.

[69] The following discussion draws on Carol H. Weiss, "Introduction," in *Using Social Research in Public Policymaking,* ed. Weiss, pp. 1–22; and Carol H. Weiss with Michael J. Bucuvalas, *Social Science Research and Decision Making* (New York: Columbia University Press, 1980).

analysis in policy making is just as complex as policy making itself. Consider this description of making a decision by Chester Barnard, a successful CEO and major contributor to the field of administration. Writing about an order, or policy, to move a telephone pole from one side of the street to the other, Barnard continues,

> It can, I think, be approximately demonstrated that carrying out that order involves perhaps 10,000 decisions of 100 men located at 15 points, requiring successive analyses of several environments, including social, moral, legal, economic, and physical facts of the environment, and requiring 9,000 redefinitions and refinements of purpose. If inquiry be made of those responsible, probably not more than half-a-dozen decisions will be recalled or deemed worthy of mention.... The others will be "taken for granted," all of a part of the business of knowing one's business.[70]

Clearly, then, the use of policy analysis is a complex process with several dimensions:[71]

- *Composition of users.* Individuals as well as collectives—for example, agencies, ministries, bureaus, courts, legislatures, parliaments—use policy analysis. When the use of analysis involves gains (or losses) in the personal utility of information, the process of use is an aspect of individual decisions (individual use). By contrast, when the process of use involves many individuals, it is an aspect of collective decisions, or policies (collective use).

- *Expected effects of use.* The use of policy analysis has cognitive as well as behavioral effects. Cognitive effects include the use of policy analysis to think about problems and solutions (conceptual use) and to legitimize preferred formulations of problems and solutions (symbolic use). By contrast, behavioral effects involve the use of policy analysis as a means or instrument for carrying out observable activities or functions (instrumental use). Conceptual and behavioral uses of information occur among individual and collective users.[72]

---

[70] Chester I. Barnard, *The Functions of the Executive* (Cambridge, MA: Harvard University Press, 1938, 1962), p. 198. Quoted by Carol Weiss, "Knowledge Creep and Decision Accretion," *Knowledge: Creation, Diffusion, Utilization* 1, no. 3 (March 1980): 403.

[71] William N. Dunn, "Measuring Knowledge Use," *Knowledge: Creation, Diffusion, Utilization* 5, no. 1 (1983): 120–33. See also Carol H. Weiss and Michael I. Bucuvalas, "Truth Tests and Utility Tests: Decision Makers' Frames of Reference for Social Science Research," *American Sociological Review* 45 (1980): 302–13; and Jack Knott and Aaron Wildavsky, "If Dissemination Is the Solution, What Is the Problem?" in *The Knowledge Cycle,* ed. Robert F. Rich (Beverly Hills, CA: Sage Publications, 1981), pp. 99–136.

[72] On distinctions between conceptual, instrumental, and symbolic use, see Carol H. Weiss, "Research for Policy's Sake: The Enlightenment Function of Social Science Research," *Policy Analysis* 3 (1977): 200–24; Weiss, "The Circuitry of Enlightenment," *Knowledge: Creation, Diffusion, Utilization* 8, no. 2 (1986): 274–81; Nathan Caplan, Andrea Morrison, and Roger Stambaugh, *The Use of Social Science Knowledge in Policy Decisions at the National Level* (Ann Arbor, MI: Institute for Social Research, Center for the Utilization of Scientific Knowledge, 1975); Robert F. Rich, "Uses of Social Science Knowledge by Federal Bureaucrats: Knowledge for Action versus Knowledge for Understanding," in *Using Social Research in Public Policy Making,* ed. Weiss, pp. 199–211; and Karin D. Knorr, "Policymakers' Use of Social Science Knowledge: Symbolic or Instrumental?" in *Using Social Research in Public Policy Making,* ed. Carol H. Weiss, pp. 165–82.

- *Scope of information used.* The scope of information used by policy makers ranges from the specific to the general. The use of "ideas in good currency" is general in scope (general use), while the use of a particular recommendation is specific (specific use).[73] Information that varies in scope is used by individuals and collectives, with effects that are conceptual and behavioral.

In practice, these three dimensions of information use overlap. As we shall see in Chapter 9, the intersection among them provides a basis for assessing and improving the uses of policy analysis.

CHAPTER SUMMARY

This chapter has presented an overview of the functions of policy analysis in policy making. Historically, the aim of policy analysis has been to provide policy makers with information that can be used to solve practical problems. Policy analysis is an intellectual activity embedded in a social process known as policy making, or the policy-making process. Although policy making can be seen as a set of phases ordered in time, the organization of these phases often resembles a garbage can or organized anarchy. Numerous models are available to describe how and why policy change occurs. All of them capture an important feature of the complex process of policy making. The role of policy analysis in policy making has two aspects. On one hand, methods of analysis are designed to produce policy-relevant information that is potentially useful in all phases of policy making. On the other, the uses of policy analysis in practice are indirect, delayed, general, and ethically controversial. This is to be expected, considering that there are many patterns of information use based on the intersection of its composition, scope, and expected effects.

LEARNING OBJECTIVES

- understand policy analysis as an intellectual activity embedded in a social process
- explain the historical development of policy analysis as a response to practical problems and crises
- contrast policy analysis, as defined in this book, with evidence-based policy making
- describe policy making as a complex, cyclic process of agenda setting, policy formulation, policy adoption, policy implementation, policy evaluation, policy adaptation, policy succession, policy termination
- compare, contrast, and assess different models of policy change
- contrast potential and actual uses of policy analysis
- distinguish the composition, scope, and expected effects of information use
- analyze a case study on the use of policy research and analysis by policy makers

---

[73] The concept of "ideas in good currency" is discussed by Donald A. Schon, "Generative Metaphor: A Perspective on Problem Setting in Social Policy," in *Metaphors and Thought,* ed. A. Ortony (Cambridge: Cambridge University Press, 1979), pp. 254–83.

KEY TERMS AND CONCEPTS

Analycentric perspective (42)
Arrow's Impossibility Theorem (49)
Bounded rationality (51)
Comprehensive rationality (48)
Critical convergence (54)
Disjointed incrementalism (51)
Erotetic rationality (53)
Evidence-based policy making (44)
Mixed scanning (52)

Policy-making process (44)
Postindustrial society (66)
Punctuated equilibrium (55)
Regulatory impact assessment (RIA) (44)
Second-best rationality (49)
Technocratic counsel (68)
Technocratic guidance (67)
Voter's Paradox (49)

REVIEW QUESTIONS

1. What does it mean to say that policy analysis is a process of producing knowledge *of* and *in* the policy-making process?
2. What is the relation between the problems faced by societies and the growth of what has been called an "analycentric" perspective?
3. Compare and contrast intellectual and social aspects of policy making. Give examples.
4. What is an "organized anarchy"? How is it related to the "garbage can" model of policy making?
5. In your experience, which model(s) of policy change are most useful? Why?
6. Considering the three dimensions of information use, how would you know when policy makers have used policy analysis? What would you do about it?
7. What are the pros and cons of evidence-based policy making? Consider concepts of "technocratic guidance" and "technocratic counsel" presented in the case study for this chapter.

DEMONSTRATION EXERCISES

After reading Case 2 (Are Policy Analysts Technocrats?), evaluate the following conclusions about "technocratic counsel" and "technocratic guidance" in policy making:
Evaluate the following statements.

- The technocratic guidance perspective presents an exaggerated assessment of the power and influence of professional policy analysts.
- The technocratic counsel perspective overestimates the symbolic importance of policy analysts in legitimizing policies made on political grounds.
- The remedy for "technocratic policy analysis" is not to abandon policy analysis, but to create new and better approaches and procedures. One approach is "democratic expertise," which proposes that analysts counteract technocratic biases "by moving from phony neutrality to thoughtful partisanship, working disproportionately to

assist have-nots in understanding and making their case. . . assisting all partisans in coping with uncertainties."[74]

After reading Case 2 (Are Policy Analysts Technocrats?), consider the following questions, which have been helpful to others in learning about the uses of research in policy making.[75]

1. Obtain a research report on a policy issue that is useful to you in your work. The report could be unpublished, posted on a Web site, or published in a professional journal, newsletter, magazine, or newspaper.

   Please use the following scale for responses to questions about the report:
   - 1 = very much
   - 2 = quite a bit
   - 3 = to some extent
   - 4 = not much
   - 5 = not at all

2. To what extent does the research contain information that is relevant to your work?

3. To what extent do you think the research is reliable (could be repeated) and valid (describes or explains what it set out to do)?

4. To what extent do the conclusions agree with your own views about the issue?

5. Please indicate the extent to which the research:
   a. deals with a high priority issue (AO)
   b. adds to theoretical knowledge in the field (TQ)
   c. adds to practical knowledge about policies or programs (AO)
   d. agrees with your ideas or values (CUE)
   e. identifies outcomes that policy makers can do something about (AO)
   f. suggests potential courses of action (AO)
   g. implies the need for major policy changes (CSQ)
   h. focuses on specific policy outcomes (AO)
   i. contains explicit recommendations for action (AO)
   j. supports your own position on the issue (CUE)
   k. provides evidence to back up recommendations (TQ)
   l. contains politically feasible implications (AO)
   m. agrees with previous knowledge about the issue (TQ)
   n. can be implemented under the present circumstances (AO)
   o. challenges existing assumptions and institutional arrangements (CSQ)
   p. raises new issues or perspectives (CSQ)
   q. is inexpensive to implement (AO)
   r. was available at the time a decision had to be made (AO)

---

[74] Edward J. Woodhouse and Dean A. Nieusma, "Democratic Expertise: Integrating Knowledge, Power, and Participation," in *Knowledge, Power, and Participation in Environmental Policy Analysis,* vol. 12, *Policy Studies Review Annual,* ed. Matthijs Hisschemoller, Rob Hoppe, William N. Dunn, and Jerry R. Ravetz (New Brunswick, NJ: Transaction Books, 2001), p. 91.

[75] These questions are drawn from Carol H. Weiss and Michael J. Bucuvalas, "The Challenge of Social Research to Decision Making," in *Using Social Research in Public Policy Making,* ed. Carol. H. Weiss (Lexington, MA: D. C. Heath, 1977), Appendix 15A and 15B, pp. 231–33. I have made slight modifications of several questions. Thanks to Carol Weiss for suggesting modifications in questions.

    s. contains novel or unexpected findings (CUE—negative coding)
    t. provides quantitative data (TQ)
    u. can be generalized to similar settings or persons (TQ)
    v. addresses in a thorough manner different factors that could explain outcomes (TQ)
    w. uses statistically sophisticated analyses (TQ)
    x. demonstrates high technical competence (TQ)
    y. presents internally consistent and unambiguous findings (TQ)
    z. takes an objective and unbiased approach (TQ)

6. Using the following categories, sum up the scaled responses (scale = numbers 1 through 5), and then average them (divide by the number of questions answered). The capital letters after each question (e.g., TQ) refer to the categories.

> *Technical Quality (TQ):*
> *Conformity to User Expectations (CUE):*
> *Action Orientation (AO):*
> *Challenge Status Quo (CSQ):*

7. Write an analysis that answers the following questions:
   - To what extent is the report of high *technical quality?*
   - To what extent does the report *conform to what you expected?*
   - To what extent is the report *actionable,* that is, has an action orientation?
   - What category is *highest? Second* highest? *Third? Last?*
   - To what extent is the report a *challenge to the status quo?*
   - Which categories are *closest together* in their rankings, that is, which tend to go together? Which are *further apart?* Why?
   - What does your analysis suggest about the reasons why research is perceived as *useful?*
   - What does your analysis suggest about the *validity of the two rival perspectives* described in the following case for this chapter (Case 2. Are Policy Analysts Technocrats?).

REFERENCES

Barber, Bernard. *Effective Social Science: Eight Cases in Economics, Political Science, and Sociology.* New York: Russell Sage Foundation, 1987.

Council for Evidence Based Policy. 1301 K Street, NW, Suite 450 West, Washington, DC 20005. www.excel-gov. org/evidence; www.evidence-basedprograms.org/

De Leon, Peter. *Advice and Consent: The Development of the Policy Sciences.* New York: Russell Sage Foundation, 1988.

Fischer, Frank. *Technocracy and the Politics of Expertise.* Newbury Park, CA: Sage Publications, 1990.

Freidson, Elliot. *Professional Powers: A Study of the Institutionalization of Formal Knowledge.* Chicago: University of Chicago Press, 1986.

Horowitz, Irving L., ed. *The Use and Abuse of Social Science: Behavioral Science and Policy Making.* 2d ed. New Brunswick, NJ: Transaction Books, 1985.

Jasanoff, Sheila. *The Fifth Branch: Science Advisors as Policymakers.* Cambridge, MA: Harvard University Press, 1990.

Kingdon, John W. *Agendas, Alternatives, and Public Policies.* Glenview, IL: Scott, Foresman, 1984.

Lerner, Daniel, ed. *The Human Meaning of the Social Sciences*. Cleveland, OH: World Publishing Company, 1959.

Lindblom, Charles E. *Inquiry and Change: The Troubled Attempt to Understand and Change Society*. New Haven, CT: Yale University Press, 1990.

Lindblom, Charles E., and David K. Cohen. *Usable Knowledge: Social Science and Social Problem Solving*. New Haven, CT: Yale University Press, 1979.

Lindblom, Charles E., and Edward J. Woodhouse. *The Policy-Making Process*. 3d ed. Englewood Cliffs, NJ: Prentice-Hall, 1993.

Machlup, Fritz. *Knowledge: Its Creation, Distribution, and Economic Significance*. Vol. 1 of *Knowledge and Knowledge Production*. Princeton, NJ: Princeton University Press, 1980.

Macrae, Duncan Jr. *The Social Function of Social Science*. New Haven, CT: Yale University Press, 1976.

Parsons, Wayne. "From Muddling Through to Muddling Up: Evidence Based Policy-Making and the Modernisation of British Government." Unpublished paper. London: University of London, 2004.

—— *Public Policy: An Introduction to the Theory and Practice of Policy Analysis*. Edward Elgar Publishing Inc, Northampton MA, 1995.

Ravetz, Jerome. *Science and Its Social Problems*. Oxford: Oxford University Press, 1971.

Sabatier, Paul A. *Theories of the Policy Process*. Boulder, CO: Westview Press, 1999.

Schmandt, Jurgen, and James E. Katz. "The Scientific State: A Theory with Hypotheses." *Science, Technology, and Human Values* 11 (1986): 40–50.

United Kingdom, House of Commons, Science and Technology Committee. *Scientific Advice, Risk and Evidence Based Policy Making*. Seventh Report of Session 2005–06, Volume I. London: HMO Printing House, 2006.

Weiss, Carol H. *Social Science Research and Decision Making*. New York: Columbia University Press, 1980.

Case 2. Are Policy Analysts Technocrats?

In the first half of the twentieth century, the involvement of social and natural scientists in policy making was largely a response to social, economic, and politico-military crises.[76] Members of the sciences and professions were ad hoc and irregular participants in government in the period of depression, dislocation, and war that stretched from the early 1930s to the late 1940s. In succeeding years, however, the social sciences and social professions—political science, sociology, economics, public administration, business management, social work, planning—became one of the main sources of full-time governmental staff, advisers, and consultants. For the first time, public agencies recruited on a regular basis specialists who had received their training and had been certified by their respective professional organizations.

---

[76] Rowland Egger, "The Period of Crises: 1933 to 1945," in *American Public Administration: Past, Present, and Future,* ed. Frederick C. Mosher (University: University of Alabama Press, 1975), pp. 49–96.

For many observers, this new era signified the advent of a new form of social and political organization in which public policy making and societal guidance were critically dependent on specialized knowledge and technologies of the sciences and professions. Emphasizing its social aspect, some referred to this new form of organization as the "knowledge society"[77] or "postindustrial society."[78] Others, focusing on its political aspect, spoke of the transition from the "administrative state" to the "scientific state."[79]

Postindustrial Society and the Scientific State

Postindustrial society, an extension of patterns of policy making and socioeconomic organization of industrial society, is increasingly dominated by an educated professional-technical class. Many of the characteristics of a postindustrial society are important to consider when we ponder the historical evolution and significance of policy analysis:[80]

- *Centrality of theoretical knowledge.* Although the earliest civilizations relied on specialized information, only in the late twentieth and twenty-first centuries are innovations in "soft" (social) and "hard" (physical) technologies directly dependent on the codification of theoretical knowledge provided by the social, physical, and biological sciences.

- *Creation of new intellectual technologies.* The improvement in mathematical and statistical techniques has made it possible to use advanced modeling, simulation, and various forms of systems analysis to find more efficient and "rational" solutions to public problems.

- *Spread of a knowledge class.* The most rapidly expanding occupational group in the United States is composed of technicians and professionals. This group, including professional managers, represented 28 percent of employed persons in 1975, 28.3 percent in 1995, and 30.3 percent in 2000. Persons in nonfarm occupations grew from 62.5 to 98.4 percent between 1900 and 1990.

- *Shift from goods to services.* In 1975, more than 65 percent of the active labor force was engaged in the production and delivery of services, a figure that exceeded 80 percent by 2000. Services are primarily human (e.g., health, education, social welfare) and professional-technical (e.g., information services, computer programming, telecommunications).

---

[77] Fritz Machlup, *The Production and Distribution of Knowledge in the United States* (Princeton, NJ: Princeton University Press, 1962).

[78] Daniel Bell, *The Coming of Post-industrial Society: A Venture in Social Forecasting* (New York: Basic Books, 1976).

[79] Jurgen Schmandt and James E. Katz, "The Scientific State: A Theory with Hypotheses," *Science, Technology, and Human Values* 11 (1986): 40–50.

[80] Bell, *Coming of Post-Industrial Society*, pp. xvi–xviii.

- *Instrumentalization of sciences.* Although the natural and social sciences have long been used as instruments for controlling the human and material environment, they have been largely open to internal criticism and protected by norms of scientific inquiry. In the present period, science and technology have become increasingly bureaucratized, subordinated to government goals, and assessed in terms of their payoffs to society. More than 95 percent of all funded research is applied research on practical problems of business, commerce, and government.

- *Scarcity of scientific and technical information.* Information has increasingly become one of society's most scarce resources. Information is a collective, not a private good, and cooperative rather than competitive strategies for its production and use are required if optimal results are to be achieved. The rapid exponential growth of the Internet and World Wide Web are vehicles for satisfying the demand for information by governments, businesses, and non-profit organizations.

The development of policy analysis and other applied sciences seems to be part of an emerging postindustrial society and scientific state. Yet, what does this development signify for issues of democratic governance, civil liberties, and privacy? How much influence do producers of policy-relevant information have? Although theoretical knowledge clearly seems to be more central than it has been in other historical periods, what does this mean for the distribution of political power? Does the proliferation of new intellectual technologies mean also that structures and processes of policy making have changed? Is the spread of a "knowledge class" commensurate with its power and influence? Considering that the aim of policy analysis and other applied sciences is to produce information for practical purposes, whose purposes are being served? In short, how are we to interpret the historical transformation of policy-oriented inquiry from earlier times to the present-day "knowledge society" and "scientific state"?

Technocratic Guidance versus Technocratic Counsel

There are several contending perspectives of these questions, two of which we consider here.[81] One perspective holds that the professionalization of policy analysis and other applied social sciences is—or should be—shifting power and responsibility from policy makers to policy analysts.[82] This perspective, *technocratic guidance,* is associated with the "analycentric turn" described earlier

---

[81] See Jeffrey D. Straussman, "Technocratic Counsel and Societal Guidance," in *Politics and the Future of Industrial Society,* ed. Leon N. Lindberg (New York: David McKay, 1976), pp. 126–66.

[82] For example, Amitai Etzioni, *The Active Society* (New York: Free Press, 1968); and Donald T. Campbell, "The Experimenting Society," in *The Experimenting Society: Essays in Honor of Donald T. Campbell,* ed. William N. Dunn (New Brunswick, NJ: Transaction Books, 1998), pp. 35–68.

in this chapter. The basic premise of the analycentric turn is that "the surest way to improve the quality of public choice is to have more analysts producing more analyses."[83] By contrast, a contending perspective, *technocratic counsel,* holds that the professionalization of policy analysis and other applied social sciences signifies new and more effective ways to enhance the influence of policy makers and other dominant groups whose positions continue to rest on power, wealth, and privilege.[84]

Strictly speaking, neither of these perspectives is wholly accurate in its interpretation of events surrounding the movement toward postindustrial society; each contains a one-sided emphasis on particular characteristics of contemporary society to the exclusion of others. Yet just as the development of nineteenth-century policy analysis was a practical response to problems of the day as viewed by dominant groups, so too is contemporary policy analysis a consequence of changes in the structure and role of government as it has attempted to grapple with new problems. "The contemporary boom in policy analysis," writes Schick, "has its primary source in the huge growth of American governments, not in the intellectual development of the social sciences."[85] Throughout the twentieth century, the expansion of government was followed by demands for more policy-relevant information. As government has grown, so too has the market for policy analysis.[86]

The development of policy analysis in this century has followed fits and starts in the growth of federal executive agencies.[87] In 1900, there were some ninety federal executive agencies. By 1940, this figure had grown to 196, and, by 1973, the total number of federal executive agencies had jumped to 394. The greatest percentage increase occurred after 1960. Some 35 percent were created after 1960. The rapid growth of the federal government was mainly a response to new problems in areas of national defense, transportation, housing, health, education, welfare, crime, energy, and the environment. There were many new "challenges" to policy making:[88] participation overload, mobilization of service sector workers, transformation of basic social values, realignment of interest groups, growing cleavages between urban and suburban citizens, and recurrent fiscal crises. Some observers, notably policy scientist Yehezkel Dror, went so far as to formulate the relationship between such problems and policy analysis in the form of a general

---

[83] Allen Schick, "Beyond Analysis," *Public Administration Review* 37, no. 3 (1977): 259.

[84] See, for example, Guy Benveniste, *The Politics of Expertise* (Berkeley, CA: Glendessary Press, 1972); and Frank Fischer, *Technocracy and the Politics of Expertise* (Newbury Park, CA: Sage Publications, 1990).

[85] Schick, "Beyond Analysis," p. 258.

[86] Schmandt and Katz, "Scientific State."

[87] Herbert Kaufman, *Are Government Organizations Immortal?* (Washington, DC: Brookings Institution, 1976), pp. 34–63.

[88] Samuel P. Huntington, "Postindustrial Politics; How Benign Will It Be?" *Comparative Politics* 6 (January 1974): 163–92; Ronald Inglehart, "The Silent Revolution in Europe: Intergenerational Change in Postindustrial Societies," *American Political Science Review,* 65 (December 1971): 991–1017; and James O'Connor, *The Fiscal Crisis of the State* (New York: St. Martin's Press, 1973).

law: "While the difficulties and dangers of problems tend to increase at a geometric rate, the number of persons qualified to deal with these problems tends to increase at an arithmetic rate."[89] Thus, the growth of policy analysis seems to be a consequence, not a cause, of changes in the structure of government and the nature and scope of social problems.

The *technocratic guidance* perspective asserts that policy-relevant knowledge is an increasingly scarce resource whose possession enhances the power and influence of policy analysts. The technocratic guidance perspective may be summarized in terms of five major propositions:[90]

- The growing interdependencies, complexity, and pace of change of contemporary society make existing knowledge obsolete, thus increasing the demand for new forms of policy-relevant knowledge.
- Problems of contemporary society may be resolved with specialized knowledge produced by policy analysts.
- The technical complexity of policy choices prompts higher levels of direct involvement of policy analysts and other applied scientists.
- Higher levels of direct involvement enhance the power of professional analysts to influence policy making, making politicians increasingly dependent on them.
- The growing dependence of politicians on professional policy analysts erodes their political power.

A rival perspective, that of *technocratic counsel,* begins from the assumption that professional policy analysts operate in settings in which policy makers, as the consumers of specialized knowledge, determine to a large extent the activities of producers. In this context, the primary role of analysts is to legitimize—that is, justify in scientific and technical terms—policy decisions made by the real holders of power. The technocratic counsel perspective may also be summarized in terms of several key propositions.[91]

- Major policy alternatives reflect conflicting values held by different segments of the community.
- Value conflicts are associated with disparities of political power.
- The choice of a given policy alternative symbolizes the victory of one segment of the community over another.
- Policy makers use scientific and technical justifications produced by analysts to suppress conflicts and legitimize choices that are actually made on political grounds.

---

[89] Yehezkel Dror, *Ventures in Policy Sciences: Concepts and Applications* (New York: American Elsevier, 1971), p. 2.

[90] Straussman, "Technocratic Counsel," pp. 150–51.

[91] Ibid., pp. 151–52.

- The credibility of scientific and technical justifications requires that policy analysis and other applied sciences be presented as value neutral, impartial, and apolitical.
- Professional analysts, although they are a source of scientific and technical justifications, are expendable. They also serve as convenient scapegoats for policies that fail.

An Assessment

If we pick our cases carefully, we can show that analysts exercised a large measure of "technocratic guidance." For example, the New York City–Rand Corporation's analysis of factors influencing the response time of city firefighters to reported fires has been credited with unusual success, even though other Rand efforts have been less effective in shaping decisions.[92] On the other hand, the use of specialized knowledge to make policy choices appears to be highly uneven. For example, in a study of 204 federal executives conducted in 1973–74, social science research was relatively unimportant as a basis for choosing among policy alternatives.[93] Moreover, the extent to which research was used depended on essentially nontechnical factors: "the level of knowledge utilization is not so much the result of a slow flow of relevant and valid information from knowledge producers to policy makers, but is due more to factors involving values, ideology, and decision-making styles."[94]

The finding that policy analysis is used for political purposes adds a measure of credibility to the technocratic counsel perspective. So does the apparent conservative character of many analyses. In this context, policy analysis has been characterized as a conservative and superficial kind of social science that fails to pose radical questions about basic social values and institutions, and neglects policy alternatives that depart significantly from existing practices.[95] Moreover, some observers see in policy analysis an ideology in disguise that suppresses ethical and value questions in the name of science.[96] Under such conditions, it is understandable that professional policy analysts might be used as instruments of everyday politics.

---

[92] On this and other cases, see Greenberger, Crenson, and Crissey, *Models in the Policy Process,* pp. 231–318.

[93] Nathan Caplan et al., *The Use of Social Science Knowledge in Policy Decisions at the National Level* (Ann Arbor, MI: Institute for Social Research, Center for Research on the Utilization of Scientific Knowledge, 1975).

[94] Nathan Caplan, "Factors Associated with Knowledge Use among Federal Executives," *Policy Studies Journal* 4, no. 3 (1976): 233. See also Robert F. Rich, *Social Science Information and Public Policy Making* (San Francisco, CA: Jossey-Bass, 1981); and David J. Webber, "The Production and Use of Knowledge in the Policy Process," in *Advances in Policy Studies since 1950,* ed. Dunn and Kelly, pp. 415–41.

[95] Charles E. Lindblom, "Integration of Economics and the Other Social Sciences through Policy Analysis," in *Integration of the Social Sciences through Policy Analysis,* ed. James C. Charlesworth (Philadelphia: American Academy of Political and Social Sciences, 1972), p. 1. For an elaboration of this critique, see Charles E. Lindblom, *Inquiry and Change: The Troubled Attempt to Understand and Change Society* (New Haven, CN: Yale University Press, 1990).

[96] Laurence H. Tribe, "Policy Science: Analysis or Ideology?" *Philosophy and Public Affairs* 2, no. 1 (1972): 66–110.

3

Structuring Policy Problems

Many people believe that policy problems are purely objective conditions that may be known by determining the "facts" in a given case. This naive view of policy problems fails to recognize that the same facts—for example, statistics that show that crime, poverty, and global warming are on the upswing—may be interpreted in different ways by different policy stakeholders. Hence, the same policy-relevant information can and often does result in conflicting definitions of a "problem." This is not so much because the facts are different but because policy stakeholders have competing interpretations of the same facts, interpretations that are shaped by diverse assumptions about human nature, the role of government, and the nature of knowledge itself. Policy problems are partly in the eye of the beholder.

This chapter provides an overview of the nature of policy problems and examines the process of problem structuring in policy analysis. After comparing and contrasting different types of policy models, all of which are products of problem structuring, we consider methods for structuring policy problems. The chapter shows that problem structuring is embedded in a political process where "the definition of alternatives is the supreme instrument of power."[1]

NATURE OF POLICY PROBLEMS

Policy problems are unrealized needs, values, or opportunities for improvement.[2] As we saw in Chapter 2, information about the nature, scope, and severity of a problem is produced by applying the policy-analytic procedure of problem structuring. Problem structuring, which is a phase of policy inquiry in which analysts search among competing problem formulations of different stakeholders, is probably the most important activity performed by policy analysts. Problem structuring is a central guidance system or steering mechanism that affects the success of all other phases of policy analysis. Regrettably, policy analysts seem to fail more often because they solve the wrong problem than because they get the wrong solution to the right problem.

Beyond Problem Solving

Policy analysis is often described as a problem-solving methodology. Although this is partly correct—and analysts do succeed in finding solutions for public problems[3]—the problem-solving image of policy analysis can be misleading. The problem-solving image wrongly suggests that analysts can successfully identify, evaluate, and recommend solutions for a problem without spending considerable prior time and effort in formulating that problem. Policy analysis is best seen as a dynamic, multilevel process in which methods of problem structuring take priority over methods of problem solving (see Figure 3.1).

Figure 3.1 shows that methods of problem structuring precede and take priority over methods of problem solving. Methods at one level are inappropriate and ineffective at the next, because the questions are different at the two levels. For example, lower-level questions about the net benefits (benefits minus costs) of alternative solutions for the control of industrial pollution already assume that industry is the problem. At the next-higher level, the question that must be answered involves the scope and severity of pollution, the conditions that cause it, and potential solutions for its reduction or elimination. Here the analyst may well find that the most appropriate formulation of the problem is closely related to the driving habits of Americans for whom petroleum fuels are comparatively cheap, by

---

[1] E. E. Schattschneider, *The Semisovereign People* (New York: Holt, Rinehart and Winston, 1960), p. 68.

[2] See David Dery, *Problem Definition in Policy Analysis* (Lawrence: University Press of Kansas, 1984).

[3] See, for example, Bernard Barber, *Effective Social Science: Eight Cases in Economics, Political Science, and Sociology* (New York: Russell Sage Foundation, 1987).

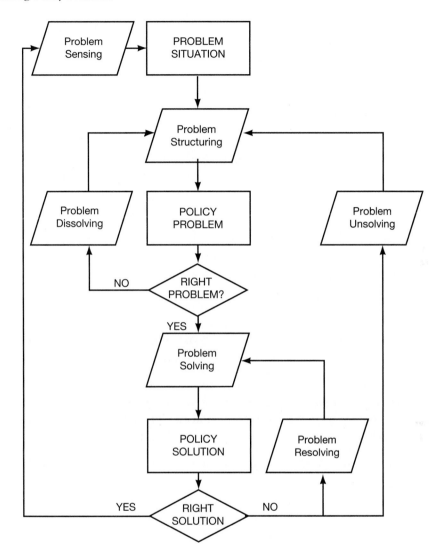

Figure 3.1   Priority of problem structuring in policy analysis.
Source: William N. Dunn, "Methods of the Second Type: Coping with the Wilderness of Conventional Policy Analysis," *Policy Studies Review* 7, no. 4 (1988): 720–37.

world standards, and heavily subsidized by the government. This is a question of problem structuring; the former is a question of problem solving. This distinction is evident from the flowchart in Figure 3.1:

- *Problem sensing versus problem structuring.* The process of policy analysis does not begin with clearly articulated problems, but a sense of diffuse worries and inchoate signs of stress.[4] These diffuse worries and inchoate signs of stress are not problems but *problem situations* that are sensed by analysts and other stakeholders. By contrast, *policy problems* "are products of thought acting on environments; they are elements of problem situations that are abstracted from these situations by analysis."[5]

- *Problem structuring versus problem solving.* Policy analysis is a multilevel process that includes higher-order methods of *problem structuring* as well as lower-order methods of *problem solving.* These higher-order methods and the questions for which they are appropriate are what some have recently discussed as policy design, or design science.[6] Higher-order methods of problem structuring are *metamethods*—that is, they are "about" and "come before" lower-order methods of problem solving. When analysts use lower-order methods to solve complex problems, they run the risk of committing errors of the third kind: solving the wrong problem.[7]

- *Problem resolving versus problem unsolving and problem dissolving.* The terms *problem resolving, problem unsolving,* and *problem dissolving* refer to three types of error-correcting processes.[8] Although the three terms come from the same root (L. *solvere,* to solve or dissolve), the error-correcting processes to which they refer occur at distinct levels (Figure 3.1). *Problem resolving* involves the reanalysis of a correctly structured problem to reduce calibrational errors, for example, reducing the probability of type I or type II errors in testing the null hypothesis that a policy has no effect on a particular policy outcome. *Problem unsolving,* by contrast, involves the abandonment of a solution based on the wrong formulation of a problem—for example, the policy of urban renewal implemented in central cities during the 1960s—and a return to problem structuring in an attempt to formulate the right problem. In turn, *problem dissolving* involves the abandonment of an incorrectly formulated problem without any effort to restructure or solve it.

---

[4] Martin Rein and Sheldon H. White, "Policy Research: Belief and Doubt," *Policy Analysis* 3, no. 2 (1977): 262.

[5] Russell A. Ackoff, *Redesigning the Future: A Systems Approach to Societal Problems* (New York: Wiley, 1974), p. 21.

[6] See Stephen H. Linder and B. Guy Peters, "From Social Theory to Policy Design," *Journal of Public Policy* 4, no. 4 (1985): 237–59; John Dryzek, "Don't Toss Coins into Garbage Cans: A Prologue to Policy Design," *Journal of Public Policy* 3, no. 3 (1983): 345–67; and Trudi C. Miller, "Conclusion: A Design Science Perspective," in *Public Sector Performance: A Turning Point,* ed. T. C. Miller (Baltimore: Johns Hopkins University Press, 1985).

[7] Howard Raiffa, *Decision Analysis* (Reading, MA: Addison-Wesley, 1968), p. 264.

[8] See Russell L. Ackoff, "Beyond Problem Solving," *General Systems* 19 (1974): 237–39; and Herbert A. Simon, "The Structure of Ill Structured Problems," *Artificial Intelligence* 4 (1973): 181–201.

Characteristics of Problems

There are several important characteristics of policy problems:

1. *Interdependence of policy problems.* Policy problems in one area (e.g., energy) frequently affect policy problems in other areas (e.g., health care and unemployment). In reality, policy problems are not independent entities; they are parts of whole systems of problems best described as *messes,* that is, systems of external conditions that produce dissatisfaction among different segments of the community.[9] Systems of problems (messes) are difficult or impossible to resolve by using an exclusively *analytic approach*—that is, one that decomposes problems into their component elements or parts—because rarely can problems be defined and resolved independently of one another. Sometimes it is easier "to solve ten interlocking problems simultaneously than to solve one by itself."[10] Systems of interdependent problems require a *holistic approach,* that is, one that views problems as inseparable and unmeasurable apart from the system of which they are interlocking parts.[11]

2. *Subjectivity of policy problems.* The external conditions that give rise to a problem are selectively defined, classified, explained, and evaluated. Although there is a sense in which problems are objective—for example, air pollution may be defined in terms of levels of CO_2 gases and particulates in the atmosphere—the same data about pollution may be interpreted in markedly different ways. The reason is that policy problems are elements of problem situations abstracted from these situations by analysts. *Problem situations* are not problems that, like atoms or cells, are partly subjective constructs.[12]

3. *Artificiality of policy problems.* Policy problems are possible only when human beings make judgments about the desirability of altering some problem situation. Policy problems are products of subjective human judgment; policy problems also come to be accepted as legitimate definitions of objective social conditions; policy problems are socially constructed, maintained, and changed.[13] Problems have no existence apart from the individuals and groups who define them, which means that there are no "natural" states of society which in and of themselves constitute policy problems.

---

[9] Russell L. Ackoff, *Redesigning the Future: A Systems Approach to Societal Problems* (New York: Wiley, 1974), p. 21.

[10] Harrison Brown, "Scenario for an American Renaissance," *Saturday Review,* December 25, 1971, 18–19.

[11] See Ian I. Mitroff and L. Vaughan Blankenship, "On the Methodology of the Holistic Experiment: An Approach to the Conceptualization of Large-Scale Social Experiments," *Technological Forecasting and Social Change* 4 (1973): 339–53.

[12] Ackoff, *Redesigning the Future,* p. 21.

[13] Compare Peter L. Berger and Thomas Luckmann, *The Social Construction of Reality,* 2d ed. (New York: Irvington, 1980).

4. *Dynamics of policy problems.* There are as many different solutions for a given problem as there are definitions of that problem. "Problems and solutions are in constant flux; hence problems *do not stay solved.* . . . Solutions to problems become obsolete even if the problems to which they are addressed do not."[14]

Problems are not discrete mechanical entities; they are *purposeful (teleological) systems* in which (1) no two members are identical in all or even any of their properties or behaviors; (2) the properties or behavior of each member has an effect on the properties or behavior of the system as a whole; (3) the properties and behavior of each member, and the way each affects the system as a whole, depend on the properties and behavior of at least one other member of the system; and (4) all possible subgroups of members have a nonindependent effect on the system as a whole.[15] What this means is that systems of problems—crime, poverty, unemployment, inflation, energy, pollution, health, security—cannot be decomposed into independent subsets without running the risk of producing the right solution to the wrong problem.

A key characteristic of systems of problems is that the whole is greater—that is, qualitatively different—than the simple sum of its parts. A pile of stones may be defined as the sum of all individual stones but also as a pyramid. Similarly, a human being

> can write or run, but none of its parts can. Furthermore, membership in the system either increases or decreases the capabilities of each element; it does not leave them unaffected. For example, a brain that is not part of a living body or some substitute cannot function. An individual who is part of a nation or a corporation is thereby precluded from doing some things he could otherwise do, and he is enabled to do others he could not otherwise do.[16]

Finally, recognition of the interdependence, subjectivity, artificiality, and dynamics of problems alerts us to the *unanticipated consequences* that may follow from policies based on the right solution to the wrong problem. Consider, for example, the problem situation confronted by Western European governments in the late 1970s. France and West Germany, seeking to expand the supply of available energy by constructing nuclear power plants on the Rhine River, defined the energy problem in a way that assumed that the production of nuclear power is independent of the other problems. Consequently, the relation of energy to wider systems of problems did not enter into the formulation of the problem. One observer went so far as to predict that

> malaria will arrive as a major epidemic in Europe within the next ten years, thanks to the decision in Germany and France to build atomic generators that

---

[14] Ackoff, *Redesigning the Future,* p. 21.

[15] Mitroff and Blankenship, "Methodology of the Holistic Experiment," pp. 341–42.

[16] Ackoff, *Redesigning the Future,* p. 13.

utilize river waters for their cooling systems and hence bring the water temperature within the range in which anopheles (the malaria-carrying mosquito) breeds.[17]

Although this forecast was incorrect, the understanding that energy policy involves a system of problems was not.

Global warming is a system of problems.

Problems versus Issues

If problems are systems, it follows that policy issues are as well. *Policy issues* not only involve disagreements about actual or potential courses of action, but they also reflect competing views of the nature of problems themselves. An apparently clear-cut policy issue—for example, whether the government should enforce air quality standards in industry—is typically the consequence of conflicting sets of assumptions about the nature of pollution:[18]

1. Pollution is a natural consequence of capitalism, an economic system where the owners of industry seek to maintain and increase profits from their investments. Some damage to the environment is a necessary price to pay for a healthy capitalist economy.

2. Pollution is a result of the need for power and prestige among industrial managers who seek promotions in large career-oriented bureaucracies. Pollution has been just as severe in socialist systems where there are no profit-seeking private owners.

3. Pollution is a consequence of consumer preferences in high mass-consumption society. In order to ensure corporate survival, owners and managers must satisfy consumer preferences for high-performance engines and automobile travel.

The ability to recognize differences among problem situations, policy problems, and policy issues is crucial for understanding the different ways that common experiences are translated into disagreements. The formulation of a problem is influenced by the assumptions that different policy stakeholders bring to a problem situation. In turn, different formulations of the problem shape the ways that policy issues are defined. In the example of environmental pollution above, assumptions about the operation of a healthy capitalist economy may result in a negative view of government enforcement of air quality standards in industry, whereas assumptions about corporate managerial behavior may result in an affirmative position. By contrast, assumptions about

---

[17] Ivan Illich in conversation with Sam Keen, reported in *Psychology Today* (May 1976).

[18] See Ritchie P. Lowry, *Social Problems: A Critical Analysis of Theories and Public Policy* (Lexington, MA: D. C. Heath and Company, 1974), pp. 23–25.

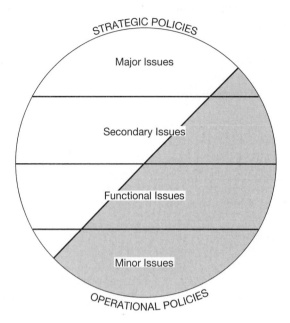

Figure 3.2 Hierarchy of types of policy issues.

consumer preferences and corporate survival may influence the view that government regulation is a nonissue, because government cannot legislate consumer demand.

The complexity of policy issues may be visualized by considering the organizational levels where they are formulated (Figure 3.2). Policy issues may be classified according to a hierarchy of types: major, secondary, functional, and minor. *Major issues* are those that are typically encountered at the highest levels of government within and between federal, state, and local jurisdictions. Major issues typically involve questions of agency mission, that is, questions about the nature and purposes of government organizations. The issue of whether the Department of Health and Human Services should seek to eliminate the conditions that give rise to poverty is a question of agency mission. *Secondary issues* are those located at the level of agency programs at the federal, state, and local levels. Secondary issues may involve the setting of program priorities and the definition of target groups and beneficiaries. The issue of how to define poverty families is a secondary issue. *Functional issues,* by contrast, are those located at both the program and the project levels and which involve such questions as budgeting, finance, and procurement. Finally, *minor issues* are those that are found most frequently at the level of specific projects. Minor issues involve personnel, staffing, employee benefits, vacation times, working hours, and standard operating procedures and rules.

As one moves up the hierarchy of types of policy issues, problems become more and more interdependent, subjective, artificial, and dynamic. Although these levels are themselves interdependent, some issues call for policies that are strategic, whereas others demand operational policies. A *strategic policy* is one where the consequences of decisions are relatively irreversible. Such issues as whether the United States should send troops to the Persian Gulf, or whether the civil service should be reorganized, call for strategic policies because the consequences of action cannot be reversed for many years. By contrast, *operational policies*—that is, policies where the consequences of decisions are relatively reversible—do not involve the risks and uncertainty present at higher levels. Although all types of policies are interdependent—for example, the realization of an agency's mission depends in part on the adequacy of its personnel practices—it is important to recognize that the complexity and irreversibility of a policy increases as one moves up the hierarchy of types of policy issues.

Three Classes of Policy Problems

There are three classes of policy problems: well-structured, moderately structured, and ill-structured problems.[19] The structure of each of these three classes is determined by the relative complexity of a problem. The differences among well-structured, moderately structured, and ill-structured problems are best illustrated by considering variations in their common elements (Table 3.1).

Well-structured problems are those that involve one or a few decision makers and a small set of policy alternatives. Utilities (values) reflect goal consensus and are clearly ranked in order of decision makers' preferences. The outcomes of each alternative are known either with complete certainty (deterministically) or within acceptable margins of probable error (risk). The prototype of the well-structured problem is the completely computerized decision problem, where all consequences of all policy alternatives are programmed in advance. Relatively low-level operational problems in public agencies provide illustrations of well-structured problems.

Table 3.1 Differences in the Structure of Three Classes of Policy Problems

	Structure of Problem		
Element	*Well Structured*	*Moderately Structured*	*Ill Structured*
Decision maker(s)	One or few	One or few	Many
Alternatives	Limited	Limited	Unlimited
Utilities (values)	Consensus	Consensus	Conflict
Outcomes	Certainty or risk	Uncertainty	Unknown
Probabilities	Calculable	Incalculable	Incalculable

[19] See Ian I. Mitroff and Francisco Sagasti, "Epistemology as General Systems Theory: An Approach to the Design of Complex Decision-Making Experiments," *Philosophy of the Social Sciences* 3 (1973): 117–34.

For example, problems of replacing agency vehicles are relatively simple ones that involve finding the optimum point at which an old vehicle should be traded for a new one, taking into account average repair costs for older vehicles and purchasing and depreciation costs for new ones.

Moderately structured problems are those involving one or a few decision makers and a relatively limited number of alternatives. Utilities (values) also reflect consensus on clearly ranked goals. Nevertheless, the outcomes of alternatives are neither certain (deterministic) nor calculable within acceptable margins of error (risk). The prototype of the moderately structured problem is the policy simulation or game, an illustration of which is the so-called "prisoner's dilemma."[20] In this game, two prisoners are held in separate cells, where each is interrogated by the prosecuting attorney, who must obtain a confession from one or both prisoners to obtain a conviction. The prosecutor, who has enough evidence to convict each prisoner of a lesser crime, tells each that if neither confesses, they will both be tried for a lesser crime carrying lesser punishment; if both confess to the more serious crime, they will both receive a reduced sentence; but if only one confesses, he will receive probation, whereas the other will receive a maximum sentence. The "optimal" choice for each prisoner, given that neither can predict the outcome of the other's decision, is to confess. Yet it is precisely this choice that will result in a five-year sentence for both prisoners, because both are likely to try to minimize their sentences. This example not only illustrates the difficulties of making decisions when outcomes are uncertain but also shows that otherwise "rational" individual choices may contribute to collective irrationality in small groups, government bureaucracies, and society as a whole.

Ill-structured problems are those that typically involve many different decision makers whose utilities (values) are either unknown or impossible to rank in a consistent fashion. Whereas well-structured and moderately structured problems reflect consensus, the main characteristic of ill-structured problems is conflict among competing goals. Policy alternatives and their outcomes may also be unknown, such that estimates of risk and uncertainty are not possible. The problem of choice is not to uncover known deterministic relations, or to calculate the risk or uncertainty attached to policy alternatives, but rather to define the nature of the problem. The prototype of the ill-structured problem is the completely intransitive decision problem, that is, one where it is impossible to select a single policy alternative that is preferred to all others. Whereas well-structured and moderately structured problems contain preference rankings that are *transitive*—that is, if alternative A_1 is preferred to alternative A_2, and alternative A_2 is preferred to alternative A_3, then alternative A_1 is preferred to alternative A_3—ill-structured problems have preference rankings that are intransitive.

Many of the most important policy problems are ill structured. One of the lessons of political science, public administration, and other disciplines is that

---

[20] See Anatol Rapoport and Albert M. Chammah, *Prisoner's Dilemma* (Ann Arbor: University of Michigan Press, 1965).

well-structured and moderately structured problems are rarely present in complex governmental settings.[21] For example, it is unrealistic to assume the existence of one or a few decision makers with uniform preferences (utilities), because public policies are sets of interrelated decisions made and influenced by many policy stakeholders over long periods of time. Consensus is rare, because public policy making typically involves conflicts among competing stakeholders. Finally, it is seldom possible to identify the full range of alternative solutions for problems, in part because of constraints on the acquisition of information, but also because it is frequently difficult to reach a satisfactory formulation of the problem. The reasons why ill-structured problems are so critical for public policy analysis have been ably summarized by a number of social scientists.[22]

PROBLEM STRUCTURING IN POLICY ANALYSIS

The requirements for solving ill-structured problems are not the same as those for solving well-structured problems. Whereas well-structured problems permit the use of conventional methods, ill-structured problems demand that *the analyst take an active and conscious part in defining the nature of the problem itself.*[23] In actively defining the nature of the problem, analysts must not only impose part of themselves on the problem situation but also exercise reflective judgment and insight. Problem solving is only one part of the work of policy analysis:

> The problem-solving image holds that the work of policy begins with articulated and self-evident problems. Supposedly, policy begins when recognizable problems appear, problems about which one can hypothesize possible courses of action and in relation to which one can articulate goals.... It is not clear problems, but diffuse worries, that appear. Political pressure groups become unusually active, or their activities become more telling; formal and informal social indicators give signs of unfavorable trends, or of trends that may be interpreted as unfavorable. There are signals, then, of a problem, but no one knows yet what the problem is.... In other words, the situation is such that the problem itself is problematic. Policy analysis contains processes for finding and construing problems; it involves problem setting [structuring] in order to interpret inchoate signs of stress in the system.[24]

---

[21] See, for example, David Braybrooke and Charles E. Lindblom, *A Strategy of Decision* (New York: Free Press, 1963); and Herbert A. Simon, "Theories of Decision-Making in Economic and Behavioral Science," *American Economic Review* 1009 (1959), 255–57.

[22] See, for example, Thomas R. Dye, *Understanding Public Policy,* 3d ed. (Englewood Cliffs, NJ: Prentice Hall, 1978), pp. 30–31; Richard O. Mason and Ian I. Mitroff, *Creating a Dialectical Social Science* (Dordrecht, The Netherlands: D. Reidel, 1981); and James G. March and Johan P. Olsen, "The New Institutionalism: Organizational Factors in Political Life," *American Political Science Review* 78, no. 3 (1984): 739–49.

[23] See John R. Hayes, *Cognitive Psychology* (Homewood, IL: Dorsey Press, 1978), pp. 210–13.

[24] Martin Rein and Sheldon H. White, "Policy Research: Belief and Doubt," *Policy Analysis* 3, no. 2 (1977): 262.

Creativity in Problem Structuring

The criteria for determining the success of problem structuring are also different from those used to judge the success of problem solving. Successful problem solving requires that analysts obtain relatively precise technical solutions for clearly formulated problems. By contrast, successful problem structuring requires that analysts produce creative solutions for ambiguous and ill-defined problems. Criteria for judging creative acts in general are also applicable to creativity in problem structuring. Problem structuring is creative to the extent that:[25] (1) the product of analysis is sufficiently *novel* that most people could not or would not have arrived at the same solution; (2) the process of analysis is sufficiently *unconventional* that it involves the modification or rejection of previously accepted ideas; (3) the process of analysis requires sufficiently *high motivation and persistence* that analysis takes place with high intensity or over long periods of time; (4) the product of analysis is regarded as *valuable* because it provides an appropriate solution for the problem; and (5) the problem as initially posed is so *ambiguous, vague, and ill defined* that the challenge is to formulate the problem itself.

Phases of Problem Structuring

Problem structuring is a process with four related phases: *problem search, problem definition, problem specification,* and *problem sensing* (Figure 3.3). A prerequisite of

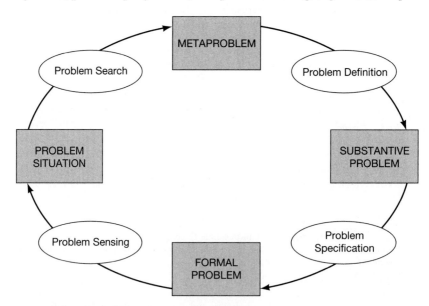

Figure 3.3 Phases of problem structuring.

---

[25] See Alan Newell, J. C. Shaw, and Herbert A. Simon, "The Process of Creative Thinking," in *Contemporary Approaches to Creative Thinking,* ed. H. F. Gruber, G. Terrell, and M. Wertheimer (New York: Atherton Press, 1962), pp. 63–119; see also the excellent monograph by James L. Adams, *Conceptual Blockbusting* (Stanford, CA: Stanford Alumni Association, 1974).

problem structuring is the recognition or "felt existence" of a *problem situation.* In moving from problem situation, the analyst engages in *problem search.* At this stage, the goal is not the discovery of a single problem (e.g., that of the client or the analyst); it is rather the discovery of many problem representations of multiple stakeholders. Practicing analysts normally face a large, tangled network of competing problem formulations that are dynamic, socially constructed, and distributed throughout the policy-making process. In effect, analysts are faced with a *metaproblem*[26]—a problem-of-problems that is ill structured because the domain of problem representations held by diverse stakeholders seems unmanageably huge.[27] The central task is to structure that metaproblem, that is, a second-order problem that may be defined as the class of all first-order problems, which are its members. Unless these two levels are distinguished, analysts run the risk of formulating the wrong problem by confusing member and class. By failing to distinguish these levels, analysts violate the rule that "whatever involves *all* of a collection must not be one of the collection."[28]

In moving from metaproblem to *substantive problem,* the analyst attempts to *define* the problem in its most basic and general terms. For example, the analyst may decide whether the problem is one of economics, sociology, political science, engineering, and so forth. If the substantive problem is conceptualized as an economic one, the analyst will treat it in terms of factors related to the production and distribution of goods and services—for example, market prices as a determinant of costs and benefits of public programs. Alternatively, if the problem is viewed as political or sociological, the analyst will approach it in terms of the distribution of power and influence among competing interest groups, elites, or classes. The choice of a conceptual framework is often similar to the choice of a worldview, ideology, or popular myth and indicates a commitment to a particular view of reality.[29]

To illustrate the importance of worldviews, ideologies, and popular myths in conceptualizing substantive problems, consider the various ways to define poverty. Poverty may be defined as a consequence of accidents or inevitable states of society, of the actions of evil persons, or of imperfections in the poor themselves.[30] These definitions of poverty contain elements of a worldview, myth, or ideology insofar as each involves a selective perception of elements of a problem situation. Worldviews, ideologies, and myths are often partly true and partly false; they may

---

[26] See Yehezkel Dror, *Design for Policy Sciences* (New York: Elsevier, 1971).

[27] Another distinguishing feature of an ill-structured problem is that its boundaries are unmanageably huge. See P. Harmon and D. King, *Expert Systems: Artificial Intelligence in Business* (New York: Wiley, 1985).

[28] Alfred North Whitehead and Bertrand Russell, *Principia Mathematica,* 2d ed., vol. I (Cambridge: Cambridge University Press, 1910), p. 101. See also Paul Watzlawick, John Weakland, and Richard Fisch, *Change: Principles of Problem Formation and Problem Resolution* (New York: W. W. Norton), p. 6.

[29] Ian Mitroff and Ralph H. Kilmann, *Methodological Approaches to Social Science* (San Francisco, CA: Jossey-Bass, 1978). See also Thomas Kuhn, *The Structure of Scientific Revolutions,* 2d ed. (Chicago: University of Chicago Press, 1971); and Ian G. Barbour, *Myths, Models and Paradigms* (New York: Harper & Row, 1976).

[30] Lowry, *Social Problems,* pp. 19–46.

be useful and dangerous at the same time. In this example, the attribution of poverty to historical accidents or to inevitability represents a *naturalistic perspective* of social problems which distorts reality by claiming that questions about the distribution of wealth are pointless, but this same myth may also sensitize analysts to the relative nature of definitions of poverty by pointing to the fact that no known society has wholly resolved the problem. Similarly, the attribution of poverty to evil or morally corrupt capitalists distorts their actual motivations. Yet this same *moralistic perspective,* which explains poverty in terms of presumed moral weaknesses, also directs attention to the ways in which private ownership promotes waste, exploitation, and social irresponsibility. Finally, to attribute poverty to imperfections in the poor themselves not only results in blaming the victim rather than responsible social forces but also points to the fact that some poor persons choose to live under conditions that the rest of society defines as "poverty." This *environmentalist perspective,* which attributes poverty and other social problems to characteristics of the immediate environment of victims, often results in a self-contradictory brand of humanitarianism known as "blaming the victim." The humanitarian can

> concentrate his charitable interest on the defects of the victim, condemn the vague social and environmental stresses that produced the defect (some time ago), and ignore the continuing effect of victimizing social forces (right now). It is a brilliant ideology for justifying a perverse form of social action designed to change, not society, as one might expect, but rather society's victim.[31]

Once a substantive problem has been defined, a more detailed and specific *formal problem* may be constructed. The process of moving from substantive to formal problem is carried out through *problem specification,* which can involve the development of a formal mathematical representation (model) of the substantive problem. At this point, difficulties may occur, because the relationship between an ill-structured substantive problem and a formal representation of that problem may be tenuous.[32] The specification of ill-structured problems in formal mathematical terms may be premature or inappropriate. The main task is not to obtain the correct mathematical solution but to define the nature of the problem itself.

Errors of the Third Type (E_{III})

A critical issue of problem structuring is how well substantive and formal problems actually correspond to the original problem situation. If problem situations contain whole systems of complex problems, then a central requirement of policy analysis is the formulation of substantive and formal problems that adequately represent that complexity. The degree of correspondence between a given problem situation and a substantive problem is determined at the problem definition phase. Here the analyst compares characteristics of the problem situation and the substantive problem. The

---

[31] William Ryan, *Blaming the Victim* (New York: Pantheon Books, 1971), p. 7.

[32] See Ralph E. Strauch, "A Critical Look at Quantitative Methodology," *Policy Analysis* 2 (1976): 121–44.

latter may be based on implicit assumptions or beliefs about human nature, time, and the possibilities for social change through government action. Equally important, however, is the degree of correspondence between the problem situation and the formal problem, which is often specified in the form of a mathematical formula or set of equations.

In the first instance (problem search), analysts who fail to engage in search, or stop searching prematurely, run the risk of choosing the wrong boundaries of the metaproblem. Important aspects of the metaproblem—for example, the formulations of problems held by those who are or will be charged with implementing the policy—simply may be left outside the boundaries of the metaproblem. In the second instance (problem definition), analysts run the risk of choosing the wrong worldview, ideology, or myth to conceptualize a problem situation when they should have chosen the right one. In the third case (problem specification), the main risk is to choose the wrong formal representation (model) of the substantive problem when the right one should have been chosen. In any case, analysts may commit *errors of the third type* (E_{III}).[33] Type III error has been described by decision theorist Howard Raiffa in the following terms:

> One of the most popular paradigms in ... mathematics describes the case in which a researcher has either to accept or reject a so-called null hypothesis. In a first course in statistics the student learns that he must constantly balance between making an error of the first kind (that is, rejecting the null hypothesis when it is true) and an error of the second kind (that is, accepting the null hypothesis when it is false) ... practitioners all too often make errors of a third kind: solving the wrong problem.[34]

The process of problem structuring raises a number of issues that are central to the methodology of policy analysis and science in general. Each phase of problem structuring requires different kinds of methodological skills and different kinds of reasoning. For example, the kinds of skills most appropriate for discovering metaproblems are observational; for substantive problems the required skills mainly conceptual. Mathematical and statistical subjects (econometrics or operations research) are primarily relevant for specifying formal problems. Problem structuring also raises questions about different meanings of rationality, because rationality is not simply a matter of finding a relatively precise formal representation of a problem situation. This is the standard technical definition of rationality criticized for its formal oversimplification of complex processes.[35] Rationality may be defined at more

---

[33] See Ian I. Mitroff and Frederick Betz, "Dialectical Decision Theory: A Meta-Theory of Decision-Making," *Management Science,* 19, no. 1 (1972): 11–24. Kimball defines type III error as "the error committed by giving the right answer to the wrong problem." See A. W. Kimball, "Errors of the Third Kind in Statistical Consulting," *Journal of the American Statistical Association* 52 (1957): 133–42.

[34] Howard Raiffa, *Decision Analysis* (Reading, MA: Addison-Wesley, 1968), p. 264.

[35] See, for example, Ida R. Hoos, *Systems Analysis in Public Policy: A Critique* (Berkeley: University of California Press, 1972).

fundamental levels, where the unconscious or uncritical choice of a worldview, ide-ology, or myth may distort the conceptualization of a substantive problem and its potential solutions. In this case, policy analysis may be an ideology in disguise.[36]

POLICY MODELS AND PROBLEM STRUCTURING

Policy models are simplified representations of a problem situation.[37] As such, the development of policy models is a form of problem structuring. Just as policy prob-lems are mental constructs based on the conceptualization and specification of ele-ments of a problem situation, policy models are constructions and reconstructions of reality. Policy models may be expressed as concepts, diagrams, graphs, or math-ematical equations and may be used not only to describe, explain, and predict elements of a problem situation but also to improve it by recommending courses of action. Policy models are never literal descriptions of a problem situation. Like policy problems, policy models are artificial devices for ordering and interpreting problem situations.

Policy models are useful and even necessary. They simplify systems of prob-lems by helping to reduce and make manageable the complexities encountered by analysts in their work. Policy models may help distinguish essential from nonessen-tial features of a problem situation, highlight relationships among important factors or variables, and assist in explaining and predicting the consequences of policy choices. Policy models may also play a self-critical and creative role in policy analy-sis by forcing analysts to make their own assumptions explicit and to challenge con-ventional ideas and methods of analysis. In any case, the use of policy models is not a matter of choice, because everyone uses some kind of model. In the words of policy modeler Jay Forrester:

> Each of us uses models constantly. Every person in his private life and in his business life instinctively uses models for decision-making. The mental image of the world around you which you carry in your head is a model. One does not have a city or a government or a country in his head. He has only selected con-cepts and relationships which he uses to represent the real system. A mental image is a model. All of our decisions are taken on the basis of models. The question is not to use or ignore models. The question is only a choice among alternatives.[38]

---

[36] Laurence Tribe, "Policy Science: Analysis or Ideology?" *Philosophy and Public Affairs* 2, no. 1 (1972): 66–110; and "Ways Not to Think about Plastic Trees," in *When Values Conflict: Essays on Environmental Analysis, Discourse, and Decision,* ed. Laurence Tribe, Corinne S. Schelling, and John Voss (Cambridge, MA: Ballinger Publishing, 1976).

[37] See Saul I. Gass and Roger L. Sisson, ed., *A Guide to Models in Governmental Planning and Operations* (Washington, DC: Office of Research and Development, Environmental Protection Agency, 1974); and Martin Greenberger, Mathew A. Crenson, and Brian L. Crissey, *Models in the Policy Process* (New York: Russell Sage Foundation, 1976).

[38] Jay W. Forrester, "Counter-Intuitive Behavior of Social Systems," *Technological Review* 73 (1971): 3.

By simplifying problem situations, models inevitably contribute to the selective distortion of reality. Models themselves cannot tell us how to discriminate between essential and nonessential questions; nor can they explain, predict, evaluate, or recommend, because these judgments are external to the model and not part of it. While models may help us to undertake these analytic tasks, the key word is "us," for it is we and not the model who provide the assumptions necessary to interpret features of reality described by a model. Finally, policy models—particularly those expressed in mathematical form—are frequently difficult to communicate to policy makers and other stakeholders for whom models are designed as an aid to better decision making.

Descriptive Models

The purpose of *descriptive models* is to explain and/or predict the causes and consequences of policy choices. Descriptive models are used to monitor the outcomes of policy actions, for example, outcomes included in the annual list of social indicators published by the Office of Management and the Budget or by Eurostat. Descriptive models are also used to forecast economic performance. For example, the Council of Economic Advisers prepares an annual economic forecast for inclusion in the President's Economic Report.

Normative Models

By contrast, the purpose of *normative models* is not only to explain and/or predict but also to provide recommendations for optimizing the attainment of some utility (value). Among the many types of normative models used by policy analysts are those that help determine optimum levels of service capacity (queuing models), the optimum timing of service and repairs (replacement models), the optimum volume and timing of orders (inventory models), and the optimum return on public investments (benefit–cost models). Normative decision models usually take the form: find the values of the manipulable (policy) variables that will produce the greatest utility, as measured by the value of outcome variables that policy makers wish to change. Often (but not always) this value is expressed as a monetary quantity such as dollars ($) or euros (€).

A simple and familiar normative model is compound interest. At one point or another in their lives, many persons have used some variation of this model to find the values of a "policy" variables (e.g., putting money in a bank versus a credit union) that will produce the greatest interest income on savings, as measured by the amount of money that one may expect after a given number of years. This is the value of the outcome variable that a person wishes to change. The analytical model for compound interest is

$$S_n = (1 + r)^n S_0$$

where S_n is the amount to which savings will accumulate in a given (n) number of years, S_0 is the initial savings, and $(1 + r)^n$ is a constant return on investment (1) plus the rate of interest (r) in the given time period (n). If an individual (policy maker) knows the interest rates of different savings institutions and wishes to optimize the return on savings, this simple normative model should permit a straightforward choice of that institution offering the highest rate of interest, provided there are no other important considerations (e.g., the security of deposits or special privileges for patrons) that should be taken into account. Note, however, that this normative model also predicts the accumulation of savings under different alternatives, thus pointing to a characteristic of all normative models: They not only permit us to estimate past, present, and future values of outcome variables but also allow us to optimize the attainment of some value.

Verbal Models

Normative and descriptive models may be expressed in three ways: verbally, symbolically, and procedurally.[39] *Verbal models* are expressed in everyday language, rather than the language of symbolic logic (if p > q and q > r, then p > r) or mathematics ($\log_{10} 10{,}000 = 3$). In using verbal models, analysts may make reasoned judgments in the form of predictions and offer recommendations. Reasoned judgments are parts of policy arguments, rather than results presented in the form of numerical values. Verbal models are relatively easily communicated among experts and laypersons alike, and their costs are low. A potential limitation of verbal models is that the reasons offered for predictions and recommendations may be implicit or hidden, making it difficult to reconstruct and critically examine arguments as a whole. The arguments for and against a blockade of the Soviet navy during the Cuban Missile Crisis of 1962 are a good example of verbal policy models. President Kennedy's own verbal model of the crisis argued, in effect, that a blockade was the United States' only real option:

> Above all, while defending our own vital interests, nuclear powers must avert those confrontations which bring an adversary to a choice of either a humiliating retreat or a nuclear war. To adopt that kind of course in the nuclear age would be evidence only of the bankruptcy of our policy—of a collective death wish for the world.[40]

Symbolic Models

Symbolic models use mathematical symbols to describe relationships among key variables that are believed to characterize a problem. Predictions or optimal solutions are obtained from symbolic models by employing methods of mathematics, statistics, and logic. Symbolic models are difficult to communicate among

---

[39] Models may also be expressed physically, as when various materials are used to construct representations of human organs, cities, or machines. The basic limitation of such models is that they cannot represent human action, which involves communication processes, social learning, and choice.

[40] Quoted in Graham T. Allison, "Conceptual Models and the Cuban Missile Crisis," *American Political Science Review* 63, no. 3 (1969): 698.

laypersons, including policy makers, and even among expert modelers, there are misunderstandings about basic elements of models.[41] The costs of symbolic models are probably not much greater than those of verbal models, provided one takes into account the time and effort expended on public debate, which is the main vehicle for expressing verbal models. A practical limitation of symbolic models is that their results may not be easily interpretable, even among specialists, because the meanings of symbols and the assumptions of symbolic models may not be adequately defined. Symbolic models may improve policy decisions, but only if

> the premises on which models are constructed are made explicit.... All too frequently what purports to be a model based on theory and evidence is nothing more than a scholar's preconception and prejudices cloaked in the guise of scientific rigor and embellished with extensive computer simulations. Without empirical verification there is little assurance that the results of such exercises are reliable, or that they should be applied for normative policy purposes.[42]

Although we have already considered a simple symbolic model designed for normative purposes (compound interest), the purpose of other symbolic models is descriptive. A frequently used symbolic model is the simple linear equation

$$Y = a + bX$$

where Y is the value of a variable the analyst seeks to predict and X is the value of a policy variable that may be manipulated by policy makers. The relation between X and Y is known as a linear function, which means that relations between X and Y will form a straight line when plotted on a graph (Figure 3.4). In this model, the symbol b denotes the amount of change in Y due to a change in X. This may be depicted by the slope of a straight line when plotted on a piece of paper (the steeper the slope, the greater the effect of X on Y). The symbol a (called an *intercept constant*) denotes the point where the straight line intercepts the vertical or Y-axis when X is zero. In Figure 3.4, all values of Y are one-half those of X along the broken line (i.e., $Y = 0 + 0.5X$), whereas along the solid line, they are equal (i.e., $Y = 0 + 1.0X$). This linear model predicts how much change in the policy variable (X) will be necessary to produce a given value of the outcome variable (Y).

Procedural Models

Procedural models represent dynamic relationships among variables believed to characterize problems and solutions. Predictions and optimal solutions are obtained by simulating and searching through sets of possible relationships—for example, economic growth, energy consumption, and food supplies in future

---

[41] See Greenberger and others, *Models in the Policy Process,* pp. 328–36.

[42] Gary Fromm, "Policy Decisions and Econometric Models," cited by Greenberger and others, *Models in the Policy Process,* p. 72.

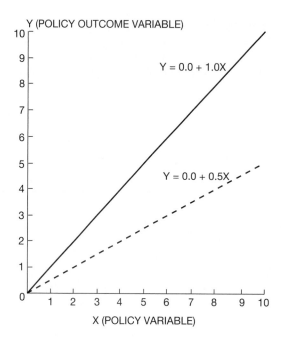

Figure 3.4 A symbolic model.

years—that cannot be adequately described because reliable data are unavailable. Simulation and search procedures are generally performed with the aid of a computer, which is programmed to yield alternative predictions under different sets of assumptions.

Procedural models also make use of symbolic modes of expression. The main difference between symbolic and procedural models is that the former often use actual data to estimate relationships among policy and outcome variables, whereas procedural models assume (simulate) such relationships. The costs of procedural models are relatively high, as compared with verbal and symbolic models, largely because of the time required to develop and run computer programs. At the same time, procedural models may be written in reasonably nontechnical language, thus facilitating communication among laypersons. Although the strength of procedural models is that they permit creative simulation and search, it is sometimes difficult to find evidence to justify model assumptions.

A simple form of procedural model is the decision tree, which is created by projecting several possible consequences of policies. Figure 3.5 illustrates a simple decision tree that estimates the probability that each of several policy alternatives will reduce pollution.[43] Decision trees are useful in comparing subjective estimates of the possible consequences of various policy choices under conditions where it is difficult to calculate risk and uncertainty on the basis of existing data.

---

[43] See Gass and Sisson, *A Guide to Models in Governmental Planning and Operations,* pp. 26–27.

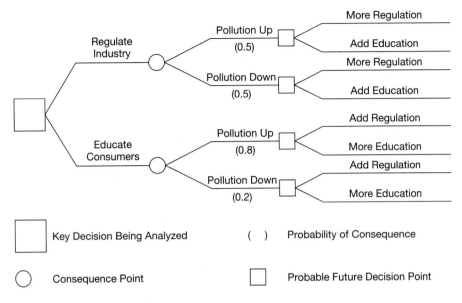

Figure 3.5 Simulation model.

Models as Surrogates and Perspectives

A final important dimension of policy models relates to their assumptions. Policy models, irrespective of their purpose or mode of expression, may be viewed as surrogates or perspectives.[44] A *surrogate model* is assumed to be a substitute for a substantive problem. Surrogate models are based, consciously or unconsciously, on the assumption that the formal problem is a valid representation of the substantive problem. By contrast, *perspective models* are viewed as one among several possible ways to structure a substantive problem. Perspective models assume that the formal problem can never be a wholly valid representation of substantive problems.

The distinction between surrogate and perspective models is particularly important in public policy analysis, where, as we have seen, many of the most important problems are ill structured. The structure of most public policy problems is sufficiently complex that the use of surrogate models significantly increases the probability of errors of the third type (E_{III})—that is, solving the wrong formulation of a problem when one should have solved the right one. This point may be clarified by considering two illustrations of formal modeling in policy analysis. The first of these illustrations is concerned with the use of symbolic models, whereas the second deals with verbal models.[45]

---

[44] Strauch, "A Critical Look at Quantitative Methodology," pp. 136–44.

[45] These illustrations are adapted from Strauch, "A Critical Look at Quantitative Methodology," pp. 131–33; and Watzlawick, Weakland, and Fisch, *Change*.

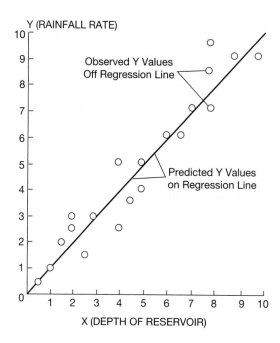

Figure 3.6   Assumed effects of X on Y.

Suppose that an analyst has constructed a simple symbolic model expressed in the form of a linear equation such as that described earlier in Figure 3.5. Using the equation $Y = a + bX$ (later we shall write this equation as $Y = b_0 + b_x$), the analyst may use observations to plot actual values of X and Y, as shown in Figure 3.6. Suppose also that the analyst assumes implicitly that the observed values of X and Y constitute a causal relationship, where the policy variable (X) is believed to produce a significant change in an outcome variable (Y). At this point, the analyst will very likely interpret the results of the formal symbolic model as a confirmation of the structure of the substantive problem. For example, the analyst will interpret the slope of the line as a measure of the effects of X on Y, whereas the correlation between observed values of Y (data points) and those predicted by the equation (those lying on the straight line) will be taken as an estimate of the accuracy of the prediction. The probable conclusion is that a change in the value of the policy variable will result in a corresponding change in the value of the outcome variable.

The point of this illustration is that the formal symbolic model itself provides no guidance in answering the question of whether X causes Y. If X happens to be unemployment and Y poverty, there may be a case for the predicted relation, provided the substantive problem has been defined in such a way as to provide plausible reasons for believing that unemployment causes poverty. Yet this information is not contained in the symbolic model; it comes from *outside* the model. The observed relation between X and Y might just as easily be interpreted as evidence of the effects of poverty on unemployment, provided the substantive problem has been defined in terms of the assumption that poverty is not an economic phenomenon but a cultural one. Poverty, for example, may be defined in terms of a "culture of poverty" that depresses the motivation to work and earn income.

The lesson of this illustration is that the conceptualization of substantive problems governs the interpretation of symbolic models. Formal representations of substantive problems are perspectives and not surrogates. To clarify this point further, let us return to the formal symbolic model previously discussed:

> Suppose, for example, that X is the mean annual depth of a reservoir and that Y is the annual rainfall in the area. . . . Because reservoir-management policies can be changed, reservoir depth is a policy variable subject to policy manipulation. Annual rainfall is a variable we might be interested in controlling, and common sense clearly suggests that the relationship between rainfall and reservoir depth is nonspecious. . . . In spite of this, however, the conclusion suggested by the analysis—that we can decrease rainfall by draining water more rapidly from the reservoir . . . seems ludicrous. This is because the causal relationship assumed in the analysis—reservoir depth causes rainfall—runs counter to our common sense understanding that rainfall determines reservoir depth.[46]

Consider now a second illustration of the difficulties that arise when we confuse surrogate and perspective models. This time we will use an illustration that makes the same point about verbal models, that is, models that are expressed in everyday language. Suppose that you are a policy analyst confronted with the following problem situation: The director of the state department of transportation has requested that a study be undertaken to recommend the least costly way to connect nine key transportation points in the central region of the state. As the agency's policy analyst you are directed to show how all nine points may be connected by four sections of highway. You are also told that these four sections of highway must be straight (no curves will be permitted) and that each new section must begin at the point where the last section stopped (the construction team will not be permitted to retrace its steps). You are then shown a map of the region (Figure 3.7) and asked to make a recommendation that will solve the director's problem.

Figure 3.7 Map of transportation points in central region.

---

[46] Strauch, "A Critical Look at Quantitative Methodology," p. 132.

Unless you were already familiar with this classic conceptual problem (called simply the "nine-dot problem"), it is very unlikely that you were able to solve it. Few people manage to find the solution by themselves, not because the problem is technically complicated (in fact it is simple) but because they almost always commit an error of the third type (E_{III}), solving the wrong formulation of a problem when they should have solved the right one. This is because most people approach the problem situation with implicit assumptions that make it impossible to solve the problem. The central point, however, is that these assumptions are introduced by analysts themselves; they are *not* part of the problem situation. In other words, analysts themselves create a substantive problem that cannot be solved.

The solution for the nine-dot problem is presented in Figure 3.8. The solution appears surprisingly simple, novel, and unconventional; that is, it has several of the key characteristics of creativity discussed earlier. In the process of analysis, it becomes suddenly clear that we have been solving the wrong problem. So long as we assume that the solution must be found within the boundaries set by our verbal model—that is, the rectangle composed of nine dots—then a solution is not possible. Yet this condition is imposed not by the formal verbal model but by the implicit assumption of "squareness" that unconsciously shaped our definition of the substantive problem. Imagine what would have occurred if we had transformed the verbal model into a symbolic one, for example, by using plane geometry to derive quantitative estimates of the distance between points. This would not only have led us further and further away from the solution; it may have also created an aura of scientific rigor and precision that would lend authority to the conclusion that the problem is "insoluble." Finally, this illustration helps convey a simple but important point about the use of verbal, symbolic, and procedural models in policy analysis. Formal models

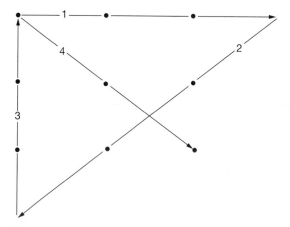

Figure 3.8 Solution for nine-dot problem.

cannot themselves tell us whether we are solving the wrong formulation of a problem when we should be solving the right one: The map is *not* the territory.

METHODS OF PROBLEM STRUCTURING

Problem structuring is the process of generating and testing alternative conceptualizations of a problem situation. As we saw in Figure 3.3, problem structuring involves four interrelated phases: problem sensing, problem search, problem definition, and problem specification. A number of methods and related techniques are helpful in carrying out problem-structuring activities in each phase. These methods, along with their respective aims, procedures, source of knowledge, and criteria of performance, are displayed in Table 3.2.

Boundary Analysis

An important task of problem structuring is estimating whether the system of individual problem formulations that we have called a *metaproblem* is relatively complete. This task is similar to the situation of the homesteaders described by Kline in his essays on the myth of certainty in mathematics.[47] The homesteaders, while clearing their land, are aware that enemies lurk in the wilderness that lies just beyond the clearing. To increase their security, the homesteaders clear a larger and larger area but never feel completely safe. Frequently, they must decide whether to clear more land or attend to their crops and domesticated animals within the boundaries of the clearing. They do their best to push back the wilderness but know full well that the enemies lurking beyond the clearing could surprise and destroy them. They hope that they will not choose to tend the crops and livestock when, instead, they should have chosen to clear more land.

The analogy of the homesteaders accentuates a key problem of problem structuring in policy analysis. Policy analysts are rarely faced with a single, well-defined problem; rather, they are faced with multiple problems that, distributed throughout the policy-making process, are defined in distinctly different ways by stakeholders whose perspectives and actions are interdependent. Under these circumstances, analysts appear as homesteaders working within unmanageable boundaries, or perhaps as modern counterparts of Diogenes, engaged in "a never-ending discourse with reality, to discover yet more facets, more dimensions of action, more opportunities for improvement."[48]

To make effective use of the methods and techniques of problem structuring described in this chapter, it is important to conduct a *boundary analysis*. Methods of

---

[47] Morris Kline, *Mathematics: The Loss of Certainty* (New York: Oxford University Press, 1980). See also the critical essays on uncertainty and creativity in modern mathematics by Michael Guillen, *Bridges to Infinity* (Ithaca, NY: Cornell University Press, 1988).

[48] Dery, *Problem Definition in Policy Analysis*, pp. 6–7.

Table 3.2 Methods of Problem Structuring

Method	Aim	Procedures	Source of Knowledge	Performance Criterion
Boundary analysis	Estimation of metaproblem boundaries	Saturation sampling, problem elicitation, and	Knowledge system	Correctness-in-limit cumulation
Classificational analysis	Clarification of concepts	Logical division and classification of concepts	Individual analyst	Logical consistency
Hierarchy analysis	Identification of possible, plausible, and actionable causes	Logical division and classification of causes	Individual analyst	Logical consistency
Synectics	Recognition of similarities among problems	Construction of personal, direct, symbolic, and fantasy analogies	Individual analyst or group	Plausibility of comparisons
Brainstorming	Generation of ideas, goals, and strategies	Idea generation and evaluation	Group	Consensus
Multiple perspective analysis	Generation of insight	Joint use of technical, organizational, and personal perspectives	Group	Improved insight
Assumptional analysis	Creative synthesis of conflicting assumptions	Stakeholder identification, assumption surfacing, challenging, pooling, and synthesis	Group	Conflict
Argumentation mapping	Assumption assessment	Plausibility and importance rating and graphing	Group	Optimal plausibility and importance

problem structuring just discussed, along with related methods that presuppose that the problem has already been structured,[49] do not themselves provide any way to know whether a set of problem formulations is relatively complete. The relative completeness of a set of problem formulations may be estimated by means of a three-step process.[50]

1. *Saturation sampling.* A saturation (or snowball) sample of stakeholders may be obtained by a multistage process that begins with a set of individuals and groups known to differ on a policy. Stakeholders in this initial set may be contacted, face-to-face or by telephone, and asked to name two additional stakeholders who agree most and least with the arguments and claims discussed. The process is continued until no *new* stakeholders are named. Provided that the set of stakeholders is not a subsample from a larger population, there is no sampling variance, because all members of the working universe of policy-relevant stakeholders in a specific area (e.g., a bill addressing health care reform or a court decision protecting the environment) have been contacted.[51]

2. *Elicitation of problem representations.* This second step is designed to elicit the alternative problem representations that Heclo has described as the "ideas, basic paradigms, dominant metaphors, standard operating procedures, or whatever else we choose to call the systems of interpretation by which we attach meaning to events."[52] The evidence required to characterize these problem representations may be obtained from face-to-face interviews or, more realistically under the time constraints facing most analysts, from telephone conversations and documents requested from stakeholders in the saturation sampling phase.

3. *Boundary estimation.* The third step is to estimate the boundaries of the metaproblem. Here the analyst constructs a cumulative frequency distribution where stakeholders are arrayed on the horizontal axis and the number of *new* problem elements—ideas, concepts, variables, assumptions, objectives, policies—are plotted on the vertical axis (Figure 3.9). As the new and nonduplicative problem elements of each stakeholder are plotted, the slope of the

---

[49] These other methods include the analytic hierarchy process, interpretive structural modeling, policy capturing, and Q-methodology. See, respectively, Thomas L. Saaty, *The Analytic Hierarchy Process* (New York: McGraw-Hill, 1980); John N. Warfield, *Societal Systems: Planning, Policy, and Complexity* (New York: Wiley, 1976); Kenneth R. Hammond, *Judgment and Decision in Public Policy Formation* (Boulder, CO: Westview Press, 1977); and Stephen R. Brown, *Political Subjectivity: Applications of Q-Methodology in Political Science* (New Haven, CT: Yale University Press, 1980). Computer software is available for applications of these methods.

[50] See William N. Dunn, "Methods of the Second Type: Coping with the Wilderness of Conventional Policy Analysis," *Policy Studies Review* 7, no. 4 (1988): 720–37.

[51] On these points as they apply to sociometric and saturation sampling in general, see Seymour Sudman, *Applied Sampling* (New York: Academic Press, 1976).

[52] Hugh Heclo, "Policy Dynamics," in *The Dynamics of Public Policy,* ed. Richard Rose (Beverly Hills, CA: Sage Publications, 1976), pp. 253–54.

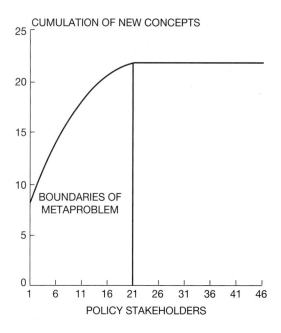

Figure 3.9 Boundaries of a metaproblem.

curve displays different rates of change. An initial rapid rate of change is followed by slow change and eventually stagnation, which is the point at which the curve becomes flat. After this point, the collection of additional information about the nature of the problem is unlikely to improve the accuracy of the collective problem representation, because the boundary of the metaproblem has been estimated.

The estimation procedures described satisfy requirements for sound inductive estimates in general: character, coordination, cost-effectiveness, and correctness-in-the-limit.[53] Applications of similar procedures in other complex areas—for example, estimates of boundaries of scientific literature, library holdings, languages, literary works, consumer preferences—suggest lawful regularities in the patterns and limits of growth in knowledge systems.[54] Boundary analysis, like other policy-analytic procedures, yields results that are plausible and not certain. In conjunction with other problem structuring methods and techniques, these boundary estimation procedures reduce the likelihood of type III errors in policy analysis.

---

[53] See Nicholas Rescher, *Induction* (Pittsburgh, PA: University of Pittsburgh Press, 1980), pp. 24–26. For the detailed argument relating these requirements to problem structuring in policy analysis, see Dunn, "Methods of the Second Type."

[54] For a brief but provocative essay on these regularities, see Herbert A. Simon, "The Sizes of Things," in *Statistics: A Guide to the Unknown,* ed. Judith M. Tanur and others (San Francisco, CA: Holden-Day, 1972), pp. 195–202.

Classificational Analysis

Classificational analysis is a technique for clarifying concepts used to define and classify problem situations.[55] In sensing a problem situation, policy analysts must somehow classify their experiences. Even the most simple descriptions of problem situations are based on the classification of experience through inductive reasoning, a process where general (abstract) concepts, such as poverty, crime, and pollution, are formed by experiencing particular (concrete) objects or situations. When we classify a problem situation in one way, we often foreclose opportunities to classify it in another way, as the nine-dot problem illustrates so well.

Classificational analysis is based on two main procedures: logical division and logical classification. When we select a class and break it down into its component parts, the process is called *logical division;* the reverse process, which involves the combination of situations, objects, or persons into larger groups or classes, is called *logical classification.* The basis of any classification depends on the analyst's purpose, which in turn depends on substantive knowledge about a problem situation.

Consider, for example, the analysis of poverty in the United States. All families in the United States may be broken down into two subclasses: those whose incomes are above and below a poverty line established by the U.S. Social Security Administration. If an analyst stops at this point in the process of logical division, he or she will reach the conclusion that poverty in the United States is gradually declining and perhaps claim that the progressive reduction of poverty is a consequence of the operation of a healthy economy. Yet when the process of logical division is carried one step further, and poverty families are divided into two additional subclasses on the basis of income before and after government transfer payments, the analyst will reach an altogether different conceptualization of the problem. Here the analyst will no doubt conclude that the reduction of poverty is a consequence of public welfare and social security programs and probably claim that problems of poverty cannot be resolved by the private enterprise system, because the number of families below the poverty line increased absolutely and relative to the total population between 1968 and 1972 (Table 3.3).

Although there is no way to know with certainty whether the bases of a classification system are the right ones, there are several rules that help ensure that a classification system is both relevant to a problem situation and logically consistent:

1. *Substantive relevance.* The basis of a classification should be developed according to the analyst's purpose and the nature of the problem situation. This rule, deceptively simple in theory, means that classes and subclasses should conform as closely as possible to the "realities" of the problem situation. Yet as what we know about a situation is partly a function of the concepts we use to experience it, there are no absolute guidelines that tell us when we have perceived a problem correctly. Poverty, for example, may be classified as a problem of inadequate income, cultural deprivation, or psychological motivation—it may be all of these and more.

---

[55] See John O'Shaughnessy, *Inquiry and Decision* (New York: Harper & Row, 1973), pp. 22–30.

Table 3.3   Number of Households Living below Poverty Level, 1965–1972[1]

Category	1965		1968		1972	
	Number (millions)	Percentage of Total	Number (millions)	Percentage of Total	Number (millions)	Percentage of Total
Pretransfer households[2]	15.6	25.7	14.9	23.2	17.6	24.8
Posttransfer households[3]	10.5	17.3	10.1	15.7	10.0	14.1

Notes:
[1] The U.S. Social Security Administration defined poverty as falling below the following income levels: $3,223 (1965), $3,553 (1968), $4,275 (1972). These levels are established for the annual cash income of a non-farm family of four.
[2] Excludes government transfers in the form of cash payments (Social Security, Public Assistance), nutrition (Food Stamps), housing, health (Medicaid, Medicare), social services (OEO), employment and manpower, and education.
[3] Includes government transfers of all forms.
Source: R. D. Plotnick and F. Skidmore, *Progress against Poverty: Review of the 1964–1974 Decade*, Institute for Research on Poverty, Poverty Policy Analysis Series No. 1 (New York: Academic Press, 1975).

2. *Exhaustiveness*. Categories in a classification system should be exhaustive. This means that all subjects or situations of interest to the analyst must be "used up," so to speak. In the above example, all families in the United States must fit into one or another of the various categories. If we discover that some families have no income, either from their own efforts or government transfers, a new category might be created.

3. *Disjointness*. Categories must be mutually exclusive. Each subject or situation must be assigned to one and only one category or subcategory. In classifying families, for example, they must fall into one or the other of the two main subcategories (income above and below the poverty line), which means that no family can be "double-counted."

4. *Consistency*. Each category and subcategory should be based on a single classificational principle. A violation of this rule leads to overlapping subclasses and is known as the fallacy of cross-division. For example, we commit the fallacy of cross-division if we classify families according to whether they are above the poverty line or receive welfare payments, because many families fall into both categories. This rule is actually an extension of rules of exhaustiveness and disjointness.

5. *Hierarchical distinctiveness*. The meaning of levels in a classification system (categories, subcategories, sub-subcategories) must be carefully distinguished. This rule, which is really a guideline for interpreting classification systems, is derived from the simple but important rule discussed previously: Whatever involves *all* of a collection must not be one of the collection. Humankind is the class of all individuals; but it is not itself an individual. Similarly, poverty as a characteristic of 14 million families cannot be understood in terms of the

behavior of one family multiplied by 14 million. A population of 14 million poor families is not just quantitatively different from a single family; it is also qualitatively different because it involves a whole system of interdependent economic, social, and political characteristics.

The rule of hierarchical distinctiveness deserves further elaboration because it is central to problem structuring. In structuring policy problems, it frequently happens that analysts ignore the distinction between member and class and that a class cannot be a member of itself. This point is best illustrated by returning to the nine-dot problem (Figure 3.7). When a person first attempts to solve this problem, the

> assumption is that the dots compose a square and that the solution must be found *within* that square, a self-imposed condition which the instructions do not contain. His failure, therefore, does not lie in the impossibility of the task, but in his attempted solution. Having now created the problem it does not matter in the least which combination of four lines he now tries, and in what order; he always finishes with at least one unconnected dot. This means that he can run through the totality of first-order change possibilities [i.e., those that are confined to the level of members of the class defined as a square] ... but will never solve the task. The solution is a second-order change [i.e., one that involves *all* of the class] which consists in leaving the field and which cannot be contained within itself because ... it involves all of a collection and cannot, therefore, be part of it.[56]

A useful approach to classificational analysis is *set thinking*.[57] Set thinking involves the study of relations of sets to each other and to subsets, where a *set* is defined as a clearly delimited collection of objects or elements. Sets and subsets are the equivalents of classes and subclasses in a classification system and are expressed visually with aid of Venn diagrams.[58] In the Venn diagram in Figure 3.10, the rectangle might be used to represent all families in the United States. In set language, it is known as the *universal set* (U). Two of its component sets, shown as circles A and

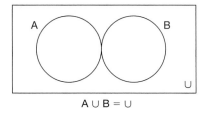

A ∪ B = U   **Figure 3.10**   Set union.

---

[56] Watzlawick and others, *Change*, p. 25. See also Gregory Bateson, *Steps to an Ecology of Mind* (New York: Ballantine Books, 1972).

[57] Set theory, created by the German mathematician-logician Georg Canter (1874–97), is the mathematical theory of collections of aggregates of entities.

[58] Venn diagrams, used extensively to illustrate set problems, are named after the English logician, John Venn (1834–1923).

B in the rectangle, might be used to represent families above and below the poverty line. If we apply rules of exhaustiveness, disjointedness, and consistency, all families will be divided into one or the other of the sets, *A* and *B,* so that the two sets reflect distinct levels of income that do not overlap. In set language, the *union* of *A* and *B* is equal to the *universe* (*U*) of all families. The symbol for union is ∪, read as "union" or "cup."

Two sets intersect to form a subset, so that the properties of the original two sets overlap, as shown in Figure 3.11. For example, the intersection (*D*) of non-poverty (*A*) and poverty (*B*) families might be used to illustrate that some families in each group receive government transfer payments. In set language, the intersection of *A* and *B* is equal to *D,* which is expressed symbolically as A ∩ B = D and read "*A* intersect (or cap) *B* equals *D.*" Union and intersection are the two most important set operations and may be used to construct classification schemes (Figure 3.12) and crossbreaks (Figure 3.13). Crossbreaks are a basic form of logical division used to organize data in tables.

Venn diagrams, classification schemes, and crossbreaks are important techniques for structuring policy problems. Procedures of classificational analysis, however, focus on the individual policy analyst, rather than groups, and use logical consistency as the primary criterion of performance in assessing how well an analyst has conceptualized the problem. While the consistency of a classification scheme is an important aspect of its adequacy, there is no way to know with confidence that the substantive basis of any category or subcategory is the right one. As different analysts frequently disagree about substantive bases of categories, the individual focus of classificational analysis may foreclose opportunities to generate alternative classification schemes. In short, classificational analysis is a technique for improving the clarity of given concepts and their relationships. Classificational analysis does not guarantee that concepts will have substantive relevance.

Hierarchy Analysis

Hierarchy analysis is a technique for identifying possible causes of a problem situation.[59] Formal logic and many social science theories provide little guidance in identifying possible causes. There is no certain way to deduce causes from effects,

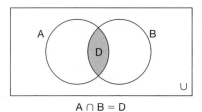

A ∩ B = D   **Figure 3.11**   Set intersection.

---

[59] See O'Shaughnessy, *Inquiry and Decision,* pp. 69–80.

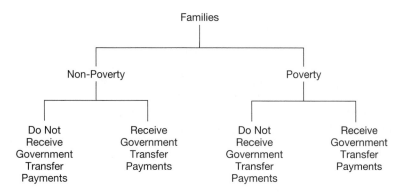

Figure 3.12 Classificational scheme.

or effects from causes, and social science theories are frequently so general or abstract as to be of little help in specific situations. In order to identify the possible causes contributing to a problem situation, it is useful to have conceptual frameworks that outline the many causes that may be operating in a given situation.

Hierarchy analysis helps the analyst to identify three kinds of causes: possible causes, plausible causes, and actionable causes. *Possible causes* are events or actions that, however remote, may contribute to the occurrence of a given problem situation. For example, resistance to work, unemployment, and the distribution of power and wealth among elites may all be taken as possible causes of poverty. By contrast, *plausible causes* are those that, on the basis of scientific research or direct experience, are believed to exert an important influence on the occurrence of a situation judged to be problematic. In the preceding example, resistance to work is unlikely to be regarded as a plausible cause of poverty, at least among experienced observers, whereas unemployment and elites are. Finally, the distribution of power and wealth among elites is unlikely to be viewed as an *actionable cause*—that is, one which is subject to control or manipulation by policy makers—because no single policy or set of policies intended to resolve problems of poverty can alter the social structure of an entire society. In this example unemployment is both a plausible and actionable cause of poverty.

	A_1	A_2
B_1	B_1A_1	B_1A_2
B_2	B_2A_1	B_2A_2

A_1 = non-poverty families
A_2 = poverty families
B_1 = do not receive transfer payments
B_2 = receive transfer payments

Figure 3.13 Crossbreak.

Political scientists Stuart Nagel and Marian Neef provide a good example of the potential uses of hierarchy analysis to structure policy problems. Many observers have been ready to accept the explanation that the major cause of overcrowded jails is the large number of persons arrested and detained in jail while awaiting trial. For this reason, a policy of pretrial release—that is, a policy that provides for the release of a certain number of those arrested (usually for less serious offenses) prior to a formal trial—has been favored by many reformers.

The difficulty with this policy, as well as the causal explanation on which it is based, is that it overlooks plea bargaining as one among several plausible causes of jail overcrowding. In plea bargaining, which is widely practiced in the U.S. judicial system, a defendant agrees to plead guilty in return for a prosecutor's agreement to reduce the charge or the sentence. When plea bargaining is taken into account along with pretrial release, the following consequences may occur:

> If the percentage of defendants released prior to trial goes up, then the percentage of successful plea bargains will probably go down.... Now, if guilty pleas go down as a result of increased pretrial release, then the number of trials will probably go up. . . . And if the number of trials increases, then the delay in going to trial will also increase, unless the system increases its quantity of prosecutors, judges, and public defenders. . . . If this delay in going to trial increases for cases in general, including defendants in jail, then the jail population may increase, since its size depends on the length of time that defendants are kept in jail as well as on the quantity of defendants who go there. Any decrease in the jail population as a result of increased pretrial release may be more than offset by the increased delay and length of pretrial detention caused by the increased pretrial release and the consequent reduction in guilty pleas and increase in trials.[60]

This example not only illustrates the potentially creative role of hierarchy analysis in structuring policy problems but also shows how hierarchy analysis can contribute to the discovery of possible unanticipated consequences of public policies whose effects seem self-evident. What could be more obvious than that pretrial release will result in a reduction of the jail population? The answer depends on having a satisfactory understanding of the plausible causes that contribute to the original problem situation. Figure 3.14 provides a simple illustration of hierarchy analysis applied to possible, plausible, and actionable causes of fires.

The rules for conducting a hierarchy analysis are the same as those used for classificational analysis: substantive relevance, exhaustiveness, disjointness, consistency, and hierarchical distinctiveness. Similarly, procedures of logical division and classification also apply to both types of analysis. The major difference between classificational analysis and hierarchy analysis is that the former involves the division and classification of concepts in general, whereas hierarchy analysis builds

---

[60] Stuart S. Nagel and Marian G. Neef, "Two Examples from the Legal Process," *Policy Analysis* 2, no. 2 (1976): 356–57.

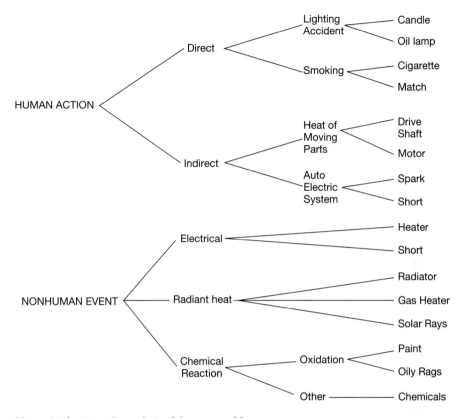

Figure 3.14 Hierarchy analysis of the causes of fires.
Source: John O'Shaughnessy, *Inquiry and Decision* (New York: Harper & Row, 1973), p. 76.

particular concepts of possible, plausible, and actionable causes. Nevertheless, both forms of analysis focus on the individual analyst and use logical consistency as the primary criterion for assessing how well a problem has been conceptualized, and neither guarantees that the correct substantive basis for concepts will be found. Thus, hierarchy analysis may also foreclose opportunities to generate alternative causal explanations by relying on the individual analyst, rather than on groups, as a source of knowledge.

Synectics

Synectics is a method designed to promote the recognition of analogous problems.[61] Synectics, which refers broadly to the investigation of similarities, helps

---

[61] See W. J. Gordon, *Synectics* (New York: Harper & Row, 1961); and Hayes, *Cognitive Psychology,* pp. 72, 241.

analysts make creative use of analogies in structuring policy problems. Many studies show that people frequently fail to recognize that what appears to be a new problem is really an old one in disguise and that old problems may contain potential solutions for problems that appear to be new. Synectics is based on the assumption that an awareness of identical or similar relationships among problems will greatly increase the problem-solving capacities of analysts.

In structuring policy problems, analysts may produce four types of analogies:

1. *Personal analogies.* In constructing personal analogies, analysts attempt to imagine themselves experiencing a problem situation in the same way as does some other policy stakeholder, for example, a policy maker or client group. Personal analogies are especially important in uncovering political dimensions of a problem situation, for "unless we are willing and able to think 'politically'—if only as a matter of role playing—we will not be able to enter the phenomenological world of the policymaker and understand the policy process."[62]

2. *Direct analogies.* In making direct analogies, the analyst searches for similar relationships among two or more problem situations. In structuring problems of drug addiction, for example, analysts may construct direct analogies from experiences with the control of contagious diseases.[63]

3. *Symbolic analogies.* In making symbolic analogies, the analyst attempts to discover similar relationships between a given problem situation and some symbolic process. For example, symbolic analogies are often drawn between servomechanisms of various kinds (thermostats, automatic pilots) and policy processes. In each case, analogous processes of adaptation are viewed as consequences of continuous feedback from the environment.[64]

4. *Fantasy analogies.* In making fantasy analogies, analysts are completely free to explore similarities between a problem situation and some imaginary state of affairs. Defense policy analysts, for example, have sometimes used fantasy analogies to structure problems of defense against nuclear attack.[65]

Synectics relies on individual analysts and groups to make appropriate analogies. The main criterion for assessing how well a problem has been conceptualized is the plausibility of comparisons, that is, the degree to which a given problem situation is actually similar to others taken as analogies.

---

[62] Raymond A. Bauer, "The Study of Policy Formation: An Introduction," in *The Study of Policy Formation,* ed. R. A. Bauer and K. J. Gergen (New York: Free Press, 1968), p. 4.

[63] See, for example, Mark H. Moore, "Anatomy of the Heroin Problem: An Exercise in Problem Definition," *Policy Analysis* 2, no. 4 (1976): 639–62.

[64] See, for example, David Easton, *A Framework for Political Analysis* (Englewood Cliffs, NJ: Prentice Hall, 1965).

[65] See, for example, Herman Kahn, *On Thermonuclear War* (Princeton, NJ: Princeton University Press, 1960). For a critique, see Philip Green, *Deadly Logic: The Theory of Nuclear Deterrence* (Columbus: Ohio State University Press, 1966).

Brainstorming

Brainstorming is a method for generating ideas, goals, and strategies that help identify and conceptualize problem situations. Originally designed by Alex Osborn as a means to enhance creativity, brainstorming may be used to generate a large number of suggestions about potential solutions for problems.[66] Brainstorming involves several simple procedures:

1. Brainstorming groups should be composed in accordance with the nature of the problem situation being investigated. This usually means the selection of persons who are particularly knowledgeable about the given situation, that is, experts.

2. Processes of idea generation and idea evaluation should be kept strictly apart, because intense group discussion may be inhibited by premature criticism and debate.

3. The atmosphere of brainstorming activities should be kept as open and permissive as possible in the idea-generating phase.

4. The idea-evaluating phase should begin only after all ideas generated in the first phase have been exhausted.

5. At the end of the idea-evaluating phase, the group should prioritize ideas and incorporate them in a proposal that contains a conceptualization of the problem and its potential solutions.

Brainstorming is a highly versatile procedure that may involve relatively structured or unstructured activities, depending on the analyst's aims and the practical constraints of the situation. Relatively unstructured brainstorming activities occur frequently in government agencies and public and private "think tanks." Here discussions of policy problems are informal and largely spontaneous, involving the interaction of generalists and specialists from several scientific disciplines or fields.[67] Brainstorming activities may also be relatively structured, with various devices used to coordinate or focus group discussions. These devices include the establishment of *continuous decision seminars* that, seeking to avoid the restrictive atmosphere of conventional committees, involve a team of highly motivated experts who meet with high frequency over a number of years.[68]

Another device for coordinating and focusing brainstorming activities is the construction of *scenarios,* which are outlines of hypothetical future events that may alter some problem situation. Scenario writing, which has been used to explore

---

[66] Alex F. Osborn, *Your Creative Power* (New York: Charles Scribner, 1948).

[67] See Edgar F. Quade, *Analysis for Public Decisions* (New York: American Elsevier Publishing, 1975), pp. 186–88; and Olaf Helmer and Nicholas Rescher. *On the Epistemology of the Inexact Sciences* (Santa Monica, CA: Rand Corporation, February, 1960).

[68] Harold D. Lasswell, "Technique of Decision Seminars," *Midwest Journal of Political Science* 4, no. 2 (1960): 213–26; and Lasswell, *The Future of Political Science* (New York: Atherton Press, 1963).

potential military and political crises, involves the constructive use of the imagination to describe some aspect of a future situation. There are two major types of scenarios: operations-analytical and free-form. In constructing a free-form scenario, the analyst is "an iconoclast, a model breaker, a questioner of assumptions, and—in rare instances—a fashioner of new criteria."[69] By contrast, an operations-analytical scenario has limited aims:

> instead of building up a picture of unrestrained fiction or even of constructing a utopian invention that the author considers highly desirable, an operations-analytical scenario starts with the present state of the world and shows how, step by step, a future state might evolve in a plausible fashion out of the present one.[70]

A good example of a relatively structured brainstorming effort is the Year 2000 Planning Program, a two and one-half year project carried out in the U.S. Bureau of the Census.[71] In this project, 120 self-selected participants from all levels and branches of the Bureau, from secretaries to division heads and the director, were asked to think as freely as possible about the future and to construct free-form scenarios, which to them indicated what the bureau should be like in the year 2000. Participants were asked to write group reports that were later integrated in a final report by an executive group composed of representatives of the individual groups. The final report was subsequently presented to the executive staff of the Census Bureau, as well as to the advisory committees of the American Statistical Association, the American Marketing Association, and the American Economic Association.

The Year 2000 Planning Program was successful on several counts. The report was received with moderate approval by all groups, and most members thought that the program should be continued in some form, perhaps permanently. Two creative products of the project were suggestions to establish an ombudsman to protect the interests of users of Census data and to create a Census University to develop and execute the bureau's continuing education programs. Those who were most positive about the report were oriented toward strategic concerns involving ill-structured problems; less positive reactions came from persons with tactical or operational orientations toward well-structured problems. The program itself was made possible by a recognition among top-level bureau staff, including the director, that the bureau was confronted by important long-range

---

[69] Seyon H. Brown, "Scenarios in Systems Analysis," in *Systems Analysis and Policy Planning: Applications in Defense*, ed. E. S. Quade and W. I. Boucher (New York: American Elsevier Publishing, 1968), p. 305.

[70] Olaf Helmer, *Social Technology* (New York: Basic Books, 1966), p. 10. Quoted in Quade, *Analysis for Public Decisions*, p. 188.

[71] See Ian I. Mitroff, Vincent P. Barabba, and Ralph II. Kilmann, "The Application of Behaviorial and Philosophical Technologies to Strategic Planning: A Case Study of a Large Federal Agency," *Management Science* 24, no. 1 (1977): 44–58.

problems whose structure was highly complex and "messy." Finally, although the program involved significant resource allocations, there did not appear to be major risks in executing the program.

The main difference between brainstorming and other techniques for problem structuring is that the focus is on groups of knowledgeables rather than individual experts. Moreover, brainstorming activities are assessed not in terms of logical consistency or the plausibility of comparisons but according to consensus among members of brainstorming groups. The major limitation of consensus as a criterion of performance in problem structuring is that conflicts about the nature of problems may be suppressed, thus foreclosing opportunities to generate and evaluate potentially appropriate ideas, goals, and strategies. While the Year 2000 Planning Program sought to create an open and permissive atmosphere, the final evaluation of the program's success was based on consensus among authoritative decision makers (agency executive staff) and experts (advisory committees of professional associations). In short, this program and other relatively structured brainstorming activities provide no explicit procedures to promote the creative use of conflict in structuring policy problems.

Multiple Perspective Analysis

Multiple perspective analysis is a method for obtaining greater insight into problems and potential solutions by systematically applying personal, organizational, and technical perspectives to problem situations.[72] Seen as an alternative to the near-exclusive emphasis on so-called rational-technical approaches in planning, policy analysis, technology assessment, social impact assessment, and other areas, multiple perspective analysis is expressly designed to address ill-structured policy problems. Although there are many characteristics of each of the three perspectives, their major features are as follows:

1. *Technical perspective.* The technical (T) perspective views problems and solutions in terms of optimization models and employs techniques based on probability theory, benefit–cost and decision analysis, econometrics, and systems analysis. The technical perspective, said to be based on a scientific–technological worldview, emphasizes causal thinking, objective analysis, prediction, optimization, and qualified uncertainty. A good example of the T perspective is provided by the decision to drop the atomic bomb on Japan. The problem was seen to be composed of five alternatives— bombing and blockade, invasion, atomic attack without warning, atomic attack after warning, and dropping the bomb on an uninhabited island.

---

[72] See Harold A. Linstone, *Multiple Perspectives for Decision Making: Bridging the Gap between Analysis and Action* (New York: North-Holland Publishing, 1984); and Linstone and others, "The Multiple Perspective Concept: With Applications to Technology Assessment and Other Decision Areas," *Technological Forecasting and Social Change* 20 (1981): 275–325.

Given the goal of unconditional surrender with a minimum loss of Allied lives and destruction of Japan, the third alternative (atomic attack without warning) was the preferred alternative.

2. *Organizational perspective.* The organizational (O) perspective views problems and solutions as part of an orderly progression (with minor but temporary crises) from one organizational state to another. Standard operating procedures, rules, and institutional routines are major characteristics of the O perspective, which is often resistant to the T perspective and only minimally concerned with achieving goals and improving performance. The decision to drop the atomic bomb provides a good example of the O perspective and how it differs from the T perspective. From an O perspective, a decision not to use the bomb raised profound organizational fears, because $2 billion in funding was expended without congressional approval. Dropping the bomb showed Congress that the funds were not wasted, and at the same time, inaugurated the Cold War by challenging the perceived Soviet threat.

3. *Personal perspective.* The personal (P) perspective views problems and solutions in terms of individual perceptions, needs, and values. Major characteristics of the personal perspective are an emphasis on intuition, charisma, leadership, and self-interest as factors governing policies and their impacts. The example of the atomic bomb also shows how the P perspective supplies insights not available from either the T or the O perspectives. In 1945 the new President Harry Truman was an outsider to the FDR establishment, which had grown and solidified during Roosevelt's three terms in office. Truman lacked the legitimacy and influence necessary to challenge the establishment, including entrenched bureaucratic interests and policies, so early in his presidency. A decision not to drop the atomic bomb would be perceived as a sign of weakness to contemporaries and to future historians. Truman, who had a strong sense of history, wanted to appear as a bold and decisive leader.

Multiple perspective analysis is relevant to any sociotechnological problem found in areas of public policy making, corporate strategic planning, regional development, and other domains. To employ multiple perspective analysis, Linstone and colleagues have developed some of the following guidelines:

- *Interparadigmatic mix.* Form teams on the basis of an interparadigmatic rather than interdisciplinary mix. For example, a team composed of a businessperson, lawyer, and writer is preferred to a team with an economist, a political scientist, and a psychologist. The interparadigmatic mix is preferable because it maximizes opportunities to find an appreciation for T, O, and P perspectives in the team.

- *Balance among perspectives.* In advance of planning and policy analysis activities, it is not possible to decide how much emphasis to place on T, O, and P perspectives. As the team engages in its work, the discovery of the proper balance among the three perspectives will permit assignments to T, O, and P tasks. In the meantime, an equal distribution is preferable.

- *Uneven replicability*. The T perspective typically employs methods (e.g., experimental design) that are replicable. The O and P perspectives are not replicable. Like a jury trial, the process is not replicable; nor are nonroutine executive decisions.

- *Appropriate communications*. Adapt the medium of communication to the message. Summaries, oral briefings, scenarios, and vignettes are appropriate for communicating with those who hold O and P perspectives. Models, data, lists of variables, and analytical routines are appropriate for those with a T perspective.

- *Deferred integration*. Leave the integration of perspectives to the client or policy maker, but point out linkages among the T, O, and P perspectives and the differing conclusions they yield.

Multiple perspective analysis has been employed extensively in the domain of technology assessment and other areas of public policy. Methods of multiple perspective analysis, developed on the basis of earlier work in foreign policy and the design of knowledge systems,[73] is a way to deal with the complexity of ill-structured problems that originate in sociotechnological systems with high scientific and technical content.

Assumptional Analysis

Assumptional analysis is a technique that aims at the creative synthesis of conflicting assumptions about policy problems.[74] In many respects, assumptional analysis is the most comprehensive of all problem-structuring methods, because it includes procedures used in conjunction with other techniques and may focus on groups, individuals, or both. The most important feature of assumptional analysis is that it is explicitly designed to treat ill-structured problems, that is, problems where policy analysts, policy makers, and other stakeholders cannot agree on how to formulate a problem. The main criterion for assessing the adequacy of a given formulation of a problem is whether conflicting assumptions about a problem situation have been surfaced, challenged, and creatively synthesized.

Assumptional analysis is designed to overcome four major limitations of policy analysis: (1) policy analysis is often based on the assumption of a single decision

---

[73] The antecedent works in foreign policy and knowledge systems design are, respectively, Graham Allison, *Essence of Decision: Conceptual Models and the Cuban Missile Crisis* (Boston, MA: Little, Brown and Company, 1962); and C. West Churchman, *The Design of Inquiring Systems* (New York: Basic Books, 1971).

[74] See Ian I. Mitroff and James R. Emshoff, "On Strategic Assumption-Making: A Dialectical Approach to Policy and Planning," *Academy of Management Review* 4, no. 1 (1979): 1–12; Richard O. Mason and Ian I. Mitroff, *Challenging Strategic Planning Assumptions: Theory, Cases, and Techniques* (New York: Wiley, 1981); and Ian I. Mitroff, Richard O. Mason, and Vincent P. Barabba, *The 1980 Census: Policymaking amid Turbulence* (Lexington, MA: D. C. Heath, 1983).

maker with clearly ordered values that may be realized at a single point in time, (2) policy analysis typically fails to consider in a systematic and explicit way strongly differing views about the nature of problems and their potential solutions, (3) most policy analysis is carried out in organizations whose "self-sealing" character makes it difficult or impossible to challenge prevailing formulations of problems, and (4) criteria used to assess the adequacy of problems and their solutions often deal with surface characteristics (e.g., logical consistency), rather than with basic assumptions underlying the conceptualization of problems.

Assumptional analysis explicitly recognizes the positive as well as the negative features of conflict and commitment. "Conflict is needed to permit the existence of maximally opposing policies to ferret out and to challenge the underlying assumptions that each policy makes. Commitment on the other hand is also necessary if the proponents for each policy are to make the strongest possible case (not necessarily the best) for their respective points of view."[75] Assumptional analysis involves the use of five procedures used in successive phases:

1. *Stakeholder identification.* In the first phase, policy stakeholders are identified, ranked, and prioritized. The identification, ranking, and prioritization of stakeholders is based on an assessment of the degree to which they influence and are influenced by the policy process. This procedure results in the identification of stakeholders—for example, dissident groups of administrators or clients—who are usually excluded in the analysis of policy problems.

2. *Assumption surfacing.* In this second phase, analysts work backward from a recommended solution for a problem to the selective set(s) of data that support the recommendation and the underlying assumptions that, when coupled with the data, allow one to deduce the recommendation as a consequence of the data. Each recommended solution put forth by policy stakeholders should contain a list of assumptions that explicitly and implicitly underlie the recommendation. By listing all assumptions—for example, that poverty is a consequence of historical accidents, elite domination, unemployment, cultural deprivation, and so on—there is an explicit specification of the problem to which each recommendation is addressed.

3. *Assumption challenging.* In the third phase, analysts compare and evaluate sets of recommendations and their underlying assumptions. This is done by systematically comparing assumptions and counterassumptions that differ maximally from their counterparts. During this process, each assumption previously identified is challenged by a counterassumption. If a counterassumption is implausible, it is eliminated from further consideration; if it is plausible, it is examined to determine whether it might serve as a basis for an entirely new conceptualization of the problem and its solution.

---

[75] Mitroff and Emshoff, "On Strategic Assumption-Making," p. 5.

4. *Assumption pooling*. When the assumption-challenging phase has been completed, the diverse proposed solutions generated in previous phases are pooled. Here assumptions (rather than recommendations) are negotiated by prioritizing assumptions in terms of their relative certainty and importance to different stakeholders. Only the most important and uncertain assumptions are pooled. The ultimate aim is to create an acceptable list of assumptions on which as many stakeholders as possible agree.

5. *Assumption synthesis*. The final phase is the creation of a composite or synthetic solution for the problem. The composite set of acceptable assumptions can serve as a basis for the creation of a new conceptualization of the problem. When issues surrounding the conceptualization of the problem and its potential solutions have reached this point, the activities of stakeholders may become cooperative and cumulatively productive.

The last four phases of assumptional analysis are illustrated in Figure 3.15, which helps visualize important features of the technique. First, the method begins with recommended solutions for problems rather than assumptions themselves. This is because most policy stakeholders are aware of proposed solutions for problems but seldom conscious of underlying assumptions. By starting with recommended solutions, the method builds on what is most familiar to stakeholders but then goes on to use familiar solutions as a point of reference for forcing an explicit consideration of underlying assumptions. A second important feature of the technique is that it attempts, as far as possible, to focus on the *same* set of data or policy-relevant information. The reason for this is that conflicts surrounding the conceptualization of policy problems are not so much matters of "fact" but matters involving conflicting interpretations of the same data. Although data, assumptions, and recommended solutions are interrelated, it is not so much the problem situation (data) that governs the conceptualization of problems but the assumptions that analysts and other stakeholders bring to the problem situation. Finally, assumptional analysis systematically addresses a major problem of policy analysis, which is that of applying some set of procedures to deal with conflict in a creative manner.

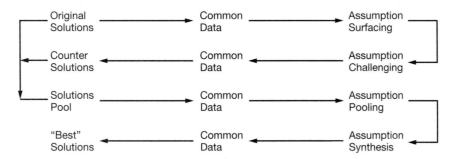

Figure 3.15   The process of assumptional analysis.

Source: Adapted from Ian I. Mitroff and James R. Emshoff, "On Strategic Assumption-Making: A Dialectical Approach to Policy and Planning." *Academy of Management Review* (1979).

The aims and procedures of assumptional analysis are intimately related to the modes of policy argument presented in Chapter 8.[76] Each mode of policy argument contains characteristically different kinds of assumptions that may be used to produce alternative conceptualizations of problem situations. Assumptional analysis is therefore a major vehicle for conducting reasoned debates about the nature of policy problems. Assumptional analysis may be used with groups of policy stakeholders who actually participate in structuring policy problems or by an individual analyst who simulates the assumptions of stakeholders in order to conduct a reasoned debate with himself. Assumptional analysis can help reduce errors of the third type (E_{III}).

Argumentation Mapping

Methods of assumptional analysis are closely related to *argumentation mapping,* which is based on the modes of policy argument presented later in Chapter 8. Modes of policy argument—authoritative, statistical, classificational, analycentric, causal, intuitive, pragmatic, and value critical—are based on distinctly different assumptions. These assumptions, when combined with the same policy-relevant information, yield conflicting knowledge claims.

An important technique of assumptional analysis is the use of graphic displays to map the plausibility and importance of elements of policy arguments. The first step in this process is to rate these elements—that is, warrants, backings, and rebuttals—on two ordinal scales. For example, recommendations to abandon the 55 mph speed limit (National Maximum Speed Law of 1973) have been based on the warrant that the opportunity costs of time lost driving at slower speeds increases risky driving among motorists with higher incomes. Conversely, it could be argued that the frequency of accidents is less among younger motorists, a claim that is based on the warrant that younger drivers earn less income, have lower opportunity costs, take fewer risks, and therefore have fewer accidents. This warrant may be rated by different stakeholders on nine-point plausibility and importance scales (1 = low, 9 = high) and plotted on a graph such as that shown in Figure 3.16.[77]

Figure 3.16 displays the plausibility and importance ratings for six stakeholders. The graph shows that stakeholders are distributed across the four quadrants, indicating substantial disagreement about the plausibility and importance of the warrant. If stakeholders are participants in a problem-structuring group, the disagreements evident in the right half of the graph (i.e., high importance) can be discussed and perhaps resolved in favor of an optimally plausible knowledge claim. The typical situation, however, is one where the analyst must identify a range of stakeholders and, on the basis of telephone interviews and documents stating the stakeholders' arguments and

---

[76] For an elaboration of assumptional analysis using the structural model of argument presented in Chapter 8, see Mitroff, Mason, and Barabba, *The 1980 Census, passim.*

[77] Computer software called *Claim Game* provides capabilities for entering, saving, storing, and accessing a system of complex policy arguments. The program enables analysts to rate each element of an argument on nine-point plausibility and importance scales and plot stakeholders and their assumptions on the coordinates formed by the intersection of the two scales.

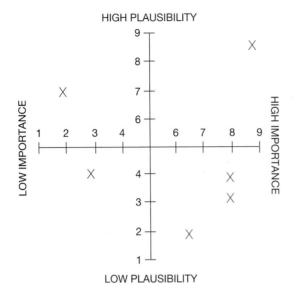

WARRANT: The opportunity costs of
driving time are less for younger drivers,
who earn less income. Younger drivers
therefore may drive slower and take fewer risks.

Figure 3.16   Distribution of warrant by plausibility and importance.

assumptions, make judgments about the plausibility and importance that stakeholders probably would attach to a warrant, backing, or rebuttal. For example, a review of documents on the 55 mph speed limit indicates that the stakeholder rating the warrant as highly plausible (P = 9) is an economist, whereas the stakeholder who ranks the warrant as having low plausibility (P = 2) is an ethnographer who specializes in the culture of young drivers and bases his/her analyses on interviews with young drivers, parents, teachers, law enforcement personnel, and other stakeholders.[78]

On the basis of reasoned arguments and evidence provided by these two sources—along with information about the assumptions of various stakeholders and available statistics on accident and fatality rates by age group—the analyst would no doubt conclude that this particular warrant has low plausibility. The warrant also has high importance—whether it is plausible or implausible, it is highly relevant to the conclusions of the argument.

---

[78] See Thomas H. Forrester, Robert F. McNown, and Larry D. Singell, "A Cost-Benefit Analysis of the 55 mph Speed Limit," *Southern Economic Journal* 50 (1984), reviewed by George M. Guess and Paul G. Farnham, *Cases in Public Policy Analysis* (New York: Longman, 1989), p. 199. For an ethnographic analysis of younger drivers and the meanings they attach to accidents and fatalities—which are different from those predicted by economic theory—see J. Peter Rothe, *Challenging the Old Order* (New Brunswick, NJ: Transaction Books, 1990).

CHAPTER SUMMARY

This chapter has provided an overview of the nature of policy problems, described the process of structuring these problems, examined relationships among policy models, and described specific methods of problem structuring. One of the most important challenges facing policy analysts is reducing the likelihood of a type III error: formulating the wrong problem.

LEARNING OBJECTIVES

- distinguish problem structuring from problem solving
- understand the subjective, systemic, and interdependent nature of policy problems
- contrast problem situations from problems
- compare and contrast relatively well-structured, moderately structured, and ill-structured problems
- distinguish different types of policy models
- discuss the strengths and limitations of different methods of problem structuring
- analyze three cases of problem structuring in policy analysis

KEY TERMS AND CONCEPTS

Argumentation mapping (114)
Assumptional analysis (111)
Blaming the victim (84)
Boundary analysis (95)
Brainstorming (107)
Classificational analysis (99)
Descriptive model (87)
Hierarchy analysis (102)
Ill-structured problem (80)
Moderately structured problem (80)
Multiple perspective analysis (109)
Normative model (87)

Perspective model (91)
Problem (72)
Problem situation (74)
Procedural model (89)
Stakeholder analysis (120)
Symbolic model (88)
Synectics (105)
Surrogate model (91)
Teleological system (76)
Type III error (84)
Verbal model (88)
Well-structured problem (79)

REVIEW QUESTIONS

1. "Our problem is not to do what is right," stated Lyndon Johnson during his years in the White House. "Our problem is to know what is right." Considering the major characteristics and types of policy problems discussed in this chapter, to what extent can we know in advance which policy is the "right" one?

2. A commonly accepted viewpoint among many policy analysts in government and in universities is that policy analysis can be objective, neutral, and impartial. Given the characteristics of ill-structured problems, consider the extent to which this viewpoint is plausible.

3. Provide two or three examples from your own experience of ways that worldviews, ideologies, and popular myths shape the formulation of policy problems.

4. There are several broad types of organizational structures in which policy formation occurs. One type is the "bureaucratic" structure, whose characteristics include
   centralization, hierarchical chain of command, specialization of tasks, and complete
   information. The bureaucratic form of organization requires consensus on preferred
   policy outcomes, as well as certainty that alternative courses of action will result in
   certain preferred outcomes (J. D. Thompson, *Organizations in Action* [New York:
   McGraw-Hill, 1967], pp. 134–35). If many of our most important policy problems
   are ill-structured ones, what does this say about the appropriateness of the bureaucratic form of organization for formulating and resolving such problems?

5. If many of our most important problems are ill-structured ones, to what extent is it
   possible to hold individual policy makers, policy analysts, and planners politically
   and morally responsible for their actions? (For a provocative discussion of this
   point, see M. M. Webber and H. W. J. Rittel, "Dilemmas in a General Theory of
   Planning," *Policy Sciences* 4, no. 2 [1973]: 155–69.)

6. The ill-structured problems described below are taken from illustrations published
   in the journal *Policy Analysis* (now the *Journal of Policy Analysis and
   Management*) under the title "Department of Unintended Consequences."

   > For several thousand years, Egyptian agriculture depended on the fertilizing
   > sediment deposited by the flood of the Nile. No longer, however. Due to
   > expensive modern technology intended to improve the age-old lot of the peas-
   > ant, Egypt's fields must be artificially fertilized. John Gall, writing in the *New
   > York Times Magazine* (December 26, 1976), reports that the Nile sediment is
   > now deposited in the Aswan Dam's Lake Nasser. Much of the dam's electrical
   > output is used to supply enormous amounts of electricity to new fertilizer
   > plants made necessary by the construction of the dam.

   > University of Illinois ecologists can explain how certain harmful field mice spread
   > from their native regions into areas where they had never before been found.
   > They are using the new, limited-access, cross-country highways, which turn out
   > to be easy escape routes with few barriers. Older highways and roads, as well as
   > railroad rights-of-way, run into towns and villages every few miles and effectively
   > deter mice migration. The Illinois group found that before interstate highways ran
   > through central Illinois, one type of mouse was limited to a single county. But in
   > six years of superhighways the four-inch-long creatures have spread sixty miles
   > south through the center of the state. The ecologists are concerned lest the mice,
   > a species that loves to chew on trees, become a threat in central and southern
   > counties where apple orchards abound (*Wall Street Journal,* December 1, 1977).

   > Edward J. Moody ... argues persuasively that worship of Satan has the effect of
   > normalizing abnormal people. Thus, to "keep secret" from ordinary people their
   > satanic power and existence, such persons are urged to behave as straight as pos-
   > sible. The effect, of course, is more effective social relations—the goal for which
   > Satan's name has been invoked in the first place! (P. E. Hammond, "Review of
   > Religious Movements in Contemporary America," *Science,* May 2, 1975, p. 442).

   > Residents of San Francisco's North Beach areas must now pay $10 for the
   > privilege of parking in their own neighborhood. A residential parking plan
   > was recently implemented to prevent commuters from using the area as a
   > daytime parking lot. But according to a story in the *San Francisco Bay
   > Guardian* (March 14, 1978), the plan has in no way improved the residential

parking situation. Numbers of commuters from outlying districts of the city have simply been changing their car registrations to North Beach addresses. A North Beach resident—now $10 poorer—still spends a lot of time driving around the block.

Choose one of these problems and write a short essay on how classificational analysis, hierarchy analysis, and synectics might be used to structure this problem.

7. Construct a scenario on the state of one of the following problem situations in the year 2050:
    Availability of public mass transit
    Arms control and national security
    Crime prevention and public safety
    Quality of the public school system
    State of the world's ecological system

8. Select two editorials on a current issue of public policy from two newspapers (e.g., *The New York Times, The Washington Post, The Economist, Le Monde*) or news magazine (e.g., *Newsweek, The New Republic, National Review*). After reading the editorial:
    a. Use the procedures for argumentation analysis (Chapter 8) to display contending positions and underlying assumptions.
    b. Rate the assumptions and plot them according to their plausibility and importance (Figure 3.16).
    c. Which arguments are the most plausible?

DEMONSTRATION EXERCISE

1. Choose a policy issue area such as crime control, national security, environmental protection, or economic development. Use the procedures for stakeholder analysis presented in Procedural Guide 3 to generate a list of stakeholders who affect or are affected by problems in the issue area you have chosen for analysis.

    After generating the list, create a cumulative frequency distribution. Place stakeholders on the horizontal axis, numbering them from 1 ... n. On the vertical axis, place the number of new (nonduplicate) ideas generated by each stakeholder (the ideas can be objectives, alternatives, outcomes, causes, etc.). Connect the total new ideas of each stakeholder with a line graph.

    • Does the line graph flatten out?
    • If so, after how many stakeholders?
    • What conclusions do you draw about the policy problem(s) in the issue area?

    Compare your work with Case Study 3 at the end of the chapter.

2. After reading Case 3, write an essay in which you compare and contrast the process of boundary analysis and estimation in the three cases. In your comparison, address these questions:

    • What are key differences in data collection, represented by the process of group interviewing and content analysis?
    • Why do the cumulative frequency graphs flatten out the way they do?
    • Evaluate the statement: "Boundary analysis is a reliable way to estimate the 'universe of meanings' in a given policy issue area."

REFERENCES

Ackoff, Russell L. *Redesigning the Future.* New York: Wiley, 1974.

Adams, James L. *Conceptual Blockbusting.* Stanford, CA: Stanford Alumni Association, 1974.

Adelman, L., T. R. Stewart, and K. R. Hammond. "A Case History of the Application of Social Judgment Theory to Policy Formulation." *Policy Sciences* 6 (1975): 137–59.

Bobrow, Davis B., and John S. Dryzek. *Policy Analysis by Design.* Pittsburgh, PA: University of Pittsburgh Press, 1986.

Brunner, Ronald D. "The Policy Movement as a Policy Problem." In *Advances in Policy Studies since 1950.* Vol. 10 of *Policy Studies Review Annual.* Edited by William N. Dunn and Rita Mae Kelly. New Brunswick, NJ: Transaction Books, 1992.

Churchman, C. West. *The Design of Inquiring Systems.* New York: Basic Books, 1971.

Dery, David. *Problem Definition in Policy Analysis.* Lawrence: University Press of Kansas, 1984.

Dror, Yehezkel. *Public Policy Making Reexamined.* Rev ed. New Brunswick. NJ: Transaction Books, 1983.

Dryzek, John S. "Policy Analysis as a Hermeneutic Activity." *Policy Sciences* 14 (1982): 309–29.

Dunn, William N. "Methods of the Second Type: Coping with the Wilderness of Conventional Policy Analysis." *Policy Studies Review* 7, no. 4 (1988): 720–37.

Dunn, William N., and Ari Ginsbero. "A Sociocognitive Approach to Organizational Analysis." *Human Relations* 39, no. 11 (1986): 955–75.

Fischhoff, Baruch. "Clinical Policy Analysis." In *Policy Analysis: Perspectives, Concepts, and Methods.* Edited by William N. Dunn. Greenwich, CT: JAI Press, 1986.

———. "Cost-Benefit Analysis and the Art of Motorcycle Maintenance," *Policy Sciences* 8 (1977): 177–202.

George, Alexander. "Criteria for Evaluation of Foreign Policy Decision Making." *Global Perspectives* 2 (1984): 58–69.

Hammond, Kenneth R. "Introduction to Brunswickian Theory and Methods." *New Directions for Methodology of Social and Behavioral Science* 3 (1980): 1–12.

Hofstadter, Richard. *Godel, Escher, Bach.* New York: Random House, 1979.

Hogwood, Brian W., and B. Guy Peters. *The Pathology of Public Policy.* Oxford: Clarendon Press, 1985.

Linder, Stephen H., and B. Guy Peters. "A Metatheoretic Analysis of Policy Design." In *Advances in Policy Studies since 1950.* Vol. 10 of *Policy Studies Review Annual.* Edited by William N. Dunn and Rita Mae Kelly. New Brunswick, NJ: Transaction Books, 1992.

Linstone, Harold A. *Multiple Perspectives for Decision Making.* New York: North-Holland, 1984.

Mason, Richard O., and Ian I. Mitroff. *Challenging Strategic Planning Assumptions.* New York: Wiley, 1981.

Meehan, Eugene J. *The Thinking Game.* Chatham, NJ: Chatham House, 1988.

Mitroff, Ian I., Richard O. Mason, and Vincent P. Barabba. *The 1980 Census: Policymaking amid Turbulence.* Lexington, MA: D. C. Heath, 1983.

Saaty, Thomas L. *The Analytic Hierarchy Process.* New York: McGraw-Hill, 1980.

Schon, Donald A. *The Reflective Practitioner.* New York: Basic Books, 1983.

Sieber, Sam. *Fatal Remedies.* New York: Plenum Press, 1981.

Warfield, John N. *Societal Systems: Planning, Policy, and Complexity.* New York: Wiley, 1976.

Watzlawick, Paul, John Weakland, and Richard Fisch. *Change: Principles of Problem Formation and Problem Resolution.* New York: W. W. Norton, 1974.

Procedural Guide 3—Stakeholder Analysis

Definition

A stakeholder is a representative or spokesperson of an individual or group that is affected by or affects a policy. Stakeholders include the president of a legislative assembly or parliament, legislative committees, organized interest and advocacy groups such as the National Association of Manufacturers, the Sierra Club, or Human Rights Watch, and policy analysts themselves. The client who commissions a policy analysis is also a stakeholder.

Assumptions

- Stakeholders are best identified by policy issue area. A policy issue area is a domain where stakeholders disagree or quarrel about policies.
- Stakeholders should have specific names and titles—for example, State Senator X, Mr. Y, Chair, House Finance Committee, or Ms. Z, a spokesperson for the National Organization of Women (NOW).
- A sociometric or "snowball" sample such as that described below is the most effective way to estimate the "population" of stakeholders.

Step 1: Using Google or a reference book such as *The Encyclopedia of Associations,* identify and list about ten stakeholders who have taken a public position on a policy. Make the initial list as heterogeneous as possible by sampling opponents as well as supporters.

Step 2: For each stakeholder, obtain a policy document (e.g., a report, news article, or e-mail or telephone interview) that describes the position of each stakeholder.

Step 3: Beginning with the first statement of the first stakeholder, list stakeholders mentioned as opponents and proponents of the policy.

Step 4: For each remaining statement, list the new stakeholders mentioned. Do not repeat.

Step 5: Draw a graph that displays statements 1, 2, ... n on the horizontal axis. On the vertical axis, display the cumulative frequency of new stakeholders mentioned in the statements. The graph will gradually flatten out, with no new stakeholders mentioned. If this does not occur before reaching the last stakeholder on the initial list, repeat steps 2–4. Add to the graph the new statements and the new stakeholders.

Step 6: Add to the estimate stakeholders who should be included because of their formal positions (organization charts show such positions) or because they are involved in one or more policy-making activities: agenda setting, policy formulation, policy adoption, policy implementation, policy evaluation, and policy succession or termination.

Retain the full list for further analysis. You now have an estimate of the "population" of key stakeholders who are affected by and affect the policy, along with a description of their positions on an issue. This is a good basis for structuring the problem.

Case 3. Problem Structuring in Mine Safety and Health, Traffic Safety, and Job Training[79]

Complex problems must be structured before they can be solved. The process of "structuring" a policy problem is the search for and specification of problem elements and their structure. The "structure" of a problem refers to the way these elements are arranged. The elements are:

> *Policy stakeholders*. Which stakeholders affect or are affected by a "problem," as perceived by the stakeholders themselves?
>
> *Policy alternatives*. What alternative courses of action may be taken to solve the perceived "problem"?
>
> *Policy actions*. Which of these alternatives should be acted on to solve the perceived "problem"?
>
> *Policy outcomes*. What are the probable outcomes of action and are they part of the solution to the perceived "problem"?
>
> *Policy values (utilities)*. Are some outcomes more valuable than others in solving the perceived "problem"?

Most policy problems are "messy" or "ill-structured." For this reason, one or more problem elements can easily be incorrectly omitted from the definition of a problem. Even when problem elements are correctly specified, relations among the elements may be unknown or obscure. This makes it difficult or impossible to determine the strength and significance, practical as well as statistical, of causal relations. For example, many causal processes that are believed to govern relations among atmospheric pollution, global warming, and climate change are obscure. The obscurity of these processes stems not only from the complexity of "nature" but also from the conflicting beliefs of stakeholders who disagree, often intensely, about the definition of problems and their potential solutions. For this reason, the possible combinations and permutations of problem elements—that is, stakeholders, alternatives, actions, outcomes, values—*appear* to be unmanageably huge.

Under these conditions, standard methods of decision theory (e.g., risk–benefit analysis), applied economics (e.g., benefit–cost analysis), and political science (e.g., policy implementation analysis) are of limited value until the "problem" has been satisfactorily defined. This is so because an adequate definition of the problem must be constructed before the problem can be solved with

---

[79] Adapted from William N. Dunn, "Using the Method of Context Validation to Mitigate Type III Errors in Environmental Policy Analysis," in *Knowledge, Power, and Participation in Environmental Policy Analysis,* ed. Matthijs Hisschemoller, Rob Hoppe, William N. Dunn, and Jerry R. Ravetz (New Brunswick, NJ: Transaction Books, 2002), pp. 417–36.

these and other standard methods. Standard methods are useful in solving relatively well-structured (deterministic) problems involving certainty, for example,
problems represented as fixed quantities in a spreadsheet. Standard methods are
also useful in solving moderately structured (probabilistic) problems involving
uncertainty, for example, problems represented as policy outcomes with different probabilities. However, ill-structured problems are of a different order.
Estimates of uncertainty, or risk, cannot be made because we do not even know
the outcomes to which we might attach probabilities. Here, the analyst is much
like an architect who has been commissioned to design a *custom* building for
which there is no *standard* plan.[80] The adoption of a standard plan, if such
existed, would almost certainly result in a type III error: solving the "wrong"
problem.

Public policies are deliberate attempts to change complex systems. The
process of making and implementing policies occurs in social systems where
many contingencies lie beyond the control of policy makers. It is these unmanageable contingencies that are usually responsible for the success and failure of
policies in achieving their objectives. The contingencies are rival hypotheses that
can challenge claims that a policy (the presumed cause) produced one or more
policy outcomes (the presumed effects). In such cases, it is usually desirable to
test, and where possible eliminate, these rival hypotheses through a process of
eliminative induction. Eliminative induction takes the general form: "Repeated
observations of policy x and outcome y confirm that x is causally relevant to the
occurrence of y. However, additional observations of $x, z,$ and y confirm that
unmanageable contingency z and not policy x is responsible for the occurrence of y."
By contrast, *enumerative* induction takes the general form: "Repeated observations confirm that the policy x is causally relevant to the occurrence of policy
outcome y."

Eliminative induction permits a critical examination of contingencies that are
beyond the control of policy makers. Because the number of these contingencies is
potentially unlimited, the process of identifying and testing rival explanations is never
complete. Yet, precisely for this reason, it seems impossible to identify and test an
unmanageably huge number of potential rival hypotheses? How is this to be done?

One answer is creativity and imagination. But creativity and imagination are
impossible to teach, because there are no rules governing the replication of creative
or imaginative solutions. Another answer is an appeal to well-established theories.
However, the bulk of theories in the social sciences are disputed and controversial.
"Well-established" theories are typically "well-defended" theories, and rival
hypotheses are rarely considered seriously, let alone tested.

A more appropriate alternative is the use of boundary analysis and estimation
to structure problems involving a large number of rival hypotheses. Boundary
analysis and estimation looks for rival hypotheses in the naturally occurring policy

---

[80] The architecture analogy is from Herbert Simon.

quarrels that take place among stakeholders. In addition to the policy analyst, these stakeholders include scientists, policy makers, and organized citizen groups. The aim of boundary estimation is to obtain a relatively complete set of rival hypotheses in a given policy context. Although boundary estimation strives to be comprehensive, it does not attempt the hopeless task of identifying and testing *all* plausible rival hypotheses. Although the range of rival hypotheses is never complete, it is possible to *estimate* the limit of this range.

Assessing the Impact of National Maximum Speed Limits

A boundary analysis was conducted with documents prepared by thirty-eight state officials responsible for reporting on the effects of the original 55 mph and later 65 mph speed limits in their states. As expected, there were sharp disagreements among many of the thirty-eight stakeholders. For example, some states were tenaciously committed to the hypothesis that speed limits are causally related to fatalities (e.g., Pennsylvania and New Jersey). Others were just as firmly opposed (e.g., Illinois, Washington, Idaho). Of direct importance to boundary estimation is that 718 plausible rival hypotheses were used by thirty-eight stakeholders to affirm or dispute the effectiveness of the 55 mph speed limit in saving lives. Of this total, 109 hypotheses were unique, in that they did not duplicate hypotheses advanced by any other stakeholder.

Here it is important to note that, from the standpoint of communications theory and language, the information-content of a hypothesis tends to be negatively related to its relative frequency or probability of occurrence. Hypotheses that are mentioned more frequently—those on which there is greater consensus—have less probative value than rarely mentioned hypotheses, because highly probable or predictable hypotheses do not challenge accepted knowledge claims.

The rival hypotheses were analyzed according the cumulative frequency of *unique* (nonduplicate) causal hypotheses. As Figure C3.1 shows, the cumulative frequency curve of unique rival hypotheses flattens out after the twenty-second stakeholder. Although the *total* number of rival hypotheses continues to increase without *apparent* limit, the boundary of *unique* rival hypotheses is reached within a small and affordable number of observations. This indicates that a satisfactory definition of the problem has probably been achieved. Indeed, of the 109 unique rival hypotheses, several variables related to the state of the economy—unemployment, the international price of oil, industrial production—explain the rise and fall of traffic fatalities better than average highway speeds and the 55 mph speed limit.

Developing an Occupational Interest Inventory: A Case in Job Training

A variant of boundary analysis was used in a 1985 project designed to elicit, map, and analyze the occupational preferences of 202 applicants for Job Training and Partnership Act (JTPA) programs in the city of Pittsburgh. Although the term "boundary analysis" was not used until later, the methodology was the same. The objective was to discover and specify the meanings attached by job trainees to a range of occupations for which jobs were available in the Pittsburgh region. The procedure used to elicit these meanings was a semiprojective interviewing

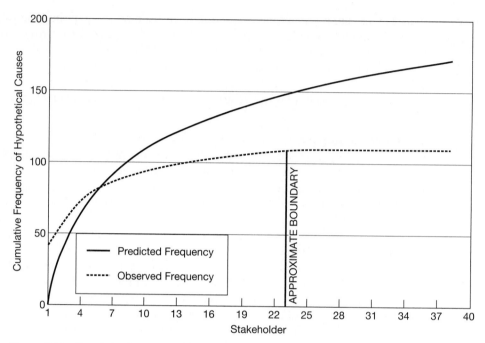

Figure C3.1 Cumulative frequency of hypothesized causes of traffic fatalities.

technique[81] that enables the generation of subjectively meaningful constructs employed to interpret any set of external objects, for example, policy options or objectives. In the present case, the external objects were drawings of occupations in an occupational interest inventory developed for persons with limited reading ability, many of whom were living at the poverty level.

Interviews with a saturation sample of 202 applicants generated a *total* of 1,411 occupational constructs, most of which were shared by two or more persons. Out of this total, 105 were *unique* (nonduplicate) constructs. The constructs were again analyzed by plotting a cumulative frequency graph of the 105 unique (nonduplicative) constructs, this time beginning with the stakeholder generating the most constructs.

This successful case of problem structuring had a major beneficial effect. Up to that point, job-training counselors had been using a standardized occupational inventory with ten dimensions of occupational choice. The counselors knew that the standardized inventory was overly simple and wanted some way to capture the range and complexity of factors that affected occupational choice. The boundary analysis, by accomplishing this purpose, reduced the likelihood of a type III error.

---

[81] The technique sometimes called the role repertory grid or "rep test" for short is based on the work of the psychologist George Kelly. His major work is *The Psychology of Personal Constructs* (Chicago, IL: W. W. Norton, 1955).

Although the cumulative frequency curve of unique rival hypotheses flattens out after the twenty-first stakeholder, the *total* number of rival hypotheses continues to increase without *apparent* limit. The boundary of *unique* rival hypotheses is reached within a small and affordable number of observations (Figure C3.2).[82]

Evaluating Research on Risk: A Case in Mine Safety and Health

In 1997, a branch of the U.S. Office of Mine Safety and Health Research began a process of strategic planning. The aim of the process was to reach consensus, if possible, on the prioritization of research projects that address different aspects of risk associated with the safety and health of miners.

Priority setting in this and other research organizations typically seeks to build consensus under conditions where researchers, research managers, and external stakeholders use conflicting criteria to evaluate the relative merits of their own and

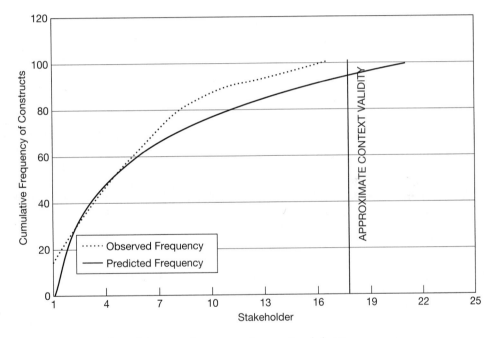

Figure C3.2   Cumulative frequency of constructs of occupational choice.

---

[82] The observed frequency distributions approximate the patterns predicted by several convergent laws predicting the distribution of information or knowledge: Lotka's inverse-square law of scientific productivity, Zipf's law of least effort, and Bradford's law of scattering. See, for example, Herbert A. Simon, "The Sizes of Things," in Judith Tanur and others, *Statistics: A Guide to the Unknown* (New York: Holden-Day, 1972); and William N. Dunn, "Probing the Boundaries of Ignorance in Policy Analysis," *American Behavioral Scientist* 40, no. 3 (1998): 277–98.

other research projects. Even when reliable and valid data are readily available—for example, quantitative data from large-sample studies of the relative frequencies of injuries and deaths—it is usually unclear whether "objective" measures of risk, by themselves, provide a sufficient basis for prioritizing research. This is so because extra-scientific as well as scientific factors affect judgments about the relative merits of research on risk.

For example, the probabilities of "black lung" disease and other high-risk conditions have been thoroughly investigated. Despite the severity and importance of the problem, additional research is not a priority. Accordingly, data on expected severity (probability × severity) do not alone provide a sufficient basis for prioritizing research problems. These same high-risk accidents, however, might be a research priority if the aim is to translate these abundant research findings into research on technologies that may improve mine safety and health. Because judgments about research priorities are based on multiple and frequently conflicting criteria, it is important to uncover and evaluate these criteria as part of an interactive process of group priority setting.

The priority-setting process had three major objectives. The first of these was to uncover hidden sources of agreement and disagreement, recognizing that *disagreement* is an opportunity for identifying alternative approaches to priority setting. Second, the process was designed to generate from stakeholders the criteria they use to evaluate research on risks affecting mine safety and health. Third, the process employed open priority-setting processes and products that included graphs, matrices, and other visual displays in order to "externalize" the criteria underlying individual judgments. The priority-setting process enabled each team member to understand and debate the varied reasons underlying the priorities used to evaluate research on risk.

Stakeholders were prompted to state the criteria they use to distinguish among twenty-five accident and health problems. Each stakeholder was presented with a form listing pre-randomized sets of three problems. One stakeholder was chosen at random to begin the process of presenting criteria to the group. The first presented 14 different criteria for evaluating research on risk, which included two criteria—severity and catastrophic potential of accidents and diseases—that were based entirely on large-sample relative frequency data. The second randomly chosen team member presented 17 additional (new) criteria. The third team member 11, the fourth 12, the fifth 6, and so on, until no additional criteria could be offered that were not mentioned before. In all, 84 criteria were generated, none after the eleventh presenter. The approximate boundary of the problem was demonstrated by displaying a cumulative frequency graph (Figure 3C.3).

The process of interactive group priority setting not only addressed the "objective" side of risk research but also captured "subjective" dimensions that go by such labels as "perceived risk," "acceptable risk," "researchable risk," and "actionable risk." The problem was successfully structured by means of an open process of generating and discussing criteria that otherwise would have interfered with consensus building because they were concealed or implicit.

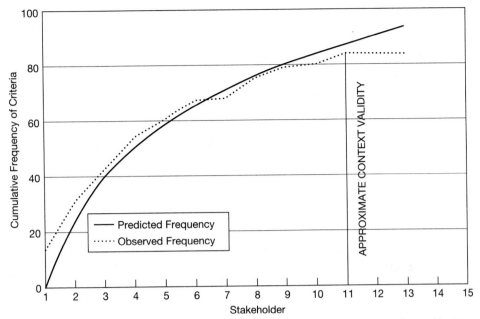

Figure C3.3   Cumulative frequency of criteria used to distinguish problems in mine safety and health.

Summary

The complexity of the social and physical systems in which policies are made creates many unmanageable contingencies that lie beyond the control of policy makers, policy analysts, and citizens. The method of boundary analysis and estimation permits us to structure problems in such a way as to lower the probability of type III errors.

4

Forecasting Expected Policy Outcomes

The capacity to forecast expected policy outcomes is critical to the success of policy analysis and the improvement of policy making. Through forecasting, we can obtain a prospective vision, or foresight, thereby enlarging capacities for understanding, control, and societal guidance. As we shall see, however, forecasts of all kinds—whether based on expert judgment, on the simple extrapolation of historical trends, or on technically sophisticated econometric models—are prone to errors based on faulty or implausible assumptions, on the error-amplifying effects of institutional incentive systems, and on the accelerating complexity of policy issue areas ranging from health, welfare, and education to science, technology, and the environment (see Figure 4.1).

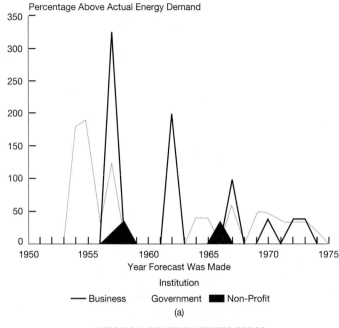

INSTITUTIONAL CONTEXT AFFECTS ERROR
Nuclear Energy Forecasts for 1975

(a)

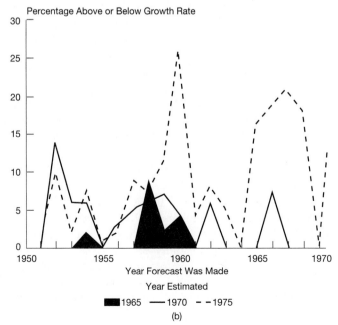

HISTORICAL CONTEXT AFFECTS ERROR
Forecasts of GNP Growth Rates

(b)

Figure 4.1 Contexts affecting forecast accuracy.

Note: Percentages are normalized errors.

Source: Adapted from William Ascher, *Forecasting: An Appraisal for Policy Makers and Planners* (Baltimore, MD: Johns Hopkins University Press, 1978).

We begin this chapter with an overview of the forms, functions, and performance of forecasting in policy analysis, stressing a range of criteria for assessing the strengths and limitations of different forecasting methods. We then compare and contrast three major approaches to creating information about expected policy outcomes: extrapolative forecasting, theoretical forecasting, and judgmental forecasting. We conclude with a presentation of methods and techniques of forecasting employed in conjunction with these three approaches.

FORECASTING IN POLICY ANALYSIS

Forecasting is a procedure for producing factual information about future states of society on the basis of prior information about policy problems. Forecasts take three principal forms: projections, predictions, and conjectures.

1. A *projection* is a forecast that is based on the extrapolation of current and historical trends into the future. Projections put forth designative claims based on arguments from method and parallel case, where assumptions about the validity of particular methods (e.g., time-series analysis) or similarities between cases (e.g., past and future policies) are used to establish the cogency of claims. Projections may be supplemented by arguments from authority (e.g., the opinions of experts) and cause (e.g., economic or political theory).

2. A *prediction* is a forecast based on explicit theoretical assumptions. These assumptions may take the form of theoretical laws (e.g., the law of diminishing utility of money), theoretical propositions (e.g., the proposition that civil disorders are caused by the gap between expectations and capabilities), or analogies (e.g., the analogy between the growth of government and the growth of biological organisms). The essential feature of a prediction is that it specifies the generative powers ("causes") and consequences ("effects"), or the parallel processes or relations ("analogs") believed to underlie a relationship. Predictions may be supplemented by arguments from authority (e.g., informed judgment) and method (e.g., econometric modeling).

3. A *conjecture* is a forecast based on informed or expert judgments about future states of society. These judgments may take the form of intuitive arguments, where assumptions about the insight, creative intellectual power, or tacit knowledge of stakeholders (e.g., "policy insiders") are used to support designative claims about the future. Judgments may also be expressed in the form of motivational arguments where present or future goals, values, and intentions are used to establish the plausibility of claims, as when conjectures about future societal values (e.g., leisure) are used to claim that the average work week will be reduced to thirty hours in the next twenty years. Conjectures may be supplemented by arguments from authority, method, and cause.

Aims of Forecasting

Policy forecasts, whether based on extrapolation, theory, or informed judgment, have several important aims. First, and most important, forecasts provide information about future changes in policies and their consequences. The aims of forecasting are similar to those of much scientific and social scientific research, insofar as the latter seek both to understand and control the human and material environment. Nevertheless, efforts to forecast future societal states are "especially related to control—that is, to the attempt to plan and to set policy so that the best possible course of action might be chosen among the possibilities which the future offers."[1]

Forecasting permits greater control through understanding past policies and their consequences, an aim that implies that the future is determined by the past. Yet forecasts also enable us to shape the future in an active manner, irrespective of what has occurred in the past. In this respect, the future-oriented policy analyst must ask what values can and should guide future action. But this leads to a second and equally difficult question: How can the analyst evaluate the future desirability of a given state of affairs?

> Even if the values underlying current actions could be neatly specified, would these values still be operative in the future? As Ikle has noted, " 'guiding predictions' are incomplete unless they evaluate the desirability of the predicted aspects of alternative futures. If we assume that this desirability is to be determined by our future rather than our present preferences...then we have to predict our values *before* we can meaningfully predict our future."[2]

This concern with future values may complement traditional social science disciplines that emphasize predictions based on past and present values. While past and present values may determine the future, this will hold true only if intellectual reflection by policy stakeholders does not lead them to change their values and behavior, or if unpredictable factors do not intervene to create profound social changes, including irreversible processes of chaos and emergent order.[3]

Limitations of Forecasting

In the years since 1985, there have been a number of unexpected, surprising, and counterintuitive political, social, and economic changes—for example, the formal abandonment of socialism in the Soviet Union, the dissolution of communist parties in Eastern Europe, the fall of the Berlin Wall, the growing uncertainty surrounding policies to mitigate global warming. These changes at once call attention to the importance and the difficulties of forecasting policy futures under conditions of

---

[1] Irene Taviss, "Futurology and the Problem of Values," *International Social Science Journal* 21, no. 4 (1969): 574.

[2] Ibid.; and Fred Charles Ikle, "Can Social Predictions Be Evaluated?" *Daedalus* 96 (summer 1967): 747.

[3] See Alasdair MacIntyre, "Ideology, Social Science, and Revolution," *Comparative Politics* 5, no. 3 (1973); and Ilya Prigogine and Isabelle Stengers, *Order Out of Chaos* (New York: Bantam Books, 1984).

increasingly complex, rapid, and even chaotic changes. The growing difficulty of forecasting, however, should be seen in light of limitations and strengths of various types of forecasts over the past three decades and more.[4]

1. *Forecast accuracy.* The accuracy of relatively simple forecasts based on the extrapolation of trends in a single variable, as well as relatively complex forecasts based on models incorporating hundreds of variables, has been limited. In the five-year period ending in 1983, for example, the Office of Management and Budget underestimated the federal budget deficit by an annual average of $58 billion. A similar record of performance tends to characterize forecasts of the largest econometric forecasting firms, which include Chase Econometrics, Wharton Econometric Forecasting Associates, and Data Resources, Inc. For example, average forecasting error as a proportion of actual changes in GNP was approximately 50 percent in the period 1971–83.[5]

2. *Comparative yield.* The accuracy of predictions based on complex theoretical models of the economy and of the energy resource system has been no greater than the accuracy of projections and conjectures made, respectively, on the basis of simple extrapolative models and informed (expert) judgment. If one of the important advantages of such models is sensitivity to surprising or counterintuitive future events, simple models have a comparative advantage over their technically complex counterparts, because developers and users of complex models tend to employ them mechanistically. Ascher's question is to the point: "If the implications of one's assumptions and hypotheses are obvious when they are 'thought out' without the aid of a model, why use one? If the implications are surprising, the strength of the complex model is in drawing from a set of assumptions these implications...."[6] Yet precisely these assumptions and implications—for example, the implication that a predicted large increase in gasoline consumption may lead to changes in gasoline taxes, which are treated as a constant in forecasting models—are overlooked or discarded because they are inconsistent with the assumptions of models.

3. *Context.* The assumptions of models and their results are sensitive to three kinds of contexts: institutional, temporal, and historical. Variations in institutional incentive systems are a key aspect of differences in institutional contexts, as represented by government agencies, businesses, and nonprofit research institutes. Forecasting accuracy tends to be greater in nonprofit research institutes than in businesses or government agencies (Figure 4.1[a]).

---

[4] A seminal work on forecasting is William Ascher, *Forecasting: An Appraisal for Policy Makers and Planners* (Baltimore and London: Johns Hopkins University Press, 1978). Also see Ascher, "The Forecasting Potential of Complex Models," *Policy Sciences* 13 (1981): 247–67; and Robert McNown, "On the Use of Econometric Models: A Guide for Policy Makers," *Policy Sciences* 19 (1986): 360–80.

[5] McNown, "On the Use of Econometric Models," pp. 362–67.

[6] Ascher, "Forecasting Potential of Complex Models," p. 255.

In turn, the temporal context of a forecast, as represented by the length of time over which a forecast is made (e.g., one quarter or year versus five years ahead), affects forecast accuracy. The longer the time frame, the less accurate the forecast. Finally, the historical context of forecasts affects accuracy. The relatively greater complexity of recent historical periods diminishes forecast accuracy, a pattern that is evident in the growth of forecasting errors since 1965 (Figure 4.1[b]).

Forecasting accuracy and comparative yield are thus closely related to the institutional, temporal, and historical contexts in which forecasts are made. The accuracy and comparative yield of forecasts are also affected, as we might expect, by the assumptions that people bring to the process. As Ascher notes, one of the difficulties of assessing the performance of forecasts lies in identifying the assumptions of forecast developers and users. In many forecasts, there is a serious problem of "assumption drag,"[7] that is, a tendency among developers and users of forecasting models to cling to questionable or plainly implausible assumptions built into a model—for example, the assumption that the pricing policies as well as the governments of petroleum-producing countries will remain stable. An important implication may be derived from the phenomenon of assumption drag—namely, that the task of structuring policy problems is central to the performance of forecasters. Indeed, the correction of errors by dissolving or unsolving problems is quite as important to forecasting as it is to other phases of policy analysis.

TYPES OF FUTURES

Policy forecasts, whether made in the form of projections, predictions, or conjectures, are used to estimate three types of future societal states: potential futures, plausible futures, and normative futures.[8] *Potential futures* (sometimes called *alternative futures*) are future societal states that may occur, as distinguished from societal states that eventually do occur. A future state is never certain until it actually occurs, and there are many potential futures. *Plausible futures* are future states that, on the basis of assumptions about causation in nature and society, are believed to be likely if policy makers do not intervene to redirect the course of events. By contrast, *normative futures* are potential and plausible futures that are consistent with an analyst's conception of future needs, values, and opportunities. The specification of normative futures narrows the range of potential and plausible futures, thus linking forecasts to specific goals and objectives (Figure 4.2).

---

[7] See William Ascher, *Forecasting: An Appraisal for Policy Makers and Planners* (Baltimore, MD: Johns Hopkins University Press, 1978).

[8] See David C. Miller, "Methods for Estimating Societal Futures," in *Methodology of Social Impact Assessment,* ed. Kurt Finsterbusch and C. P. Wolf (Stroudsburg, PA: Dowden, Hutchinson & Ross, 1977), pp. 202–10.

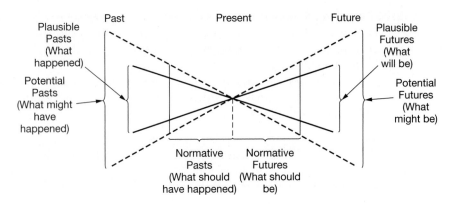

Figure 4.2   Three types of societal futures: potential, plausible, and normative.

Goals and Objectives of Normative Futures

An important aspect of normative futures is the specification of goals and objectives. But today's values are likely to change in the future, thus making it difficult to define normative futures on the basis of existing preferences. The analyst must, therefore, be concerned with future changes in the ends as well as means of policy. In thinking about the ends of policy, it is useful to contrast goals and objectives. Although goals and objectives are both future oriented, goals express broad purposes while objectives set forth specific aims. Goals are rarely expressed in the form of operational definitions—that is, definitions that specify the set of operations necessary to measure something—while objectives usually are. Goals are not quantifiable; but objectives may be and often are. Statements of goals usually do not specify the time period in which policies are expected to achieve desired consequences, while statements of objectives do. Finally, goals define target populations in broad terms, while objectives define target populations specifically. Contrasts between goals and objectives are illustrated in Table 4.1.

Table 4.1   Contrasts between Goals and Objectives

Characteristic	Goals	Objectives
Specification of purposes	1. Broadly stated (. . . to upgrade the quality of health care . . .)	1. Concrete (. . . to increase the number of physicians by 10 percent . . .)
Definition of terms	2. Formal (. . . the quality of health care refers to accessibility of medical services . . .)	2. Operational (. . . the quality of health care refers to the number of physicians per 100,000 persons . . .)
Time period	3. Unspecified (. . . in the future . . .)	3. Specified (. . . in the period 1990–2000 . . .)
Measurement procedure	4. Nonquantitative (. . . adequate health insurance . . .)	4. Frequently quantitative (. . . the number of persons covered per 1,000 persons . . .)
Treatment of target groups	5. Broadly defined (. . . persons in need of care . . .)	5. Specifically defined (. . . families with annual incomes below $19,000 . . .)

The definition of normative futures not only requires that we clarify goals and objectives, it also requires that we identify which sets of policy alternatives are relevant for the inachievement. Although these questions may appear simple, they are in fact difficult. Whose goals and objectives should the analyst use as a focal point of forecasts? How does an analyst choose among a large number of alternatives to achieve given goals and objectives? If analysts use existing policies to specify goals, objectives, and alternatives, they run the risk of applying a conservative standard. If, on the other hand, they propose new goals, objectives, and alternatives, they may be charged with imposing their own beliefs and values or making choices that are closer to the positions of one stakeholder than another.

Sources of Goals, Objectives, and Alternatives

One way to select goals, objectives, and alternatives is to consider their possible sources. Alternatives imply goals and objectives, just as goals and objectives imply policy alternatives. Sources of policy alternatives, goals, and objectives include the following:

1. *Authority.* In searching for alternatives to resolve a problem, analysts may appeal to experts. For example, the President's Commission on the Causes and Prevention of Violence may be used as a source of policy alternatives (registration of firearms, restrictive licensing, increased penalties for the use of guns to commit crime) to deal with the problem of gun controls.[9]

2. *Insight.* The analyst may appeal to the intuition, judgment, or tacit knowledge of persons believed to be particularly insightful about a problem. These "knowledgeables," who are not experts in the ordinary sense of the word, are an important source of policy alternatives. For example, various stakeholders from the Office of Child Development, a division of the Department of Education, have been used as a source of informed judgments about policy alternatives, goals, and objectives in the area of child welfare.[10]

3. *Method.* The search for alternatives may benefit from innovative methods of analysis. For example, new techniques of systems analysis may be helpful in identifying alternatives and rank-ordering multiple conflicting objectives.[11]

4. *Scientific theories.* Explanations produced by the natural and social sciences are also an important source of policy alternatives. For example, social psychological

---

[9] See National Commission on the Causes and Prevention of Violence, Final Report, *To Establish Justice, to Ensure Domestic Tranquility* (Washington, DC: U.S. Government Printing Office, 1969).

[10] See, for example, Ward Edwards, Marcia Guttentag, and Kurt Snapper, "A Decision-Theoretic Approach to Evaluation Research," in *Handbook of Evaluation Research,* vol. 1, ed. Elmer L. Struening and Marcia Guttentag (Beverly Hills, CA: Sage Publications, 1975), pp. 159–73.

[11] An excellent example is Thomas L. Saaty and Paul C. Rogers, "Higher Education in the United States (1985–2000): Scenario Construction Using a Hierarchical Framework with Eigenvector Weighting," *Socio-Economic Planning Sciences,* 10 (1976): 251–63. See also Thomas L. Saaty, *The Analytic Hierarchy Process* (New York: Wiley, 1980).

theories of learning have served as one source of early childhood education programs, such as Head Start and Follow Through.

5. *Motivation*. The beliefs, values, and needs of stakeholders may serve as a source of policy alternatives. Alternatives may be derived from the goals and objectives of particular occupational groups, for example, workers whose changing beliefs, values, and needs have created a new "work ethic" involving demands for leisure and flexible working hours.

6. *Parallel case*. Experiences with policy problems in other countries, states, and cities are an important source of policy alternatives. The experiences of New York and California with financial reforms have served as a source of financial policies in other states.

7. *Analogy*. Similarities between different kinds of problems are a source of policy alternatives. Legislation designed to increase equal employment opportunities for women has been based on analogies with policies adopted to protect the rights of minorities.

8. *Ethical systems*. Another important source of policy alternatives is ethical systems. Theories of social justice put forward by philosophers and other social thinkers serve as a source of policy alternatives in a variety of issue areas.[12]

APPROACHES TO FORECASTING

Once goals, objectives, and alternatives have been identified, it is possible to select an approach to forecasting. By selecting an approach we mean three things. The analyst must (1) decide what to forecast, that is, determine what the *object* of the forecast is to be; (2) decide how to make the forecast, that is, select one or more *bases* for the forecast; and (3) choose *techniques* that are most appropriate for the object and base selected.

Objects

The *object* of a forecast is the point of reference of a projection, prediction, or conjecture. Forecasts have four objects:[13]

1. *Consequences of existing policies*. Forecasts may be used to estimate changes that are likely to occur if no new government actions are taken. The status quo, that is, doing nothing, is an existing policy. Examples are population

---

[12] John Rawls, *A Theory of Justice* (Cambridge, MA: Harvard University Press, 1971). On ethical systems as a source of policy alternatives, see Duncan MacRae Jr., *The Social Function of Social Science* (New Haven, CT: Yale University Press, 1976).

[13] See William D. Coplin, *Introduction to the Analysis of Public Policy Issues from a Problem-Solving Perspective* (New York: Learning Resources in International Studies, 1975), p. 21.

projections of the U.S. Bureau of the Census and projections of female labor force participation in 1985 made by the U.S. Bureau of Labor Statistics.[14]

2. *Consequences of new policies.* Forecasts may be used to estimate changes in society that are likely to occur if new policies are adopted. For example, energy demand in 1995 may be projected on the basis of assumptions about the adoption of new policies to regulate industrial pollution.[15]

3. *Contents of new policies.* Forecasts may be used to estimate changes in the content of new public policies. The Congressional Research Service, for example, forecasts the possible adoption of a four-week annual paid vacation on the assumption that the government and labor unions will follow the lead of European countries, most of which have adopted four- or five-week annual paid vacations for workers.[16]

4. *Behavior of policy stakeholders.* Forecasts may be used to estimate the probable support (or opposition) to newly proposed policies. For example, techniques for assessing political feasibility may be used to estimate the probability that different stakeholders will support a policy at various stages of the policy process, from adoption to implementation.[17]

Bases

The *basis* of a forecast is the set of assumptions or data used to establish the plausibility of estimates of consequences of existing or new policies, the content of new policies, or the behavior of stakeholders. There are three major bases of forecasts: trend extrapolation, theoretical assumptions, and informed judgment. Each of these bases is associated with one of the three forms of forecasts previously discussed.

Trend extrapolation is the extension into the future of trends observed in the past. Trend extrapolation assumes that what has occurred in the past will also occur in the future, provided that no new policies or unforeseen events intervene to change the course of events. Trend extrapolation is based on *inductive logic,* that is, the process of reasoning from particular observations (e.g., time-series data) to general conclusions or claims. In trend extrapolation, we usually start with a set of time-series data, project past trends into the future, and then invoke assumptions about regularity and persistence that justify the projection. The logic of trend extrapolation is illustrated in Figure 4.3.

---

[14] See, for example, Howard N. Fullerton Jr. and Paul O. Flaim, "New Labor Force Projections to 1990," *Monthly Labor Review* (December 1976).

[15] See Barry Hughes, *U.S. Energy, Environment and Economic Problems: A Public Policy Simulation* (Chicago: American Political Science Association, 1975).

[16] See Everett M. Kassalow, "Some Labor Futures in the United States," Congressional Research Service, Congressional Clearing House on the Future, Library of Congress (January 31, 1978).

[17] See Michael K. O'Leary and William D. Coplin, *Everyman's "Prince"* (North Scituate, MA: Duxbury Press, 1976).

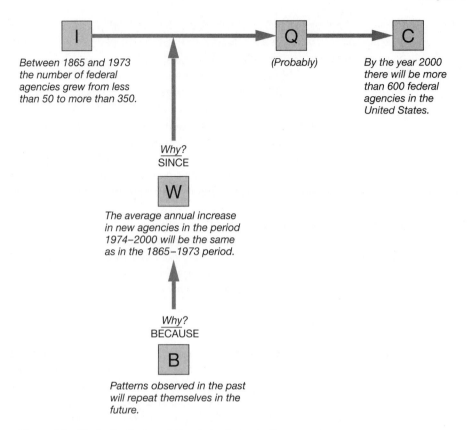

Figure 4.3 The logic of extrapolation: inductive reasoning.

Theoretical assumptions are systematically structured and empirically testable sets of laws or propositions that make predictions about the occurrence of one event on the basis of another. Theoretical assumptions are causal in form, and their specific role is to explain and predict. The use of theoretical assumptions is based on *deductive logic,* that is, the process of reasoning from general statements, laws, or propositions to particular sets of information and claims. For example, the proposition that in "postindustrial" society the knowledge of policy analysts is an increasingly scarce resource which enhances their power may be used to move from information about the growth of professional policy analysis in government to the predictive claim that policy analysts will have more power than policy makers in coming years (Figure 4.4).

Informed judgments refer to knowledge based on experience and insight, rather than inductive or deductive reasoning. These judgments are usually expressed by experts or knowledgeables and are used in cases where theory

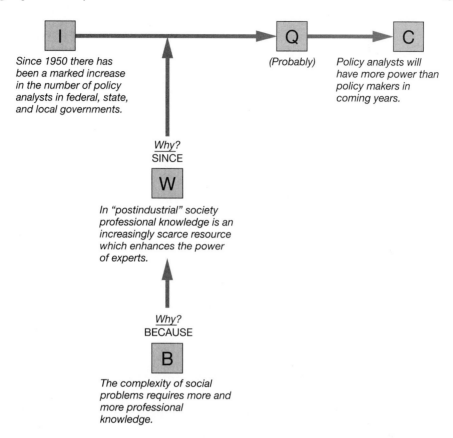

Figure 4.4   The logic of theoretical prediction: deductive reasoning.

and/or empirical data are unavailable or inadequate. Informed judgments are often based on *retroductive logic,* that is, the process of reasoning that begins with claims about the future and then works backward to the information and assumptions necessary to support claims. A good example of informed judgment as a basis of forecasts is the use of scientists or other knowledgeables to make conjectures about future changes in technology. Through retroductive logic, experts may construct a scenario that claims that there will be automated high-ways with adaptive automobile autopilots in the year 2000. Experts then work backward to the information and assumptions needed to establish the plausibility of the claim (Figure 4.5).

In practice the boundaries between inductive, deductive, and retroductive reasoning are often blurred. Retroductive reasoning is often a creative way to explore ways in which potential futures may grow out of the present, while inductive and

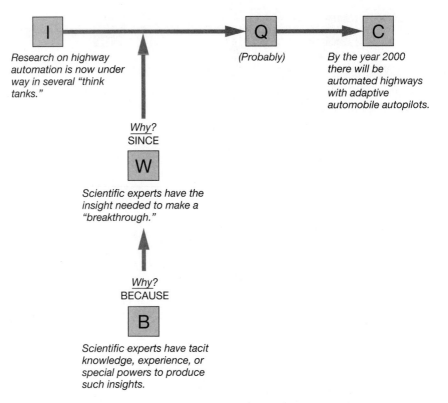

Figure 4.5   The logic of informed judgment: retroductive reasoning.

deductive reasoning yield new information and theories that lead to claims about future societal states. Nevertheless, inductive and deductive reasoning are potentially conservative, because the use of information about past events or the application of established scientific theories may restrict consideration of potential (as distinguished from plausible) futures. A good example of the restrictive influence of past events and established scientific theories comes from the well-known astronomer William H. Pickering (1858–1938):

> The popular mind pictures gigantic flying machines speeding across the Atlantic and carrying innumerable passengers in a way analogous to our modern steamships.... It seems safe to say that such ideas must be wholly visionary, and even if a machine could get across with one or two passengers the expense would be prohibitive.[18]

18 Quoted in Brownlee Haydon, *The Year 2000* (Santa Monica, CA: Rand Corporation, 1967).

Table 4.2   Three Approaches to Forecasting with Their Bases, Appropriate Methods and Techniques, and Products

Approach	Basis	Appropriate Technique(s)	Product
Extrapolative forecasting	Trend extrapolation	Classical time-series analysis Linear trend estimation Exponential weighting Data transformation Catastrophe methodology	Projections
Theoretical forecasting	Theory	Theory mapping Causal modeling Regression analysis Point and interval estimation Correlational analysis	Predictions
Judgmental forecasting	Informed judgment	Conventional Delphi Policy Delphi Cross-impact analysis Feasibility assessment	Conjectures

Choosing Methods and Techniques

While the selection of an object and basis helps guide the analyst toward appropriate methods and techniques, there are literally hundreds of forecasting methods and techniques to choose from.[19] A useful way to think about these methods and techniques is to group them according to the bases of forecasts discussed earlier. Table 4.2 outlines the three approaches to forecasting, their bases, appropriate methods, and products. This table serves as an overview of the rest of the chapter.

EXTRAPOLATIVE FORECASTING

Methods and techniques of extrapolative forecasting enable analysts to make projections of future societal states on the basis of current and historical data. Extrapolative forecasting is usually based on some form of *time-series analysis,* that is, on the analysis of numerical values collected at multiple points in time and presented sequentially. Time-series analysis provides summary measures (averages) of the amount and rate of change in past and future years. Extrapolative forecasting has been used to project economic growth, population decline, energy consumption, quality of life, and agency workloads.

---

[19] See, for example, Daniel P. Harrison, *Social Forecasting Methodology* (New York: Russell Sage Foundation, 1976); Denis Johnston, "Forecasting Methods in the Social Sciences," *Technological Forecasting and Social Change* 2 (1970): 120–43; Arnold Mitchell and others, *Handbook of Forecasting Techniques* (Fort Belvoir, VA: U.S. Army Engineer Institute for Water Resources, December 1975); and Miller, "Methods for Estimating Societal Futures."

When used to make projections, extrapolative forecasting rests on three basic assumptions:

1. *Persistence.* Patterns observed in the past will persist in the future. If energy consumption has grown in the past, it will do so in the future.
2. *Regularity.* Past variations in observed trends will regularly recur in the future. If wars have occurred every twenty or thirty years in the past, these cycles will repeat themselves in the future.
3. *Reliability and validity of data.* Measurements of trends are reliable (i.e., relatively precise or internally consistent) and valid (i.e., measure what they purport to be measuring). For example, crime statistics are relatively imprecise measures of criminal offenses.

When these three assumptions are met, extrapolative forecasting may yield insights into the dynamics of change and greater understanding of potential future states of society. When any one of these assumptions is violated, extrapolative forecasting techniques are likely to yield inaccurate or misleading results.[20]

Classical Time-Series Analysis

When making extrapolative forecasts, we may use *classical time-series analysis,* which views any time series as having four components: secular trend, seasonal variations, cyclical fluctuations, and irregular movements. *Secular trend* is a smooth long-term growth or decline in a time series. Figure 4.6 shows a secular trend in the growth of crimes per 1,000 persons in Chicago over a thirty-year period. By convention, the time-series variable is plotted on the *Y*-axis (also called the *ordinate*) and years are plotted on the *X*-axis (also called the *abscissa*). A straight-line trend has been used to summarize the growth of total arrests per 1,000 persons between 1940 and 1970. In other cases (e.g., mortality), the straight-line trend shows a long-term decline, while still other cases (e.g., consumption of coal oil) shows a *curvilinear trend,* that is, a trend where the numerical values in a time-series display a convex or concave pattern.

Seasonal variation, as the term suggests, is the variation in a time series that recurs periodically within a one-year period or less. The best examples of seasonal variations are the ups and downs of production and sales that follow changes in weather conditions and holidays. The workloads of social welfare, health, and public utilities agencies also frequently display seasonal variations as a result of weather conditions and holidays. For example, the consumption of home heating fuels increases in the winter months and begins to decline in March of each year.

---

[20] Fidelity to these and other methodological assumptions has no guarantee of accuracy. In this author's experience, the less of two or more forecasts is frequently based on strict adherence to technical assumptions. This is why judgment is so important to all forms of forecasting, including complex modeling.

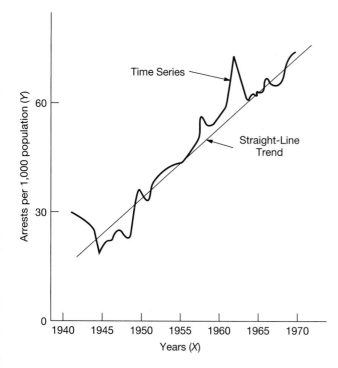

Figure 4.6 Demonstration of secular trend; total arrests per 1,000 population in Chicago, 1940–70.

Source: Adapted from Ted R. Gurr, "The Comparative Analysis of Public Order," in *The Politics of Crime and Conflict,* ed. Ted R. Gurr, Peter N. Grabosky, and Richard C. Hula (Beverly Hills, CA: Sage Publications, 1977), p. 647.

Cyclical fluctuations are also periodic but may extend unpredictably over a number of years. Cycles are frequently difficult to explain, because each new cyclical fluctuation may be a consequence of unknown factors. Total arrests per 1,000 population in Chicago, displayed over a period of more than a hundred years, show at least three cyclic fluctuations (Figure 4.7). Each of these cycles is difficult to explain, although the third cyclical fluctuation coincides with the Prohibition Era (1919–33) and the rise of organized crime. This example points to the importance of carefully selecting an appropriate time frame, because what may appear to be a secular trend may in fact be part of some larger long-term pattern of cyclical fluctuations. Note also that total arrests per 1,000 persons were higher in the 1870s and 1890s than in most years from 1955 to 1970.

The interpretation of cyclical fluctuations is frequently made more difficult by the presence of *irregular movements,* that is, unpredictable variations in a time series that appear to follow no regular pattern. Irregular movements may be the result of many factors (changes in government, strikes, natural disasters). As long as these factors are unaccounted for, they are treated as random error, that is, unknown sources of variation that cannot be explained in terms of secular trend, seasonal variations, or cyclical fluctuations. For example, the irregular movement in total arrests that occurred after 1957 (Figure 4.7) might be regarded as an unpredictable variation in the time series that follows no regular pattern. On closer inspection, however, the sharp temporary upswing in arrests may be explained by

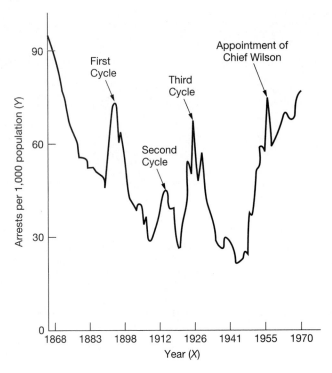

Figure 4.7 Demonstration of cyclical fluctuations: total arrests per 1,000 population in Chicago, 1868–1970.

Source: Ted R. Gurr, "The Comparative Analysis of Public Order," in *The Politics of Crime and Conflict,* ed. Ted R. Gurr, Peter N. Grabosky, and Richard C. Hula (Beverly Hills, CA: Sage Publications, 1977), p. 647.

the changes in record keeping that came into effect when Orlando Wilson was appointed chief of police.[21] This example points to the importance of understanding the sociohistorical and political events underlying changes in a time series.

Linear Trend Estimation

A standard technique for extrapolating trends is *linear trend estimation,* a procedure that uses regression analysis to obtain statistically reliable estimates of future societal states on the basis of observed values in a time series. Linear regression is based on assumptions of persistence, regularity, and data reliability. When linear regression is used to estimate trend, it is essential that observed values in a time series are not curvilinear, because any significant departure from linearity will produce forecasts with sizable errors. Nevertheless, linear regression may also be used to remove the linear trend component from a series that displays seasonal variations or cyclical fluctuations.

---

[21] See Donald T. Campbell, "Reforms As Experiments," in *Readings in Evaluation Research,* ed. Francis G. Caro (New York: Russell Sage Foundation, 1971), pp. 240–41.

There are two important properties of regression analysis:

1. *Deviations cancel.* The sum of the differences between observed values in a
    time series and values lying along a computed straight-line trend (called a
    regression line) will always equal zero. Thus, if the trend value (Y_t) is subtracted
    from its corresponding observed value (Y) for all years in a time series, the total
    of these differences (called *deviations*) will equal zero. When the observed
    value for a given year lies *below* the regression line, the deviation $(Y - Y_t)$ is
    always *negative*. By contrast, when the observed value is *above* the regression
    line, the deviation $(Y - Y_t)$ is always *positive*. These negative and positive values
    cancel each other out, such that $\Sigma(Y - Y_t) = 0$.

2. *Squared deviations are a minimum.* If we square each deviation (i.e., multiply
    each deviation value by itself) and add them all up, the sum of these squared
    deviations will always be a minimum or least value. This means that linear
    regression minimizes the distances between the regression line and all
    observed values of Y in the series. In other words, it is the most efficient way
    to draw a trend line through a series of observed data points.

These two properties of regression analysis are illustrated with hypothetical
data in Figure 4.8.

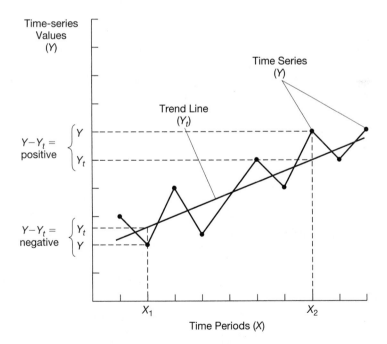

Figure 4.8   Two properties of linear regression.
Note: $\Sigma(Y - Y_t) = 0$; $\Sigma(Y - Y_t)^2 =$ a minimum (least) value.

The computation of linear trend with regression analysis is illustrated in Table 4.3 with data on energy consumption. In column (3) note that years in the series may be coded by calculating the numerical distance (x) of each year from the middle of the entire period (i.e., 1973). The middle of this series is given a coded value of zero and treated as the origin. The values of x range from -3 to $+3$ and are deviations from the origin. Observe also the computational procedures used in columns (4) and (5) of Table 4.3. The value of xY is calculated by multiplying values of energy consumption (Y) by each coded time value (x), as shown in column (4). The value of x^2, shown in column (5), is calculated by multiplying each value of x by itself, that is, squaring all the x values in column (3). Finally, column (6) contains trend values of the time-series variable (Y_t). These trend values, which form a straight line, are calculated according to the following equation:

$$Y_t = a + b(x)$$

where

Y_t = the trend value for a given year
a = the value of Y_t when $X = 0$
b = the slope of the trend line representing the change in Y_t for each unit of time
x = the coded time value for any year, as determined by its distance from the origin

Once the values of a and b have been calculated, estimates of total energy consumption may be made for any year in the *observed* time series or for any *future* year. For example, Table 4.3 shows that the trend value for energy consumption in 1972 is 70.27 quadrillion BTUs. To project total energy consumption for 1980, we set the value of x at 7 (i.e., seven time periods away from 1973, the origin) and solve the equation $Y_{t(1980)} = a + b(x)$. The formula for computing the value of a is

$$a = \frac{\Sigma Y}{n}$$

where

ΣY = the sum of observed values in the series
n = the number of years in the observed time series

The formula for computing the value of b is

$$b = \frac{\Sigma(xY)}{\Sigma(x^2)}$$

where

$\Sigma(xY)$ = the sum of the products of the coded time values and the observed values in the series [see column (4) of Table 4.3]
$\Sigma(x^2)$ = the sum of the squared coded time values [see column (5) of Table 4.3]

Table 4.3 Time-Series Data on Total Energy Consumption Used in Linear Regression

Years (X) (1)	Energy Consumption (Y) (2)	Coded Time Value (x) (3)	Columns (2) By (3) (xY) (4)	Column (3) Squared (x²) (5)	Trend Value for Energy Consumption (Yₜ) (6)
1970	66.9	−3	−200.7	9	68.35
1971	68.3	−2	−136.6	4	69.31
1972	71.6	−1	−71.6	1	70.27
1973	74.6	0	0	0	71.24
1974	72.7	1	72.7	1	72.20
1975	70.6	2	141.2	4	73.17
1976	74.0	3	222.0	9	74.13
$n = 7$	$\Sigma Y = 498.7$	$\Sigma x = 0$	$\Sigma(xY) = 27.0$	$\Sigma(x^2) = 28$	$\Sigma Y_t = 498.7$

$$Y_t = a + b(x)$$

$$a = \frac{\Sigma Y}{n} = \frac{498.7}{7} = 71.243$$

$$b = \frac{\Sigma(xY)}{\Sigma(x^2)} = \frac{27.0}{28.0} = 0.964$$

$$Y_t = 71.24 + 0.964(x)$$

$$Y_{t(1980)} = 71.24 + 0.964(7) = 77.99 \text{ quadrillion BTUs}$$

The calculations in Table 4.3 not only permit us to compute trend values for energy consumption in the observed series, they also enable us to project total energy consumption for any given year in the future. Thus, the estimate of total energy consumption in 1980 [$Y_{t(1980)}$] is 77.99 quadrillion BTUs.

In illustrating the application of linear regression, we have used a time series with an odd number of years. We treated the middle of the series as the origin and coded it as zero. Obviously, there are many time series that contain an even number of years, and a different procedure may be used for determining each coded time value (x), because there is no middle year. The procedure used with even-numbered time series is to divide the series into two equal parts and code the time values in intervals of two (rather than in intervals of one, as in odd-numbered series). Each year in Table 4.4 is exactly two units away from its neighbor, and the highest and lowest coded time values are +7 and −7, rather than +3 and −3. Note that the size of the interval need not be 2; it could be 3, 4, 5, or any number provided that each year is equidistant from the next one in the series. Increasing the size of the interval will not affect the computation of results.

Despite its precision in extrapolating secular trend, linear regression is limited by several conditions. First, the time series must be *linear,* that is, display a constant increase or decrease in values along the trend line. If the pattern of observations is

Table 4.4 Linear Regression with an Even-Numbered Series

Years (X) (1)	Energy Consumption (Y) (2)	Coded Time Value (x) (3)	Columns (2) By (3) (xY) (4)	Column (3) Squared (x²) (5)	Trend Value for Energy Consumption (Yₜ) (6)
1969	64.4	−7	−450.8	49	66.14
1970	66.9	−5	−334.5	25	67.36
1971	68.3	−3	−204.9	9	68.57
1972	71.6	−1	−71.6	1	69.78
1973	74.6	1	74.6	1	71.00
1974	72.7	3	218.1	9	72.21
1975	70.6	5	353.0	25	73.43
1976	74.0	7	518.0	49	74.64
$n = 8$	$\Sigma Y = 563.1$	$\Sigma x = 0$	$\Sigma(xY) = 101.9$	$\Sigma(x^2) = 168$	$\Sigma Y_t = 563.1$

$$Y_t = a + b(x)$$

$$a = \frac{\Sigma Y}{n} = \frac{563.1}{8} = 70.39$$

$$b = \frac{\Sigma(xY)}{\Sigma(x^2)} = \frac{101.9}{168} = 0.607$$

$$Y_t = 70.39 + 0.607(x)$$

$$Y_{t(1980)} = 70.39 + 0.607(15) = 79.495 \text{ quadrillion BTUs}$$

nonlinear (i.e., where the amounts of change increase or decrease from one time period to the next), other techniques must be used. Some of these techniques require fitting various types of curves to nonlinear time series. Second, plausible arguments must be offered to show that historical patterns will *persist* in the future, that is, continue in much the same form in subsequent years as they have in past ones. Third, patterns must be *regular,* that is, display no cyclical fluctuations or sharp discontinuities. Unless all of these conditions are present, linear regression should not be used to extrapolate trend.

The SPSS output for the regression analyses computed by hand in Tables 4.3 and 4.4 is displayed in Exhibit 4.1. As may be seen by comparing Table 4.3 in the text with the SPSS output (Table 4.3 in Exhibit 4.1), the results are identical. The SPSS output identifies the dependent variable (which was named "ENCONS" for energy consumption), the number of observations in the sample (n = 7), the correlation coefficient expressing the strength of the relationship between time and energy consumption (R:.729), and the squared correlation coefficient (SQUARED MULTIPLE R:.531), which expresses the proportion of variance in the dependent variable ("ENCONS") explained by the independent variable ("TIMECODE").

Exhibit 4.1   SPSS Output for Tables 4.3 and 4.4

Model Summary[b]

Model	R	R Square	Adjusted R Square	Std. Error of the Estimate	Durbin Watson
1	.729[a]	.531	.437	2.14575994	1.447

a. Predictors: (Constant), TIMECODE
b. Dependent Variable: ENCONS

ANOVA[b]

Model		Sum of Squares	df	Mean Square	F	Sig.
1	Regression	26.036	1	26.036	5.655	.063[a]
	Residual	23.021	5	4.604		
	Total	49.057	6			

a. Predictors: (Constant), TIMECODE
b. Dependent Variable: ENCONS

Coefficients[a]

Mode		Unstandardized Coefficients		Standardized Coefficients		
		B	Std. Error	Beta	t	Sig.
1	(Constant)	71.243	.811		87.843	.000
	TIMECODE	.964	.406	.729	2.378	.063

a. Dependent Variable: ENCONS

Residuals Statistics[a]

	Minimum	Maximum	Mean	Std. Deviation	N
Predicted Value	68.349998	74.135712	71.242857	2.08309522	7
Residual	−2.571429	3.3571429	8.120E-15	1.95880187	7
Std. Predicted Value	−1.389	1.389	.000	1.000	7
Std. Residual	−1.198	1.565	.000	.913	7

a. Dependent Variable: ENCONS

For present purposes, the most important part of the SPSS output gives the coefficient for the constant, a, which is 71.243—this is the value of Y, energy consumption, when X equals zero. Line 5 gives the coefficient for the slope of the regression line, b, which is 0.964—this is the amount of change in Y, energy consumption, for each unit change in X, the years. This part of the output enables us to write the regression equation and, using the coefficients in this equation, forecast the value of energy consumption for any future year. The regression equation for Table 4.3 is

$$Y_t = 71.243 + 0.964(X)$$

The regression equation for Table 4.4, which has eight rather than seven years in the time series, is

$$Y_t = 70.388 + 0.607(X)$$

Note how much of a difference there is in the slopes after adding only one year to the series.

Many time-series data of concern to policy analysts—for example, data on crime, pollution, public expenditures, urbanization—are nonlinear. A variety of techniques have been developed to fit nonlinear curves to patterns of change that do not display a constant increase or decrease in the values of an observed time series. Although these techniques are not presented in detail, we discuss some of their properties and underlying assumptions. Readers who wish to investigate these forecasting techniques in greater depth should consult advanced texts on time-series analysis.[22]

Nonlinear Time Series

Time series that do not meet conditions of linearity, persistence, and regularity fall into five main classes (Figure 4.9):

1. *Oscillations*. Here there are departures from linearity, but only *within* years, quarters, months, or days. Oscillations may be persistent and regular (e.g., most police arrests occur between 11 P.M. and 2 P.M. throughout the year) but not show a constant increase or decrease within the period under examination (Figure 4.9[a]). Oscillations *within* years may occur in conjunction with long-term secular trends *between* years. Examples include seasonal variations in unemployment, monthly variations in agency workloads, and daily variations in levels of pollutants.

2. *Cycles*. Cycles are nonlinear fluctuations that occur between years or longer periods of time. Cycles may be unpredictable or occur with persistence and regularity. While the overall pattern of a cycle is always nonlinear, segments of a given cycle may be linear or curvilinear (Figure 4.9[b]). Examples are business cycles and the "life cycles" of academic fields, scientific publications, and civilizations.

3. *Growth curves*. Departures from linearity occur *between* years, decades, or some other unit of time. Growth curves evidence cumulative *increases* in the rate of growth in a time series, cumulative *decreases* in this rate of growth, or some *combination* of the two (Figure 4.9[c]). In the latter case, growth curves are S-shaped and called *sigmoid* or *logistic* curves. Growth curves, which developed out of studies of biological organisms, have been used to forecast the growth of

---

[22] See G. E. P. Box and G. M. Jenkins, *Time Series Analysis: Forecasting and Control* (San Francisco, CA: Holden-Day, 1969); and S. C. Wheelwright and S. Makridakis, *Forecasting Methods for Management* (New York: Wiley, 1973).

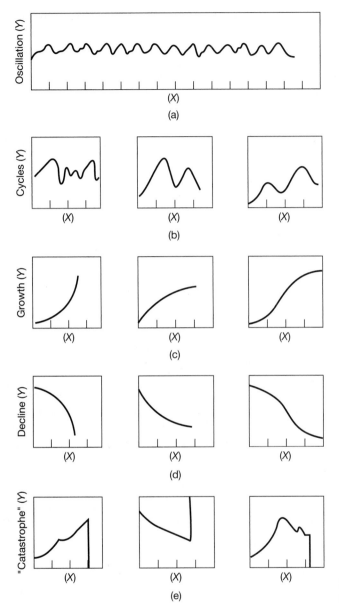

Figure 4.9 Five classes of nonlinear time series.

industry, urban areas, population, technology, and science. Although growth curves are not linear, they are nevertheless persistent and regular.

4. *Decline curves.* Here departures from linearity again occur *between* years, decades, or longer periods. In effect, decline curves are the counterpart of growth curves. Decline curves evidence either cumulative increases or

decreases in the rate of decline in a time series (Figure 4.9[d]). Increasing and decreasing rates of decline may be combined to form curves with different shapes. Patterns of decline are sometimes used as a basis for various dynamic or "life-cycle" perspectives of the decline of civilizations, societies, and urban areas. Decline curves are nonlinear but regular and persistent.

5. *"Catastrophes."* The main characteristic of time-series data that are "catastrophic" is that they display sudden and sharp discontinuities. The analysis of catastrophic change, a field of study founded by the French mathematician René Thom, not only involves nonlinear changes over time, it also involves patterns of change that are discontinuous (Figure 4.9[e]). Examples include sudden shifts in government policy during war (surrender or withdrawal), the collapse of stock exchanges in times of economic crisis, and the sudden change in the density of a liquid as it boils.[23]

The growth and decline curves illustrated in Figures 4.9(c) and (d) cannot be described by a straight-line trend. Patterns of growth and decline display little or no cyclical fluctuation, and the trend is best described as *exponential growth* or *decline,* that is, growth or decline where the values of some quantity increase or decrease at an increasing rate. The growth of federal government organizations between 1789 and 1973 (Figure 4.10) is an example of exponential growth. After 1789 the total number of organizations began to grow slowly, until about 1860 when the growth rate began to accelerate. Clearly, this growth trend is very different from the secular trends and cyclical variations examined so far.[24]

Techniques for fitting curves to processes of growth and decline are more complex than those used to estimate secular trend. While many of these techniques are based on linear regression, they require various transformations of the time-series variable (Y). Some of these transformations of the time-series variable (Y) involve roots $(\sqrt[n]{Y})$, while others require logarithms $(\log Y)$ or exponents (e^x). In each case, the aim is to express mathematically changes in a time series that increase by increasing or decreasing amounts (or, conversely, decrease by increasing or decreasing amounts). While these techniques will not be presented here, their logic is sufficiently important for public policy analysis to warrant further illustration.

A simple illustration will serve best to clarify techniques for curve fitting. Recall the model of compound interest. This model states that

$$S_n = (1 + r)^n S_0$$

---

[23] See C. A. Isnard and E. C. Zeeman, "Some Models from Catastrophe Theory in the Social Sciences," in *The Use of Models in the Social Sciences,* ed. Lyndhurst Collins (Boulder, CO: Westview Press, 1976), pp. 44–100.

[24] The outstanding work on processes of growth in science and other areas is Derek de Sólla Price, *Little Science, Big Science* (New York: Columbia University Press, 1963).

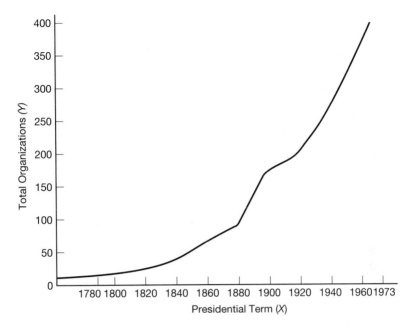

Figure 4.10   Growth of federal government organizations in the United States by presidential term, 1789–1973.

Source: Herbert Kaufman, *Are Government Organizations Immortal?* (Washington, DC: Brookings Institution, 1976), p. 62.

where

S_n = the amount to which a given investment will accumulate in a given (n) number of years

S_0 = the initial amount of the investment

$(1 + r)^n$ = a constant return on investment (1.0) plus the rate of interest (r) in a given (n) number of years

Imagine that the manager of a small municipality of 10,000 persons is confronted by the following situation. In order to meet immediate out-of-pocket expenses for emergencies, it was decided in 1970 that a sum of $1,000 should be set aside in a special checking account. The checking account is very handy but earns no interest. In 1971 and subsequent years, because of rising inflation, the manager began to increase the sum in the special account by $100 per year. The increase in funds, illustrated in Figure 4.11(a), is a good example of the kind of linear trend we have been examining. The time series increases by constant amounts ($100 per year) and by 1980, there was $2,000 in the special account. In this case, the time-series values (Y) are identical to the trend values ($Y_t = Y$), because all values of Y are on the trend line.

Now consider what would have occurred if the manager had placed the funds in a special interest-bearing account (we will assume that there are no legal restrictions and that withdrawals can be made without penalties). Assume that the annual

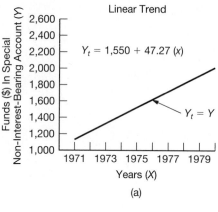

(a)

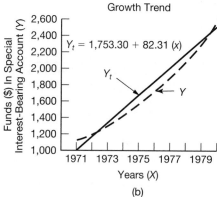

(b)

Figure 4.11 Linear versus growth trends.

rate of interest is 10 percent compounded annually. Assume also that only the original $1,000 was left in the account for the ten-year period, that is, no further deposits were made. The growth of city funds, illustrated in Figure 4.11(b), is a good example of the kind of growth trend we have been discussing. City funds increased by increasing amounts over the ten-year period (but at a constant interest rate compounded annually), and the total funds available at the end of 1980 was $2,594, compared with $2,000 in the non-interest-bearing account (Figure 4.11[a]). Note that in the first case (no interest) it takes ten years to double the original amount. No accumulation above the original $1,000 comes from interest. In the second case, it takes a little more than seven years to double the original amount, and all of the additional ($1,594) accumulation comes from interest. The values used to calculate accumulation at the end of 1980 are

$$S_n = (1 + r)^n S_0$$
$$= (1 + r)^{10}(\$1,000) = (2.5937)(\$1,000)$$
$$S_{10} = \$2,594$$

Note that accumulation for any given year (e.g., 1975 as the fifth year) may be calculated simply by substituting the appropriate values in the formula $S_5 = (1 + r)^5$ ($1,000) = (1.6105)($1,000) = $1,610.51.

Consider now the limitations of linear regression in estimating growth trends such as that illustrated in Figure 4.11(b). The linear regression equation of Figure 4.11(b) [$Y_t = 1,753.30 + 82.31(x)$] will produce an inaccurate forecast. For example, a 1990 forecast using the linear regression equation yields a trend estimate of $4,140.29 [$Y_{t(1990)} = 1,753.30 + 82.31(29) = $4,140.29$]. By contrast, the compound interest formula, which exactly represents the nonlinear growth in accumulated funds, produces a 1990 estimate of $6,727.47 [$S_{20} = (1.1)^{20}($1,000) = $6,727.47$].[25] The linear regression estimate is therefore highly inaccurate.

Fortunately, the linear regression technique may be adapted to estimate growth trends. For regression to do this, however, it is necessary to change our original linear equation [$Y_t = a + b(x)$] to a nonlinear one. Although there are many ways to do this, two of the most common procedures are exponential weighting and data transformation.

Exponential Weighting

In *exponential weighting* the analyst may raise one of the terms in the regression equation to a power, for example, square the value of (x), or add another term, also raised to a power, to the equation [e.g., $c(x^2)$]. The more pronounced the increase (or decrease) in the observed growth pattern, the higher the power necessary to represent it. For example, if we have slowly increasing amounts of change, such as those illustrated by the compound interest formula (Figure 4.11[b]), we might add to the original linear regression equation a third term [$c(x^2)$] that has been raised to a power by squaring the coded time value (x). The equation (called a second-degree parabola) then reads

$$Y_t = a + b(x) + c(x^2)$$
$$= 1753.30 + 82.31(x) + 1.8(x^2)$$

Note that the only part of this equation that is not linear is the squared time value (x^2). This means that any value of x computed for given years will increase by a power of 2 (e.g., coded values of -5 and $+9$ become 25 and 81, respectively). The higher the original x value, the greater the amount of change, because the squares of larger numbers produce disproportionately larger products than do the squares of smaller numbers. Whereas a coded time value (x) of 9 is three times the value of 3 in the linear regression equation, in the second-degree parabola the same year is nine times the value of the corresponding year

---

[25] Note that the coded time values for this even-numbered series are two units apart (see Table 4.6 below). The year 1990 is 29 units away from 1976. Note that there are other ways to code time (e.g., 1; 2;...h) that are cumbersome for the hand-calculations required here.

$$\frac{9}{3} = 3 \ \text{and} \ \frac{9^2}{3^2} = 9$$

It is now easier to visualize what it means to say that growth processes exhibit increasing increases in a time series.

Data Transformation

A second procedure used to adapt linear regression techniques to processes of growth and decline is *data transformation*. Whereas exponential weighting involves the writing of a new and explicitly nonlinear regression equation [e.g., $Y_t = a + b(x) + c(x^2)$], the transformation of data permits analysts to work with the simple linear equation [$Y_t = a + b(x)$], but only after values of the time-series variable (Y) have been appropriately transformed. One way to transform the time-series variable is to take its square root ($\sqrt{Y}$). Another way to transform data is to take the natural *logarithm* of values of the time-series variable. The common (base 10) logarithm of a number is the power to which 10 must be raised to produce that number. For example, 2 is the logarithm of 100, because 10 must be raised to the power of 2 to produce 100 ($10 \times 10 = 10^2 = 100$). The natural (base e) logarithm of a number is the power to which the base e, which equals 2.71828, must be raised to produce that number. For example, the natural logarithm of 100 is 4.6052, because 2.71828 raised to the power 4.6052 equals 100. The abbreviation for base 10 logarithms is log, and the abbreviation for base e logarithms is ln. For readers with no experience with logarithms and roots, it is easier to grasp the nature of these transformations if we study a hypothetical time series that exhibits extremely rapid growth (Table 4.5). We can then observe the consequences of taking roots and logarithms of the time-series variable before solving the simple linear regression equation.

Note that all computations used in Table 4.5 are identical to those already used in applying linear regression to estimate trend. The only difference is that values of Y have been transformed, either by taking their square roots or by taking their common (base 10) logarithms. Observe that the linear regression procedure is wholly inappropriate for describing the sharp growth trend that progresses by multiples of 10 in each period [column (2), Table 4.5]. The linear equation [$Y_t = a + b(x)$] produces a 1981 forecast of 85,227, when the actual value of the series will be 1,000,000! (We are assuming, of course, that the series will grow by a factor of 10 in 1981 and subsequent years.) The linear equation based on the square root transformation [$\sqrt{Y_t} = a + b(x)$] helps very little with this explosive time series. The transformation results in a 1981 estimate of 94,249, hardly much of an improvement.

Only the logarithmically transformed linear equation [log $Y = a + b(x)$] gives us the exact value for 1981. In effect, what we have done is "straighten out" the growth trend by taking the common logarithm of Y, thus permitting the use of linear regression to extrapolate trend. This does *not* mean that the trend is actually linear (obviously, it is not). It only means that we can use linear regression to make a precise forecast of the value of the *nonlinear* trend in 1981 or any other year.

Table 4.5 Square Root and Logarithm of a Time Series Exhibiting Rapid Growth

Year (X)	Original Value of Time-Series Variable (Y)	Square Root of Time-Series Variable $(\sqrt{Y})_t$	Logarithm of Time-Series Variable (log Y)	Coded Time Value (x)	Time Value Squared (x^2)	Columns (2) by (5) (xY)	Columns (3) by (5) $(x\sqrt{Y})_t$	Columns (4) by (5) $(x \log Y)$	Trend Estimates Y_t	Trend Estimates $\sqrt{Y}_t$	Trend Estimates $\log Y_t$
(1)	(2)	(3)	(4)	(5)	(6)	(7)	(8)	(9)	(10)	(11)	(12)
1976	10	3.16	1.0	-2	4	-20	-6.32	-2	-19,718	-51.0	1.0
1977	100	10.00	2.0	-1	1	-100	-10.0	-2	1,271	20.6	2.0
1978	1,000	31.62	3.0	0	0	0	0	0	22,260	92.2	3.0
1979	10,000	100.00	4.0	1	1	10,000	100.00	4	43,249	163.8	4.0
1000	100,000	316.23	5.0	2	4	200,000	632.46	10	64,238	235.4	5.0
5	111,300	461.01	15.0	0	10	209,880	716.14	10.0	11,300	461.01	15.0

$Y_t = a + b(x)$

$a = \dfrac{\Sigma Y}{n} = \dfrac{111,300}{5} = 22,260$

$b = \dfrac{\Sigma(xY)}{\Sigma(x^2)} = \dfrac{209,880}{10} = 20,988$

$Y_t = 22,260 + 20,988(x)$

$Y_{t(1981)} = 22,260 + 20,988(3)$

$= 85,224$

$\sqrt{Y}_t = a + b(x)$

$a = \dfrac{\Sigma\sqrt{Y}}{n} = \dfrac{461.01}{5} = 92.2$

$b = \dfrac{\Sigma(x\sqrt{Y})}{\Sigma(x^2)} = \dfrac{716.14}{10} = 71.6$

$\sqrt{Y}_t = 92.2 + 71.6(x)$

$Y_{t(1981)} = [92.2 + 71.6(3)]^2$

$= 94,249$

$\log Y = a + b(x)$

$a = \dfrac{\Sigma \log Y}{n} = \dfrac{15}{5} = 3.0$

$b = \dfrac{\Sigma(x\log Y)}{\Sigma(x^2)} = \dfrac{10}{10} = 1.0$

$\log Y = 3.0 + 1.0(x)$

$Y_{t(1981)} = \text{antilog } 3.0 + 1.0(3)$

$= \text{antilog } 6.0$

$= 1,000,000$

Note, however, that to make a trend estimate for 1981, we must convert the logarithmic value (6.0) back into the original value of the Y variable. This is done (Table 4.5) by taking the *antilogarithm* of 6.0 (abbreviated "antilog 6.0"), which is 1,000,000 (an antilogarithm is the number corresponding to the logarithm, e.g., antilog 2 = 100, antilog 3 = 1,000, antilog 4 = 10,000, and so on). Note also that roots must also be reconverted by raising the trend estimate by the appropriate power (see Table 4.5).

Now that we understand some of the fundamentals of estimating growth trends, let us return to our example of the manager of the small municipality and the problem of compound interest. We know from the compound interest model that $1,000 invested at an interest rate of 10 percent (compounded annually) will accumulate to $6,727.47 by the end of 1990. That is,

$$S_n = (1 + r)^n S_0$$
$$= (1 + 0.10)^{20}(\$1,000)$$
$$S_{20} = \$6,727.50$$

If we use the linear regression equation to extrapolate to 1990, we will obtain $4,140.29. This is $2,587.18 in error ($6,727.47 − 4,140.29 = $2,587.18). But what can we do about this sizable error, given that we would like to use the linear regression model to forecast the growth trend? The easiest way to deal with this problem is to find the base 10 logarithms of all values of Y and use these with the linear regression equation. This has been done in Table 4.6, which shows that the 1990 trend estimate based on the logarithmic transformation is log $Y_{t(1990)} = 3.828$. When we take the antilogarithm of this value, we find that it equals approximately $6,730, an estimate that is very close to that produced by the compound interest formula (note: small errors are due to rounding). Hence, through a logarithmic transformation of the time-series variable, we have applied linear regression to a nonlinear growth process. The same kinds of logarithmic transformations are regularly used in public policy analysis to extrapolate other important growth trends, including national income, population, and government expenditures.

Catastrophe Methodology

No matter how successfully we adapt linear regression to problems of forecasting growth and decline, there is one condition that must be present: The processes we seek to understand and extrapolate must be smooth and continuous. Yet as we have seen (Figure 4.9[e]), many time series are discontinuous. It is here where catastrophe methodology, a field within the special branch of mathematics called topography, provides useful insights. *Catastrophe methodology,* which involves the systematic study and mathematical representation of discontinuous processes, is specifically designed to forecast trends where small changes in one variable (e.g., time) produce sudden large changes in another variable. The point where a small change in one variable results in a sudden and dramatic shift in another variable is called a

Table 4.6 Linear Regression with Logarithmic Transformation of Time Series

Years (X) (1)	Time Series Variable (Y) (2)	Logarithm of Time Series Variable (log Y) (3)	Coded Time Value (x) (4)	Squared Time Value (x²) (5)	Columns (3) By (4) (x log Y) (6)	Trend Estimate (log Yₜ) (7)
1971	1100	3.041	−9	81	−27.369	3.0413
1972	1210	3.083	−7	49	−21.581	3.0827
1973	1331	3.124	−5	25	−15.620	3.1241
1974	1464	3.165	−3	9	−9.495	3.1655
1975	1611	3.207	−1	1	−3.207	3.2069
1976	1772	3.248	1	1	3.248	3.2483
1977	1949	3.290	3	9	9.870	3.2897
1978	2144	3.331	5	25	16.655	3.3311
1979	2358	3.373	7	49	23.611	3.3725
1980	2594	3.414	9	81	30.726	3.4139
10	17533	32.276	0	330	6.838	32.2760

$$\log Y_t = a + b(x)$$

$$a = \frac{\Sigma \log Y}{n} = \frac{32.276}{10} = 3.2276$$

$$b = \frac{\Sigma(x \log Y)}{\Sigma(x^2)} = \frac{6.838}{330} = 0.0207$$

$$\log Y_t = 3.2276 + 0.0207(x)$$

$$\log Y_{t(1990)} = 3.2276 + 0.0207(29) = 3.828$$

$$Y_{t(1990)} = \text{antilog } 3.828 = \$6{,}745.27$$

catastrophe, a term that refers to a mathematical theorem that classifies discontinuous processes into five major types rather than to any sense of impending doom or disaster. According to its founder, René Thom, it is a methodology (not a theory) for studying the elementary types of discontinuity in nature and society.[26]

Catastrophe methodology is much too complex to survey here. We should nevertheless be aware of some of its major assumptions and applications to public policy analysis:

1. *Discontinuous processes.* Many of the most important physical, biological, and social processes are not only curvilinear, they are also abrupt and discontinuous. An example of discontinuous processes in the social realm is the sudden shifts in public attitudes that sometimes follow smooth and gradually evolving changes in public opinion.

---

[26] See Isnard and Zeeman, "Some Models from Catastrophe Theory in the Social Sciences." René Thom's major work is *Stabilite structurelle et morphogenese,* trans. D. II. Fowler (New York: W. A. Benjamin, 1975). Related to catastrophe methodology is work on chaos theory, which offers explanations of discontinuous change. See Prigogine and Stengers, *Order Out of Chaos.*

2. *Systems as wholes.* Social systems as a whole frequently exhibit changes that are not the simple sum of their parts. Sudden shifts may occur in the structure of a social system as a whole, even though the system's parts may have changed gradually and smoothly. For example, public opinion on major policy issues may suddenly diverge, making for an intense debate or confrontation, while at the same time the opinions of individual citizens evolve gradually. Similarly, public policies may shift abruptly, even though the direction of public opinion has changed gradually.

3. *Incremental delay.* In attempting to maintain or build public support, policy makers tend to choose policies that involve incremental changes of existing routines and practices. Incremental choice involves "the continual successive comparison of the adopted policy with all nearby alternatives."[27] Delay is a consequence of many factors: incomplete information; the prevalence of intuitive (ordinary common sense) forms of analysis; political loyalties and commitments; institutional inertia; and historical precedent.

4. *Catastrophic policy change.* Incremental policy making delays catastrophic change until the last possible moment, partly because smoothly evolving changes in the opinion of contending groups do not appear to require abrupt changes of direction. At a given point in time, policy makers are compelled to make sudden and discontinuous shifts in policy in order to retain popular support.

So far, the primary application of catastrophe methodology in public policy analysis has been to the area of public opinion.[28] A sudden and discontinuous shift in West German energy policy, for example, has been explained by using catastrophe methodology to show how gradual changes in public opinion, together with incremental delay, produced a decision to suddenly terminate plans for the construction of a nuclear power plant in Kaiserstuhl, an agricultural area situated on the Rhine River in the state of Baden Wurttemberg.[29] Following public hearings, construction was begun on the plant, only to be followed by sit-ins and the forcible removal of demonstrators from the site. Throughout this period, public opinion gradually shifted in favor of the farming population in the region. Finally, after a number of incremental policy changes and considerable cost to the government, the project was abruptly abandoned.[30]

---

[27] Isnard and Zeeman, "Some Models from Catastrophe Theory," p. 52. Incremental delay is normally labeled the "Delay Rule" (change policy in the direction that locally increases support). Other rules are "Maxwell's Rule" (change policy to where support is maximum) and the "Voting Rule" (change policy to where the *base,* rather than the maximum, support is greatest).

[28] See Isnard and Zeeman, "Some Models from Catastrophe Theory," pp. 45–60.

[29] See Rob Coppock, "Decision-Making When Public Opinion Matters," *Policy Sciences,* 8 (1977): 135–46.

[30] For a similar case, although presented in terms of "speculative augmentation" rather than catastrophe methodology, see Charles O. Jones, *Clean Air* (Pittsburgh, PA: University of Pittsburgh Press, 1975). Interestingly, Jones challenges the explanatory value of "disjointed incrementalism" (see Chapter 2), while Isnard and Zeeman see it as a major factor contributing to catastrophic change.

Catastrophe methodology provides concepts and techniques for understanding discontinuous policy processes. Yet it is a set of concepts and methods, rather than a "theory." As such it rests on the assumption that discontinuous processes observed in the past will repeat themselves in the future. While catastrophe methodology attempts to provide sound theoretical reasons for the occurrence of future events (as contrasted with simple beliefs that patterns observed in the past will repeat themselves in the future), catastrophe methodology is best viewed as a form of extrapolative forecasting. It is more a way to think about discontinuous policy futures than to make predictions derived from theory, for example, "chaos theory" (see note 26).

THEORETICAL FORECASTING

Theoretical forecasting methods help analysts to make *predictions* of future societal states on the basis of theoretical assumptions and current and historical data. In contrast to extrapolative forecasting, which uses assumptions about historical recurrence to make *projections,* theoretical forecasting is based on assumptions about cause and effect contained in various theories. Whereas the logic of extrapolative forecasting is essentially inductive, the logic of theoretical forecasting is essentially deductive.

Deductive logic, as you will recall, is a form of reasoning where certain general statements (axioms, laws, propositions) are used to show the truth or falsity of other more specific statements, including predictions. In policy analysis, deductive reasoning is most frequently used in connection with arguments from cause that seek to establish that if one event (X) occurs, another event (Y) will follow it. While the distinguishing feature of theoretical forecasting is that predictions are deduced from theoretical assumptions, it should be emphasized that deduction and induction are interrelated. The persuasiveness of a deductive argument is considerably increased if theoretically deduced predictions are observed time after time through empirical research. Similarly, an isolated empirical generalization ("The enemy chose to withdraw when threatened") is much more persuasive if backed by one or more assumptions contained in a theory ("The greater the costs of an alternative, the less likely that it will be chosen").[31]

In this section, we consider several procedures that assist analysts in making theoretical forecasts: theory mapping, causal modeling, regression analysis, point and interval estimation, and correlational analysis. Some of these procedures (theory mapping) are concerned with ways to identify and systemize theoretical assumptions, while others (regression) provide better estimates of future societal states predicted from theory. Before we begin, however, it is essential to recognize that none of these

---

[31] The classic discussion of relations between theory and empirical data (generalizations) in the social sciences is Robert K. Merton, *Social Theory and Social Structure,* rev. ed. (Glencoe, IL: Free Press, 1957), pp. 95–99.

techniques actually makes predictions; only theory can make predictions. In the words of a key contributor to the area of theoretical modeling,

> Owing to the inherent nature of the scientific method, there is a gap between the languages of theory and research. Causal inferences belong on the theoretical level, whereas actual research can only establish covariations and temporal sequences . . . . As a result, we can never actually demonstrate causal laws empirically.[32]

Theory Mapping

Theory mapping is a technique that helps analysts to identify and arrange key assumptions within a theory or causal argument.[33] Theory mapping can assist in uncovering four types of causal arguments: convergent, divergent, serial, and cyclic. *Convergent arguments* are those in which two or more assumptions about causation are used to support a conclusion or claim. *Divergent arguments* are those in which a single assumption supports more than one claim or conclusion. By contrast, in *serial arguments* one conclusion or claim is used as an assumption to support a series of further conclusions or claims. Finally, *cyclic arguments* are serial arguments in which the last conclusion or claim in a series is connected with the first claim or conclusion in that series. The consequences of a cyclic argument may be positively or negatively self-reinforcing. These four types of causal arguments are illustrated in Figure 4.12.

A theory may contain a mixture of convergent, divergent, serial, and cyclic arguments. Several procedures may be used to uncover the overall structure of an argument or theory: (1) separate and number each assumption, which may be an axiom, law, or proposition; (2) underline the words that indicate claims ("therefore," "thus," "hence") or assumptions used to warrant claims ("since," "because," "for"); (3) when specific words ("therefore," and so on) have been omitted, but are clearly implied, supply the appropriate logical indicators in brackets; and (4) arrange numbered assumptions and claims in an arrow diagram that illustrates the structure of the causal argument or theory.

Let's apply these procedures to an important theory about public policy making. This theory, called "public choice," is concerned with the institutional conditions underlying efficient (and inefficient) government administration.[34] Public choice theorists have attempted to show on theoretical grounds how various institutional arrangements, particularly democratic forms of administration, will result in greater efficiency and public accountability. Public choice theory is also controversial, because it

---

[32] Hubert M. Blalock Jr., *Causal Inferences in Nonexperimental Research* (Chapel Hill: University of North Carolina Press, 1964), p. 172.

[33] Adapted from John O'Shaughnessy, *Inquiry and Decision* (New York: Harper & Row, 1973), pp. 58–61; and M. C. Beardsley, *Thinking Straight* (Englewood Cliffs, NJ: Prentice-Hall, 1950).

[34] See Vincent Ostrom, *The Intellectual Crisis in American Public Administration,* rev. ed. (University: University of Alabama Press, 1974).

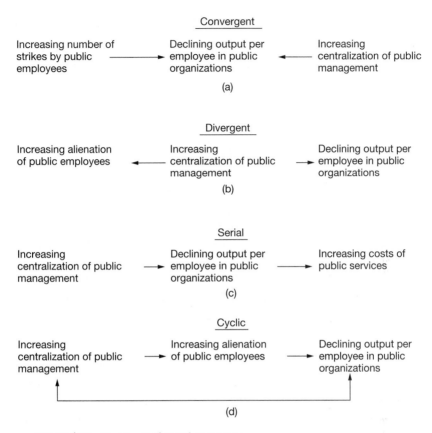

Figure 4.12 Four types of causal arguments.

suggests that major problems of American government (inefficiency, inequity, unresponsiveness) are partly a consequence of the teachings of public administration, a discipline that for fifty and more years has emphasized centralization, hierarchy, and the consolidation of administrative powers.

In an effort to explain the inefficiency of governmental institutions, one public choice theorist, Vincent Ostrom, offers the following argument, which has been mapped by underlining key words and supplying logical indicators in brackets:

> Gordon Tullock in *The Politics of Bureaucracy* (1965) analyzes the consequences which follow when [IT IS ASSUMED THAT] rational, self-interested individuals pursue maximizing strategies in very large public bureaucracies. Tullock's "economic man" is [THEREFORE] an ambitious public employee who seeks to advance his career opportunities for promotions within a bureaucracy. *Since* career advancement depends upon favorable recommendations by his superiors, a career-oriented public servant will act so as to please his superiors. [THEREFORE] Favorable information will be forwarded; unfavorable information

will be repressed. [SINCE] Distortion of information will diminish control and create expectations which diverge from events generated by actions. Large-scale bureaucracies will *thus* become error-prone and cumbersome in adapting to rapidly changing conditions. [SINCE] Efforts to correct the malfunctioning of bureaucracy by tightening control will simply magnify errors. A decline in return to scale can [THEREFORE] be expected to result. [BECAUSE] The larger the organization becomes, the smaller the percent of its activities will relate to output and the larger the proportion of its efforts will be expended on management.[35]

In the argument just quoted, we have already used procedures (2) and (3) of theory mapping. We have underlined words that indicate claims or assumptions underlying claims and supplied missing logical operators in brackets. Observe that the argument begins with an assumption about human nature ("economic man"), an assumption so fundamental that it is called an axiom. Axioms are regarded as true and self-evident; that is, they are believed to require no proof. Note also that this is a complex argument whose overall structure is difficult to grasp simply by reading the passage.

The structure of the argument can be more fully described when we complete steps (1) and (4). Using procedure (1), we separate and number each claim and its warranting assumption, changing some of the words to improve the clarity of the original argument.

[SINCE]	1. Public employees working in very large public bureaucracies are rational, self-interested individuals who pursue maximizing strategies ("economic man").
[AND]	2. The desire for career advancement is a consequence of rational self-interest.
[THEREFORE]	3. Public employees strive to advance their career opportunities.
[SINCE]	4. The advancement of career opportunities is a consequence of favorable recommendations from superiors.
[AND]	5. Favorable recommendations from superiors are a consequence of receiving favorable information from subordinates.
[THEREFORE]	6. Subordinates striving to advance their careers will forward favorable information and suppress unfavorable information.
[SINCE]	7. The repression of unfavorable information creates errors by management, reducing their flexibility in adapting to rapidly changing conditions.

---

[35] Ibid., p. 60. Underlined words and bracketed insertions have been added for purposes of illustrating theory-mapping procedures.

[AND]	8. The repression of unfavorable information diminishes managerial control.
[THEREFORE]	9. Managers compensate for their loss of control by attempting to tighten control. Compensatory attempts to tighten control further encourage the repression of unfavorable information and (6) the magnification of management errors (7). Further (8) loss of control produces attempts to tighten control.
[AND]	10. Compensatory tightening of control is a consequence of the size of public bureaucracies.
[SINCE]	11. Compensatory tightening of control requires the expenditure of a larger proportion of effort on management activities, and a smaller proportion of output activities.
[THEREFORE]	12. The larger the public bureaucracy, the smaller the proportion of effort expanded on output activities in relation to size, that is, the less the return to scale.

By separating and numbering each claim and warranting assumption, we have begun to expose the logical structure of the argument. Note that there are different types of causal arguments in this theory of governmental inefficiency. The first part of the quotation contains a serial argument that emphasizes the influence of employee motivation on information error and managerial control. The second part of the quotation contains another serial argument, but one that stresses the importance of the size of public bureaucracies. In addition, there is one cyclic argument (error magnification) and several divergent and convergent arguments.

The structure of the overall argument cannot be satisfactorily exposed until we complete procedure (4) and draw an arrow diagram that depicts the causal structure of the argument (Figure 4.13). Observe, first, that there are two serial arguments: (1, 2, 3) and (5, 4, 3). The second of these (5, 4, 3) can stand by itself and does not require the first (1, 2, 3), which rests exclusively on deductions from the axiom of "economic man." Second, there is one divergent argument (5, 4, 6) that indicates that the same factor (5) has multiple consequences. There are also three convergent arguments (4, 2, 3), (3, 5, 6), and (8, 10, 9), which suggest in each case that there are two factors that explain the occurrence of the same event.

The arrow diagram also exposes two central features of this theoretical argument. It makes explicit an important potential relationship, denoted by the broken line between (10) and (6), which suggests that the size of public bureaucracies may independently affect the tendency to forward or suppress information. At the same time, the arrow diagram helps identify a cyclic argument (6, 7, 8, 9) that is crucial to this theory. This part of the theory argues, in effect, that we may expect a cumulative increase in the amount of management error as a result of the self-reinforcing relationship among information suppression (6), management error (7), loss of

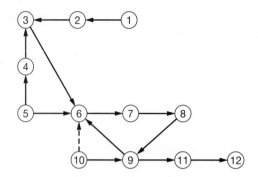

1. Rational Self-Interest (RSA)
2. Desire for Career Advancement (DCA)
3. Striving to Advance Career Opportunities (SAC)
4. Favorable Recommendations for Superiors (FRS)
5. Favorable Information from Subordinates (FIS)
6. Suppression of Unfavorable Information (SUI)
7. Management Error (ME)
8. Loss of Managerial Control (LMC)
9. Compensatory Tightening of Control (CTC)
10. Size of Public Bureaucracies (SPB)
11. Expenditures on Management (EM)   **Figure 4.13**   Arrow diagram illustrating the
12. Return to Scale (RS)   causal structure of an argument.

management control (8), compensatory tightening of control (9), consequent further encouragement of information suppression (6), and so on. This cyclic argument, also known as a *positive feedback loop* (positive because the values of variables in the cycle continue to grow), suggests that any forecast based on public choice theory will predict a curvilinear pattern of growth in management error and government inefficiency.

If we had not used theory mapping procedures, it is doubtful that we would have uncovered the mixture of convergent, divergent, serial, and cyclic arguments contained in the structure of the theory. Particular causal assumptions—for example, the assumption that the size of public bureaucracies may combine with compensatory tightening of control to repress unfavorable information—are not clearly stated in the original passage. Because theory mapping makes the structure of claims and assumptions explicit, it provides us with opportunities to use techniques of theoretical modeling.

Theoretical Modeling

Theoretical modeling refers to a broad range of techniques and assumptions for constructing simplified representations (models) of theories. Modeling is an essential part of theoretical forecasting, because analysts seldom make theoretical forecasts directly from theory. While analysts may begin with theories, they must develop models of these theories before they can actually forecast future events. Theoretical modeling is essential because theories are frequently so complex that they must be simplified before they may be applied to policy problems, and because the process of analyzing data to assess the plausibility of a theory involves constructing and testing models of theories, not the theories themselves.

In the last chapter, we compared and contrasted models in terms of their aims (descriptive, normative), forms of expression (verbal, symbolic, procedural), and methodological functions (surrogates, perspectives). The majority of theoretical forecasting models are primarily descriptive, because they seek to predict rather than optimize some valued outcome. For the most part, these models are also expressed symbolically, that is, in the form of mathematical symbols and equations. Note that we have already used several symbolic models in connection with extrapolative forecasting, for example, the regression equation or model $[Y_t = a + b(x)]$. Although it is not a causal model (because no explicit causal arguments are offered), it is nevertheless expressed symbolically.

In public policy analysis, there are a number of standard forms of symbolic models which assist in making theoretical forecasts: causal models, linear programming models, input–output models, econometric models, microeconomic models, and system dynamics models.[36] As it is beyond the scope of this book to detail each of these model forms, we confine our attention to causal models. In our review, we outline the major assumptions, strengths and limitations, and applications of causal modeling.

Causal Modeling

Causal models are simplified representations of theories that attempt to explain and predict the causes and consequences of public policies. The basic assumption of causal models is that covariations between two or more variables—for example, covariations that show that increases in per capita income occur in conjunction with increases in welfare expenditures in American states—are a reflection of underlying generative powers (causes) and their consequences (effects). The relation between cause and effect is expressed by laws and propositions contained within a theory and modeled by the analyst. Returning to our illustration from public choice theory, observe that the statement "The proportion of total effort invested in management activities is determined by the size of public organizations" is a theoretical proposition. A model of that proposition might be $Y = a + b(X)$, where Y is the ratio of management to nonmanagement personnel, a and b are constants, and X is the total number of employees in public organizations of different sizes.

---

[36] For a discussion of these and other standard model forms, see Martin Greenberger and others, *Models in the Policy Process* (New York: Russell Sage Foundation, 1976), Chapter 4; and Saul I. Gass and Roger L. Sisson, eds., *A Guide to Models in Governmental Planning and Operations* (Washington, DC: U.S. Environmental Protection Agency, 1974). While these models are here treated as descriptive and symbolic (using the definitions of these terms provided in Chapter 3), some (e.g., linear programming) are often treated as normative. Similarly, others (e.g., system dynamics) are typically treated as procedural (or simulation) models. This should accentuate the point that the distinctions among types of models are relative and not absolute.

The strength of causal models is that they force analysts to make causal assumptions explicit. The limitation of causal models lies in the tendency of analysts to confuse covariations uncovered through statistical analysis with causal arguments. Causal inferences always come from *outside* a model, that is, from laws, propositions, or assumptions within some theory. In the words of Sewall Wright, one of the early pioneers in causal modeling, causal modeling procedures are "not intended to accomplish the impossible task of deducing causal relations from the values of the correlation coefficients."[37]

Causal modeling has been used to identify the economic, social, and political determinants of public policies in issue areas ranging from transportation to health, education and welfare.[38] One of the major claims of research based on causal modeling is that differences in political structures (e.g., single versus multiparty polities) do not directly affect such policy outputs as educational and welfare expenditures. On the contrary, differences in levels of socioeconomic development (income, industrialization, urbanization) determine differences in political structures, which in turn affect expenditures for education and welfare. This conclusion is controversial because it appears to contradict the commonly shared assumption that the content of public policy is determined by structures and processes of politics, including elections, representative mechanisms, and party competition.

One of the main statistical procedures used in causal modeling is *path analysis,* a specialized approach to linear regression that uses multiple (rather than single) independent variables. In using path analysis, we hope to identify those independent variables (e.g., income) that singly and in combination with other variables (e.g., political participation) determine changes in a dependent variable (e.g., welfare expenditures). An independent variable is presumed to be the cause of a dependent variable, which is presumed to be its effect. Estimates of cause and effect are called path coefficients, which express one-directional (recursive) causal relationships among independent and dependent variables.

A standard way of depicting causal relationships is the path diagram. A path diagram looks very much like the arrow diagram used to map public choice theory, except that a path diagram contains estimates of the strength of the effects of independent on dependent variables. A path diagram has been used to model part of public choice theory in Figure 4.14. The advantage of path analysis and causal modeling is that they permit forecasts that are based on explicit theoretical assumptions about causes (the number of employees in individual public organizations) and their consequences (the ratio of managerial to nonmanagerial staff and costs in tax dollars per unit of public service). The limitation of these procedures, as already

---

[37] Sewall Wright, "The Method of Path Coefficients," *Annals of Mathematical Statistics* 5 (1934): 193; quoted in Fred N. Kerlinger and Elazar J. Pedhazur, *Multiple Regression in Behavioral Research* (New York: Holt, Rinehart and Winston, 1973), p. 305.

[38] For a review, see Thomas R. Dye and Virginia H. Gray, "Symposium on Determinants of Public Policy: Cities, States, and Nations," *Policy Studies Journal 7,* no. 4 (summer 1979): 279–301.

1.Employees Per Public Organization (EPO)
2.Ratio of Managers to Non-Managers (RMN)
3.Costs in Tax Dollars Per Unit of Service (CUS)

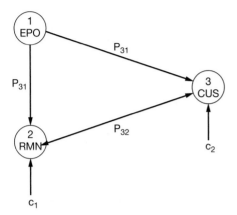

Figure 4.14 Path diagram illustrating a model of public choice theory.

Note: The symbol p designates a causal path and the subscripts specify the direction of causation. p_{31} means that variable 3 is caused by variable 1. Variables that have no antecedent cause are called exogenous variables (i.e., their cause is external to the system), while all others are called endogenous (i.e., their cause is internal to the system). The symbol e (sometimes designated as u) is an error term, defined as the unexplained (residual) variance in an endogenous variable that is left over after taking into account the effects of the endogenous variable that precedes it in the path diagram. Error terms should be uncorrelated with each other and with other variables.

noted, is that they are not designed for the impossible task of inferring causation from estimates of relationships among variables. Although the absence of a relationship may be sufficient to infer that causation is *not* present, only theory permits us to make causal inferences and, hence, predictions.

Regression Analysis

A useful technique for estimating relationships among variables in theoretical forecasting models is regression analysis. *Regression analysis,* which has already been considered in slightly modified form in our discussion of trend estimation, is a general statistical procedure that yields estimates of the pattern and magnitude of a relationship between a dependent variable and one or more independent variables. When regression analysis is performed with one independent variable, it is called *simple regression;* if there are two or more independent variables, it is called *multiple regression*. While many theoretical forecasting problems require multiple regression, we limit ourselves to simple regression in the remainder of this section.[39]

Regression analysis is particularly useful in theoretical modeling. It provides summary measures of the pattern of a relationship between an independent and dependent variable. These summary measures include a regression line, which permits us to estimate values of the dependent variable simply by knowing values of the independent variable, and an overall measure of the vertical distances of observed values from the regression line. A summary measure of these distances, as we shall see, permits us to calculate the amount of error contained in a forecast. Because

---

[39] For a thorough and readable treatment of multiple regression and related techniques, see Kerlinger and Pedhazur, *Multiple Regression in Behavioral Research*.

regression analysis is based on the principle of *least squares,* it has a special advantage already noted in connection with linear trend estimation. It provides the one best "fit" between data and the regression line by ensuring that the squared distances between observed and estimated values represent a minimum or least value.[40]

A second advantage of regression analysis is that it forces the analyst to decide which of two (or more) variables is the cause of the other, that is, to specify the independent (cause) and dependent (effect) variable. To make decisions about cause and effect, however, analysts must have some theory as to why one variable should be regarded as the cause of another. Although regression analysis is particularly well suited to problems of predicting effects from causes, the best that regression analysis can do (and it does this well) is to provide *estimates* of relationships predicted by a theory. Yet it is the theory and its simplified representation (model), and not regression analysis, that do the predicting. Regression analysis can only provide estimates of relationships between variables that, because of some theory, have been stated in the form of predictions.[41] For this reason, analysts should employ theory-mapping procedures before using regression analysis.

To illustrate the application of regression analysis to problems of theoretical forecasting, let us suppose that municipal policy makers wish to determine the future maintenance costs of police patrol vehicles under two alternative policies. One policy involves regular police patrols for purposes of traffic and crime control. In 1980 the total maintenance costs for the ten patrol cars were $18,250, or $1,825 per vehicle. The total mileage for the ten vehicles was 535,000 miles, that is, 53,500 miles per vehicle. A new policy now being considered is one that would involve "high-impact" police patrols as a way to create greater police visibility, respond more rapidly to citizens' calls for assistance, and, ultimately, deter crime by increasing the probability that would-be offenders are apprehended.[42]

Local policy makers are interested in any means that will reduce crime. Yet there are increasing gaps between revenues and expenditures, and several citizens' groups have pressed for a cutback in municipal employees. Policy makers need some way to forecast, on the basis of their own mileage and maintenance records, how much it will cost if several of the ten vehicles are driven an additional 15,000 miles per year.

This forecasting problem may be effectively dealt with by using regression analysis. The relationship between cause and effect is reasonably clear, and the primary determinant of maintenance costs is vehicle usage as measured by miles

---

[40] If this point is not clear, you should return to the section on extrapolative forecasting and review Figure 4.8.

[41] Recall the distinction between surrogate and perspective models in Chapter 3 and the example of the annual rainfall rate and reservoir depth. This and other examples show vividly that regression analysis, apart from its superiority in making estimates, cannot answer questions about which variable predicts another.

[42] Under the sponsorship of the Law Enforcement Assistance Administration, high-impact patrolling has been used, with mixed success, in a number of large municipalities. See Elinor Chelimsky, "The Need for Better Data to Support Crime Control Policy," *Evaluation Quarterly* 1, no. 3 (1977): 439–74.

driven.[43] A municipal policy analyst might therefore plot the values of the independent (X) and dependent (Y) variables on a *scatter diagram (scatterplot)*, which will show the pattern of the relationship (linear–nonlinear), the direction of the relationship (positive–negative), and the strength of the relationship (strong–moderate–weak) between annual mileage per vehicle and annual maintenance costs per vehicle (Figure 4.15). We assume that the pattern, direction, and strength of the relationship is linear, positive, and strong, as shown in Figure 4.15(a).

Regression analysis assumes that variables are related in a linear pattern. While linear regression analysis may also be used with negative linear relationships (Figure 4.15[b]), it will produce serious errors if applied to curvilinear patterns such as those illustrated in Figures 4.15(c) and (d). In such cases, as we saw earlier in the discussion of curve fitting, we must either use nonlinear regression or transform values of variables (e.g., by taking their logarithms) prior to applying conventional linear regression techniques. Regression analysis will yield less reliable estimates when data are widely scattered, as in Figure 4.15(e). If data indicate no pattern or relationship (Figure 4.15[f]), the best estimate of changes in Y due to X is the average (mean) of values of Y.

Recall from our discussion of trend estimation that the straight line describing the relationship between X and Y variables is called a *regression line*. The equation used to fit the regression line to observed data in the scatter diagram is identical to that used to estimate linear trend, with several minor differences. The symbol Y_t (the subscript t refers to a trend value) is replaced with Y_c (the subscript c refers to a computed, or estimated, value). These different subscripts remind us that here, regression is applied to two substantive variables, whereas in linear trend estimation one of the variables is time. The formula for the regression equation is

$$Y_c = a + b(X)$$

where

a = the value of Y_c when $X=0$, called the *Y intercept* because it shows where the computed regression line intercepts the Y-axis

b = the value of changes in Y_c due to a change of one unit in X, called the *slope* of the regression line because it indicates the steepness of the straight line

X = a given value of the independent variable

A second minor difference between the regression and trend equations is the computation of values of a and b. In regression analysis, we do not work with original values of Y and coded time values of X but with *mean deviations*. A mean deviation is simply the difference between a given value of X or Y and the average

---

[43] The question of causation is never certain, as illustrated by this example. Under certain conditions, maintenance costs may affect miles driven, for example, if cost-conscious managers or policemen limit vehicle use in response to knowledge of high expenses. Similarly, annual mileage for certain vehicles may mean larger patrol areas, which in turn may be situated where road conditions are better (or worse) for cars.

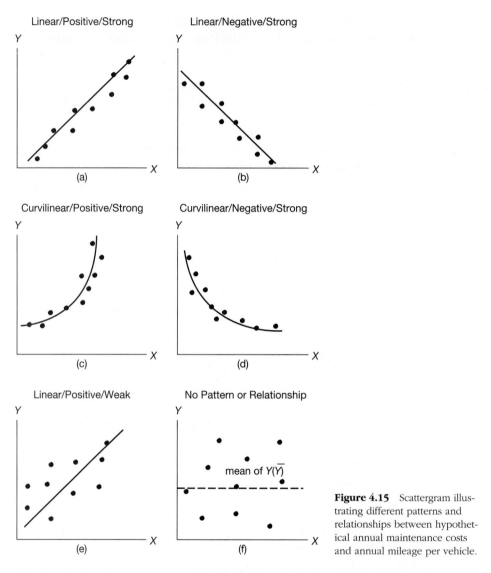

Figure 4.15 Scattergram illustrating different patterns and relationships between hypothetical annual maintenance costs and annual mileage per vehicle.

(mean) of all values of X or Y. The formulas necessary to calculate the mean and mean deviations for X and Y are

$$\text{mean of } X = \bar{X} = \frac{\Sigma X}{n}$$

$$\text{mean of } Y = \bar{Y} = \frac{\Sigma Y}{n}$$

$$\text{mean deviation of } X = x = X - \bar{X}$$

$$\text{mean deviation of } Y = y = Y - \bar{Y}$$

The values of a and b in the regression equation are computed with the following formulas:

$$b = \frac{\Sigma(xy)}{\Sigma(x^2)}$$

$$a = \bar{Y} - b(\bar{X})$$

Let us now return to the forecasting problem facing our municipal policy analyst. All data needed to solve the regression equation are provided in Table 4.7. Observe that column (1) lists the ten vehicles in the municipal fleet. Annual mileage (X) and maintenance costs (Y) are expressed in thousands of miles and dollars [columns (2) and (3)] for ease of calculation. At the bottom of columns (1) and (2), we have also calculated the sums of X (X) and Y (ΣY) and their respective means ($\bar{X} = \Sigma X/n = 53.6$ and $\bar{Y} = \Sigma Y/n = 1.785$). Columns (4) and (5) contain the deviations of each X and Y value from its respective mean. These mean deviations ($x = \bar{X} - X$) and ($y = Y - \bar{Y}$) show us the spread of each X and Y value about its own mean. Note that the values of the mean deviation sum to zero [bottom of columns (4) and (5)]. This is because the means of X and Y are averages, which guarantee that values above the mean will cancel those below the mean.

The mean deviations (x and y) exhibit the spread of each value around the X and Y means. Nevertheless, they cannot be used as a summary measure of this spread, because they sum to zero. For this reason, mean deviations are squared [columns (7) and (8)], thus eliminating negative signs, and summed. These sums, called the *sums of squares* (which is a shortened form of "sums of the squares of mean deviations"), provide an overall summary of the spread of X and Y values around their means. Finally, in column (6) we have multiplied the mean deviations (x and y), obtaining *deviation cross-products* (xy). These cross-products are an expression of the pattern and strength of relationship between X and Y, but one that takes into account the spread of X and Y scores.

To estimate future maintenance costs under the high-impact police patrol program, we first solve the regression equation

$$Y_c = a + b(X)$$

by substituting calculations from the worksheet into formulas for a and b. Hence

$$b = \frac{\Sigma(xy)}{\Sigma(x^2)} = \frac{179.54}{5610.5} = 0.032$$

$$a = \bar{Y} - b(\bar{X}) = 1.785 - 0.032(53.6) = 0.07$$

$$Y_c = 0.07 + 0.032(X)$$

This regression equation means that the regression line intercepts the Y-axis at 0.07 thousand dollars (i.e., $70) and that maintenance costs increase by 0.032 thousand dollars (i.e., $32) for every 1,000 miles driven. On the basis of this

Table 4.7 Worksheet for Estimating Future Maintenance Costs from Annual Mileage per Vehicle

Vehicle Number (1)	Mileage per Vehicle (Thousands of Miles) (X) (2)	Maintenance Costs per Vehicle (Thousands of Dollars) (Y) (3)	X Mean Deviation $(X-\bar{X})$ (x) (4)	Y Mean Deviation $(Y-\bar{Y})$ (y) (5)	Deviation Cross-Product (xy) (6)	X Mean Deviation Squared (x^2) (7)	Y Mean Deviation Squared (y^2) (8)	Estimated Values of (Y_c) (9)
1	24	0.45	−29.5	−1.335	39.38	870.25	1.7820	0.838
2	23	1.25	−30.5	−0.585	17.84	930.25	0.3420	0.806
3	30	0.85	−23.5	−0.985	23.15	552.25	0.9700	1.030
4	40	1.15	−13.5	−0.685	9.25	182.25	0.4690	1.400
5	48	1.95	−5.5	0.115	−0.633	30.25	0.0130	1.606
6	65	1.85	11.5	0.015	0.173	132.25	0.0002	2.150
7	65	2.35	11.5	0.515	5.923	132.25	0.2650	2.150
8	60	2.65	6.5	0.815	5.298	42.25	0.6640	1.990
9	90	2.55	36.5	0.715	26.098	1332.25	0.5110	2.950
10	91	3.25	37.5	1.415	53.063	1406.25	2.0020	2.982
$n=10$	$\Sigma X=536$	$\Sigma \bar{Y}=17.85$	0.0	0.0	$\Sigma(xy)=179.54$	$\Sigma(x^2)=5610.5$	$\Sigma(y^2)=7.02$	$\Sigma Y_c=17.85$
	$\bar{X}=53.6$	$\bar{Y}=1.785$						

$$b = \frac{\Sigma(xy)}{\Sigma(x^2)} = \frac{179.54}{5610.50} = 0.032$$

$$a = \bar{Y} - b(\bar{X}) = 1.785 - 0.032(53.6) = 0.0698 \text{ or } 0.07$$

$$Y_c = a + b(X) = 0.07 + 0.032(X)$$

$$Y_{150} = 0.07 + 0.032(150) = 4.87 = \$4,870$$

information, we can make precise estimates of maintenance costs on the basis of knowledge of annual miles per vehicle. Computed values (Y_c) for each original value of X [column (9)] may be plotted on a graph to create the regression line. Finally, our forecast indicates that the city will incur an additional \$4,870 in expenses by adopting high-impact patrolling, because an additional 150,000 miles will result in $Y_{150} = 0.07+0.032(150) = \$4.87$ thousand dollars.

Point and Interval Estimation

Regression analysis, as we have seen, enables us to fit a regression line to data in such a way that the squared distances between data points and the regression line are a minimum or least value (see Figure 4.8). This means that regression analysis not only uses (rather than loses) information about variations in costs and mileage, it also permits us to make a sound estimate of the central tendency in a relationship and compare this estimate with observed values in a scatter diagram. Because the distances between the regression line and individual data points are minimized, the regression estimate contains less error than other kinds of estimates, for example, those calculated on the basis of average costs per mile driven. Regression analysis also allows us to calculate the probable error in our estimate. This may be done in several ways (Table 4.8). One way is simply to subtract each value of Y_c [column (3)] from its corresponding observed value [column (2)]. This tells us how much distance there is between each pair of estimated and observed values. The error of a regression estimate, expressed by the distance between values of Y and Y_c, increases in direct proportion to the amount of scatter. The greater the scatter, the less accurate the estimate.

Another way to calculate error is to sum and average these distances. Because one of the properties of linear regression is that these distances equal zero when they are added up [i.e., $\Sigma(Y - Y_c) = 0$], we must square them before we divide by the number of cases to find the average. Column (4) of Table 4.8 shows that the average squared error (also called the variance of an estimate) is 1.304. This expression of error, while useful for certain calculations to be described in a moment, is difficult to interpret. Fortunately, the square root of this value is a good approximation of the error that will occur about two-thirds of the time in a regression estimate.[44] The square root of the average squared error, called the *standard error of estimate,* is calculated with the following formula:[45]

$$S_{y.x} = \sqrt{\frac{\Sigma(Y - Y_c)^2}{n}}$$

[44] For readers who recall the normal curve, the standard error is the standard deviation of the average squared error. One standard error is one standard deviation unit to the left or right of the mean of a normal distribution and therefore includes the middle 68.3 percent of all values in the distribution. In the example above, we have assumed for purposes of illustration that data are normally distributed.

[45] Note that we divide by n, because the 10 vehicles constitute the entire population of vehicles under analysis. If we were working with a sample, we would divide by $n - 1$. This is a way of providing an unbiased estimate of the variance in the population sampled. Most packaged computer programs use $n - 1$, even though sampling may not have occurred.

Table 4.8   Calculation of Standard Error of Estimated Maintenance Costs

Vehicle Number (1)	Observed Maintenance Costs (Y) (2)	Estimated Maintenance Costs (Y_c) (3)	Observed Minus Estimated Costs $(Y - Y_c)$ (4)	Observed Minus Estimated Costs Squared $(Y - Y_c)^2$ (5)
1	0.45	0.838	−0.388	0.151
2	1.25	0.806	0.394	0.155
3	0.85	1.030	−0.230	0.053
4	1.15	1.400	−0.300	0.090
5	1.95	1.606	0.294	0.086
6	1.85	2.150	−0.350	0.123
7	2.35	2.150	0.150	0.023
8	2.65	1.990	0.610	0.372
9	2.55	2.950	−0.450	0.203
10	3.25	2.982	0.218	0.048
$n = 10$	$\Sigma Y = 17.85$	$\Sigma Y_c = 17.85$	$\Sigma(Y-Y_c) = 0$	1.304

$$S_{y.x} = \sqrt{\frac{\Sigma(Y - Y_c)^2}{n}} = \sqrt{\frac{\Sigma(Y - Y_c)^2}{10}} = \sqrt{\frac{1.304}{10}} = 0.36111$$

$$Y_i = Y_c \pm Z(S_{y.x})$$

$$Y_{i(150)} = 4.87 \pm 2(0.3611) = 4.87 \pm 0.72222$$

$$= 4.14778 \text{ to } 5.59222$$

$$= \$4{,}147.78 \text{ to } \$5{,}592.22$$

where

$(Y - Y_c)^2$ = the squared difference between observed and estimated values of the dependent variable

n = the number of cases

In the example above, the standard error of estimate is

$$S_{y.x} = \sqrt{\frac{\Sigma (Y - Y_c)^2}{n}} = \sqrt{\frac{1.304}{10}}$$

$$= \sqrt{.1304} = 0.3611 \text{ thousand}$$

$$= \$361.11 \text{ in annual maintenance costs}$$

What this means is that any actual value of maintenance costs is likely to be $361.11 above or below an estimated value about two-thirds of the time. The figure of $361.11 is one standard error (1 × $361.11); two standard errors are $722.22 (2 × $361.11); and three standard errors are $1,083.33 (3 × $361.11). The standard error gives us a *probability interpretation* of these values, because one standard error unit will occur about two-thirds (actually 68.3 percent) of the time; two standard error units will occur about 95 percent (actually 95.4 percent) of the time; and three standard error units will occur about 99 percent (actually 99.7 percent) of the time.

The standard error of estimate allows us to make estimates that take error into account systematically. Rather than make simple *point estimates*—that is, estimates that produce a single value of Y_c—we can make *interval estimates* that yield values of Y_c expressed in terms of one or more standard units of error. If we want to be 95 percent confident that our estimate is accurate (this is usually regarded as a minimum standard of accuracy), we will want to express our estimate in terms of two intervals above and below the original point estimate. We can use the following formula to find out how much error we might expect in our point estimate of $4,870 [$Y_{150}$=0.07+0.032(150)=4.87 thousand dollars] 95 percent of the time:

$$Y_i = Y_c + Z(S_{y.x})$$

$$= 4.87 \pm 2(0.3611)$$

$$= 4.87 \pm 0.72222 = 4.14778 \text{ to } 5.59222$$

$$= \$4,147.78 \text{ to } \$5,592.22$$

where

Y_c = the point estimate of Y
Z = a standard error unit, which takes the value of 2 (95% confidence) in this case
$S_{y.x}$ = the value (0.3611) of one standard error unit
Y_i = an interval estimate of Y (±0.72222)

Correlational Analysis

Regression analysis has an additional feature of importance to theoretical forecasting: It permits us to use *correlational analysis* to interpret relationships. Recall that different scatter diagrams not only exhibit the pattern of a relationship but also its direction and strength (see Figure 4.15). Yet it is desirable that we have measures of the direction and strength of these relationships, not just the visual images contained in scatter diagrams. Two measures that yield such information can be calculated from the worksheet already prepared for estimating future maintenance costs (Table 4.7). The first of these measures is the *coefficient of determination* (r^2), which is a summary measure or index of the amount of variation in the dependent variable explained by the independent variable. The second is the *coefficient of correlation* (r), which is the square root of the coefficient of determination. The coefficient of correlation, which varies between -1.0 and $+1.0$, tells us whether the direction of the relationship is positive or negative and how strong it is. If r is 0, there is no relationship, whereas a value of ± 1.0 (i.e., positive or negative) indicates a maximal relationship. Unlike the coefficient of correlation (r), the coefficient of determination (r^2) takes a positive sign only and varies between 0.0 and 1.0. The formulas for both coefficients are applied below to our data on maintenance costs and mileage (see Table 4.7).

$$r^2 = \frac{b(\Sigma xy)}{\Sigma(y^2)} = \frac{0.032(179.54)}{7.02} = 0.818 \text{ or } 0.82$$

$$r = \sqrt{r^2} = \sqrt{0.818} = 0.90$$

The analysis carried out by hand in Tables 4.7 and 4.8 has been done with SPSS (Exhibit 4.2). Identical results have been obtained, but with greater accuracy and efficiency. When we inspect the SPSS output, we see that the correlation coefficient (r), designated in the output as R, is 0.905. We also see that the coefficient of determination (r^2), designated as R SQUARE, is 0.818. All coefficients are in agreement with our hand calculations. The output also provides the value of the intercept (CONSTANT = 0.07), which conforms to the output in Table 4.7, as does the slope of the regression line ($B = 0.032$) for the variable annual miles per vehicle. Finally, the ANOVA (Analysis of Variance) table provides a breakdown of that part of the total sum of squares due to the effects of regressing the dependent variable on the independent variable (regression = 5.746). The output also provides that part of the sum of squares due to error, that is, residual = 1.275. If we add the regression and residual sum of squares and divide this total into the regression sum of squares, we obtain the coefficient of determination (R). Thus,

$$\frac{5.746}{5.746 + 1.275} = 0.818 = 0.82$$

These coefficients tell us that 82 percent of the variance in annual maintenance costs is explained by annual mileage ($r^2 = 0.82$) and that the direction and strength of the relationship between these two variables is positive and strong ($r = 0.90$). Regression analysis, when supplemented by interval estimation and coefficients of determination and correlation, provides more information of direct relevance to policy makers than other forms of estimation. For example, simple estimates of average costs per mile, apart from their relative inaccuracy, neither provide summary measures of the direction and strength of relationships nor anticipate forecasting errors in a systematic way. In this and many other cases, regression analysis can assist policy makers in dealing with the uncertainties that accompany efforts to predict the future.

Exibit 4.2   SPSS Output for Table 4.7

Variables Entered/Removed[b]

Model	Variables Entered	Variables Removed	Method
1	Annual Miles Per Vehicle (000s)[a]		Enter

a. All requested variables entered

b. Dependent Variable: Annual Maintenance Costs Per Vehicle ($000)

Model Summary

Model	R	R Square	Adjusted R Square	Std. Error of the Estimate
1	.905[a]	.818	.796	.39917721

a. Predictors: (Constant), Annual Miles Per Vehicle (000s)

ANOVA[b]

Model		Sum of Squares	df	Mean Square	F	Sig.
1	Regression	5.746	1	5.746	36.058	.000[a]
	Residual	1.275	8	.159		
	Total	7.020	9			

a. Predictors: (Constant), Annual Miles Per Vehicle (000s)

b. Dependent Variable: Annual Maintenance Costs Per Vehicle ($000)

Coefficients[a]

Model		Unstandardized Coefficients		Standardized Coefficients		
		B	Std. Error	Beta	t	Sig.
1	(Constant)	6.973E-02	.312		.223	.829
	Annual Miles Per Vehicle (000s)	3.200E-02	.005	.905	6.005	.000

a. Dependent Variable: Annual Maintenance Costs Per Vehicle ($000)

JUDGMENTAL FORECASTING

In contrast to extrapolative and theoretical forecasting techniques, where empirical data and/or theories play a central role, judgmental forecasting techniques attempt to elicit and synthesize informed judgments. Judgmental forecasts are often based on arguments from insight, because assumptions about the creative powers of persons making the forecast (and not their social positions per se) are used to warrant claims about the future. The logic of intuitive forecasting is essentially retroductive, because analysts begin with a conjectured state of affairs (e.g., a normative future such as world peace) and then work their way back to the data or assumptions necessary to support the conjecture. Nevertheless, inductive, deductive, and retroductive reasoning are never completely separable in practice. Judgmental forecasting is therefore often supplemented by various extrapolative and theoretical forecasting procedures.[46]

In this section, we review three intuitive forecasting techniques: Delphi technique, cross-impact analysis, and the feasibility assessment technique. These and other techniques, most of which have been widely used in government and industry, are particularly well suited to the kinds of problems we described (Chapter 3) as messy, ill structured, or squishy. Because one of the characteristics of ill-structured problems is that policy alternatives and their consequences are unknown, it follows that in such circumstances there are no relevant theories and/or empirical data to make a forecast. Under these conditions, judgmental forecasting techniques are particularly useful and even necessary.

The Delphi Technique

Delphi technique is a judgmental forecasting procedure for obtaining, exchanging, and developing informed opinion about future events. Delphi technique (named after Apollo's shrine at Delphi, where Greek oracles sought to foresee the future) was developed in 1948 by researchers at the Rand Corporation and has since been used in many hundreds of forecasting efforts in the public and private sectors. Originally, the technique was applied to problems of military strategy, but its application gradually shifted to forecasts in other contexts: education, technology, marketing, transportation, mass media, medicine, information processing, research and development, space exploration, housing, budgeting, and the quality of life.[47] While the technique originally emphasized the use of experts to verify forecasts based on empirical data, Delphi began to be applied to problems of values forecasting in the 1960s.[48] The Delphi technique has been used by analysts in countries ranging from the United States, Canada, and the United Kingdom to Japan and the Soviet Union.

Early applications of Delphi were motivated by a concern with the apparent ineffectiveness of committees, expert panels, and other group processes. The technique was designed to avoid several sources of distorted communication found in groups: domination of the group by one or several persons; pressures to conform to peer group opinion; personality differences and interpersonal conflict; and the difficulty of publicly opposing persons in positions of authority. To avoid these

---

[46] In fact, even large-scale econometric models are dependent on judgment. The best sources on this point are Ascher, *Forecasting;* Ascher, "The Forecasting Potential of Complex Models"; and McNown, "On the Use of Econometric Models."

[47] Thorough accounts may be found in Harold Sackman, *Delphi Critique* (Lexington, MA: D. C. Heath and Company, 1975); and Juri Pill, "The Delphi Method: Substance, Contexts, a Critique and an Annotated Bibliography," *Socio-Economic Planning Sciences* 5 (1971): 57–71.

[48] See, for example, Nicholas Rescher, *Delphi and Values* (Santa Monica, CA: Rand Corporation, 1969).

problems, early applications of the Delphi technique emphasized five basic principles: (1) *anonymity*—all experts or knowledgeables respond as physically separated individuals whose anonymity is strictly preserved; (2) *iteration*—the judgments of individuals are aggregated and communicated back to all participating experts in a series of two or more rounds, thus permitting social learning and the modification of prior judgments; (3) *controlled feedback*—the communication of aggregated judgments occurs in the form of summary measures of responses to questionnaires; (4) *statistical group response*—summaries of individual responses are presented in the form of measures of central tendency (usually the median), dispersion (the interquartile range), and frequency distributions (histograms and frequency polygons); and (5) *expert consensus*—the central aim, with few exceptions, is to create conditions under which a consensus among experts is likely to emerge as the final and most important product.

These principles represent a characterization of conventional Delphi. *Conventional Delphi*, which dominated the field well into the late 1960s, should be contrasted with policy Delphi. *Policy Delphi* is a constructive response to the limitations of conventional Delphi and an attempt to create new procedures that match the complexities of policy problems. In the words of one of its chief architects,

> Delphi as it originally was introduced and practiced tended to deal with technical topics and seek a consensus among homogeneous groups of experts. The Policy Delphi, on the other hand, seeks to generate the strongest possible opposing views on the potential resolution of a major policy issue...a policy issue is one for which there are no experts, only informed advocates and referees.[49]

While policy Delphi is based on two of the same principles as conventional Delphi (iteration and controlled feedback), it also introduces several new ones:

1. *Selective anonymity.* Participants in a policy Delphi remain anonymous only during the initial rounds of a forecasting exercise. After contending arguments about policy alternatives have surfaced, participants are asked to debate their views publicly.

2. *Informed multiple advocacy.* The process for selecting participants is based on criteria of interest and knowledgeableness, rather than "expertise" per se. In forming a Delphi group, investigators therefore attempt to select as representative a group of informed advocates as may be possible in specific circumstances.

3. *Polarized statistical response.* In summarizing individual judgments, measures that purposefully accentuate disagreement and conflict are used. While conventional measures may also be used (median, range, standard deviation),

---

[49] Murray Turoff, "The Design of a Policy Delphi," *Technological Forecasting and Social Change* 2, no. 2 (1970): 149–71. See also Harold A. Linstone and Murray Turoff, eds., *The Delphi Method: Techniques and Applications* (New York: Addison-Wesley, 1975).

policy Delphi supplements these with various measures of polarization among individuals and groups.

4. *Structured conflict.* Starting from the assumption that conflict is a normal feature of policy issues, every attempt is made to use disagreement and dissension for creatively exploring alternatives and their consequences. In addition, efforts are made to surface and make explicit the assumptions and arguments that underlie contending positions. The outcomes of a policy Delphi are nevertheless completely open, which means that consensus as well as a continuation of conflict might be results of the process.

5. *Computer conferencing.* Where possible, computer consoles are used to structure a continuous process of anonymous interaction among physically separated individuals. Computer conferencing eliminates the need for a series of separate Delphi rounds.

A policy Delphi may be conducted in a number of different ways, depending on the context and the skill and ingenuity of the persons using the technique. Because policy Delphi is a major research undertaking, it involves a large number of technical questions, including sampling, questionnaire design, reliability and validity, and data analysis and interpretation. Although these questions are beyond the scope of this chapter,[50] it is important to obtain an overall understanding of the process of conducting a policy Delphi. A policy Delphi can best be visualized as a series of interrelated steps.[51]

Step 1: *Issue specification.* Here the analyst must decide what specific issues should be addressed by informed advocates. For example, if the area of concern is national drug abuse policy, one of the issues might be "The personal use of marijuana should or should not be legalized." One of the central problems of this step is deciding what proportion of issues should be generated by participants, and what proportion should be generated by the analyst. If the analyst is thoroughly familiar with the issue area, it is possible to develop a list of issues prior to the first round of the Delphi. These issues may be included in the first questionnaire, although respondents should be free to add or delete issues.

Step 2: *Selection of advocates.* Here the key stakeholders in an issue area should be selected. To select a group of advocates who represent conflicting positions, however, it is necessary to use explicit sampling procedures. One

---

[50] Unfortunately, there are few shortcuts to developing methodologically sound questionnaires for use in policy Delphis. On questionnaire construction, the best short introduction is Earl R. Babbie, *Survey Research Methods* (Belmont, CA: Wadsworth, 1973). On reliability and validity, see Fred N. Kerlinger, *Foundations of Behavioral Research,* 3d ed. (New York: Holt, Rinehart and Winston, 1985), pp. 442–78. A useful general-purpose handbook on these questions is Delbert C. Miller, *Handbook of Research Design and Social Measurement,* 5th ed. (Newbury Park, CA: Sage Publications, 1991).

[51] See Turoff, "The Design of a Policy Delphi," pp. 88–94.

way to do this is to use "snowball" sampling. Here the analyst begins by identifying one advocate, usually someone who is known to be influential in the issue area, and asking that person to name two others who agree and disagree most with his or her own position. These two persons are asked to do the same thing, which results in two more persons who agree and disagree maximally, and so on (hence the term "snowball" sample). Advocates should be as different as possible, not only in terms of positions attributed to them but also in terms of their relative influence, formal authority, and group affiliation. The size of the sample might range from ten to thirty persons, although this depends on the nature of the issue. The more complex the issue, and hence the more heterogeneous the participants, the larger the sample must be to be representative of the range of advocates.

Step 3: *Questionnaire design.* Because a policy Delphi takes place in a series of rounds, analysts must decide which specific items will go in questionnaires to be used in the first and subsequent rounds. Yet the second-round questionnaire can only be developed after the results of the first round are analyzed; the third-round questionnaire must await results of the second round; and so on. For this reason, only the first-round questionnaire can be drafted in advance. Although the first-round questionnaires may be relatively unstructured (with many open-ended items), they may also be relatively structured, provided the analyst has a good idea of the major issues. First-round questionnaires may include several types of questions: (1) *forecasting items* requesting that respondents provide subjective estimates of the probability of occurrence of particular events, (2) *issue items* requesting respondents to rank issues in terms of their importance, (3) *goal items* that solicit judgments about the desirability and/or feasibility of pursuing certain goals, and (4) *options items* requesting that respondents identify alternative courses of action that may contribute to the attainment of goals and objectives.

Several types of scales are available to measure responses to each of these four types of items. One procedure is to use different scales with different types of items. For example, a certainty scale may be used primarily with forecast items; an importance scale with issue items; desirability and feasibility scales with goal items; and some combination of these scales with options items. The best way to show what is involved is to illustrate the way in which items and scales are presented in a policy Delphi questionnaire. This has been done in Table 4.9.

Observe that the scales in Table 4.9 do not permit neutral answers, although "No Judgment" responses are permitted for all items. This restriction on neutral responses is designed to bring out conflict and disagreement, an important aim of the policy Delphi. An important part of the construction of questionnaires is pretesting among a sample of advocates and determining the reliability of responses.

Table 4.9 **Types of Items and Scales Used in a Policy Delphi Questionnaire**

Type of Item	Item	Scale				
Forecast	According to a recent projection by researchers at the National Institute of Mental Health, the number of marijuana users per 1,000 persons in the general population will double between 1980 and 1990. How certain are you that this projection is reliable?	Certainly Reliable 1 □	Reliable 2 □	Risky 3 □	Unreliable 4 □	No Judgment 0 □
Issue	The Personal use of marijuana *should/should not be* legalized. How important is this issue relative to others?	Very Important 1 □	Important 2 □	Slightly Important 3 □	Unimportant 4 □	No Judgment 0 □
Goal	One goal of national policy might be to increase public awareness of the difference between drug use (responsible) and abuse (irresponsible). How *desirable* is this objective?	Very Desirable 1 □	Desirable 2 □	Undesirable 3 □	Very Undesirable 4 □	No Judgment 0 □
Options	It has been suggested that drug abuse education programs contribute to the reduction of potential users in the general population. How *feasible* is this policy option?	Definitely Feasible 1 □	Possibly Feasible 2 □	Possible Unfeasible 3 □	Definitely Unfeasible 4 □	No Judgment 0 □

Note: For additional information, see Irene Ann Jillson, "The National Drug Abuse Policy Delphi: Progress Report and Findings to Date," in *The Delphi Method: Techniques and Applications*, ed. Harold A. Linstone and Murray Turoff (New York: Addison-Wesley, 1975), pp. 124–59.

Step 4: *Analysis of first-round results.* When the questionnaires are returned after the first round, analysts attempt to determine the initial positions on forecasts, issues, goals, and options. Typically, some items believed to be desirable or important are also believed to be unfeasible, and vice versa. Because there will be conflicting assessments among the various advocates, it is important to use summary measures that not only express the central tendency in the set of responses but also describe the extent of dispersion or polarization. These summary measures not only eliminate items that are uniformly important, undesirable, unfeasible and/or uncertain, but also serve in the second-round questionnaire as a means to communicate to participants the results of the first round.

The calculation and subsequent presentation of these summary measures of central tendency, dispersion, and polarization are best illustrated graphically. Assume for purposes of illustration that ten advocates in the first round of a hypothetical policy Delphi provided different assessments of the desirability and feasibility of two drug-control goals: to reduce the supply of illicit drugs and to increase public awareness of the difference between responsible and irresponsible drug use. Let us imagine that the responses were those presented in Table 4.10.

Table 4.10 Hypothetical Responses in First-Round Policy Delphi: Desirability and Feasibility of Drug-Control Objectives

Advocate	Goal 1 (Reduce Supply)		Goal 2 (Public Awareness)	
	Desirability	*Feasibility*	*Desirability*	*Feasibility*
1	1	4	1	1
2	4	1	2	2
3	3	3	2	1
4	4	2	1	2
5	1	4	2	1
6	2	3	2	1
7	1	4	1	1
8	4	2	1	2
9	4	1	2	2
10	1	4	1	2
	$\Sigma = 25$	$\Sigma = 28$	$\Sigma = 15$	$\Sigma = 15$
	Md = 2.5	Md = 3.0	Md = 1.5	Md = 1.5
	Md = 2.5	Md = 2.8	Md = 1.5	Md = 1.5
	Range = 3.0	Range = 3.0	Range = 1.0	Range = 1.0

Note: The median (Md) in a set of scores is the value of the score that falls in the middle when the scores are arranged in order of magnitude. If the number of scores is even (as above), the median is the value of the score which is halfway between the two middle scores. The median is normally used in place of the mean (Mn) when we do not know if the intervals between measures (e.g., the intervals between 1 and 2 and 3 and 4) are equidistant.

Observe that some respondents (advocates 2, 8, and 9) believe that the goal of reducing the supply of illicit drugs is very undesirable but possibly or definitely feasible, while others (advocates 1, 5, 7, and 10) believe that this goal is very desirable but definitely unfeasible. When we compare these inconsistencies between desirability and feasibility with responses under goal 2 (public awareness), we find much less inconsistency in the latter set of scores. All of this suggests that the responses to goal 1, while much lower in average desirability and feasibility, also reflect the kinds of important conflicts that policy Delphi is specially designed to address. In this case, analysts would not want to eliminate this item. Rather they would want to report these conflicts as part of the second-round instrument, requesting that respondents provide the reasons, assumptions, or arguments that led them to positions that were so different. Another way to bring out such disagreements is to construct and report an average *polarization measure,* which may be defined as the absolute difference among scores for all combinations of respondents answering a particular question.[52]

Step 5: *Development of subsequent questionnaires.* Questionnaires must be developed for second, third, fourth, or fifth rounds (most policy Delphis involve three to five rounds). As indicated previously, the results of prior rounds are used as a basis for subsequent ones. One of the most important aspects of policy Delphi occurs in these rounds, because it is here that advocates have an opportunity to observe the results of immediately preceding rounds and offer explicit reasons, assumptions, and arguments for their respective judgments. Note that later rounds do not simply include information about central tendency, dispersion, and polarization; they also include a summary of arguments offered for the most important conflicting judgments. In this way, the policy Delphi promotes a reasoned debate and maximizes the probability that deviant and sometimes insightful judgments are not lost in the process. By the time the last round of questionnaires is completed, all advocates have had an opportunity to state their initial positions on forecasts, issues, goals, and options; to examine and evaluate the reasons why their positions differ from those of others; and to reevaluate and change their positions.

Step 6: *Organization of group meetings.* One of the last tasks is to bring advocates together for a face-to-face discussion of the reasons, assumptions, and arguments that underlie their various positions. This face-to-face meeting,

---

[52] Ibid., p. 92; and Jerry B. Schneider, "The Policy Delphi: A Regional Planning Application," *Technological Forecasting and Social Change* 3, no. 4 (1972). The total number of combinations (C) is calculated by the formula $C = k(k - 1)/2$, where k is the number of responses to a particular item. The average difference is obtained by computing the numerical distance between all combinations, adding them up, and dividing by the number of respondents. This requires that we ignore the signs (plus or minus). Another procedure is to retain the signs, square each difference (eliminating minus signs), sum, and average.

because it occurs after all advocates have had a chance to reflect on their positions and those of others, may create an atmosphere of informed confidence that would not be possible in a typical committee setting. Face-to-face discussions also create conditions where advocates may argue their positions intensely and receive immediate feedback.

Step 7: *Preparation of final report.* There is no guarantee that respondents will have reached consensus but much reason to hope that creative ideas about issues, goals, options, and their consequences will be the most important product of a policy Delphi. The report of final results will therefore include a review of the various issues and options available, taking care that all conflicting positions and underlying arguments are presented fully. This report may then be passed on to policy makers, who may use the results of the policy Delphi as one source of information in arriving at decisions.

Cross-Impact Analysis

Delphi technique is closely related to another widely used judgmental forecasting technique called cross-impact analysis. *Cross-impact* analysis, developed by the same Rand Corporation researchers responsible for early applications of conventional Delphi,[53] is a technique that elicits informed judgments about the probability of occurrence of future events on the basis of the occurrence or nonoccurrence of related events. The aim of cross-impact analysis is to identify events that will facilitate or inhibit the occurrence of other related events. Cross-impact analysis was expressly designed as a supplement to conventional Delphi. In the words of two of its early developers,

> A shortcoming of [Delphi] and many other forecasting methods... is that potential relationships between the forecasted events may be ignored and the forecasts might well contain mutually reinforcing or mutually exclusive items. [Cross-impact analysis] is an attempt to develop a method by which the probabilities of an item in a forecasted set can be adjusted in view of judgments relating to the potential interactions of the forecasted items.[54]

The basic analytical tool used in cross-impact analysis is the *cross-impact matrix,* a symmetrical table that lists potentially related events along row and column headings (Table 4.11). The type of forecasting problem for which cross-impact analysis is particularly appropriate is one involving a series of interdependent events. Table 4.11, for example, expresses the interdependencies among events that follow the mass production of automobiles. Observe the string of direct positive effects

---

[53] These researchers include Olaf Helmer, T. J. Gordon, and H. Hayward. Helmer is credited with coining the term *cross-impact.* See T. J. Gordon and H. Hayward, "Initial Experiments with the Cross-Impact Matrix Method of Forecasting," *Futures* 1, no. 2 (1968): 101.

[54] Ibid., p. 100.

Table 4.11 Cross-Impact Matrix Illustrating Consequences of Mass Automobile Use

	Events (E)						
Events (E)	E_1	E_2	E_3	E_4	E_5	E_6	E_7
E_1		+	0	0	0	0	0
E_2	⊕		+	0	0	0	0
E_3	⊕	0		+	0	0	0
E_4	0	0	0		+	0	0
E_5	0	0	0	0		+	0
E_6	0	0	0	0	0		+
E_7	0	0	0	⊕	⊕	0	

E_1 = mass production of automobiles

E_2 = ease of travel

E_3 = patronization of large suburban stores

E_4 = alienation from neighbors

E_5 = high social-psychological dependence on immediate family members

E_6 = inability of family members to meet mutual social-psychological demands

E_7 = social deviance in form of divorce, alcoholism, juvenile delinquency

Note: A plus (+) indicates direct one-way effects; a zero (0) indicates no effect; a circled plus sign indicates positive feedback effects.

Source: Adapted from Joseph Coates, "Technology Assessment: The Benefits, the Costs, the Consequences," *Futurist 5,* no. 6 (December 1971).

(represented by "+" signs) directly above the blank cells in the main diagonal. These effects are first-, second-, third-, fourth-, fifth-, and sixth-order impacts of mass automobile production. Note also the positive feedback effects of $(E_2 - E_1)$, $(E_3 - E_1)$, $(E_7 - E_4)$, and $(E_7 - E_5)$. These positive feedback effects suggest that ease of travel and patronization of large suburban stores may themselves affect the mass production of automobiles, for example, by increasing demand. Similarly, various forms of social deviance may intensify existing levels of alienation from neighbors and create even greater social-psychological dependence on family members.

This illustration purposefully oversimplifies linkages among events. In many other situations, the linkage of one event with another is not unambiguously positive; nor do events follow one another so neatly in time. Moreover, many events may be negatively linked. For this reason, cross-impact analysis takes into account three aspects of any linkage:

1. *Mode (direction) of linkage.* This indicates whether one event affects the occurrence of another event and, if so, whether the direction of this effect is positive or negative. Positive effects occur in what is called the *enhancing mode,* while

negative ones fall into a category called the *inhibiting mode*. A good example of linkages in the enhancing mode is increased gasoline prices provoking research and development on synthetic fuels. The arms race and its effects on the availability of funds for urban redevelopment are an illustration of linkages in the inhibiting mode. The *unconnected mode* refers to unconnected events.

2. *Strength of linkage.* This indicates how strongly events are linked, whether in the enhancing or inhibiting mode. Some events are strongly linked, meaning that the occurrence of one event substantially changes the likelihood of another's occurring, while other events are weakly linked. In general, the weaker the linkage, the closer it comes to the unconnected mode.

3. *Elapsed time of linkage.* This indicates the amount of time (weeks, years, decades) between the occurrence of linked events. Even though events may be strongly linked, either in the enhancing or inhibiting modes, the impact of one event on the other may require a considerable period of time. For example, the linkage between the mass production of automobiles and social deviance required an elapsed time of several decades.

Cross-impact analysis works on the principle of conditional probability. Conditional probability states that the probability of occurrence of one event is dependent on the occurrence of some other event, that is, the two events are not independent. Conditional probabilities may be denoted by $P(E_1/E_2)$, which is read "The probability of the first event (E_1), given the second event (E_2)." For example, the probability (P) of being elected president (E_1) after a candidate has received the party nomination (E_2) may be 0.5, that is, there is a fifty–fifty chance of winning the election $[P(E_1/E_2) = 0.50]$. However, the probability (P) of being elected (E_1) without the party's nomination (E_3) is low, because party nomination is almost a prerequisite for the presidency $[P(E_1/E_3) = 0.20]$.

This same logic is extended to cross-impact analysis. The construction of a cross-impact matrix begins with the question: "What is the probability that a certain event (E) will occur prior to some specified point in time?" For example, an extrapolative forecast using time-series analysis may provide an interval estimate that claims that there is a 90 percent (0.9) probability that total energy consumption will exceed 100.0 quadrillion BTUs by 1995. The next question is "What is the probability that this event (E_2) will occur, given that another event (E_1) is certain to precede it?" For example, if presently unpredictable factors (new agreements, political turmoil, accidents) result in a doubling of oil prices (E_1) by 1995, the probability of energy consumption at the level of 100.0 quadrillion BTUs may be reduced to 0.5. In this case, note that "objective" data used to make the original extrapolative forecast are combined with a "subjective" judgment about the conditional probability of the originally projected event, given the prior occurrence of the first.

The construction of a cross-impact matrix for any reasonably complex problem involves many thousands of calculations and requires a computer. Many applications of cross-impact analysis in areas of science and technology policy, environmental policy, transportation policy, and energy policy have involved more than 1,000 separate iterations (called "games" or "plays") to determine the consistency of the cross-impact matrix, that is, to make sure that every sequence of conditional probabilities has been taken into account before a final probability is calculated for each event. Despite the technical complexity of cross-impact analysis, the basic logic of the technique may be readily grasped by considering a simple illustration.

Suppose that a panel of experts assembled for a conventional Delphi provides estimates of the probability of occurrence of four events $(E_1 \ldots E_4)$ for future years. Suppose further that these four events are an increase in the price of gasoline to $3 per gallon (E_1), the "gentrification" of central city neighborhoods by former suburbanites (E_2), a doubling of reported crimes per capita (E_3), and the mass production of short-distance battery-powered autos (E_4). The probabilities attached to these four events are, respectively, $P_1 = 0.5$, $P_2 = 0.5$, $P_3 = 0.6$, and $P_4 = 0.2$. Given these subjective estimates, the forecasting problem is this: Given that one of these events occurs (i.e., $P = 1.0$, or 100%), how will the probabilities of other events change?[55]

Table 4.12 illustrates the first round (play) in the construction of a cross-impact matrix. Observe that the assumption that gasoline per gallon will go to $3 produces revised subjective probabilities for "gentrification" (an increase from 0.5 to 0.7), reported crimes per capita (an increase from 0.6 to 0.8), and the mass manufacture of

Table 4.12   Hypothetical Illustration of the First Round (Play) in a Cross-Impact Matrix

If this Event Occurs (P=1.0)	Then the Changed Probability of Occurrence of these Events Is:			
	E_1	E_2	E_3	E_4
E_1 Gas to $3 per gallon		0.7	0.8	0.5
E_2 "Gentrification"	0.4		0.7	0.4
E_3 Crime doubles	0.5	0.4		0.1
E_4 Electric autos	0.4	0.5	0.7	

Events	Original Probabilities (P)
E_1	$P_1 = 0.5$
E_2	$P_2 = 0.5$
E_3	$P_3 = 0.6$
E_4	$P_4 = 0.2$

[55] Alternatively, we can ask the same question about the *nonoccurrence* of an event. Therefore, it is usually necessary to construct two matrices: one for occurrences and one for nonoccurrences. See James F. Dalby, "Practical Refinements to the Cross-Impact Matrix Technique of Technological Forecasting," in *Industrial Applications of Technological Forecasting* (New York: Wiley, 1971), pp. 259–73.

electric autos (an increase from 0.2 to 0.5). These changes reflect the *enhancing link-ages* discussed earlier. By contrast, other linkages are *inhibiting*. For example, the gentrification of central cities makes it less likely that gasoline will increase to $3 per gallon (note the decrease from 0.5 to 0.4), on the assumption that oil companies will become more price competitive when former suburbanites drive less. Finally, there are also *unconnected linkages*. Increased crime and mass-produced electric autos exert no influence on the probability of gas prices increasing to $3 per gallon or on the process of gentrification (note that original probabilities remain constant at 0.5).

The advantage of the cross-impact matrix is that it enables the analyst to discern interdependencies that otherwise may have gone unnoticed. Cross-impact analysis also permits the continuous revision of prior probabilities on the basis of new assumptions or evidence. If new empirical data become available for some of the events (e.g., crime rates), the matrix may be recalculated. Alternatively, different assumptions may be introduced—perhaps as a consequence of a policy Delphi that yields conflicting estimates and arguments—to determine how sensitive certain events are to changes in other events. Finally, information in a cross-impact matrix may be readily summarized at any point in the process.

Cross-impact matrices may be used to uncover and analyze those complex interdependencies that we have described as ill-structured problems. The technique is also consistent with a variety of related approaches to intuitive forecasting, including technology assessment, social impact assessment, and technological forecasting.[56] As already noted, cross-impact analysis is not only consistent with conventional Delphi but actually represents its adaptation and natural extension. For example, while cross-impact analysis may be done by single analysts, the accuracy of subjective judgments may be increased by using Delphi panels.

Cross-impact analysis, like the other forecasting techniques discussed in this chapter, has its limitations. First, the analyst can never be sure that all potentially interdependent events have been included in the analysis, which again calls attention to the importance of problem structuring (Chapter 3). There are other techniques to assist in identifying these events, including variations of theory mapping (see Table 4.9) and the construction and graphic presentation of networks of causally related events called *relevance trees* (see Figure 3.14). Second, the construction and "playing" of a cross-impact matrix is a reasonably costly and time consuming process, even with the advent of packaged computer programs and high-performance computer technology. Third, there are technical difficulties associated with matrix calculations (e.g., nonoccurrences are not always analyzed), although many of these problems have been resolved.[57] Finally, and most important, existing applications of cross-impact analysis suffer from one of the same weaknesses as conventional Delphi, namely, an unrealistic emphasis on consensus among experts. Most of the forecasting

---

[56] On these related approaches, see François Hetman, *Society and the Assessment of Technology* (Paris: Organization for Economic Cooperation and Development, 1973); and Kurt Finsterbusch and C. P. Wolf, eds., *Methodology of Social Impact Assessment* (Stroudsburg, PA: Dowden, Hutchinson & Ross, 1977).

[57] See Dalby, "Practical Refinements to Cross-Impact Matrix Technique," pp. 265–73.

problems for which cross-impact analysis is especially well suited are precisely the kinds of problems where conflict, and not consensus, is widespread. Problem-structuring methods are needed to surface and debate the conflicting assumptions and arguments that underlie subjective conditional probabilities.

Feasibility Assessment

The final judgmental forecasting procedure we consider in this chapter is one that is expressly designed to produce conjectures about the future behavior of policy stakeholders. This procedure, most simply described as the *feasibility assessment technique,* assists analysts in producing forecasts about the probable impact of stakeholders in supporting or opposing the adoption and/or implementation of different policy alternatives.[58] The feasibility assessment technique is particularly well suited for problems requiring estimates of the probable consequences of attempting to legitimize policy alternatives under conditions of political conflict and the unequal distribution of power and other resources.

The feasibility assessment technique may be used to forecast the behavior of stakeholders in any phase of the policy-making process, including policy adoption and implementation. What makes this technique particularly useful is that it responds to a key problem that we have already encountered in reviewing other intuitive forecasting techniques: Typically, there is no relevant theory or available empirical data that permit us to make predictions or projections about the behavior of policy stakeholders. While social scientists have proposed various theories of policy-making behavior that are potentially available as a source of predictions, most of these theories are insufficiently concrete to apply in specific contexts.[59]

The feasibility assessment technique is one way to respond to a number of concerns about the lack of attention to questions of political feasibility and policy implementation in policy analysis. While problems of policy implementation play a large part in most policy problems, much of contemporary policy analysis pays little attention to this question. What is needed is a systematic way to forecast "the capabilities, interests, and incentives of organizations to implement each alternative."[60] In practical terms, this means that the behavior of relevant stakeholders must be forecasted along with the consequences of policies themselves. Only in this way

---

[58] The following discussion draws from but modifies Michael K. O'Leary and William D. Coplin, "Teaching Political Strategy Skills with 'The Prince,' " *Policy Analysis* 2, no. 1 (winter 1976): 145–60. See also O'Leary and Coplin, *Everyman's "Prince."*

[59] These theories deal with elites, groups, coalitions, and aggregates of individuals and leaders. See, for example, Raymond A. Bauer and Kenneth J. Gergen, eds., *The Study of Policy Formation* (New York: Free Press, 1968); and Daniel A. Mazmanian and Paul A. Sabatier, *Implementation and Public Policy* (Lanham, MD: University Press of America, 1989).

[60] Graham T. Allison, "Implementation Analysis: 'The Missing Chapter' in Conventional Analysis: A Teaching Exercise," in *Benefit–Cost and Policy Analysis: 1974,* ed. Richard Zeckhauser (Chicago: Aldine Publishing Company, 1975), p. 379.

can the analyst ensure that organizational and political factors which may be critical to the adoption and implementation of a policy are adequately accounted for.

The feasibility assessment technique, like other intuitive forecasting procedures, is based on subjective estimates. The feasibility assessment technique may be used by single analysts, or by a group of knowledgeables, much as in a Delphi exercise. Feasibility assessment focuses on several aspects of political and organizational behavior:

1. *Issue position.* Here the analyst estimates the probability that various stakeholders will support, oppose, or be indifferent to each of two or more policy alternatives. Positions are coded as supporting (+1), opposing (−1), or indifferent (0). A subjective estimate is then made of the probability that each stakeholder will adopt the coded position. This estimate (which ranges from 0 to 1.0) indicates the saliency or importance of the issue to each stakeholder.

2. *Available resources.* Here the analyst provides a subjective estimate of the resources available to each of the stakeholders in pursuing their respective positions. Available resources include prestige, legitimacy, budget, staff, and access to information and communications networks. Because stakeholders nearly always have positions on other issues for which part of their resources are necessary, available resources should be stated as a fraction of total resources held by the stakeholder. The resource availability scale, expressed as a fraction, varies from 0 to 1.0. Note that there may be a high probability that a given stakeholder will support a policy (e.g., 0.9), yet that same stakeholder may have little capability to affect the policy's adoption or implementation. This is typically the result of an overcommitment of resources (prestige, budget, staff) to other issue areas.

3. *Relative resource rank.* Here the analyst determines the relative rank of each stakeholder with respect to its resources. Relative resource rank, one measure of the "power" or "influence" of stakeholders, provides information about the magnitude of political and organizational resources available to each stakeholder. A stakeholder who commits a high fraction (say, 0.8) of available resources to support a policy may nevertheless be unable to affect significantly a policy's adoption or implementation. This is because some stakeholders have few resources to begin with.

Because the purpose of feasibility assessment is to forecast behavior under conditions of political conflict, it is essential to identify as representative and powerful a group of stakeholders as possible. The analyst may identify representative stakeholders from various organizations and organizational levels with different constituencies and with varying levels of resources and roles in the policy-making process.

An illustration of the feasibility assessment technique has been provided in Table 4.13. In this example, a policy analyst in a large municipality has completed a study that shows that local property taxes must be raised by an average of 1 percent in order to cover expenditures for the next year. Alternatively, expenditures for municipal services must be cut by a comparable amount, an action that will result in

Table 4.13 Feasibility Assessment of Two Fiscal Policy Alternatives in a Hypothetical Municipality

(a) Alternative 1 (Tax Increase)

Stakeholder (1)	Coded Position (2)	Probability (3)	Fraction of Resources Available (4)	Resource Rank (5)	Feasibility Score (6)
Mayor	+1	0.2	0.2	0.4	0.016
Council	−1	0.6	0.7	0.8	−0.336
Taxpayers' association	−1	0.9	0.8	1.0	−0.720
Employees' union	+1	0.9	0.6	0.6	0.324
Mass meida	+1	0.1	0.5	0.2	0.010
					$\Sigma F = -0.706$

Index of total feasibility (TF) $= \dfrac{\Sigma F}{n} = \dfrac{-0.706}{5} = -0.14$

Adjusted total feasibility (TF$_{ADJ}$) $= $ TF$(5/2) = -0.14(2.5) = -0.35$

(b) Alternative 2 (Budget Cut)

Stakeholder (1)	Coded Position (2)	Probability (3)	Fraction of Resources Available (4)	Resource Rank (5)	Feasibility Score (6)
Mayor	+1	0.8	0.2	0.4	0.192
Council	+1	0.4	0.5	0.8	0.160
Taxpayers' association	+1	0.9	0.7	1.0	0.630
Employees' union	−1	0.9	0.8	0.6	−0.432
Mass media	−1	0.1	0.5	0.2	−0.010
					$\Sigma F = 0.54$

Index if total feasibility (TF) $= \dfrac{\Sigma F}{n} = \dfrac{0.54}{5} = 0.11$

Adjusted total feasibility (TF$_{ADJ}$)TF$(5/3) = 0.11(5/3) = 0.11(1.66) = 0.183$

the firing of fifteen hundred employees. Because most public employees are union-ized, and there has been a threat of a strike for more than two years, the mayor is extremely hesitant to press for a cutback in services. At the same time, local taxpay-ers' groups are known to be strongly opposed to yet another tax increase, even if it means the loss of some services. Under these conditions, the mayor has requested that the analyst provide a feasibility assessment of the policy alternatives.

Table 4.13 shows that a tax increase is unfeasible. In fact the negative sign of the indices (simple and adjusted) at the bottom of the table indicates that there is more opposition than support for a tax increase. By contrast, the index of total feasibility (adjusted) for the budget cut is positive and in the weak range. The index of total feasibility ranges from −1.0 to +1.0, which means that the feasibility of different policy alternatives is directly comparable. Observe, however, that there is an adjusted total feasibility index. The adjustment is necessary because the maximum value that the index can take depends on its sign (positive or negative) and the number of positive (or negative) positions taken.

In Table 4.13(a), for example, the maximum negative value of the index depends on the number of negative positions in relation to positive ones. Imagine that the two negative feasibility scores were "perfect" (i.e., −1.0) and that all other stakeholders were indifferent, giving them feasibility scores of 0.0. In this case, the maximum value of the sum of individual feasibility scores would be −2.0. If we then divide by the total number of stakeholders ($n = 5$), we produce an index value of −0.40, even though there is maximum opposition to the alternative. For this reason, we must compute a maximum value of TF, which in this case is $TF_{MAX} = 2/5 = 0.40$. To find the adjusted value of the index (TF_{ADJ}), we simply divide the original value of TF by its maximum value, that is, $TF/TF_{MAX} = TF_{ADJ} = -0.40/0.40 = -1.0$. The same procedure was used to find the maximum and adjusted positive values of TF in Table 4.13(b).

The feasibility assessment technique forces the analyst to make explicit subjective judgments, rather than treat political and organizational questions in a loose or arbitrary fashion. Feasibility assessment also enables analysts to systematically consider the sensitivity of issue positions and available resources to changes in policy alternatives. In the previous example, a smaller tax increase, combined with austerity measures and a plan to increase the productivity of municipal employees, would probably evoke altogether different levels of feasibility.

The limitations of the feasibility assessment technique are similar to those already encountered with other judgmental forecasting techniques. The feasibility assessment technique, like conventional Delphi and cross-impact analysis, provides no systematic way of surfacing the assumptions and arguments that underlie subjective judgments. Perhaps the best way to resolve this difficulty is to adopt procedures from policy Delphi, or use assumptional analysis (Chapter 3). A second limitation of the technique is that it assumes that the positions of stakeholders are independent and that they occur at the same point in time. These assumptions are unrealistic, because they ignore processes of coalition formation over time and the fact that one stakeholder's position is frequently determined by changes in the position of another. To capture the interdependencies of issue positions as they shift over time, we can employ some adaptation of cross-impact analysis. Finally, the feasibility assessment technique, like other judgmental forecasting techniques discussed in this chapter, is most useful under conditions where the complexity of a problem cannot easily be grasped by using available theories or empirical data. For this reason, any attempt to outline its limitations should also consider its potential as a source of creative insight and surprising or counterintuitive findings.

In concluding this chapter, it is important to stress that different approaches to forecasting are complementary. The strength of one approach or technique is very often the weakness or limitation of another, and vice versa. All of this is to say that the logical foundations of each approach are interdependent. Improvements in forecasting are therefore likely to result from the creative combination of different approaches and techniques, that is, from *multimethod forecasting*. Multimethod forecasting combines multiple forms of logical reasoning (inductive, deductive, retroductive), multiple bases (extrapolation, theory, judgment), and multiple objects (the content and consequences of new and existing policies and the behavior of policy stakeholders). Multimethod forecasting recognizes that neither precision nor creativity is an end in itself. What appears to be a creative or insightful conjecture may lack plausibility and turn out to be pure speculation or quackery, while highly precise projections or predictions may simply answer the wrong question. The ultimate justification for a forecast is whether it provides plausibly true results. In the words of an accomplished policy analyst and former assistant secretary in the Department of Defense, "It is better to be roughly right than exactly wrong."[61]

CHAPTER SUMMARY

This chapter has provided an overview of the process of forecasting, highlighting the nature, types, and uses of forecasting in policy analysis. After comparing approaches based on inductive, deductive, and retroductive reasoning, the chapter presents specific methods and techniques. These include methods and techniques of extrapolative, theoretical, and judgmental forecasting. The ultimate justification for a forecast is whether it yields plausibly true beliefs about the future, not whether it is based on a particular type of method, quantitative or qualitative. In this and other respects, it is better to be approximately right than exactly wrong.

LEARNING OBJECTIVES

- distinguish projections, predictions, and conjectures
- understand the effects of temporal, historical, and institutional contexts on forecast accuracy
- contrast potential, plausible, and normative futures
- describe objects, bases, methods, and products of forecasts

- contrast and evaluate extrapolative, theoretical, and judgmental forecasting methods and techniques
- use statistical software to make point and interval estimates of future policy outcomes
- analyze a case in policy forecasting involving issues of environmental justice

---

[61] Alain C. Enthoven, "Ten Practical Principles for Policy and Program Analysis," in *Benefit–Cost and Policy Analysis: 1974*, ed. Zeckhauser, p. 459.

KEY TERMS AND CONCEPTS

catastrophe (158)
chaos theory (161)
conjecture (130)
cross-impact matrix (187)
deductive reasoning (139)
extrapolative forecasting (141)
goal (134)
inductive reasoning (138)
judgmental forecasting (179)
linearity (136)

nonlinearity (150)
normative futures (133)
objective (134)
plausible futures (133)
political feasibility (192)
potential futures (133)
prediction (130)
projection (130)
retroductive reasoning (139)
theoretical forecasting (161)

REVIEW QUESTIONS

1. What are the three forms of forecasting and how are they related to bases of forecasts?
2. In addition to promoting greater understanding of the future, what other aims can be achieved through forecasting?
3. To what extent are econometric methods more accurate than methods of extrapolative and judgmental forecasting? Explain.
4. How do the institutional, temporal, and historical contexts of forecasts affect their accuracy?
5. Distinguish potential, plausible, and normative futures.
6. List the main differences between goals and objectives. Provide examples.
7. Contrast inductive, deductive, and retroductive reasoning. Do the same for theoretical and judgmental forecasting.
8. List and describe techniques used in the three main types of forecasts. Provide examples.
9. Whether they are linear or nonlinear, most forecasts are based on assumptions of persistence and regularity. To what extent are these assumptions plausible?
10. Many forecasts employ linear regression analysis, also known as the classical linear regression (CLR) model. What are the main assumptions of the CLR model when used to make forecasts?
11. What corrective actions can be taken when assumptions of the CLR model are violated?
12. Is it better to be approximately right, rather than exactly wrong? How does your answer affect the choice of a forecasting method?

DEMONSTRATION EXERCISE

1. After reading Case 4, use SPSS or a similar statistical program (e.g., Excel) to perform a forecast in which you estimate the value of the Metropolitan Atlanta Rapid Transit Authority (MARTA) receipts in the years 1997–2001. Assume you are conducting the analysis in January 1997, as a consultant to MARTA. The client has hired you because MARTA needs an accurate estimate of future receipts. The estimate will be used to

make decisions about fare increases that have become a focal point of debates about environmental justice. Although you could not have known it at the time, the Atlanta City Council opposed a fare increase in 2000 and 2001, amidst considerable political turmoil. MARTA's actual operating budget in 2001 was $307 million, which required a significant fare increase and generated opposition from community groups, who contended that the fare increase violated principles of environmental justice.

Perform the following SPSS analyses, which are based on the procedures for extrapolative forecasting covered in the chapter.

- Enter the data from Table 4.14 (Payments to MARTA, 1973–96) into the SPSS Data Editor. Click on *Variable View* and complete the rows by entering the

Table 4.14   Payments to MARTA, 1973–96 (000s)

Year	Receipts	Econometric Forecast	Average Change Forecast
1973	$43,820		
1974	$50,501		
1975	$50,946		
1976	$52,819		
1977	$57,933		
1978	$66,120		
1979	$75,472		
1980	$88,342		
1981	$99,836		
1982	104,685		
1983	112,008		
1984	123,407		
1985	134,902		
1986	147,149		
1987	148,582		
1988	158,549		
1989	162,543		
1990	165,722		
1991	168,085		
1992	167,016		
1993	181,345		
1994	198,490		
1995	222,475		
1996		251,668	239,100
1997		272,407	257,000
1998		281,476	276,300
1999		290,548	297,100
2000		306,768	319,400
2001		322,573	343,000

Note: The actual operating budget adopted for 2001 was $307 million.

Source: Guess and Farnham (2000), pp. 185, 187, 204. Payments composed of receipts and user fees. The econometric forecast was done in October 1996 by the Economic Forecasting Center of Georgia State University. The average (proportionate) change forecast was done by Guess and Farnham (Table 4.6) on the basis of 1973–95 data.

Names, Types, Labels, and so on, for the variables YEAR and PAYMENTS. Be sure to indicate that the value of PAYMENTS is in thousands of dollars.

- On the pull-down menu, click on *Graphs* and *Sequence* to create a sequence (time-series) graph. Move PAYMENTS into the *Variables:* box. You do not need to fill in the *Time Axis Label* box. Click *OK* and inspect and interpret the graph. Does the series meet assumptions of the linear regression model? Click on the *Natural Log Transform* button. Click *OK* and reinterpret.
- On the pull-down menu, click on *Analyze, Regression,* and *Linear.* Enter the dependent (PAYMENTS) and independent (YEAR) variables. Click on *Statistics* and on *Durbin-Watson.* Also click on *Save* and then on *Unstandardized Predicted Values, Residuals,* and the 95 percent *Confidence Interval for Mean.* Click *OK* to run the regression. Calculate by hand the point estimate for 2001. Interpret the interval estimate printed on the SPSS output.
- Rerun the regression after using a logarithmic transformation of PAYMENTS (use the menu for *Transform* and *Compute*). Rerun the regression again. Recalculate. Interpret the interval estimate. You must take the antilog first.
- Interpret the point and interval estimates provided in the output.

2. How accurate are your estimates? How do they compare with those of the econometric and average change forecasts in Table 4.14? Identify and describe your "best" five-year forecast for 2001. What does it suggest about the need to raise fares? How sure are you?

3. Write a policy memo to MARTA in which you explain and justify your five-year forecast for the year 2001, and make a policy recommendation about options for increasing fares (including no increase). Relate your memo to the issue of environmental justice.

REFERENCES

Allen, T. Harrell. *New Methods in Social Science Research: Policy Sciences and Futures Research.* New York: Frederick A. Praeger, 1978.

Ascher, William. *Forecasting: An Appraisal for Policy Makers and Planners.* Baltimore, MD: Johns Hopkins University Press, 1978.

———. "The Forecasting Potential of Complex Models." *Policy Sciences* 13 (1981): 247–67.

Bartlett, Robert V., ed. *Policy through Impact Assessment: Institutionalized Analysis as a Policy Strategy.* New York: Greenwood Press, 1989.

Box, G. E. P., and G. M. Jenkins. *Time Series Analysis: Forecasting and Control.* San Francisco, CA: Holden-Day, 1969.

Dror, Yehezkel. *Policymaking under Adversity.* New Brunswick, NJ: Transaction Books, 1986.

Finsterbusch, Kurt, and C. P. Wolf, eds. *Methodology of Social Impact Assessment.* Stroudsburg, PA: Dowden, Hutchinson & Ross, 1977.

Gass, Saul I., and Roger L. Sisson, eds. *A Guide to Models in Governmental Planning and Operations.* Washington, DC: U.S. Environmental Protection Agency, 1974.

Guess, George M., and Paul G. Farnham. *Cases in Public Policy Analysis.* New York: Longman, 1989, ch. 3, "Forecasting Policy Options," pp. 49–67.

Harrison, Daniel P. *Social Forecasting Methodology.* New York: Russell Sage Foundation, 1976.

Liner, Charles D. "Projecting Local Government Revenue." In *Budget Management: A Reader in Local Government Financial Management.* Edited by W. Bartley Hildreth and Gerald J. Miller. Athens: University of Georgia Press, 1983, pp. 83–92.

Linstone, Harold A., and Murray Turoff, eds. *The Delphi Method: Techniques and Applications.* Reading, MA: Addison-Wesley, 1975.

Marien, Michael. *Future Survey Annual: A Guide to the Recent Literature of Trends, Forecasts, and Policy Proposals.* Bethesda, MD: World Future Society, published annually.

———— "The Scope of Policy Studies: Reclaiming Lasswell's Lost Vision." In *Advances in Policy Studies since 1950,* Vol. 10 of *Policy Studies Review Annual.* Edited by William N. Dunn and Rita Mae Kelly. New Brunswick, NJ: Transaction Books, 1992, pp. 445–88.

McNown, Robert. "On the Use of Econometric Models: A Guide for Policy Makers." *Policy Sciences* 19 (1986): 360–80.

O'Leary, Michael K., and William D. Coplin. *Everyman's "Prince."* North Scituate, MA: Duxbury Press, 1976.

Schroeder, Larry D., and Roy Bahl. "The Role of Multi-year Forecasting in the Annual Budgeting Process for Local Governments." *Public Budgeting and Finance* 4, no. 1 (1984): 3–14.

Thomopoulos, Nick T. *Applied Forecasting Methods.* Englewood Cliffs, NJ: Prentice Hall, 1980.

Toulmin, Llewellyn M., and Glendal E. Wright, "Expenditure Forecasting." In *Handbook on Public Budgeting and Financial Management.* Edited by Jack Rabin and Thomas D. Lynch. New York: Marcel Dekker, 1983, pp. 209–87.

U.S. General Accounting Office. *Prospective Evaluation Methods: The Prospective Evaluation Synthesis.* Washington, DC: U.S. General Accounting Office, Program Evaluation and Methodology Division, July 1989.

Case 4. Political Consequences of Forecasting: Environmental Justice and Urban Mass Rapid Transit

In the case that follows, policy makers responsible for the performance of the MARTA have frequently hired consultants who have used simple as well as complex forecasting techniques. Even with reasonably accurate estimates of future revenues from sales tax receipts and user fees (a reasonably accurate forecast will lie within ±10 percent of the observed value), MARTA policy makers could not avoid making politically unpopular and controversial policy decisions that involved raising fares and cutting back services to cover shortfalls. In the MARTA case, the accuracy of forecasts is directly related to issues of environmental justice raised primarily by relatively poor and disadvantaged minorities in the Atlanta region (see below).

The following materials are excerpted from Vol. 2, No. 1 (summer 2000) of *Transportation Equity: A Newsletter of the Environmental Justice Resource Center at Clark Atlanta University* (see www.ejrc.cau.edu.).

Box 4.1 Transit Equity: A Look at MARTA[*]

What Is Transportation Important?	Other than housing, Americans spend more on transportation than any other household expense. The average American household spends one-fifth of its income on transportation.
What Counties Support MARTA?	The Metropolitan Atlanta Rapid Transit Authority (MARTA) serves just two counties, Fulton and DeKalb, in the ten-county Atlanta region. In the 1960s, MARTA was hailed as the solution to the region's growing traffic and pollution problems. The first referendum to create a five-county rapid rail system failed in 1968. However, in 1971, the City of Atlanta, Fulton County and DeKalb County, approved a referendum for a 1-percent sales tax to support a rapid rail and feeder bus system. Cobb County and Gwinnett County voters rejected the MARTA system.
Who Pays for MARTA?	MARTA's operating budget comes from sales tax (46%), fares (34%), and the Federal Transit Administration and other sources (20%). Only Fulton and DeKalb County residents pay for the upkeep and expansion of the system with a one-cent MARTA sales tax. Revenues from bus fares generated $5 million more revenue than taken in by rail in 1997. In 1999, the regular one-way fare on MARTA was $1.50, up from $1 in 1992.
Who Rides MARTA?	A recent rider survey revealed that 78 percent of MARTA's rail and bus riders are African American and other people of color. Whites make up 22 percent of MARTA riders.
Where Do MARTA Riders Live?	Over 45 percent of MARTA riders live in the city of Atlanta, 14 percent live in the remainder of Fulton County, 25 percent live in DeKalb County, and 16 percent of MARTA riders live outside MARTA's service area.
Where Are Weekday MARTA Riders Headed?	The majority (58%) of MARTA's weekday riders are on their way to work. The second highest use of MARTA was for getting to medical centers and other services (21%). Other MARTA riders use the system for attending special events (8%), shopping (7%), and school.

(continued)

Box 4.1 Transit Equity: A Look at MARTA* (continued)

How Much Is MARTA's Proposed Fare Increase?

MARTA proposed raising one-way fares from $1.50 to $1.75, a 17-percent increase. The increase is proposed to offset a $10 million shortfall associated with the openings of the Sandy Springs and North Springs stations. The proposal also calls for increasing the weekly transit pass from $12 to $13 and the monthly pass from $45 to $52.50.

Who Would Be Most Impacted by the Proposed MARTA Fare Increase?

While the increase of $7.50 a month may not seem like a lot at first glance, it could do irreparable harm to a $5.25 per hour minimum-wage transit user. These fare increases would fall heaviest on the transit dependent, low-income households, and people of color who make up the lion's share of MARTA users.

How Can the Public Comment on the Proposed MARTA Fare Increase?

Because MARTA receives federal transportation dollars, it is required to hold public hearings before any fare increase takes effect.

How Has MARTA Grown?

MARTA has grown from thirteen rail stations in 1979 to thirty-six rail stations in 2000. Two additional stations (Sandy Springs and North Springs) along the north line were under construction. These two new northern stations opened in early 2001. With its $270.4 million annual budget, MARTA operates 700 buses and 240 rail cars. The system handles over 534,000 passengers on an average weekday. MARTA operates 154 bus routes that cover 1,531 miles and carry 275,000 passengers on an average weekday. MARTA's rail lines cover 46 miles with rail cars carrying 259,000 passengers on an average weekday.

Who Uses MARTA's Parking Spaces?

MARTA provides nearly 21,000 parking spaces at twenty-three of its thirty-six transit stations. Parking at MARTA lots is free except for the overnight lots that cost $3 per day. MARTA provides 1,342 spaces in four overnight lots. All of the overnight lots are MARTA's North Line. It is becoming increasingly difficult to find a parking space in some MARTA lots. A recent license tag survey, "Who Parks-and-Rides," covering the period 1988–97, revealed that 44 percent of the cars parked at MARTA lots were from outside the MARTA Fulton/DeKalb County service area.

What Are the Similarities between Atlanta and Los Angeles?	A similar transit proposal in Los Angles sparked a grassroots movement. In 1996, the Labor Community Strategy Center and the Bus Riders Union (a grassroots group of transit users) sued the Los Angeles MTA over its plan to raise bus fares and build an expensive rail system at the expense of bus riders, who made up 95 percent of transit users. The MTA bus system, comprised largely of low-income persons and people of color, only received 30 percent of the MTA's transit dollars. Grassroots organizing and the Bus Riders Union's legal victory resulted in $1.5 billion for new clean-fuel buses, service improvements, lower fares, a landmark Civil Rights Consent Decree, and a vibrant multiracial grassroots organization of over 2,000 dues-paying members.
Where Can I Get More Information on Transportation Equity?	Contact the Environmental Justice Resource Center at Clark Atlanta University, 223 James P. Brawley Drive, Atlanta, GA 30314, (404) 880–6911 (ph), (404) 880–6909 (fx), E-mail: ejrc@cau.edu. Web site: http//:www.ejrc.cau.edu.

*Prepared by the Environmental Justice Resource Center at Clark Atlanta University under its Atlanta Transportation Equity Project (ATEP). The ATEP is made possible by grants from the Turner Foundation and Ford Foundation. See http//:www.ejrc.cau.edu.

Race and Public Transportation in Metro Atlanta: A Look at MARTA

By Robert D. Bullard

Race still operates at the heart of Atlanta's regional transportation dilemma. For years, I-20 served as the unofficial racial line of demarcation in the region, with blacks located largely to the south and whites to the north. The bulk of the region's growth in the 1990s occurred in Atlanta's northern suburbs, areas where public transit is inadequate or nonexistent.

The ten-county Atlanta metropolitan area has a regional public transit system only in name. In the 1960s, the Metropolitan Atlanta Rapid Transit Authority or MARTA was hailed as the solution to the region's growing traffic and pollution problems, but today, MARTA serves just two counties, Fulton and DeKalb. For years, MARTA's acronym was jokingly referred to as "Moving Africans Rapidly Through Atlanta." African Americans currently make up 75 percent of MARTA's riders.

The first referendum to create a five-county rapid rail system failed in 1968, and the vote was largely along racial lines. However, in 1971, the City of Atlanta,

Fulton and DeKalb counties (political jurisdictions with the largest minority concentration in the region), approved a referendum for a 1-percent sales tax to support a rapid rail and feeder bus system, but the mostly white suburban Cobb County and Gwinnett County voters rejected the MARTA system. People of color represent 29 percent of the population in the ten-county region.

Nevertheless, MARTA has since grown from thirteen rail stations in 1979 to thirty-six rail stations in 1999, and two additional stations—Sandy Springs and North Springs—along the north line were under construction and opened in early 2001. MARTA operates 154 bus routes that cover 1,541 miles. Its rail lines cover 46 miles. In 1999, MARTA was responsible for 553,000 daily passenger trips (50.1% bus and 49.9% rail).

Just how far MARTA lines extend has proved to be a thorny issue. Politics will likely play a major role in determining where the next MARTA lines go. Even who pays the tab for MARTA is being debated. MARTA's operating budget comes from sales tax (46%), fares (34%), and the Federal Transit Administration and other sources (20%). But only Fulton and DeKalb County residents pay for the upkeep and expansion of the system with a one-cent MARTA sales tax.

A recent rider survey revealed that 78 percent of MARTA's rail and bus riders are African Americans and other people of color. Whites make up 22 percent of MARTA riders. More than 45 percent of MARTA riders live in the city of Atlanta, 14 percent live in the remainder of Fulton County, 25 percent live in DeKalb County, and 16 percent live outside MARTA's service area.

Parking at MARTA's twenty-three lots is free except for the 1,342 overnight parking slots that cost $3 per day. All of the overnight lots are located on MARTA's North Line where they serve affluent, mostly white suburban communities. For example, the far-north stops on the orange lines (Doraville and Dunwoody Stations) have proven to be popular among suburban air travelers. It is becoming increasingly difficult to find a parking space in some MARTA lots.

A license tag survey covering the period 1988–97 revealed that 44 percent of the cars parked at MARTA lots were from outside the Fulton/DeKalb County service area. It appears that Fulton and DeKalb County tax payers are subsidizing people who live in outlying counties and who park their cars at the park-and-ride lots and ride on MARTA trains into the city and to Hartsfield Atlanta Airport, the busiest airport in the nation. Both the Doraville and Dunwoody stations (and the Sandy Springs and North Springs stations opened in early 2001) provide fast, comfortable, traffic-free rides to Hartsfield Atlanta International Airport. By paying only $1.50 (the fare increased to $1.75 on January 1, 2001) for the train ride (and no one-cent MARTA sales tax), many suburbanites who live outside Fulton and DeKalb Counties get an added bonus by not having to park in airport satellite parking lots that range from $6 and up.

Atlanta and Fulton County Adopt Resolutions Opposing Fare Increase

On May 1, the Atlanta City Council voted unanimously to approve a resolution opposing MARTA's fare increase. The Fulton County Commission, on April 5, 2000, also adopted a resolution in opposition to the fare hike. Both resolutions expressed that the fare increase would have a disproportionately negative impact on low-income MARTA riders, the vast majority of whom reside in Atlanta, Fulton and

DeKalb counties, and who already pay a 1-percent sales tax, which subsidizes the other metro users. The MARTA board was urged to consider alternatives to the fare increase in order to "provide equity to the residents of Atlanta, Fulton and DeKalb counties" and to "more effectively spread the financial burden of operating the system to other users in the Metropolitan Atlanta area."

Several MARTA Board appointees representing Atlanta and Fulton County apparently ignored the resolutions passed by the elected officials from these districts. These appointees voted for a resolution adopting the MARTA budget with the fare increase on May 25, 2000, which failed by one vote and again on June 18, 2000, which was passed by the MARTA Board. The resolution adopted by the MARTA Board called for implementation of the fare increase on January 1, 2001. Atlanta and Fulton County appointees to the MARTA Board who voted for the fare hike are as follows: Dr. Walter Branch (Atlanta), Amos Beasley (Atlanta), Frank Steinemann (Atlanta), and Arthur McClung (Fulton County).

South DeKalb Leaders Hold Transportation Town Hall Meeting

May 9, 2000, Atlanta, GA—Nearly a hundred residents turned out for a town hall meeting held at the Georgia Perimeter College—South Campus. The meeting was organized and chaired by State Senator Connie Stokes and Representative Henrietta Turnquest. Senator Stokes explained why the town hall meeting was called. "The purpose of this meeting is to provide South DeKalb residents with the initial goals, objectives, and future transportation plans in the Atlanta region, including those of MARTA and GRTA" stated Stokes. Representative Turnquest registered her concern with the historical treatment of the South DeKalb area: "South DeKalb residents have not been active participants in the Atlanta metropolitan transportation decision-making process. This must change."

The meeting led off with a panel that included Robert Bullard (Clark Atlanta University), Catherine Ross (Georgia Regional Transportation Authority), William Mosley (MARTA Board chair), and Arthur Barnes (Georgia Rail Passenger Authority). Much of the panel discussion revolved around existing public transit service inequities, the MARTA fare increase, and regional transportation investments. During the question and answer period, South DeKalb residents expressed concern about the growing North–South economic divide in their county and the role of transportation agencies in developing plans that are inclusive of low-income and people of color communities. Jennifer Parker, editor of the *South DeKalb Crossroads* magazine, expressed the view of many local residents: "You can't get there on MARTA." Parker urged MARTA to concentrate on improving services and take care of its loyal customers.

Residents Stage Mass Walkout at MARTA Board Meeting

May 25, 2000, Atlanta, GA—Atlanta residents waited more than an hour for the MARTA Board members to show up for the scheduled 1:15 P.M. board meeting. The meeting room at MARTA headquarters was filled with customers whose yellow signs urged the board to "Vote NO" on the fare hike. The residents complained that this was not a way to run a $300 million business. William R. Moseley, chair of the MARTA Board, opened the meeting with a resolution to adopt the Fiscal Year 2001 operating and capital funds budget and was immediately interrupted by John Evans,

President of DeKalb NAACP. Evans asked the board to move to the public comment period before the vote on the fare increase. Moseley refused to do so. He also asked Evans to not disrupt the meeting or he would have him removed from the room. While Moseley and Evans were engaged in a heated debate, most of the residents walked out of the meeting. After about ten minutes, a MARTA staff person came outside and told the residents that the MARTA board voted on the proposed fare hike. The budget measure was defeated by one vote.

Two-Mile Rail Extension Costs Whopping $464 Million

MARTA officials claim the fare hike is needed to offset a projected $10 million shortfall associated with the opening of two new suburban train stations on its North line. The two new Sandy Springs and North Springs stations, scheduled to open in December, 2000, add just two miles of track at the cost of $464 million in construction. They will cost an additional $4 million to operate annually. The $464 million North Springs and Sandy Springs stations are projected to increase MARTA's ridership by approximately 5 percent. On the other hand, the fare increase is projected to decrease ridership by 5 percent. Compared with the "new" riders, the "lost" riders are far more likely to be low-income, transit-dependent, and people of color who reside and pay sales tax in Fulton and DeKalb Counties. Currently, African Americans make up 75 percent of MARTA's riders.

MARTA Board Approves Fare Increase

June 19, 2000, Atlanta, GA—MARTA recently approved a $307 million operating bud-get that raises its one-way cash fare from $1.50 to $1.75—a 17-percent increase. The weekly transit pass will jump from $12 to $13, monthly passes will increase from $45 to $52.50, and half-price senior citizens passes will go from 75 cents to 85 cents. A sim-ilar budget proposal came before the MARTA board on May 25, but failed by one vote. Although split, the board approved its FY01 budget, which included the whopping fare hike. In an effort to save face, the board passed a "rabbit-out-of-the-hat" amendment that instructed the MARTA staff to seek alternatives over the next 120 days to cut $2 million from the administration, take $2 million from its reserve fund, and request another $2 million from various city, county, state, and federal governments.

MARTA officials will be hard pressed to get any extra funds from the Atlanta City and Fulton County governments since both entities voted unanimously against the fare hike. Citizens of Atlanta, Fulton, and DeKalb have invested twenty-five years in a one-cent sales tax in building the Metropolitan Atlanta Rapid Transit Authority or MARTA. For the past four months, a host of community leaders, civil rights activists, academics, local elected officials, and transit riders have called for MARTA to increase ridership, trim its bloated administrative staff, and seriously con-sider alternative revenue sources such as advertising, concession, and parking fees.

Equity Coalition Holds Press Conference on "Juneteenth"

June 19, 2000, Atlanta, GA—A dozen local community leaders, representing the Metropolitan Atlanta Transportation Equity Coalition or MATEC, held a press conference in front of the MARTA headquarters (2424 Piedmont Road, N.E.) on Monday June 19th (before the MARTA board meeting). It is ironic that the questionable fare increase passed on "Juneteenth," a date celebrated by millions of African Americans across the nation. Although formed less than a year ago, MATEC has steadily expanded its membership. It has also sharpened its focus on transportation inequities in the region.

The ethnic coalition now includes an array of environmental justice organizations, civil rights groups, churches, service organizations, labor unions, homeowners associations, neighborhood planning units, elected officials, and academic institutions who have come together under a common theme of dismantling transportation racism in metropolitan Atlanta.

What People Are Saying about the Fare Increase

There are clear equity impacts related to the proposed MARTA fare hike. Without a doubt, poor people and black people will be hit the hardest. In lieu of fare hikes, the MARTA should initiate an aggressive plan to expand ridership, streamline its administrative staff, acquire more state, regional, and federal funding for public transit, and explore the feasibility of a fare reduction" (Dr. Robert D. Bullard, Director of the Environmental Justice Resource Center at Clark Atlanta University and author of the 1997 book *Just Transportation: Dismantling Race and Class Barriers to Mobility*).

"MARTA is not in serious need to increase the fares, but because of the two new stations (Sandy Springs and North Springs) soon to be on line, now would be the perfect timing for a fare increase" (Terry L. Griffis, VP of Finance and Administration for MARTA; statement made at a Metropolitan Atlanta Rapid Transit Overview Committee [MARTOC] meeting held on May 12, 2000).

"MARTA will not be in violation of either the 35% Operating Ratio nor the 50% Operating Funding tests for its fiscal year 2001 (FY01) or Fiscal Year (FY02) Budget if it does not impose the recommended fare increase. Atlantans already pay a high one-way cash fare. Going to a $1.75 fare would definitely set MARTA apart from the pack. Therefore, if the objective is to carry more passengers, a fare decrease is likely to be the most productive and cost-effective methodology available by a wide margin" (Thomas A. Rubin, CPA and nationally known transportation consultant).

"I find it unfortunate that MARTA feels they must increase their fare at a time when we are trying to get more and more people out of their cars and on to mass transit. In addition to the negative effects on our air quality and traffic congestion, a fare increase at this time could limit some low-income people's access to the transit system and their places of employment. While I pledge to continue working for more federal money for MARTA, I believe that a certain percentage of state gas tax revenue should be dedicated to MARTA, and I hope that MARTA will work to find other fiscal solutions to their budget without increasing fares at this time" (Cynthia McKinney, U.S. Congresswoman).

"This whole thing is about race. Cobb, Gwinnett and Clayton don't want MARTA and poor or black people. I can't imagine MARTA saying we will raise the fare on the core of this proposed regional transportation system we plan to have" (James E. "Billy" McKinney, State Senator).

"MARTA should ensure that all avenues have been exhausted before initiating a fare increase. There presently are many questions as to whether that has been done" (Vernon Jones, State Representative).

"South DeKalb residents have not been active participants in the Atlanta metropolitan transportation decision-making process. This must change." (Henrietta Turnquest, State Representative).

"The impact of a MARTA fare increase on the working poor would be disastrous. MARTA should work to ensure that all alternatives have been exhausted, and work with state, local and federal officials to find resources for MARTA" (Vincent Fort, State Senator).

"I can appreciate the fiscal situation that MARTA finds itself in. But in all fairness to working class and poor people who are the financial mainstay of the MARTA System, I along with my other Atlanta City Council colleagues urge MARTA not to raise their fare but to look at alternative ways of financing. Some of these initiatives could include parking fees or other creative initiatives" ("Able" Mable Thomas, Atlanta City Councilwoman).

"MARTA's fare increase is a complete disrespect for those who depend on mass transportation for their mode of transportation. I would like to see our state legislators take the leadership to remove Gwinnett and Clayton members off the MARTA Board" (John Evans, DeKalb NAACP).

"By insisting on this fare increase, MARTA has violated the trust placed in it by the citizens of Fulton and DeKalb counties to have an affordable and safe transit system. We had to resort to public protests to alert citizens about the proposed fare increase" (Flora M. Tommie, a MARTA rider since 1983 and an active member of Atlanta's NPU-X).

"MARTA riders have already adjusted to the $1.50 fare. People on fixed incomes definitely cannot afford a 25 cents increase in one-way cash fare. The MARTA Board needs to address the existing inadequate services in minority communities especially in Southwest Atlanta e.g., no benches at bus stops, no kiosks during inclement weather, overcrowded buses, buses running late, and old broken-down buses" (Ester B. McCrary, a transit-dependent rider).

"Environmental Defense opposes the proposed fare increase for MARTA because it would be inefficient, environmentally destructive and inequitable. Rather than increasing fares, MARTA should be contemplating lower fares to encourage people to use transit. Higher transit use would result in less congestion, cleaner air, and less consumption of natural resources like gasoline" (Robert Garcia, Senior Attorney and Director, Environmental Defense—formerly known as Environmental Defense Fund—Los Angeles Project Office).

The fare increase reportedly will raise approximately $12 million per year for MARTA. However, any benefit to the agency is likely to be outweighed by the substantial losses of income and mobility for the transit-dependent that will result in the loss of employment and housing, and the inability to reach medical care, food sources, educational opportunities, and other basic needs of life.

The fare hike would have the greatest impact on low-income riders who pay with cash. MARTA's transit-dependent riders are typically children and elderly, lower-income, carless, large households, residents who live near transit stations, and generally people of color. On the other hand, MARTA's northern-tier ridership will likely increase regardless of fare hikes. MARTA should encourage affluent white suburbanites to get out of their cars and use its system. At the same time, the agency should not balance this initiative on the backs of those customers who can least afford to pay.

Many Atlantans do not take kindly when people compare their city with Los Angeles' smog, traffic, gridlock, or sprawl problem. However, Los Angeles beats out

Atlanta when it comes to affordable public transit. Despite the higher median household income and higher cost of living in Los Angeles, Atlantans now pay more to ride public transit than Los Angeles residents. MARTA's one-way cash fare was $1.50 (scheduled to increase to $1.75 in January 1, 2001). At that time, the Los Angeles MTA one-way cash fare was $1.35.

The Environmental Justice Resource Center (EJRC) retained the services of Thomas A. Rubin, an Oakland, California-based transportation consultant, to assist with the analysis of MARTA's fare structure and financial status. Rubin has worked on a number of national transportation equity and civil rights cases, including the Los Angeles MTA case. On June 1, 2000 the EJRC submitted its legal analysis and Rubin's budget analysis to the MARTA board.

The fare increase raises serious equity questions under Title VI of the Civil Rights Act of 1964 and its regulations for the following reasons: (1) The fare increase would adversely impact African Americans, (2) there is no business necessity for a fare increase, and (3) MARTA has less discriminatory alternatives to a fare increase. The Title VI regulations prohibit an agency that receives federal funding from engaging in actions that have an adverse disparate impact on protected classes (race, color, national origin) for which there is no business necessity and for which there are less discriminatory alternatives.

MARTA's 2000 fare of $1.50 is the second highest of all major U.S. urban transit operators. An increase of one-quarter would make MARTA's $1.75 adult cash fare the highest in the nation. Considering costs of living, MARTA's cash fare is the highest in the nation now.

MARTA's 34.2-percent farebox recovery ratio is the highest of comparable Sun Belt transit systems. Since the 15-cent fare ended in 1979, MARTA's adult cash fare has increased tenfold. Factoring in cost of living changes, it has increased over 300 percent. MARTA will be in full compliance with all statutory requirements for both FY01 and FY02 without a fare increase. MARTA has absolutely no shortage of cash. Rubin concludes that the fare increase is not necessary, justified, or wise.

Federal Court Blocks Regional Transportation Plan

Atlanta, GA, July 20, 2000—The 11th U.S. Circuit Court of Appeals of Atlanta on Tuesday blocked metro Atlanta's effort to regain use of federal road-building funds. The region is a nonattainment area for ground level ozone. The action, which places metro Atlanta's regional transportation plan on hold, was a result of a lawsuit filed by a coalition of environmental groups. The regional transportation plan proposed to spend $36 billion over twenty-five years on roads, transit, sidewalks, bike paths, and HOV lanes in the thirteen-county region. The court granted a stay to the coalition who sued the EPA in April, charging the agency with illegally extending the region's deadline for meeting federal clean air standards. The coalition also charged the regional transportation plan with using flawed data. The court is not expected to hear the case at least until September, thereby delaying the final approval of metro Atlanta's regional transportation plan until later in the fall.

MARTA Ignores Its Spanish-Speaking Customers
By Angel O.Torres

The Atlanta metro area looks a lot different today than it did twenty-five years ago when MARTA first began its service. However, one would not know it from observing the May 3rd public hearings held at MARTA headquarters. Two other public hearings were held the same day at Atlanta City Hall and in Decatur. The lack of Latino participation in the events was alarming. During the three hearings, not a single member of Atlanta's Latino community testified. The Latino community was not informed about the meeting. Ironically, the largest Latino community within the city limits is located within close proximity to the MARTA headquarters at the Lindbergh station.

MARTA has not responded proactively to the changing demographics of its Fulton and DeKalb service district. For example, the public hearing notices ran in the Atlanta Journal-Constitution in English only. The advertisement was also posted on MARTA's Web page, also in English only. MARTA did not take the time to properly alert Latinos in metro Atlanta of the proposed fare changes. Even calling MARTA's customer service Hot Line for information in Spanish proved fruitless. After maneuvering through the available choices in Spanish on the Hot Line, the customer is offered an opportunity to listen to the Olympic route bus schedule.

The translation equipment for Spanish-speaking individuals was requested well in advance of the May 3 and June 19 MARTA board meetings. A MARTA customer service representative assured me that the agency was prepared to handle Spanish-English translation. However, while at the June 19th MARTA board meeting, I was informed that if individuals needed this kind of assistance, it is MARTA's policy that the individual should bring his or her own translator to the meeting. Several Latino (non-English speaking) MARTA customers who attended the June 19th board meeting needed translation. I volunteered. Soon after beginning my new duties as a translator, I was quickly informed that I could not talk while the Board was in session. This ended my tenure as a translator after less than two minutes. This policy must change. It effectively renders MARTA's Spanish-speaking customers invisible and voiceless.

There are measures that MARTA could take to remedy this problem. MARTA could begin by requesting a meeting with Latino community leaders and attempt to understand its next-door neighbors. This task should not be hard to achieve because many organizations serving Latinos can be easily found in the Atlanta's Hispanic Yellow Pages. Another step toward this goal could be establishing a meaningful and inclusive community outreach program to the Latino community. It would also help if the Latino representation were added to the MARTA board. Other cities have faced the same challenge that Atlanta faces today. City and county leaders need to follow the examples set by cities such as Los Angeles, Chicago, Miami, and New York, to name a few. Atlanta is no longer the city "too busy to hate"; it is just "too busy to care" about its new residents.

Resources

Books
Bullard, Robert D., Glenn S. Johnson, and Angel O. Torres, eds. *Sprawl City: Race, Politics, and Planning in Atlanta*. Washington, DC: Island Press, 2000; $30.

A serious but often overlooked impact of the random, unplanned growth—commonly known as "sprawl"—that has come to dominate the American landscape is its effect on economic and racial polarization. Sprawl-fueled growth pushes people further apart geographically, politically, economically, and socially. Atlanta, Georgia, is experiencing one of the most severe cases of sprawl in the country, and offers a striking example of sprawl-induced stratification. *Sprawl City: Race, Politics, and Planning in Atlanta* uses a multidisciplinary approach to analyze and critique the emerging crisis resulting from urban sprawl in the ten-county Atlanta Metropolitan region. Local experts, including sociologists, lawyers, urban planners, economists, educators, and health care professionals, consider sprawl-related concerns as core environmental justice and civil rights issues. All the contributors examine institutional constraint issues that are embedded in urban sprawl, considering how government policies, including housing, education, and transportation policies, have aided and in some cases subsidized separate but unequal economic development, segregated neighborhoods, and spatial layout of central cities and suburbs.

Contributors offer analysis of the causes and consequences of urban sprawl, and outline policy recommendations and an action agenda for coping with sprawl-related problems, both in Atlanta and around the country. The book illuminates the rising class and racial divisions underlying uneven growth and development, and provides an important source of information for anyone concerned with these issues, including the growing environmental justice movement as well as planners, policy analysts, public officials, community leaders, and students of public policy, geography, planning, and related disciplines. *Sprawl City* (Island Press, Summer 2000, ISBN: 1–55963–790–0) is edited by Robert D. Bullard, Glenn S. Johnson, and Angel O. Torres. To view book description, use http://www.islandpress.org/books/bookdata/sprawlcity.html. The book can be ordered from Island Press at 1–800–828–1302 or orders@islandpress.org.

Bullard, Robert D., and Glenn S. Johnson, eds. *Just Transportation: Dismantling Race and Class Barriers to Mobility*. Gabriola Island, BC: New Society Publishers, 1997, $15.95.

Racism continues to dominate America, media and public debate, but the subtle ways in which institutionalized racism affects us are still unexamined. Does our public transportation reinforce segregation and discrimination? How do transportation policies affect where we live and work, the health, education, and public service benefits we have access to—our social and economic mobility? *Just Transportation* moves beyond denouncing gross bigotry and offers provocative insight into the source of pervasive racism and social apartheid in America.

From Harlem to Los Angeles, and cities in-between, *Just Transportation* examines how the inequitable distribution of transportation benefits creates subtle, yet profound obstacles to social and economic mobility for people of color and those on the lower end of the socioeconomic spectrum. While the automobile culture has been spurred on by massive government investments in roads and highways, federal commitment to public transportation—which serves mostly the poor and minorities—appears to have reached an all-time low, allowing urban mass transit systems to fall into disrepair.

With a Foreword by Congressman John Lewis, an original Freedom Rider and a champion of civil rights in the U.S. Congress, and essays by a wide range of environmental and transportation activists, lawyers, and scholars, *Just Transportation* traces the historical roots of transportation struggles in our civil rights history. From Rosa Parks and the Freedom Riders to modern-day unjust transportation practices, *Just Transportation* persuasively illustrates how the legacy of "separate but equal" is still with us. *Just Transportation* (New Society Publishers, 1997, ISBN 0–86571–357–X) is edited by Robert D. Bullard and Glenn S. Johnson. See book description at http://www.newsociety.com/aut.html. The book can be ordered from New Society Publishers at 1–800–567–6772 or info@newsociety.com.

Web Sites

Community Transportation Association of America. http://www.ctaa.org/. The Community Transportation Association of American (CTAA) is a nonprofit membership association with members who are devoted to mobility for everyone, regardless of economic status, disability, age, or accessibility. Community transportation is a practical alternative that picks up where the private auto and mass transit leave off.

Environmental Justice Resource Center. http://www/ejrc.cau.edu. The Environmental Justice Resource Center (EJRC) at Clark Atlanta University was formed in 1994 to serve as a research, policy, and information clearinghouse on issues related to environmental justice, race and the environment, civil rights, facility siting, land use planning, brownfields, transportation equity, suburban sprawl, and Smart Growth. The center is multidisciplinary in its focus and approach. It serves as a bridge among the social and behavioral sciences, natural and physical sciences, engineering, management, and legal disciplines to solve environmental problems.

Federal Transit Administration. http://www.fta.dot.gov/wtw. The federal government through the Federal Transit Administration (FTA) provides financial and technical assistance to the local transit systems. The National Transit Library is a repository of reports, documents, and data generated by professionals and lay persons from around the country. The library is designed to facilitate documents sharing among people interested in transit and transit-related topics.

Southern Resource Center. http://www.fhwa.dot.gov/resourcecenters/ southern. The Southern Resource Center (SRC) is designed to facilitate transportation decision making and choices. The choices made by SRC will help the Federal Highway Administration, state, and local officials in achieving FHA's National Strategic Plan goals and performance measures.

TEA-21. http://www.fhwa.dot/tea21/index.htm. The Transportation Equity Act for the twenty-first century was enacted June 9, 1998, as Public Law 105–178. TEA-21 authorizes the federal surface transportation programs for highways, highway safety, and transit for the six-year period 1998–2003, and provided technical corrections to the original law. This Web site is a reflection of the combined effect of these two laws and refers to this combination as TEA-21.

5

Recommending Preferred Policies

Forecasting does not offer explicit reasons why we should value one expected outcome over another. While it answers questions of the form, What is likely to occur? it does not permit answers to the question, What should be done?[1] To answer this kind of question, we require methods of recommendation, which help produce information about the likelihood that future courses of action will result in consequences that are valuable to some individual, group, or society as a whole.

RECOMMENDATION IN POLICY ANALYSIS

The procedure of recommendation involves the transformation of information about expected policy outcomes into information about preferred policies. To recommend a preferred policy requires prior information about the future consequences of acting

---

[1] As we saw in Chapter 1, answers to this question require a normative approach, or normative (versus descriptive) policy analysis.

on different alternatives. Yet making policy recommendations requires that we also determine which policies are most valuable and why. For this reason, the policy-analytic procedure of recommendation is normative. It is closely related to ethical and moral questions.[2]

Recommendation and Multiple Advocacy

Should the United States increase its economic commitment to less developed countries by raising levels of foreign aid and technical assistance? Should the Congress pass legislation that will strictly curtail the pollution of the atmosphere and waterways by industry? Should state governments provide low-cost home-heating fuel to the poor? Should the city council raise local taxes to build a community recreation center? Should the federal government provide a minimum annual income for all citizens or invest in a cure for cancer?

All these issues call for policy recommendations that answer the question: What should be done? Any answer to this question requires an approach that is normative, rather than one that is merely empirical or merely evaluative, because the question is one of right action. Questions of action demand that analysts choose among multiple advocative claims about what should be done.[3]

Advocative claims have several distinctive characteristics. Advocative claims are

1. *Actionable.* Advocative claims focus on actions that may be taken to resolve a policy problem. Although advocative claims require prior information about what will occur and what is valuable, they go beyond questions of "fact" and "value" and include arguments about what should be done to solve a problem.

2. *Prospective.* Advocative claims are prospective, because they occur prior to the time that actions are taken (*ex ante*). While policy-analytic procedures of monitoring and evaluation are retrospective, because they are applied after actions are taken (*ex post*), forecasting and recommendation are both applied prospectively (*ex ante*).

3. *Value laden.* Advocative claims depend as much on "facts" as they do on "values." To claim that a particular policy alternative should be adopted requires not only that the action being recommended will have the predicted consequences; it also requires that the predicted consequences are valued by individuals, groups, or society as a whole.

4. *Ethically complex.* The values underlying advocative claims are ethically complex. A given value (e.g., health) may be regarded as both intrinsic

---

[2] For a synthesis of literature on ethical aspects of policy analysis, see William N. Dunn, "Values, Ethics, and Standards in Policy Analysis," in *Encyclopedia of Policy Studies,* ed. Stuart S. Nagel (New York: Marcel Dekker, 1983), pp. 831–66.

[3] On multiple advocacy, see Alexander George, *Presidential Decision Making in Foreign Policy: The Effective Use of Information and Advice* (Boulder, CO: Westview Press, 1980).

and extrinsic. *Intrinsic values* are those that are valued as ends in themselves; *extrinsic values* are those that are valued because they will produce some other value. Health may be regarded as an end in itself and as a condition necessary for the attainment of other values, including security, freedom, and self-actualization. Similarly, democratic participation may be valued as an end in itself (intrinsic value) and a means to political stability (extrinsic value).

The idea of multiple advocacy should be sharply contrasted with the view that the function of policy analysis is to support a predetermined political position by mustering as much information as possible on behalf of the client's cause. Multiple advocacy is an approach to the systematic comparison and critical assessment of a number of potential solutions, not a way to defend single positions at any cost. To be sure, analysts eventually arrive at single set of recommendations—but only after critically assessing the pros and cons of multiple potential solutions for a problem. Multiple advocacy is just as much an approach to problem structuring as problem solving.[4] When policy analysts follow guidelines of multiple advocacy, they are less likely to fall into what is commonly known as the *over-advocacy trap* (Box 5.1), a trap that often results in recommending the wrong solution because we have formulated the wrong problem. Indeed, the process of making plausible policy recommendations often requires that we move backward to problem structuring before we can move forward to a solution.

Simple Model of Choice

Advocative claims are possible only when the analyst is confronted by a situation of choice between two or more alternatives. In some situations, the choice is between a new course of action and the status quo. In other situations, choice may be complex, because there may be many alternatives to choose from.

In its simplest terms, choice may be represented as a process of reasoning that involves three interrelated components: (1) the definition of a problem requiring action; (2) the comparison of consequences of two or more alternatives to resolve the problem; and (3) the recommendation of the alternative that will result in a preferred outcome, that is, the alternative that best satisfies some need, value, or opportunity. For example, choice may be described as a process of reasoning where the first alternative (A_1) yields one outcome (O_1), the second alternative (A_2) yields another outcome (O_2), and the value of O_1 is greater than O_2 $(O_1 > O_2)$. Having this information, the analyst will find no difficulty in recommending A_1 as the preferred alternative. The analyst reasons as follows: The first alternative leads to one result,

---

[4] Ian I. Mitroff, Richard O. Mason, and Vincent P. Barabba, *The 1980 Census: Policymaking amid Turbulence* (Lexington, MA: D.C. Heath, 1983), see multiple advocacy as a methodology for problem structuring, which has features similar to their own dialectical approach.

Box 5.1   The Over-Advocacy Trap

In *Presidential Decision Making and Foreign Policy: The Effective Use of Information and Advice* (1980), Alexander George has listed many shortcomings and weaknesses of policy advice that, applicable to domestic and foreign policy alike, are best described as the *over-advocacy trap.*[*] The over-advocacy trap occurs when

- The client and the analyst agree too readily on the nature of the problem and responses to it.
- Disagreements among policy advocates incorporated in an analysis do not cover the full range of policy alternatives.
- The analyst ignores advocates for unpopular policy alternatives.
- The analyst fails to communicate recommendations requiring that the client face up to a difficult or unpopular decision.
- The analyst is dependent on a single source of information.
- The client is dependent on a single analyst.
- Assumptions of a policy are evaluated only by advocates of that policy—including the trapped analyst or client.
- The client dismisses the results of analysis simply because they are perceived as negative or counterintuitive.
- The client or the analyst uncritically accepts consensus findings without probing the basis for the consensus and how it was achieved.

[*]Alexander George, *Presidential Decision Making in Foreign Policy* (Boulder, CO: Westview Press, 1980), pp. 23–24. I have changed some of George's language to show the relevance of his points to policy analysis (e.g., the term *adviser* has been replaced with *analyst*).

---

while the second leads to another. The first result is more valuable than the second. Therefore A1, the first course of action, should be recommended (Figure 5.1).

This simple process of reasoning contains two essential elements of choice: factual and value premises. The first decision premise states that A_1 will result in O_1 while the second decision premise states that A_2 will result in O_2. These are *factual premises;* that is, assumptions that in principle may be shown to be true or false on the basis of factual knowledge. The third premise, however, is a *value premise,* that is, an assumption that may be shown to be good or bad on the basis of some set of values or system of ethics. This value premise states that O_1 is preferable to O_2 on some scale of values. Such premises cannot be proved right or wrong by appealing

$$A_1 \longrightarrow O_1$$
$$A_2 \longrightarrow O_2$$
$$O_1 > O_2$$
$$\therefore A_1$$

Figure 5.1   Simple model of choice.

to factual premises, because questions of value require reasoned arguments about why the outcome in question is good or right for some person, group, or society as a whole. All choices contain both factual and value premises.

This simple model has the advantage of pointing out that factual and value premises are present in all choice situations. The disadvantage of this simple model is that it obscures the complexity of choice. Consider, for example, the conditions that must be present for this model of choice to be a valid one.[5]

1. *Single decision maker.* The choice must be confined to a single person. If choices are affected by or in turn affect more than one person, there are likely to be conflicting sets of factual and value premises.

2. *Certainty.* The outcomes of choice must be known with certainty. Yet the outcomes of choice are seldom known with certainty. People who affect and are affected by the choice often disagree about factual and value premises. Moreover, alternative courses of action are not the only causes of outcomes because there are many uncontrollable factors that enhance or inhibit the occurrence of a given outcome.

3. *Immediacy of consequences.* Results of a course of action must occur immediately. In most choice situations, however, outcomes of action occur over long periods of time. Because outcomes do not occur immediately the values that originally prompted action change with time.

Imagine now that our simple model of choice involves the issue of whether to provide minimum wages to unskilled workers. Assume that unskilled workers are not now covered by minimum wage legislation. On the basis of this information, we conclude that maintaining the status quo (no minimum wage laws) will result in an annual average income of \$4,000 for unskilled workers. We might also forecast that a minimum wage of \$4.50 per hour will result in an annual average income of \$7,000 for unskilled workers covered by the proposed policy. If we assume that more income is better than less income, we will have no difficulty in choosing as follows:

$$A_1 \rightarrow O_1(\$4,000)$$
$$A_2 \rightarrow O_2(\$7,000)$$
$$O_2 > O_1$$
$$\therefore A_2$$

This case fails to satisfy the three conditions necessary for the simple model of choice. First, there are multiple decision makers, not simply one. Many stakeholders—for example, legislators, voters, administrators, employers—affect and are affected by

---

[5] See, for example, Richard Zeckhauser and Elmer Schaefer, "Public Policy and Normative Economic Theory." in *The Study of Policy Formation,* ed. Raymond A. Bauer and Kenneth J. Gergen (New York: Free Press, 1968), p. 28.

the issue of minimum wages. Each of these stakeholders brings different factual and value premises to the choice situation, so there is likely to be considerable conflict about what should be done and why. For example, certain legislators may want to increase the income of unskilled workers while constituents may want to reduce the tax burden that will accompany the enactment and implementation of minimum wage legislation. Second, there is considerable uncertainty about the consequences of minimum wage legislation. Many factors other than the legislation—for example, the availability of college students as an alternative source of unskilled labor—may determine whether or not employers will actually pay the minimum wage. Finally, the consequences of the legislation will occur over a relatively long period of time, which means that values may also change. For example, if the cost of living increases dramatically as a result of inflation, some groups who formerly supported a $4.50 per hour minimum wage may decide that such a level will not produce enough of an increase in real wages to justify the effort. If an alternative policy providing for a $5 per hour minimum wage is proposed, employers may be much more likely to hire college students than pay their unskilled employees the new minimum wage. In short, the simple model of choice provides a distorted picture of the actual issues involved in setting minimum wages for unskilled workers.

Complex Model of Choice

Suppose that a more thorough effort were made to gather relevant information about the policy issue of minimum wages. In addition to the original alternatives (minimum wages and the status quo), a third alternative may have been identified, for example, personnel training. This third alternative may have been proposed on the assumption that the problem is not low wages but an absence of skills necessary to qualify workers for available higher-paying jobs. After adding this third alternative, we might forecast the following consequences: The first alternative (A_1 or the status quo) will produce by 1991 an average annual income of $4,000 for some 12,000 unskilled workers; the second alternative (A_2 or a $4.50 per hour minimum wage) will produce by 1991 an average annual income of $7,000 for 6,000 unskilled workers, with the remaining workers entering the ranks of the unemployed because they will be replaced by college students; the third alternative (A_3 or personnel training) will produce by 1991 an average annual income of $4,000 for some 10,000 formerly unskilled workers who will find jobs.

Each of these three alternatives will also have different consequences for stakeholders. For example, Congress members who will vote on the issue must be attentive to their prospects for reelection. Maintaining the status quo will result in the loss of fifty seats in districts where labor and welfare rights organizations are very powerful. Minimum wage legislation will result in no electoral changes, because the costs of the program will be passed on to owners of small businesses, who have little influence in the legislature. Finally, personnel training will result in a loss of ten seats in districts with strong opposition to any new tax increase. Furthermore, the full benefits of training will not be felt for several years, because the real earning capacity of trainees will increase gradually, reaching an average annual level of $5,000 for 12,000 workers by 1993. The real incomes of unskilled workers receiving the minimum wage will remain constant and may even decline as a result of inflation. Finally, the three alternatives have different costs that will be borne unequally by various stakeholders. The first alternative (the status quo) involves no new costs, but the second will require that owners of small businesses pay the additional wages. The third alternative will distribute costs among taxpayers who will foot the bill for training programs.

The simple model of choice has quickly become considerably more complex as a result of multiple stakeholders, uncertainty about outcomes, and time. If we diagram the choice situation in its new and complex form (Table 5.1), we find that the choice is more difficult to make. If we are concerned only with immediate monetary results in 1991, there is no difficulty. A_1 is the preferred alternative, because O_1 is greater than O_4 and O_7. But if we consider future monetary results in 1993, A_3 is the preferred alternative, because O_8 is greater than O_2, which in turn is greater than O_5. Finally, if we are concerned with political consequences in 1994, A_2 is the preferred alternative, because O_6 is greater (i.e., produces more retained seats) than A_9 and A_3.

The problem with this complex choice is that we cannot make a satisfactory recommendation that combines the values of all stakeholders at multiple points in time. A situation such as this, where it is impossible to consistently rank alternatives according to two or more attributes, is termed *intransitive*. Intransitive choice typically involves multiple conflicting objectives and should be contrasted with situations involving transitive choices. A *transitive* choice is one where alternatives can be consistently ranked according to one or more attributes: If A_1 is preferable to A_2 in the choice set (A_1, A_2) and A_2 is preferable to A_3 in the choice set (A_2, A_3), then A_1 is preferable to A_3 in the set (A_1, A_3). Transitive choices can be constructed by assigning values to each alternative, so that if A_1 is preferred to A_2 and A_3, it is assigned a higher value. The person making a choice is said to maximize utility

Table 5.1 Complex Model of Choice

A_1 (status quo)	O_1 ($48,000 income in 1991)	O_2 ($48,000 income in 1993)	O_3 (retain 150 seats in 1994)
A_2 (minimum wages)	O_4 ($42,000 income in 1991)	O_5 ($36,000 income in 1993)	O_6 (retain 200 seats in 1994)
A_3 (personnel training)	O_7 ($40,000 income in 1991)	O_8 ($60,000 income in 1993)	O_9 (retain 190 seats in 1994)

$$O_1 > O_4 > O_7; \therefore A_1$$
$$O_8 > O_2 > O_5; \therefore A_3$$
$$O_6 > O_9 > O_3; \therefore A_2$$

Table 5.2   Transitive and Intransitive Choice

(a) Transitive

| Alternative | Outcome | | |
	1981 Income	1983 Income	1982 Elections
A_1	1st	1st	1st
A_2	2nd	2nd	2nd
A_3	3rd	3rd	3rd

(b) Intransitive

| Alternative | Outcome | | |
	1981 Income	1983 Income	1982 Elections
A_1	1st	2nd	3rd
A_2	2nd	3rd	1st
A_3	3rd	1st	2nd

(value) by selecting the alternative that yields the greatest value. Transitive and intransitive choice situations are illustrated in Table 5.2.

Forms of Rationality

In principle, any situation of choice can yield a recommendation that is preferred to all others because it will result in desired outcomes. Yet most choice situations involve multiple stakeholders, uncertainty, and consequences that change over time. In fact, conflict and disagreement are essential characteristics of most policy issues:

> Difficult choice problems in which attribute rankings conflict lie at the core of the decisions that must be made by public policy makers. These difficulties may arise because their decisions affect many individuals. Though policy A might be better for one group in our society, policy B might be better for another. If time is a crucial element we may find, for example, that policy B will be better twenty years from today. In a third context, policy A might be superior if some uncertain events turn out favorably but policy B might be a better hedge against disaster.[6]

For these and similar reasons, it may appear that the process of making policy recommendations is not and cannot be "rational." Tempting as this conclusion might be, our inability to satisfy the conditions of the simple model of choice does not mean that the process of recommendation is not and cannot be rational. If by *rationality* we mean a self-conscious process of using reasoned arguments to make

---

[6] Ibid., p. 30.

and defend advocative claims, we will find not only that many choices are rational, but we will also see that most are *multirational*. This means that there are multiple rational bases underlying most policy choices.[7]

1. *Technical rationality*. Technical rationality is a characteristic of reasoned choices that involve the comparison of alternatives according to their capacity to promote *effective* solutions for public problems. Choices between solar and nuclear energy technologies are an example of technical rationality.

2. *Economic rationality*. Economic rationality is a characteristic of reasoned choices that involve the comparison of alternatives according to their capacity to promote *efficient* solutions for public problems. Choices involving the comparison of alternative medical care systems in terms of their total costs and benefits to society may be characterized in terms of economic rationality.

3. *Legal rationality*. Legal rationality is a characteristic of reasoned choices that involve the comparison of alternatives according to their *legal conformity* to established rules and precedents. Choices that involve the award of public contracts according to whether companies comply with laws against racial and sexual discrimination are an example of legal rationality.

4. *Social rationality*. Social rationality is a characteristic of reasoned choices that involve the comparison of alternatives according to their capacity to maintain or improve valued social institutions, that is, promote *institutionalization*. Choices involving the extension of rights to democratic participation at work are an example of social rationality.

5. *Substantive rationality*. Substantive rationality is a characteristic of reasoned choices that involve the comparison of *multiple forms of rationality*—technical, economic, legal, social—in order to make the most appropriate choice under given circumstances. For example, many issues of government information policy involve questions about the usefulness of new computer technologies, their costs and benefits to society, their legal implications for rights to privacy, and their consistency with democratic institutions. Debates about these issues may be characterized in terms of substantive rationality.

Criteria for Policy Recommendation

The several types of rational choice may be viewed in terms of specific decision criteria used to advocate solutions for policy problems. By *decision criteria* we mean explicitly stated values that underlie recommendations for action. Decision criteria are of six main types: effectiveness, efficiency, adequacy, equity, responsiveness, and appropriateness.[8]

---

[7] See Paul Diesing, *Reason and Society* (Urbana: University of Illinois Press, 1962).

[8] On decision criteria, see Theodore H. Poister, *Public Program Analysis: Applied Research Methods* (Baltimore, MD: University Park Press, 1978), pp. 9–15.

Effectiveness refers to whether a given alternative results in the achievement of a valued outcome (effect) of action, that is, an objective. Effectiveness, which is closely related to technical rationality, is often measured in terms of units of products or services or their monetary value. If nuclear generators produce more energy than solar collection devices, the former are regarded as more effective, because nuclear generators produce more of a valued outcome. Similarly, an effective health policy is one that provides more quality health care to more people, assuming that quality health care is a valued outcome (objective).

Efficiency refers to the amount of effort required to produce a given level of effectiveness. Efficiency, which is synonymous with economic rationality, is the relationship between effectiveness and effort, with the latter often measured in terms of monetary costs. Efficiency is often determined by calculating the costs per unit of product or service (for example, dollars per gallon of irrigation water or dollars per medical examination), or by calculating the volume of goods or services per unit of cost (e.g., 10 gallons of irrigation water per dollar or 50 medical examinations per $1,000). Policies that achieve the greatest effectiveness at least cost are said to be efficient.

Adequacy refers to the extent to which any given level of effectiveness satisfies the needs, values, or opportunities that gave rise to a problem. The criterion of adequacy specifies expectations about the strength of a relationship between policy alternatives and valued outcomes. The criterion of adequacy may refer to four types of problems (Table 5.3):

1. *Type I problems.* Problems of this type involve fixed costs and variable effectiveness. When maximum allowable budgetary expenditures result in fixed costs, the aim is to maximize effectiveness within the limits of available resources. For example, given a fixed budget of $1 million for each of two programs, a health policy analyst will recommend the alternative that results in the greatest improvement in the quality of health care in the community. The response to type I problems is called *equal-cost analysis,* because analysts compare alternatives that vary in effectiveness but whose costs are treated as equal. Here the most adequate policy is one that maximizes the attainment of objectives while remaining within the limits of fixed costs.

2. *Type II problems.* Problems of this type involve fixed effectiveness and variable costs. When the level of valued outcomes is fixed, the aim is to minimize costs. For example, if public transportation facilities must serve at least 100,000 persons annually, the problem is to identify those alternatives—bus, monorail,

Table 5.3   Criteria of Adequacy: Four Types of Problems

Effectiveness	Costs	
	Fixed	*Variable*
Fixed	Type IV	Type II
	(equal-cost-equal-effectiveness)	(equal-effectiveness)
Variable	Type I	Type III
	(equal-cost)	(variable-cost-variable-effectiveness)

subways—that will achieve this fixed level of effectiveness at least cost. The response to type II problems is called *equal-effectiveness analysis*, because analysts compare alternatives that vary in costs but whose effectiveness is equal. Here the most adequate policy is one that minimizes costs while achieving fixed levels of effectiveness.

3. *Type III problems*. Problems of this type involve variable costs and variable effectiveness. For example, the choice of an optimal budget to maximize the attainment of agency objectives is a type III problem. The response to type III problems is called *variable-cost-variable-effectiveness analysis*, because costs and effectiveness are free to vary. Here the most adequate policy is one that maximizes the ratio of effectiveness to costs.

4. *Type IV problems*. Problems of this type involve fixed costs as well as fixed effectiveness. Type IV problems, which involve *equal-cost-equal-effectiveness analysis*, are often especially difficult to resolve. Analysts are not only limited by the requirement that costs not exceed a certain level but also limited by the constraint that alternatives satisfy a predetermined level of effectiveness. For example, if public transportation facilities must serve a minimum of 100,000 persons annually—yet costs have been fixed at an unrealistic level—then any policy alternative must either satisfy both constraints or be rejected. In such circumstances, the only remaining alternative may be to do nothing.

The different definitions of adequacy contained in these four types of problems point to the complexity of relationships between costs and effectiveness. For example, two programs designed to provide municipal services (measured in units of service to citizens) may differ significantly in terms of both effectiveness and costs (Figure 5.2). Program I achieves a higher overall level of effectiveness than program II, but program II is less costly at lower levels of effectiveness. Should the analyst recommend the program that maximizes effectiveness (program I), or the program that minimizes costs at the same level of effectiveness (program II)?

To answer this question, we must look at the relation between costs and effectiveness, rather than view costs and effectiveness separately. Yet this is where the complications begin (see Figure 5.2). (1) If we are dealing with a type I (equal-cost) problem and costs are fixed at $20,000 ($C_2$), program II is more adequate because it achieves the highest level of effectiveness while remaining within the fixed-cost limitation. (2) If we are confronted with a type II (equal-effectiveness) problem and effectiveness is fixed at 6,000 units of service (E_2), program I is more adequate. (3) If, on the other hand, we are dealing with a type III (variable-cost-variable-effectiveness) problem, where costs and effectiveness are free to vary, program II is more adequate, because the ratio of effectiveness to costs (called an *effectiveness–cost ratio*) is greatest at the intersection of E_1 and C_1. Here program II produces 4,000 units of service for $10,000, that is, a ratio of 4,000 to 10,000 or 0.4. By contrast, program II has an effectiveness–cost ratio of 0.32 (8,000 units of service

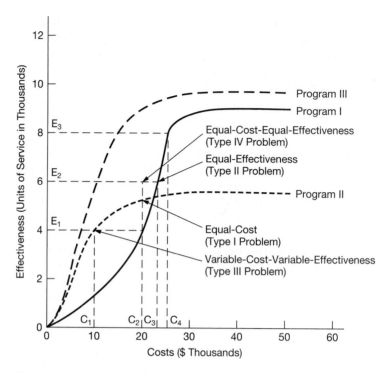

Figure 5.2 Cost–effectiveness comparisons using four criteria of adequacy.

Source: Adapted from E. S. Quade, *Analysis for Public Decisions* (New York: American Elsevier, 1975), p. 93.

divided by $25,000 = 8,000/25,000 = 0.32$).[9] Finally, (4) if we are dealing with a type IV (equal-cost-equal-effectiveness) problem, where both effectiveness and costs are fixed at E_2 and C_2, neither program is adequate. This dilemma, which permits no adequate solution, is known as *criterion overspecification*.

The lesson of this illustration is that it is seldom possible to choose between two alternatives on the basis of *either* costs *or* effectiveness. While it is sometimes possible to convert measures of effectiveness into dollar benefits, which permits us to calculate net income benefits by subtracting monetary costs from monetary benefits, it is frequently difficult to establish convincing dollar equivalents for many of the most important policy outcomes. What is the dollar equivalent of a life saved through traffic safety programs? What is the dollar value of international peace and security promoted by United Nations educational, scientific, and cultural activities? What is the dollar value of natural beauty preserved through environmental protection legislation? While such questions will be examined further when we discuss

---

[9] A simple way to display effectiveness–cost ratios graphically is to draw a straight line from the *origin* (i.e., lower left-hand corner) of a graph to the *knee* of the effectiveness-cost curve (i.e., the point where the straight line touches the curvature but does not pass through it). The more that the line moves leftward toward the vertical effectiveness scale, the greater the ratio between effectiveness and costs.

cost–benefit analysis, it is important to recognize that the measurement of effectiveness in dollar terms is a complex and difficult problem.[10]

Sometimes it is possible to identify an alternative that simultaneously satisfies all criteria of adequacy. For example, the broken-line curve in Figure 5.2 might represent a third program that adequately meets fixed-cost as well as fixed-effectiveness criteria and also has the highest ratio of effectiveness to costs. As this situation is rare, it is almost always necessary to specify the level of effectiveness and costs that are regarded as adequate. Yet this is a matter of reasoned judgment about what constitutes an adequate level of effectiveness, given the costs.

Questions of adequacy cannot be resolved by arbitrarily adopting a single criterion. For example, net income benefits (dollars of effectiveness minus dollar costs) are *not* an appropriate criterion when costs are fixed and a single program with the highest benefit-cost ratio can be repeated many times within total fixed-cost limits. This is illustrated in Table 5.4, where program I can be repeated 10 times up to a fixed-cost limit of $40,000, with total net benefits of $360,000 (i.e., $36,000 × 10). Program I, as it can be repeated 10 times, has the highest benefit–cost ratio. But if program I cannot be repeated—that is, if only one of the three programs must be selected—program III should be recommended. Program III produces the greatest net benefits, even though it has the lowest benefit–cost ratio.

The criterion of *equity* is closely related to legal and social rationality and refers to the distribution of effects and effort among different groups in society. An equitable policy is one where effects (e.g., units of service or monetary benefits) or efforts (e.g., monetary costs) are fairly or justly distributed. Policies designed to redistribute income, educational opportunity, or public services are sometimes recommended on the basis of the criterion of equity. A given program might be effective, efficient, and adequate—for example, the benefit–cost ratio and net benefits may be superior to all other programs—yet it might still be rejected on grounds that it will produce an inequitable distribution of costs and benefits. This could happen under several conditions: those most in need do not receive services in proportion to their numbers; those who are least able to pay bear a disproportionate share of costs; or those who receive most of the benefits do not pay the costs.

Table 5.4 Comparison of Benefit–Cost Ratio and Net Benefits as Criteria of Adequacy (in Thousands of Dollars)

Program	Benefits	Costs	Benefit–Cost Ratio	Net Benefits
I	40	4	10	36
II	64	8	8	56
III	100	40	2.5	60

Source: Adapted from Richard Zeckhauser and Elmer Schaefer, "Public Policy and Normative Economic Theory," in *The Study of Policy Formation,* ed. R. A. Bauer and K. J. Gergen (New York: The Free Press, 1968), p. 73.

---

[10] See, for example, Richard Zeckhauser, "Procedures for Valuing Lives," *Public Policy* (fall 1975): 419–64; and Baruch Fischhoff, "Cost-Benefit Analysis and the Art of Motorcycle Maintenance," *Policy Sciences* 8 (1977): 177–202.

The criterion of equity is closely related to competing conceptions of justice or fairness and to ethical conflicts surrounding the appropriate basis for distributing resources in society. Such problems of "distributive justice," which have been widely discussed since the time of the ancient Greeks, may occur each time a policy analyst recommends a course of action that affects two or more persons in society. In explicitly defining objectives for society as a whole, the analyst may actually be seeking a way to measure *social welfare,* that is, the aggregate satisfaction experienced by members of a community. Yet, as we know, individuals and groups have different values. What satisfies one person or group often does not satisfy another. Under these circumstances, the analyst must consider a fundamental question: How can a policy maximize the welfare of society, and not just the welfare of particular individuals or groups? The answer to this question may be pursued in several different ways:

1. *Maximize individual welfare.* The analyst can attempt to maximize the welfare of all individuals simultaneously. This requires that a single transitive preference ranking be constructed on the basis of all individual values. *Arrow's impossibility theorem,* as we have seen, demonstrates that this is impossible even in cases where there are two persons and three alternatives.

2. *Protect minimum welfare.* Here the analyst can attempt to increase the welfare of some persons while still protecting the positions of persons who are worst off. This approach is based on the *Pareto criterion,* which states that one social state is better than another if at least one person is better off, and no one is worse off. A *Pareto optimum* is a social state in which it is not possible to make any person better off without also making another person worse off. The Pareto criterion is seldom applicable, because most policy decisions involve the provision of services to persons who are made better off by taxing those who are made worse off.

3. *Maximize net welfare.* Here the analyst attempts to increase net welfare (e.g., total benefits less total costs) but assumes that the resulting gains could be used to compensate losers. This approach is based on the *Kaldor–Hicks criterion:* One social state is better than another if there is a net gain in efficiency (total benefits minus total costs) and if those who gain can compensate losers. For all practical purposes, this criterion, which does not require that losers actually be compensated, avoids the issue of equity. The Kaldor–Hicks criterion is one of the foundations of traditional cost–benefit analysis.

4. *Maximize redistributive welfare.* Here the analyst attempts to maximize redistributional benefits to selected groups in society, for example, the racially oppressed, poor, or sick. One redistributive criterion has been put forth by philosopher John Rawls: one social state is better than another if it results in a gain in welfare for members of society who are worst off.[11]

---

[11] John Rawls, *A Theory of Justice* (Cambridge, MA: Harvard University Press, 1971).

Rawls's formulation attempts to provide an ethical foundation for the concept of justice. It does so by requesting that we imagine ourselves in an "original" state, where there is a "veil of ignorance" about the future distribution of positions, statuses, and resources in a civil society yet to be established. In this "original" state, individuals will choose a social order on the basis of the redistributive criterion just described, because it is in everyone's individual interest to establish a society in which they will not be worst off.

By postulating this "original" condition, it becomes possible to reach consensus on a just social order. This "original" condition should be contrasted with the conditions of present societies, where vested interests make it impossible to reach consensus on the meaning of justice. The weakness of Rawls's formulation is its oversimplification or avoidance of conflict. The redistributive criterion is appropriate for well-structured problems and not for the types of problems typically encountered by public policy analysts. While this does not mean that the redistributive criterion cannot be used to make choices, it does mean that we have still not reached a single basis for defining social welfare.

None of these criteria of equity is fully satisfactory. The reason is that conflicting views about the rationality of society as a whole (social rationality) or of the appropriateness of legal norms guaranteeing rights to property (legal rationality) cannot be resolved simply by appealing to formal economic rules (e.g., the Pareto or Kaldor–Hicks criteria) or to formal philosophical principles (e.g., Rawls's redistributive criterion). Questions of equity, fairness, and justice are political ones; that is, they are influenced by processes involving the distribution and legitimation of power in society. While economic theory and moral philosophy can improve our capacity to critically assess competing criteria of equity, they cannot replace the political process.

Responsiveness refers to the extent that a policy satisfies the needs, preferences, or values of particular groups. The criterion of responsiveness is important because an analyst can satisfy all other criteria—effectiveness, efficiency, adequacy, equity—yet still fail to respond to the actual needs of a group that is supposed to benefit from a policy. A recreation program might result in an equitable distribution of facilities but be unresponsive to the needs of particular groups (e.g., the elderly). In effect, the responsiveness criterion asks a practical question: Do criteria of effectiveness, efficiency, adequacy, and equity actually reflect the needs, preferences, and values of particular groups?

The final criterion to be discussed here is that of appropriateness. The criterion of *appropriateness* is intimately related to substantive rationality, because questions about the appropriateness of a policy are not concerned with individual sets of criteria but two or more criteria taken together. Appropriateness refers to the value or worth of a program's objectives and to the tenability of assumptions underlying these objectives. While all other criteria take objectives for granted—for example, the value neither of efficiency nor of equity is questioned—the criterion of appropriateness asks whether these objectives are proper ones for society. To answer this question, analysts may consider all criteria together—that is, reflect on the relations among multiple forms of rationality—and apply higher-order criteria (metacriteria) that are logically prior to those of effectiveness, efficiency, adequacy, equity, and responsiveness.[12]

The criterion of appropriateness is necessarily open ended, because by definition it is intended to go beyond any set of existing criteria. For this reason, there is not and cannot be a standard definition of criteria of appropriateness. The best we can do is consider several examples:

1. *Equity and efficiency.* Is equity as redistributional welfare (Rawls) an appropriate criterion when programs designed to redistribute income to the poor are so inefficient that only a small portion of redistributional benefits actually reaches them? When such programs are viewed as a "leaky bucket" used to carry benefits to the poor, analysts may question whether equity is an appropriate criterion.[13]

2. *Equity and entitlement.* Is equity as minimum welfare an appropriate criterion when those who receive additional benefits have not earned them through socially legitimate means? Analysts may question the appropriateness of the Pareto criterion when those who gain (even though none lose) have done so through corruption, fraud, discrimination, and unearned inheritance.[14]

3. *Efficiency, equity, and humanistic values.* Are efficiency and equity appropriate criteria when the means required to achieve an efficient or just society conflict with democratic processes? Analysts may challenge the appropriateness of efficiency or equity when efforts to rationalize decision making for these purposes subvert conditions required for emancipation, individuation, or self-actualization.[15] Efficiency, equity, and humanism are not necessarily equivalent. Alienation, as Marx and other social thinkers have recognized, is not automatically eliminated by creating an abundant society of equals.

4. *Equity and reasoned ethical debate.* Is equity as redistributive welfare (Rawls) an appropriate criterion when it subverts opportunities for reasoned ethical debate? This criterion of equity can be challenged on grounds that it presupposes an individualistic conception of human nature where ethical claims are no longer derived from reasoned arguments but are "the contractual composite of arbitrary (even if comprehensible) values individually held and either biologically or socially shaped. The structure of the Rawlsian argument thus corresponds closely to that of instrumental rationality; ends are exogenous, and

---

[12] On similar metacriteria, including generality, consistency, and clarity, see Duncan MacRae Jr., *The Social Function of Social Science* (New Haven, CT: Yale University Press, 1976).

[13] See Arthur M. Okun, *Equality and Efficiency* (Washington, DC: Brookings Institution, 1975).

[14] See, for example, Peter Brown, "Ethics and Policy Research," *Policy Analysis* 2 (1976): 325–40.

[15] See, for example, Jurgen Habermas, *Toward a Rational Society* (Boston, MA: Beacon Books, 1970); and *Legitimation Crisis* (Boston, MA: Beacon Books, 1975).

the exclusive office of thought in the world is to ensure their maximum realization. [Rawls's premises] reduce all thought to the combined operations of formal reason and instrumental prudence in the service of desire."[16]

APPROACHES TO RECOMMENDATION

In making policy recommendations, the analyst typically addresses a number of interrelated questions. Whose needs, values, and opportunities are at issue, and what alternatives are available for their satisfaction? What goals and objectives should be attained, and how should they be measured? How much will it cost to attain objectives and what kinds of constraints—budgetary, legal, administrative, political—may impede their attainment? Are there side effects, spillovers, and other anticipated and unanticipated consequences that should be counted as costs or benefits? How will the value of costs and benefits change over time? How certain is it that forecasted outcomes will occur? What should be done?

Public versus Private Choice

Answers to these questions are designed to enhance our capabilities for making persuasive policy recommendations. Although these questions are just as relevant for policy making in the private as in the public sector, there are several important differences between these sectors that should be kept in mind.[17]

1. *Nature of public policy processes.* Policy making in the public sector involves bargaining, compromise, and conflict among citizens' groups, legislative bodies, executive departments, regulatory commissions, businesses, and many other stakeholders. There is no single producer or consumer of goods and services whose profits or welfare is to be maximized. The presence of numerous stakeholders with competing or conflicting values makes problems of choice more complex in the public than in the private sector.

2. *Collective nature of public policy goals.* Policy goals in the public sector are collective ones that are supposed to reflect society's preferences or some broad "public interest." The specification of these collective goals, as we have seen, often involves multiple conflicting criteria, from effectiveness, efficiency, and adequacy to equity, responsiveness, and appropriateness.

3. *Nature of public goods.* Public and private goods may be divided into three groups: specific goods, collective goods, and quasi-collective goods. *Specific goods* are exclusive, because the person who owns them has the legal right to

---

[16] See Laurence H. Tribe, "Ways Not to Think about Plastic Trees," in Tribe and others, *When Values Conflict* (Cambridge MA: Ballinger, 1976), p. 77.

[17] See H. H. Hinrichs and G. M. Taylor, *Systematic Analysis: A Primer on Benefit-Cost Analysis and Program Evaluation* (Pacific Palisades, CA: Goodyear Publishing, 1972), pp. 4–5.

exclude others from their benefits. The allocation of specific goods (for example, cars, houses, or physicians' services) is often made on the basis of market prices, which are determined by supply and demand. *Collective goods* are nonexclusive, because they may be consumed by everyone. No person can be excluded from the consumption of clean air, water, and roads provided by the government. It is frequently impossible to allocate collective goods on the basis of market prices, because normal relationships between supply and demand do not operate in the public sector. *Quasi-collective goods* are specific goods whose production has significant spillover effects for society. Although elementary education can be provided by the private sector, the spillovers are regarded as so important that the government produces great quantities at a cost affordable by all.

Organizations in the public and private sectors produce each of these three types of goods. Nevertheless, the public sector is primarily occupied with the provision of such collective and quasi-collective goods as defense, education, social welfare, public safety, transportation, environmental protection, recreation, and energy conservation. By contrast, the private sector is chiefly concerned with the production of such specific goods as food, appliances, machinery, and housing. Contrasts between the production of these goods in the public and private sectors are illustrated in Figure 5.3.

Because the nature of these three types of goods differs, so do the procedures for estimating their value to producers and consumers. The primary aim of a private firm producing specific goods for the market is to make profits, that is, to maximize the difference between the total revenues earned by selling a product and the total costs required for its production. When a private firm is faced with a choice

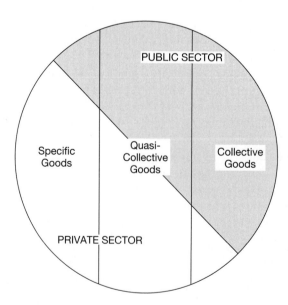

Figure 5.3 Three types of goods in the public and private sectors.

Source: H. H. Hinrichs and G. M. Taylor, *Systematic Analysis: A Primer on Benefit-Cost and Program Evaluation* (Pacific Palisades, CA: Goodyear Publishing, 1972), p. 5.

between two or more products that differ in the revenues they will earn and the costs required for their production, the firm will choose that product that maximizes profits, defined as total revenue minus total costs. If the firm should decide to invest in a product that yields lower profits, either in the short or in the long run, we can estimate the opportunity cost of the decision. *Opportunity cost* refers to the benefits sacrificed by investing resources to produce one product when another more profitable alternative might have been chosen.

Supply and Demand

Opportunity costs in the private sector can be estimated by using market prices as a measure of costs and benefits. Market prices of specific goods are determined by supply and demand. If we look at various combinations of the price and quantity of a specific good, we observe that (1) consumers will demand greater quantities (Q) of a product as the price (P) for that product decreases; and (2) producers will supply greater quantities (Q) of a product as the price (P) of that product increases (Figure 5.4). Finally, (3) the combination of price and quantity that yields a single level of consumer demand and producer supply—that is, the point where supply and demand intersect (P_eQ_e in Figure 5.4)—indicates the price and quantity of specific goods that will be sold on the market. Graphic representations of the various combinations of price and quantity where consumers and producers are willing to buy and sell a product are called a *demand curve* and *supply curve,* respectively. The point where demand and supply curves intersect is called the *equilibrium price–quantity combination.*

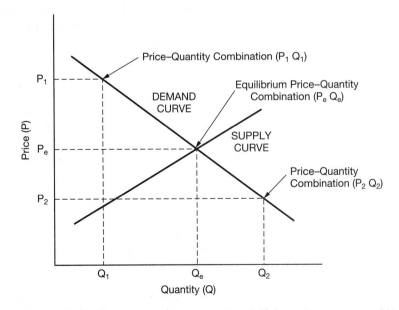

Figure 5.4 Supply and demand curves and the equilibrium price–quantity combination.

The equilibrium price–quantity combination represents that point where consumers and producers, if they are completely free to choose what they will buy and sell, will produce and consume equal quantities of a good at a given price. If we know the equilibrium price–quantity combination for a specific good (e.g., electric toothbrushes), we can determine the profit of a given investment by subtracting the total costs required to produce a specific good from the total revenues earned by selling the product at the equilibrium price (P_e) and equilibrium quantity (Q_e). By knowing the profits that can be earned from alternative investments, it is possible to estimate the benefits sacrificed by investing resources to produce one product when another more profitable investment might have been made. For example, if a firm producing electric toothbrushes (a specific good) and earning an annual profit of $1 million finds that it could have earned a profit of $2 million by producing electric drills at the same cost (including costs for any additional labor, technology, or marketing facilities), the opportunity cost of the investment in electric toothbrush production is $1 million.

The logic of profit maximization in the private sector can be extended to public policy. We can view public programs as if they were private firms attempting to maximize profits on investments. Instead of using profits (total revenue minus total cost) as a criterion for recommending alternatives, we can use net benefits (total benefits minus total costs). We can also apply the concept of opportunity costs by viewing public programs as investments in the production of goods that might have been made by private firms. For example, if government invests $50 million in the construction of a dam that will yield $10 million in net benefits to farmers and other beneficiaries, it must extract these investment resources from private citizens who could have invested the $50 million elsewhere. If private investment would have yielded $20 million in net benefits (profits) to private citizens, the opportunity cost of building the dam is $10 million (net private benefits of $20 million minus net public benefits of $10 million).

Public Choice

This logic begins to break down when we consider differences between public and private choice, including contrasts among specific, quasi-collective, and collective goods. While the logic of profit maximization can be applied to certain kinds of public goods (e.g., the production of hydroelectric power), there are important reasons why concepts of profit, net benefits, and opportunity costs are difficult to apply to problems of public choice:

1. *Multiple legitimate stakeholders*. Public policy making involves multiple stakeholders whose claims on public investments are frequently guaranteed by law. While there are also multiple stakeholders in private policy making, none except owners and stockholders can legitimately make claims on investments. In the public sector, with its many legitimate stakeholders, it is difficult to know whose benefits should be maximized and who should bear the costs of public investments.

2. *Collective and quasi-collective goods.* Because most public goods are collective (e.g., clean air) or quasi-collective (e.g., education), it is difficult or impossible to sell them on the market, where transactions are made on the basis of ability to pay. For this reason, market prices are frequently unavailable as a measure of net benefits or opportunity costs. Even where prices are based on interview surveys among citizens, some persons may falsely indicate no willingness to pay for a public good but later use the good at a price lower than that they are actually willing to pay. This is called the *free-rider problem.*

3. *Limited comparability of income measures.* Even when the net benefits of public and private investments can be expressed in dollars as a common unit of measure, private investments with higher net benefits are not always preferable to public ones with lower (or even zero or negative) net benefits. For example, a private investment in a new office building that yields $1 million in net benefits is unlikely to be preferred over a public investment in a cure for cancer that yields zero or negative net benefits. Even where comparisons are confined to public investments, the use of income measures to recommend alternatives implies that the goal of increasing aggregate income "is more important than good health or better education, or the elimination of poverty, and that these other goals are legitimate only to the extent that they increase future income."[18]

4. *Public responsibility for social costs and benefits.* Private firms are responsible for their own *private costs* and *private benefits* but not for social ones, except as prescribed by law (e.g., antipollution legislation) or moral convention. By contrast, the costs and benefits of public programs are socialized, thus becoming *social costs* and *social benefits* that go much beyond the need to satisfy private stockholders. Social costs and social benefits (e.g., the costs of destroying the natural environment by building highways) are difficult to quantify and often have no market price. Such social costs and social benefits are called intangibles.

Contrasts between public and private choice do not mean that the logic of profit maximization is wholly inapplicable to public problems. Contrasts do mean, however, that there are limitations to such logic when applied to public problems. These strengths and limitations are evident when we consider two of the most important approaches to recommendation in policy analysis: cost–benefit and cost–effectiveness analysis.

Cost–Benefit Analysis

Cost–benefit analysis is an approach to policy recommendation that permits analysts to compare and advocate policies by quantifying their total monetary costs and total monetary benefits. While cost–benefit analysis may be used to recommend policy

---

[18] Alice Rivlin, *Systematic Thinking for Social Action* (Washington, DC: Brookings Institution, 1971), p. 56.

actions, in which case it is applied prospectively (*ex ante*), it may also be used to evaluate policy performance. In this case, it is applied retrospectively (*ex post*). Much of modern cost–benefit analysis is based on that field of economics that treats problems of how to maximize social welfare, that is, the aggregate economic satisfaction experienced by members of a community.[19] This field is called *welfare economics,* because it is especially concerned with the ways that public investments may contribute to the maximization of net income as a measure of aggregate satisfaction (welfare) in society.

Cost–benefit analysis has been applied to many different kinds of public programs and projects. The earliest applications of cost–benefit analysis were in the area of dam construction and the provision of water resources, including efforts to analyze the costs and benefits of hydroelectric power, flood control, irrigation, and recreation. Other more recent applications include transportation, health, manpower training, and urban renewal.

When used to make recommendations in the public sector, cost–benefit analysis has several distinctive characteristics:

1. Cost–benefit analysis seeks to measure *all* costs and benefits to society that may result from a public program, including various intangibles that cannot be easily measured in terms of monetary costs and benefits.

2. Traditional cost–benefit analysis epitomizes *economic rationality,* because the criterion most frequently employed is global economic efficiency. A policy or program is said to be efficient if its *net benefits* (i.e., total benefits minus total costs) are greater than zero and higher than those net benefits that would have resulted from an alternative public or private investment.

3. Traditional cost–benefit analysis uses the *private marketplace* as a point of departure in recommending public programs. The opportunity costs of a public investment are often calculated on the basis of what net benefits might have been gained by investing in the private sector.

4. Contemporary cost–benefit analysis, sometimes called *social cost–benefit analysis,* can also be used to measure redistributional benefits. As social cost–benefit analysis is concerned with criteria of equity, it is consistent with *social rationality.*

Cost–benefit analysis has a number of strengths. First, *both* costs and benefits are measured in dollars as a common unit of value. This permits analysts to subtract costs from benefits, a task that is not possible with cost–effectiveness analysis. Second, cost–benefit analysis permits us to go beyond the confines of a single policy or program and link benefits to the income of society as a whole. This is possible because the results of individual policies and programs can be expressed in monetary terms, at

---

[19] For comprehensive treatments of cost–benefit analysis, see, for example, Edward J. Mishan, *Cost-Benefit Analysis* (New York: Frederick A. Praeger, 1976); and Edward M. Gramlich, *Benefit-Cost Analysis of Public Programs,* 2d ed. (Englewood Cliffs, NJ: Prentice Hall, 1990).

least in principle. Finally, cost–benefit analysis allows analysts to compare programs in widely differing areas (e.g., health and transportation), because net efficiency benefits are expressed in terms of dollars. This is not possible when effectiveness is measured in terms of units of service, because the number of persons treated by physicians cannot be directly compared with the number of miles of roads built.

Cost–benefit analysis, in both its traditional and its contemporary forms, also has several limitations. First, an exclusive emphasis on economic efficiency can mean that criteria of equity are meaningless or inapplicable. In practice, the Kaldor–Hicks criterion simply ignores problems of redistributional benefits, while the Pareto criterion seldom resolves conflicts between efficiency and equity. Second, monetary value is an inadequate measure of responsiveness, because the actual value of income varies from person to person. For example, an extra $100 of income is far more significant to the head of a poverty household than to a millionaire. This problem of *limited interpersonal comparisons* often means that income is an inappropriate measure of individual satisfaction and social welfare. Third, when market prices are unavailable for important goods (e.g., clean air or health services), analysts are often forced to estimate *shadow prices,* that is, subjective estimates of the price that citizens might be willing to pay for goods and services. These subjective judgments may simply be arbitrary expressions of the values of analysts.

Cost–benefit analysis, even when it takes into account problems of redistribution and social equity, is closely tied to income as a measure of satisfaction. For this reason, it is difficult to discuss the appropriateness of *any* objective that cannot be expressed in monetary terms. The exclusive concentration on net income or redistributional benefits often inhibits reasoned debates about the ethical or moral bases of alternative policies. Cost–benefit analysis is therefore limited in its capacity to consider relations among alternative forms of reason (technical, economic, social, legal) as part of an overall effort to establish the substantive rationality of policies and programs. Hence, cost–benefit analysis may come very close to providing us with "the price of everything and the value of nothing."

Types of Costs and Benefits

In using cost–benefit analysis, it is essential to consider *all* costs and benefits that may result from a policy or program. While such a comprehensive inventory of costs and benefits is quite difficult to achieve in practice, it can help reduce errors that occur when we omit some costs and benefits from our analysis. One of the best ways to guard against such errors is to classify costs and benefits: inside ("internal") versus outside ("external"); directly measurable ("tangible") versus indirectly measurable ("intangible"); primary ("direct") versus secondary ("indirect"); and net efficiency ("real") versus distributional ("pecuniary"). These types of costs and benefits, and the questions they are based on, are illustrated in Figure 5.5.

Inside versus outside costs and benefits. Here the question is whether a given cost or benefit is internal or external to a given target group or jurisdiction. Inside or

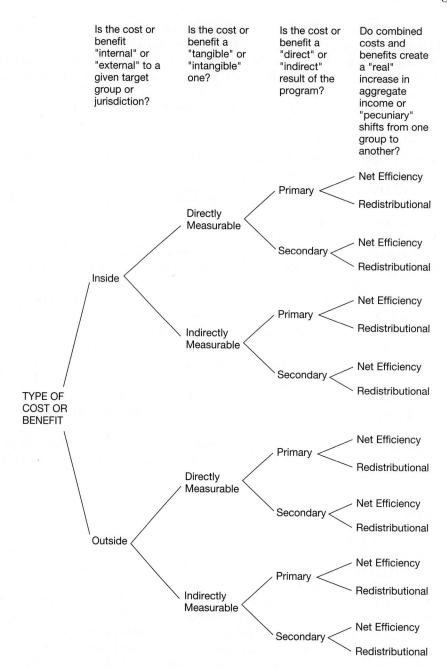

Figure 5.5 Classification of costs and benefits according to four types of questions.

internal costs and benefits are called *internalities,* while outside or external ones are called *externalities.* What is an inside cost or benefit (internality) in one case will be an outside one (externality) in another. The difference depends on how the analyst draws boundaries around the target group or jurisdiction. If the boundary is society as a whole, there may be no externalities. If, however, the boundary is a particular target group or jurisdiction, there will be internalities as well as externalities. Externalities are the positive and negative spillovers outside the boundaries of the jurisdiction or target group. For example, the construction of high-rise apartments in a central-city area as part of an urban renewal program has certain costs and benefits within the urban jurisdiction, including expenditures on construction and income derived from rents. The same urban renewal program also has external costs to suburban jurisdictions that must provide additional fire and police services in areas where vagrants or criminals have resettled because they can no longer afford to live in the central-city area.

Directly measurable versus indirectly measurable costs and benefits. The question here is whether the cost or benefit is a "tangible" or "intangible" one. *Tangibles* are costs and benefits that are directly measurable in terms of known market prices for goods and services, while *intangibles* are costs and benefits that are indirectly measurable in terms of estimates of such market prices. When dealing with intangibles, such as the price of clean air, the analyst may attempt to estimate shadow prices by making a subjective judgment about the dollar value of costs and benefits. In the urban renewal example, the analyst may try to estimate the opportunity costs that various groups might be willing to pay for the destruction of the sense of community resulting from urban renewal.

Primary and secondary costs and benefits. Here the question is whether the cost or benefit is a "direct" or "indirect" result of a program. A *primary cost or benefit* is one that is related to the most highly valued program objectives, while a *secondary cost or benefit* is one that is related to objectives that are less valued. For example, an urban renewal program may have as its most important objective the provision of low-cost housing to the poor, in which case the primary costs and benefits would include expenditures for construction and income from rents. Secondary costs and benefits would involve lesser objectives, including intangible costs, such as the destruction of a sense of community, or tangible benefits, such as reduced costs of police and fire services because of better street lighting and fire-resistant construction.

Net efficiency versus redistributional benefits. Here the question is whether combined costs and benefits create an increase in aggregate income or result merely in shifts in income or other resources among different groups. *Net efficiency benefits* are those that represent a "real" increase in net income (total benefits minus total costs), while *redistributional benefits* are those that result in a "pecuniary" shift in the incomes of one group at the expense of another but without increasing net efficiency benefits. Such changes are called *real benefits* and *pecuniary benefits,* respectively.

For example, an urban renewal project may produce $1 million in net efficiency benefits. If urban renewal also results in increased sales in small grocery stores in the immediate area—and decreased sales in stores that are more distant from new high-rise apartments—the benefits and the costs of income gained and lost are "pecuniary." They cancel each other out without producing any change in net efficiency benefits.

To call one type of benefit "real" and the other merely "pecuniary" can introduce considerable bias: Is an increase in the disposable income of the poor less "real" than an improvement in the net benefits of the community? For this reason, it is best to drop the categories of "real" versus "pecuniary" altogether, provided that we do not *add* any increase in redistributional benefits to net efficiency benefits without also *subtracting* the costs of redistribution to those whose income or other benefits were reduced. This error, called *double counting,* can produce invalid estimates of net efficiency benefits.

Observe that answers to these four questions can result in many combinations of costs and benefits. A given inside cost or benefit may be directly measurable (tangible) or indirectly measurable (intangible). An intangible cost or benefit may in turn be primary or secondary, depending on the relative importance of different objectives. A primary or secondary objective may itself be defined in terms of net efficiency or redistribution. Typically, either net efficiency or redistribution must be a primary objective, because it is seldom possible to create higher net efficiency benefits *and* redistributional benefits at the same time. In other words, these two types of benefits conflict. They represent a situation requiring *trade offs,* that is, conscious efforts to determine how much of one objective should be sacrificed to obtain another.

Tasks in Cost–Benefit Analysis

In conducting a cost–benefit analysis, most of the following tasks (Table 5.5) are important for making maximally plausible recommendations.

Problem structuring. The search for alternative formulations of the problem and the definition of the boundaries of the metaproblem (see Figure 3.9) are essential tasks of cost–benefit analysis. Problem structuring does not occur once, at the beginning of the cost–benefit analysis, but occurs at many points throughout the analysis. Problem structuring yields information about the potentially relevant goals, objectives, alternatives, criteria, target groups, costs, and benefits to guide the analysis. Problem structuring also may result in dissolving, resolving, and unsolving the problem many times during the cost–benefit analysis (see Figure 3.1).

Specification of objectives. Analysts usually begin with general aims or goals, for example, controlling cocaine addiction. Goals, as we have seen, must be converted into objectives that are temporally specific and measurable (see Table 4.1). The goal of controlling cocaine addiction may be converted into a number of specific objectives, for example, a 50 percent reduction in the supply of cocaine within five years. Objectives usually imply policy alternatives. The reduction in supply implies a policy

Table 5.5 Ten Tasks in Conducting a Cost–Benefit Analysis

Task	Description
Problem structuring	Formulation of metaproblem by defining boundaries of goals, objectives, alternatives, criteria, target groups, costs, and benefits
Specification of objectives	Conversion of general aims (goals) into temporally specific and measurable aims (objectives)
Specification of alternatives	Selection of most promising policy alternatives from a larger set of potential solutions defined at the problem structuring phase
Information search, analysis, and interpretation	Location, analysis, and interpretation of information needed to forecast the outcomes of specified policy alternatives
Identification of target groups and beneficiaries	Listing of all groups (stakeholders) that are a target of action (e.g., regulation) or inaction (status quo), or which will benefit from action or inaction
Estimation of costs and benefits	Estimation in units of monetary value the specific benefits and costs of each alternative in all classes (internal and external, directly and indirectly measurable, primary and secondary, efficiency and redistributional)
Discounting of costs and benefits	Conversion of monetary costs and benefits into their present value on the basis of a specified discount factor
Estimation of risk and uncertainty	Use of sensitivity and a *fortiori* analysis to estimate probabilities that benefits and costs will occur in future
Choice of decision criterion	Choice of criterion for selecting among alternatives: Pareto improvement, net efficiency improvement, distributional improvement, internal rate of return
Recommendation	Selection of alternative that is most plausible, considering rival ethical and causal hypotheses

of drug interdiction, whereas another objective—for example, a 50 percent reduction in the demand for cocaine—not only implies a policy of drug interdiction to raise the price of cocaine and lower demand, but also suggests drug rehabilitation as a way to decrease the number of addicts and, in turn, lower demand. In this and other cases, the relation between objectives and policy alternatives rests on causal assumptions that may prove to be questionable or plainly mistaken.

Identification of alternative solutions.   Once objectives have been specified, the analyst's assumptions about the causes of a problem and its potential solutions are almost inevitably transformed into alternative policies to achieve these objectives. The way a problem has been structured—for example, the problem of cocaine may be formulated as a demand problem requiring the interdiction of the flow of drugs from South America—thus governs the policies perceived to be appropriate and effective. If problem search has been severely restricted, inadvertently or for explicit political and ideological reasons, the policy metaproblem will exclude otherwise promising policy alternatives. Eventually, problem unsolving may be necessary (see Figure 3.1).

Information search, analysis, and interpretation. The task here is to locate, analyze, and interpret information relevant for forecasting the outcomes of policy alternatives. At this point, the principal objects of a forecast are the costs and benefits of policy alternatives already identified at the previous stage of analysis. Here, information may be acquired from available data on costs and benefits of similar existing programs. For example, prior to the establishment of the Drug Enforcement Administration, published budgetary data on the costs of drug enforcement activities of the U.S. Customs Service was used to estimate some of the costs of new drug interdiction policies. The benefits of interdiction in the form of decreased supply and demand were based on economic and administrative assumptions that eventually proved to be highly questionable or plainly wrong.[20]

Identification of target groups and beneficiaries. Here the task is to conduct a stakeholder analysis which lists all groups that have a stake in the policy issue because they will be affected, negatively and positively, by the adoption and implementation of policy recommendations. Target groups are the objects of new regulations or restrictions that typically involve the loss of freedom or resources—for example, regulations restricting the choice of women to terminate pregnancies or new tax schedules that increase the tax burden on the middle class. By contrast, beneficiaries are groups that will gain from the adoption and implementation of recommendations, for example, commercial truckers who receive increased net income as a consequence of some forty states moving from the 55 mph to the 65 mph speed limit in the late 1980s.

Estimation of costs and benefits. This task, perhaps the most difficult in cost–benefit analysis, requires the estimation in monetary terms of all benefits and costs that are likely to be experienced by target groups and beneficiaries. As we have seen (Figure 5.5), the types of benefits and costs are several: internal and external, directly and indirectly measurable, primary and secondary, net efficiency and redistributional. In many areas of public policy, it is difficult and even practically impossible to estimate costs or benefits. For example, the monetary benefits of a fatality averted through mandatory seat belt laws, obligatory state vehicle inspections, or breast cancer screening programs are subject to broad disagreement, especially when the costs of these fatality-averting policies are subtracted from the benefits of a human life. The validity, reliability, and appropriateness of such measures are often disputed.

Discounting of costs and benefits. If a certain level of costs and benefits is projected for a future time period, estimates must adjust for the decreasing real value of money due to inflation and future changes in interest rates. The real value of costs and benefits is usually based on the technique of discounting, a procedure that

---

[20] See George M. Guess and Paul G. Farnham, *Cases in Public Policy Analysis,* Chapter 5, "Coping with Cocaine" (New York: Longman, 1989), pp. 7–48; and Constance Holden, "Street-Wise Crack Research." *Science* 246 (December 15, 1989): 1376–81. As of 1992, the Bush administration had made no "effort to" unsolve the problem.

expresses future costs and benefits in terms of their present value. For example, the value of human life is sometimes expressed as an hourly wage rate multiplied by life expectancy. If the human life being valued is that of a twenty year old with low earning capacity—and if the discount factor used is 10 percent—the present value of that person's life can amount to no more than a few thousand dollars. This raises critical ethical questions about the comparability of values attached to the lives of young and old, poor and rich, rural and urban populations.

Estimation of risk and uncertainty.   The task here is to employ sensitivity analysis, a generic term that refers to procedures that test the sensitivity of conclusions to alternative assumptions about the probability of occurrence of different costs and benefits, or to different discount factors. It is difficult to develop reliable probabilistic estimates because different forecasts of the same future outcome often have widely differing levels of accuracy that stem from differences in institutional, temporal, and historical contexts.

Choice of a decision criterion.   Here the task is to specify a decision criterion or rule for choosing between two or more alternatives with different mixes of costs and benefits. These criteria are of six types: efficiency, effectiveness, adequacy, equity, responsiveness, and appropriateness. Among efficiency criteria are net efficiency improvement (the net present value after discounting costs and benefits to their present value must exceed zero) and internal rate of return (the rate of return on a public investment must be greater than that which could be earned at the actual rate of interest paid). Effectiveness criteria include the marginal effectiveness of graduated levels of public investment in producing the greatest volume of some valued good or service (e.g., access to medical treatment per dollar invested in health maintenance organizations versus traditional health care providers). Distributional and redistributional criteria, respectively, include Pareto improvement (at least one group gains while none loses) and Rawlsian improvement (those worst off become better off). The choice of a decision criterion has important ethical implications, because decision criteria are grounded in very different conceptions of moral obligation and the just society.

Recommendation.   The final task in cost–benefit analysis is to make a recommendation by choosing between two or more policy alternatives. The choice of alternatives is seldom clear and unequivocal, which calls for a critical analysis of the plausibility of recommendations, taking into account rival causal and ethical hypotheses that may weaken or invalidate a recommendation. For example, a recommendation based on Pareto improvement may be weakened by establishing that the rich will benefit at the expense of the middle and lower classes. In retrospect, this has been the actual history of social and economic policy in the United States over the last twenty years.[21]

---

[21] See, for example, Frank Levy, *Dollars and Dreams: The Changing American Income Distribution* (New York: Russell Sage Foundation, 1987).

Cost–Effectiveness Analysis

Cost–effectiveness analysis is an approach to policy recommendation that permits analysts to compare and advocate policies by quantifying their total costs and effects. In contrast to cost–benefit analysis, which attempts to measure all relevant factors in a common unit of value, cost–effectiveness analysis uses two different units of value. Costs are measured in monetary units, while effectiveness is typically measured in units of goods, services, or some other valued effect. In the absence of a common unit of value, cost–effectiveness analysis does not permit net effectiveness or net benefit measures, because it makes no sense to subtract total costs from total units of goods or services. It is possible, however, to produce cost–effectiveness and effectiveness–cost ratios, for example, ratios of costs to units of health service or units of health service to costs.

These ratios have an altogether different meaning than cost–benefit ratios. Whereas effectiveness–cost and cost–effectiveness ratios tell us how much of a good or service is produced per dollar expended—or, alternatively, how many dollars are expended per unit produced—benefit–cost ratios tell us how many times more benefits than costs are produced in a given instance. Benefit–cost ratios must be greater than 1 if there are any net benefits at all. For example, if total benefits are $4 million and total costs are $6 million, then the benefit–cost ratio is 4 to 6, or 0.66, and total net benefits are minus $2 million. If total net benefits are zero ($4 million minus $4 million equals zero), then the benefit–cost ratio is always 1 (4/4 = 1). By definition, then, a benefit–cost ratio must exceed 1 for there to be any net benefits. This is not true of effectiveness–cost ratios, which have a different meaning from one case to the next.

Cost–effectiveness analysis, like its cost–benefit counterpart, may be applied prospectively (*ex ante*) as well as retrospectively (*ex post*). In contrast to cost–benefit analysis, cost–effectiveness analysis grew out of work done for the Defense Department in the early 1950s, and not from work in the field of welfare economics. Much of the early development of cost–effectiveness analysis was carried out by the Rand Corporation in projects designed to evaluate alternative military strategies and weapons systems. In the same period, cost–effectiveness analysis was applied to problems of program budgeting in the Department of Defense and was extended in the 1960s to other government agencies.[22]

Cost–effectiveness analysis is particularly appropriate for questions involving the most efficient way to use resources to attain objectives that cannot be expressed in terms of income. Cost–effectiveness analysis has been used to recommend alternative policies and programs in criminal justice, manpower training, transportation, health, defense, and other areas.

---

[22] See, for example, David Novick, *Efficiency and Economy in Government through New Budgeting and Accounting Procedures* (Santa Monica, CA: Rand Corporation, February 1954); Roland J. McKean, *Efficiency in Government through Systems Analysis* (New York: Wiley, 1958); Charles J. Hitch and Roland J. McKean, *The Economics of Defense in the Nuclear Age* (New York: Atheneum, 1965); and T. A. Goldman, ed., *Cost-Effectiveness Analysis* (New York: Frederick A. Praeger, 1967).

Cost–effectiveness analysis, when used to make recommendations in the public sector, has several distinguishing characteristics:

1. Cost–effectiveness analysis, because it avoids problems of measuring benefits in monetary terms, is more easily applied than cost–benefit analysis.

2. Cost–effectiveness analysis epitomizes *technical rationality*, because it attempts to determine the utility of policy alternatives but without relating their consequences to global economic efficiency or aggregate social welfare.

3. Cost–effectiveness analysis, because it relies minimally on market prices, is less dependent on the logic of profit maximization in the private sector. Cost–effectiveness analysis, for example, frequently makes no attempt to determine whether benefits exceed costs or whether alternative investments in the private sector would have been more profitable.

4. Cost–effectiveness analysis is well suited to the analysis of externalities and intangibles, because these types of effects are difficult to express in dollars as a common unit of measure.

5. Cost–effectiveness analysis typically addresses fixed-cost (type I) or fixed-effectiveness (type II) problems, whereas cost–benefit analysis typically addresses variable-cost-variable-effectiveness (type III) problems.

The strengths of cost–effectiveness analysis are its comparative ease of application, its capacity to treat collective and quasi-collective goods whose values cannot be estimated on the basis of market prices, and its appropriateness for analyzing externalities and intangibles. The main limitation of cost–effectiveness analysis is that recommendations are less easily related to questions of aggregate social welfare. Unlike cost–benefit analysis, efforts to measure costs and effectiveness are confined to given programs, jurisdictions, or target groups and cannot be used to calculate net income benefits as a measure of the aggregate satisfaction experienced by members of a community.

Cost–effectiveness analysis also attempts to consider all costs and benefits of policies and programs, with the exception that benefits are not measured in monetary terms. Many of the same types of costs and benefits as those discussed previously are important in cost–effectiveness analysis: inside versus outside; directly measurable versus indirectly measurable; and primary versus secondary. While it is not possible to calculate net efficiency benefits, redistributional effects may be analyzed.

The tasks in conducting a cost–effectiveness analysis are similar to those required in cost–benefit analysis (Table 5.5), with two exceptions. Only costs are discounted to their present value and criteria of adequacy differ from those normally used in cost–benefit analysis. In cost–effectiveness analysis, two criteria of adequacy are most often employed:

1. *Least-cost criterion*. After establishing a desired level of effectiveness, the costs of programs with equal effectiveness are compared. Programs with less than the fixed level of effectiveness are dropped, while the program which meets the fixed level of effectiveness at least cost is recommended.

2. *Maximum-effectiveness criterion.* After establishing an upper level of permissible costs (usually a budgetary constraint), programs with equal costs are compared. Programs that exceed the upper cost limit are dropped, while the program that meets the fixed-cost level with the maximum effectiveness is recommended.

3. *Marginal effectiveness.* If units of some service or good as well as the costs of that service or good can be expressed on two continuous scales, the marginal effectiveness of two or more alternatives can be calculated. For example, the costs of providing security services by municipal police and by private security firms contracted by municipalities can be expressed on two continuous scales: a graduated scale of costs associated with each hour of patrols and the number of crimes against property reported, deterred, investigated, and cleared. A continuous cost–effectiveness function may be established for each type of service provider. The provider with the highest effectiveness–cost ratio at any point along the function beyond some minimum level of effectiveness has the greater marginal effectiveness—that is, the highest effectiveness achieved at the last dollar expended at the margin between the last dollar and the subsequent dollar cost (see point $E_1 - C_1$ in Figure 5.2).

4. *Cost–effectiveness.* The cost–effectiveness of two or more alternatives is the cost per unit of goods or services. For example, the 55 mph and 65 mph speed limits involve different costs per fatality averted, with the latter ranking slightly lower in cost–effectiveness. If the 55 mph and 65 mph speed limits have approximately equal costs (the denominator), but the latter averts slightly fewer fatalities (the numerator), then the average cost per fatality averted will be greater for the 65 mph speed limit. Effectiveness–cost ratios, in contrast to the benefit-cost ratios used in cost–benefit analysis, may not take into account all costs (e.g., the value of lives lost driving at the higher speed limit). For this reason, simple effectiveness–cost ratios may yield biased estimates of the actual costs of a given service or good, although the exclusion of costs is by no means an inherent limitation of cost–effectiveness analysis.

METHODS AND TECHNIQUES FOR RECOMMENDATION

A range of methods and techniques are available for making recommendations with cost–benefit and cost–effectiveness analysis (Table 5.6). These methods and techniques are most easily understood if they are viewed as tools for carrying out tasks of cost–benefit analysis described above (see Table 5.5). Cost–benefit and cost–effectiveness analysis, as we saw earlier, differs in certain important respects. These differences, however, are mainly related to the choice of decision criteria—for example, net efficiency improvement cannot be estimated with cost–effectiveness analysis because benefits are not expressed in monetary terms. With few exceptions (e.g., calculating the present value of future benefits), methods and techniques of cost–benefit analysis are also appropriate for cost–effectiveness analysis.

Table 5.6   Methods and Techniques for Recommendation Classified by Tasks of Cost–Benefit Analysis

Task	Method/Technique
Problem structuring[1]	Boundary analysis
	Classificational analysis
	Hierarchy analysis
	Multiple perspective analysis
	Argumentation analysis
	Argumentation mapping
Specification of objectives	Objectives mapping
	Value clarification
	Value critique
Information search, analysis, and interpretation	Boundary analysis[2]
Identification of target groups and beneficiaries	Boundary analysis
Estimation of costs and benefits	Cost element structuring
	Cost estimation
	Shadow pricing
Discounting of costs and benefits	Discounting
Estimation of risk and uncertainty	Feasibility assessment[3]
	Constraints mapping
	Sensitivity analysis
	A *fortiori* analysis
Choice of decision criterion	Value clarification
	Value critique
Recommendation	Plausibility analysis

Notes:
[1]See Chapter 3 for these methods and techniques.
[2]See Chapter 3.
[3]See Chapter 4.

Objectives Mapping

A frequent difficulty experienced in making policy recommendations is knowing what objectives to analyze. *Objectives mapping* is a technique used to array goals and objectives and their relationship to policy alternatives. Goals, objectives, and alternatives that have been identified by one or more methods of problem structuring (Chapter 3) may be depicted in the form of an *objectives tree,* which is a pictorial display of the overall structure of objectives and their relationships.[23] The objectives, when mapped in the form of a tree diagram, often form a hierarchy in which certain objectives that are necessary for the attainment of other objectives

---

[23] See T. Harrell Allen, *New Methods in Social Science Research: Policy Sciences and Futures Research* (New York: Frederick A. Praeger, 1978), pp. 95–106.

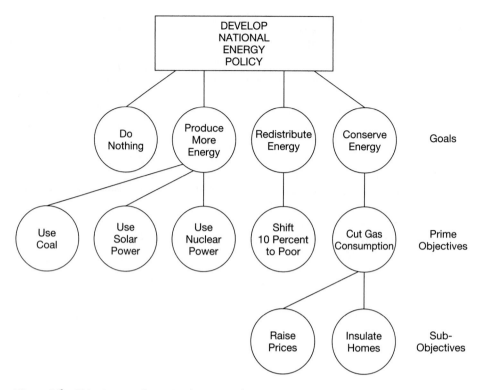

Figure 5.6   Objectives tree for national energy policy.

are arranged vertically. An objectives tree for the development of a national energy policy is illustrated in Figure 5.6.

In constructing an objectives tree, the analyst may start with existing objectives or may generate new ones. If it is necessary to generate new objectives, there are several problem-structuring techniques available for this purpose, including hierarchy analysis, classificational analysis, brain-storming, and argumentation analysis (see Chapter 3). Once a set of objectives has been obtained, it is possible to arrange them hierarchically in a tree such as that provided in Figure 5.6. Objectives trees are more general at the top and progressively more detailed as one moves lower in the hierarchy. Typically, the uppermost part of an objectives tree contains broad purposes, while lower levels represent goals, prime objectives, and subobjectives. Observe that when we read downward, we answer the question "*How* should we accomplish this objective?" When we read upward, we answer the question "*Why* should we pursue this objective?" Objectives mapping is therefore useful, not only for purposes of mapping the complexities of policy implementation (i.e., "how" questions), but also for clarifying the ends of action (i.e., "why" questions). Finally, most objectives can be regarded as both ends and means.

Value Clarification

Value clarification is a procedure for identifying and classifying value premises that underlie the selection of policy objectives. The need for value clarification in making policy recommendations is most evident when we consider competing criteria for recommendation (effectiveness, efficiency, adequacy, responsiveness, equity, appropriateness) and the multiple forms of rationality from which these criteria are derived. Value clarification helps answer such questions as the following: What value premises underlie the choice of policy objectives? Are these value premises those of policy analysts, of policy makers, of particular social groups, or of society as a whole? What circumstances explain the fact that certain groups are committed to these value premises and objectives, while others are opposed? Finally, what reasons are offered to justify particular value premises and objectives?

There are several major steps in value clarification:[24]

1. Identify all relevant objectives of a policy or program. Objectives may simply be listed or displayed in the form of an objectives tree (Figure 5.6).

2. Identify all stakeholders who affect and are affected by the attainment or nonattainment of the objectives. Be sure to include yourself, as policy analyst, in the list of stakeholders.

3. List the value premises that underlie each stakeholder's commitment to objectives. For example, environmentalists may value energy conservation because it preserves the esthetic qualities of the natural environment, while suburban homeowners may value energy conservation because it provides for a more secure material existence.

4. Classify value premises into those that are simply expressions of personal taste or desire (*value expressions*); those that are statements about the beliefs of particular groups (*value statements*); and those that are judgments about the universal goodness or badness of the actions or conditions implied by the objective (*value judgments*). For example, you as policy analyst may express a personal desire for more energy consumption, environmental groups may state their belief in energy conservation, and oil producers may offer judgments about increased energy production that are based on beliefs in universal rights to use private property as owners see fit.

5. Further classify value premises into those that provide a *basis for explaining* objectives (e.g., environmentalists seek to conserve energy because this is consistent with their belief in the inviolability of nature), and those that provide a *ground for justifying* objectives (e.g., energy conservation is an appropriate objective because nature and humanity alike are entitled to rights of self-protection).

---

[24] For background material, see Chapter 7.

The advantage of value clarification is that it enables us to go beyond the analysis of objectives as if they were merely expressions of personal desire or taste. Value clarification also takes us one step beyond the explanation of circumstances that explain objectives. While the *bases* of values are important—for example, it is important to know that the poor favor greater social equity—ethical and moral disputes cannot be resolved without examining the *grounds* for justifying objectives.

Value Critique

Value critique is a set of procedures for examining the persuasiveness of conflicting arguments offered in the course of a debate about policy objectives. Whereas value clarification enables us to classify values according to their form, context, and function, value critique allows us to examine the role of values in policy arguments and debates. Value clarification focuses on the objectives and underlying values of individual stakeholders. By contrast, value critique focuses on conflicts among the objectives and underlying values of different stakeholders. Value clarification also has a static quality, while value critique looks toward changes in values that may result from reasoned debates.

Procedures for value critique are an extension of the ethical mode of policy argument discussed in Chapter 8. In conducting a value critique, it is necessary to

1. Identify one or more advocative claims, that is, claims that set forth a recommendation for action.
2. List all stakeholders who will affect and be affected by the implementation of the recommendation.
3. Describe each stakeholder's argument for and against the recommendation.
4. Identify each element in the debate: information (I), claim (C), qualifier (Q), warrant (W), backing (B), and rebuttal (R).
5. Assess the *ethical persuasiveness* of each argument and determine whether to retain, alter, or reject the recommendation.

To illustrate the process of value critique, imagine a policy analyst who has completed a cost–benefit analysis of low-cost home insulation. The recommendation or claim (C) is that the government should adopt the low-cost home insulation program. Information (I) indicates that the net benefits of the program are $50 million and the benefit–cost ratio is 5 to 1. As the program will result in considerable energy savings, it is almost certainly justified (Q). But after the arguments of each stakeholder have been analyzed, the recommendation seems less persuasive (Figure 5.7). The original warrant (W) used to support the recommendation is that of increased social welfare, a warrant that in turn might be backed (B) by the Pareto or Kaldor–Hicks criteria. The rebuttal (R) is that the program will not benefit the poor and the elderly. This rebuttal is backed by the Rawls criterion that persons who are worst off should gain.

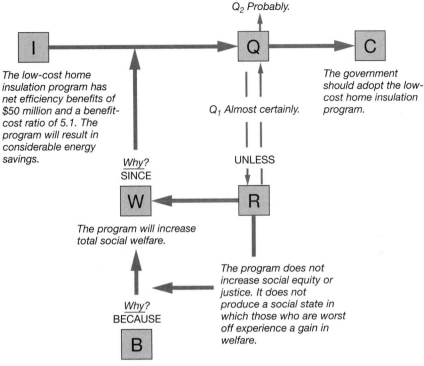

Figure 5.7 Value-critical debate.

Note that this debate is both economic and ethical, because it involves questions of efficiency and of justice at the same time. One result of the debate might be to modify the recommendation in such a way that the government would provide low-cost home insulation on a graduated-cost basis. Those who cannot afford it might pay nothing, while those in higher income brackets would pay most. Yet this would make the program less attractive to those who use most heat. If equal costs were maintained across the board (with the exception of the poor and the elderly, who would pay nothing), the total net benefits may well be negative. While value critique cannot finally answer the question of how much efficiency should be sacrificed for a given increase in social equity, it does make it possible to conduct a reasoned ethical debate about such questions, rather than expect cost–benefit analysis to provide answers to questions for which it is not suited. Economics is not ethics any more than price is value.

Cost Element Structuring

The concept of cost is central to the process of making policy recommendations, because the pursuit of one objective almost always requires that we sacrifice another. *Opportunity costs,* as we have seen, are the benefits that could otherwise be obtained by investing resources in the attainment of some other objective. In other words, costs are benefits forgone or lost, while net benefits (total benefits minus total costs) are a measure of the costs that would have been paid if resources had been invested in the pursuit of some other objective.

Cost element structuring is a procedure for classifying and describing all costs that will be incurred by establishing and operating a program.[25] The cost element structure is a list of functions, equipment, and supplies that require the expenditure of resources. The purpose of cost element structuring is to create a list of functions, equipment, and supplies that is exhaustive and mutually exclusive. If the list is exhaustive, no important costs will be overlooked. If the list contains mutually exclusive items, no costs will be *double counted.*

A cost element structure contains two main divisions: *primary* (direct) and *secondary* (indirect) costs. Primary costs are subdivided into three categories: *one-time fixed costs, investment costs,* and *recurrent (operating and maintenance) costs.*[26] A typical cost element structure is illustrated in Table 5.7.

Cost Estimation

Cost estimation is a procedure that provides information about the dollar value of items in a cost element structure. While the cost element structure indicates what elements should be measured, cost estimation actually measures them. A *cost–estimating relationship* is an explicit measure of the relationship between the quantity of functions, materials, or personnel and their costs. The simplest type of cost-estimating relationship is cost per unit, for example, the cost per acre of land, per square foot of facilities, or per worker in a given job category. More complex cost-estimating relationships involve the use of linear regression and interval estimation (Chapter 4). For example, linear regression may be used to provide an interval estimate of vehicle maintenance costs, using miles driven as the independent variable.

Cost-estimating relationships are central to the process of making recommendations, because explicit measures of the relationship between the quantity of functions, materials, or personnel and their costs permit analysts to compare two or more policy alternatives in a consistent manner. Cost-estimating relationships are used to construct cost models that represent some or all of the costs that will be

---

[25] See H. G. Massey, David Novick, and R. E. Peterson, *Cost Measurement: Tools and Methodology for Cost-Effectiveness Analysis* (Santa Monica, CA: Rand Corporation, February 1972).

[26] Poister, *Public Program Analysis,* pp. 386–87; and H. P. Hatry, R. E. Winnie, and D. M. Fisk, *Practical Program Evaluation for State and Local Government* (Washington, DC: Urban Institute, 1973).

Table 5.7 Cost Element Structure

I. Primary (direct) costs
   1. One-time fixed costs
      Research
      Planning
      Development, testing, and evaluation
   2. Investment costs
      Land
      Building and facilities
      Equipment and vehicles
      Initial training
   3. Recurring (operating and maintenance) costs
      Salaries, wages, and fringe benefits
      Maintenance of grounds, vehicles, and equipment
      Recurrent training
      Direct payments to clients
      Payments for extended support services
      Miscellaneous materials, supplies, and services
II. Secondary (indirect) costs
   1. Costs to other agencies and third parties
   2. Environmental degradation
   3. Disruption of social institutions
   4. Other

required to initiate and maintain a program. A simplified cost model for initial investment is illustrated in Figure 5.8.

Shadow Pricing

Shadow pricing is a procedure for making subjective judgments about the monetary value of benefits and costs when market prices are unreliable or unavailable. Market prices might be distorted (i.e., not represent the actual social value of costs and benefits) for a number of reasons. These reasons include unfair competition, monopolistic or oligopolistic practices, and government price support programs. In such cases, upward (or downward) adjustments can be made in the actual market price of a good or service. In other cases, market prices are simply unavailable. This is often the case with certain collective goods (e.g., clean air or a sense of community) that we discussed earlier as *intangibles*. Analysts can use several procedures to estimate the price of such intangibles.[27]

   1. *Comparable prices.* Here the analyst uses prices for comparable or similar items in the market. For example, in estimating the economic benefits of time saved by the construction of a mass rapid transit system, the analyst might use

[27] Poister, *Public Program Analysis,* pp. 417–19.

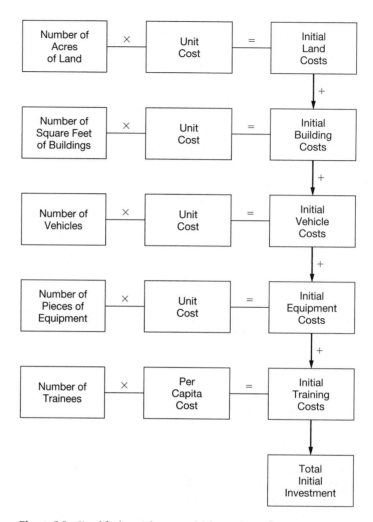

Figure 5.8 Simplified partial cost model for total initial investment.

area wage rates as a measure of the monetary value of time saved by using the new transportation facilities. This equation of work time and leisure time is based on the questionable assumption that time saved in travel could have been used to earn income.

2. *Consumer choice.* Here the analyst estimates the value of intangibles (e.g., travel time) by observing consumer behavior in situations where individuals are forced to choose between a given intangible and money. For example, estimates of the value of time can be made by observing actual choices made between low-cost and time-consuming versus high-cost and time-reducing modes of travel. This may help to determine how much consumers are willing

to pay for reduced travel time, although it assumes that consumers have complete information about the relation between time and costs and that both alternatives are equal in all respects, save time and cost.

3. *Derived demand.* Here the value of intangibles for which there are no market prices (e.g., satisfaction with government parks and recreation areas that charge no fees) can be estimated on the basis of the indirect costs paid by visitors. A demand curve (i.e., a curve that displays the various price–quantity combinations at which consumers will use a service) can be derived from the costs paid by consumers in traveling to the park. These indirect costs are taken to be actual prices paid for the use of parks and recreation areas. This procedure assumes that the sole purpose of the travel is to use the park or recreation area.

4. *Survey analysis.* Here the analyst surveys citizens by interviewing them or asking them to complete mailed questionnaires. Respondents indicate at what level of costs they will be willing to pay for a given service (e.g., bus transportation). One weakness of this procedure is the so-called *free-rider problem,* that is, a situation where consumers will claim that they are not willing to pay for a service in the hope that they will benefit from the service while others pay for it.

5. *Cost of compensation.* Here the analyst estimates the value of intangibles—particularly those that occur in the form of unwanted outside costs (negative externalities)—by obtaining prices for actions required to correct them. For example, the costs of environmental damage might be estimated by basing dollar values on the prices of programs for water purification, noise abatement, or reforestation. Similarly, the benefits of an antipollution enforcement program might be estimated on the basis of medical costs that will be avoided because people contract less lung cancer, emphysema, and other chronic diseases.

Constraint Mapping

Constraint mapping is a procedure for identifying and classifying limitations and obstacles that stand in the way of achieving policy and program objectives. Generally, constraints fall into six categories:

1. *Physical constraints.* The attainment of objectives may be limited by the state of development of knowledge or technology. For example, the reduction of pollution through the use of solar energy is constrained by the present low level of development of solar technology.

2. *Legal constraints.* Public law, property rights, and agency regulations often limit attempts to achieve objectives. For example, social programs designed to redistribute resources to the poor are frequently constrained by reporting requirements.

3. *Organizational constraints.* The organizational structure and processes available to implement programs may limit efforts to achieve objectives. For example, excessive centralization, poor management and low morale limit the effectiveness and efficiency of public programs.[28]

4. *Political constraints.* Political opposition may impose severe limitations on the implementation as well as the initial acceptance of programs. Such opposition is reflected in organizational inertia and tendencies to avoid problems by practicing incremental decision making. For example, certain problems (consumer protection, environmental protection, energy conservation) may take years even to be placed on the formal agenda of public bodies.[29]

5. *Distributional constraints.* Public programs designed to provide social services efficiently are often limited by the need to ensure that benefits and costs are equitably distributed among different groups. Programs that achieve the highest net efficiency benefits, as we have seen, are frequently those that produce least social equity, and vice versa.

6. *Budgetary constraints.* Government budgets are limited, thus requiring that objectives be considered in light of scarce resources. Fixed budgets create type I problems, where analysts are forced to consider alternatives that maximize effectiveness within the limits of available resources.

An effective way to identify and classify constraints is to construct a *constraints tree,* which is a graphic display of limitations and obstacles that stand in the way of achieving objectives. A constraints tree involves the superimposition of constraints on an objectives tree (see Figure 5.6). A simplified constraints tree for national energy policy is illustrated in Figure 5.9.

Cost Internalization

Cost internalization is a procedure for incorporating all relevant outside costs (externalities) into an internal cost element structure. Costs as well as benefits can be internalized by considering significant positive and negative spillovers of public policies and programs. When costs are fully internalized, there are no externalities because, by definition, all costs are internal ones. This means that a variety of important external costs—for example, costs of pollution, environmental degradation, or social dislocation—are explicitly built into the process of recommendation.

In general, there are four kinds of spillovers or externalities to which policy analysts should pay particular attention.[30]

---

[28] For a general treatment of these organizational constraints, see Vincent Ostrom, *The Intellectual Crisis in American Public Administration* (University: University of Alabama Press, 1974).

[29] See, for example, Roger W. Cobb and Charles D. Elder, *Participation in American Politics: The Dynamics of Agenda-Building* (Boston, MA: Allyn and Bacon, 1972).

[30] Hinrichs and Taylor, *Systematic Analysis,* pp. 18–19.

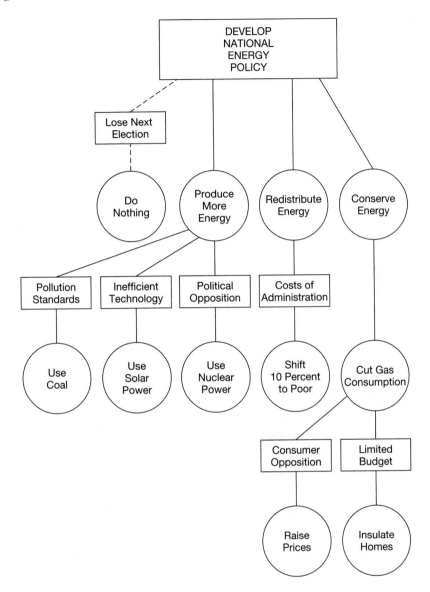

Figure 5.9 Constraints map for national energy policy.

1. *Production-to-production spillovers.* The products of a program serving one target group or jurisdiction may affect (positively or negatively) the products of another. For example, successful alcoholism and drug-treatment programs may result in a decrease of law enforcement activities in the surrounding community.

2. *Production-to-consumption spillovers.* The products of a particular program may affect the quality and quantity of goods consumed by members within another target group or jurisdiction. For example, publicly funded highway projects may displace residents from their homes or change the demand for goods and services in neighboring areas.

3. *Consumption-to-consumption spillovers.* The consumption activities of public programs in one area may affect consumption patterns within adjacent target groups or jurisdictions. For example, the construction of a large government office facility may make it impossible for local citizens to find adequate parking.

4. *Consumption-to-production spillovers.* The consumption activities of public programs in one area may affect the production activities of public and private programs in adjacent areas. For example, the construction of a public housing project may improve the market for local businesses.

The importance of cost internalization is evident in Table 5.8, which shows total, outside, and inside costs for three programs designed to provide maternal care. If all three programs are equally effective, an analyst at the state level who has not internalized federal cost sharing will recommend program I, because it satisfies the least-cost criterion. If federal costs are internalized, program III will be recommended, because total costs are least. This example calls attention to the relative nature of internal and external costs, because what is an externality to one party is not to another.

Discounting

Discounting is a procedure for estimating the present value of costs and benefits that will be realized in the future. Discounting is a way to take into account the effects of time when making policy recommendations. Time is important because

Table 5.8 Internal, External, and Total Costs of Alternative Maternal Care Programs (Costs per Patient)

	Program					
Type of Cost	Maternal and Infant Care Project I		Neighborhood Health Center II		Private Physician III	
Cost to state (internal)	$31	10%	$96	48.3%	$85	48.3%
Cost to federal government (external)	282	90	103	51.7	90	51.7
Total cost	$313	100%	$199	100%	$175	100%

Source: Adapted from M. R. Burt, *Policy Analysis: Introduction and Applications to Health Programs* (Washington, DC: Information Resources Press, 1974), p. 35.

future costs and benefits have less value than present ones. A dollar spent today is more valuable than a dollar spent one or two years from now, since today's dollar can be invested so that it will generate $1.12 one year from now (at 12% interest). Apart from interest earnings, many people prefer to consume now rather than later, since the future is uncertain and it is hard to delay the consumption that produces immediate satisfaction.

Many policies and programs generate different levels of costs and benefits that flow forward into time. These flows of costs and benefits, called *cost (or benefit) streams,* are unevenly distributed in time. For this reason, each cost and benefit stream must be discounted to its present value. For example, two health programs with equal effectiveness and identical total costs over a five-year period would appear to be equally recommendable. Yet in one of these programs (program I), costs are heavily concentrated in the first year, while in the other (program II), they are concentrated in the last year. If we assume that the dollar is losing value at the rate of 10 percent per year, then program II achieves the same level of effectiveness at least cost. If we do not take time and the changing value of money into account, there is no basis for distinguishing the two programs (Figure 5.10).

The present value of a future benefit or cost is found by using a *discount factor,* which expresses the amount by which the value of future benefits and costs should be decreased to reflect the fact that present dollars have more value than future ones. Once we know the discount factor, we simply multiply this factor by the known dollar value of a future benefit or cost. This was what was done in Figure 5.8. Given a certain *discount rate,* that is, the rate at which the value of future benefits and costs should be reduced, the discount factor may be calculated by

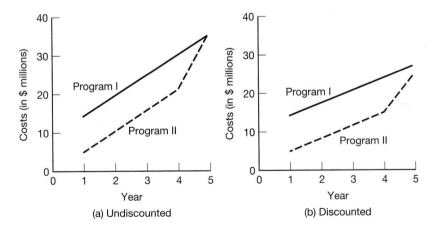

Figure 5.10 Comparison of discounted and undiscounted costs cumulated for two programs with equal effectiveness.

knowing the number of years over which future benefits and costs must be discounted. The formula for the discount factor is

$$DF = \frac{1}{(1 + r)^n}$$

where r is the discount rate and n is the number of years over which benefits or costs are discounted.[31] For example, to calculate the discount factor (DF) for a discount rate of 10 percent at five years, we make the following computations:

$$DF = \frac{1}{(1 + r)^n}$$

$$= \frac{1}{(1 + 0.10)^5} = \frac{1}{(1.1)^5}$$

$$= \frac{1}{(1.61)}$$

$$= 0.621$$

If we want to discount the value of $100 in costs incurred in the fifth year, we simply multiply this cost by the discount factor, that is, $100 × 0.621 = $62.10. In other words, the present value of $100 in costs incurred in the fifth year at a discount rate of 10 percent is $62.10. *Present value* is the dollar value of future costs or benefits that have been multiplied by the appropriate discount factor. The formula for the present value of a stream of costs or benefits is

$$PV = \Sigma(FV \cdot DF)$$

where FV designates the future value of costs or benefits, DF is the discount factor, and the symbol Σ (sigma) tells us to sum or add up all the products of costs or benefits times the discount factor for all years in the cost (or benefit) stream.[32]

The calculation of the present value of a cost stream is illustrated in Table 5.9. Observe that the future value of all undiscounted costs is $180 million, while the present value of the discounted cost stream is $152.75 million. Assume that the present value of the *benefit* stream is $175 million. If we were using the net benefit criterion

---

[31] The discount factor assumes that future dollar values in a cost (or benefit) stream are unequal (for example, heavy costs at the beginning of a period decrease over time). If the future dollar values in a cost (or benefit) stream are identical from year to year (e.g., $1 million in costs every year for five years), it is customary to use a shortcut, called an *annuity factor* (annuity means annually, or regularly over a number of years). The formula for the annuity factor is

$$AF = 1 - \left(\frac{1}{1 + r}\right) n/r.$$

Stated more concisely, $AF = 1 - DF/r$.

[32] Another formula for present value, which gives identical results, is $PV = FV/(1 + r)^n$, where FV is future costs or benefits, r is the discount rate, and n is the number of years over which costs or benefits must be discounted.

Table 5.9   Calculation of Present Value of Cost Stream over Five Years at 10 Percent Discount Rate (in Millions of Dollars)

Year	Future Value (FV)	Discount Rate (r)	Number of Years (n)	Discount Factor (DF) $[1/(1+r)^n]$	Present Value (PV) [FV·DF]
1991	$100	0.10	1	0.909	$90.90
1992	50	0.10	2	0.826	41.30
1993	10	0.10	3	0.751	7.51
1994	10	0.10	4	0.683	6.83
1995	10	0.10	5	0.621	6.21
	$180.0				$152.75

to make a recommendation (i.e., net benefits must be greater than zero), the undiscounted costs would result in a rejection of the program ($175 – 180 = –$5). By contrast, when we discount the cost stream, our recommendation would be positive, because net benefits are $22.5 million ($175 – 152.75 = $22.5).

Once we know the appropriate discount rate, it is a simple matter to calculate the discount factor and the present value of a cost (or benefit) stream. The problem is that the choice of a discount rate depends on judgments that reflect the ethical values of analysts, policy makers, or particular social groups. For example, the higher the rate at which we discount future benefits, the more difficult it is to obtain net benefits and benefit–cost ratios that justify public programs. If discount rates are uniformly high, this leads to a minimal role for government investments and a maximal one for private ones. If, on the other hand, discount rates are uniformly low, this encourages an expanded role for government in society. For this reason, it is important to recognize competing bases for selecting a discount rate:

1. *Private discount rates.* Here the selection of a discount rate is based on judgments about the appropriate rate of interest charged for borrowing money in the private sector. The argument for using private rates is that public investments are made with the tax monies of citizens who could have invested in the private sector. The private rate of discount therefore measures the benefits that would have been obtained if funds had been left in the private sector. These are the opportunity costs of public (versus private) investment. The arguments against private rates are that private rates differ widely (from 5 to 20%) because of market distortions; private rates do not reflect the external social costs of private investment (for example, pollution); and private rates reflect narrow individual and group preferences and not those of society as a whole.

2. *Social discount rates.* Here the selection of a discount rate is based on judgments about the social time preference of society as a whole. The *social time preference* refers to the collective value that society attaches to benefits or costs realized in some future time period. This collective value is not simply the sum of individual preferences, because it reflects a collective sense of what is

valuable for the community as a whole. The *social rate of discount,* that is, the rate at which future collective benefits and costs should be discounted, is generally lower than the private rate. The arguments for a social rate of discount are that the social rate compensates for the narrowness and short-sightedness of individual preferences; it takes into account external social costs of private investment (for example, the depletion of finite natural resources); and it reflects a concern with the security, health, and welfare of future generations. Arguments against the social rate of discount are that it is economically inefficient or "irrational" and that the social rate of discount should be *higher* than the private rate. The assumption here is that the private rate actually underestimates the value of future benefits, because individuals habitually underestimate the extent to which rapid technological progress promotes future income.

3. *Government discount rates.* Here a discount rate is selected on the basis of the current costs of government borrowing. The problem is that the rate at which federal, state, and local governments may borrow money varies considerably. While the Office of Management and Budget (OMB) has advocated a 10 percent discount rate for government programs, this standard rate does not reflect the opportunity cost of investments when lower interest rates are available within a given state, region, or community.

The selection of a discount rate is a matter of reasoned judgment and ethical discourse. Conflicts surrounding the choice of a discount rate cannot be resolved by pretending that market prices will produce value consensus. The choice of a discount rate is closely connected to competing views of the proper role of government in society and to the different forms of rationality discussed earlier. Under these circumstances, the analyst must examine the sensitivity of net benefits and benefit–cost ratios to alternative discount rates and the assumptions that justify their selection. Alternatively, the analyst can calculate the *internal rate of return* on investment, a procedure used to recommend alternatives when the rate of undiscounted benefits returned for each discounted dollar of costs exceeds the actual rate at which investment funds are borrowed. Here, as elsewhere, it is essential to examine the underlying assumptions and ethical implications of any choice based on the internal rate of return.

Sensitivity Analysis

Sensitivity analysis is a procedure for examining the sensitivity of results of cost–benefit or cost–effectiveness analysis to alternative assumptions about the likelihood that given levels of costs or benefits will actually occur. In comparing two or more policy alternatives, there may be considerable uncertainty about the probable outcomes of action, even though a single overall measure of costs and benefits (e.g., an effectiveness–cost ratio) may have been calculated. In such circumstances, the analyst may introduce alternative assumptions about future costs—for example, assumptions about high, medium, and low costs—and compute separate ratios under each of these assumptions. The point is to see how "sensitive" the ratios are to these different assumptions.

For example, in comparing two personnel training programs, the analyst may examine the sensitivity of transportation costs to possible changes in the price of gasoline. Here the analyst may introduce assumptions that the price of gasoline will increase by 10 percent, 20 percent, and 30 percent over the life of the program. As program I is situated in a semirural area, trainees must drive a longer distance to reach the training site than trainees in program II, which is located in the city. A marked increase in gasoline prices could result in recommending the most costly of the two programs. An example of this kind of sensitivity analysis is provided in Table 5.10. Another type of sensitivity analysis, and one we already discussed in Chapter 4, involves the use of regression analysis to make interval estimates of the values of costs or benefits.

A *Fortiori* Analysis

A fortiori analysis is a procedure used to compare two or more alternatives by resolving all uncertainties in favor of an alternative that is generally preferred on intuitive grounds but which appears after preliminary analysis to be the weaker of the two alternatives. The analyst may deliberately resolve a major cost uncertainty in favor of the weaker, but intuitively favored, alternative. If the stronger alternative still dominates the intuitively favored one, there is an even stronger case for the competing alternative. Note that *a fortiori* means "with even greater strength."

Plausibility Analysis

Plausibility analysis is a procedure for testing a recommendation against rival claims. Plausibility analysis, a form of critical multiplism used to examine rival causal and ethical claims, may be presented as a policy debate. There are at least ten types of rival claims, each of which is a threat to the plausibility of recommendations based on cost–benefit analysis. These threats to the plausibility of policy

Table 5.10 Sensitivity Analysis: Effects of Possible Increases in Gasoline Prices on Costs of Two Training Programs (in Thousands of Dollars)

	Price Increase		
Program	*10%*	*20%*	*30%*
I. Semirural			
Total costs	$4400	$4800	$5200
Trainees	$5000	$5000	$5000
Costs per trainee	$0.88	$0.96	$1.04
II. Urban			
Total costs	$4500	$4800	$5100
Trainees	$5000	$5000	$5000
Costs per trainee	$0.90	$0.96	$1.02

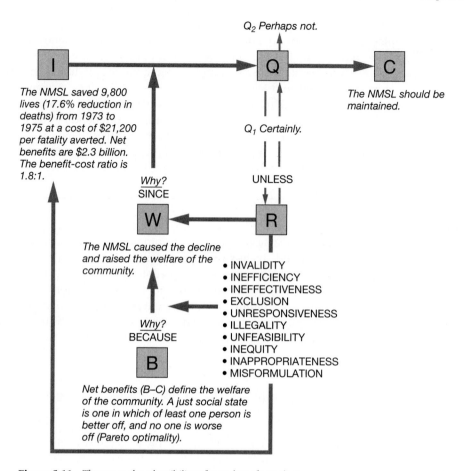

Q_2 *Perhaps not.*

I — **Q** → **C**

The NMSL saved 9,800 lives (17.6% reduction in deaths) from 1973 to 1975 at a cost of $21,200 per fatality averted. Net benefits are $2.3 billion. The benefit-cost ratio is 1.8:1.

The NMSL should be maintained.

Q_1 *Certainly.*

Why?
SINCE

UNLESS

W ← **R**

The NMSL caused the decline and raised the welfare of the community.

- INVALIDITY
- INEFFICIENCY
- INEFFECTIVENESS
- EXCLUSION
- UNRESPONSIVENESS
- ILLEGALITY
- UNFEASIBILITY
- INEQUITY
- INAPPROPRIATENESS
- MISFORMULATION

Why?
BECAUSE

B

Net benefits (B–C) define the welfare of the community. A just social state is one in which of least one person is better off, and no one is worse off (Pareto optimality).

Figure 5.11 Threats to the plausibility of cost–benefit analysis.

recommendations are illustrated (Figure 5.11) with examples drawn from debates about the efficacy of the 55 mph speed limit in saving lives.

- *Invalidity.* A policy recommendation is based on an invalid assumption about the causal relation between a policy and its outcomes. For example, debates about the efficacy of the 55 mph speed limit (National Maximum Speed Law of 1973) have focused on the extent to which enforcing a maximum speed on all intercity highways is responsible for the observed decline in traffic fatalities after 1973. The claim that the new maximum speed (55 mph) was responsible for the decline of 9,800 fatalities between 1973 and 1975 has been challenged on grounds that the decline was due to the new compressed range or standard deviation of speeds; improvements in automobile and highway safety; the interaction of maximum speed with population density; and the effects of recession, unemployment, and declining gasoline prices on miles driven and, consequently, fatality rates.[33]

- *Inefficiency.* Estimates of the net efficiency benefits of the 55 mph speed limit vary markedly, depending on the value attached to human lives and the costs of time lost by driving at 55 mph rather than 65 mph. One estimate of net efficiency benefits is $2.3 billion, while another is minus $3.4 billion.[34]

- *Ineffectiveness.* Estimates of the cost–effectiveness of the 55 mph speed limit also vary markedly. The costs per fatality averted range from approximately $1,300 to $21,000, depending on assumptions about what should be included as costs and benefits.[35]

- *Exclusion.* The exclusion of legitimate costs and benefits will produce implausibly high or low net efficiency benefits. For example, costs of time lost by driving at 55 mph or benefits in the form of the monetary value of human lives may be excluded.

- *Unresponsiveness.* The costs of time and other resources are often based on assumptions that individuals would be willing to pay the average wage rate to engage in a timesaving activity. The average wage rate is typically unresponsive to the price individuals are actually willing to pay. For example, approximately half of drivers are engaged in recreational activities, not commerce or business. The average wage rate, which markedly increases the estimated costs of the 55 mph speed limit, is therefore unresponsive to the perceived costs of driving at 55 mph.

- *Illegality.* In some cases, the legality of a recommendation may be challenged. It is not appropriate to count as costs (or benefits) income earned through illegality, fraud, or unlawful discrimination. In cases involving the comparable worth of jobs held by men, women, and minorities, illegality is a major factor. In the case of the 55 mph speed limit, it is not.

- *Unfeasibility.* Policy recommendations can be challenged on grounds that they are not feasible because of political, budgetary, and administrative constraints. The implementation of the 55 mph speed limit varies across states because of differing capacities for implementing or enforcing speed laws. Implementational capacity is generally greater in states with high population density.

- *Inequity.* Recommendations may be challenged on ethical grounds involving alternative conceptions of social equity and justice. The group that pays a

---

[33] See Duncan MacRae Jr. and James Wilde, *Policy Analysis for Public Decisions* (North Scituate, MA: Duxbury Press, 1979), pp. 133–52; Edward R. Tufte, *Data Analysis for Politics and Policy* (Englewood Cliffs, NJ: Prentice Hall, 1974), pp. 5–18; Charles T. Clotfelter and John C. Hahn, "Assessing the National 55 mph Speed Limit," *Policy Sciences* 9 (1978): 281–94; and Charles A. Lave and Lester B. Lave, "Barriers to Increasing Highway Safety," in *Challenging the Old Order: Toward New Directions in Traffic Safety Theory*, ed. J. Peter Rothe (New Brunswick, NJ: Transaction Books, 1990), pp. 77–94. The author has tested the effects of unemployment and gasoline prices on mileage and fatality rates, explaining over 90 percent of the variance in mileage death rates.

[34] See Grover Starling, *Strategies for Policy Making* (Chicago: Dorsey Press, 1988), pp. 407–10; and Guess and Farnham, *Cases in Public Policy Analysis,* pp. 177–203.

[35] Starling, *Strategies for Policy Making,* pp. 409–11; see also references in footnote 33.

disproportionately high cost in terms of lives lost is younger drivers. The median age of traffic fatalities is approximately twenty-nine years, which means that half of traffic deaths are relatively young persons. The Rawlsian conception of justice of fairness—that is, those worst off should benefit—may be used to challenge policies designed to reduce fatalities through speed laws rather than through educational and driver training programs that specially target young drivers.[36]

- *Inappropriateness.* Recommendations based on estimates of the value of human lives sometimes employ discounted lifetime earnings as a measure of value. Efforts to establish the cost (discounted or undiscounted) of a human life may be challenged on grounds that it is inappropriate to calculate a price for human lives, which are not commodities on an open market.[37]

- *Misformulation.* A standing challenge to recommendations based on cost–benefit analysis is that the problem has been misformulated. In the case of the 55 mph speed limit, saving fuel during the oil crisis of 1970–73 was the original problem for which the National Maximum Speed Law was a recommended solution. The definition of the problem shifted to averting fatalities after the oil crisis passed. The existing formulation of the problem (averting traffic fatalities) may be challenged on grounds that the problem should be formulated as one of saving a nonrenewable resource, mitigating the emission of pollutants, and averting fatalities by a significant increase in taxes on gasoline, which in constant dollars cost less per gallon in 1990 than in 1974.

These threats to the plausibility of policy recommendations do not apply solely to cost–benefit and cost–effectiveness analyses. As all policy recommendations are based on causal as well as ethical premises, these threats to plausibility are relevant to almost any policy that seeks to achieve reforms through the regulation, allocation, or reallocation of resources.[38]

In concluding this chapter, it is important to emphasize that the policy-analytic method of recommendation involves many uncertainties. The most important of these has to do with the role of values and ethics in policy analysis. The purpose of a policy recommendation is not simply to forecast or predict some future outcome but to advocate a course of action whose consequences are also *valuable* to members of a community. Yet, as we have seen, there are severe difficulties in using economic theory and the tools of cost–benefit analysis to justify claims about what is best for society as a whole. For this reason, uncertainties about values are best treated as a matter for reasoned ethical argument and debate and not as technical economic questions.

A second source of uncertainty stems from incomplete knowledge about the effects of policies on valued outcomes. Even if there were total consensus on all important social values, we would still not know with certainty which policies and

---

[36] On this question, see, especially, Rothe, *Challenging the Old Order.*

[37] See the discussion in Guess and Farnham, *Cases in Public Policy Analysis.*

[38] See Dunn, "Policies as Arguments"; and Frank Fischer, *Politics, Values, and Public Policy: The Problem of Methodology* (Boulder, CO: Westview Press, 1980).

programs work best under different conditions. Some of this uncertainty is a result of the poor quality of data available to measure costs and benefits. Many cost–benefit analyses, for example, are based on incomplete information about the range of costs and benefits that must be considered in a reasonably thorough analysis. An even more important source of uncertainty stems from the inaccuracy of measurement procedures and the consequent need to exercise judgment in matters involving the estimation of shadow prices or the selection of an appropriate discount rate.

CHAPTER SUMMARY

In this chapter, we have provided an overview of the nature and role of recommendation in policy analysis, compared and contrasted two major approaches to recommendation, and described specific techniques used in conjunction with these approaches. As we have seen, policy recommendations answer the question: What should be done? For this reason, policy recommendations require an approach that is normative, and not one that is merely empirical or merely evaluative. All policy recommendations involve claims about action, rather than claims that are simply designative (as in forecasting) or simply evaluative (as in evaluation).

Two major approaches to recommendation in policy analysis are cost–benefit analysis and cost–effectiveness analysis. While both approaches seek to measure all costs and benefits to society, only cost–benefit analysis measures costs as well as benefits in dollars as a common unit of value. Costs and benefits are of several types: inside versus outside; tangible versus intangible; primary versus secondary; and real versus pecuniary. In conducting a cost–benefit analysis, it is necessary to complete a series of interrelated tasks: specification of objectives; identification of alternatives; collection, analysis, and interpretation of information; specification of target groups; identification of types of costs and benefits; discounting of costs and benefits; specification of criteria for recommendation; and recommendation itself. The criteria of adequacy most frequently employed in traditional cost–benefit analysis are net benefits and benefit–cost ratios. In contemporary cost–benefit analysis, these criteria are supplemented by redistributional criteria.

LEARNING OBJECTIVES

- distinguish policy recommendation from other policy-analytic methods
- list and describe criteria employed to make reasoned choices among two or more alternatives
- contrast the Pareto criterion, the Kaldor–Hicks criterion, and the Rawls criterion
- compare and contrast comprehensive rationality and disjointed incrementalism as models of choice

- describe six types of rationality
- list and describe the steps in conducting benefit–cost and cost–effectiveness analyses
- discuss the main sources of uncertainty in making recommendations
- list and describe threats to the plausibility of policy recommendations
- use a case study to perform a critical analysis of assumptions and procedures of benefit–cost analysis

KEY TERMS AND CONCEPTS

decision criteria (221)
collective goods (230)
externalities (237)
Kaldor-Hicks criterion (226)
net efficiency benefits (237)
over-advocacy trap (216)
Pareto criterion (226)

present value (256)
public choice (232)
quasi-collective goods (232)
Rawls criterion (227)
redistributional benefits (237)
transitive choice (219)
types of rationality (221)

REVIEW QUESTIONS

1. The late Milton Friedman, Nobel Laureate in economics from the University of Chicago, argued for a *positive* (rather than normative) economics that focuses on the study of the factual premises underlying policy choices.

   "Differences about economic policy among disinterested citizens derive predominantly from different predictions about the economic consequences of taking action—differences that in principle can be eliminated by the progress of positive economics—rather than from fundamental differences in basic values, differences about which men can only fight" [*Essays in Positive Economics* (Chicago: University of Chicago Press, 1953), p. 5].

   Write a short essay that outlines the strengths and weaknesses of this position. In your answer refer to contrasts between descriptive and normative analysis (Chapter 1).

2. "If individuals can order their preferences in a transitive fashion, it should be possible to use majority rule to obtain a collective preference ranking which is also transitive." Do you agree? Disagree? Why?

3. Is rational choice possible? Write an essay on this question. In your answer distinguish different types of rationality.

4. How are different types of rationality related to different criteria for recommendation?

5. Indicate how you would measure the effectiveness of efforts to achieve the following goals:
   Close the gap between municipal revenues and expenditures
   Deter the commission of serious crimes in urban areas
   Enhance the national security of the country
   Improve the quality of life of citizens
   Reduce national unemployment
   Increase the income of poverty families

6. Return to Question 4. Indicate how you would measure the *efficiency* of efforts to achieve these goals.

7. Many economists argue that equality and efficiency are competing objectives. For this reason, the relation between equality and efficiency is one that requires a trade-off where gains in equality must be sacrificed for gains in efficiency, and vice versa [see Arthur M. Okun, *Equality and Efficiency: The Big Trade-Off* (Washington, DC: Brookings Institution, 1975)]. Other economists [see Jaroslav Vanek, *The Participatory Economy* (Ithaca, NY: Cornell University Press, 1970)] and political scientists [see Carole Pateman, *Participation and Democratic Theory* (Cambridge,

MA: Cambridge University Press, 1970)] argue that the "trade-off" between equality and efficiency is a consequence of the limited forms of democratic participation in politics and work. These writers argue that equality and efficiency do not have to be "traded" when politics and economics are fully democratic. What does this controversy imply about the appropriateness of some of the central concepts of modern cost–benefit analysis, including "opportunity costs," "pecuniary" versus "real" costs and benefits, and "net efficiency" versus "redistributional" benefits?

8. Return to Figure 5.2 and consider the following criteria for recommendation:
   a. Maximize effectiveness at least cost [*Note:* Be careful—this is a tricky question].
   b. Maximize effectiveness at a fixed cost of $10,000.
   c. Minimize costs at a fixed-effectiveness level of 4,000 units of service.
   d. Achieve a fixed-effectiveness level of 6,000 units of service at a fixed cost of $20,000.
   e. Assuming that each unit of service has a market price of $10, maximize net benefits.
   f. Again assuming that each unit of service has a market price of $10, maximize the ratio of benefits to costs.

   Indicate which of the two main programs (program I and program II) should be selected under each of these criteria, and describe the conditions under which each criterion may be an adequate measure of the achievement of objectives.

9. The estimation of risk and uncertainty is an essential aspect of making policy recommendations. While it seems obvious that the best way to obtain valid estimates of risk and uncertainty is to use the most highly qualified experts, there is evidence that "people who know the most about various topics are not consistently the best at expressing the likelihood that they are correct" [Baruch Fischoff, "Cost-Benefit Analysis and the Art of Motorcycle Maintenance," *Policy Sciences* 8 (1977): p. 184]. How can a policy analyst resolve this apparent dilemma?

10. Discuss various ways to obtain shadow prices for clean air.

11. Use procedures of value clarification and value critique to analyze value premises that underlie the following claim: "Increased energy production is essential to the continued growth of the economy. The government should therefore make massive investments in research and development on new energy technologies." Treat the first sentence as information (*I*) and the second as the claim (*C*).

12. Calculate the discount factor (DF) at ten years for a 5, 10, and 12 percent discount rate.

13. Calculate the present value (PV) of the following cost and benefit streams (in millions of dollars) for two health programs. Use a discount rate of 6 percent. Which program has the highest present net efficiency benefits? Why?

			Year			
Program	*1990*	*1995*	*2000*	*2005*	*2010*	*Total*
I Costs	$60	$10	$10	$10	$10	$100
Benefits	10	20	30	40	50	150
II Costs	20	20	20	20	20	100
Benefits	10	20	30	40	50	150

DEMONSTRATION EXERCISE

After re-reading Case 1 (*Saving Lives and Saving Time*) and Case 5 (*Saving Time, Lives, and Gasoline: Benefits and Costs of the National Maximum Speed Limit*), prepare a short analysis in which you answer these questions:

- What assumptions govern estimates of the value of time lost driving? Are some assumptions more tenable than others? Why?
- What is the best way to estimate the value of time? Justify your answer.
- What is the best way to estimate the cost of a gallon of gasoline? Justify your answer.
- Driving speeds and miles per gallon estimates may be based on official statistics on highway traffic from the Environmental Protection Agency and the Department of Energy, or on engineering studies of the efficiency of gasoline engines. Which is the more reliable? Why? What are the consequences of using one source rather than another?
- What is the value of a life saved? Why?
- Which policy is preferable, the 55 mph speed limit, or the 65 mph limit that was abandoned in 1974?

REFERENCES

Fischhoff, Baruch, "Cost-Benefit Analysis and the Art of Motorcycle Maintenance," *Policy Sciences* 8, (1977): 177–202.

Gramlich, Edward M., *Benefit-Cost Analysis of Public Programs,* 2d ed. Englewood Cliffs, NJ: Prentice Hall, 1990.

Haveman, Robert H., and Julius Margolis, eds., *Public Expenditure and Policy Analysis,* 3d ed. Boston: Houghton Mifflin, 1988.

Mishan, Edward J., *Cost-Benefit Analysis.* New York: Praeger, 1976.

Whittington, Dalf, and Duncan MacRae Jr. "The Issue of Standing in Cost-Benefit Analysis," *Journal of Policy Analysis and Management* 5 (1986): 665–82.

Case 5. Saving Time, Lives, and Gasoline: Benefits and Costs of the National Maximum Speed Limit [39]

Conducting a benefit–cost analysis is not only a technical matter of economic analysis, but it is also a matter of identifying, and if necessary challenging, the assumptions on which benefit–cost analysis is based. This can be seen most clearly if we examine the case of the National Maximum Speed Limit of 1974.

Table 5.11 describes steps in benefit–cost analysis and comments on the assumptions of these steps. The case shows, among other things, that the final step of calculating benefit–cost ratios and net benefits is very sensitive to these assumptions.

---

[39] From Grover Starling, *Strategies for Policy Making* (Chicago: Dorsey, 1988), pp. 407–10.

Table 5.11   Measuring the Costs and Benefits of the 55 mph Speed Limit: A Critical Appraisal

Steps	Comments
Costs	
1. The major cost of the National Maximum Speed Law (NMSL) was the additional time spent driving as a result of slower speeds. To calculate the number of hours spent driving in 1973, divide the total number of vehicle miles by the average highway speed (65 mph) and then multiply by the average occupancy rate per vehicle. Next, find the number of hours spent driving in 1974 by dividing total vehicle miles by the average highway speed in 1974 (58 mph). The NMSL caused some people to cancel trips and others to find alternative modes of transportation, and as a result, time calculations based on 1974 mileage would be an underestimate. Therefore, we should use 1973 mileage. Using the following formula, where *VM* is vehicle miles, *S* is average speed, *R* is a average occupancy rate, and *H* is the number of hours lost, $$H = \left(\frac{VM_{1973}}{S_{1974}} - \frac{VM_{1973}}{S_{1973}} \right) \times R$$	*Why use 1973 mileage without any adjustment? The average growth rate in travel before 1973 was 4 percent. Therefore, the formula should be* $$H = \left(\frac{1.04\,VM_{1973}}{S_{1974}} - \frac{VM_{1973}}{S_{1973}} \right) \times R$$
The number of hours lost driving in 1974 based on this equation, is estimated to be 1.72 billion.	*Using the above formula, the estimated number of hours lost should be 1.95 billion—not 1.72 billion.*
2. To estimate the value of this time, begin with the average wage rate for all members of the labor force in 1974—$5.05. The value of one hour's travel is not $5.05 per hour because very few persons would pay this sum to avoid an hour of travel. We estimate that the people will pay up to 33 percent of their average hourly wage rate to avoid an hour of commuting. The value of time spent traveling is therefore about $1.68 per hour.	*Why take a percentage of the $5.05 figure based on what commuters would pay to avoid an hour of travel? We should avoid reducing the value of people's time for two reasons. First, the value of time in cost to society is equal to what society will pay for productive use of that time. Time's value is not what a commuter will pay to avoid commuting because commuting has other benefits, such as solitude for thinking or the advantages of suburban living. Second, the value of time spent driving for a trucker is many times the industrial wage rate. Discounting would greatly underestimate the value of commercial drivers.*
3. Application of the cost figure ($1.68) to the time lost figure (1.72 billion hours) results in an estimated travel cost of $2.89 billion.	*Applying the value of one hour's time to the hours lost as calculated above (1.95 billion) results in an estimated travel cost of $9.85 billion.*
4. The NMSL also has some enforcement costs. Total enforcement costs for signs, advertising, and patrolling are about $810,000.	*Total enforcement cost should be about $12 million—not $810,000.*
a. New signs were posted. Cost estimates from twenty-five states for modification of speed limit signs totaled $707,000; for fifty states, this results in an estimated $1.23 million. Spread out over the three-year life of traffic signs, we get an estimate of $410,000.	*OK.*

(continued)

Table 5.11   Measuring the Costs and Benefits of the 55 mph Speed Limit: A Critical Appraisal (*continued*)

Steps	Comments
b. The federal government engaged in an advertising campaign encouraging compliance. The Federal Highway Administration's advertising budget for 1974 was $2 million. About 10 percent of this, or $200,000, was spent to encourage compliance with the NMSL. Assume that an additional amount of public service advertising time was donated, for a total of $400,000.	*Not OK. The Federal Highway Administration does other advertising; not all $2 million should be counted part of NMSL. Public service advertising estimate also seems low.*
c. Compliance costs are difficult to estimate. The cost of highway patrols cannot be used because these persons were patrolling highways before the NMSL. Assume that states did not hire additional personnel solely for enforcement of the NMSL. Therefore, we assume that enforcement of the NMSL will not entail any additional costs above enforcement of previous speed limits.	*Compliance costs pose some problems, but they can be estimated. In 1973, some 5,711,617 traffic citations jumped by 1,713,636 to over 7.4 million. Each additional traffic citation includes an opportunity cost to society. If a law enforcement officer were not issuing traffic tickets, he could be solving other crimes. Assuming that it requires fifteen minutes for a law enforcement officer to issue a speeding ticket, the total cost of law enforcement is $2.9 million. This figure is based on the average cost of placing a law enforcement officer on the streets at $6.75 per hour. This figure is clearly an underestimate because it does not count time lost waiting to catch speeders.*
	Approximately 10 percent of all speeders will demand a court hearing. Estimating an average of thirty minutes for each hearing and an hourly court cost of $45 results in an additional cost to society of $3.8 million for 171,000 cases. Given the overloaded court dockets, this opportunity cost may be even higher.

Benefits

| 1. The most apparent benefit of the NMSL is the amount of gasoline saved. The average gasoline economy improves from 14.9 miles per gallon at 65 miles per hour to 16.1 at .58 miles per hour. Use this information to estimate the number of gallons of gasoline saved by traveling at lower speeds. Gallons saved will be calculated by the following formula $$G = \frac{VM_{1973}}{MPG_{1973}} - \frac{VM_{1973}}{MPG_{1974}}$$ $$= \frac{697 \text{ b } - \text{ gals.}}{14.9 \text{ mgal.}} - \frac{697 \text{ b } - \text{ gals.}}{16.1 \text{ mgal.}}$$ $$= 3.487 \text{ billion gallons}$$ | *Why estimate gasoline saved by comparing 1973 and 1974 miles-per-gallon figures in relation to vehicle miles traveled? The federal figures for average miles per hour are estimates based on several assumptions. Given the conflict between industry estimates, Environmental Protection Agency estimates, and Energy Department estimates, any miles-per-hour estimate must be considered unreliable. The number of vehicle miles traveled is also based on gallons of fuel sold multiplied by average miles per hour. Hence, this figure is also subject to error.* |
| | *Studies of the efficiency of gasoline engines show that the effect of reducing the average speed of free-flow interstate highways would save 2.57 percent of the normal gas used. In 1979, American motorists consumed 106.3 billion gallons of gasoline. Saving 2.57 percent would total 2.73 billion gallons.* |

Table 5.11   Measuring the Costs and Benefits of the 55 mph Speed Limit: A Critical Appraisal (*continued*)

Steps	Comments
In 1974, the average price of gasoline was 52.8 cents per gallon. This market price, however, does not reflect the social cost of gasoline, due to government price controls on domestic oil. The marginal (or replacement) cost of crude oil is the price of foreign oil. Therefore, the price of gasoline must reflect the higher cost of foreign oil. Use the market price of gasoline in the absence of price controls, which is about 71.8 cents per gallon. This figure yields an estimate of $2.50 billion in benefits through gasoline saved.	*Why not use the market price? There is no way to determine whether a marginal gallon of gasoline will be imported or come from domestic reserves. In addition, the costs and benefits of the NMSL should not be distorted simply because the U.S. government does not have a market-oriented energy policy. In 1974, gasoline cost 52.8 cents per gallon, and therefore, a gallon of gasoline saved was worth 52.8 cents.*
2. A major second-order benefit of the 55-miles-per-hour limit was a large drop in traffic fatalities, from 55,087 in 1973 to 46,049 in 1974. Part of the gain must be attributable to reduction in traffic speeds. Studies by the National Safety Council estimate that up to 59 percent of the decline in fatalities was the result of the speed limit. Applying this proportion to the decline in fatalities provides an estimated 5,332 lives saved. The consensus of several studies is that a traffic fatality costs $240,000 in 1974 dollars. Using this figure, the value of lives saved in 1974 is estimated at $1,279.7 million.	*OK.*
3. The NMSL also resulted in a reduction of nonfatal injuries. Use the 59 percent figure found in the fatality studies. Between 1973 and 1974, nonfatal traffic injuries declined by 182,626. Applying the estimated percentages results in 107,749 injuries avoided. Generally, three levels of injuries are indentified: (1) permanent total disability, (2) permanent partial disability and permanent disfigurement, and (3) nonpermanent injury. In 1971, the proportion of traffic injuries that accounted for injuries in each category was .2 percent, 6.5 percent, and 93.3 percent, respectively. The National Highway Traffic Safety Administration estimated that in 1971 the average cost of each type of injury was $260,300, $67,100, and $2,465, respectively. The average injury, therefore, cost $8,745 in 1974 dollars. Applying this figure to our injury estimate results in $942.3 million as the social benefit of injury reduction.	*OK.*

(continued)

Table 5.11 Measuring the Costs and Benefits of the 55 mph Speed Limit: A Critical Appraisal (*continued*)

Steps	Comments
4. The final benefit of the reduction in property damage fell from 25.8 million to 23.1 million. About 50 percent of this reduction was the result of lower speeds. The NMSL saved 1.3 million cases of property damage at an average cost of $363. Therefore, the total benefits from property damage prevented is $472 million.	*OK.*

Conclusion

Our estimates of the costs and benefits of the
NMSL result in the following figures (in millions):

A better estimate would be as follows:

Costs			Costs	
Time spent traveling	$2,890.0		*Time spent traveling*	*$9,848.0*
Enforcement	.8		*Enforcement*	*12.0*
	$2,890.8			*$9,860.0*
Benefits			*Benefits*	
Gasoline saved	$2,500.0		*Gasoline save*	*$1,442.0*
Lives saved	1.297.7		*Lives saved*	*998.0*
Injuries prevented	942.3		*Injuries prevented*	*722.0*
Property damage averted	472.0		*Property damage adverted*	*236.0*
	$5,212.0			*$3,398.0*
Net benefits: $2,321.2 million			*Net benefits: −$6,462 million*	
Benefits to costs ratio: 1.8			*Benefits to costs ratio: .345*	

Source: The steps and data were suggested by Charles T. Clotfelter and John C. Hahn, "Assessing the National 55 m.p.h. Speed Limit," *Policy Sciences* 9 (1978): 281–94. The critical comments are based on Charles A. Lave, "The Costs of Going 55," *Car and Driver.* May 1978, p. 12.

6

Monitoring Observed Policy Outcomes

The consequences of policies are never fully known in advance. For this reason, it is essential to monitor policies after they have been implemented. In this context, policy recommendations may be viewed as hypotheses about the relation between policies and their outcomes: If policy P is taken at time *t,* outcome O will result at time *t* + 1. Usually, there are reasons to believe that policies will work; otherwise they would be blind speculation or pure ideology. Nevertheless, "policy hypotheses" must be tested against subsequent experience.

MONITORING IN POLICY ANALYSIS

Monitoring is the policy-analytic procedure used to produce information about the causes and consequences of policies. Because monitoring helps describe relationships between policy-program operations and their outcomes, it is the primary source of knowledge about the effectiveness of policy implementation.[1] Monitoring is therefore primarily concerned with establishing factual premises about public policy. While factual and value premises are in continuous flux, and "facts" and "values" are interdependent, only monitoring produces factual claims before and after policies have been adopted and implemented, that is, ex post facto. By contrast, forecasting seeks to establish factual premises in advance of action, that is, *ex ante*.

Monitoring plays an essential methodological role in policy analysis. When information about policy actions is transformed through monitoring into information about policy outcomes, we may experience *problem situations*. Problem situations, as we saw in Chapter 3, are external environments that interact with thought, and not external environments themselves. Problem situations described through monitoring are transformed into problems through problem structuring. Information about policy outcomes is also transformed through evaluation into information about policy performance.

Monitoring performs at least four major functions in policy analysis: explanation, accounting, auditing, and compliance.

1. *Compliance*. Monitoring helps determine whether the actions of program administrators, staff, and other stakeholders are in compliance with standards and procedures imposed by legislatures, regulatory agencies, and professional bodies. For example, the Environmental Protection Agency's Continuous Air Monitoring Program (CAMP) produces information about pollution levels that helps determine whether industries are complying with federal air quality standards.

2. *Auditing*. Monitoring helps determine whether resources and services intended for certain target groups and beneficiaries (individuals, families, municipalities, states, regions) have actually reached them. For example, by monitoring federal revenue sharing, we can determine the extent to which funds are reaching local governments.[2]

3. *Accounting*. Monitoring produces information that is helpful in accounting for social and economic changes that follow the implementation of broad sets of public policies and programs over time. For example, changes in the quality of life may be monitored with such social indicators as average education, percentage of the population below the poverty line, and average annual paid vacations.[3]

---

[1] The best general source on implementation is Daniel A. Mazmanian and Paul A. Sabatier, *Implementation and Public Policy,* rev. ed. (Lanham, MD: University Press of America, 1989).

[2] Richard P. Nathan and others, *Monitoring Revenue Sharing* (Washington, DC: Brookings Institution, 1975).

[3] See, for example, Office of Management and the Budget, *Social Indicators, 1973* (Washington, DC: U.S. Government Printing Office, 1974); and U.S. Department of Labor, *State Economic and Social Indicators,* Bulletin 328 (Washington, DC: U.S. Government Printing Office, 1973).

4. *Explanation*. Monitoring also yields information that helps to explain why the outcomes of public policies and programs differ. For example, social experiments in criminal justice, education, and social welfare help us find out what policies and programs work best, how they work, and why.[4]

Sources of Information

To monitor public policies in any given issue area, we require information that is relevant, reliable, and valid. If we want to know about the consequences of programs designed to provide educational opportunity for disadvantaged children, we need information that not only documents problems of achieving educational opportunity in general but information that yields answers about specific factors that policy makers may manipulate to induce greater opportunity. The first type of information is appropriately termed *macronegative,* while the latter is best described as *micropositive*. Information acquired through monitoring must also be reliable, which means that observations should be reasonably precise and dependable. For example, we know that information on crime is unreliable by a factor of about 2:5 to 1; that is, there are some two to three times more crimes actually committed than reported to police.[5] Finally, we also want to know whether information about policy outcomes is actually measuring what we think it is, that is, whether it is valid information. If we are interested in violent crimes, for example, information on crimes in general (which includes auto theft and white-collar crimes) will not be a valid measure of the kinds of policy outcomes in which we are interested.[6]

　　　Information on policy outcomes is regularly collected at various points in time at considerable cost to federal, state, and local governments, private research institutes, and universities. Some of this information is general—for example, information about the social, economic, and demographic characteristics of the population as a whole—and some is more specific because it deals with regions, states, municipalities, and other subpopulations within society. Consider, for example, the following sources of information about policy outcomes published by the U.S. Bureau of the Census, the U.S. Bureau of Labor Statistics, offices and clearinghouses attached to federal agencies and institutes, several nonprofit research centers, and agencies of the European Union and the United Nations.[7]

　　　In addition to these sources federal, state, and municipal agencies produce reports on special programs and projects in education, health, welfare, labor, employment,

---

[4] See Alice Rivlin, *Systematic Thinking for Social Action* (Washington, DC: Brookings Institution, 1971); and George W. Fairweather and Louis G. Tornatzky, *Experimental Methods for Social Policy Research* (Oxford and New York: Pergamon Press, 1977).

[5] See R. H. Beattie, "Criminal Statistics in the United States," *Journal of Criminal Law, Criminology, and Police Science* 51 (May 1960): 49–51.

[6] See Wesley G. Skogan, "The Validity of Official Crime Statistics: An Empirical Investigation," *Social Science Quarterly* 55 (June 1974): 25–38.

[7] For guides to available statistics, see Delbert C. Miller, *Handbook of Research Design and Social Measurement,* 3d ed. (Chicago: David McKay, 1977); "Guide to the U.S. Census and Bureau of Labor Statistics: Data References and Data Archives," pp. 104–23; and "Social Indicators," pp. 267–80.

Historical Statistics of the United States	United States Census of Population by States (www.census.gov)
Statistical Abstract of the United States (www.fedstats.gov)	Congressional District Data Book
County and City Data Book Census Use Study	National Opinion Research Center (NORC) General Social Survey
Social and Economic Characteristics of Students	National Clearinghouse for Mental Health Information
Educational Attainment in the United States	National Clearinghouse for Drug Abuse Information
Current Population Reports	National Criminal Justice Reference Service
The Social and Economic Status of the Black Population in the United States	Child Abuse and Neglect Clearinghouse Project
Female Family Heads Monthly Labor Review	National Clearinghouse on Revenue Sharing
Handbook of Labor Statistics	Social Indicators, 1973
Congressional Quarterly	Social Indicators, 1976
Law Digest	State Economic and Social Indicators
Current Opinion	Statistics of the European Union (www.eurostat.eu)

crime, energy, pollution, foreign affairs, and other areas. Research centers, institutes, and universities also maintain data archives that contain a wide variety of political, social, and economic data, and there is a large stock of books, monographs, articles, and reports written by applied researchers throughout the country. Much of this information can now be accessed through several computerized information retrieval systems, including *United States Political Science Documents,* the *National Technical Information Service,* and the various information clearinghouses and reference services previously listed. When data and other types of information are not available from existing sources, monitoring may be carried out by some combination of questionnaires, interviewing, field observation, and the use of agency records.[8]

Types of Policy Outcomes

In monitoring policy outcomes, we must distinguish between two kinds of consequences: outputs and impacts. *Policy outputs* are the goods, services, or resources received by target groups and beneficiaries. Per capita welfare expenditures and

---

[8] A review of applied research methods is beyond the scope of this book. For reference materials, see Miller, *Handbook of Research Design and Social Measurement;* Clair Selltiz and others, *Research Methods in Social Relations* (New York: Holt, Rinehart and Winston, 1976); and David Nachmias, *Public Policy Evaluation: Approaches and Methods* (New York: St. Martin's Press, 1979).

units of home food service received by the elderly are examples of policy outputs. *Policy impacts,* by contrast, are actual changes in behavior or attitudes that result from policy outputs. For example, while units of home food service (meals) provided to the elderly is an appropriate output indicator, the average daily protein intake of elderly persons is a measure of impact. Similarly, the number of hospital beds per 1,000 persons might be a good indicator of policy output. To monitor policy impact, however, we would have to determine how many members of a particular target group actually use available hospital beds when they are ill.

In monitoring policy outputs and impacts, it is important to recognize that target groups are not necessarily beneficiaries. *Target groups* are individuals, communities, or organizations on whom policies and programs are designed to have an effect, while *beneficiaries* are groups for whom the effects of policies are beneficial or valuable. For example, industrial and manufacturing firms are the targets of federal programs administered by the Occupational Safety and Health Administration (OSHA), but workers and their families are the beneficiaries. At the same time, the strict enforcement of health and safety standards may result in higher production costs and consequent cutbacks in employment. In this case, certain groups (e.g., unskilled and marginally employed workers) may be laid off, so that they are neither target groups nor beneficiaries. Finally, today's target groups and beneficiaries are not necessarily tomorrow's, because future generations are affected in different ways by present-day policies and programs. A good example is the effort to minimize the risk of cancer in adult life by protecting children from harmful chemicals and pollutants.

Types of Policy Actions

To account satisfactorily for variations in policy outputs and impacts, it is necessary to trace them back to prior policy actions. Generally, policy actions have two major purposes: regulation and allocation. *Regulative actions* are those designed to ensure compliance with certain standards or procedures, for example, those of the Environmental Protection Agency or the Federal Aeronautics Administration. By contrast, *allocative actions* are those that require inputs of money, time, personnel and equipment. Regulative and allocative actions may have consequences that are distributive as well as redistributive.[9] The regulation of liquor licenses by state liquor control boards affects the distribution of business opportunities, while the allocation of resources to the Social Security Administration results in the distribution of benefits to retired persons. By contrast, the allocation of resources to federal revenue-sharing programs is designed in part to redistribute revenues from

---

[9] Theodore Lowi categorizes the impacts of public policies as regulatory, distributive, and redistributive. These categories may be treated as attributes of either actions or outcomes, depending on how various stakeholders perceive needs, values, and opportunities (i.e., policy problems) in particular contexts. See Theodore J. Lowi, "American Business, Public Policy Case Studies, and Political Theory," *World Politics* 16 (July 1964): 689–90; and Charles O. Jones, *An Introduction to the Study of Public Policy,* 2d ed. (North Scituate, MA: Duxbury Press, 1977), pp. 223–25. In the scheme used here, all regulative action is also distributive or redistributive, no matter what the intent of the regulative action.

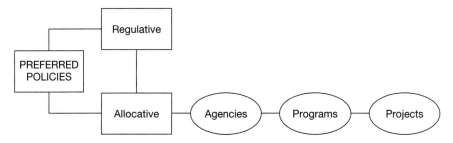

Figure 6.1 Regulative and allocative actions and their implementation through agencies, programs, and projects.

states to municipalities. Note, however, that all regulative actions require resource inputs. For example, federal occupational health and safety regulations require large resource allocations for effective enforcement. Regulative and allocative actions are implemented by federal, state, and municipal agencies in the form of programs and projects (Figure 6.1).

Policy actions may also be further subdivided into policy inputs and policy processes. *Policy inputs* are the resources—time, money, personnel, equipment, supplies—used to produce outputs and impacts. One of the best examples of policy inputs is the program budget, which contains a systematic account of resources allocated for program activities and tasks. By contrast, *policy processes* are the administrative, organizational, and political activities and attitudes that shape the transformation of policy inputs into policy outputs and impacts. For example, conflicts among agency staff and management, dissatisfaction with working conditions, or inflexible decision-making procedures may explain why programs that have the same resource inputs produce lower levels of outputs and impacts. The important point is to distinguish between inputs and processes, on the one hand, and outputs and impacts on the other. To fail to do so is akin to measuring "the number of times a bird flaps its wings without any attempt to determine how far the bird has flown."[10] Types of policy actions and outcomes are illustrated in three policy issue areas (Table 6.1).

Definitions and Indicators

Our success in obtaining, analyzing, and interpreting data on policy outcomes depends on our capacity to construct reliable and valid measures. One way to construct measures is to specify the variables we are interested in monitoring. A *variable* is any characteristic of a person, event, or object that takes on different numerical values, while a *constant* is a characteristic that does not vary. For example, policy-impact variables include educational opportunity, public safety, and air quality. One difficulty with public policy analysis is that frequently we do not have precise definitions of these and other variables. For this reason, it is useful to think about two

---

[10] Edward A. Suchman, *Evaluative Research: Principles and Practice in Public Service and Social Action Programs* (New York: Russell Sage Foundation, 1969), p. 61.

Table 6.1 Types of Policy Actions and Policy Outcomes: Inputs, Processes, Outputs, and Impacts in Three Issue Areas

	Policy Actions	Policy Outcomes		
Issue Area	*Inputs*	*Processes*	*Outputs*	*Impacts*
Criminal justice	Dollar expenditures for salaries, equipment, maintenance	Illegal arrests as percentages of total arrests	Criminals arrested per 100,000 known crimes	Criminals convicted per 100,000 known crimes
Municipal services	Dollar expenditures for sanitation workers and equipment	Morale among workers	Total residences served	Cleanliness of streets
Social welfare	Number of social workers	Rapport with welfare recipients	Welfare cases per social worker	Standard of living of dependent children

kinds of definitions of variables: constitutive and operational definitions. *Constitutive definitions* give meaning to words used to describe variables by using other synonymous words. For example, educational opportunity may be constitutively defined as "the freedom to choose learning environments consistent with one's abilities." Such definitions, while essential, provide us with no concrete rules or guidelines for actually monitoring changes in educational opportunity. In fact, it is impossible to measure educational opportunity directly, because constitutive or "dictionary" definitions provide only the most tenuous links with the "real world" of policy making.

We experience policy actions and outcomes only indirectly, by using operational definitions and indicators of variables. An *operational definition* gives meaning to a variable by specifying the operations required to experience and measure it. For example, we can go much beyond our constitutive definition of educational opportunity by specifying that educational opportunity is "the number of children from families with less than $6,000 annual income who attend colleges and universities, as documented by census data." In this case, our definition is operational because it specifies the operation required to experience and measure educational opportunity. Here we are directed to locate and read those sections of the census on family income and educational levels of children. In so doing, we experience educational opportunity indirectly. With this information in hand, we can proceed to monitor the impact of public policies.

Operational definitions not only specify procedures required to experience and measure something but they also help specify indicators of input, process, output, and impact variables. *Indicators* of variables—for example, average school enrollment, the number of drug addicts, or the amount of sulfur dioxide in the air—are directly observable characteristics that are substituted for indirectly observable or unobservable characteristics. We do not directly observe job satisfaction, quality of life, or economic progress.

There are many alternative indicators that may be used to operationally define the same variable. This creates problems of interpretation. For example, it may be quite difficult to know whether one, several, or all of the following indicators are adequate measures of the impact of crime-control policies: arrests per officer, arrests per known crime, the ratio of false to total arrests, number of crimes cleared, number of convictions, numbers of citizens reporting victimization by criminals, citizens' feelings of personal safety. Because the relationship between variables and indicators is complex, it is often desirable to use multiple indicators of the same action or outcome variable.[11] Sometimes it is possible to construct an *index,* that is, a combination of two or more indicators that together provide a better measure of actions and outcomes than any one indicator does by itself. Among the many types of indexes used in policy analysis are indices of cost of living, pollution, crime severity, energy consumption, health care, administrative centralization, and the quality of life.[12]

APPROACHES TO MONITORING

Monitoring is central to policy analysis. Yet there are so many ways to monitor outputs and impacts that it is sometimes difficult to distinguish monitoring from social research in general. Fortunately, monitoring can be broken down into several identifiable approaches: social systems accounting, social experimentation, social auditing, and research and practice synthesis. These approaches may be contrasted in terms of two major properties (Table 6.2):

1. *Types of controls.* Approaches to monitoring differ in terms of the ways they exercise control over variations in policy actions. Only one of the approaches (social experimentation) involves direct controls over policy inputs and policy processes. The other three approaches "control" inputs and processes by determining after the fact how much of an observed variation in outcomes is due to inputs and processes, as compared to extraneous factors that are not directly connected with policy actions.

2. *Types of information required.* Approaches to monitoring differ according to their respective information requirements. Some approaches (social experimentation and social auditing) require the collection of new information. Social systems accounting may or may not require new information, while research and practice synthesis relies exclusively on available information.

[11] The general case for multiple indicators may be found in Eugene Webb and others, *Unobtrusive Measures: Nonreactive Research in the Behavioral Sciences* (Chicago: Rand McNally, 1966). For applications to criminal justice and other areas, see Roger B. Parks, "Complementary Measures of Police Performance," in *Public Policy Evaluation,* ed. Kenneth M. Dolbeare (Beverly Hills, CA: Sage Publications, 1975), pp. 185–218.

[12] On various kinds of indices, see references in Miller, *Handbook of Research Design and Social Measurement,* pp. 207–460; James L. Price, *Handbook of Organizational Measurement* (Lexington, MA: D. C. Heath and Company, 1972); Dale G. Lake and others, *Measuring Human Behavior* (New York: Columbia University Teachers College Press, 1973); Paul N. Cheremisinoff, ed., *Industrial Pollution Control: Measurement and Instrumentation* (Westport, CT: Technomic Press, 1976); Leo G. Reader and others, *Handbook of Scales and Indices of Health Behavior* (Pacific Palisades, CA: Goodyear Publishing, 1976); Lou E. Davis and Albert B. Cherns, *The Quality of Working Life,* vol. I (New York: Free Press, 1975); and Albert D. Biderman and Thomas F. Drury, eds., *Measuring Work Quality for Social Reporting* (New York: Wiley, 1976).

Table 6.2 Main Contrasts among Four Approaches to Monitoring

Approach	Types of Control	Type of Information Required
Social systems accounting	Quantitative	Available and/or new information and New information
Social experimentation	Direct manipulations quantitative	
Social auditing	Quantitative and/or qualitative	New information
Research and practice synthesis	Quantitative and/or qualitative	Available information

Each of these four approaches also has certain common features. First, each is concerned with monitoring *policy-relevant outcomes*. Therefore, each approach deals with variables that are relevant to policy makers because they are indicators of policy outputs and/or impacts. Some policy-relevant variables can be manipulated by policy makers (e.g., resource inputs or new processes for delivering services), while others cannot. These nonmanipulable variables include preconditions, which are present before actions are taken (e.g., the average age or the cultural values of a target group), as well as unforeseen events that occur in the course of policy implementation (e.g., sudden staff turnover, strikes, or natural disasters).

A second common feature of these approaches is that they are *goal-focused*. This means that policy outcomes are monitored because they are believed to enhance the satisfaction of some need, value, or opportunity—that is, outcomes are seen as ways to resolve a policy problem. At the same time, some policy outcomes are monitored because they may inhibit the satisfaction of some need, value, or opportunity.[13] Note also that nonmanipulable variables, that is, policy preconditions and unforeseen events, are also goal-focused to the extent that they are known to affect policy outcomes.

A third feature common to these approaches is that they are *change-oriented*. Each approach seeks to monitor change, by analyzing changes in outcomes over time; by comparing such changes across two or more programs, projects, or localities; or by using some combination of the two. While some approaches (social systems accounting) are oriented toward macrolevel changes in societies, states, regions, and communities, other approaches (social auditing and social experimentation) are primarily oriented toward microlevel changes in programs and projects.

A fourth common feature of these approaches is that they permit the *cross-classification* of outputs and impacts by other variables, including variables used to monitor policy inputs and policy processes.[14] For example, such outputs as per

---

[13] There is also the special case in which outputs and impacts are neither enhancing nor inhibiting, but neutral. In this context, one of the objections to an exclusive concern with social indicators that have "direct normative interest" is that what is relevant to today's goals may not be so in later years. See Eleanor B. Sheldon and Howard E. Freeman, "Notes on Social Indicators: Promises and Potential," *Policy Sciences* 1 (April 1970): 97–98. Note that if a goal-focused outcome is defined in terms of its potential effect on a policy problem—and if policy problems are artificial, dynamic, and interdependent (see Chapter 3)—then all outcomes, including "neutral" ones, may someday be of direct normative interest.

[14] Ibid., p. 97.

pupil educational expenditures may be cross-classified with input variables (e.g., teachers' salaries) and those intended to measure processes (e.g., class sizes). Outputs and impacts may also be cross-classified by types of preconditions (e.g., the average income of community residents) and unforeseen events (e.g., frequency of strikes).

Finally, each approach is concerned with *objective as well as subjective* measures of policy actions and outcomes. For example, all approaches provide measures of such objective outcomes as units of health care received as well as such subjective outcomes as satisfaction with medical and health services. Objective indicators are frequently based on available data (e.g., census materials), while subjective ones are based on new data acquired through sample surveys or field studies. In some instances, objective and subjective measures are based both on available and new information. For example, past studies may be repeated (replicated) to obtain new information that may then be compared with old information in an effort to monitor the direction and pace of social change.[15]

Each of these common features contributes to a general definition of monitoring as the process of obtaining policy-relevant information to measure changes in goal-focused social conditions, both objective and subjective among various target groups and beneficiaries.[16] Social conditions include policy actions and outcomes as well as policy preconditions and unforeseen events that affect actions and outcomes in the course of implementation. Impacts may be immediate (first-order impacts) or secondary (second-, third-, and *n*th-order impacts), as when policy actions produce "side effects" and "spillovers" beyond their intended effects. Side effects and spillovers may enhance or inhibit the satisfaction of needs, values, and opportunities. Elements of this general definition of monitoring are diagrammed in Figure 6.2, which represents a general framework for monitoring in policy analysis.

Social Systems Accounting

With this general framework in mind, we can proceed to contrast the four approaches to monitoring. *Social systems accounting* is an approach and set of methods that permit analysts to monitor changes in objective and subjective social conditions over time.[17] The term *social systems accounting* comes from a report published by the National Commission on Technology, Automation, and Economic Progress, a body

---

[15] This combination of old and new information is called *replication of baseline studies*. See Otis Dudley Duncan, *Toward Social Reporting: Next Steps* (New York: Russell Sage Foundation, 1969).

[16] Compare the definition of social indicators offered by Kenneth C. Land, "Theories, Models, and Indicators of Social Change," *International Social Science Journal* 25, no. 1 (1975): 14.

[17] Much of the following account is based on Kenneth C. Land and Seymour Spilerman, eds., *Social Indicator Models* (New York: Russell Sage Foundation, 1974); and Land, "Theories, Models, and Indicators of Social Change," pp. 7–20.

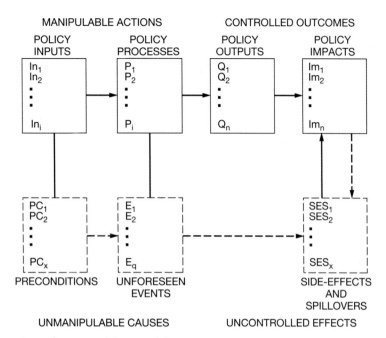

Figure 6.2 General framework for monitoring.

Note: The solid lines indicate effects on manipulable actions and controlled outcomes. The broken lines indicate unforeseen events, side effects and spillovers. Side effects and spillovers are uncontrollable secondary impacts that may enhance or inhibit the satisfaction of needs, values, and opportunities.

established in 1964 to examine the social consequences of technological development and economic growth. The commission's report recommended that the federal government establish a "system of social accounts" that would serve as a counterpart to national economic accounts.[18] Several years earlier, a project undertaken by the American Academy of Arts and Sciences for the National Aeronautics and Space Administration explored the second-order impacts of the space program. One result of this project was the development of methods for monitoring social and political, as well as economic trends, and a major book was published in 1966 under the title *Social Indicators*.[19] While these efforts to develop social systems accounting occurred in the 1960s, they actually represent a continuation of work begun in 1933 under the auspices of the President's Research Committee on Social Trends. Under the direction

[18] National Commission on Technology, Automation, and Economic Progress, *Technology and the American Economy* (Washington, DC: U.S. Government Printing Office, 1966). A primary influence on the Commission's recommendations was Daniel Bell, whose major work (*Toward Post-Industrial Society: A Venture in Social Forecasting*) was described in Case Study 2.

[19] Raymond A. Bauer, ed., *Social Indicators* (Cambridge, MA: MIT Press, 1966). Chapter 3, by Bertram M. Gross, is titled "The State of the Nation: Social Systems Accounting."

of sociologist William F. Ogburn, the Committee produced a two-volume report, *Recent Social Trends,* before its work was abandoned during the depression.[20]

Work on social systems accounting continued throughout the 1960s and 1970s. Some of the major products of this period were produced by social scientists interested in objective and subjective indicators of social change.[21] Other major initiatives came from federal agencies, including the Department of Health, Education, and Welfare, the Office of Management and the Budget, and the Department of Labor.[22] In addition, several international organizations (the United Nations and the Organization for Economic Cooperation and Development) have undertaken work on social indicators, as have the governments of France, the United Kingdom, West Germany, Canada, Norway, Sweden, and Japan.[23]

The major analytic element of social systems accounting is the *social indicator.* While there are various definitions of this term, the most useful is that which defines social indicators as "statistics which measure social conditions and changes therein over time for various segments of a population. By social conditions, we mean both the external (social and physical) and the internal (subjective and perceptional) contexts of human existence in a given society."[24] Social indicators, as has been suggested, are both objective and subjective, because they help monitor such objective conditions as urbanization, as well as such subjective conditions as satisfaction with municipal services. Social indicators are used to monitor change at the national, as well as state and municipal levels.[25] Social indicators are also

---

[20] President's Research Committee on Social Trends, *Recent Social Trends* (New York: McGraw-Hill, 1933). Ogburn's major work was *Social Change: With Respect to Culture and Original Nature* (New York: B. W. Huebsch, 1922).

[21] Two companion volumes were devoted, respectively, to objective and subjective dimensions of social change. See Eleanor B. Sheldon and Wilbert E. Moore, eds., *Indicators of Social Change: Concepts and Measurements* (New York: Russell Sage Foundation, 1968); and Angus Campbell and Philip E. Converse, eds., *The Human Meaning of Social Change* (New York: Russell Sage Foundation, 1972). For a recent review, see "America in the Seventies: Some Social Indicators," *Annals of the American Academy of Political and Social Science* 435 (January 1978).

[22] Relevant publications are U.S. Department of Health, Education, and Welfare, *Toward a Social Report* (Washington, DC: U.S. Government Printing Office, 1969); Executive Office of the President, Office of Management and Budget, *Social Indicators, 1973* (Washington, DC: U.S. Government Printing Office, 1974); and U.S. Department of Labor, *State Economic and Social Indicators* (Washington, DC: U.S. Government Printing Office, 1973). In 1974 the National Science Foundation funded a Center for the Coordination of Research on Social Indicators, administered under the Social Science Research Council. The Center publishes *Social Indicators Newsletter.*

[23] For a comprehensive annotated bibliography, see Leslie D. Wilcox and others, *Social Indicators and Societal Monitoring: An Annotated Bibliography* (New York: American Elsevier Publishing, 1974). The major international journal is *Social Indicators Research: An International and Interdisciplinary Journal for Quality of Life Measurement*, published since 1974.

[24] Land, "Theories, Models, and Indicators of Social Change," p. 15.

[25] On social indicators at the community level, see Terry N. Clark, "Community Social Indicators: From Analytical Models to Policy Applications," *Urban Affairs Quarterly* 9, no. 1 (September 1973): 3–36. On urban social indicators, see M. J. Flax, *A Study in Comparative Urban Indicators: Conditions in 18 Large Metropolitan Areas* (Washington, DC: Urban Institute, 1972).

Table 6.3   Some Representative Social Indicators

Area	Indicator
Health and illness	Persons in state mental hospitals[1]
Public safety	Persons afraid to walk alone at night[2]
Education	High school graduates aged 25 and older[1]
Employment	Labor force participation rate for women[1]
Income	Percent of population below poverty line[1]
Housing	Households living in substandard units[2]
Leisure and recreation	Average annual paid vacation in manufacturing[1]
Population	Actual and projected population[2]
Government and politics	Quality of public administration[3]
Social values and attitudes	Overall life satisfaction and alienation[4]
Social mobility	Change from father's occupation[1]
Physical environment	Air pollution index[5]
Science and technology	Scientific discoveries[6]

Sources:

[1] U.S. Department of Health, Education and Welfare, *Toward a Social Report* (Ann Arbor: University of Michigan Press, 1970).

[2] Office of Management and Budget, *Social Indicators, 1973* (Washington, DC: U.S. Government Printing Office, 1974).

[3] U.S. Department of Labor, *State Economic and Social Indicators* (Washington, DC: U.S. Government Printing Office, 1973).

[4] Angus Campbell, Philip Converse, and Willard Rodgers, *The Quality of American Life* (New York: Russell Sage Foundation, 1976).

[5] Otis Dudley Duncan, *Toward Social Reporting: The Next Steps* (New York: Russell Sage Foundation, 1969).

[6] National Science Board, *Science and Engineering Indicators* (Washington, DC) (Biennial). National Science Foundation.

available to monitor special aspects of social change such as pollution, health care, and the quality of working life.[26]

A list of representative social indicators is presented in Table 6.3. These representative indicators, drawn from several major sources, are grouped by area. Note, first, that many indicators are designed to monitor objective social states, for example, persons in state mental hospitals. Other indicators depend on subjective responses, for example, persons afraid to walk alone at night. Second, most indicators are expressed in units of time and are cross-classified by various segments of the population, for example, persons afraid to walk alone at night are arranged in a time series from 1965 to 1972 and cross-classified by race, age, education, and income. Third, some indicators are expressed in terms of present experience, while others are stated as future goals. For example, average annual

---

[26] See footnote 12. The most complete source on policy-relevant social indicators is Duncan MacRae Jr., *Policy Indicators* (Chapel Hill: University of North Carolina Press, 1985).

paid vacation in manufacturing is expressed in terms of the 1967 value (two weeks) and a 1976–79 goal (four weeks). Finally, many indicators are related to outputs and impacts of public policies. For example, the labor force participation rate for women aged thirty-five to sixty-four may be taken as an indicator of impacts of equal employment opportunity-affirmative action policies, while indices of air pollution may be used to monitor the impact of programs implemented by the Environmental Protection Agency. In short, most social indicators are policy-relevant, goal-focused, change-oriented, cross-classified, and expressive of objective and subjective social conditions.

In using social indicators for purposes of monitoring, it is frequently necessary to make assumptions about the reasons for change in a social indicator. For example, if reported crime is used to monitor the output of crime control policies, official statistics from the Federal Bureau of Investigation (*Uniform Crime Reports*) indicate that reported crimes per 100,000 inhabitants declined by three-tenths of 1 percent between 1975 and 1976 but increased by 76.2 percent between 1967 and 1976. To attribute the decrease or increase to criminal justice policies, it is necessary to make the assumption that changes in crime are a consequence of policy actions undertaken by federal, state, and local law enforcement authorities. This assumption is highly questionable, even when we have accurate data on resource inputs (expenditures for personnel and equipment), because we ignore uncontrollable factors (a more youthful population following the postwar "baby boom") as well as the processes used to transform inputs into outputs. In effect, we are forced to treat the relation between inputs and outputs as a kind of "black box," that is, an unknown area that symbolizes what we don't know (and therefore must assume) about the relation between inputs into outputs.

The use of social indicators has several advantages. First, efforts to develop indicators appropriate for monitoring policy outcomes may alert us to areas where there is insufficient information. For example, while there is much information about municipal services, much of this information deals with outputs, that is, the number and types of services provided per capita. Information about the impacts of municipal service policies on citizens—for example, impacts measured in terms of satisfaction with transportation, sanitation, and recreational facilities—is inadequate in most cases.[27] Second, when social indicators provide reliable information about the impacts of policies on target groups, it becomes possible to modify policies and programs. Social indicators also provide information that helps structure policy problems and modify existing policy alternatives. We may find, for example, that the number of high school graduates aged twenty-five and over has increased, but that the social mobility of the educated population has not changed. In this case, we may wish to restructure the problem of social inequality

---

[27] See, for example, the Urban Institute, *Measuring the Effectiveness of Basic Municipal Services* (Washington, DC: Urban Institute, 1974).

in a way that places less emphasis on educational opportunity as a vehicle for social mobility.[28]

Social indicators also have various limitations. The choice of certain indicators (e.g., percent of households below the poverty line) reflects particular social values rather than others and may convey the political biases of analysts.[29] Given that policy problems are themselves artificial and subjective, it is doubtful that any social indicator can be totally free of the values of those who develop and apply it for purposes of monitoring. Second, social indicators may not be directly useful to policy makers faced with practical choices. One study of federal policy makers, for example, finds that social indicators are not seen as having great instrumental value.[30] Hence, while social indicators may help to conceptualize or structure problems, they are often so general that they cannot be used to find specific solutions for particular problems.

Second, most social indicators are based on available data about objective social conditions. While it is easier to use available data on objective conditions than it is to collect new information about subjective conditions, it may be just as important to monitor subjective conditions as it is to monitor objective ones.[31] For example, reported crimes per 100,000 inhabitants may decrease, yet citizens' sense of personal insecurity may remain the same or even increase. Similarly, the number of poverty families may decrease without any appreciable change in perceptions of the quality of life.

Finally, social indicators provide little information about the various ways that policy inputs are transformed into policy outcomes. Claims about variations in policy outputs and impacts are based on observed correlations between policy inputs and outcomes, rather than on knowledge about the processes by which resource inputs are transformed into outputs and impacts. Policy inputs are measured, policy outputs are measured, and the two are related by establishing the degree of their association. Concurrently, efforts are made to determine whether preconditions and unforeseen events—that is, factors apart from the original policy inputs—enhance or inhibit the production of some output. Yet the process of accounting for these nonpolicy effects takes place after policy outputs have been produced and is based on the use of statistical controls, that is, techniques that permit analysts to observe the effects of inputs on outputs under carefully specified conditions. For example, the effects of educational expenditures on school achievement will be analyzed for poor and middle-class families separately.

---

[28] See Christopher Jencks and others, *Inequality: A Reassessment of the Effect of Family and Schooling in America* (New York: Basic Books, 1972).

[29] Thomas R. Dye, *Understanding Public Policy*, 3d ed. (Englewood Cliffs, NJ: Prentice Hall, 1978), pp. 324–25.

[30] Nathan Caplan and others, *The Use of Social Science Information by Policy-Makers at the Federal Level* (Ann Arbor: Institute for Social Research. Center for Research on the Utilization of Scientific Knowledge, University of Michigan, 1975).

[31] Vijai P. Singh, "Indicators and Quality of Life: Some Theoretical and Methodological Issues," paper presented at the Annual Meeting, American Sociological Association, August 25–29, 1975.

Social Experimentation

One of the consequences of using social indicators is that it may take a very large number of successes and failures to find out what works best and why. Such an approach has been called random innovation and contrasted with systematic experimentation.[32] *Random innovation* is the process of executing a large number of alternative policies and programs whose inputs are neither standardized nor systematically manipulated. Because there is no direct control over policy actions, the outcomes of policies cannot easily be traced back to known sources. By contrast, *social experimentation* is the process of systematically manipulating policy actions in a way that permits more or less precise answers to questions about the sources of change in policy outcomes. Social experimentation, of which there are many varieties—for example, laboratory experimentation, field experimentation, quasi-experimentation—is advocated as a way to find solutions for social problems by deliberately maximizing the differences between types of policy actions in a small and carefully selected group of programs and assessing their consequences prior to making large-scale investments in untested programs.[33]

Social experimentation is based on adaptations of procedures used in classical laboratory experiments in the physical sciences:[34]

- *Direct control over experimental treatments (stimuli).* Analysts who use social experimentation directly control experimental treatments (policy actions) and attempt to maximize differences among them in order to produce effects that differ as much as possible.

- *Comparison (control) groups.* Two or more groups are used in social experiments. One group (called the experimental group) receives the experimental treatment, while other groups (called control groups) receive no treatment or a significantly different treatment than that received by the experimental group.

- *Random assignment.* Potential sources of variation in policy outcomes other than those produced by the experimental treatment are eliminated by randomly selecting members of the policy experiment, by randomly dividing them into experimental and control groups, and by randomly assigning the "treatment" (policy or program) to these groups. Random assignment minimizes biases in the selection of members and groups who may respond differently to the experimental treatment. For example, children from

---

[32] Rivlin, *Systematic Thinking for Social Action*; and Rivlin, "How Can Experiments Be More Useful?" *American Economic Review* 64 (1974): 346–54.

[33] See, for example, Fairweather and Tornatzky, *Experimental Methods for Social Policy Research.*

[34] See Donald T. Campbell and Julian C. Stanley, *Experimental and Quasi-experimental Designs for Research* (Chicago: Rand McNally, 1966); and Campbell, "Reforms as Experiments," in *Handbook of Evaluation Research*, vol. 1, ed. Elmer I., Struening and Marcia Guttentag (Beverly Hills, CA: Sage Publications, 1965), pp. 71–100.

middle-class families may respond to a special education program in a more positive way than children from poor families. This would mean that factors other than the program itself are responsible for such outputs as higher reading scores. These selection biases are reduced or eliminated through randomization.

Social experiments and quasi-experiments have been advocated as a way to monitor the outcomes of public policy since the New Deal years of the 1930s.[35] In the post-World War II period, social experiments have been conducted in many areas of public policy: public health, compensatory education, welfare, criminal justice, drug and alcohol abuse, population control, nutrition, highway safety, and housing.[36] One of the best known social experiments is the New Jersey–Pennsylvania Graduated Work Incentives Experiment, funded by the Office of Economic Opportunity to answer questions surrounding the reform of the social welfare system in the 1960s. A random sample of able-bodied men aged fifteen to fifty-eight from low-income families was selected from three sites in New Jersey (Trenton, Paterson–Passaic, and Jersey City) and one in Pennsylvania (Scranton). In each city, some families received various levels of guaranteed income and tax breaks, while others received none. Altogether, some 1,350 families participated in the experiment.

Critics of welfare reform expected that income supplements and tax breaks (called a negative income tax) would induce men from low-income families to work less. This expectation was not substantiated by the original experiment, which indicated that the experimental (income maintenance) and control (no income maintenance) groups did not differ significantly in their employment behavior, as reflected by changes in earnings before and after the experiment. In fact, the earnings of the experimental groups showed a slightly higher increase than those of the control group.

Social experimentation has the potential of showing in precise terms whether certain policy actions (e.g., the provision of income maintenance) result in certain outcomes (e.g., family earnings). The capacity of experiments and quasi-experiments to produce valid causal inferences about the effects of actions on outcomes is called *internal validity*. The greater the internal validity, the more confidence we have that policy outputs are a consequence of policy inputs. Threats to validity are special conditions of persons, policies, or contexts, or methodological features of the experiment itself, that compromise or diminish the validity of claims about policy outcomes. In fact, procedures for social experimentation are a way to reduce threats

---

[35] A. Stephen "Prospects and Possibilities: The New Deal and New Social Research," *Social Forces* 13 (1935): 515–21. See Robert S. Weiss and Martin Rein, "The Evaluation of Broad-Aim Programs: A Cautionary Case and a Moral," in *Readings in Evaluation Research*, ed. Francis G. Caro (New York: Russell Sage Foundation, 1971), pp. 37–42.

[36] See Carl A. Bennett and Arthur A. Lumsdaine, eds., *Evaluation and Experiment* (New York: Academic Press, 1975); and Fairweather and Tornatzky, *Experimental Methods for Social Policy Research*.

to the internal validity of claims about policy outcomes.[37] Among these threats to internal validity, the most important are the following:

1. *History.* A number of unforeseen events can occur between the time a policy is implemented and the point at which outcomes are measured. For example, public disturbances, strikes, or sudden shifts in public opinion may represent a plausible rival explanation of the causes of variations in policy outcomes.

2. *Maturation.* Changes within members of groups, whether these be individuals, families, or larger social units, may exert an independent effect on policy outcomes. For example, with the passage of time, individual attitudes may change, learning may occur, or geographical units may grow or decline. Such maturation may make it difficult to explain policy outcomes.

3. *Instability.* Fluctuations in a time series may produce unstable variations in outcomes that are a consequence of random error or procedures for obtaining information and not a result of policy actions. Because most time series are unstable, causal inferences about the effects of actions on outcomes are often problematic.

4. *Testing.* The very fact of conducting an experiment and measuring outcomes may sensitize members of experimental and control groups to the aims and expectations of the experiment. When this occurs, policy outcomes may be a result of the meaning attributed to policy actions by participants, and not the actions (e.g., income guarantees) themselves.[38]

5. *Instrumentation.* Changes is the system or procedures for measuring an outcome, rather than variations in the outcome itself, may be the reason for the success (or failure) of a policy.

6. *Mortality.* Some of the experimental or control groups, or their members, may drop out of the experiment before it is completed. This makes it more difficult to make causal inferences. For example, in the New Jersey–Pennsylvania experiment some families broke up before the experiment was over.

7. *Selection.* In many situations random sampling is not possible, thus requiring a quasi-experimental design that does not fully eliminate biases in selecting respondents. For example, if one group of children in a quasi-experimental program designed to improve reading skills is drawn primarily from upper-class families where regular reading is more prevalent, the difference between reading scores before and after the program will be less pronounced than with

---

[37] For a fuller discussion of threats to internal validity, see Campbell and Stanley, *Experimental and Quasi-experimental Designs for Research*, pp. 5–6.

[38] The effects of interpretation and testing are sometimes known as the "Hawthorne effect," named after a series of experiments conducted in the Western Electric Company's Hawthorne Plant in Chicago, Illinois in 1927–31. The output of workers increased after working conditions and other factors (inputs) were changed. Later, output continued to increase even after working conditions (rest pauses, lighting, and so on) were changed back to their original state, largely because the experiment itself provided opportunities for workers' participation. See Paul Blumberg, *Industrial Democracy: The Sociology of Participation* (London: Constable, 1968).

those of children drawn from lower-class families. This may make the program look less effective than it really is and, in some cases, can even make the experiment look harmful.[39]

8. *Regression artifacts.* When members of experimental and control groups are selected on the basis of extreme characteristics (e.g., poor children selected for an experimental reading program may be high achievers), artificial changes in reading scores may occur as a result of what is known as *regression toward the mean.* Regression toward the mean is the statistical phenomenon where extreme values of some characteristic of a population automatically regress toward or "go back to" the average of the population as a whole. For example, the height of children of very tall or very short parents tends to regress toward the arithmetic mean of all parents. Children of very tall and very short parents tend, respectively, to be shorter and taller than their fathers and mothers.

There are many ways to increase the internal validity of social experiments and quasi-experiments by carefully designing research. Generally, such research involves random selection, repeated measures of outcome variables over time, and measurement of the preprogram outcome measures for some of the experimental and control groups but not others. The latter procedure eliminates the possibility of testing effects for some groups, whose outcome measures after the program can be compared with those of equivalent groups whose outcomes have been measured both before and after receiving inputs.[40]

Social experimentation is weakest in the area of *external validity,* which refers to the generalizability of causal inferences outside the particular setting in which an experiment is conducted. Important threats to the external validity of claims about policy outputs are similar to those that threaten internal validity, including interpretation, testing, and selection. In addition, other threats are important to the generalizability of claims. The most important of these is artificiality. Conditions under which a social experiment is carried out may be atypical or unrepresentative of conditions elsewhere. For example, conditions in New Jersey and Pennsylvania are different from those present in San Francisco, Seattle, and Anchorage, making generalizations problematic.

Social experimentation is frequently unsuccessful in monitoring policy processes, including patterns of interaction among staff and clients and their changing attitudes and values. Many of the most important policies and programs are so complex that social experimentation results in the oversimplification of policy processes. For example, social experimentation is not well suited to broad-aim programs that involve high levels of conflict among stakeholders, or contexts where

---

[39] See Donald T. Campbell and A. E. Erlebacher, "How Regression Artifacts in Quasi-experimental Evaluations Can Mistakenly Make Compensatory Education Look Harmful," in *Compensatory Education: A National Debate,* vol. III, ed. J. Hellmuth (New York: Brunner-Mazel, 1970), pp. 185–225.

[40] The design described here is the "Solomon 4-group design." The best overview of alternative research designs and their role in reducing threats to internal validity is Fred N. Kerlinger, *Foundations of Behavioral Research,* 2d ed. (New York: Holt, Rinehart and Winston, 1973), pp. 300–77.

the same inputs of personnel, resources, and equipment are perceived in altogether different ways by different groups.[41] For these and other reasons, various qualitative methods for obtaining the subjective judgments of stakeholders have been used to uncover otherwise neglected aspects of policy processes. These methods—which range from participant observation and the use of logs or diaries to group sessions that resemble a policy Delphi—may be viewed as a way to complement or replace social experimentation.[42]

Social Auditing

One of the limitations of social systems accounting and social experimentation—namely, that both approaches neglect or oversimplify policy processes—is partly overcome in social auditing. *Social auditing* explicitly monitors relations among inputs, processes, outputs, and impacts in an effort to trace policy inputs "from the point at which they are disbursed to the point at which they are experienced by the ultimate intended recipient of those resources."[43] Social auditing, which has been used in areas of educational and youth policy by analysts at the Rand Corporation and the National Institute of Education, helps determine whether policy outcomes are a consequence of inadequate policy inputs or a result of processes that divert resources or services from intended target groups and beneficiaries.

The essential differences between social auditing and other approaches to monitoring are most easily seen if we compare social auditing with social systems accounting and social experimentation. Variations of the latter approaches have been used to monitor educational policies in two important studies, *Equality of Educational Opportunity* and the Westinghouse Learning Corporation's evaluation of the Head Start program.[44] In the former case, a variation of social systems accounting, the effectiveness of various levels of school resources was monitored by measuring the relation between resource inputs (teachers, textbooks, school facilities) and outcomes, measured in terms of the achievement levels of students. In the Head Start study, which had several characteristics of a social experiment, the relations between special reading and skill-development activities (inputs) and

---

[41] See Robert S. Weiss and Martin Rein, "The Evaluation of Broad-Aim Programs: A Cautionary Case and a Moral," in *Readings in Evaluation Research*, ed. Caro, pp. 287–96; and Ward Edwards, Marcia Guttentag, and Kurt Snapper, "A Decision-Theoretic Approach to Evaluation Research," in *Handbook of Evaluation Research*, vol. 1, ed. Stuening and Guttentag, pp. 139–82.

[42] See M. G. Trend, "On the Reconciliation of Qualitative and Quantitative Analysis: A Case Study," *Human Organization* 37, no. 4 (1978): 345–54; and M. Q. Patton, *Alternative Evaluation Research Paradigm* (Grand Forks: University of North Dakota Study Group on Evaluation, 1976).

[43] James S. Coleman, *Policy Research in the Social Sciences* (Morristown, NJ: General Learning Press, 1972), p. 18. See also Michael Q. Patton, *Utilization-Focused Evaluation* (Beverly Hills, CA: Sage Publications, 1978).

[44] See James S. Coleman and others, *Equality of Educational Opportunity* (Washington, DC: U.S. Government Printing Office, 1966): and Victor Cicarelli and others, *The Impact of Head Start: An Evaluation of the Effects of Head Start on Children's Cognitive and Affective Development* (Washington, DC: U.S. Government Printing Office, 1969).

cognitive and affective skills (outputs) of children exposed to the program were studied in a number of cities. The essential feature of these two approaches is that

> the policy inputs are measured, policy outcomes are measured, and the two are related (with, of course, the use of experimental or statistical controls to neutralize the effect of situational variables). Whatever institutional structure intervenes is taken in effect as a black box into which the input resources go and out of which the desired outcomes and side effects come. In the first research mentioned above [*Equality of Educational Opportunity*], the school was the black box. Inputs to it were teacher salaries, pupil-teacher ratio, age of textbooks, size of library, and a variety of other traditional measures of school resources. Outputs studied were achievement of students in verbal and mathematical skills. In the second study, the resource inputs were the additional resources provided by Head Start; the outputs were cognitive and affective measures on the children.[45]

In monitoring policy processes, social auditing provides important information about what goes on inside the "black box." The processes monitored in a social audit are of two main types: resource diversion and transformation.[46] In *resource diversion,* original inputs are diverted from intended target groups and beneficiaries as a result of the passage of resources through the administrative system. For example, the total expenditures for two manpower training programs may be equal, yet one program may expend a higher percentage of funds on salaries and other personnel costs, thus resulting in fewer staff members per dollar and a diversion of services from beneficiaries. Far more important is the process of *resource transformation.* Here resources and their actual receipt by target groups may be identical, yet the *meaning* of these resources to program staff and target groups may be altogether different. If the meaning of resources is in fact different, then resources may have been transformed in such a way as to enhance (or retard) their impact on beneficiaries. For this reason, quantitative methods may be supplemented by *qualitative methods* designed to provide information about the subjective interpretations of policy actions by stakeholders who affect and are affected by the implementation of policies.[47]

A good example of the supplementary use of qualitative methods to monitor policy processes is that provided by a housing experiment conducted in 1972 by the U.S. Department of Housing and Urban Development (HUD). This particular experiment was designed to find out whether direct cash payments for housing would help low-income families to obtain adequate housing on the open market.[48]

---

[45] Coleman, *Policy Research in the Social Sciences*, p. 18.

[46] The following account of social auditing differs from that of Coleman, which is confined to "resource loss." Coleman's account does not include resource transformation and is based on the restrictive assumption that social auditing is appropriate only for policies involving resource distribution.

[47] The best expositions of qualitative methodology are Barney G. Glaser and Anselm L. Strauss, *The Discovery of Grounded Theory: Strategies for Qualitative Research* (Chicago: Aldine Publishing, 1967); and Norman K. Denzin, *The Research Act* (Chicago: Aldine Publishing, 1970).

[48] See Trend, "On the Reconciliation of Qualitative and Quantitative Analyses: A Case Study."

In this case, quantitative measures of inputs and outputs not only forced some analysts to treat policy-program processes as a "black box," initially, it also prevented them from seeing that certain factors—for example, spontaneous assistance by housing counselors—accounted for program impacts. The supplementary use of qualitative methods yielded strikingly different results than those that might have been produced by focusing exclusively on quantitative measures of inputs and outputs. This case also shows that alternative approaches to monitoring are potentially complementary. Social experimentation and quantitative measurement were successfully combined with social auditing and the qualitative description of policy processes.

Research and Practice Synthesis

Social auditing and social experimentation require the collection of new information about policy actions and outcomes. Social systems accounting, while based chiefly on available information, also requires new data insofar as information about subjective social conditions is out of date or unavailable. In contrast to each of these approaches, *research and practice synthesis* is an approach to monitoring that involves the systematic compilation, comparison, and assessment of the results of past efforts to implement public policies. It has been used to synthesize information in a number of policy issue areas that range from social welfare, agriculture, and education to municipal services and science and technology policy.[49] It has also been employed to assess the quality of policy research conducted on policy processes and policy outcomes.[50]

There are two primary sources of available information relevant to research and practice syntheses: case studies of policy formulation and implementation, and research reports that address relations among policy actions and outcomes. When research and practice synthesis is applied to case studies, it may be based on the *case survey method,* a set of procedures used to identify and analyze factors that account for variations in the adoption and implementation of policies.[51] The case

---

[49] See, for example, Jack Rothman, *Planning and Organizing for Social Change: Action Principles from Social Science Research* (New York: Columbia University Press, 1974); Gerald Zaltman, Robert Duncan, and James Holbek, *Innovations and Organizations* (New York: Wiley-Interscience, 1973); Everett Rogers and F. Floyd Shoemaker, *The Communication of Innovations* (New York: Free Press, 1971); Robert K. Yin and Douglas Yates, *Street-Level Governments: Assessing Decentralization and Urban Services* (Santa Monica, CA: Rand Corporation, October, 1974); U.S. General Accounting Office, *Designing Evaluations* (Washington, DC: U.S. GA Office, July 1984); and Richard J. Light and David B. Pillemer, *Summing Up: The Science of Reviewing Research* (Cambridge, MA: Harvard University Press, 1984).

[50] See, for example, Ilene N. Bernstein and Howard E. Freeman, *Academic and Entrepreneurial Research: The Consequences of Diversity in Federal Evaluation Programs* (New York: Russell Sage Foundation, 1975).

[51] See Robert K. Yin and Kenneth Heald, "Using the Case Survey Method to Analyze Policy Studies," *Administrative Science Quarterly* 20, no. 3 (1975): 371–81; William A. Lucas, *The Case Survey Method: Aggregating Case Experience* (Santa Monica, CA: Rand Corporation, October 1974); and Yin, *Case Study Analysis* (Beverly Hills, CA: Sage Publications, 1985).

survey method requires that the analyst first develop a *case-coding scheme,* a set of categories that capture key aspects of policy inputs, processes, outputs, and impacts. In one such case survey, analysts sought to determine the influence of political participation and other process variables on the delivery of municipal services, an output variable.[52] Other case surveys, focusing on public agencies and private corporations, have attempted to determine what factors account for successful and unsuccessful efforts to implement and utilize a variety of management innovations.[53] Representative indicators and coding categories from a typical case-coding scheme are illustrated in Table 6.4.

When research and practice synthesis is applied to available research reports, it is based on the *research survey,* research synthesis, or evaluation synthesis, a set of procedures used to compare and appraise results of past research on policy actions and outcomes.[54] Some of the more important applications of the research survey method have yielded insights into factors associated with the diffusion and communication of innovations, planned social change, and the outputs and impacts

Table 6.4   Case-Coding Scheme: Representative Indicators and Coding Categories

Type of Indicator	Indicator	Coding Categories
Input	Adequacy of resources	[ ] Totally adequate [ ] Mostly adequate [ ] Not adequate [ ] Insufficient information
Process	Involvement of policy analyst(s) in defining problem	[ ] Makes decisions [ ] Influences decisions [ ] No influence [ ] Insufficient information
Output	Utilization of results of policy research	[ ] High [ ] Moderate [ ] Low [ ] None [ ] Insufficient information
Impact	Perceived resolution of problem(s)	[ ] Complete [ ] Partial [ ] No resolution [ ] Insufficient information

---

[52] Yin and Yates, *Street Level Governments.*

[53] William N. Dunn and Frederic W. Swierczek, "Planned Organizational Change: Toward Grounded Theory," *Journal of Applied Behavioral Science* 13, no. 2 (1977): 135–58.

[54] See Rothman, *Planning and Organizing for Social Change;* U.S. General Accounting Office, *Designing Evaluations;* and Light and Pillemer, *Summing Up.*

of public policies and programs.[55] The research survey method provides several kinds of information: empirical generalizations about sources of variation in policy outcomes; summary assessments of the confidence researchers have in these generalizations; and policy alternatives or action guidelines that are implied by these generalizations. Sample results of one application of the research survey method are illustrated in Table 6.5.

The research survey method, like the case survey method, requires the construction of a format for extracting information about research reports. The typical research report form includes a number of items that help analysts to summarize the research and appraise its quality. These items include variables measured, the type of research design and methods used, the issue area in which the

Table 6.5   Sample Results of the Research Survey Method: Empirical Generalizations, Action Guidelines, and Levels of Confidence in Generalizations

Generalization[1]	Action Guidelines[2]	Confidence in Generalization[3]
1. Current resource expenditures are strongly associated with past resource expenditures.	In determining the receptivity to new policies and programs, analysts should seek out situations where substantial resource expenditures have occurred in the past.	3
2. Policy outcomes are associated with the level of economic development of the municipality, state, or region where policy actions are undertaken.	In determining the receptivity to new policies and programs, analysts should focus attention on wealthy, urban, and industrial areas.	4
3. Outputs of educational policies in municipalities with professional city managers (reform governments) are greater than in municipalities without professional managers (nonreform governments).	Analysts should adjust recommendations according to information about the type of municipality where policy actions are intended to take effect.	2

Notes:

[1] Empirical generalizations are based on available research reports, including scholarly books, articles and government reports.

[2] Action guidelines are derived from empirical generalizations. The same generalization frequently implies multiple action guidelines.

[3] The numbers used to express the degree of confidence in a generalization are based on the number of reliable and valid studies that support generalization.

Source: Adapted from Jack Rothman, *Planning and Organizing for Social Change: Action Principles from Social Science Research* (New York: Columbia University Press, 1974), pp. 254–65.

---

[55] Rogers and Shoemaker, *The Communication of Innovations*; Gerald Zaltman, *Toward a Theory of Planned Social Change: A Theory-in-Use Approach,* prepared for the Second Meeting of the Network of Consultants on Knowledge Transfer, Denver, Colorado, December 11–13, 1977; and Rothman, *Planning and Organizing for Social Change,* ch. 6, pp. 195–278.

1. Title of Report _____

2. Authors of Report _____

3. Abstract of Report (conceptual framework, hypotheses, research methodology, major findings)

4. Issue Area (for example, health, labor, criminal justice):
   _____

5. Major Variables Measured (Describe):
   (a) Input _____
   (b) Process _____
   (c) Output _____
   (d) Impact _____

6. Empirical Generalizations (List):
   _____
   _____
   _____
   _____

7. Research Design (for example, case study, social experiment, cross-sectional study)
   _____

8. Research Quality (reliability of data, internal validity, external validity)
   _____

Figure 6.3   Sample research survey form.

research was carried out, and an overall assessment of the reliability and validity of the research findings. A sample research survey form is presented in Figure 6.3.

There are several major advantages of research and practice synthesis as an approach to monitoring. First, the case survey and research survey methods are comparatively efficient ways to compile and appraise an increasingly large body of cases and research reports on policy implementation.[56] Whether the focus is upon cases or research reports, research and practice synthesis allows analysts to systematically and critically examine different empirical generalizations and their implications. Second, the case survey method is one among several ways to uncover different dimensions of policy processes that affect policy outcomes. Generalizations about policy processes may be used to support arguments from parallel case and analogy, for example, by showing that policies and programs carried out under similar circumstances have similar outcomes. Finally, the case survey method is a good way to examine objective as well as subjective social conditions. The case survey method is an inexpensive and effective way to obtain information about the subjective perceptions of policy processes held by different stakeholders.[57]

---

[56] On case materials, see the Electronic Hallway, a repository of many hundreds of cases in public administration and policy. This case repository, housed and managed at the Evans School at the University of Washington, is the product of a consortium of public policy schools.

[57] See Zaltman, *Toward a Theory of Planned Social Change*; and Dunn and Swierczek, "Planned Organizational Change: Toward Grounded Theory."

The main limitations of research and practice synthesis are related to the reliability and validity of information. Cases and research reports not only vary in quality and depth of coverage but are often self-confirming.

For example, most available cases and research reports contain no explicit discussion of the limitations and weaknesses of the study, and frequently they put forth only one point of view. Similarly, available cases often report only "successful" efforts to implement policies and programs. Despite these limitations, research and practice synthesis is a systematic way to accumulate knowledge about policy actions and outcomes in many issue areas. Because it relies exclusively on available information, it is less expensive than social auditing, social experimentation, and social systems accounting. At the same time, these other approaches to monitoring have their own distinctive advantages and limitations. The strengths of one approach are often the weaknesses of another. For this reason, the most persuasive generalizations about policy outcomes are those that have multiple foci (inputs, processes, outputs, impacts), use different types of controls (direct manipulation, quantitative analysis, qualitative analysis), and are based on a combination of available and new information about objective and subjective conditions.

TECHNIQUES FOR MONITORING

Monitoring, unlike other policy analytic methods, does not involve procedures that are clearly associated with alternative approaches. Many of the same techniques are therefore appropriate for each of the four approaches: social systems accounting, social auditing, social experimentation, and social research cumulation. Techniques appropriate for the four approaches to monitoring are illustrated in Table 6.6.

Graphic Displays

Much information about policy outcomes is presented in the form of *graphic displays,* which are pictorial representations of the values of one or more action or

Table 6.6   Techniques Appropriate to Four Approaches to Monitoring

Approach	Graphic Displays	Tabular Displays	Index Numbers	Interrupted Time-Series Analysis	Control-Series Analysis	Regression-Discontinuity Analysis
Social systems accounting	✕	✕	✕	✕		O
Social auditing	✕	✕	✕	✕	✕	O
Social experimentation	✕	✕	✕	✕	✕	✕
Research and practice synthesis	✕	✕	O	O	O	O

Note: ✕, technique appropriate to approach; O, technique not appropriate to approach.

outcome variables. A graphic display can be used to depict a single variable at one or more points in time, or to summarize the relationship between two variables. In each case, a graph displays a set of data points, each of which is defined by the coordinates of two numerical scales. The horizontal scale of a graph is called the *abscissa* and the vertical scale is called the *ordinate*. When a graph is used to display a causal relationship, the horizontal axis is reserved for the independent variable (*X*) and called the *X*-axis, while the vertical axis is used to display the dependent variable (*Y*) and called the *Y*-axis. Because one of the main purposes of monitoring is to explain how policy actions affect policy outcomes, we usually place input and process variables on the *X*-axis and output and impact variables on the *Y*-axis.

One of the most simple and useful kinds of graph is the *time-series graph,* which displays an outcome variable on the vertical axis and time on the horizontal axis. If we wish to monitor the effects of police traffic control activities on motor vehicle deaths between 1970 and 1977, we might use time-series graphs like the ones presented in Figures 6.4(a) and (b). Note that graph (a) has a vertical scale marked off in units of 1,000 motor vehicle deaths and an origin of 44,000 (the origin is the point where the horizontal and vertical axes intersect). By contrast, graph (b) is marked off in units of 5,000 deaths and has an origin of zero. While both graphs display the same data—which show a decrease in deaths after the implementation of the 55-mph speed limit in 1973—the decline in deaths is more dramatic in graph (a) than in graph (b). This example shows how the stretching or

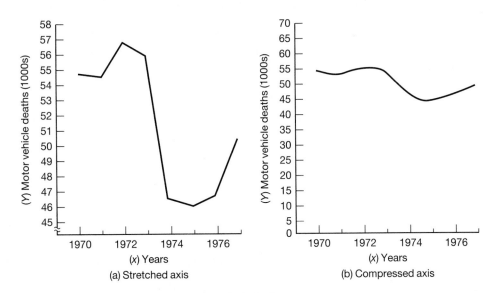

Figure 6.4 Two graphic displays of motor vehicle deaths, 1970–77.

Note: Deaths include those involving collisions between motor vehicles and collisions between motor vehicles and trains, cycles, and fixed objects.

Source: National Safety Council.

compression of values on the vertical axis can distort the significance of data. Because there is no clear rule to follow in selecting the size of intervals, it is essential to examine the underlying meaning of changes depicted in graphs.

Graphs may also be used to depict relationships between two or more variables at one point in time. Graphs of this kind, called *scatter diagrams,* were discussed in Chapter 4. We may use a scatter diagram to find out if one variable changes in the same direction as another, that is, whether two variables are correlated. If one of the variables precedes the other in time (e.g., a new program precedes changes in the target population), or if there is a persuasive theory that explains the correlated variables (e.g., economic theory posits that greater income results in a higher propensity to save), then we may be warranted in claiming that there is a *causal relationship* between the variables. Otherwise, variables are simply *correlated*—that is, the values of two variables covary or "go with" each other—and one variable cannot be assumed to be the cause of the other.

A common problem in using graphs is *spurious interpretation,* a situation where two variables that appear to be correlated are actually each correlated with some other variable. A good example of spurious interpretation is that of the analyst who observes from an examination of data on municipal firefighting activities that the number of fire engines present at the scene of a fire (input variable) is positively correlated with the amount of fire damage (output variable). This observed correlation might be used to claim that the number of fire engines deployed does not reduce fire damage, because no matter how many fire engines are present, the amount of fire damage continues to rise at the same rate. This interpretation is spurious (false) because a third variable—the size of fires—is not taken into account. Once we include this variable in our analysis, we find that the size of fires is correlated both with the number of fire trucks deployed and fire damage. The original correlation disappears when we include this third variable in our analysis, and our interpretation is plausible, rather than spurious (Figure 6.5). Spurious interpretation is a serious problem because we can never be completely certain that we have identified all relevant variables that may be affecting the original two-variable relationship.

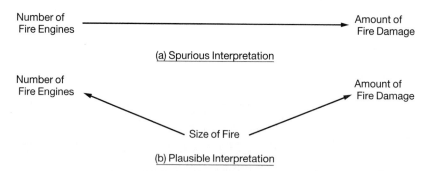

Figure 6.5   Spurious and plausible interpretations of data on municipal firefighting activities.

Source: Example adapted from H. W. Smith, *Strategies of Social Research: The Methodological Imagination* (Englewood Cliffs, NJ: Prentice Hall, 1975), pp. 325–26.

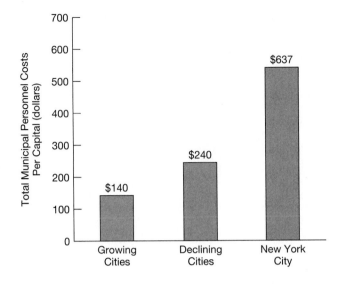

Figure 6.6 Bar graph showing total municipal personnel costs per capita for cities with growing and declining populations and for New York City.

Note: Total personnel costs are for 1973. The growth and decline of population is based on a 1960–73 average.

Source: Thomas Muller, *Growing and Declining Urban Areas: A Fiscal Comparison* (Washington, DC: Urban Institute, 1975).

Another means for displaying data on policy outcomes is the *bar graph,* a pictorial representation that presents data in the form of separated parallel bars arranged along the horizontal (or vertical) axis. The bar graph presented in Figure 6.6 was used to display data on policy inputs (total municipal personnel costs per capita) as part of an analysis of the fiscal crisis of U.S. cities. Note that cities with growing population have the lowest per capita personnel costs, while cities that are losing population have higher costs. The bar graph also shows the somewhat special position of New York City in 1973.

Information about policy outcomes is often available in the form of *grouped frequency distributions,* in which the numbers of persons or target groups in particular categories (e.g., age or income) are presented graphically. For example, if we want to monitor the number of persons below the poverty line in various age groups, we might begin with the data in Table 6.7. These data can then be converted into two kinds of graphic displays: histograms and frequency polygons.

A *histogram* is a kind of bar graph that organizes information about a grouped frequency distribution of an action or outcome variable at one point in time. In a histogram, the width of the bars along the horizontal axis is equal, and there is no space between the bars. The height of the bars in a histogram shows the frequency of occurrence in each group (called a class interval). The histogram illustrated in Figure 6.7(a) shows the numbers of persons below the poverty threshold in several age categories in 1977. The histogram can be easily converted into a frequency polygon (Figure 6.7[b]) by using the midpoints of each class interval as data points and connecting all points with a line. The difference between a histogram and a frequency polygon is that the latter uses a series of lines to represent the frequency distribution.

Another way to display information about policy outcomes is the *cumulative frequency polygon,* a graph that shows the cumulative frequencies of a distribution along the vertical axis. As one moves from left to right along the horizontal axis, the

Table 6.7   Grouped Frequency Distribution: Number of Persons Below the Poverty Threshold by Age Group in 1977

Age Groups	Number of Persons Below The Poverty Threshold
Under 14	7,856,000
14 to 21	4,346,000
22 to 44	5,780,000
45 to 54	1,672,000
55 to 59	944,000
60 to 64	946,000
65 and over	3,177,000
Total	24,721,000

Note: The poverty threshold is based on an index that takes into account consumption requirements based on sex, age, and residence in farm or nonfarm areas. Poverty thresholds are updated to reflect changes in the Consumer Price Index. In 1977 the poverty threshold for all persons, irrespective of age and place of residence, was $3067 annually.

Source: U.S. Department of Commerce, Bureau of the Census.

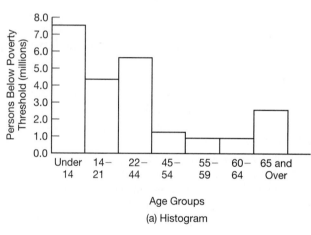

(a) Histogram

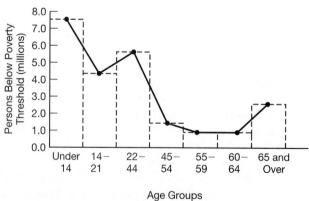

(b) Frequency Polygon

Figure 6.7   Histogram and frequency polygon: number of persons below the poverty threshold by age group in 1977.

Source: U.S. Department of Commerce, Bureau of the Census.

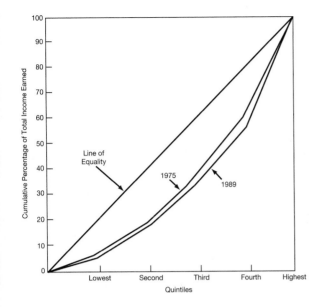

Figure 6.8 Lorenz curve showing distribution of family personal income in the United States in 1989 and 1975.

Source: U.S. Department of Commerce, Bureau of the Census.

frequency of persons (or families, cities, states) in the first group is plotted on the vertical axis; the frequency of persons in the first and second groups is then plotted; and so on until we reach the end of the horizontal scale, which is the sum of all frequencies. In monitoring the effects of policies designed to alleviate poverty, a useful type of cumulative frequency polygon is the *Lorenz curve,* which can be used to display the distribution of income, population, or residential segregation in a given population.[58] For example, a Lorenz curve enables us to compare the share of total income earned by each successive percentage group in the population. These percentage groups are called *quintiles* or *deciles,* which are groups comprised of one-fifth or one-tenth of the population, respectively. Figure 6.8 shows the distribution of family personal income in the United States in 1947 and 1975. As the Lorenz curve moves closer to the diagonal (which represents perfect equality), family incomes become more equitably distributed. The curve shows that the distribution of family personal income was more equitable in 1975 than it was in 1947.

The Gini Index

The Lorenz curve illustrated in Figure 6.8 displays the distribution of income among families at two points in time. Lorenz curves may also be used to display the distribution of population or certain types of activities (e.g., crime or racial segregation) among spatially organized units such as cities.[59] Lorenz curves can also be

---

[58] The original exposition of the Lorenz curve may be found in M. O. Lorenz, "Methods of Measuring the Concentration of Wealth," *Quarterly Publications of the American Statistical Association* 9, no. 70 (1905): 209–19.

[59] For other indices, see Jack P. Gibbs, ed., *Urban Research Methods* (Princeton, NJ: Van Nostrand, 1961).

Table 6.8 **Computation of Gini Concentration Ratio for Violent Crimes Known to Police per 100,000 Population in 1976**

Size of City	Number of Cities (1)	Violent Crimes (2)	Proportion Cities (3)	Proportion Crimes (4)	Cumulative Proportion Cities (Y_i) (5)	Cumulative Proportion Crimes (X_i) (6)	$X_i Y_{i+1}$ (7)	$X_{i+1} Y_i$ (8)
250,000 and over	59	1,095	0.008	0.379	0.008	0.379	0.0087	0.0046
100,000–249,999	110	573	0.015	0.198	0.023	0.577	0.0340	0.0166
50,000–99,999	265	416	0.036	0.144	0.059	0.721	0.1016	0.0494
25,000–49,999	604	338	0.082	0.117	0.141	0.838	0.2774	0.1306
10,000–24,999	1,398	254	0.190	0.088	0.331	0.926	0.9260	0.331
Under 10,000	4,925	216	0.669	0.074	1.000	1.000		
Totals	7,361	2,892	1.000	1.000			$\Sigma = 1.3477$	$\Sigma = 0.5322$

$$\text{Gini concentration ratio (GI)} = \frac{[(\Sigma X_i Y_{i+1}) - (\Sigma X_{i+1} Y_i)]}{\Sigma X_i Y_{i+1}}$$

$$= \frac{1.3477 - 0.5322}{1.3477} = \frac{0.8155}{1.3477}$$

$$= 0.605 = 0.61 \text{ (rounded)}$$

Source: Federal Bureau of Investigation, *Uniform Crime Reports for the United States,* 1976.

expressed in the form of the *Gini concentration ratio* (sometimes called simply the Gini index), which measures the proportion of the total area under the diagonal that lies in the area between the diagonal and the Lorenz curve. The formula for calculating this proportion is

$$\text{GI} = \frac{[(\Sigma X_i Y_{i+1}) - (\Sigma X_{i+1} Y_i)]}{\Sigma X_i Y_{i+1}}$$

where

X_i = the cumulative percentage distribution of the number of areas (e.g., cities)
Y_i = the cumulative percentage distribution of the population or of some activity (e.g., crime)

To illustrate the calculation of the Gini index, let us consider an example from the area of criminal justice policy. Suppose that we wish to depict the concentration of violent crimes in cities of various sizes in 1976. We would use the following procedures, illustrated in Table 6.8.

1. Place the number of cities and the total violent crimes reported for each class-size of cities in columns (1) and (2).

2. Compute the proportionate distribution of cities from column (1) and place in column (3). For example, $59 \div 7361 = 0.008$.

3. Compute the proportionate distribution of violent crimes from column (2) and place in column (4). For example, $1095 \div 2892 = 0.379$.

4. Cumulate the proportions of column (3) downward and place the results in column (5). For example, $0 + 0.008 = 0.008$, $0.008 + 0.015 = 0.23$, and so on.

5. Cumulate the proportions of column (4) downward and place the results in column (6). For example, $0 + 0.379 = 0.379$, $0.379 + 0.198 = 0.577$, and so on.

6. Multiply the first line in column (6) by the second line in column (5), the second line by the third line, and so on. For example, $0.379 \times 0.023 = 0.0087$, $0.577 \times 0.059 = 0.0340$, and so on. Place the results in column (7).

7. Multiply the first line in column (5) by the second line in column (6), and so on. For example, $0.008 \times 0.577 = 0.0046$, $0.023 \times 0.721 = 0.0166$, and so on. Place the results in column (8).

8. Sum column (7) and record the total (i.e., 1.3477). Sum column (8) and record the total (i.e., 0.5322).

9. Subtract the total of column (8) from the total of column (7) and then divide by the total of column (7). That is, $1.3477 - 0.5322 \div 1.3477 = 0.8155 \div 1.3477 = 0.605 = 0.61$. This result is the Gini index.

The Gini index shows the proportion of the area under the diagonal that lies between the diagonal and the Lorenz curve. It can be used to depict the concentration of wealth, income, population, ethnic groups, urban residents, crime, and other social conditions. The advantage of Gini index is that it is a precise measure of concentration that supplies much more information than the pictorial representation provided by the Lorenz curve. Furthermore, the Gini index ranges from zero (no concentration at all) to 1.0 (maximum concentration). In the example of the concentration of violent crimes, note that approximately 2 percent of the largest cities (100,000 and up) have almost 58 percent of the violent crimes. If violent crimes were more or less equally distributed among cities of all class sizes, the Gini index would be approximately zero. In fact, however, violent crimes are heavily concentrated in large cities. The Gini index value of 0.61 shows that 61 percent of the total area is between the diagonal and the Lorenz curve. This is a substantial concentration with important implications for criminal justice policy in the United States.

Tabular Displays

Another useful way to monitor policy outcomes is to construct tabular displays. A *tabular display* is a rectangular array used to summarize the key features of one or more variables. The simplest form of tabular display is the one-dimensional table, which presents information about policy outcomes in terms of a single dimension of interest, for example, age, income, region, or time. In monitoring changes in energy demand in the United States over the period 1950–70, an analyst might use a one-dimensional tabular display.

Information may also be arranged in tables with two dimensions, for example, levels of education by income, target groups by levels of education, or the income

Table 6.9   Race of Families Below the Poverty Level in the United States in 1959 and 1968
(Thousands of Families)

	Year		Change (1959–68)	
Race of Family	1959	1968	Number	Percent
Black and other minorities	2,135	1,431	−704	−33.0
White	6,185	3,616	−2,569	−41.0
Total	8,320	5,047	−3,273	−39.3

Note: The threshold poverty level for a nonfarm family of four in 1968 was $3,553 annual gross income. Data in 1959 and 1968 have been standardized to reflect changes in the definition of the poverty threshold in 1964.

Source: U.S. Bureau of the Census, *Current Population Reports*, Series P-60, No. 68, "Poverty in the United States: 1959–1968" (Washington, DC: U.S. Government Printing Office, 1969).

of target groups by time periods. An analyst concerned with the impact of the War on Poverty may wish to monitor changes in the number and percentage of families below the poverty level in the United States between 1959 and 1968. The following two-dimensional table (Table 6.9) would provide relevant information.

Another type of two-dimensional table involves the analysis of two or more groups by levels of some outcome variable, which might be employment, services received, or earnings. For example, social experiments are based on comparisons of groups that have received a particular type of treatment (experimental group) and groups that have not (control group). Table 6.9 was used to assess whether groups participating in a publicly funded alcoholism treatment program differed in the number of arrests following treatment (Table 6.10). The results indicate that a court-ordered policy of forced short-term referrals for treatment has no discernible positive effect on target groups.

In monitoring policy outcomes, data may also be arranged in three-dimensional tables. For example, a three-dimensional table can be used to display the change between 1959 and 1968 in the number and percent of black and white families below the poverty threshold, while also taking into account the age of the head of household

Table 6.10   Number of Drunk Rearrests among 241 Offenders in Three Treatment Groups

	Treatment Group			
Rearrests	Alcoholism Clinic	Alcoholics Anonymous	No Treatment	Total
None	26 (32.0)	27 (31.0)	32 (44.0)	85
One	23 (28.0)	19 (22.0)	14 (19.0)	56
Two or more	33 (40.0)	40 (47.0)	27 (37.0)	100
Total	82 (100.0)	86 (100.0)	73 (100.0)	241

Source: John P. Gilbert, Richard J. Light, and Frederick Mosteller, "Assessing Social Innovations: An Empirical Base for Policy," in *Evaluation and Experiment: Some Critical Issues in Assessing Social Programs*, ed. Carl A. Bennett and Arthur A. Lumsdaine (New York: Academic Press, 1975), pp. 94–95.

Table 6.11 Change in Families Below the Poverty Level in the United States in 1959 and 1968 by Race and Age

Family Race and Age	Year		Change (1959–68)	
	1959	*1968*	*Number*	*Percent*
Black and other races	2,135	1,431	−704	−33.0
Head 65 years and over	320	219	−101	−31.6
Head under 65 years	1,815	1,212	−603	−33.2
White	6,185	3,616	−2,569	−41.5
Head 65 years and over	1,540	982	−558	−36.2
Head under 65 years	4,654	2,634	−2,011	−43.3
Total	8,320	5,047	−3,273	−39.3

Source: U.S. Bureau of the Census, *Current Population Reports*, Series P-60, No. 68, "Poverty in the United States: 1959–1968" (Washington, DC: U.S. Government Printing Office, 1969).

(the inclusion of age is called "controlling" for a third variable). The following three-dimensional display (Table 6.11) might be used to monitor the consequences of poverty policy between 1959 and 1968. The table shows that more white families than black families moved above the poverty threshold but also that the relative improvement of white families with a head under sixty-five years was considerably greater than any of the other three groups. This suggests that the position of black and elderly white families changed more slowly than that of younger white families.

Index Numbers

A useful way to monitor changes in outcome variables over time is to construct index numbers. *Index numbers* are measures of how much the value of an indicator or set of indicators changes over time relative to a base period. Base periods are arbitrarily defined as having a value of 100, which serves as the standard for comparing subsequent changes in the indicators of interest. Many index numbers are used in public policy analysis. These include index numbers used to monitor changes in consumer prices, industrial production, crime severity, pollution, health care, quality of life, and other important policy outcomes.

Index numbers differ in their focus, complexity, and degree of explicitness. Index numbers may focus on changes in prices, quantities, or values. For example, changes in the price of consumer items are summarized in the form of the Consumer Price Index (CPI), while changes in the quantity of pollutants are measured by various air pollution indices. Relatedly, changes in the value of goods produced by industry are summarized with the Index of Industrial Production. Whether they focus on price, quantity, or value, index numbers may be simple or composite. *Simple index numbers* are those that have only one indicator (e.g., the quantity of crimes per 100,000 persons), while *composite index numbers* include many different indicators. A good example of composite index numbers are two CPIs used to measure the costs of some four hundred goods and services. One index includes all urban consumers, while the other includes urban wage earners and clerical workers.[60]

Index numbers may be *implicitly weighted* or *explicitly weighted.* In the former case, indicators are combined with no explicit procedure for establishing their value. For example, an air pollution index may simply aggregate various kinds of pollutants (carbon monoxide, oxidants, sulfur oxides) without taking into account the different costs in impaired health that result from some of these pollutants (e.g., carbon monoxide). An explicitly weighted index takes such factors into account by establishing the relative value or significance of each indicator.

There are two general procedures for constructing index numbers: aggregation and averaging. Aggregative indices are constructed by summing the values of indicators (e.g., consumer prices) for given periods. Averaging procedures (or the so-called average of relatives method) require the calculation of average changes in the value of an indicator over time, while aggregative procedures do not. A useful and simple aggregative price index is the *purchasing power index,* which measures the real value of earnings in successive periods. A purchasing power index may be used to monitor the impact of wage agreements on the real income of employees as part of public sector collective bargaining activities. A purchasing power index is constructed by using values of the CPI. This is done by locating the year (e.g., 1977) for which we wish to determine the purchasing power of wages and converting this value into a *price relative,* that is, a value that expresses the price of goods and services in the year of interest (1977) relative to a base year (e.g., 1967). If we then divide this price relative into one (this is called a *reciprocal*), we will obtain the purchasing power of wages in 1967 dollars.

In the following illustration (Table 6.12), the values of the purchasing power index for given years indicate how much every dollar is worth in real terms, relative to the CPI base year of 1967. For example, in 1977 every dollar in wages buys about 55 cents of goods and services when compared with the purchasing power of one

Table 6.12   Computation of Purchasing Power Index

	Consumer Price Index (1)	Price Relative (2)	Reciprocal (3)	Purchasing Power Index (4)
1967	100.0	$100.0 \div 100.0 = 1.0$	$1.0 \div 1.0 = 1.0$	$\times 100 = 100.0$
1970	116.3	$116.3 \div 100.0 = 1.163$	$1.0 \div 1.163 = .859$	$\times 100 = 85.9$
1975	161.2	$161.2 \div 100.0 = 1.612$	$1.0 \div 1.612 = .620$	$\times 100 = 62.0$
1977	181.5	$181.5 \div 100.0 = 1.815$	$1.0 \div 1.815 = .551$	$\times 100 = 55.1$

Source: U.S. Department of Labor, Bureau of Labor Statistics.

---

[60] In January 1978 the Consumer Price Index was revised. Since that time, two indices have been produced. A new index includes All Urban Consumers, irrespective of whether they are employed, and covers 80 percent of the noninstitutional population. The old index includes Urban Wage Earners and Clerical Workers and covers approximately 50 percent of persons in the new index.

Table 6.13   Computation of Real Gross Average Weekly Earnings in the Textile Industry

Year	Nominal Earnings (1)	Purchasing Power Index (2)	Reciprocal (3)	Real Wages (4)
1967	$87.70	100.0 ÷ 100 =	1.000 × $87.70 =	$87.70
1970	97.76	85.9 ÷ 100 =	0.859 × 97.76 =	83.98
1975	133.28	62.0 ÷ 100 =	0.620 × 133.28 =	82.63
1977	160.39	55.1 ÷ 100 =	0.551 × 160.39 =	88.37

Source: U.S. Department of Labor, Bureau of Labor Statistics.

dollar in 1967. The purchasing power index can be directly converted into real wages by taking the nominal wages for given years and multiplying by the purchasing power index. This has been done in Table 6.13, which shows the real value of gross average weekly earnings in the textile industry for 1970, 1975, and 1977. Note that real wages in the textile industry declined until 1977, when a slight increase was evident.

Another useful aggregative index is the Index of Pollutant Concentration developed under the CAMP of the Environmental Protection Agency. The concentration of various kinds of pollutants, measured in parts per million (ppm) or micrograms per cubic meter of air (mg/m^3), are punched into a recording tape every five minutes in various locations across the country. Pollutants fall into two main categories: gases and suspended particulates. The maximum concentrations of pollutants reported in Chicago, San Francisco, and Philadelphia for two averaging times (five minutes and one year) in 1964 are displayed in Table 6.14. An averaging time of one year is the total quantity of pollutants reported in all five-minute intervals over a year's period divided by the total number of five-minute intervals for the year. An averaging time of five minutes is simply the maximum concentration of pollutants registered in any five-minute period. An implicitly weighted aggregative-quantity index can be developed to monitor the concentration of pollutants over time. The formula for this index is

$$QI_n = \frac{\Sigma q_n}{q_0} \cdot 100$$

where

QI_n = the quantity index for gaseous pollutants in a given time period n

q_n = the quantity of gaseous pollutants in period n of a time series

q_0 = the quantity of gaseous pollutants in the base period 0 of a time series

On the basis of this formula, we can calculate index numbers to monitor changes in levels of pollutants (measured in millions of tons) between 1970 and 1975. We would begin by selecting 1970 as the base period (q_0) and calculate values of the

Table 6.14 Maximum Concentration of Pollutants Reported in Chicago, Philadelphia, and San Francisco for Averaging Times of Five Minutes and One Year

City and Averaging Time	Gases[1]							Suspended Particulates[2]		
	Carbon Monoxide	Hydro-Carbons	Nitric Oxide	Nitrogen Dioxide	Nitrogen Oxides	Oxident	Sulfur Dioxide	Lead	Organic (Benzene Soluble)	Sulfate
Chicago										
5 minutes	64.0	20.0	0.97	0.79	1.12	0.17	1.62	NA	NA	NA
1 year	12.0	3.0	0.10	0.05	0.15	0.02	0.18	0.6	15.1	16.6
Philadelphia										
5 minutes	43.0	17.0	1.35	0.37	1.50	0.25	1.00	NA	NA	NA
1 year	7.0	2.0	0.04	0.04	0.08	0.02	0.09	0.8	12.2	19.8
San Francisco										
5 minutes	47.0	16.0	0.68	0.38	0.91	0.29	0.26	NA	NA	NA
1 year	7.0	3.0	0.09	0.05	0.14	0.02	0.02	NA	9.2	6.2

Type of Pollutant

Notes:

[1] Gaseous pollutants measured in parts per million (ppm) of air in 1964.

[2] Suspended particulates measured in micrograms per cubic meter (mg/m^3) of air in 1964.

Source: N. D. Singpurwalla, "Models in Air Pollution," in *A Guide to Models in Governmental Planning and Operations,* ed. Saul I. Gass and Roger L. Sisson (Washington, DC: U.S. Environmental Protection Agency, 1975), pp. 69–71.

Table 6.15 **Implicitly Weighted Aggregative Quantity Index to Measure Changes in Pollutants in the United States, 1970–75**

	Quantity			
Pollutant	*1970*	*1973*	*1974*	*1975*
Carbon monoxide	113.7	111.5	104.2	96.2
Sulfur oxides	32.3	32.5	31.7	32.9
Hydrocarbons	33.9	34.0	32.5	30.9
Particulates	26.8	21.9	20.3	18.0
Nitrogen oxides	22.7	25.7	25.0	24.2
	229.4	225.6	213.7	202.2
Quantity index (1970 = 100)	100.0	98.34	93.16	88.14

$$QI_n = \frac{\Sigma q_n}{\Sigma q_0} \cdot 100$$

$$QI_{1970} = \frac{\Sigma 113.7 + 32.3 + 33.9 + 26.8 + 22.7}{\Sigma 113.7 + 32.3 + 33.9 + 26.8 + 22.7} \cdot 100$$

$$= \frac{229.4}{229.4} \cdot 100 = 100.0$$

$$QI_{1973} = \frac{\Sigma 111.5 + 32.5 + 34.0 + 21.9 + 25.7}{\Sigma 113.5 + 32.3 + 33.9 + 26.8 + 22.7} \cdot 100$$

$$= \frac{225.6}{229.4} \cdot 100 = 98.34$$

Note: In millions of tons of pollutants (gases and particulates).

Source: U.S. Environmental Protection Agency.

quantity index for 1973, 1974, and 1975. These values are provided in Table 6.15, which shows that total pollutant emissions have declined since 1970.

The weakness of this implicitly weighted aggregative-quantity index of pollution is that it does not take into account variations in the concentrations of pollutants or their relative damage to health. By contrast, the index developed as part of the Environmental Protection Agency's CAMP provides explicit weights, because it permits analysts to examine the maximum concentration of pollutants in given periods (averaging times) and relate these concentrations to known health hazards. For example, while the overall quantity of pollutants has declined since 1970, some cities have registered very high levels of pollution in particular periods. Data on these periods are not reflected in the implicitly weighted quantity index illustrated in Table 6.15. Most important, the concentration of different types of pollutants per time period creates different kinds of health hazards. An explicitly weighted quantity index takes into account both the concentration of pollutants per time period (averaging times) and potential health hazards. While we will not construct an explicitly

Table 6.16 **Duration of Exposure to Pollutants and Consequent Damage to Health and the Environment**

Duration of Exposure	Consequence	Pollutant			
		Carbon Monoxide	Oxidants	Particulates	Sulfur Oxides
1 second	Sensation				
	Odor	−	+	−	+
	Taste	−	−	−	+
	Eye irritation	−	+	−	−
1 hour	Athletic performance impaired	−	+	−	−
	Visibility reduced	−	+	+	+
8 hours	Judgment impaired	+	−	−	−
	Stress to heart patients	+	−	−	−
1 day	Health impaired	+	−	+	+
4 days	Health impaired	+	−	+	+
1 year	Vegetation damaged	−	−	+	+
	Corrosion	−	−	+	+

Note: A minus (−) indicates no damaging consequences. A plus (+) indicates damaging consequence.

Source: N. D. Singpurwalla, "Models in Air Pollution," in *A Guide to Models in Governmental Planning and Operations,* ed. Saul I. Gass and Roger L. Sisson (Washington, DC: U.S. Environmental Protection Agency, 1975), p. 66.

weighted aggregative-quantity index on the basis of averaging times reported by the CAMP, it is important to consider relationships between the duration of exposure to pollutants and damage to health and the environment (Table 6.16).

There are several indexes widely used to monitor changes in policy outcomes. These include the two CPIs already noted above (one for all urban consumers and the other for urban wage earners and clerical workers); the Producer Price Index (PPI)—before 1978 called the Wholesale Price Index (WPI)—which is used to measure changes in the prices of all commodities produced in the economy; and the Index of Industrial Production (IIP)—published monthly by the Federal Reserve System—which is used to measure changes in the outputs of plants, mines, and utilities companies. The base period for all these indexes is 1967. In addition to these indexes, there are those that measure the severity of crime, the quality of life, the quality of health care, and the quality of the environment.

Index numbers have several limitations. First, explicit weighting procedures often lack precision. For example, estimates of the damage caused by different kinds of pollutants are partly subjective, and it is difficult to attach dollar costs to resultant health problems. Second, it is difficult to obtain sample data for indexes that are equally meaningful for all groups in society. The CPI, for example, is based on a sample of more than four hundred consumer goods and services purchased by urban residents. The sample is selected monthly from fifty-six urban areas, and data thus obtained are used to construct a composite national index. While the development of the two-part CPI in 1978 makes index numbers more meaningful to retired, elderly, and unemployed persons, as well as to wage earners and clerical workers, the CPI does not reflect price differences in many urban and rural areas. Finally, index numbers do not always reflect qualitative changes in the meaning or significance of index items over time. For example, as we learn more about the effects of various kinds of pollutants (e.g., lead particulates or asbestos), their significance changes. The simple quantity of pollutants may not reflect the changing social value (or disvalue) attached to them in different time periods.

Index numbers may be used to monitor a wide variety of changes. Yet these techniques provide no systematic way of relating changes in policy outcomes to prior policy actions. We now consider three sets of techniques that permit analysts to make systematic judgments about the effects of policy actions on policy outcomes: interrupted time-series analysis, control-series analysis, and regression-discontinuity analysis.[61] These procedures are used in conjunction with graphic displays and based on correlation and regression techniques discussed in the chapter on forecasting (Chapter 4). Although two of these procedures (interrupted time-series and control-series analysis) are equally applicable to social systems accounting, social auditing, and social experimentation, one of them (regression-discontinuity analysis) is exclusively applicable to social experiments.

Interrupted Time-Series Analysis

Interrupted time-series analysis is a set of procedures for displaying in graphic and statistical form the effects of policy actions on policy outcomes. Interrupted time-series analysis is appropriate for problems where an agency initiates some action that is put into effect across an entire jurisdiction or target group, for example, in a particular state or among all families below the poverty threshold. Because policy actions are limited to persons in the jurisdiction or target group, there is no opportunity for comparing policy outcomes across different jurisdictions or among different categories of the target group. In this situation, the only basis of comparison is the record of outcomes for previous years.

The graphing of interrupted time series is a powerful tool for assessing the effects of a policy intervention on a measure of some policy outcome (e.g., highway death rates, persons receiving medical assistance, job trainees employed, hospital mortality rates). As Figure 6.9 shows, some policy interventions have genuine effects on policy outcomes, while others do not. Interventions (a) and (b) indicate that the policy intervention is plausibly related to the increase in some valued outcome, because there is a practically significant jump in the value of the measured policy outcome after the intervention. Intervention (b), however, shows that the valued outcome was not durable—it began to "fade" after the fifth time period.

Intervention (c) also lacks durability, but it was also preceded by an extreme high in the measured policy outcome before the intervention. This suggests that

---

[61] The following discussion is based on Campbell, "Reforms As Experiments."

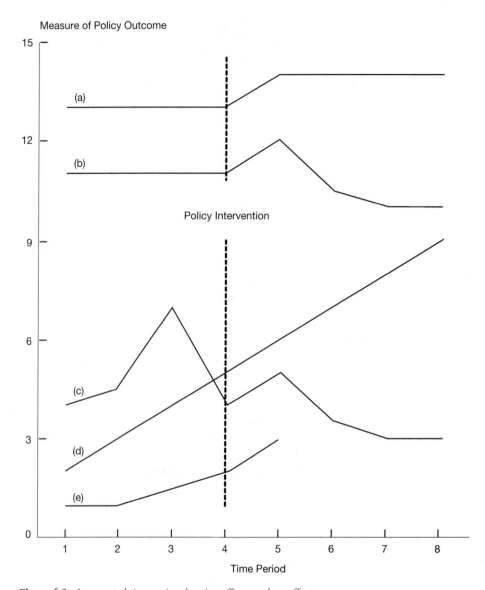

Figure 6.9   Interrupted time series showing effects and no effects.

Source: Donald T. Campbell and Julian C. Stanley, *Experimental and Quasi-experimental Designs for Research* (Chicago: Rand McNally, 1967).

there probably was "regression" toward the average value of the time series after the intervention—that is, the increase between the fourth and fifth period probably would have occurred anyway (see below). Intervention (d) shows that the intervention had no effect because there is no difference in the rate of change in the value of the measured outcome variable. Finally, intervention (e) shows a slight increase in the measured policy outcome but one that was preceded by an increase already in progress. This weak effect is not sufficient to conclude that the intervention was responsible for the increase between the fourth and fifth periods. If data on subsequent time periods were available, the postintervention increase might prove to lack durability, or might increase at an increasing rate. Here it is simply not possible to know.

Interrupted time-series analysis is one among many approaches to social experimentation that are called "quasi-experimental." *Quasi-experimental* refers to experiments that have many but not all characteristics of a genuine experiment: random selection of subjects, random assignment of subjects to experimental and control groups, random assignment of a "treatment" (a policy or program) to experimental and control groups, and measurement of outcomes before and after the experimental treatment (policy or program). The only feature that interrupted time-series analysis does not have is random selection of participants or subjects. The other three characteristics are present in many quasi-experiments designed to "test" policies and programs to determine whether they make a difference in producing some outcome of interest.

The best way to visualize interrupted time-series analysis is to consider a concrete illustration.[62] In 1956, after a record high number of traffic fatalities in 1955, the governor of Connecticut (Abraham Ribicoff) implemented a severe crackdown on violators of the state's speeding laws. At the end of 1956, there were 284 traffic deaths, as compared with 324 deaths the year before. Governor Ribicoff interpreted the outcomes of the crackdown on speeding in the following way: "With the saving of 40 lives in 1956, a reduction of 12.3 percent from the 1955 motor vehicle death toll, we can say that the program is definitely worthwhile." The apparent results of the speeding crackdown are displayed graphically in Figure 6.10. The values on the vertical scale have been deliberately stretched to exaggerate the magnitude of effects.

If we wish to monitor the outcomes of the Connecticut crackdown on speeding using interrupted time-series analysis, we will follow several steps:

1. Compress the values along the vertical axis so that the apparent observed effect is not so dramatic. Here we will use intervals of twenty-five rather than ten deaths.

2. Obtain values of traffic deaths in multiple years before and after the implementation of the policy and plot them on the graph. This creates an extended time series from 1951 through 1959.

3. Draw a vertical line that interrupts the time series at the beginning of the year when the policy was implemented, that is, in 1956 (hence, an "interrupted time series"). Note that intervals used to display years in a time series denote the middle of each year (July 1), so that any point midway between two intervals is the value of the time series on January 1.

---

[62] See Campbell, "Reforms as Experiments," pp. 75–81; and Donald T. Campbell and H. Lawrence Ross, "The Connecticut Crackdown on Speeding: Time-Series Data in Quasi-experimental Analysis," *Law and Society Review* 3, no. 1 (1968): 33–53.

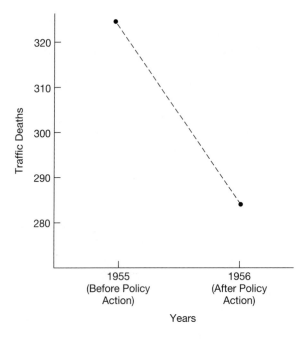

Figure 6.10 Connecticut traffic deaths before and after the 1956 crackdown on speeding.

Source: Donald T. Campbell, "Reforms as Experiments," in *Handbook of Evaluation Research*, vol. 1, ed. Elmer L. Struening and Marcia Guttentag (Beverly Hills, CA: Sage Publications, 1975), p. 76.

The results of following these procedures are displayed in Figure 6.11, which is called an interrupted time-series graph. Observe that this graph creates an altogether different visual image of policy outcomes than that presented in Figure 6.10.

The main advantage of interrupted time-series analysis is that it enables us to consider systematically various threats to the validity of causal inferences about policy outcomes. The importance of these threats to validity can be easily seen when we compare policy outcomes (traffic deaths) displayed in the interrupted time-series graph and Governor Ribicoff's causal inference that the speeding crackdown definitely resulted in lowered traffic fatalities. Let us now examine several threats to the validity of this claim by considering the data displayed in Figures 6.10 and 6.11.

1. *Maturation*. Changes within the members of groups (in this case, drivers) may exert effects on policy outcomes apart from those of policy actions. For example, death rates in Connecticut may have been declining for a number of years as a result of increased social learning among drivers who have been exposed to drivers' education programs or to public safety campaigns. The simple pre-policy–postpolicy graph (Figure 6.10) does not allow us to examine such possible independent effects. The interrupted time-series graph (Figure 6.11) enables us to rule out maturation as a plausible rival explanation, because the time series does not show a long-term secular decline in traffic fatalities.

2. *Instability*. All time series are to some degree unstable. The interrupted time-series graph permits us to display this instability, which is rather pronounced. The decline between 1955 and 1956 is only slightly greater than declines in 1951–52 and 1953–54, thus suggesting that the policy outcome may be a

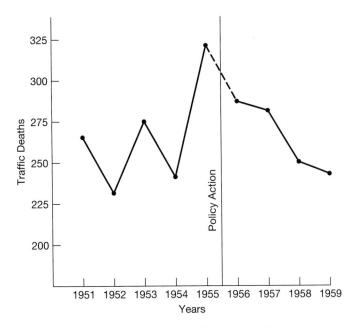

Figure 6.11 Interrupted time-series graph displaying Connecticut traffic fatalities before and after the 1956 crackdown on speeding.

Source: Adapted from Donald T. Campbell, "Reforms as Experiments," in *Handbook of Evaluation Research*, vol. 1, ed. Elmer L. Struening and Marcia Guttentag (Beverly Hills, CA: Sage Publications, 1975), p. 76.

consequence of instability, and not the policy action. On the other hand, there are no increases in traffic fatalities after 1956. Although this lends persuasiveness to the governor's claim, this argument would not have been possible without the interrupted time-series graph of Figure 6.11.

3. *Regression artifacts.* In monitoring policy outcomes, it is often difficult to separate the effects of policy actions from effects exerted by the persons or groups selected for a program. If traffic fatalities for 1955 represent an extreme—as might be the case if we only have Figure 6.10 to go on—then the decline in traffic deaths in 1956 may simply reflect the tendency of extreme scores to regress toward the mean or general trend of a time series. Fatalities in 1955 are in fact the most extreme ones in the series. For this reason, part of the decline from 1955 to 1956 may be attributed to regression artifacts, together with the instability of the time series. Regression artifacts are a particularly important threat to the validity of claims about policy outcomes for one important reason: policy makers tend to take action when problems are most acute or extreme.

Control-Series Analysis

Control-series analysis involves the addition of one or more control groups to an interrupted time-series design in order to determine whether characteristics of different groups exert an independent effect on policy outcomes, apart from the original policy action. The logic of control-series analysis is the same as interrupted time-series analysis. The only difference is that a group or groups that were not exposed to the policy actions in question are added to the graph. Figure 6.12 shows the original data from Connecticut along with data on traffic fatalities from control states.

Control-series analysis helps further to scrutinize the validity of claims about the effects of policy actions on policy outcomes. For example, rival claims based on history (sudden changes in weather conditions) and maturation (safety habits learned by drivers) would appear to be partly supported by the control-series data. Hence Connecticut and the control states show a similar general pattern of successive increases and decreases in traffic deaths between 1952 and 1955. Yet it is also evident that Connecticut traffic fatalities declined much more rapidly than control states after 1955. The control-series graph not only enables us to assess more critically the governor's claim about the success of his policy, but in this case allows us to rule out plausible rival interpretations. This has the effect of providing much firmer grounds for policy claims.

The use of interrupted time-series and control-series analyses, together with the various threats to internal and external validity, may be viewed as a policy

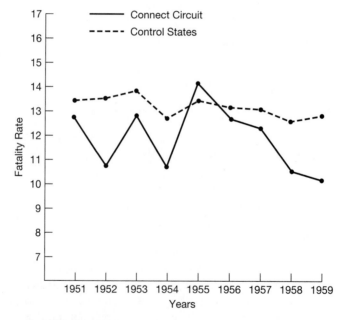

Figure 6.12   Control-series graph displaying traffic fatalities in Connecticut and control states, 1951–59.

Note: The fatality rate is a population-based measure that represents deaths per 100,000 persons in the population of states.

Source: Donald T. Campbell, "Reforms as Experiments," in *Handbook of Evaluation Research*, vol. 1, ed. Elmer L. Struening and Marcia Guttentag (Beverly Hills, CA: Sage Publications, 1975), p. 84.

argument. The original data on the decline in traffic fatalities between 1955 and 1956 represent information (I), while the policy claim (C) is "the program is definitely worthwhile." The qualifier (Q) expresses maximum certainty, as indicated by the term "definitely," and the *implicit* warrant (W) necessary to carry information to claim is that the policy action caused the reduction in traffic fatalities. What is important in the present case is the series of rebuttals (R) that may be advanced on the basis of the various threats to internal and external validity: history, maturation, instability, testing, instrumentation, mortality, selection, regression artifacts. These threats to the validity of claims have been put in the form of a policy argument in Figure 6.13.

The final procedure to be discussed in this chapter is an extension of regression and correlational procedures. Because linear regression and correlation

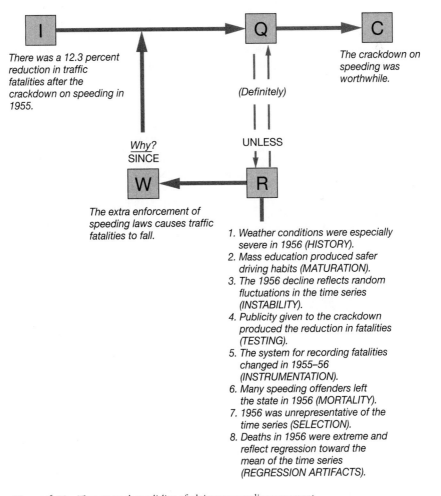

Figure 6.13 Threats to the validity of claims as a policy argument.

have already been described in some detail, we will not repeat the discussion of these techniques here, except to note that they are applicable to problems of monitoring as well as forecasting. Regression analysis may be used to explain past outcomes, rather than predict future ones, and the results of analysis are sometimes called "postdictions" to emphasize that we are predicting past events. Even where regression analysis is used to predict future events, the analysis is necessarily based on information acquired by monitoring past policy outcomes.

Imagine that we have obtained information about dollar investments in five manpower training programs, together with information about the subsequent employment of trainees who have completed these programs. The problem can be stated in the following way: How does the level of investment in manpower training programs affect the subsequent employment of trainees? A worksheet necessary to compute the regression equation $[Y_c = a + b(x)]$, the coefficient of determination (r^2), the simple correlation coefficient (r), the standard error of estimate $(S_{y.x})$, and an interval estimate (Y_i) is provided in Table 6.17. The SPSS results, displayed below as Exhibit 6.1, should be self-explanatory. If they are not, you should return to Chapter 4 and review the section on correlation and regression.

Exhibit 6.1   SPSS Output for Table 6.11

			Model Summary	
Model	**R**	**R Square**	**Adjusted R Square**	**Std. Error of the Estimate**
1	.900[a]	.810	.747	7.95822426

a. Predictors: (Constant), PROGINV

		ANOVA[b]				
Model		**Sum of Squares**	**df**	**Mean Square**	**F**	**Sig.**
1	Regression	810.000	1	810.000	12.789	.037[a]
	Residual	190.000	3	63.333		
	Total	1000.000	4			

a. Predictors: (Constant), PROGINV
b. Dependent Variable: PERCEMP

		Coefficients[a]				
		Unstandardized Coefficients		**Standardized Coefficients**		
Model		**B**	**Std. Error**	**Beta**	**t**	**Sig.**
1	(Constant)	−6.000	10.677		−.562	.613
	PROGINV	9.000	2.517	.900	3.576	.037

a. Dependent Variable: PERCEMP

Table 6.17 Worksheet for Regression and Correlation: Investment in Training Programs and Subsequent Employment of Trainees

Program	Percent of Trainees Employed (Y)	Program Investment (Millions of Dollars)(X)	$Y-\bar{Y}$ (y)	$X-\bar{X}$ (x)	xy	y^2	x^2	Y_c	$Y-Y_c$	$(Y-Y_c)^2$
A	10	2	−20	−2	40	400	4	12	−2	4
B	30	3	0	−1	0	0	1	21	9	81
C	20	4	−10	0	0	100	0	30	−10	100
D	50	6	20	2	40	400	4	48	2	4
E	40	5	10	1	10	100	1	39	1	1
	150	20	0	0	90	4000	10	150	0	190
	$\bar{Y}=30$	$\bar{X}=4$								

$$b = \frac{\sum(xy)}{\sum(x)^2} = \frac{90}{10} = 9$$

$$a = \bar{Y} - b(\bar{X}) = 30 - 9(4) = -6$$

$$Y_c = a + b(X) = -6 + 9(X)$$

$$r^2 = \frac{b(\sum xy)}{\sum y^2} = \frac{9(90)}{1000} = 0.81$$

$$r = \sqrt{r^2} = 0.90$$

$$S_{yx} = \sqrt{\frac{\sum(Y - Y_c)^2}{n - 2}} = \sqrt{\frac{190}{3}} = 7.96$$

$$Y_{t(6)}(95\%) = Y_{c(6)} \pm 2Z(s_{y.x}) = 48 \pm 1.96(7.96)$$

$$= 48 \pm 15.6 = 63.6 \text{ to } 32.4$$

Regression-Discontinuity Analysis

Having reviewed computational procedures for correlation and regression analysis, we are now in a position to consider regression-discontinuity analysis. *Regression-discontinuity analysis* is a set of graphic and statistical procedures used to compute and compare estimates of the outcomes of policy actions undertaken among two or more groups, one of which is exposed to some policy treatment while the other is not. Regression-discontinuity analysis is the only procedure discussed so far that is appropriate solely for social experimentation. In fact, regression-discontinuity analysis is designed for a particularly important type of social experiment, namely, an experiment where some resource input is in such scarce supply that only a portion of some target population can receive needed resources. Such experiments involve "social ameliorations that are in short supply, and that therefore cannot be given to all individuals."[63] At the same time, randomization may be politically unfeasible and morally unjustifiable, because some of those who are most in need (or most capable) will be eliminated through random selection. For example, limited resources for job training cannot be allocated randomly among a sample of unskilled persons, because job training is intended for the most needy. Similarly, a limited number of scholarships cannot be distributed randomly among a sample of applicants of varying abilities, because it is the most meritorious student (and not the needy one) who is believed to deserve scholarship funds. Although randomization would help determine the effects of manpower training or of scholarships on the subsequent behavior of typical or representative members of a target population, randomization frequently violates principles of need or merit and is thus politically and morally unacceptable.

The advantage of regression-discontinuity analysis is that it allows us to monitor the effects of providing a scarce resource to the most needy or most deserving members of a target population that is larger than a given program can accommodate. Imagine a situation where large numbers of deserving persons (e.g., those who obtain high scores on a law school entrance examination) are to be selected to receive some scarce resource (e.g., a scholarship to law school). One of the aims of the admission policy is to select those persons who will succeed later in life, with "success" defined in terms of subsequent income. Only the most deserving applicants are awarded a scholarship, thus satisfying the principle of merit. But the most deserving students would probably be successful in later life even if they received no scholarship. Under these circumstances, it is difficult to determine whether late success in life is a consequence of receiving a scholarship or of other factors, including the family backgrounds of applicants or their social position. Do scholarships affect subsequent success in life?

One way to answer this question is to conduct an experiment (called a "tie-breaking" experiment) where scarce resources are randomly allocated to a small number of persons who are identical or "tied" in their abilities or level of need. The easiest way to visualize a tie-breaking experiment is to imagine five individuals, all of

---

[63] Campbell, "Reforms as Experiments," pp. 86–87.

whom have scored 100 on an examination. The problem here is to give awards to two of the most deserving students. Because all students are equally deserving, some procedure must be used to break the tie. One such procedure is randomization.

This same logic is extended to social experimentation through regression-discontinuity analysis. In a tie-breaking experiment, we take a narrow band of merit or need (e.g., as determined by entrance examination scores or family income) above some point that marks the cutoff between those who qualify for some resource and those who do not. To illustrate, imagine that this narrow band of ability is between 90 and 95 percent correct on a law school entrance examination. Persons with scores of 89 percent or less will not be given a scholarship, and persons with scores of 96 percent or more will be given a scholarship. But persons falling into the 90–95 interval (i.e., the narrow band of ability) will be randomly divided into two groups. One group will receive a scholarship and the other will not. Note that this procedure can be justified only under conditions where there are more deserving or needy persons seeking a valued resource than can be accommodated within existing resource constraints.

Without this "tie-breaking equipment," we would be forced to choose only the top students. Under these conditions, we would expect to find entrance examination scores to be strongly and positively correlated with subsequent success in life, as shown by the broken line in Figure 6.14. But by randomly selecting persons from the narrow band of ability (i.e., the 90–95 interval), admitting some and rejecting others (the exact number depends on how many students can be accommodated in any given year), we can find out whether scholarships have an effect on later achievement over and above that of family background and social position. If entrance examination scores do have this augmenting effect, they will be displayed in the form of a discontinuous solid line that separates those who received scholarships from those who did not (Figure 6.14).

Regression-discontinuity analysis is based on principles of correlation and regression. The main difference is that regression-discontinuity analysis requires that we compute a regression equation $[Y_c = a + b(x)]$ for each of two groups, one of which receives some valued resource while the other does not. The standard error of estimate $(S_{y.x})$, the coefficient of determination (r^2), and the simple correlation coefficient (r) may also be computed for each group. Note that the standard errors of regression estimates for the experimental and control groups can be converted into interval estimates that establish the significance of any discontinuity, for example, that displayed by the solid line in Figure 6.14.

Let us now use another hypothetical example to illustrate the application of regression-discontinuity analysis. Imagine that we want to monitor the effects of enforcement policies of the Environmental Protection Agency on the reduction of air pollution levels in various cities. Because enforcement is costly, it is not possible to mount programs in every city where pollution is a significant problem. A random sample of cities is not politically feasible because those areas with the greatest need for enforcement efforts would be eliminated simply by chance. At the same time, we want to find out whether enforcement activities, as compared with no enforcement at all, reduce pollution.

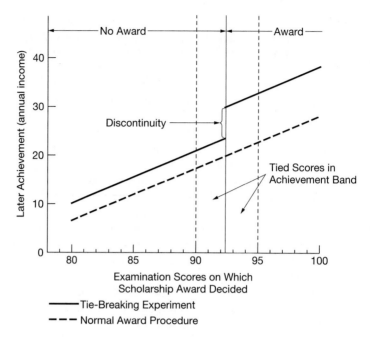

Figure 6.14 Tie-breaking experiment and regression-discontinuity analysis.
Source: Adapted from Donald T. Campbell, "Reforms as Experiments," in *Handbook of Evaluation Research*, vol. 1, ed. Elmer L. Struening and Marcia Guttentag (Beverly Hills, CA: Sage Publications, 1975), p. 87.

Assume that twenty cities with moderate to high pollution levels have been selected for the enforcement experiment. These cities are ranked according to data on pollutants provided by the CAMP. The distribution of these cities by an index of pollution severity (100 = highest) is illustrated in Table 6.18.

Six cities in the interval between 81 and 85 have been identified as the "tie-breaking" group for purposes of the enforcement experiment. Three of these cities have been selected at random to receive the enforcement program, while the remaining three cities receive no program. Because these cities were chosen solely on the basis of chance, it is unlikely that charges of favoritism will be advanced against policy makers, even though pollution severity scores for two of the control cities are slightly above those of the experimental cities. Imagine that air pollution levels in all twenty cities (ten each in the experimental and control groups) were monitored by CAMP one year before and one year after the conclusion of the enforcement experiment. Hypothetical results, displayed in Table 6.19, provide all data necessary to compute regression equations, standard errors of estimates, coefficients of determination, and simple correlation coefficients. Note that these calculations are made separately for the experimental and control groups. The SPSS output is displayed in Exhibit 6.2.

Table 6.18 Distribution of Cities by Scores on a Hypothetical Index of Pollution Severity

Pollution Severity		Number of Cities
97		1
95		1
92		1
90		1
89		1
87		1
86		1
85		2
84		1
83	"Tie-breaking" group	1
82		1
81		1
80		1
79		1
78		1
76		1
74		1
71		1
67		1
		Total 20

Source: Fictitious data.

The results of the regression-discontinuity analysis help answer several questions about the outcomes of the enforcement experiment. First, observe the pre- and postenforcement means for the experimental and control cities. The pollution levels for both groups are lower in the postenforcement period, even though the control group received no enforcement program. Nevertheless, the difference between the pre- and postenforcement means is larger for the experimental cities (88.6 − 84.7 = 3.9) than for the control cities (77.5 − 76.7 = 0.8), suggesting that the enforcement program contributed to the decrease in pollution. Second, experimental cities have a stronger coefficient of determination ($r^2 = 0.971$) and simple correlation coefficient ($r = 0.986$) than those for control cities ($r^2 = 0.932$, $r = 0.961$). The standard error of estimate for the experimental cities ($S_{y.x} = 0.76$) is also lower than that for the control cities ($S_{y.x} = 2.27$). Hence, there is less error in the estimated relationship between enforcement and pollution levels for the experimental cities.

Finally, there is a partial discontinuity between the regression lines for the two groups. If we calculate interval estimates for the two "tie-breaking" cities with identical preenforcement scores of 85, we obtain the following results:

$$Y_i \text{ (experimental city 8)} = Y_{c(85)} \pm 1.96(0.76)$$
$$= 81.33 \pm 1.49$$
$$= 79.8 \text{ to } 82.8$$

Table 6.19 Results of Regression-Discontinuity Analysis for Hypothetical Experimental and Control Cities

Experimental Cities

City	Preenforcement Pollution Level (X)	Postenforcement Pollution Level (Y)	x	y	x^2	y^2	xy	Y_c	$(Y-Y_c)^2$
1	97	93	8.4	8.3	70.56	68.89	69.72	92.56	0.19
2	95	91	6.4	6.3	40.96	39.69	40.32	90.69	0.10
3	92	87	3.4	2.3	11.56	5.29	7.82	87.88	0.77
4	90	87	1.4	2.3	1.96	5.29	3.22	86.01	0.98
5	89	84	0.4	-0.7	0.16	0.49	-0.28	85.07	1.15
6	87	82	-1.6	-2.7	2.56	7.29	4.32	83.20	1.44
7	86	83	-2.6	-1.7	6.76	2.89	4.42	82.27	0.53
8	85	82	-3.6	-2.7	12.96	7.29	9.72	81.33	0.45
9	84	80	-4.6	-4.7	21.16	22.09	21.62	80.39	0.15
10	81	78	-7.6	-6.7	57.76	44.89	50.92	77.59	0.17
	$\bar{X} = 88.6$	$\bar{Y} = 84.7$	0	0	226.40	204.10	211.80	847.00	5.74

$$b = \frac{\sum(xy)}{\sum(x^2)} = \frac{211.80}{226.40} = 0.936 \qquad a = \bar{Y} - b(\bar{X}) = 84.7 - 0.936(88.6) = 1.8$$

$$Y_c = a + b(X) = 1.8 + 0.936(X)$$

$$S_{y \cdot x} = \sqrt{\frac{(Y - Y_c)^2}{n - 2}} = \sqrt{\frac{5.74}{8}} = 0.86$$

$$r^2 = \frac{b(\sum xy)}{\sum(y^2)} = \frac{936(211.80)}{204.10} = 0.97$$

$$r = \sqrt{r^2} = 0.98$$

Control Cities

City	Preenforcement Pollution Level (X)	Postenforcement Pollution Level (Y)	x	y	x^2	y^2	xy	Y_c	$(Y-Y_c)^2$
11	85	88	7.5	11.3	56.25	127.69	84.75	87.2	4.84
12	83	84	5.5	7.3	30.25	53.29	40.15	84.4	1.96
13	82	86	4.5	9.3	20.25	86.49	41.85	83.0	1.00
14	80	78	2.5	1.3	6.25	1.69	3.25	80.2	0.04
15	79	75	1.5	-1.7	2.25	2.89	-2.55	78.8	0.04
16	78	77	0.5	0.3	0.25	0.09	0.15	77.4	0.36
17	76	75	-1.5	-1.7	2.25	2.89	2.55	74.6	1.96
18	74	73	-3.5	-3.7	12.25	13.69	12.95	71.8	4.84
19	71	71	-6.5	-5.7	42.25	32.49	37.05	67.6	11.56
20	67	60	-10.5	-16.7	110.25	278.89	175.35	62.0	25.00
	$\bar{X}=77.5$	$\bar{Y}=76.7$	0	0	282.50	600.10	395.50	767.0	51.60

$$b = \frac{\sum(xy)}{\sum(x^2)} = \frac{395.5}{282.5} = 1.4 \qquad a = \bar{Y} - b(\bar{X}) = 76.7 - 1.4(77.5) = -31.8$$

$$Y_c = a + b(X) = -31.8 + 1.4(X)$$

$$S_{y.x} = \sqrt{\frac{(Y-Y_c)^2}{n-2}} = \sqrt{\frac{51.60}{8}} = 2.41$$

$$r^2 = \frac{b(\sum xy)}{\sum(y^2)} = \frac{1.4(395.5)}{600.10} = 0.923$$

$$r = \sqrt{r^2} = 0.961$$

Exhibit 6.2   SPSS Output for Tables 6.13 and 6.14

Model Summary

Model	R	R Square	Adjusted R Square	Std. Error of the Estimate
1	.985[a]	.971	.967	.86302379

a. Predictors: (Constant), PREENF

ANOVA[b]

Model		Sum of Squares	df	Mean Square	F	Sig.
1	Regression	198.142	1	198.142	266.030	.000[a]
	Residual	5.958	8	.745		
	Total	204.100	9			

a. Predictors: (Constant), PREENF
b. Dependent Variable: POSTENF

Coefficients[a]

Model		Unstandardized Coefficients		Standardized Coefficients	t	Sig.
		B	Std. Error	Beta		
1	(Constant)	1.814	5.089		.356	.731
	PREENF	.936	.057	.985	16.310	.000

a. Dependent Variable: POSTENF

Model Summary

Model	R	R Square	Adjusted R Square	Std. Error of the Estimate
1	.961[a]	.923	.913	2.40831892

a. Predictors: (Constant), PREENFC

ANOVA[b]

Model		Sum of Squares	df	Mean Square	F	Sig.
1	Regression	553.700	1	553.700	95.466	.000[a]
	Residual	46.400	8	5.800		
	Total	600.100	9			

a. Predictors: (Constant), PREENFC
b. Dependent Variable: POSTENFC

Exhibit 6.2   SPSS Output for Tables 6.13 and 6.14 (continued)

		Coefficients[a]				
		Unstandardized Coefficients		Standardized Coefficients		
Model		B	Std. Error	Beta	t	Sig.
1	(Constant)	−31.800	11.131		−2.857	.021
	PREENFC	1.400	.143	.961	9.771	.000

a. Dependent Variable: POSTENFC

$$Y_i \text{ (control city 11)} = Y_{c(85)} \pm 1.96(2.27)$$
$$= 87.2 \pm 4.45$$
$$= 82.8 \text{ to } 91.7$$

These interval estimates mean that the highest pollution level that is likely to occur 95 percent of the time in experimental city 8 is 82.8, while the lowest that is likely to occur 95 percent of the time in control city 11 is also 82.8. In other words, when we take the highest and lowest pollution levels that are likely to occur 95 percent of the time, the experimental city equals the control city. At the same time, the point estimates are closer for experimental city 10 (77.59) and control city 14 (80.2), indicating that the discontinuity is not as great for some cities.

Note that this kind of comparison would not have been possible without regression-discontinuity analysis. By randomly assigning "tied" scores to experimental and control groups, we are able to determine the effects of the enforcement program on cities that are identical or very similar in their preenforcement pollution levels. The results of the regression-discontinuity analysis are more readily visualized if we display them in graphic form. In Figure 6.15, a partial discontinuity between the two groups is evident.

Regression-discontinuity analysis is a highly useful technique for monitoring the outcomes of social experiments that involve the distribution of some scarce resource. While our hypothetical example illustrates some of the calculations required to apply the technique, it also avoids some of its complexities. The application of the technique normally requires a much larger number of cases than that used here. For example, as many as two hundred cases might have been required to do the kind of analysis just described. The need for a relatively large sample of cases is one of several conditions that must be satisfied in order to obtain valid results. These conditions, which include variables that are normally distributed, are discussed in available statistics texts.[64]

---

[64] See, for example, William Mendenhall and James E. Reinmuth, *Statistics for Management and Economics*, 3d ed. (North Scituate, MA: Duxbury Press, 1978), ch. 11.

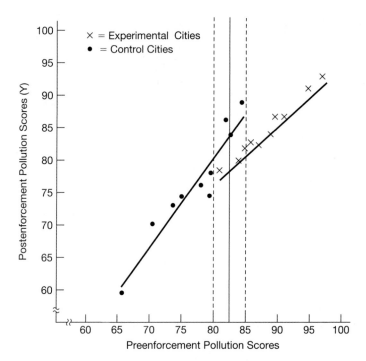

Figure 6.15   Graphic display of results of regression-discontinuity analysis for hypothetical experimental and control cities.

CHAPTER SUMMARY

This chapter has provided an overview of the nature and functions of monitoring in policy analysis, compared and contrasted four approaches to monitoring, and described and illustrated the application of techniques used in conjunction with these approaches.

LEARNING OBJECTIVES

- distinguish monitoring from other policy-analytic methods
- list the main functions of monitoring
- distinguish policy outcomes, impacts, processes, and inputs
- compare and contrast social systems accounting, social experimentation,

- social auditing, and research and practice synthesis
- describe threats to internal and external validity
- perform interrupted time-series and control-series analyses on a case involving highway safety

KEY TERMS AND CONCEPTS

case survey method (294)
constitutive (formal) definition (279)
control-series analysis (317)
external validity (291)
Gini Index (303)
internal validity (290)
interrupted time-series analysis (313)
Lorenz curve (303)
operational definition (279)

purchasing power index (308)
regression-discontinuity analysis (322)
research survey method (295)
social auditing (292)
social experimentation (288)
social systems accounting (281)
spurious interpretation (300)
threats to validity (rival hypotheses) (290)

REVIEW QUESTIONS

1. How is monitoring related to forecasting?
2. What is the relationship between ill-structured problems and approaches to monitoring?
3. What is the relationship between monitoring and the types of policy claims discussed in Chapter 8?
4. Construct constitutive and operational definitions for any five of the following action and outcome variables:

    Program expenditure Equality of educational opportunity
    Personnel turnover National security
    Health services Work incentives
    Quality of life Pollution
    Satisfaction with municipal services Energy consumption
    Income distribution Rapport with clients

5. Listed below are several policy problems. For five of these problems, provide an indicator or index that would help determine whether these problems are being resolved through government action.

    Work alienation School dropouts
    Crime Poverty
    Energy crisis Fiscal crisis
    Inflation Racial discrimination

6. The following table reports the number of criminal offenses known to the police per 100,000 population. Known offenses are broken down into two categories—total crimes against person and total crimes against property—over the period 1965–89. Construct two curved-line graphs that display trends in crime rates over the period. Label the two graphs appropriately. What do these graphs suggest about crime as a policy problem?

Crime Rates in the United States: Offenses Known to Police per 100,000 Population, 1960–76

	1965	1970	1975	1980	1985	1989
Violent	200	364	482	597	556	663
Property	2,249	3,621	4,800	5,353	4,651	5,077

Source: Harold W. Stanley and Richard G. Niemi, *Vital Statistics on American Politics,* 3d ed. (Washington, DC: Congressional Quarterly Press, 1992), p. 401.

7. In the following table are data on the percentage distribution of family income by quintiles in 1975 and 1989. Use these data to construct two Lorenz curves that depict changes in the distribution of income between 1975 and 1989. Label the two curves and the two axes.

Percentage Distribution of Family Personal Income in the United States by Quintiles, 1975 and 1989

Quintiles	1975	1989
Highest	41.0	46.7
Second	24.0	24.0
Third	17.6	15.9
Fourth	12.0	9.6
Lowest	5.4	3.8
Total	100.0	100.0

Source: U.S. Bureau of the Census, *Current Population Reports,* Series P-60.

8. Calculate the Gini concentration ratio for 1975 and 1989 data in study suggestion 7. What do the Lorenz curves and Gini coefficients suggest about poverty as a policy problem? If poverty and other problems are "artificial" and "subjective," how valid is the information displayed by the Lorenz curves? Why?

9. Policy issue: Should average monthly benefits paid to mothers under the Aid to Families with Dependent Children (AFDC) program be increased?

Year	Average Monthly Benefit	Consumer Price Index (1982–84 = 100)
1970	$183.13	38.8
1975	219.44	53.8
1980	280.03	82.4
1985	342.15	107.6
1988	374.07	118.3

Prepare a policy memo that answers this question. Before writing the memo:
a. Prepare a purchasing power index for all years in the series, using 1970 as the base year.
b. Convert the average monthly benefits into real benefits for these years.
c. Repeat the same procedures, using 1980 as the base year.

10. The War on Drugs was initiated in 1981 during the Reagan administration and continued under President Bush. Although another policy—mandatory drug education in schools—had successfully eliminated the country's first cocaine epidemic at the turn of the twentieth century, the central focus of the Reagan–Bush policy is the interdiction of cocaine and crack cocaine before it enters the United States from other countries, especially South America. It is widely acknowledged that the policy has not reduced the quantity of cocaine and crack entering the country and that the street price of these drugs has actually declined since the early 1980s.

    The following table provides data on some key policy outcome measures relevent to the War on Drugs. On the basis of these data, write a policy memo to the chief of the Drug Enforcement Administration that assesses the effectiveness of the War on Drugs.

Percentage of Cocaine Users in Past Month and Cocaine-Related Emergency Room Visits and Deaths Among Different Groups

Group	1982	1985	1988
High school seniors	5.0	6.7	3.4
College undergraduates	17.3	17.1	10.0
Age in general population			
12–17 years	1.6	1.5	1.1
18–25 years	6.8	7.6	4.5
26+ years	1.2	2.0	0.9
Emergency room visits			
Cocaine	NA	10,099	46,835
Crack	NA	1,000	15,306
Emergency room deaths	NA	717	2,163

Source: Drug Abuse and Drug Abuse Research (Washington, DC: National Institute on Drug Abuse, 1991).

11. Imagine that you are examining the effects of ten scholarship awards on the subsequent performance of disadvantaged youths in college. There are fewer awards than applicants, and awards must be based on merit. Therefore, it is not possible to provide all disadvantaged students with awards, nor is it politically feasible to select students randomly because this conflicts with the principle of merit. You decide to allocate the ten awards according to the following rules: No student will receive an award without scoring at least 86 on the examination; five awards will be given automatically to the top students in the 92–100 interval; and the remaining five awards will be given to a random sample of students in the 86–91 interval.

    One year later, you obtain information on the grade point averages of the ten award students and ten other disadvantaged students who did not receive an award. You have college entrance examination scores for all twenty students. Does the provision of scholarship awards to disadvantaged students improve subsequent achievement in college?

Award Group		Nonaward Group	
Examination Scores	*Grade Point Average*	*Examination Scores*	*Grade Point Average*
99	3.5	88	3.2
97	3.9	89	3.2
94	3.4	90	3.3
92	3.0	86	3.0
92	3.3	91	3.5
86	3.1	85	3.1
90	3.3	81	3.0
89	3.2	79	2.8
88	3.2	84	3.0
91	3.4	80	2.6

a. Construct a regression-discontinuity graph that displays examination scores and grade point averages for the award and nonaward groups. Use Xs and Os to display data points for the experimental (X) and control (O) groups.

b. Construct a worksheet and compute for each group the values of a and b in the equation $Y_c = a + b(X)$.

c. For each group, write the regression equation that describes the relation between merit (examination scores) and subsequent achievement (grade point averages).

d. Compute the standard error of estimate at the 95 percent estimation interval (i.e., two standard errors) for each group.

e. Compute r^2 and r.

f. Interpret information contained in (a) through (e) and answer the question: Does the provision of scholarship awards to disadvantaged students improve subsequent achievement in college? Justify your answer.

12. Subtract 0.5 from each student's grade point average in the nonaward (control) group above.

a. Does the Y intercept change for the control group? Why?

b. Does the slope of the regression line change for the control group? Why?

c. Does the standard error of estimate change for the control group? Why?

d. Does r^2 and r change for the control group? Why?

e. What do your answers show about the appropriateness of correlation and regression analysis for problems where pretest and posttest scores are highly correlated?

f. What, then, are the special advantages of regression-discontinuity analysis?

13. Using at least four threats to validity, construct rebuttals to the following argument: (*B*) The greater the cost of an alternative, the less likely it is that the alternative will be pursued. (*W*) The enforcement of the maximum speed limit of 55 mph increases the costs of exceeding the speed limit. (*I*) The mileage death rate fell from 4.3 to 3.6 deaths per 100 million miles after the implementation of the 55-mph speed limit. (*C*) The 55-mph speed limit (National Maximum Speed Law of 1973) has been definitely successful in saving lives. Study Figure 6.13 before you begin.

DEMONSTRATION EXERCISE

As we know, the simple (bivariate) linear regression equation is written as

$$Y = a + b(x)$$

OR

$$y = b_0 + b_1 x \tag{6.1}$$

When we use this equation to estimate the value of a variable in a *time series*, the equation is written as

$$y_t = b_0 + b_1 x_t \tag{6.2}$$

In Equation 6.1, the values of the variables y and x are not ordered in time. For example, the price and age of automobiles would be unrelated to the time at which price and age were measured. By contrast, Equation 6.2 expresses price as a function of time, for example, the year in which price was measured. The data would be arrayed like this:

CASE	PRICE (Y_t)	YEAR (x_t)	
1	$10,000	1985	NOTE: Years may be coded as 1,
2	10,200	1986	2,..., T, or as $-1, -2,..., 0, 1, 2,..., $ T.
3	10,300	1987	
4	10,600	1988	
5	10,500	1989	
6	11,100	1990	
7	11,100	1991	
8	11,200	1992	
9	11,500	1993	

Equation 6.2 is a time-series regression equation. It is frequently used to forecast the value of a variable in future years, for example, the price of Nissans in the year 2000.

Another type of time-series regression equation is one where there are two or more independent (predictor) variables, $X_{1t} \ldots x_{kt}$, which are presumed to be causes of a dependent (response) variable, y_t, which is presumed to be the effect (because regression analysis has nothing to do with causality, per se, the term "presumed" is used here). The equation is written as

$$y_t = b_0 + b_1 x_{1t} + b_2 x_{2t} + b_k x_{kt} \tag{6.3}$$

When using time-series regression analysis, it is important to remember the following points, which will be discussed in class:

1. We often want to estimate the effects of a policy intervention on a policy outcome. We do this by creating a so-called "dummy (categorical) variable," which takes the values of 0 before the policy intervention and 1 after the policy intervention. For example, a dummy variable may be symbolized as x_{2t} when the dummy variable is the second predictor variable. The first variable is time, x_{1t}, measured in years. The policy intervention regression equation would be written:

$$y_t \text{ (policy outcome)} = b_0 + b_1 x_{1t} \text{ (time)} + b_2 x_{2t} \text{ (policy intervention)} \tag{6.4}$$

2. In linear regression, we must satisfy assumptions of linearity and homoskedasticity. An additional assumption must be satisfied in time-series analysis: The observations

of y in the time series must be independent (uncorrelated). This is called the non-autocorrelation assumption. Note that, just as there are *tests for linearity* (e.g., plotting the y values against normal scores in a normal probability plot), there are *tests for autocorrelation*. One of these is the Durbin–Watson (D-W) test. We can apply this test with SPSS and other statistical packages.

3. If the autocorrelation coefficient, r, is statistically significant at a specified level of α (usually $p = 0.05$), we reject the null hypothesis that adjacent observations in a time series are uncorrelated—and we thereby accept the alternative hypothesis that adjacent observations *are* autocorrelated. When there is statistically significant autocorrelation, we often can eliminate most of its effects by regressing the values of y_t on their lagged values, y_{t-1}. This is a lag of one time period (e.g., one year). The lagged values (one or more time periods) of a variable can be easily computed with SPSS and other statistical packages.

The regression equation with a lagged dependent variable (in this case, one year) is written as follows:

$$y_t = b_0 + b_1 y_{t-1} \tag{6.5}$$

Equations 6.4 and 6.5 can be combined to express the effects of a lagged policy outcome variable (y_{t-1}), time (x_{t1}), and a policy intervention (x_{t2}) on a policy outcome variable (y_t). Here is the combined equation:

$$y_t = b_0 + b_1 y_{t-1}\text{(lag 1 period)} + b_2 x_{2t}\text{(time)}$$
$$+ b_3 x_{3t}\text{(policy intervention)} \tag{6.6}$$

In this demonstration exercise, we will be using a data file from the Fatal Accident Reporting System of the National Highway Traffic Safety Administration to perform the tasks described below.

1. Estimate the effect of time on fatalities before (1966–73) and after (1974–2000) the adoption of the 55-mph speed limit. Run two separate regressions. Interpret the two regression estimates.

2. Estimate the effect of employment on fatalities. Forecast traffic fatalities for 2000, using the actual value of employment, which is 125,331,000. Note that we either have to assume the 2000 values for unemployment or use time-series analysis to forecast the 2000 value. Interpret the computer printout and compare the forecast with actual fatalities for 2000.

3. Estimate the effect of time (years) and the policy intervention (55-mph speed limit) on fatalities, using a dummy variable. Assess whether the effect of the policy intervention is statistically significant and interpret the computer output.

4. Reestimate the equation in part 3 above. This time, control for the effect of autocorrelation by adding Y_{t-1} (the lagged value of the dependent variable) as a third predictor. Interpret the output and compare it to output obtained in part 3.

5. Estimate the effect of the policy intervention on fatalities, after including miles traveled and employment as additional predictor variables. In this regression, do not include time as a predictor variable. Interpret your computer output.

6. Create SPSS graphs that display an interrupted time series for (a) the United States; (b) for European countries that adopted 48- and 54-mph (80- and 90-kph) speed limits; and (c) for European countries that did not adopt a speed limit. Interpret the graphs.

REFERENCES

Bartlett, Robert V., ed. *Policy through Impact Assessment: Institutionalized Analysis as a Policy Strategy*. New York: Greenwood Press, 1989.

Campbell, Donald T. *Methodology and Epistemology for Social Science: Selected Papers*, ed. E. Samuel Overman. Chicago: University of Chicago Press, 1989.

Cook, Thomas D., and Charles S. Reichardy, eds. *Qualitative and Quantitative Methods in Evaluation Research*. Beverly Hills, CA: Sage Publications, 1979.

Light, Richard J., and David B. Pillemer. *Summing Up: The Science of Reviewing Research*. Cambridge, MA: Harvard University Press, 1984.

MacRae, Duncan Jr. *Policy Indicators: Links between Social Science and Public Debate*. Chapel Hill: University of North Carolina Press, 1985.

Miles, Matthew B., and A. Michael Huberman. *Qualitative Data Analysis: A Sourcebook of New Methods*. Beverly Hills, CA: Sage Publications, 1984.

Shadish, William, Thomas D. Cook, and Donald T. Campbell. *Experimental and Quasi-Experimental Design for External Validity*. Boston, MA: Houghton Mifflin, 2002.

Trochim, William M. K. *Research Design for Program Evaluation: The Regression-Discontinuity Approach*. Beverly Hills, CA: Sage Publications, 1984.

U.S. General Accounting Office. *Designing Evaluations*. Methodology Transfer Paper 4. Washington, DC: Program Evaluation and Methodology Division, U.S. General Accounting Office, July 1984.

Yin, Robert K. *Case Study Analysis*. Beverly Hills, CA: Sage Publications, 1985.

Case 6. Rival Explanations of Policy Outcomes: The Political Economy of Traffic Fatalities in Europe and the United States

The 55-mph speed limit, adopted in 1974 as a means to reduce gasoline consumption during the 1973–74 OPEC oil embargo, was unexpectedly followed by a sharp decline in traffic fatalities. Between January 1, 1974, and December 31, 1975, there was a decline of 9,100 fatalities, a 16.8 percent drop. Despite continuing opposition from rural Western states and the trucking industry, there was broad support for the policy among policy makers, policy analysts, and the general public. And, clearly, the problem is not unimportant or trivial. Traffic fatalities represent the leading cause of death among persons thirty-five years of age and younger. Average annual highway deaths since 1974 are equivalent to a fully loaded 767 aircraft crashing with no survivors every third day of the week.

On April 2, 1987, Congress enacted the Surface Transportation and Uniform Relocation Assistance Act of 1987, overriding President Reagan's veto. Provisions of this bill permitted individual states to experiment with speed limits up to 65 mph on rural interstate highways. By July 1988, forty states had raised the speed limit to 60 or 65 mph on 89 percent of rural interstate roads. Senator John C. Danforth, an influential supporter of the 55-mph speed limit, argued against the new policy. The 65-mph speed limit, said Danforth, would save an average of one minute per day per driver, but result in an annual increase of 600 to 1,000 deaths. *The Washington Post* joined the opponents. "The equation is in minutes versus lives. It's not even close.... A hundred miles at 55 mph take about 17 minutes longer than at 65. That's the price of those lives. It ought to be the easiest vote the House takes this year." Eight years later, in a November 1995 press release, U.S. Secretary of Transportation Federico Pena reaffirmed the Clinton administration's opposition to the higher speed limits (see Chapter 1, Case 1). The National Maximum Speed Limit was officially abandoned the same year.

Many analysts who have evaluated the effects of the intervention, along with elected officials from the ten northeastern states that retained the 55-mph speed limit until its repeal, affirm that the 1974 law was responsible for the decline in traffic fatalities. However, the evidence suggests that they may have failed to consider rival hypotheses—which had they been identified and tested—would have resulted in a different explanation of traffic deaths and, consequently, a different policy recommendation.

Here are data on U.S. traffic fatalities and other variables for the period 1966–2000 (Exhibit 6.3). In addition, fatality rates in the U.S. and European countries are provided in a separate SPSS file (Exhibit 6.4). Use the data for the demonstration exercise.

Exhibit 6.3

	year	years_	fat	bimi	uempr	licd	rveh
1	1966	1.00	50,894	926	3.2	100,998	95,703
2	1967	2.00	50,724	964	3.1	103,172	98,859
3	1968	3.00	52,725	1,016	2.9	105,410	102,987
4	1969	4.00	53,543	1,062	2.8	108,306	107,412
5	1970	5.00	52,627	1,110	4.4	111,543	111,242
6	1971	6.00	52,542	1,179	5.3	114,426	116,330
7	1972	7.00	54,589	1,260	5.0	118,414	122,557
8	1973	8.00	54,052	1,313	4.2	121,546	130,025
9	1974	9.00	45,196	1,281	4.9	125,427	134,900
10	1975	10.00	44,525	1,328	7.9	129,791	125,402
11	1976	11.00	45,523	1,402	7.1	134,036	130,731
12	1977	12.00	47,878	1,467	6.3	138,121	134,887
13	1978	13.00	50,331	1,545	5.3	140,844	140,978
14	1979	14.00	51,093	1,529	5.1	143,284	144,805
15	1980	15.00	51,091	1,527	6.9	145,295	146,845
16	1981	16.00	49,301	1,553	7.4	147,075	149,330
17	1982	17.00	43,945	1,595	9.9	150,234	151,148

Exhibit 6.3 (continued)

18	1983	18.00	42,589	1,653	9.9	154,389	153,830
19	1984	19.00	44,257	1,720	7.4	155,424	158,900
20	1985	20.00	43,825	1,774	7.0	156,868	165,382
21	1986	21.00	46,087	1,835	6.9	159,487	168,137
22	1987	22.00	46,390	1,921	6.2	161,818	172,366
23	1988	23.00	47,087	2,026	5.5	162,853	176,752
24	1989	24.00	45,582	2,096	5.2	165,555	180,792
25	1990	25.00	44,599	2,144	5.6	167,015	183,934
26	1991	26.00	41,508	2,172	7.0	168,995	186,052
27	1992	27.00	39,250	2,247	7.8	173,125	184,864
28	1993	28.00	40,150	2,297	7.2	173,149	188,453
29	1994	29.00	40,716	2,360	6.1	175,403	192,213
30	1995	30.00	41,817	2,423	5.6	176,628	197,096
31	1996	31.00	41,907	2,469	5.4	.	.
32	1997	32.00	42,013	2,560	4.9	179,539	201,631
33	1998	33.00	41,471	2,619	4.5	182,709	203,568
34	1999	34.00	41,611	.	4.2	.	.
35	2000	35.00	.	.	4.0	.	.

Note: fat = fatalities; bimi = billions of miles traveled on all roads; uempr = unemployment rate; licd = licensed drivers; rveh = registered vehicles; emp = employment (thousands); pop = population of U.S. (thousands); remp = rate of employment.

	emp	pop	remp
1	72,895	195,578	96.80000
2	74,372	197,457	96.90000
3	75,920	199,399	97.10000
4	77,902	201,385	97.20000
5	78,627	203,984	95.60000
6	79,120	206,827	94.70000
7	81,702	209,284	95.00000
8	84,409	211,357	95.80000
9	85,936	213,342	95.10000
10	84,783	215,465	92.10000
11	87,485	217,561	92.90000
12	90,546	219,758	93.70000
13	94,373	222,093	94.70000
14	96,945	224,569	94.90000
15	97,722	227,255	93.10000
16	98,878	229,637	92.60000
17	98,047	231,996	90.10000
18	99,347	234,284	90.10000
19	103,413	236,477	92.60000
20	105,613	237,924	93.00000
21	107,860	240,133	93.10000
22	110,634	242,289	93.80000

(continued)

Exhibit 6.3 (continued)

	emp	pop	remp
23	113,153	244,499	94.50000
24	115,453	246,819	94.80000
25	116,660	249,403	94.40000
26	115,657	252,138	93.00000
27	116,395	255,039	92.20000
28	118,149	257,800	92.80000
29	121,999	260,350	93.90000
30	124,766	262,755	94.40000
31	125,311	265,284	94.60000
32	129,558	267,744	95.05000
33	131,463	270,299	94.47000
34	133,488	.	.
35	135,208	.	.

Exhibit 6.4

	year	us	eurexp	eurc	uk	fin	fr	den
1	1970	25.8	21.9	24.3	14.3	24.8	23.5	25
2	1971	25.4	22.8	24.7	14.8	25.9	25.4	25
3	1972	26.1	22.8	25.0	14.6	25.2	27.4	24
4	1973	25.6	22.1	23.5	14.7	23.8	25.6	24
5	1974	21.2	17.4	21.3	13.0	18.0	22.5	16
6	1975	20.1	17.6	20.2	11.9	19.0	24.0	17
7	1976	20.9	18.3	18.8	12.0	20.0	26.0	17

Note: eurexp = European "experimental" states that adopted a 90 kph (54 mph) speed limit in 1972; eurcon = European "control" states. Other names refer to countries.

7

Evaluating Policy Performance

Monitoring is primarily concerned with "facts," whereas evaluation is primarily concerned with "values." Monitoring answers the question: How and why did a policy outcome occur? Evaluation answers a related but different question: Of what value is the outcome?

The purpose of this chapter is to address this important question by considering the policy-analytic method of evaluation. We first review several ways in which ethics and values are important for public policy and several frameworks for thinking about values, ethics, and metaethics (metaethics is the philosophical study of ethical reasoning). Second, we examine the nature, aims, and functions of evaluation in policy analysis, showing how evaluation as a form of ethical appraisal helps produce information about policy performance. By contrast, monitoring as a type of causal appraisal helps produce information about policy outcomes. We then compare and contrast three approaches to evaluation and examine methods and techniques employed in conjunction with these approaches.

ETHICS AND VALUES IN POLICY ANALYSIS

Some policy analysts believe that policy evaluation should concentrate on explanation and prediction, as distinguished from the analysis of ethics and values.[1] Policy disagreements would diminish or disappear, they argue, if analysts could only explain and predict with greater certainty. There is no point spending much time on differences in basic values, because they are always subject to dispute and difficult to resolve.[2]

This view of policy analysis, known as logical positivism or "positivism" for short, makes a strict separation between facts and values. The acquisition of facts is seen as positive, because facts affirm what is, as distinguished from values, which speculate on what might be. Logical positivism[3] was developed in Europe in the 1920s by a group of physicists and philosophers of science called the Vienna Circle. The original Vienna Circle positivists, and later their followers in the social sciences, believed that questions of ethics and morality are not proper subjects of science. Because observation, explanation and prediction are deemed to be the only legitimate aims of science, ethical and value judgments are seen as unscientific or antiscientific. Science and values should be kept strictly apart. In the social sciences, analysts should confine their work to explaining and predicting policy outcomes, limiting themselves to the observation and analysis of what "is" rather than what "ought" to be.

Thinking about Values

Positivism was abandoned in philosophy by the late 1950s. It is no longer regarded as a tenable model of science. The consensus today is that science, which is subject to a great many social, cultural, economic, political, and psychological influences, does not work the way positivists said it does. Because analysts need to look critically at the relation (not separation) between facts and values, it is important to understand what we mean when we use the terms "values" and "ethics."

The term values is often defined in a comprehensive way, so that it includes any wants, needs, interests, or preferences.[4] Here, values represent "objects" along a broad spectrum of behaviors involving choice. In this view, which refers to *values-as-objects* (e.g., the preference for efficiency), values are anything of interest to those who make evaluations. Given this broad conception, policy analysts can be

---

[1] For example, Edith Stokey and Richard Zeckhauser, *A Primer for Policy Analysis* (New York: W. W. Norton, 1978), p. 261.

[2] This is a paraphrase from Milton Friedman, *Essays in Positive Economics* (Chicago: University of Chicago Press, 1953), p. 5. Friedman is speaking about "positive economics."

[3] Logical positivism is also called logical empiricism, and sometimes scientific empiricism.

[4] Stephen C. Pepper, *The Sources of Value* (Berkeley: University of California Press, 1958).

seen to address a sweeping array of values. It is in this broad sense that policy choices involve "the authoritative allocation of values."[5]

A second, more specific conception of values refers to *values-as-criteria*. Here, the concern is not only with values as objects but also with the criteria used to choose values. This second meaning of values incorporates decision rules or criteria employed to choose between two or more values. A broad definition of values leads to statements such as "The majority of citizens want government programs to be more efficient." A more specific definition specifies the criterion or rule: "The majority of citizens want to vote for programs according to the rule: Select the program that produces the greatest net benefit (i.e., benefits – costs)."

These two usages of the term values are related to the different contexts—personal, standard, and ideal—in which values arise.[6] In the personal context, values are *expressed* in the form of preferences, wants, and needs. A value expression is "I prefer public to private schools." By contrast, the standard context involves *statements* about some (standard) individual or group that holds certain values, for example, "School busing for racial integration is a bad policy in the eyes of middle-class citizens." Finally, the ideal context involves *value judgments* that are not reducible to value expressions offered in the personal context, or to value statements in the standard context.

Value judgments are unique because they justify criteria such as net efficiency improvement, or decision rules such as: Select the policy that maximizes net benefits. It is the role of value judgments to warrant or justify such criteria and decision rules when they are used in the process of ethical argumentation (see Chapters 1 and 8). For example, "Policy A is preferable to policy B, because it produces the greatest net benefit, thereby increasing the aggregate satisfaction of members of the community—that is, the greatest good for the greatest number." This value judgment goes beyond the description of personal preferences and the values of a particular group, for example, economists who seem to believe that the rule "Maximize net benefits!" is a self-evident moral imperative, when it is a decision rule in need of ethical justification. Although we can describe values and apply criteria and decision rules, we can also supply grounds for their justification, and this is the special role of value judgments.[7]

In addition to differences in the contexts of values, there are other important distinctions.

- *Value versus values.* Because people express values that we can describe and explain, it does not follow that such value expressions refer to things that are of value. The value of something cannot be established on the basis of observation alone, because it is always possible to ask: "Are these values good?"

---

[5] This definition, well known to political scientists, is that of David Easton in *The Political System* (Chicago: Alfred Knopf, 1953).

[6] Abraham Kaplan, *The Conduct of Inquiry* (San Francisco, CA: Chandler, 1964), pp. 387–97.

[7] Ibid., pp. 387–89.

Consider the quip attributed to Oscar Wilde: "An economist is a man who knows the price of everything and the value of nothing."

- *Values versus needs.* Although values may be a source of needs, as when the value of health justifies attempts to satisfy unmet needs for minimum nutritional standards, values are not the same as needs. A perceived deficiency that gives rise to a need (e.g., nutrition as a material need) may be relatively independent of such values as security, order, justice, and equality. Complex relationships between needs and values create conceptual and methodological issues for analysts who conduct "needs assessments," because needs are not the same as values.

- *Values versus norms.* Whereas norms are rules of conduct applicable in specific contexts, values are standards of achievement applicable in many or all contexts. Values of power, respect, rectitude, affection, well-being, wealth, and enlightenment[8] may each result in the establishment of separate sets of norms intended to regulate relationships between analyst and politician, analyst and analyst, analyst and journalist, analyst and client, or analyst and the public at large. Conversely, the norm of public accountability may involve power, respect, well-being, and other values. Although values provide grounds for justifying norms, the more general the norm, the more difficult it is to distinguish it from a value. Codes of conduct for regulating the behavior of planners, policy analysts, and public managers contain norms that are sufficiently general to be virtually indistinguishable from values.[9]

- *Valuation versus evaluation.* Another important distinction is between valuation and evaluation.[10] Evaluation as a general social process involving many forms of appraisal should be distinguished from valuation, a special process involving efforts to establish the grounds on which appraisals are made. Whereas evaluation requires that two or more alternatives be appraised—for example, according to the criterion of efficiency improvement—valuation requires that the criterion itself be justified, for example, in terms of the utilitarian philosophy of the greatest good for the greatest number. Disputes surrounding the aims and nature of policy and program evaluation often turn on the distinction between valuation and evaluation.[11]

---

[8] See Harold D. Lasswell and Abraham Kaplan, *Power and Society* (New Haven, CT: Yale University Press, 1950).

[9] For illustrations, see Elizabeth Howe and Jerome Kaufman, "Ethics and Professional Practice in Planning and Related Policy Professions," *Policy Studies Journal* 9, no. 4 (1981): 585–94.

[10] See John Dewey, "Theory of Valuation," *International Encyclopedia of Unified Science* 11, no. 4 (1939).

[11] See, for example, Ernest House, *Evaluating with Validity* (Beverly Hills, CA: Sage Publications, 1980); and Deborah Stone, "Conclusion: Political Reason," in *Policy Paradox: The Art of Political Decision Making* (New York: W. W. Norton, 2002), pp. 384–415.

- *Valuation versus prescription.* Value judgments, which are products of valuation, should not be confused with nonrational emotional appeals, ideological exhortations, or doctrinaire forms of policy advocacy. This confusion is related to the notion that policy analysis must be value-neutral,[12] for so long as valuation is mistakenly believed to be subjective and nonrational, value-neutrality is the only protection against analyses that are seen as unscientific and arbitrary. Many analysts fail to recognize that value judgments are not "commands, prescriptions, or other forms of telling people to do things . . . telling people what they should do is not telling or exhorting them to do it . . . it is purporting to give them sound solutions to their practical problems."[13]

Ethics and Metaethics

The term ethics refers to the reflective study of moral choice, whereas metaethics refers to the reflective study of ethics itself. The term ethics is often applied to habitual or customary behavior, as in the "ethics of policy makers." This everyday usage derives etymologically from the Greek and Latin *ethos* and *mores,* which refer to habits or customs. Although it is primarily this everyday usage that has guided the development of ethical codes for public managers, planners, and policy analysts,[14] these efforts at professional standard setting are based on implicit ethical and moral judgments. "Even when 'customary morality' is spoken of, the reference of the term is not merely to the customs as such—in the sense of regular, repeated sequences of behavior—but also to the view, at least implicitly held by the participants, that what they regularly do is in some way right; it is not merely what is done, it is also what is to be done."[15] As can be seen, the term ethics has two different but related meanings. Descriptive ethics, which involves the analysis of descriptions of customary morality, should be contrasted with normative ethics. Normative ethics is concerned with the analysis, evaluation, and development of normative statements that provide guidance to those trying to solve practical problems.

Normative ethics is concerned with the appraisal of criteria for justifying normative statements. The central questions of normative ethics are of the form: What criteria justify normative claims about the rightness, goodness, or justice of public actions? By contrast, metaethics is concerned with the nature and meaning of normative claims in general. Questions of metaethics are of the form: What (metaethical) criteria warrant the choice of (normative ethical) criteria employed to justify claims about the rightness, goodness, or justice of public policies? In this and other cases, the term "meta" signifies something that is "about" or "of" something else.

---

[12] Stokey and Zeckhauser, *A Primer for Policy Analysis,* pp. 4–5.

[13] Kurt Baier, "What Is Value? An Analysis of the Concept," in *Values and the Future,* ed. Kurt Baier and Nicholas Rescher (New York: Free Press, 1969), p. 53.

[14] For example, Herman Mertins, *Professional Standards and Ethics: A Workbook for Public Administrators* (Washington, DC: American Society for Public Administration, 1979).

[15] Louis A. Gewirth, *Reason and Morality* (Chicago: University of Chicago Press, 1978), p. 67.

"Metapolicy," for example, is making policy about policies,[16] and "metaevaluation" is the evaluation of evaluations, because it develops and applies criteria to evaluate program and policy evaluations.[17]

There has been a growing concern with the role of normative ethics and metaethics in public policy analysis. An emphasis on the reflective evaluation of criteria employed to justify normative claims may be found in the general literature of policy analysis.[18] In addition, there have been specialized attempts to examine metaethical questions that are ontological (Does ethical knowledge exist?), epistemological (What criteria, if any, govern the truth or falsity of ethical claims?), and practical (What is the relation between ethics and moral action?). Michalos, for example, argues that widely accepted but mistaken assumptions about the existence of two mutually exclusive realms of experience ("facts" and "values") leads analysts to the false conclusion that ethical claims are "scientifically incorrigible."[19] Dallmayr, drawing on critical theory and the work of Jurgen Habermas and other members of the Frankfurt School, argues that "policy evaluation requires a critically reflective 'practical discourse' open not only to experts or policy analysts but to the public at large . . . recovery of a fully non-instrumental 'practical' judgment presupposes an evaluation not only of concrete policies but of the status of 'policy' itself."[20]

Distinctions among descriptive ethics, normative ethics, and metaethics are applicable to issues of social equity and justice. Issues of distributive justice are often addressed by describing the consequences of adopting one or more of the following neo-utilitarian decision criteria: net efficiency improvement (maximize total benefits minus total costs), Pareto improvement (maximize total benefits minus total costs up to that point where it is not possible to make any person better off without also making another person worse off), and Kaldor-Hicks improvement or "virtual Pareto improvement" (maximize total benefits minus total costs, provided that winners may in principle compensate losers).

At the level of descriptive ethics, the satisfaction of the above criteria can be addressed by comparing a measure of inequality such as the Gini Index (see Chapter 6), which is used to measure differences in the distribution of income. By

---

[16] Yehezkel Dror, *Public Policymaking Reexamined* (New York: Elsevier, 1968).

[17] Thomas D. Cook and Charles Gruder, "Metaevaluation Research," *Evaluation Quarterly* 2 (1978): 5–51. MacRae has developed an important original application of metaethics to the normative ethics of policy analysis. Duncan MacRae Jr., *The Social Function of Social Science* (New Haven, CT: Yale University Press, 1976).

[18] For example, MacRae, *The Social Function of Social Science;* Frank Fischer, *Evaluating Public Policy* (Chicago: Nelson-Hall, 1995).

[19] Alex C. Michalos, "Facts, Values, and Rational Decision Making," *Policy Studies Journal* 9, no. 4 (1981): 544–51.

[20] Fred R. Dallmayr, "Critical Theory and Public Policy," *Policy Studies Journal* 9, no. 4 (1981): 523. Daneke makes a general case for the introduction of metaethics into the curricula of schools of public policy and management. Gregory Daneke, "Beyond Ethical Reductionism in Public Policy Education," in *Ethics, Values, and the Practice of Policy Analysis,* ed. William N. Dunn (Lexington, MA: D. C. Heath, 1982).

contrast, at the level of normative ethics, the justifiability of these criteria may be addressed by normative theories of justice, for example, John Rawls's theory of justice-as-fairness.[21] In a pre–civil society in which discrepancies of power, wealth, and privilege are as yet unknown—a society under a "veil of ignorance"—citizens would accept a decision criterion different from all those mentioned above. The Rawlsian decision criterion is to maximize the welfare of members of society who are worst off. The justifiability of this criterion can be addressed at a more basic, metaethical level. In this context, the Rawlsian theory has been challenged on metaethical grounds that it presupposes an individualistic conception of human nature where normative commitments are no longer products of reasoned social discourse but are

> the contractual composite of arbitrary (even if comprehensible) values individually held and either biologically or socially shaped. . . . The structure of the Rawlsian argument thus corresponds closely to that of instrumental rationality; ends are exogenous, and the exclusive office of thought in the world is to ensure their maximum realization. . . . [Rawls's arguments] reduce all thought to the combined operations of formal reason and instrumental prudence in the service of desire.[22]

Standards of Conduct

The standards of conduct or norms of "customary morality" that guide the behavior of analysts are variable. In part, this variability may be attributed to the diverse approaches to teaching of ethics and values in schools of public policy and management.[23] Government policy analysts and planners are themselves divided along methodological as well as ethical lines.[24] Efforts to reduce this variability have drawn on several sources of standards: social values and norms, including equity, honesty, and fairness, which may guide the actions of policy analysts as well as citizens at large; scientific values and norms, including objectivity, neutrality, and institutionalized self-criticism; professional codes of conduct, including formally stated obligations, duties, and prescriptions; and legal and administrative procedures, including mechanisms for securing informed consent by seeking the formal approval of institutional review boards.

The communication of social values and norms are central to the research and teaching activities of individual scholars, whereas the communication of scientific

---

[21] John Rawls, *A Theory of Justice* (Cambridge, MA: Harvard University Press, 1968).

[22] Laurence H. Tribe, "Ways Not to Think about Plastic Trees," in *When Values Conflict,* ed. L. H. Tribe, C. S. Schelling, and J. Voss (Cambridge, MA: Ballinger, 1976), p. 77.

[23] Joel L. Fleishman and Bruce L. Payne, *Ethical Dilemmas and the Education of Policymakers* (Hastings-on-Hudson, NY: Hastings Center, 1980).

[24] Elizabeth Howe and Jerome Kaufman, "The Ethics of Contemporary American Planners," *Journal of the American Planning Association* 45 (1979): 243–55; and "Ethics and Professional Practice in Planning and Related Planning Professions," *Policy Studies Journal* 9, no. 4 (1981): 585–94.

and professional norms has occurred largely through the curriculum development efforts of the National Association of Schools of Public Affairs and Administration (NASPAA) and through the traditional conference and publications activities of the Policy Studies Organization (PSO), the Association for Public Policy and Management (APPAM), and the American Society for Public Administration (ASPA). In addressing the need for a code of professional conduct, but stopping short of the formal codification of standards, ASPA has published and disseminated a pamphlet titled *Professional Standards and Ethics: A Workbook for Public Administrators*. By contrast, legal and administrative procedures to regulate the conduct of research involving human subjects and research integrity generally are products of government initiatives rather than those of professional associations or universities.

DESCRIPTIVE ETHICS, NORMATIVE ETHICS, AND METAETHICS

Theories of ethics and values may be conveniently classified according to their functions: the description, classification, measurement of ethics and values (descriptive theories); the development and application of criteria to assess ethical behaviors (normative theories); and the development and application of additional criteria to assess normative ethical theories themselves (metaethical theories). This classification has important subdivisions—for example, teleological versus deontological normative theories, or cognitivist versus noncognitivist metaethical theories.

Descriptive Value Typologies

The work of Rokeach[25] represents a major synthesis of descriptive theories of values undertaken since the 1930s. The scope and depth of his concern is evident in the claim that

> the concept of values, more than any other, is the core concept across all the social sciences. It is the main dependent variable in the study of culture, society, and personality, and the main independent variable in the study of social attitudes and behavior. It is difficult for me to conceive of any problem social scientists might be interested in that would not deeply implicate human values.[26]

One of Rokeach's contributions is the development of a basic typology for developing and testing descriptive theories of values. The basic typology has two major dimensions: terminal and instrumental values. Terminal values, which are both personal and social, are beliefs about desirable end-states of existence. Instrumental values are beliefs about desirable modes of conduct. Table 7.1 presents Rokeach's list of 18 terminal and instrumental values.

---

[25] Milton Rokeach, *The Nature of Human Values* (New York: Free Press, 1973).

[26] Ibid., p. ix.

Table 7.1   Basic Value Typology: Terminal and Instrumental Values

Terminal Value	Instrumental Value
A comfortable life	Ambitious
An exciting life	Broadminded
A sense of accomplishment	Capable
A world at peace	Cheerful
A world of beauty	Clean
Equality	Courageous
Family security	Forgiving
Freedom	Helpful
Happiness	Honest
Inner harmony	Imaginative
Mature love	Independent
National security	Intellectual
Pleasure	Logical
Salvation	Loving
Self-respect	Obedient
Social recognition	Polite
True friendship	Responsible
Wisdom	Self-controlled

Source: Milton Rokeach *The Nature of Human Values* (New York: Free Press, 1973), Table 2.1, p. 28. Test-retest reliability coefficients and parenthetical qualifiers have been omitted.

Howe and Kaufman have employed a similar typology in their study of the ethics of professional planners.[27] Distinguishing between "ends-oriented" and "means-oriented" ethics regarding the importance of a large number of values reported in existing literature, Howe and Kaufman draw two classes of ethical principles from the 1962 *Code of Professional Responsibility and Rules of Procedure of the American Institute of Planners*. Among the major findings of the study are that professional and personal ethical norms are often inconsistent and that a commitment to certain ends (e.g., social equity) affects ethical judgments about the use of particular means (e.g., leaking information to low income groups). Although this study is essentially exploratory, it addresses important competing principles: good ends justify the selection of means[28] versus means should be justified in their own terms.[29]

Developmental Value Typologies

Basic typologies can serve as a basis for examining theories of individual and collective value change and development. For example, Rokeach tests a theory of cognitive inconsistency with data organized according to the typology of terminal

---

[27] Howe and Kaufman "The Ethics of Contemporary American Planners."

[28] See Saul Alinsky, *Rules for Radicals* (New York: Random House, 1971).

[29] See Sissela Bok, *Lying: Moral Choice in Public and Private Life* (New York: Pantheon, 1978).

and instrumental values.[30] He also identifies a variety of developmental patterns based on age differences, concluding that values change not only during adolescence but also throughout life.[31] These patterns are related to the stage theory of moral development created and tested by Kohlberg.[32] Kohlberg's developmental typology distinguishes three levels in the development of moral reasoning: preconventional, conventional, and postconventional. Because each level has two stages, the typology yields six stages in all: stage 1 (punishment and obedience orientation); stage 2 (instrumental relativist orientation); stage 3 (interpersonal concordance orientation); stage 4 (law-and-order orientation); stage 5 (social-contract legalistic orientation); and stage 6 (universal ethical principle orientation).

Kohlberg's developmental typology is of great potential importance for assessing the role of ethical norms and principles in policy analysis. The six stages are claimed to represent an invariant sequence whereby individuals progress in their *capacity* for moral judgment. Because the sequence is invariant and sequential, developmental transitions can occur only between adjacent stages. Accordingly, individuals cannot be expected to move directly from an egocentric market society (stage 2) to a society based on universal ethical principles (stage 6), for example, from a concern with an ethic of income maximization to an ethic of the type outlined by Rawls. Because Kohlberg's theory is based on relatively firm (although imperfect) empirical grounds, it has an important bearing on questions surrounding possibilities for normative ethical discourses in contemporary society: "Any conception of what moral judgment ought to be must rest on an adequate conception of what is. The fact that our conception of the moral 'works' empirically is important for its philosophic adequacy."[33]

Normative Theories

Normative theories of value, or normative ethics, may be divided into three main types: deontological, teleological, and practical. Deontological normative theories claim that certain kinds of actions are inherently right or obligatory (the Greek *deontos* means "of the obligatory"), or right because they conform to some formal principle. Teleological normative theories, by contrast, hold that certain actions are right because they result in good of valuable ends (the Greek *teleios* means "brought to its end or purpose"). Finally, practical normative theories hold that certain actions are right because they conform to principles, or result in consequences, whose rightness or goodness has been established through reasoned

---

[30] Rokeach, *Nature of Human Values,* pp. 215–34.

[31] Ibid., p. 81.

[32] Lawrence Kohlberg, *Stages in the Development of Moral Thought and Action* (New York: Holt, Rinehart, and Winston, 1961).

[33] Lawrence Kohlberg, "From Is to Ought: How to Commit the Naturalistic Fallacy and Get Away with It in the Study of Moral Development," in *Cognitive Development and Epistemology,* ed. T. Mischel (New York: Academic Press, 1971), pp. 151–235. The "naturalistic fallacy" is the fallacy of deriving an "ought" from an "is."

discourses or transactions (the Greek *praktikos* means "to experience, negotiate, or transact") among those who affect and are affected by the creation and application of moral rules.

Deontological normative theories rest on "deontic" concepts and principles, as distinguished from concepts and principles based on the goodness of consequences. Theories of justice such as that offered by Rawls are mainly deontological because they employ formal principles of obligation (a pre-civil social contract executed under a "veil of ignorance") to justify arguments about distributive justice ("justice as fairness") and a just society (a society that maximizes the welfare of those who are worst off). By contrast, teleological theories evaluate actions according to the goodness of their consequences. A prominent form of teleological theory, one that has deeply affected policy analysis through modern welfare economics, is utilitarianism. The classical utilitarian theories of Jeremy Bentham and John Stuart Mill held that right actions are those that promote the maximum or greatest good for everyone. Policy analysts who use cost-benefit analysis are utilitarians to the degree that they base policy recommendations on the criterion of maximizing net income benefits, a criterion presumed to reflect the aggregate satisfaction experienced by members of society.

The main properties of teleological theories, including modern neo-utilitarian theories, are most easily visualized by comparing them with deontological theories.[34]

- Teleological theories justify actions because of their consequences (e.g., maximization of net income benefits), whereas deontological theories justify actions because they conform to some principle (e.g., procedural fairness) or because they are deemed to be inherently right (e.g., truth-telling).
- Teleological theories set forth conditional obligations (e.g., freedom might be compromised in the interests of national security), whereas deontological theories set forth absolute obligations (e.g., freedom is a generic right that cannot be justified in terms of any higher principle).
- Teleological theories advance material or substantive criteria (e.g., pleasure, happiness, or satisfaction), whereas deontological theories advance formal or relational criteria (e.g., social equity or administrative impartiality).
- Teleological theories supply aggregate criteria (e.g., social welfare as the total satisfaction experienced by members of a community), whereas deontological theories supply distributive criteria regulating the allocation of goods (e.g., educational opportunities or a living wage) or evils (e.g., exposure to toxic wastes and carcinogens).

Practical normative theories stress reflective moral action as a process for discovering the criteria on which values and ethics may be known. Practical normative theories have stressed reasoned moral discourse as a process for creating and

---

[34] See Louis A. Gewirth, *Reason and Morality* (Chicago: University of Chicago Press, 1978).

evaluating ethical as well as scientific knowledge.[35] Sometimes called "good reasons" theories, these theories are "practical" to the extent that actions are deemed right or valuable because they conform to principles, or result in consequences, that have been established on the basis of reasoned transactions (Greek *praktikos*: "to experience, negotiate, or transact") among persons who affect and are affected by the development and application of moral rules.

Metaethical Theories

The function of normative ethical theories in policy analysis is to answer the question: According to what criteria can we determine whether public actions are right or wrong? Answers to this question, as we saw earlier, may be based on one or more types of normative ethical criteria: teleological, deontological, practical. The function of metaethical theories, by contrast, is to answer questions about normative ethical claims themselves: Can we determine the truth and falsity of normative ethical claims? Does normative ethics produce a kind of knowledge and, if so, what kind of knowledge is it? If normative ethics is not capable of being true and false, what kinds of noncognitive results are produced?

Metaethical theories differ in terms of their assumptions about the epistemological status of normative ethical theories—for example, so-called "cognitivist" metaethics affirms that normative ethical theories are capable of being true or false and, therefore, that normative ethics constitutes a kind of knowledge. This is denied by "noncognitivist" metaethical theories. Metaethical theories are associated with normative ethical theories. Thus, for example, the growth of logical positivism in the social sciences has contributed to noncognitivist metaethical doctrines that, in turn, have resulted in the devaluation of normative ethical discourse and an inability to recognize that putative empirical theories (welfare economics) and analytic routines (cost-benefit analysis) are based on controversial ethical premises. In this case, a particular metaethical doctrine (noncognitivism) has exerted a direct and logically constraining effect on normative ethics by preempting opportunities for reflective normative discourse and the development of new ethical knowledge.

EVALUATION IN POLICY ANALYSIS

Descriptive, normative, and metaethical theories provide a foundation for evaluation in policy analysis, where evaluation refers to the production of information about the value or worth of policy outcomes. When policy outcomes do in fact have

---

[35] See P. W. Taylor, *Normative Discourse* (Englewood Cliffs, NJ: Prentice Hall, 1971); Stephen Toulmin, *The Place of Reason in Ethics* (Oxford: Oxford University Press, 1950); Stephen Toulmin, *The Uses of Argument* (Cambridge: Cambridge University Press, 1958); Kurt Baier, *The Moral Point of View* (Ithaca, NY: Cornell University Press, 1965); Frank Fischer, *Politics, Values, and Public Policy* (Boulder, CO: Westview Press, 1980).

value, it is because they contribute to goals and objectives. In this case, we say that a policy or program has attained some significant level of performance.

The Nature of Evaluation

The main feature of evaluation is that it results in claims that are evaluative in character. Here the main question is not one of facts (Does something exist?) or of action (What should be done?) but one of values (Of what worth is it?). Evaluation therefore has several characteristics that distinguish it from other policy-analytic methods:

1. *Value focus.* Evaluation, as contrasted with monitoring, focuses on judgments regarding the desirability or value of policies and programs. Evaluation is primarily an effort to determine the worth or social utility of a policy or program, and not simply an effort to collect information about the anticipated and unanticipated outcomes of policy actions. As the appropriateness of policy goals and objectives can always be questioned, evaluation includes the evaluation of goals and objectives themselves.

2. *Fact-value interdependence.* Evaluation depends as much on "facts" as it does on "values." To claim that a particular policy or program has attained a high (or low) level of performance requires not only that policy outcomes are valuable to some individual, group, or society as a whole, but it also requires that policy outcomes are actually a consequence of actions undertaken to resolve a particular problem. Hence, monitoring is a prerequisite of evaluation.

3. *Present and past orientation.* Evaluative claims, as contrasted with advocative claims produced through recommendation, are oriented toward present and past outcomes, rather than future ones. Evaluation is retrospective and occurs after actions have been taken (*ex post*). Recommendation, while also involving value premises, is prospective and occurs before actions have been taken (*ex ante*).

4. *Value duality.* The values underlying evaluative claims have a dual quality, because they may be regarded as ends and means. Evaluation is similar to recommendation insofar as a given value (e.g., health) may be regarded as intrinsic (valuable in itself) as well as extrinsic (desirable because it leads to some other end). Values are often arranged in a hierarchy that reflects the relative importance and interdependency of goals and objectives.

Functions of Evaluation

Evaluation performs several main functions in policy analysis. First, and most important, evaluation provides reliable and valid information about *policy performance,* that is, the extent to which needs, values, and opportunities have been realized through public action. In this respect, evaluation reveals the extent to which particular goals (e.g., improved health) and objectives (e.g., a 20% reduction of chronic diseases by 1990) have been attained.

Second, evaluation contributes to the *clarification* and *critique* of values that underlie the selection of goals and objectives. Values are clarified by defining and operationalizing goals and objectives. Values are also critiqued by systematically questioning the appropriateness of goals and objectives in relation to the problem being addressed. In questioning the appropriateness of goals and objectives, analysts may examine alternative sources of values (e.g., public officials, vested interests, client groups) as well as their grounds in different forms of rationality (technical, economic, legal, social, substantive).

Third, evaluation may contribute to the application of other policy-analytic methods, including *problem structuring* and *recommendation*. Information about inadequate policy performance may contribute to the restructuring of policy problems, for example, by showing that goals and objectives should be redefined. Evaluation can also contribute to the definition of new or revised policy alternatives by showing that a previously favored policy alternative should be abandoned and replaced with another one.

Criteria for Policy Evaluation

In producing information about policy performance, analysts use different types of criteria to evaluate policy outcomes. These types of criteria have already been discussed in relation to policy recommendation (Chapter 5). The main difference between criteria for evaluation and criteria for recommendation is the time at which criteria are applied. Criteria for evaluation are applied retrospectively (*ex post*), whereas criteria for recommendation are applied prospectively (*ex ante*). These criteria are summarized in Table 7.2.

Table 7.2   Criteria for Evaluation

Type of Criterion	Question	Illustrative Criteria
Effectiveness	Has a valued outcome been achieved?	Units of service
Efficiency	How much effort was required to achieve a valued outcome?	Unit cost Net benefits Cost-benefit ratio
Adequacy	To what extent does the achievement of a valued outcome resolve the problem?	Fixed costs (type I problem) Fixed effectiveness (type II problem)
Equity	Are costs and benefits distributed equitably among different groups?	Pareto criterion Kaldor-Hicks criterion Raw's criterion
Responsiveness	Do policy outcomes satisfy the needs, preferences or values of particular groups?	Consistency with citizen surveys
Appropriateness	Are desired outcomes (objectives) actually worthy or valuable?	Public programs should be equitable as well as efficient

Note: See Chapter 5 for extended descriptions of criteria.

APPROACHES TO EVALUATION

Evaluation, as we saw earlier, has two interrelated aspects: the use of various methods to monitor the outcomes of public policies and programs and the application of some set of values to determine the worth of these outcomes to some person, group, or society as a whole. Observe that these two interrelated aspects point to the presence of factual and value premises in any evaluative claim. Yet many activities described as "evaluation" in policy analysis are essentially *nonevaluative*—that is, they are primarily concerned with the production of designative (factual) claims rather than evaluative ones. In fact, each of the four approaches to monitoring described in Chapter 6 is frequently mislabeled as approaches to "evaluation research" or "policy evaluation."[36]

Given the present lack of clarity about the meaning of evaluation in policy analysis, it is essential to distinguish among several different approaches to policy evaluation: pseudo-evaluation, formal evaluation, and decision-theoretic evaluation. These approaches and their aims, assumptions, and major forms are illustrated in Table 7.3.

Table 7.3 Three Approaches to Evaluation

Approach	Aims	Assumptions	Major Forms
Pseudo-evaluation	Use descriptive methods to produce reliable and valid information about policy outcomes	Measures of worth or value are self-evident or uncontroversial	Social experimentation Social systems accounting Social auditing Research and practice synthesis
Formal evaluation	Use descriptive methods to produce reliable and valid information about policy outcomes that have been formally announced as policy-program objectives	Formally announced goals and objectives of policy makers and administrators are appropriate measures of worth or value	Developmental evaluation Experimental evaluation Retrospective process evaluation Retrospective outcome evaluation
Decision-theoretic evaluation	Use descriptive methods to produce reliable and valid information about policy outcomes that are explicitly valued by multiple stakeholders	Formally announced as well as latent goals and objectives of stakeholders are appropriate measures of worth or value	Evaluability assessment Multiattribute utility analysis

[36] See, for example, the description of "evaluation" research in Marcia Guttentag and Elmer Struening, ed., *Handbook of Evaluation Research,* 2 vols. (Beverly Hills, CA: Sage Publications, 1975); and Leonard Rutman, ed., *Evaluation Research Methods: A Basic Guide* (Beverly Hills, CA: Sage Publications, 1977).

Pseudo-evaluation

Pseudo-evaluation is an approach that uses descriptive methods to produce reliable and valid information about policy outcomes, without attempting to question the worth or value of these outcomes to persons, groups, or society as a whole. The major assumption of pseudo-evaluation is that measures of worth or value are self-evident or uncontroversial.

In pseudo-evaluation, the analyst typically uses a variety of methods (quasi-experimental design, questionnaires, random sampling, statistical techniques) to explain variations in policy outcomes in terms of policy input and process variables. Yet any given policy outcome (e.g., number of employed trainees, units of medical services delivered, net income benefits produced) is taken for granted as an appropriate objective. Major forms of pseudo-evaluation include the approaches to monitoring discussed in Chapter 6: social experimentation, social systems accounting, social auditing, and research and practice synthesis.

Formal Evaluation

Formal evaluation is an approach that uses descriptive methods to produce reliable and valid information about policy outcomes but evaluates such outcomes on the basis of policy-program objectives that have been formally announced by policy makers and program administrators. The major assumption of formal evaluation is that formally announced goals and objectives are appropriate measures of the worth or value of policies and programs.

In formal evaluation, the analyst uses the same kinds of methods as those employed in pseudo-evaluation and the aim is identical: to produce reliable and valid information about variations in policy outputs and impacts that may be traced to policy inputs and processes. The difference, however, is that formal evaluations use legislation, program documents, and interviews with policy makers and administrators to identify, define, and specify formal goals and objectives. The appropriateness of these formally announced goals and objectives is not questioned. In formal evaluations, the types of evaluative criteria most frequently used are those of effectiveness and efficiency.

One of the major types of formal evaluation is the *summative evaluation,* which involves an effort to monitor the accomplishment of formal goals and objectives after a policy or program has been in place for some period of time. Summative evaluations are designed to appraise products of stable and well-established public policies and programs. By contrast, a *formative evaluation* involves efforts to continuously monitor the accomplishment of formal goals and objectives. The differences between summative and formative evaluation should not be overemphasized, however, because the main distinguishing characteristic of formative evaluation is the number of points in time at which policy outcomes are monitored. Hence, the difference between summative and formative evaluation is mainly one of degree.

Formal evaluations may be summative or formative, but they may also involve direct or indirect controls over policy inputs and processes. In the former case, evaluators can directly manipulate expenditure levels, the mix of programs, or the characteristics of target groups—that is, the evaluation may have one or more characteristics of social experimentation as an approach to monitoring (Chapter 6). In the case of indirect controls, policy inputs and processes cannot be directly manipulated; rather they must be analyzed retrospectively on the basis of actions that have already occurred. Four types of formal evaluation—each based on a different orientation toward the policy process (summative versus formative) and type of control over action (direct versus indirect)—are illustrated in Table 7.4.

Varieties of Formal Evaluation

Developmental evaluation refers to evaluation activities that are explicitly designed to serve the day-to-day needs of program staff. Developmental evaluation is useful "for alerting the staff to incipient weaknesses or unintended failures of a program and for insuring proper operation by those responsible for its operation."[37] Developmental evaluation, which involves some measure of direct control over policy actions, has been used in a wide variety of situations in the public and private sectors. Thus, for example, businesses frequently use developmental evaluations to distribute, test, and recall new products. In the public sector, developmental evaluations have been used to test new teaching methods and materials in public education programs, such as *Sesame Street* and *Electric Company*. Such programs are systematically monitored and evaluated by showing them to audiences composed of children within specified age limits. Subsequently, they are "revised many times on the basis of systematic observations of which program features achieved attention and on the basis of interviews with the children after viewing the program."[38] Developmental evaluations, as they are both formative and involve direct controls, can be used to adapt immediately to new experience acquired through systematic manipulations of input and process variables.

Table 7.4 Types of Formal Evaluation

	Orientation Toward Policy Process	
Control Over Policy Actions	*Formative*	*Summative*
Direct	Developmental evaluation	Experimental evaluation
Indirect	Retrospective process evaluation	Retrospective outcome evaluation

---

[37] Peter H. Rossi and Sonia R. Wright, "Evaluation Research: An Assessment of Theory, Practice, and Politics," *Evaluation Quarterly* 1, no. 1 (February 1977): 21.

[38] Ibid., p. 22.

Retrospective process evaluation involves the monitoring and evaluation of programs after they have been in place for some time. Retrospective process evaluation, which often focuses on problems and bottlenecks encountered in the implementation of policies and programs, does not permit the direct manipulation of inputs (e.g., expenditures) and processes (e.g., alternative delivery systems). Rather it relies on *ex post facto* (retrospective) descriptions of ongoing program activities, which are subsequently related to outputs and impacts. Retrospective process evaluation requires a well-established internal reporting system that permits the continuous generation of program-related information (e.g., the number of target groups served, the types of services provided, and the characteristics of personnel employed to staff programs). Management information systems in public agencies sometimes permit retrospective process evaluations, provided they contain information on processes as well as outcomes.

Title I of the Elementary and Secondary Education Act (1965) was subjected to a form of retrospective process evaluation by the Office of Education, but with disappointing results. Title I provided funds to local school systems in proportion to the number of pupils from poor or deprived families. Local school districts submitted inadequate and marginally useful information, thus making it impossible to evaluate and implement programs concurrently. Retrospective process evaluations presuppose a reliable and valid information system, which is often difficult to establish.

Experimental evaluation involves the monitoring and evaluation of outcomes under conditions of direct controls over policy inputs and processes. The ideal of experimental evaluation has generally been the "controlled scientific experiment," where all factors that might influence policy outcomes except one—that is, a particular input or process variable—are controlled, held constant, or treated as plausible rival hypotheses. Experimental and quasi-experimental evaluations include the New Jersey–Pennsylvania Income Maintenance Experiment, the California Group Therapy-Criminal Recidivism Experiment, the Kansas City Preventive Patrol Experiment, Project Follow Through, the Supported Work Demonstration Project, and various experiments in educational performance contracting.

Experimental evaluations must meet rather severe requirements before they can be carried out:[39] (1) a clearly defined and directly manipulable set of "treatment" variables that are specified in operational terms; (2) an evaluation strategy that permits maximum generalizability of conclusions about performance to many similar target groups or settings (*external validity*); (3) an evaluation strategy that permits minimum error in interpreting policy performance as the actual result of manipulated policy inputs and processes (*internal validity*); and (4) a monitoring system that produces reliable data on complex interrelationships among preconditions, unforeseen events, inputs, processes, outputs, impacts, and side effects and spillovers (see Figure 6.2). As these demanding methodological requirements are

---

[39] Walter Williams, *Social Policy Research and Analysis* (New York: Elsevier, 1971), p. 93.

rarely met, experimental evaluations typically fall short of the "true" controlled experiment, and are referred to as "quasi-experimental."

Retrospective outcome evaluations also involve the monitoring and evaluation of outcomes but with no direct control over manipulable policy inputs and processes.[40] At best controls are indirect or statistical—that is, the evaluator attempts to isolate the effects of many different factors by using quantitative methods. In general, there are two main variants of retrospective process evaluation: cross-sectional and longitudinal studies. *Longitudinal studies* are those that evaluate changes in the outcomes of one, several, or many programs at two or more points in time. Many longitudinal studies have been carried out in the area of family planning, where fertility rates and changes in the acceptance of contraceptive devices are monitored and evaluated over reasonably long periods of time (five to twenty years). *Cross-sectional studies,* by contrast, seek to monitor and evaluate multiple programs at one point in time. The goal of the cross-sectional study is to discover whether the outputs and impacts of various programs are significantly different from one another; and if so, what particular actions, preconditions, or unforeseen events might explain the difference.

Two prominent examples of retrospective outcome evaluations that are cross-sectional in nature are Project Head Start, a program designed to provide compensatory education to preschool children, and the Coleman Report. Indeed,

> almost every evaluation of the national compensatory education programs started during the middle 1960s has been based on cross-sectional data. Pupils enrolled in compensatory education programs were contrasted to those who were not, holding constant statistically such sources of competing explanations as family backgrounds, ethnicity, region, city size, and so on.[41]

Decision-Theoretic Evaluation

Decision-theoretic evaluation is an approach that uses descriptive methods to produce reliable and valid information about policy outcomes that are explicitly valued by multiple stakeholders. The key difference between decision-theoretic evaluation, on the one hand, and pseudo-and formal evaluation on the other, is that decision-theoretic evaluation attempts to surface and make explicit the latent as well as manifest goals and objectives of stakeholders. This means that formally announced goals and objectives of policy makers and administrators are but one source of values, because all parties who have a stake in the formulation and implementation of a policy (e.g., middle- and lower-level staff, personnel in other agencies, client groups) are involved in generating the goals and objectives against which performance is measured.

---

[40] Note that three of the approaches to monitoring discussed in Chapter 8—that is, social systems accounting, social auditing, and research and practice synthesis—may also be considered as forms of retrospective outcome evaluation. Similarly, cost-benefit and cost-effectiveness analysis (Chapter 5) may be viewed as particular forms of retrospective outcome evaluation.

[41] Rossi and Wright, "Evaluation Research," p. 27.

Decision-theoretic evaluation is a way to overcome several deficiencies of pseudo-evaluation and formal evaluation:[42]

1. *Underutilization and nonutilization of performance information.* Much of the information generated through evaluations is underutilized or never used to improve policy making. In part, this is because evaluations are not sufficiently responsive to the goals and objectives of parties who have a stake in formulating and implementing policies and programs.

2. *Ambiguity of performance goals.* Many goals of public policies and programs are vague. This means that the same general goal—for example, to improve health or encourage better conservation of energy—can and do result in specific objectives that conflict with one another. This is evident when we consider that the same goal (e.g., improved health) may be operationalized in terms of at least six types of evaluation criteria: effectiveness, efficiency, adequacy, equity, responsiveness, and appropriateness. One of the purposes of decision-theoretic evaluation is to reduce the ambiguity of goals and make conflicting objectives explicit.

3. *Multiple conflicting objectives.* The goals and objectives of public policies and programs cannot be satisfactorily established by focusing on the values of one or several parties (e.g., Congress, a dominant client group, or a head administrator). In fact, multiple stakeholders with conflicting goals and objectives are present in most situations requiring evaluation. Decision-theoretic evaluation attempts to identify these multiple stakeholders and surface their goals and objectives.

One of the main purposes of decision-theoretic evaluation is to link information about policy outcomes with the values of multiple stakeholders. The assumption of decision-theoretic evaluation is that formally announced as well as latent goals and objectives of stakeholders are appropriate measures of the worth or value of policies and programs. The two major forms of decision-theoretic evaluation are evaluability assessment and multiattribute utility analysis, both of which attempt to link information about policy outcomes with the values of multiple stakeholders.

Evaluability assessment is a set of procedures designed to analyze the decision-making system that is supposed to benefit from performance information and to clarify the goals, objectives, and assumptions against which performance is to be measured.[43] The basic question in evaluability assessment is whether a policy

---

[42] For accounts of these and other deficiencies, see Carol H. Weiss, *Evaluation Research* (Englewood Cliffs, NJ: Prentice Hall, 1972); Ward Edwards, Marcia Guttentag, and Kurt Snapper, "A Decision-Theoretic Approach to Evaluation Research," in *Handbook of Evaluation Research,* ed. Guttentag and Struening, pp. 139–81; and Martin Rein and Sheldon H. White, "Policy Research: Belief and Doubt," *Policy Analysis* 3, no. 2 (1977): 239–72.

[43] On evaluability assessment, see Joseph S. Wholey and others, "Evaluation: When Is It Really Needed?" *Evaluation* 2, no. 2 (1975): 89–94; and Wholey, "Evaluability Assessment," *Evaluation Research Methods,* ed. Rutman, pp. 41–56.

or program can be evaluated at all. For a policy or program to be evaluable, at least three conditions must be present: a clearly articulated policy or program; clearly specified goals and/or consequences; and a set of explicit assumptions that link policy actions to goals and/or consequences.[44] In conducting an evaluability assessment, analysts follow a series of steps that clarify a policy or program from the standpoint of the intended users of performance information and the evaluators themselves:[45]

1. *Policy-program specification.* What federal, state, or local activities and what goals and objectives constitute the program?
2. *Collection of policy-program information.* What information must be collected to define policy-program objectives, activities, and underlying assumptions?
3. *Policy-program modeling.* What model best describes the program and its related objectives and activities, from the point of view of intended users of performance information? What causal assumptions link actions to outcomes?
4. *Policy-program evaluability assessment.* Is the policy-program model sufficiently unambiguous to make the evaluation useful? What types of evaluation studies would be most useful?
5. *Feedback of evaluability assessment to users.* After presenting conclusions about policy-program evaluability to intended users, what appear to be the next steps that should (or should not) be taken to evaluate policy performance?

A second form of decision-theoretic evaluation is *multiattribute utility analysis.*[46] Multiattribute utility analysis is a set of procedures designed to elicit from multiple stakeholders subjective judgments about the probability of occurrence and value of policy outcomes. The strengths of multiattribute utility analysis are that it explicitly surfaces the value judgments of multiple stakeholders; it recognizes the presence of multiple conflicting objectives in policy-program evaluation; and it produces performance information that is more usable from the standpoint of intended users. The steps in conducting a multiattribute utility analysis are the following:

1. *Stakeholder identification.* Identify the parties who affect and are affected by a policy or program. Each of these stakeholders will have goals and objectives that they wish to maximize.
2. *Specification of relevant decision issues.* Specify the courses of action or inaction about which there is a disagreement among stakeholders. In the simplest case, there will be two courses of action: the status quo and some new initiative.

---

[44] See Rutman, *Evaluation Research Methods,* p. 18.
[45] Wholey, "Evaluability Assessment," pp. 43–55.
[46] See Edwards, Guttentag, and Snapper, "A Decision-Theoretic Approach," pp. 148–59.

3. *Specification of policy outcomes.* Specify the range of consequences that may follow each course of action. Outcomes may be arranged in a hierarchy where one action has several consequences, each of which itself has further consequences. A hierarchy of outcomes is similar to an objectives tree (Chapter 5), except that outcomes are not objectives until they have been explicitly valued.

4. *Identification of attributes of outcomes.* Here the task is to identify all relevant attributes that make outcomes worthy or valuable. For example, each outcome may have different types of benefits and costs to different target groups and beneficiaries.

5. *Attribute ranking.* Rank each value attribute in order of importance. For example, if increased family income is an outcome of a poverty program, this outcome may have several value attributes: sense of family well-being; greater nutritional intake; and more disposable income for health care. These attributes should be ranked in order of their relative importance to one another.

6. *Attribute scaling.* Scale attributes that have been ranked in order of importance. To do so, arbitrarily assign the least important attribute a value of ten. Proceed to the next most important attribute, answering the question: How many times more important is this attribute than the next-least-important one? Continue this scaling procedure until the most important attribute has been compared with all others. Note that the most important attribute may have a scale value 10, 20, 30, or more times that of the least important attribute.

7. *Scale standardization.* The attributes that have been scaled will have different maximum values for different stakeholders. For example, one stakeholder may give attribute *A,* a value of 60; attribute *B,* a value of 30; and attribute *C,* a value of 10. Another stakeholder, however, may give these same attributes values of 120, 60, and 10. To standardize these scales, sum all original values for each scale, divide each original value by its respective sum, and multiply by 100. This results in separate scales whose component values sum to 100.

8. *Outcome measurement.* Measure the degree that each outcome is likely to result in the attainment of each attribute. The maximum probability should be given a value of 100; the minimum probability should be given a value of 0 (i.e., there is no chance that the outcome will result in the attainment of the attribute).

9. *Utility calculation.* Calculate the utility (value) of each outcome by using the formula:

$$U_i = \Sigma w_i u_{ij}$$

where

U_i = the aggregate utility (value) of the *i*th outcome
w_j = the standardized scale value of the *j*th attribute
u_{ij} = the probability of occurrence of the *i*th outcome on the *j*th attribute

10. *Evaluation and presentation.* Specify the policy outcome with the greatest overall performance, and present this information to relevant decision makers.

The strength of multiattribute utility analysis is that it enables analysts to deal systematically with conflicting objectives of multiple stakeholders. This is possible, however, only when the steps just described are carried out as part of a *group process* involving relevant stakeholders. Hence, the essential requirement of multiattribute utility analysis is that stakeholders who affect and are affected by a policy or program are active participants in the evaluation of policy performance.

METHODS FOR EVALUATION

A number of methods and techniques can assist analysts in evaluating policy performance. Nearly all of these techniques, however, may also be used in conjunction with other policy-analytic methods, including problem structuring, forecasting, recommendation, and monitoring. Thus, for example, argumentation analysis (chapter 8) may be used to surface assumptions about expected relationships between policy actions and objectives. Cross-impact analysis (Chapter 4) may prove useful in identifying unanticipated policy outcomes that work against the achievement of policy-program objectives. Similarly, discounting (Chapter 5) may be as relevant to policy-program evaluation as it is to recommendation, given that cost-benefit and cost-effectiveness analysis may be used retrospectively (*ex post*) as well as prospectively (*ex ante*). Finally, techniques that range from graphic displays and index numbers to control-series analysis (Chapter 6) may be essential for monitoring policy outcomes as a prelude to their evaluation.

The fact that various techniques may be used with more than one policy-analytic method points to the interdependence of problem structuring, forecasting, recommendation, monitoring, and evaluation in policy analysis. Many methods and techniques are relevant to pseudo-evaluation, formal evaluation, and decision-theoretic evaluation (Table 7.5).

Only one of the techniques listed in Table 7.5 has not already been described. *User-survey analysis* is a set of procedures for collecting information about the evaluability of a policy or program from intended users and other stakeholders.[47] User surveys are central to the conduct of evaluability assessments and other forms of decision-theoretic evaluation. The major instrument for collecting information is an interview protocol with a series of open-ended questions. Responses to these questions provide the information required to complete the several steps in an evaluability assessment previously described: policy-program specification; policy-program modeling; policy-program assessment; and presentation of evaluability assessment to users. A sample interview protocol for a user survey analysis is presented in Table 7.6.

---

[47] See Wholey, "Evaluability Assessment," pp. 44–49.

Table 7.5   Techniques for Evaluation by Three Approaches

Approach	Technique
Pseudo-evaluation	Graphic displays
	Tabular displays
	Index numbers
	Interrupted time-series analysis
	Control-series analysis
	Regression-discontinuity analysis
Formal evaluation	Objectives mapping
	Value clarification
	Value critique
	Constraint mapping
	Cross-impact analysis
	Discounting
Decision-theoretic evaluation	Brainstorming
	Argumentation analysis
	Policy Delphi
	User-survey analysis

Table 7.6   Interview Protocol for User-Survey Analysis

Step in Evaluability Assessment	Questions
Policy-program specification	1. What are the objectives of the policy or program?
	2. What would be acceptable evidence of the achievement of policy-program objectives?[1]
Policy-program modeling	3. What policy actions (for example, resources, guidelines, staff activities) are available to achieve objectives?[2]
	4. Why will action A lead to objective O?[2]
Policy-program evaluability assessment	5. What do various stakeholders (for example, Congress, OMB, state auditor general, mayor's office) expect of the program in terms of performance? Are these expectations consistent?
	6. What is the most serious obstacle to achieving objectives?
Feedback of evaluability assessment to users	7. What performance information do you need on the job? Why?
	8. Are present sources of performance information adequate? Why? Why not?
	9. What is the most important source of performance information you will need in the next year?
	10. What key issues should any evaluation address?

Notes:

[1]Answers to this question yield operational measures of objectives.

[2]Answers to these questions yield causal assumptions about the relation between actions and objectives.

Source: Adapted from Joseph S. Wholey, "Evaluability Assessment," in *Evaluation Research Methods: A Basic Guide,* ed. Leonard Rutman (Beverly Hills, CA: Sage Publications, 1977), Fig. 3, p. 48.

CHAPTER SUMMARY

This chapter has provided an overview of the process of evaluation, contrasted three approaches to evaluation, and presented specific methods and techniques used in conjunction with these approaches. The process of valuation is then distinguished from evaluation, and alternative ethical and metaethical theories are examined. Normative ethics and metaethics provide rationales for selecting criteria to evaluate policy performance.

LEARNING OBJECTIVES

- compare and contrast processes of monitoring and evaluation
- list characteristics that distinguish evaluation from other methods of analysis
- describe and illustrate criteria for evaluating policy performance
- contrast decision-theoretic evaluation and metaevaluation

- distinguish values, ethics, and metaethics
- describe and illustrate descriptive, normative, and metaethical theories
- analyze a case in "living wage" policies that involves issues of economic inequality

KEY TERMS AND CONCEPTS

decision-theoretic evaluation (359)
multiattribute utility analysis (361)
evaluability assessment (360)
user survey analysis (363)
values (342)
norms (344)

teleological (utilitarian) theory (351)
deontolological theory (351)
metaethics (345)
normative ethics (345)
practical ethics (350)

REVIEW QUESTIONS

1. Compare and contrast evaluation and recommendation in terms of time and the types of claims produced by each policy-analytic method.
2. Many policy-program evaluations fail to recognize the latent purposes of evaluation, including a desire (a) to make programs look good by focusing on their surface characteristics ("eyewash"); (b) to cover up program failures ("white-wash"); (c) to destroy a program ("submarine"); (d) to engage in evaluation merely as a ritual that must be practiced to receive funding ("posture"); and (e) to postpone attempts to resolve problems ("postponement"). See Edward A. Suchman, "Action for What? A Critique of Evaluative Research," in *Evaluating Action Programs,* ed. Carol H. Weiss (Boston: Allyn and Bacon, 1972), p. 81. What problems does this raise for defining the objectives against which performance is to be evaluated?

3. Compare and contrast formative and summative evaluation. Which of these two types of evaluation provides performance information that is likely to be of most use to policymakers? Why?

4. What are the strengths and limitations of cost-benefit analysis as an approach to evaluation? (see Chapter 15). In your answer refer to contrasts among pseudo-evaluation, formal evaluation, and decision-theoretic evaluation.

5. Select a policy or program that you would like to evaluate. (a) Outline the specific steps you would take to conduct an evaluability assessment. (b) Outline the steps you would take in doing a multiattribute utility analysis of the same policy or program. (c) Indicate which of the two procedures is likely to yield the most reliable, valid, and useful results.

6. Select a program with which you are familiar, either because you have read about it or because you were actually involved. Prepare a short paper that outlines a plan, strategy, and procedures for evaluating this program. Refer to Appendix 1 in preparing your answer.

DEMONSTRATION EXERCISE

Issues of a "living wage" turn on questions of poverty, inequality, and the distribution of income, wealth, and other social goods. Inequalities of various kinds have increased in the past twenty-five years, including the years in which Bill Clinton was president. Although conservatives refer to American society as an "opportunity society," it may also be described as an "inequality society."

Issues of economic inequality are particularly salient for education, at all levels. As the distribution of family income has become less equitable, families at the top of the income hierarchy invested five times as much in their children as their counterparts at the bottom. The low level of governmental support for child care, as compared with subsidies for public universities, means that in many cases it costs more to send a four year old to an early childhood education program than to send an eighteen year old to college. And most children who start out near the bottom of the income hierarchy end up there. Approximately 60 percent of children from poor families remain there.

Attempts to define inequality often use the analogy of a cake that can be cut into slices of differing sizes according to different rules.[48] These rules, along with their underlying justifications, deal with the distribution of such social goods as income, wealth, energy, education, and health care.

Some of the rules are the basis of theories of justice put forth by well-known political and ethical theorists including John Rawls[49] and Robert Nozick.[50] Rawls has given us a theory of justice that is largely, though not exclusively, based on what he sees as a fair distribution of social goods. For Rawls, the fundamental rule of fairness is "allocate social goods so that those worse off are made better off." Nozick, by contrast, has a theory of justice based on what he sees as a fair process for achieving social goods. Here, the rule is "allocate social goods in accordance with the rule that everyone has an equal

[48] For example, Deborah Stone, *Policy Paradox: The Art of Political Decision Making*. Rev ed. (New York: W. W. Norton, 2002), Chapter 2: Equity, pp. 39–60, and Chapter 3: Efficiency, pp. 61–85.

[49] John Rawls, *A Theory of Justice* (Cambridge, MA: Harvard University Press, 1971).

[50] Robert Nozick, *Anarchy, State, and Utopia* (New York: Basic Books, 1974).

opportunity to acquire such goods." Both theorists have had a significant influence on the way that many people think about values, ethics, and public policy.

The task in this demonstration exercise is, first, to choose one rule from each of the following three sets, A, B, and C:

SET A: RULES FOR DISTRIBUTING SOCIAL GOODS BASED ON WHO BENEFITS

1. Divide the cake equally among members of society (e.g., all workers will receive the same health benefits for themselves and their families).
2. Divide the cake so that the higher the rank, the larger the slice, although persons of the same rank receive equal slices (e.g., persons who achieve higher occupational rank because of merit will receive higher salaries).
3. Divide the cake so that different groups in society receive equal slices (e.g., minority groups who have suffered historical discrimination will receive preferences in admission to colleges and universities, so that student bodies are more representative of the proportion of minorities in the population).

SET B: RULES FOR DISTRIBUTING SOCIAL GOODS BASED ON WHAT IS BEING DISTRIBUTED

1. Divide the cake so that persons with caloric intake below some recommended daily standard receive larger pieces of cake to compensate for the caloric deficit (e.g., affirmative action programs give preference to minorities and women because they have suffered past discrimination in hiring and wages).
2. Divide the cake so that persons with preferences for carbohydrates, fats, vitamins, and other kinds of nutrients receive pieces large or small enough to satisfy these preferences (e.g., in single-payer health insurance policyholders can choose their own physician, according to their own preferences, whereas in a managed-care health insurance system administrators assign a primary care physician to each policyholder).

SET C: RULES FOR DISTRIBUTING SOCIAL GOODS BASED ON THE PROCESS FOR DISTRIBUTING THE GOOD

1. Divide the cake according to a competitive process in which each person has a fair chance to obtain as many pieces as he wishes, with some having a competitive advantage or disadvantage at the start (e.g., all workers in a competitive market economy have an equal opportunity to compete for higher paying jobs).
2. Divide the cake according to a random process (lottery) in which each person has an equal probability of being selected to receive one or more[51] pieces of the cake

---

[51] Random sampling with replacement (a person selected is returned to the pool and can be selected again) permits the same person to receive more than one piece. Random sampling without replacement (a person selected is not returned to the pool) limits each person to one piece, if selected.

(e.g., scarce social goods such as potentially effective anticancer drugs are distributed randomly in the course of a randomized clinical trial).

3. Divide the cake according to an electoral process in which the majority gets the entire cake (e.g., in a popular election with majority voting one and only one candidate is elected).

After choosing three of the above rules—one each from sets A, B, and C—apply each rule to the issue of whether or not the "living wage" policies described in Case 7 are justifiable. Justify your selection of each rule by drawing on normative ethical and metaethical theories of the kinds described in this chapter. Summarize the results of your analysis in a two-page policy memo addressed to a mayor or member of Congress in one of the cities or regions covered in the case.

REFERENCES

Dolbeare, Kenneth, ed. *Public Policy Evaluation*. Beverly Hills, CA: Sage Publications, 1975.

Dunn, William N. "Assessing the Impact of Policy Analysis: The Functions of Usable Ignorance." In *Advances in Policy Studies since 1950*. Vol. 10 of *Policy Studies Review Annual*. Edited by William N. Dunn and Rita Mae Kelly. New Brunswick, NJ: Transaction Books, 1992, pp. 419–44.

Guttentag, Marcia, and Elmer L. Struening, eds. *Handbook of Evaluation Research*. 2 vols. Beverly Hills, CA: Sage Publications, 1975.

Case 7. Living Wage Policies in the United States

Millions of American families do not have sufficient income to meet basic needs for child care, housing, health insurance, and affordable housing. For many families, employment alone is insufficient to meet basic needs. Although "welfare-to-work" has been advocated as a solution, it appears that a more adequate social safety net may be needed.

Federal minimum wage policy and local policies designed to provide a "living wage" are potential solutions. Local living wage policies in the form of municipal ordinances have been adopted in more than forty U.S. cities.[52] Living wage policies set a wage floor above the federal minimum wage for designated workers. They are usually government workers and workers employed by businesses that receive government grants, contracts, or subsidies. The wage floor is based either on a percentage (usually about 200%) of the federal poverty threshold or on a model family budget that recommends amounts necessary for a minimally adequate standard of living. For example, in Pittsburgh and Allegheny County, Pennsylvania, estimates

---

[52] See Jared Bernstein, Chauna Brocht, and Maggie Spade-Aguilar, "How Much Is Enough?" in *Basic Family Budgets for Working Families* (Washington, DC: Economic Policy Institute, 2000).

for a "living budget" that provides for a minimally adequate standard of living include expense floors for food, utilities including telephone, housing, health insurance, child care, transportation, and taxes. In 1996, the recommended minimal family budget for a two-parent family with two children was $2,598 per month, or $31,176 annually.[53] As of October 2001, there were living wage ordinances for seventy-one cities and regions (see Table 7.7). Following the table is an article on problems and issues surrounding the living wage movement.

Table 7.7   Twelve Living Wage Ordinances in Place in October 2001

City and Year Enacted	Wages and Benefits	Employees Covered
1. Alexandria, VA; 2000	$10.21 index annually to the poverty line for a family of 4 with cost for health insurance	City employees, contracts, and subcontracts and other firms who benefit from over $75,000
2. Baltimore, MD; 1994	$6.10 in 1996 to $7.70 in 1999, $8.20 in 2000	Service contractors; construction contracts over $5,000; includes subcontractors
3. Boston, MA; 1997	$7.49; adjusted annually by the higher of the federal poverty line for a family of four, CPI or 110% of the federal minimum wage	Subsidies (grant, loan, tax incentive, bond financing) over $100,000 for for-profits with over 25 employees and nonprofits with over 100 employees; includes subcontractors and leaseholders or renters of beneficiaries; exemptions for hardship
4. Chicago, IL; 1998	$7.60	Service contracts with over 25 employees; includes subcontractors; exemptions for nonprofits
5. Cleveland, OH; 2000	$8.20, increased to $9.20 Oct. 2002 (indexed accordingly thereafter on annual basis)	Contrast and subsidies over $75,000 with at least 20 employees (profit) and 50 employees for nonprofit with a wage ratio grater than 5:1
6. Detroit, MI; 1998	100% of poverty line for a family of 4 with health benefits; 125% of poverty line without benefits	Service contracts or subsidies (federal grant programs, revenue bond financing, planning assistance, tax increment financing, tax credits) over $50,000; includes subcontractors and leaseholders

(continued)

---

[53] Ralph Bangs, Cheryl Z. Kerchis, and Laurel S. Weldon, *Basic Living Cost and Living Wage Estimates for Pittsburgh and Allegheny County* (Pittsburgh, PA: University Center for Social and Urban Research, University of Pittsburgh, 1997). Figures are for 1996.

Table 7.7   Twelve Living Wage Ordinances in Place in October 2000 (*continued*)

City and Year Enacted	Wages and Benefits	Employees Covered
7. Gary, IN; 1991	Prevailing wage for similar occupations in the county and health care for employees working over 25 hr/wk	Subsidies (industrial revenue bonds, economic grants or other economic development incentives); includes subcontractors
8. Los Angeles, CA; 1997	$7.50 with benefits; $8.50 without benefits; 12 paid days for vacation, sick or personal leave	Service contracts over $25,000 and a term over 3 months; includes subcontractors; exemptions for first time recipients of financial assistance and employers with fewer than 5 employees
9. Miami Beach, FL; 2001	$8.56 with health, $9.81 without benefits	City, and certain city service contract over $100,000
10. New York, NY; 1996	Prevailing wage of similar occupations in the city	Service contracts; includes subcontractors; exemptions for nonprofits
11. Oakland, CA; 1998	$8.00 with health benefits; $9.25 without benefits; adjusted yearly by regional CPI; 12 days paid leave	Service contracts over $25,000 or subsidies over $100,000; includes subcontractors
12. Pittsburgh, PA; 2001	$9.12 with health, $10.62 without	City, certain service contractors, recipients of subsidies and certain leaseholders (profit, at least 10 employees; nonprofit, at least 25)
13. San Francisco, CA; 2000	$10 followed by 2.5% increases for the next 3 years and health insurance or penalty payments to City's public health system fund	City service contracts, nonprofits, and leaseholders at the San Francisco International Airport

Source: "Living Wage Successes." Association of Community Organizations for Reform Now, http://www.acorn.org/. Last updated October 2001.

*The Living Wage Movement: Pointing the Way toward the High Road**

By Jared Bernstein

Despite a surging economy, many low-income working families continue to struggle. Their average income, adjusted for inflation, is 11 percent lower than it was in 1979, and, at $14,900 in 1997, was about $1,300 below that year's poverty line for a two-parent family with two children. For working families in the bottom of the

---

*This piece originally appeared in the spring 1999 issue of *Community Action Digest*. Copyright © 2000 by The Economic Policy Institute. Economic Policy Institute, "Viewpoints." Washington, D.C.: Economic Policy Institute, 2000 (http://www.epinet.org/webfeatures.html).

income scale, the major cause of this negative trend is the decline in their rates of pay. They are working as much or more than ever, but their paychecks are failing to keep up with the rest of the growing economy. The result: the economic gap between the haves and have-nots currently stands at its highest level in the post-World War II era.

Things are particularly tough in some of our cities, where quality jobs for low-wage workers have been disappearing, only to be replaced by service sector jobs with low pay and few benefits. There are numerous reasons why urban workers have lost ground over the past few decades, including declining unions, the shift from manufacturing to services, urban flight, and reduced political support for cities. But two important and growing problems that have gotten less attention are (1) an increase in the use of tax incentives to draw firms to the area and (2) the privatization of services formerly provided by the public sector. A third issue facing low-wage urban workers is pressure on the low-wage labor market caused by the welfare-to-work component of welfare reform.

The first problem-tax incentives that do not deliver is described in great detail in a fascinating piece of economic journalism by Donald Bartlett and James Steele in a recent *Time* magazine series on corporate welfare. You have got to read this series for yourself, but to sum it up, they present an air-tight case showing that, far from a solution, these tax incentives are a big part of the problem. All too often, they show, cities are sacrificing crucial resources to lure firms, with little payback in the way of quality jobs.

The second problem, privatization, is exemplified in the following anecdote. A friend from a New York City suburb told me that in her town, in order to accommodate a local tax cut, the trash removal service was privatized, which, in this case simply meant that a private firm bought the city's dump trucks, painted the firm's name on them, and charged residents a rate that was a bit less than the tax cut (the other change was that now my friend had to bring the trash to the end of the driveway herself). I have no idea if the guys picking up the trash were the same folks who used to work for the city, but you can bet they were paid less. You can also bet that this shift from public to private service provision is taking place throughout the land.

What can we do to combat these trends?
Enter the living wage movement. Although living wage ordinances come in a variety of flavors, they all amount to the same thing: they force employers who receive contracts or tax benefits from the locality to pay their workers a wage rate a few bucks over the minimum. The message and purpose are quite simple: if you as an employer have benefited from some form of incentive, then you ought to give a little something back to your workforce.

Sounds simple, right? Well, anytime you are talking about mandating a wage increase, you can bet somebody will squawk, and those who benefit from privatization and tax giveaways have predictably been squawking pretty loudly. What's more, their warnings about the negative consequences of living wage ordinances are not only the predictable response of vested interests; some of these arguments are well-grounded and deserve careful consideration.

This essay will explore the debate around this relatively new movement. First, we will look at the different types of living wage ordinances that are currently in place. Next we shall take a brief tour through the arguments of the opposition. Then we shall examine some of the evidence regarding the impact of current living wage ordinances and finally reflect on the relevance of the living wage movement in the larger economic context.

What Are "Living Wage" Ordinances?

The living wage movement takes as it theme the reasonable position that no one who works for a living should be poor. Thus, wages paid to even the lowest wage workers, should, with full-time work, lift them out of poverty. But how does the movement achieve this goal?

Perhaps the most obvious way to meet this objective would be to push for a federal minimum wage that was high enough to lift full-time workers up to a decent standard of living. However, although those in the living wage movement certainly support a higher federal minimum, given their limited resources, community organizing backgrounds, and recognition of current political realities, most of their energies have been directed at municipal ordinances.

Essentially, these are rules that set a wage level below which certain employers cannot pay their workers. Thus, they are a close relative of federal minimum wage regulations, which set a national floor on wages (some states set their minimum wage above the federal level, but they cannot set it lower than the current $5.15 per hour). What is different about living wage ordinances (besides the obvious fact that they set a wage level above the federal minimum) is that they are much more narrowly targeted than the federal law. In all cases, the ordinances currently in place cover a subset of a city's workforce. They usually cover those employed by city contracts and, in some cases, those employed by firms who have benefited from some form of favorable tax treatment by the locality.

A good example is the living wage law passed in the city of Baltimore in 1994. Under this law, firms under contract with the city had to pay those workers who were performing the duties under the contract an hourly wage of $6.10 in 1996, rising incrementally to $7.70 in 1999. Note that only those workers actually working under the city contract are covered by the ordinance. Other workers in the firm are not subject to the living wage ordinance, even if they work at the same site. Another example is the Los Angeles living wage proposal, passed in March 1997. In this case, covered workers are those under service contracts (or subcontracts) with the city of $25,000 or more, firms with concession agreements, or firms receiving subsidies from the city at least $100,000 annually must be paid an hourly wage of at least $7.25.

So Who Could Object to That?

Sounds fair, you are thinking? Well it will not come as a shock that employers who benefit from city contracts or tax breaks are not enthusiastically signing onto the living wage movement. Some of those who argue against living wages are simply ideologues who oppose any mandates on the private sector. Others are bound to oppose any policy that will cut into their profits. But opponents of the policy also include employers who genuinely fear that the mandated wage increase will hurt their ability to compete in the marketplace; similarly, city officials worry that if there is a wage ordinance in their city, businesses considering relocation will simply look elsewhere, at the cost of local employment opportunities. Both of these counter-arguments maintain that the ordinances, by raising the cost of doing business to city contractors and entrepreneurs, will cost the city jobs and thus hurt the very people they are designed to help.

How well-founded are these fears? First, even those of us who support living wage ordinances should accept that these arguments cannot be rejected out of hand. In fact, two fundamentals of economic theory support these concerns about the ordinances. The first fundamental is that people are generally paid what they are worth, that is, their hourly compensation is about as valuable as the goods they produce or the services they perform in that hour. The second, and related, fundamental is that if you raise the price of something, people will buy less of it. In classical economics, this principle holds as much for the bananas you purchase at the supermarket as for the privately contracted refuse worker who carts away your banana peels. A third piece of economic theory relevant to our discussion is that mobile capital will seek the highest return (i.e., firms will seek to locate where they can make the most profits), but more on this one later.

If you believe these theoretical propositions, then you are likely to be troubled about mandated wage increases. After all, if workers are by definition being paid their worth, raising their "price" (their hourly wage) can only be bad (as in wasteful and inefficient) for the economy, and ultimately harmful to the worker herself, who, now overpriced, will have to be let go. The result, as contractors leave the market, will be fewer city contracts and less jobs for low-wage workers. The plan to help them has backfired.

But what if these reasonable sounding propositions do not hold? What if workers are not always paid what they are worth, and what if employers—the buyers of labor services—respond differently to price increases than do shoppers buying bananas? Then these arguments against the living wage have to be reevaluated.

There is actually an extensive literature in labor economics that examines the validity of these theories, and, at least as far as the labor market goes, finds them lacking. The literature that evaluates the impact of minimum wage increases is particularly germane, and it universally finds that the job-loss predictions of opponents of the policy never materialize. This is not to imply that no one single worker is unemployed by the mandated wage hike; nor is it meant to imply that a huge wage mandate would not wreak havoc. But, contrary to the predictions of the economic "laws" stated above, it does show that the vast majority of low-wage workers have benefited from the moderate increases in the minimum wage we have implemented.

So are the theories wrong? In the case of the labor market, it appears that, if not wrong, they are pretty unreliable in predicting the impact of mandated wage hikes. The reasons why are not hard to fathom. First, most workers are not paid exactly what they are worth. Wages are set by a number of factors, including the skill, race, and gender of the worker, the conditions of the local labor market (if there are a lot of excess workers, the wage will tend to fall), the nature of the industry and occupation in which the job is located, and, importantly, the bargaining ability of the worker him/herself.

Second, employers will not always respond to the wage hike by laying off workers, for there are other, less disruptive ways they can absorb the price increase. After all, workers are not bananas, and it is much more difficult for an employer to restructure her workforce than for a shopper to switch to oranges until the price of bananas goes back down. As much as they might not want to, employers might find it in their interest to cut their profit margins, or they might try to pass the increase onto their customers through higher prices. Or, instead of laying off their workforce, they are likely to try to get them to increase their productivity, and thus absorb the increase through more efficient production.

That said, there is still an important difference between the federal minimum wage and the municipal living wage. The federal policy is national in scope; thus, no one employer can escape the wage increase by relocating. Recall the third "law" given above: mobile capital seeks the highest return. As the living wage ordinance applies to a specific geographical area, can't employers simply relocate to avoid paying the higher wage rate?

This is the motivation for rigorous opposition of living wages by anxious city officials who may have been elected to office on the promise of creating X-million jobs. They reasonably fear that if MoneyBags Enterprises is trying to decide where to build their next factory, stadium, and so on, a living wage ordinance is not exactly a draw.

This argument also calls for serious consideration. First, we should acknowledge that this mode of thinking is clearly a blueprint for a race to the bottom. You could probably get every factory and sports team in the world to move to your town if you cut them every tax and environmental break available. But, while you might create some jobs, you are just as likely to ruin your community. What's more, you will create an incentive for neighboring communities to compete on the same basis with you, ultimately lowering regional living standards. On the other hand, you would be just as harmful a leader if you raised environmental regulations to impossible levels, taxed profits at 95 percent, and insisted that all employees be paid like Michael Jordan.

Sound municipal policy calls for a middle ground. Some taxes and regulations need to be in place to avoid the race to the bottom, and to preserve both the city's tax base and living standards. What's more, despite their claims to the contrary, employers and contractors will not flee the minute a new regulation is reduced. Instead, they will calculate what the regulation will cost them and, as discussed above, try to figure out ways to absorb the cost increase. And if they can continue to make a profit by doing business with the city, they will stay. The next section provides some evidence on these matters from existing living wage ordinances.

What Does the Evidence Show?

As contemporary living wage ordinances have not been around for very long, there is as yet little evidence of their impact on jobs or economic activity. But what evidence there is shows that the opponents' dire predictions were once again unwarranted.

The most thorough evaluations (of which I am aware) are two separate studies of the Baltimore living wage ordinance, which was approved by the city council in December 1994. These studies are by no means the last word on the issue; like all empirical studies, they have limitations, particularly regarding sample size. But they are still very instructive. Their main findings are:

- As far as these studies could discern, the cost increase to the city after the living wage ordinance went into effect was less than the rate of inflation.
- Again, given data limitations, these studies found no evidence of job loss in response to the wage increases.
- There was a small decrease-concentrated among smaller firms—in the number of bids per contract after the ordinance went into effect; this small decline, however, did not appear to lower competitiveness or raise contract costs.
- Interviews and case studies with affected employers suggests some absorption of labor cost increases through efficiency gains, particularly lower turnover.
- Although there is evidence that the ordinance raised wages for those at the bottom of the wage scale, the affected group appears to be small (less than 2,000).
- Given their low levels of hours worked, the income/poverty-reducing effect was also small; other benefits include some "spillover" increases to workers above the new wage floor.
- Non-compliance on the part of covered employers "remains a significant problem."

Both of these evaluations create the strong impression that the Baltimore living wage ordinance has so far had little impact on either the city's contracting and budget process, or its business environment. Both studies find a real (inflation-adjusted) decrease in contract costs of the contracts in their sample. But they also (the Johns Hopkins study, in particular) leave the impression that few workers were affected, because of both the limited coverage requirements of the ordinance and the fact that most of the covered workers already earn above the living wage (not to mention non-compliance). In cases where more workers fell into the covered wage range, for example, among public school bus aides, the work tended to be seasonal and part-time.

Summing Up

So, at least given the extensive evidence we have on minimum wages and the early returns on living wage ordinances, they appear to be exactly what the doctor ordered to counteract some of the negative economic trends affecting low-wage workers. They force some redistribution of economic resources to those whose boats have not been lifted by the rising economic tide, and do so without creating distortions in the local economy.

There are other advantages as well. The ordinances also have the potential to counteract the destructive race to the bottom, as cities try to undercut each other. The more pervasive these ordinances are, the less firms shopping around for the cheapest locality will be able to do so on the basis of cutting wages. This point should not be minimized. There is already evidence (given in the *Time* magazine series and the Pollin and Luce book cited earlier) that urban competition has hurt cities more than it has helped them. Living wages can help begin to reverse this destructive policy development.

Living wage campaigns also are useful and productive organizing tools. In numerous cities, low-wage urban residents have responded very positively to these campaigns, apparently viewing them as an opportunity to take action against negative trends that directly affect their living standards. In this sense, the campaigns have provided an all too rare opportunity for low-income communities to become actively involved in their economic fates.

Finally, there is a larger lesson from the living wage movement—a lesson about the nature of the labor market. The movement forces you to step back from the narrow economic arguments for and against the living wage and ask yourself the following question: Why does America, the largest and one of the most productive economies in the world, need to subsidize wages so that full-time, adult workers performing essential tasks can achieve a dignified life style? These workers are taking our kids to school, picking up our trash, and maintaining our public infrastructure. How is it possible that our economy has devolved to the point where we have to subsidize these essential services?

Part of the answer is that we have allowed and even encouraged firms to "take the low-road" in terms of their business practices. Instead of creating incentives to be good corporate actors, to play a positive roll in the economic life of the communities wherein they reside, our policies encourage them to minimize their contributions and maximize their personal gain. This may be a profitable strategy in the short-run, but it will ultimately serve to corrode some of our most valuable resources. The living wage movement, by pointing the way to the high road, offers a timely and progressive alternative route.

Jared Bernstein is a labor economist at the Economic Policy Institute. He specializes in income and wage inequality issues.

8

Developing Policy Arguments

What most policy makers understand and many analysts forget is that policy argumentation is central to policy analysis and the policy-making process. Because policy argumentation is the main vehicle for communicating the results of analysis, it is a major factor in the use of policy-relevant information. The analysis and evaluation of policy argumentation are also central to the process of critical thinking that we began to examine in the first part of this book.

In contexts of practice, argumentation is not limited to the kinds of reasoning employed in the social sciences and professions, for example, reasoning based on quantitative models of economic or political behavior, or reasoning based on statistical inferences from a random sample to a population. In the world of policy making, many other modes of reasoning and types of evidence coexist and compete for the attention of policy makers. In this context, analysts who want to improve policies are unlikely to succeed unless they can translate the specialized technical vocabularies of the sciences and professions into arguments that can be understood by policy makers and other participants in policy making. Analysts also should be able to critically assess and, where appropriate, challenge the information and assumptions that underlie their own arguments. This chapter presents tools for developing and evaluating policy arguments, a subject that was introduced in Chapter 1.

THE STRUCTURE OF POLICY ARGUMENTS

A policy argument is the product of argumentation, which is the process. In real-life policy settings, arguments are complex and prone to misunderstanding. For this reason, conceptual models are useful in identifying and relating the elements of policy arguments and examining conditions under which they change. One such model is the structural model of argument developed by Stephen Toulmin.[1] The structural model of argument is designed to investigate structures and processes of practical reasoning. Arguments based on practical reasoning, as distinguished from those based on the formal reasoning of mathematics and deductive logic, lack the certainty of formally valid syllogisms, for example, if A affects B, and B affects C, then A affects C.

The conclusions of *practical arguments* are always uncertain, as are the reasons and evidence that lead to these conclusions. Reasons, including underlying assumptions, are often not stated explicitly. Even when they are stated, they are always incomplete or inconclusive. Practical reasoning yields conclusions "about which we are not entirely confident by relating them back to other information about which we have greater assurance."[2] Because policy arguments are based on practical reasoning, they are always uncertain and almost never deductive.

Types of Knowledge Claims

A knowledge claim is the conclusion of a policy argument. There are three main types of knowledge claims: designative, evaluative, and advocative. Procedure 8.1 provides guidelines for distinguishing among these three types of claims. Designative claims, associated with empiricism and the investigation of policy causation, are concerned with questions of *fact:* What are the observed outcomes of a policy and why did they occur? Evaluative claims, closely related to ethics, are concerned with questions of *value:* Was the policy worthwhile? Advocative claims, which are explicitly normative, are concerned with questions of *right action:* Which policy should be adopted?

Policy arguments, as we saw in Chapter 1, contain six elements: information *I,* claim *C,* warrant *W,* backing *B,* rebuttal *R,* and qualifier *Q* (see Figure 8.1a). The

---

[1] Stephen Toulmin, *The Uses of Argument* (Cambridge: Cambridge University Press, 1958); and Stephen Toulmin, Robert Rieke, and Alan Janik, *An Introduction to Reasoning,* 2d ed. (New York: Macmillan, 1984). Other models of reasoning and argument are Hayward Alker Jr., "The Dialectical Logic of Thucydides' Melian Dialogue," *American Political Science Review* 82, no. 3 (1988): 805–20; Michael Scriven, *Reasoning* (New York: McGraw Hill, 1977); D. R. Des Gasper, "Structures and Meanings: A Way to Introduce Argumentation Analysis in Policy Studies Education," *Africanus* (University of South Africa) 30, no. 1 (2000): 49–72; and D. R. Des Gasper, "Analyzing Policy Arguments," *European Journal of Development Research* 8, no. 1 (1996): 36–62.

[2] Toulmin, *Uses of Argument,* p. 127.

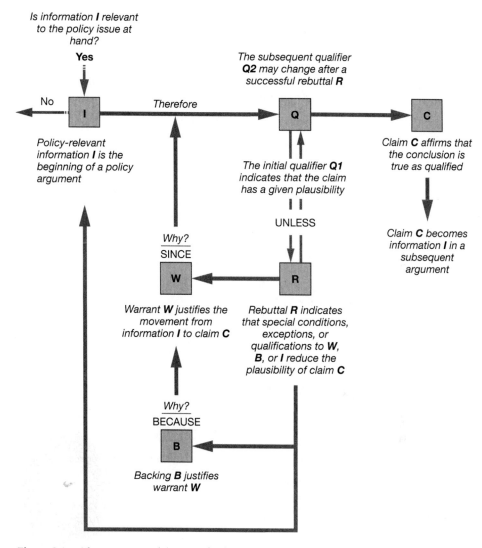

Figure 8.1a The structure and process of policy argumentation.

first four of these elements are present in any policy argument. The claim **C** is the conclusion or "output" of an argument, which is supported by policy-relevant information **I,** which is the beginning or "input" of the argument. The warrant **W** is the justification, or reason, for concluding **C** from **I.** The qualifier indicates that **C** has a given truth or plausibility. Consider the following example:

> The Senator supports the privatization of the federal highway system, which will bring significant gains in efficiency and a reduction in taxes. Considering that the

privatization of public services has been successful in other areas, this is definitely a "no brainer." Besides, this is the same conclusion as a panel of experts
on privatization.

Now let's diagram the argument by breaking it down into its basic
elements (Figure 8.1b): *"The Senator supports the privatization of the federal highway system (**I**), which will bring significant gains in efficiency and a reduction in
taxes (**C**). Considering that the privatization of public services has been successful in*

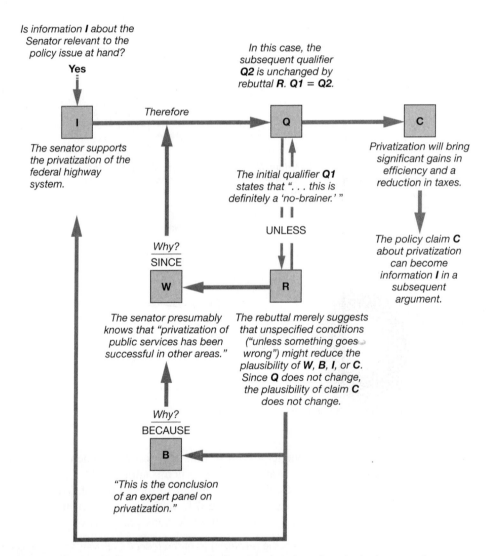

Figure 8.1b   The structure and process of policy argumentation—the privatization example.

*other areas (**W**), this is definitely a 'no brainer'"* (**Q**). Additional elements can be introduced to strengthen the argument. For instance, a backing **B** has been added (*"This is the conclusion of an expert panel on privatization."*). Here, as elsewhere, the **B** provides additional reasons or evidence to support **W**. Finally, the rebuttal **R** states any special conditions, exceptions, or qualifications that may reduce the strength of **Q**, which states the plausibility, or approximate truth, of the conclusion **C**. In this example, the rebuttal **R** merely suggests a possible exception: "Unless something goes wrong." In this case, **R** is general, nonspecific, and ineffective. It fails to challenge the original qualifier **Q1**, which is absolute ("this is definitely a 'no brainer'"). Accordingly, the conclusion **C** is unaffected, because **Q2** is the same: *"this is definitely a 'no brainer' . . . the privatization of the federal highway system . . . will mean significant gains in efficiency and a reduction in taxes."*

The Underdetermination of Conclusions by Information

One of the important features of policy argumentation is that policy-relevant information (or data) does not fully determine the conclusions of policy arguments. One way to say this is "Policy arguments are always underdetermined by data."[3] Another way is "Information does not speak for itself." Identical information can and often does lead to different conclusions, which we call policy *claims* to emphasize the fallible and indeterminate character of arguments. For example, an important document in the history of educational policy in the United States is the Coleman Report (*Equality of Educational Opportunity,* 1966), which among other things provided policy-relevant information about the effects of differences between black and white schools in the achievement of equality of educational opportunity. The same policy-relevant information, however, led to different policy claims (Figure 8.2). Given the information that "Black students attending primarily black schools had lower achievement test scores than black students attending primarily white schools," the claims (with italicized qualifiers in brackets) are as follows:

- *Designative claim and qualifier:* "Since schools in large urban areas are primarily black, the hopes of blacks for higher educational achievement [*simply*] cannot be realized."
- *Evaluative claim and qualifier:* "The Coleman Report is [*clearly*] a racist document based on ethnically biased achievement tests."
- *Advocative claim and qualifier:* "[*There is no question*] that a national policy of compulsory school busing ought to be adopted to achieve integrated schools."

---

[3] This is a paraphrase of philosophers of science such as W. V. O. Quine, Norwood Hanson, Karl Popper, Thomas Kuhn, and many others, who affirm that all data (and information) are theory-dependent. I am glossing distinctions between information and data.

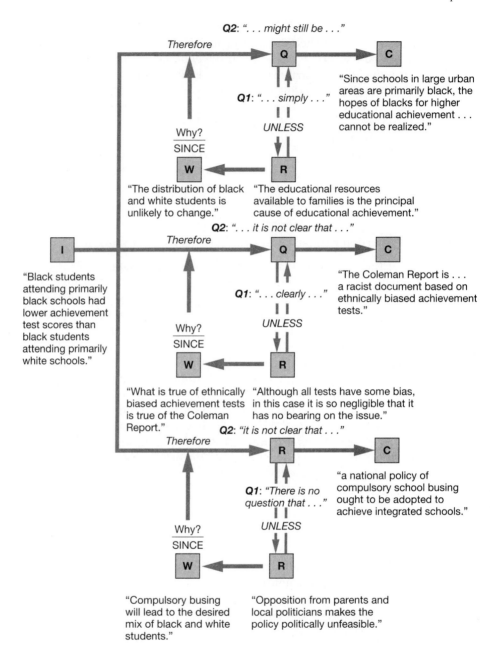

Figure 8.2 The same information leads to different types of claims—as warrants are challenged, the initial qualifier changes.

Procedural Guide 8.1 Identifying Types of Policy Claims

The first and most important step in developing, analyzing, or evaluating a policy argument is to identify the claim or conclusion. To identify the three types of claims, divide statements into three sets. Use the following rules:

1. *Designative claims.* If the claim asserts that some aspect of a policy has been or can be observed, or if observations are used to make causal inferences, then the claim is designative. Look for words that describe observed or observable characteristics: became, originated, linked, caused, effected, consequence, prediction. Some terms that seem to be designative are really evaluative: "He is a good liberal." "That country is undemocratic." "The evil empire (or axis of evil) is the enemy of all." Claims using these and other "appraising" descriptions are evaluative, not designative, although it may be possible to make observations relevant to the appraisals. A good example is an index of democracy included in a questionnaire. Designative claims rest on warrants that are "factual."

2. *Evaluative.* If the claim asserts that some aspect of a policy has or does not have value or worth, it is evaluative. Look for words such as good, bad, right, wrong, beneficial, costly, efficient, responsive, equitable, just, fair, secure. Examples: "The policy will bring about a 'living wage,' thus moving society toward equity and responsiveness." "The program is less efficient than expected." "The policy compromises the health of the economy." Some evaluative claims refer to states (e.g., a just society) and some to processes (e.g., fair procedures). Evaluative claims often rest on warrants that involve "facts" as well as "values."

3. *Advocative.* If the claim asserts that a government or division within it should take action, the claim is advocative. Look for words such as "ought," "needs to," "must," "is required." Examples: "The World Bank should terminate its structural adjustment program." "Congress should pass the Equal Rights Amendment." "The United States should sign the Kyoto Treaty." "Auto manufacturers should be provided with incentives to produce more fuel efficient vehicles." Advocative claims rest on warrants that involve "facts" as well as "values."

Warrants and Rebuttals

Although each of the above claims begins with the same information, very different conclusions are drawn. The reason for these differences is *not* the information—information ("facts") never "speaks for itself." Differences are due, rather, to the role of the warrants in justifying (plausibly or implausibly) the claims on the basis of the information supplied. Some of these warrants are listed below. Although rebuttals apply to backings and information as well, the list shows rebuttals to the warrants only. In this case, the rebuttals diminish the plausibility of the original qualified claims.

Procedural Guide 8.2 Identifying and Arranging Elements of a Policy Argument

There are six elements of a policy argument: information, claim, qualifier, warrant, backing, and rebuttal. The following guidelines are useful in identifying and arranging these elements.

1. If you can, do a stakeholder analysis (Chapter 3) before you analyze an argument. This is the main source of elements *C, I, Q, W, B,* and *R*.
2. Start by locating the major claim *C,* which is the endpoint or output of the argument. *C* is always more general than *I. C* involves an "inferential leap" beyond information.
3. Look for language that indicates the degree of credibility the arguer attaches to *C*—this is the qualifier *Q*.
4. Look for the *I* that supports *C*. The *I* answers two questions: "What does the arguer have to go on? Is it relevant to the case at hand?"
5. Look for *W,* which also supports *C*. The *W* answers the question "Why is the arguer justified in making claim *C* on the basis of *I?*" Respond with "Since. . ." or "Because. . ." and then identify *W*.
6. Repeat the same procedure with *B*. If there is a question whether a statement is a *B* or a *W,* look for the one that is more general. This is the *B*.
7. Remember that a *W* or *B* may be implicit and unstated—do not expect arguments to be entirely transparent. They are rarely so.
8. Look to the arguments of other stakeholders to find *R*s. You will not be able to do this competently by yourself, because it requires someone who actually believes in them.
9. Remember that elements can be rules, principles, statements, or entire arguments. Arguments are complex.
10. An isolated *argument* is static; *argumentation,* which involves at least two stakeholders, is dynamic. The initial *Q* usually changes when *R* challenges the argument.
11. Most *Q*s become weaker, although some stay the same. Some grow stronger (a fortiori) by withstanding challenges.
12. Argumentation produces "trees" and "chains" involving many processes of argumentation among many stakeholders arrayed through time.

- *Warrant and rebuttal for designative claim.* "The distribution of black and white students is unlikely to change" (*W*). *Unless* (*R*): "The educational resources available to families is the principal cause of educational achievement." The plausibility of the claim is reduced from the qualifier *Q1* ("simply"—which is another word for "absolutely" or "without question") to *Q2* ("might still be" realized).

- *Warrant and rebuttal for evaluative claim.* "What is true of ethnically biased achievement tests is true of the Coleman Report" (**W**). *Unless* (**R**): "Although all tests have some bias, in this case it is so negligible that it has no bearing on the issue." Here, the qualifier **Q1** changes from "clearly" to **Q2** "it is not clear that."

- *Warrant and rebuttal for advocative claim.* "Compulsory busing will lead to the desired mix of black and white students" (**W**). *Unless* (**R**): "Opposition from parents and local politicians makes the policy politically unfeasible." Here, the qualifier **Q1** changes from "there is no question" to **Q2** "to the extent feasible."

MODES OF POLICY ARGUMENTATION

Modes of policy argumentation are the characteristic routes followed by information as it is transformed into policy claims. The several different modes of argument involve reasoning from authority, method, generalization, classification, intuition, cause, sign, motivation, analogy, parallel case, and ethics.[4] Each of these eleven modes of argument has a different type of warrant, and multiple modes can be found in any policy argument. The warrants are the reasons offered by the proponent or opponent of a policy to justify a claim, or inference, based on the information supplied. Modes of policy argumentation and their characteristic patterns of reasoning are summarized in Table 8.1.

Argumentation from Authority

In the authoritative mode, claims are based on arguments from authority. Policy-relevant information consists of factual reports or expressions of opinion. The function of the warrant is to affirm the reliability or trustworthiness of the source of the information. Depending on the social context, authorities may be kings, magicians, or religious leaders, or they may occupy roles as presidents, legislators, agency heads, scientists, professors, writers, or news reporters.

In authoritative arguments, the policy claim reiterates the information that has been provided by the authority, whose reliability, status, sagacity, and so forth, has been underwritten by the warrant. To illustrate (see Figure 8.3), let us imagine that a policy analyst advising the National Security Council at the height of the 1999 U.S.–NATO attack on Yugoslavia made the designative claim **C**: "though Western leaders continue to deny it, there can be little doubt that the bombing campaign

---

[4] Some of the modes presented here draw from Wayne Brockriede and Douglas Ehninger, "Toulmin or Argument: An Interpretation and Application," *Quarterly Journal of Speech* 1006 (1960): 45–53; and Toulmin, Rieke, and Janik, *Introduction to Reasoning*, 2d ed., pp. 213–37. I have added additional modes.

Table 8.1   Modes of Policy Argumentation and Characteristic Reasoning Patterns

Mode	Reasoning Pattern
Authority	Reasoning from authority is based on warrants having to do with the achieved or ascribed statuses of producers of policy-relevant information, for example, experts, insiders, scientists, pecialists, gurus, power brokers. Footnotes and references are disguised authoritative arguments.
Method	Reasoning from method is based on warrants about the approved status of methods or techniques used to produce information. The focus is on the achieved or ascribed status or "power" of procedures, rather than persons. Examples include approved statistical, econometric, qualitative, ethnographic, and hermeneutic methods and techniques.
Generalization	Reasoning from generalization is based on similarities between samples and populations from which samples are selected. Although samples can be random, generalizations can also be based on qualitative comparisons. The assumption is that what is true of members of a sample will also be true of members of the population not included in the sample. For example, random samples of $n \geq 30$ are taken to be representative of the (unobserved and often unobservable) population of elements from which the sample is drawn.
Classification	Reasoning from classification has to do with membership in a defined class. The reasoning is that what is true of the class of persons or events described in the warrant is also true of individuals or groups which are members of the class described in the information. An example is the untenable ideological argument that because a country has a socialist economy it must be undemocratic, because all socialist systems are undemocratic.
Cause	Reasoning from cause is about the activity of generative powers ("causes") and their consequences ("effects"). For example, a claim may be made based on general propositions, or laws, of economics that state invariant relations between cause and effect. Other causal claims are based on observing conditions that must be satisfied to infer that a policy has a specified effect. Most argumentation in the social and natural sciences is based on reasoning from cause.
Sign	Reasoning from sign is based on signs, or indicators, and their referents. The presence of a sign indicates the presence of an event or condition, because the sign and what it refers to occur together. Examples are indicators of institutional performance such as "organizational report cards" and "benchmarks," or indicators of economic performance such as "leading economic indicators." Signs are not causes, because causality must satisfy additional requirements not expected of signs.
Motivation	Reasoning from motivation is based on the motivating power of goals, values, and intentions in shaping individual and collective behavior. For example, a claim that citizens will support the strict enforcement of pollution standards might be based on reasoning that, since citizens are motivated by the desire to achieve the goal of clean air and water, they will act to offer their support.
Intuition	Reasoning from intuition is based on the conscious or preconscious cognitive, emotional, or spiritual states of producers of policy-relevant information. For example, the awareness that an advisor has some special insight, feeling, or "tacit knowledge" may serve as a reason to accept his judgment.
Analogy	Reasoning from analogies is based on similarities between relations found in a givenase and relations characteristic of a metaphor, analogy, or allegory. For example, the claim that government should "quarantine" a country by interdicting illegal drugs—with the illegal drugs seen as an "infectious disease"—is based on reasoning that, since quarantine has been effective in cases of infectious diseases, interdiction will be effective in the case of illegal drugs.
Parallel Case	Reasoning from parallel case is based on similarities among two or more cases of policy making. For example, a reason that a local government should strictly enforce pollution standards is that a parallel policy was successfully implemented in a similar local government elsewhere.

Table 8.1   Modes of Policy Argumentation and Characteristic Reasoning Patterns (*continued*)

Mode	Reasoning Pattern
Ethics	Reasoning from ethics is based on judgments about the rightness or wrongness, goodness or badness, of policies or their consequences. For example, policy claims are frequently based on moral principles stating the conditions of a "just" or "good" society, or on ethical norms prohibiting lying in public life. Moral principles and ethical norms go beyond the values and norms of particular individuals or groups. In public policy, many arguments about economic benefits and costs involve unstated or implicit moral and ethical reasoning.

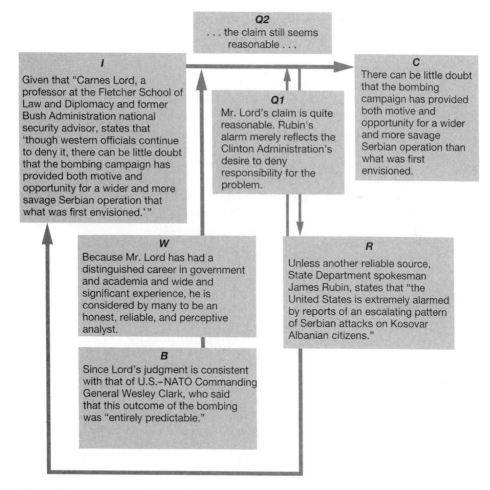

Figure 8.3   Argumentation from authority: consequences of the U.S.–NATO attack on Yugoslavia.

has provided both motive and opportunity for a wider and more savage Serbian operation than what was first envisioned."[5]

The information *I* is from of a statement by Carnes Lord, a professor at the Fletcher School of Law and Diplomacy and former Bush administration national security advisor. The warrant *W* affirms Lord's reliability and is backed *B* by an additional authoritative argument designed to add to the persuasiveness of the argument. The rebuttal *R* challenges the initial warrant, without weakening the claim's credibility, as stated in the original qualifier *Q1*. Therefore *Q2* does not differ from *Q1*. Note that this and other figures were developed with easy-to-use and widely available graphics programs, which provide an efficient and flexible way to represent complex arguments.[6]

Argumentation from Method

Argumentation from method is based on warrants about the approved status of methods or techniques used to produce information. Policy-relevant information may consist of factual statements or reports. The role of the warrant is to provide a reason for accepting the claim based on the information by associating the latter with the use of an approved method or rule. Usually, the claim is that the event, condition, or object described in the information should be regarded as valuable (or worthless), because of the method used to produce it. Consider the following public investment problem. An analyst has information *I* that the production of energy per dollar is greater in nuclear power plants than in hydroelectric plants, which in turn produce more energy per dollar than solar power plants. The claim *C* is that the government should invest in nuclear energy rather than solar energy. The warrant *W* associates the information *I* with claim *C* by invoking the transitivity rule of mathematical economics.[7] The warrant is backed *B* by the presumption that transitivity is a "universal selection rule" that guarantees the rationality of choice. The rebuttal *R* challenges the presumption about the universal validity of transitivity by pointing to the presence of cyclical preferences. The original qualifier *Q1* is reduced from "very likely" to *Q2* "quite uncertain" (Figure 8.4).

In argumentation from method, claims are assessed in terms of the achieved or ascribed status of general procedures (methods) and specialized ones (techniques), along with the rules guiding their use. The methods and techniques can be "analytic," in the sense of the dictionary definition of analysis as the separation or breaking up of

---

[5] *Boston Globe*, April 4, 1999. Quoted in Noam Chomsky, *Rogue States: The Rule of Force in World Affairs* (Cambridge, MA: South End Press, 2000), p. 35.

[6] The program is Microsoft Draw, which is part of Microsoft Word. Other graphics alternatives include Decision Programming Language software. See *DPL 4.0: Professional Decision Analysis Software—Academic Edition* (Pacific Grove, CA: Duxbury, 1998). Using these and similar graphics programs responds to the criticism that hand-drawn figures are inflexible and overly simple. See Des Gasper and George, "Analyzing Argumentation."

[7] On rules expressing transitive and cyclical preferences, see, for example, Norman Frohlich and Joe A. Oppenheimer, *Modern Political Economy* (Englewood Cliffs, NJ: Prentice Hall, 1978), pp. 6–13.

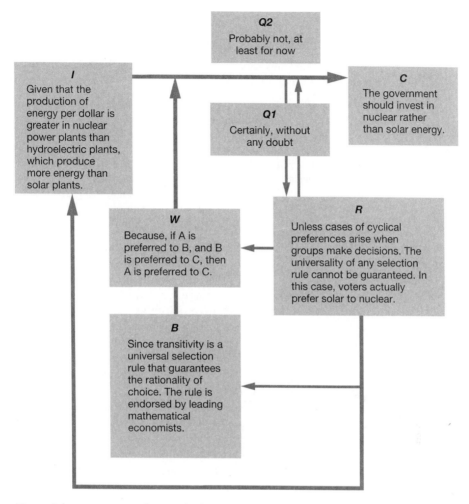

Figure 8.4 Argumentation from method—contested claims about the authority of the transitivity rule.

a whole into its fundamental elements or constituent parts. Policy analysts who accept the authority of analytic methods such as econometrics, benefit–cost analysis, or decision analysis sometimes seem to believe that the use of such methods actually "sets the policy agenda and its directions, that useful analysis will be used analysis."[8]

The authority of methods need not be derived from rules of formal logic or mathematics, as the history of qualitative as well as quantitative methods shows. Many qualitative methods used by policy analysts originate in the hermeneutic tradition, which evolved from the interpretation of biblical texts. The authority of qualitative

---

[8] Allen Schick, "Beyond Analysis," *Public Administration Review* 37, no. 3 (1977): 259.

methods, like any other, stems from the professional and scientific communities that create definitions of the purpose, scope, and proper application of approved methods.[9] These communities are extra-scientific sources of authority.

The transitivity rule and other basic axioms of mathematics have also arisen from extra-scientific sources:

> Consider the axiom which asserts the transitivity of preference: if A is preferred to B, and B to C, then A is (or rationally must be) preferred to C. The intuitive appeal of this assertion is so great that few if any economists feel the urge to build formal economic systems in which the axiom fails. Geometry...is the classic example; the intuitive strength of Euclid's "postulates" was so great that for two thousand years geometers played their games strictly within the domain...which Euclid had laid down. Even when non-Euclidean geometries were discovered in the early nineteenth century, most mathematicians never thought of them as valid.[10]

Adherence to approved methods is wrongly believed to make policy decisions somehow more "rational." A rational choice is thought to be possible if the analyst can order all consequences associated with action, if the ordering of consequences is transitive, and if the analyst can consistently and in a transitive fashion choose the alternative that will bring the greatest benefit in relation to cost.[11] Challenges to this argument may be made on authoritative, intuitive, and ethical grounds. New schools of analysis may serve as a source of approved methods, new axioms providing for nontransitive preferences may come to be accepted on intuitive grounds, and rules that run counter to moral principles and ethical norms may be replaced with new ones.[12] Challenges may also be made on pragmatic grounds, for example, by arguing that the transitivity rule does not actually promote better decisions in policy settings characterized by incomplete information, value conflicts, multiple competing objectives, partisan mutual adjustment, and "organized anarchy."[13] In the last analysis, a successful argument from method must demonstrate only that the results of using particular rules are superior to those that occur without them and that the observed improvement is a consequence of using the rule or procedure.[14]

---

[9] Approved methods are part of Kuhn's disciplinary matrix. Thomas Kuhn, *The Structure of Scientific Revolutions,* 2d ed. (Chicago: University of Chicago Press, 1971), p. 103.

[10] C. West Churchman, *The Design of Inquiring Systems: Basic Concepts of Systems and Organization* (New York: Basic Books, 1971), p. 25.

[11] Joseph L. Bower, "Descriptive Decision Theory from the 'Administrative' Viewpoint," in *The Study of Policy Formation,* ed. Raymond A. Bauer and Kenneth J. Gergen (New York: Free Press, 1968), pp. 104–6.

[12] See the discussion of the evolution of welfare economics in Duncan MacRae Jr., *The Social Function of Social Science* (New Haven, CT: Yale University Press, 1976), pp. 107–57.

[13] See Chapter 2.

[14] Bower, "Descriptive Decision Theory from the 'Administrative' Viewpoint," p. 106. See Nicholas Rescher's essays on methodological pragmatism, for example, *Induction* (Pittsburgh, PA: University of Pittsburgh Press, 1980).

Argumentation from Generalization

Arguments from generalization frequently involve samples. Policy-relevant information consists of events, conditions, persons, groups, organizations, or societies that are taken to be representative of a larger population of the same elements. The function of the warrant is to affirm that what is true of the elements in the sample is also true of the unobserved (and often unobservable) elements in the population. The policy claim rests on the assumption that the sample is an adequate or satisfactory representation of the population.

To illustrate, consider the director of a community food bank who wants to know whether persons receiving food are getting an adequate daily allowance of calcium, one of the most important minerals in the body (Figure 8.5). The director, who is attentive to reasons that might justify additional funding for the food bank, makes the claim *C* that it is "pretty likely" that food bank clients are receiving sufficient calcium—specifically, given that the observed amount of 755 milligrams (mg) of calcium could have occurred by chance 9 times out of 100, it is not reliably different than the Recommended Daily Allowance (RDA) of 800 mg, an amount prescribed by the Food and Nutrition Board of the National Academy of Sciences.

In this case, the information *I* describes the average daily intake of calcium (755 mg) measured in a random sample (sometimes inappropriately called a "scientific sample" in policy circles) of fifty clients. The information *I* indicates that the difference between 755 mg and 800 mg could occur by chance 9 times out of 100, a conclusion reached on the basis of a statistical test (a "two-sample test"). The probability value (p = 0.09) is included in the qualifier *Q* in the ordinary language of "pretty likely." The warrant *W* that provides the reason for moving from information *I* to claim *C* has two parts: the rule that a random sample of at least 30 is adequate in such cases to generalize to the population from which the sample is selected and the practice of accepting a level of statistical significance of p = 0.05 (5 times out of 100) as an "acceptable" level of risk. When pressed for additional justification, the director checks her statistics text to find the appropriate theoretical backing *B* for the rule $n \geq 30$. The backing *B* is the Central Limit Theorem of probability theory.

A member of the director's staff responsible for distributing the food is sensitive to criticism and resistant to the idea that clients served by the food bank may have a calcium deficiency. He therefore challenges the claim with several rebuttals *R*: A 9 percent margin of error leaves too much room for chance, including a 91 percent (100–9) chance of a "false negative" conclusion of no difference (Type II error); another random sample could result in another conclusion; and, in any case, the difference between 755 and 800 mg of calcium is *practically* significant and should be looked at carefully. The rebuttals are very plausible, and we would guess that the director's qualifier *Q1* changed from "pretty likely" to *Q2* "not likely" that clients are receiving their minimum RDA of calcium. On balance, the director's original claim—that calcium intake is

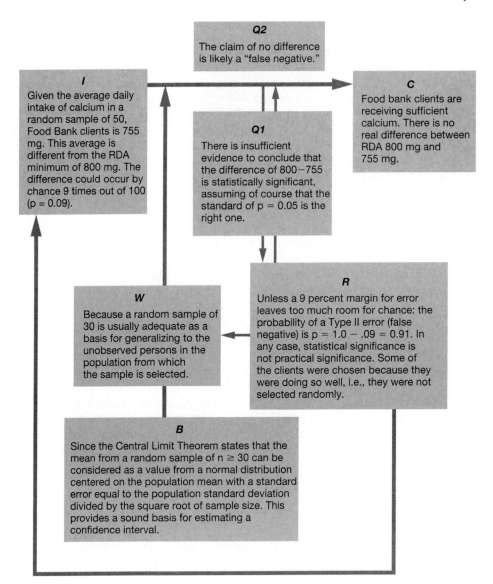

Figure 8.5 Argumentation from generalization—a statistical claim about the nutritional status of food bank clients is a "false negative."

probably adequate—is diminished by the rebuttals of the well-meaning and critical staff member.

Arguments from generalization are not always statistical, in the specific sense that statistics are estimates of population values (called parameters). Nonrandom samples—for example, purposive samples, theoretical samples, and sociometric (snowball) samples—do not permit statistical estimates. They are nevertheless useful in making claims about populations.[15] Even case studies (where $n = 1$) may be used to generalize to wider populations by means of various pattern-matching methods.[16]

Argumentation from Classification

Argumentation from classification focuses on membership in a defined class. The reasoning is that what is true of the class of persons or events described in the warrant is also true of individuals or groups which are members of the class, as they are described in the information. To illustrate, consider the following argument about the relationship between regime type and the control of terrorism (Figure 8.6). The information *I* is Iran, Iraq, and the Palestinian Authority are authoritarian dictatorships. The claim *C* is that Iran, Iraq, and the Palestinian Authority control terrorism within their borders. The warrant *W* is that authoritarian regimes exercise firm control of terrorists and other armed groups within their territories. The backing *B* has two parts. The first is that firm control exercised by authoritarian dictatorships is possible because such regimes do not permit the private use of weapons without the express or tacit approval of the government. The second is that the theory of authoritarian dictatorship was developed and tested by distinguished scholars at Harvard University. The rebuttal *R* is that one or more of the Middle Eastern regimes permit the private use of weapons and, in fact, is a democracy. It does not fit the classification. The original qualifier *Q1* (certainly) is reduced to *Q2* (it is not clear).

The plausibility of classificational arguments depends on the completeness and internal consistency of the properties employed to define a class. Various classes of political regimes—authoritarian dictatorship, totalitarian democracy, socialist democracy, capitalist democracy—are much less homogeneous and

---

[15] See, for example, Delbert C. Miller, *Handbook of Research Design and Social Measurement*, 4th ed. (Newbury Park, CA: Sage Publications, 1991). Generalizability (external validity) in experimental and quasi-experimental research is essentially nonstatistical. See William R. Shadish, Thomas D. Cook, and Donald T. Campbell, *Experimental and Quasi-Experimental Designs for Generalized Causal Inference* (Boston, MA: Houghton Mifflin, 2002).

[16] See William N. Dunn, "Pattern Matching: Methodology," *International Encyclopedia of the Social and Behavioral Sciences* (New York: Elsevier, 2002).

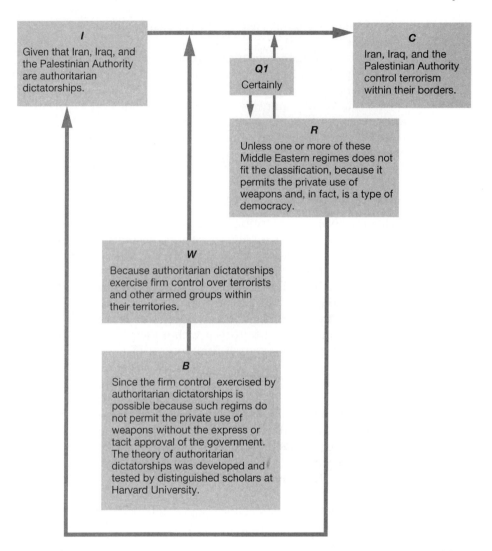

Figure 8.6 Argumentation from classification—challenging claims about authoritarian rule and the control of terrorism.

internally consistent than popular classifications suggest. The same is true for classes of policies (e.g., "privatization"), organizations (e.g., "bureaucracy"), political doctrines (e.g., "liberal" and "conservative"), and groups (e.g., "lower class," "middle class," "upper class"). Many apparently simple classifications turn out to be complex, not simple, and often they are ideologies in disguise.

Argumentation from Cause

Argumentation from cause focuses on the causes and effects of public policies.[17] In causal arguments, information consists of one or more evidently factual statements or reports about a policy environment, a policy stakeholder, or a policy. The warrant transforms these statements or reports by relating them to generative powers (causes) and their results (effects). The claim relates these causes and effects back to the information supplied.

The role of causal arguments in transforming policy-relevant information into policy claims may be illustrated by Allison's well-known causal explanations of foreign policy behavior during the Cuban missile crisis in October 1962.[18] Showing how different models yield alternative explanations of foreign policy, Allison argues that (1) government policy analysts think about problems of foreign policy in terms of implicit conceptual models that shape their thought; (2) most analysts explain the behavior of governments in terms of one basic model, one that assumes the rationality of political choices (*rational policy model*); and (3) alternative models, including those that emphasize organizational processes (*organizational process model*) and bureaucratic politics (*bureaucratic politics model*), provide bases for improved explanations of foreign policy behavior.

In contrasting alternative models, Allison wants to assess U.S. foreign policy during the Cuban missile crisis by reviewing explanatory arguments derived from the three conceptual models. In 1962, the policy alternatives open to the United States ranged from no action and diplomatic pressures to secret negotiations, invasion, surgical air strike, and blockade. The alternatives are examined in terms of rival explanations of foreign policy behavior. The structure of these explanations conforms to a type of causal explanation that philosophers call deductive-nomological (D-N)

---

[17] Causal argumentation has dominated efforts of political scientists to explain policy making. Recent examples include contributors to Sabatier, *Theories of the Policy Process.* Other examples are James E. Anderson, *Public Policy-Making* (New York: Praeger Publishers, 1975); Thomas R. Dye, *Understanding Public Policy,* 3d ed. (Englewood Cliffs, NJ: Prentice Hall, 1978); Robert Eyestone, *The Threads of Public Policy: A Study in Policy Leadership* (Indianapolis, IN: Bobbs-Merrill, 1971); Jerald Hage and J. Rogers Hollingsworth, "The First Steps toward the Integration of Social Theory and Public Policy," *Annals of the American Academy of Political and Social Science,* 434 (November 1977): 1–23; Richard I. Hofferbert, *The Study of Public Policy* (Indianapolis, IN: Bobbs-Merrill, 1974); Charles O. Jones, An *Introduction to the Study of Public Policy,* 2d ed. (North Scituate, MA: Duxbury Press, 1977); Robert L. Lineberry, *American Public Policy: What Government Does and What Difference It Makes* (New York: Harper & Row, 1977); Austin Ranney, ed., *Political Science and Public Policy* (Chicago: Markham, 1968); Richard Rose, ed., *The Dynamics of Public Policy: A Comparative Analysis* (Beverly Hills, CA: Sage Publications, 1976); Ira Sharkansky, ed., *Policy Analysis in Political Science* (Cambridge, MA: Markham, 1970); and Peter Woll, *Public Policy* (Cambridge, MA: Winthrop Publishers, 1974).

[18] Graham T. Allison, "Conceptual Models and the Cuban Missile Crisis," *American Political Science Review* 3002, no. 3 (1969): 689–718.

explanation, which holds that valid explanations are possible only when general theoretical propositions or laws link prior circumstances with subsequent events.[19]

Among the several advocative claims made at the time of the Cuban missile crisis, let us consider the policy recommendation actually adopted by the United States: "The United States should blockade Cuba." In this case, the policy-relevant information **I** is "The Soviet Union is placing offensive missiles in Cuba." To carry information **I** to claim **C,** a warrant **W** answers the question: Why is it plausible, given the information provided, to claim that the United States should blockade Cuba? The warrant provides the answer by stating *since* "the blockade will force the withdrawal of missiles by showing the Russians that the United States is determined to use force." In providing additional reasons to accept the claim, the backing **B** answers the question: Why would the blockade have this effect? The backing answers the question by stating *because* "[a]n increase in the cost of an alternative reduces the likelihood of that alternative being chosen."[20] The backing **B** represents a general theoretical proposition, or law, within the rational policy model (Figure 8.7). In this case, **Q1** (probably) changes to **Q2** (probably not) after the rebuttal **R** has successfully challenged the warrant **W.**

The primary purpose of Allison's account is not to demonstrate the inherent superiority of one or another of the three explanatory models. It is rather to show that the use of multiple competing models can result in improved explanations of foreign policy behavior. The use of multiple models moves policy analysis from a self-contained and static single argument about the relation between information and claim to a new stage of dynamic debate. In this context, the organizational, process model provides a rebuttal **R** in the form of a competing causal argument. The rebuttal states *unless* "Russian leaders are unable to force their own organizational units to depart from assigned tasks and routines." This can be expected to occur *because* "[m]ajor lines of organizational behavior are straight, that is, behavior at one time is marginally different from that behavior at t-1."[21] The backing **B** for the rebuttal **R** is again a general proposition or law within the organizational process model.

The case of the Cuban missile crisis illustrates some of the limitations of causal argumentation based on D-N explanation. First, several competing causal arguments are equally compatible as general propositions or laws. These arguments, each backed by scientific theories, cannot be confirmed or refuted solely on the basis of this or any other information or data.[22] Second, a given causal argument, however persuasive, cannot directly lead to an advocative claim or

---

[19] See Carl G. Hempel, *Aspects of Scientific Explanation* (New York: Free Press, 1965).

[20] Allison, "Conceptual Models," p. 694.

[21] Ibid., p. 702.

[22] Georg H. von Wright, *Explanation and Understanding* (Ithaca, NY: Comell University Press, 1970), p. 145; and Kuhn, *Structure of Scientific Revolutions.*

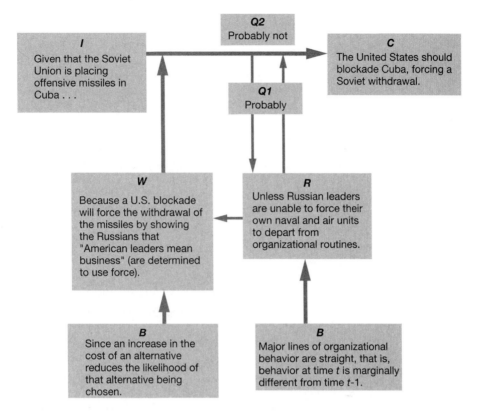

Figure 8.7 Argumentation from cause: rival theoretical explanations of foreign policy behavior during the Cuban missile crisis.

recommendation, because traditional causal explanations do not themselves contain value premises.[23] In the example below, there is a suppressed value premise, which is that U.S. leaders are motivated by the value of security from the Soviet military presence in the western hemisphere. If some other value had motivated policy makers, either of the two competing causal explanations would have supported altogether different claims, for example, that the United States should invade and occupy Cuba.

---

[23] This is not to say that they do not imply values, because empirical theories in the social and natural sciences rest on unstated value premises. See, for example, M. Gunther and K. Reshaur, "Science and Values in Political 'Science,'" *Philosophy of Social Sciences* 1 (1971): 113–21; J. W. Sutherland, "Axiological Predicates in Scientific Enterprise," *General Systems* 19 (1974): 3–14; and Ian I. Mitroff, *The Subjective Side of Science: A Philosophical Inquiry into the Psychology of the Apollo Moon Scientists* (New York: American Elsevier Publishing, 1974).

Causal argumentation based on the D-N model of scientific explanation attempts to develop and test general propositions about the causes and effects of public policy.[24] Carl Hempel has elaborated D-N explanation as follows:

> We divide explanation into two major constituents, the *explanandum* and the *explanans*. By the explanandum, we understand the sentence describing the phenomenon to be explained (not that phenomenon itself); by the explanans the class of those sentences which are adduced to account for the phenomenon. . . . [Scientific explanation] answers the question, "Why did the explanandum-phenomenon occur?" by showing that the phenomenon resulted from particular circumstances, specified in $C_1, C_2, \ldots, C_k$, in accordance with laws $L_1, L_2, \ldots, L_r$. By pointing this out, the argument shows that, given the particular circumstances and the laws in question, the occurrence of the phenomenon was to be *expected;* and it is in this sense that the explanation enables us to understand why the phenomenon occurred.[25]

A simple example illustrates traditional causal (D-N) explanation.[26] If I leave my car outside overnight and the temperature drops below freezing, my full radiator (without antifreeze) will burst. Why will this happen? "My radiator burst" (*explanandum*). "My radiator was full of water, the cap was tightly fastened, and the temperature outside dropped below freezing" (circumstances, or C_k, in the *explanans*). And, "the volume of water expands when it freezes" (general proposition or law, L_r in the explanans).[27] In this example, knowledge of prior circumstances and the appropriate law permits a prediction of the resultant event.

Questions have been raised about the suitability of D-N explanation in history and the social sciences.[28] These questions arise, among other reasons, because policy analysis and other social sciences are partly evaluative and advocative (normative) in character. Every advocative claim contains both factual and value premises, whereas in traditional causal explanations we evidently find only factual premises. Traditional causal explanations also require that the *explanans* precede (or accompany) the *explanandum*. Yet many advocative claims reverse this sequence, insofar as circumstances that explain action are situated in the future. Future circumstances, including intentions, goals, and desires, explain present actions to the extent that actions cannot occur without the motivation provided by such intentions, goals, and desires.[29] Finally, any correspondence between the results of acting on an advocative claim and the conclusions of a causal argument

---

[24] Allison, "Conceptual Models," p. 690 (note 4) tells us that Hempel's D-N (deductive-nomological) explanation is the basis (backing) for his three models.

[25] Hempel, *Aspects of Scientific Explanation,* pp. 247–58.

[26] See von Wright, *Explanation and Understanding,* p. 12.

[27] Ibid., p. 12.

[28] Ibid., p. 11.

[29] Ibid., pp. 74–124; G. E. M. Anscombe, *Intention* (London: Basil Blackwell, 1957); and W. H. Dray, *Laws and Explanation in History* (London: Oxford University Press, 1957).

may be purely coincidental. In policy making, predictions based on D-N explanations will fail if policy actors employ intelligent reflection to change their behavior, or if unpredictable factors deriving from creative thought intervene.[30]

D-N explanation is not the sole legitimate form of causal argumentation in public policy. Another form is hypothetico-deductive (H-D) explanation, which involves the deduction of hypotheses from theories that do not involve propositions about invariant causal relations or laws. Often the hypotheses of interest are those dealing with policy or program actions designed to achieve some practical outcome.[31] The relation between action and outcome, however, is not certain. If it were, it would conform to the following requirements, usually called the "essentialist" view of causation:

- The policy, x, must precede the outcome, y, in time.
- The occurrence of the policy, x, must be necessary for the occurrence of y, the outcome, which must not occur in the absence of the policy, x.
- The occurrence of the policy, x, must be sufficient for the occurrence of y, the outcome, which must occur when the policy, x, is present.

If these requirements were met, the relation between a policy action and an outcome would be certain. This requirement is virtually never satisfied in real-life policy settings. Instead, what occurs is that other conditions—uncontrolled contingencies that lie beyond the control of policy makers—make it impossible to know definitely whether a policy is necessary or sufficient for the occurrence of an outcome. The uncontrolled contingencies are plausible rival hypotheses that must be taken into account and, where possible, eliminated as competing explanations of a policy outcome. Here, the best that may be expected is an optimally plausible claim, that is, an approximately valid causal inference.[32] Figure 8.8 displays causal argumentation in the quasi-experimental tradition founded by Donald T. Campbell, a tradition based on the fundamental premise that causal argumentation in real-life policy settings requires the formulation, testing, and elimination of rival hypotheses.[33] Figure 8.8 shows that rival hypotheses used to challenge the W and I change the initial qualifier from "definitely" (**Q1**) to "doubtful" (**Q2**).

---

[30] Alasdair MacIntyre, "Ideology, Social Science, and Revolution," *Comparative Politics* 5, no. 3 (1973): 334.

[31] See the discussion of the "activity theory of causation" in Thomas D. Cook and Donald T. Campbell, *Quasi-Experimentation: Design and Analysis Issues for Field Settings* (Boston, MA: Houghton Mifflin, 1979), ch. 1.

[32] The preeminent source on validity questions in the social and behavioral sciences is William R. Shadish, Thomas D. Cook, and Donald T. Campbell, *Experimental and Quasi-Experimental Designs for Generalized Causal Inference* (Boston, MA: Houghton Mifflin, 2002).

[33] Rival hypotheses are also known as "threats to validity." See Donald T. Campbell, *Methodology and Epistemology for Social Science: Collected Papers,* ed. E. S. Overman (Chicago: University of Chicago Press, 1988). The example is from Campbell's "Reforms as Experiments," in the Overman edition cited above.

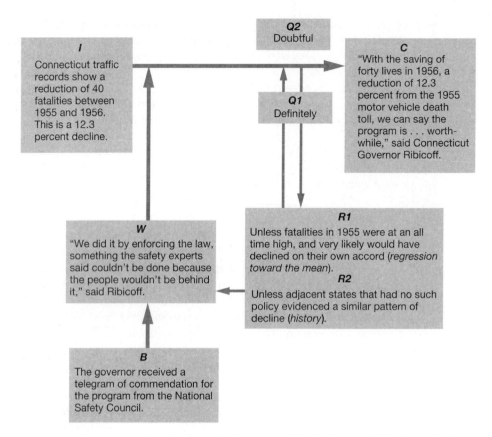

Figure 8.8 Argumentation from cause: rival explanations of the decline in traffic fatalities after the 1955 Connecticut crackdown on speeding.

Argumentation from Sign

Reasoning from sign is based on indicators and their referents. The presence of a sign indicates the presence of an event, condition, or process, because the sign and what it refers to occur together. Examples are indicators of institutional performance such as "organizational report cards," "benchmarks," and "best practices."[34] Another example is the widely used set of indicators (actually indices) of economic performance—"leading," "lagging," and "coincident" economic indicators—published periodically by the Conference Board. Signs are not causes. As we saw above, causality must satisfy additional requirements not expected of signs. Figure 8.9 displays an argumentation from sign based on a correlation coefficient and probability value (p-value).

---

[34] For example, William T. Gormley Jr. and David L. Weimer, *Organizational Report Cards* (Cambridge, MA: Harvard University Press, 1999).

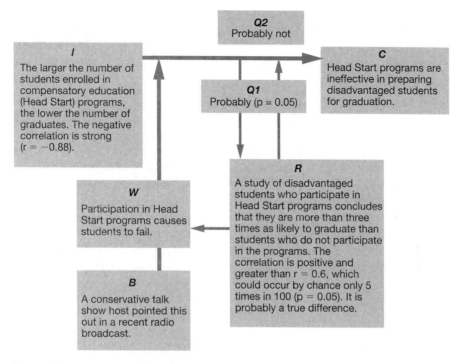

Figure 8.9 Argumentation from sign—quantitative indicators such as correlation coefficients and p-values are not sufficient to show causality.

Figure 8.9 makes an important distinction between signs and causes. In modern statistical analysis, measures of correlation, regression, and statistical significance (e.g., chi-square, t, and F values) are signs that refer to covariation. Covariation is a necessary but not sufficient condition of causation. In Figure 8.9, the **R** states a causal relation between participation in Head Start programs and increased graduation rates. It is a causal relation because students who participated had higher graduation rates; those who did not had lower graduation rates; the program came before the graduation in time; and there was, in addition, a positive correlation between participation and graduation. It is positive, moderate in strength ($r = 0.61$), and statistically significant ($p = 0.05$). The **R** successfully challenges the argument from sign, which mistakenly infers that Head Start is ineffective. The initial qualifier **Q1** ("probably") becomes **Q2** ("unlikely").

Arguments from sign—whether presented as organizational report cards, benchmarks, or correlation and regression coefficients—are at best statements of covariation or coincidence. Although covariation must be present for a causal relation to exist, causation requires that we fulfill certain conditions. John Stuart Mill, the nineteenth-century English philosopher, presented a set of methods (sometimes called "canons") of inductive inference designed to discover causal relations. *Mills's methods* are broadly employed today in the social and behavioral sciences, policy analysis, and program evaluation.[35] The methods are those of *agreement, difference, agreement and difference* (the so-called "joint method"), *concomitant variation,* and *residues.* The basic idea of the first three methods is as follows:

- If on two or more occasions a presumed effect has only one antecedent condition in common, then that condition is probably the cause of the presumed effect. If on the first occasion, presumed effect Y is preceded by conditions X_1, X_3, and X_5, and on the second occasion the presumed effect Y is preceded by conditions X_2, X_3, and X_6, then X_3 is probably the cause of Y.
- If a presumed effect and a presumed noneffect share every antecedent condition except one, which occurs along with the presumed effect, then that condition is probably the cause of the presumed effect. If the presumed effect Y and the presumed noneffect ~ Y share antecedent conditions X_1, X_2, X_5, and X_6, but do not share condition X_3, which occurs along with presumed effect Y, then X_3 is probably the cause of Y.
- If two or more occasions when a presumed effect occurs have only one antecedent in common, while two or more occasions when a presumed effect does not occur have nothing in common except the absence of that antecedent condition, then the antecedent condition in which the presumed effects and presumed noneffects differ is probably the cause. If on two or more occasions when presumed effect Y occurs it is accompanied solely by antecedent condition X_3, while two or more occasions when presumed effect Y does not occur have nothing in common except the absence of antecedent condition X_3, then X_3 is probably the cause of Y.

The method of concomitant variation, which we know today as correlation (covariation, association), does not require additional comment here, except to say that it is a necessary condition of causation. The method of residues is similar to what we now call the analysis of residual (error) variance in multivariate statistics and econometrics. The logic is that what is "left over" when we have explained the effects of all the (presumed) causes of a phenomenon are the "residues" of other possible (and usually unknown) causes. To know whether we are analyzing causation or correlation, however, requires that we first employ the first three methods, because no statistical analyses, however advanced, are sufficient to establish causation. Statistics provides signs, not causes.

---

[35] Quasi-experimental design in program evaluation is based very largely on Mill's methods. The best example is Cook and Campbell, *Quasi-Experimentation,* ch. 1, who critique and go beyond Mill's methods. For another critique and reformulation, see William N. Dunn, "Pragmatic Eliminative Induction," *Philosophica* 60, no. 2 (1997), Special issue honoring Donald T. Campbell. Comparative political science, comparative sociology, comparative public policy, and experimental psychology have also drawn on Mill's methods.

Argumentation from Motivation

In motivational arguments, claims assert that an action should be adopted because of the motivating power of intentions, goals, or values. Motivational arguments seek to demonstrate that the intentions, goals, or values underlying a recommended course of action are such as to warrant its acceptance, adoption, or performance. It is often sufficient to know that large or important groups actually desire to follow the course of action stated in the claim.

Argumentation from motivation represents a form of reasoning that philosophers since Aristotle have called the practical syllogism, or practical inference. In practical inference, the major premise or warrant *W* describes some desired state or end of action, while the minor premise or information *I* relates a course of action to this desired state as a means to an end. The conclusion or claim *C* consists of a recommendation act in a certain way to secure the desired state or end. Whereas in *theoretical inference* (argumentation from cause) acceptance of a general proposition or law leads to the conclusion or claim, in *practical inference* (argumentation from motivation) acceptance of a premise about goals, values, or intentions leads a conclusion or claim about actions that are in accordance with them.[36] Claims in practical inference are usually designed to *understand actions,* whereas claims in theoretical inference seek to *explain events.*[37]

Practical reasoning is of great importance to policy analysis, where one of the chief problems is to explain actions in terms of goals, values, and intentions:

> the practical syllogism provides the sciences of man with something long missing from their methodology: an explanation model in its own right which is a definite alternative to the subsumption-theoretic covering law model [i.e., deductive-nomological explanation—*author*]. Broadly speaking, what the subsumption-theoretical model is to causal explanation and explanation in the natural sciences, the practical syllogism is to teleological explanation and explanation in history and the social sciences.[38]

Motivational argumentation not only provides an alternative explanatory model for policy analysis, but also compels us to conceptualize policy making as a political process. Arguments from motivation force analysts to think in terms of the goals, values, and intentions of policy actors, and "enter the phenomenological world of the policy maker."[39] Motivational arguments also bring us closer to questions of values and ethics, which in other modes of policy argumentation are frequently and

---

[36] von Wright, *Explanation and Understanding,* pp. 22–27.

[37] Ibid., pp. 22–24. See also Fred R. Dallmayr and Thomas A. McCarthy, eds., *Understanding and Social Inquiry* (Notre Dame, IN: University of Notre Dame Press, 1977); and Rein, *Social Science and Public Policy,* pp. 14–15, 139–70.

[38] *von Wright, Explanation and Understanding,* p. 27.

[39] Bauer, *Study of Policy Formation,* p. 4.

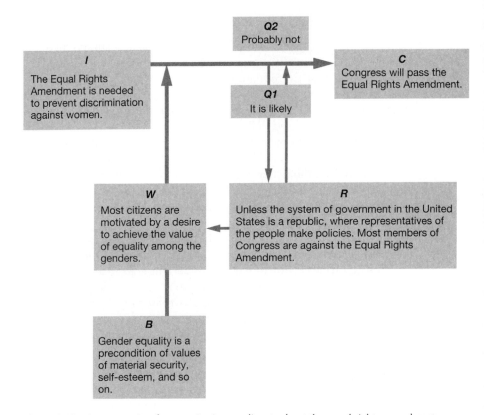

Figure 8.10   Argumentation from motivation—a dispute about the equal rights amendment.

regrettably kept separate from evidently "factual" matters. Figure 8.10 presents an argument from motivation that is challenged by another argument from motivation and an argument from classification. In this example, **Q1** ("it is likely") becomes **Q2** ("probably not") after the rebuttal.

Argumentation from Intuition

In reasoning from intuition, policy claims are based on premises or assumptions about the insight of participants in the policy-making process. Policy-relevant information consists of factual reports or expressions opinion. The function of the warrant is to affirm that inner mental states (insight, judgment, understanding) of producers of information make them specially qualified to offer opinions or advice. The policy claim may simply reiterate the report or opinion supplied in the information. Consider this example of early military policy:

> When in 1334 the Duchess of Tyrol, Margareta Maultasch, encircled the castle of Hochosterwitz in the province of Carinthia, she knew only too well that the fortress, situated on an incredibly steep rock rising high above the valley floor,

was impregnable to direct attack and would yield only to a long siege. In due course, the situation of the defenders became critical: they were down to their last ox and had only two bags of barley corn left. Margareta's situation was becoming equally pressing, albeit for different reasons: her troops were beginning to be unruly, there seemed to be no end to the siege in sight, and she had similarly urgent military business elsewhere. At this point the commandant of the castle decided on a desperate course of action, which to his men must have seemed sheer folly; he had the last ox slaughtered, had its abdominal cavity filled with the remaining barley, and ordered the carcass thrown down the steep cliff onto a meadow in front of the enemy camp. Upon receiving this scornful message from above, the discouraged duchess abandoned the siege and moved on.[40]

Figure 8.11 serves to emphasize some of the unique advantages of insight, judgment, and tacit knowledge in developing creative solutions to policy problems. However, it also points to difficulties. Although policy scholars urge that

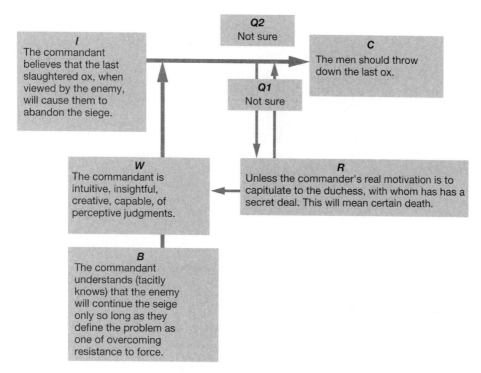

Figure 8.11 Intuitive argumentation—perceptive military leadership is unsuccessfully challenged by reasoning from motivation.

---

[40] Quoted in Paul Watzlawick, John Weakland, and Richard Fisch, *Change: Principles of Problem Formation and Problem Resolution* (New York: W. W. Norton & Company, 1974), p. xi.

intuition, judgment, and tacit knowledge be incorporated into policy analysis,[41] it is seldom possible to identify in advance the methods or forms of reasoning that are likely to yield insight or creativity. A creative act, observes Churchman, "is an act that cannot be designed beforehand, although it may be analyzable in retrospect. If this is the correct meaning of creativity, then no intelligent technician can be creative."[42]

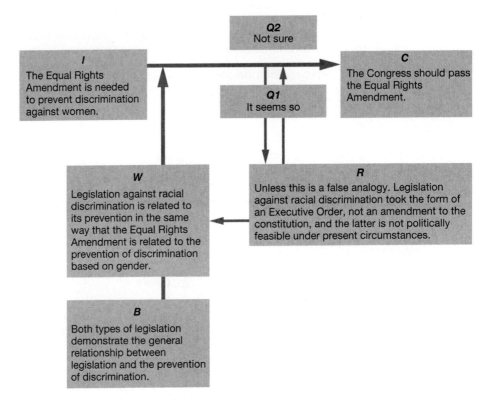

Figure 8.12 Argumentation from analogy—a false analogy diminishes the plausibility of the initial claim about the equal rights amendment.

---

[41] For example, Yehezkel Dror, *Ventures in Policy Sciences* (New York: American Elsevier Publishing, 1971), p. 52; Sir Geoffrey Vickers, *The Art of Judgment: A Study of Policy Making* (New York: Basic Books, 1965); and Edgar S. Quade, *Analysis for Public Decisions* (New York: American Elsevier, 1975), pp. 4–5. Some observers have also commented favorably on the possibility of drug-induced changes in the mental states of policy makers. See Kenneth B. Clark, "The Pathos of Power: A Psychological Perspective," *American Psychologist* 26, no. 12 (1971): 1047–57.

[42] Churchman, *Design of Inquiring Systems,* p. 17.

Argumentation from Analogy

Reasoning from analogies and metaphors is based on similarities between (Figure 8.12) relationships found in a given case and relationships found in a metaphor, analogy, or allegory. For example, the claim that government should "quarantine" a country by interdicting illegal drugs—with the illegal drugs presented as an "infectious disease"— is based on reasoning that, because quarantine has been effective in cases of infectious diseases, interdiction will be effective in the case of illegal drugs. In arguments from analogy, claims are based on assumptions that relationships among two or more cases (not cases themselves) are essentially similar. For example, claims about the desirability of adopting policies to mitigate air pollution have been based on beliefs about the success of water pollution policies. In making claims about ways to reduce employment discrimination against women, the reasoning is sometimes based on assumptions about the success or failure of policies designed to reduce discrimination against ethnic minorities.[43]

Argumentation from Parallel Case

Reasoning from parallel case focuses on similarities among two or more (Figure 8.13) cases of policy making. For example, a reason that a local government should strictly enforce pollution standards is that a parallel policy was successfully implemented in a similar local government elsewhere. Policy claims are based on assumptions that the results of policies adopted in similar circumstances are worthwhile or success-ful. Government agencies in the United States and abroad often face similar prob-lems, and policy claims may be based on their common experiences. The British experiences with comprehensive medical care and city planning ("new towns"), and the Dutch and Swiss approaches to the decriminalization of illegal drugs, have influenced debates about drug policy in the United States. The experience of some states in adopting taxation, open housing, and equal employment opportunity poli-cies has been used as a basis for policy at the federal level.[44] A variation of argu-mentation from parallel case is an argument based on the experience of the same agency over time. Past policies in the same agency are used as a basis for claims that the agency should adopt particular courses of action, usually those that are marginally different from the status quo. Claims about federal and state budgetary policies typically derive from assumptions about similarities with past policies adopted in the same agency.[45]

---

[43] Robert L. Lineberry, *American Public Policy: What Government Does and What Difference It Makes* (New York: Harper and Row, 1977), p. 28.

[44] Ibid.

[45] See, for example, Aaron Wildavsky's now classic treatment of incremental policy making in *The Politics of the Budgetary Process* (Boston: Little, Brown and Company, 1964). See also the discussion of models of policy change in Chapter 2.

Argumentation from Ethics

Reasoning from ethics is based on the rightness or wrongness, goodness (Figure 8.14) or badness, of policies or their consequences. For example, policy claims are frequently based on moral principles stating the conditions of a "just" or "good" society, or on ethical norms prohibiting lying in public life. Moral principles and ethical norms go beyond the values and norms of particular individuals or groups. In public policy, many arguments about economic benefits and costs involve unstated or implicit moral and ethical reasoning. The warrant in an argument from ethics provides reasons for accepting a claim by associating it with some moral principle or ethical rule. The claim is that the person, situation, or condition referred to in the information should be regarded as valuable or worthless, or that a policy described in the information should or should not be adopted.

To illustrate ethical argumentation, consider Figure 8.13. Here, the evaluative claim **C** is that "the existing distribution of income in the United States is unjust." The information **I** supplied is that "in 1975, the top 20 percent of American families

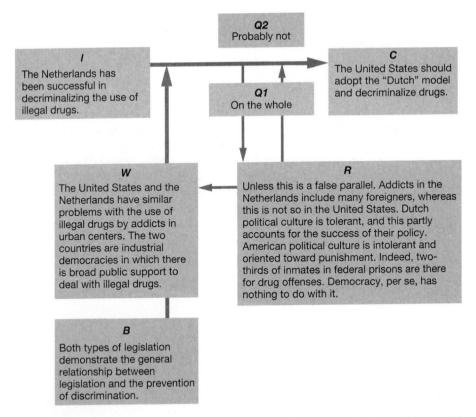

Figure 8.13 Argumentation from parallel case—challenges often come in the form of false parallels.

received 41 percent of all income, while the bottom 20 percent received 5.4 percent. In 1989, the top 20 percent received 46.7 percent, while the bottom 20 percent received 3.8 percent. By 2000, the gap between rich and poor had widened even further. In the period 1969–2000, the real income of everyone increased by about 3 percent." The warrant **W** is the *Pareto rule,* named after the Italian economist and sociologist Wilfredo Pareto (1848–1923).

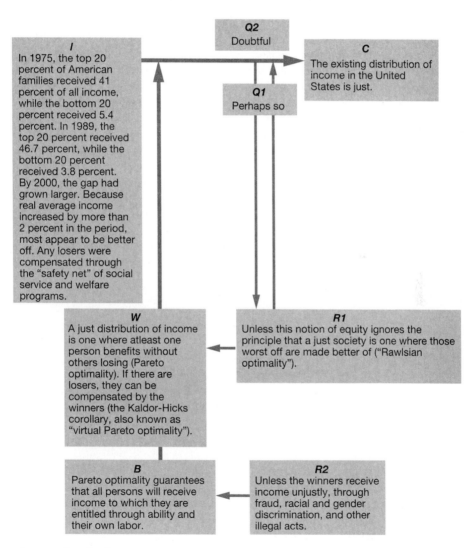

Figure 8.14 Ethical argumentation—exceptions and special conditions weaken the credibility of the Pareto rule as a criterion of justice.

The Pareto rule is a simple ethical rule that enjoys broad consensus among policy economists.[46] The rule states that "[a]n optimum distribution of income in society is one where some individuals benefit without others losing." The backing **B** for the warrant is "Pareto optimality guarantees that all persons retain income to which they are justly entitled by ability and work." The rebuttal **R** is "Pareto optimality does not reflect unjust entitlements to income based on fraud, racial discrimination, and other illegal behaviors" (Figure 8.13).

Figure 8.13 shows how ethical argumentation may be conducted in policy analysis. The example of Pareto optimality shows that a widely accepted ethical rule, while it supports claims about a just society, does not apply to situations involving fraud, discrimination, and other illegal behaviors (we could add inheritance, insofar as it is not based on ability and work). The systematic analysis of underlying ethical and moral reasoning compels parties in a debate to clarify the meaning of key concepts, such as "entitlement," which are more complex than may be apparent at first glance. Parties making a claim also may be compelled to consider whether a particular ethical rule, such as Pareto optimality, violates their own moral convictions. Proponents of the Pareto Rule may see that its application violates moral convictions about the necessity of basing principles of entitlement on ability and work. If this is done for welfare recipients, why not for heirs? In short, the process of ethical argumentation can help develop ethical rules that are general in their applicability to various situations and internally consistent.[47] Ethical argumentation, it should be emphasized, differs from each of the other modes of reasoning in one essential respect: Whereas each of the other modes takes values as a "given"—for example, by describing values by means of opinion surveys—the process of ethical argumentation attempts to discover whether there are *good reasons* to hold various ethical positions.

EVALUATING POLICY ARGUMENTS

The evaluation of policy arguments is a central aspect of thinking critically about public policy. So far, we have looked at the structure of arguments, the process of argumentation, and some of the many types of reasoning employed to make policy claims. This enables us to identify hidden or tacit assumptions and investigate the extent to which the plausibility of a claim **C,** as represented by its qualifier **Q,** changes as a result of rebuttals **R** introduced in the course of policy argumentation.

We now turn to guidelines for evaluating parts of arguments and arguments as a whole. Some of these guidelines come from formal logic, a discipline that offers criteria for determining—without qualification and with deductive certainty—the

---

[46] See Peter G. Brown, "Ethics and Policy Research," *Policy Analysis* 2 (1976): 332–35.

[47] MacRae, *Social Function of Social Science,* pp. 92–94.

formal validity of arguments.[48] However, most guidelines originate in an evolving body of standards for assessing the approximate *informal* validity of arguments.[49] Other guidelines come from procedures employed by qualitative methodologists who work in the hermeneutics tradition. This tradition has long been concerned with discovering and accurately representing the meaning of human action, whether expressed in the form of a written text or as the action represented by a written text.[50] Still other guidelines originate in philosophical pragmatism, a philosophy of science and methodology that is useful for evaluating the plausibility of entire systems of arguments.[51]

Some Hermeneutic Guidelines

Hermeneutics investigates the meanings of human texts. It is perhaps the most comprehensive and systematic of the qualitative methods. The term "qualitative," contrary to a common misunderstanding that pervades the social sciences,[52] is not the simple negative of "quantitative" (in the sense that qualitative refers to that which is not quantitative). Rather, qualitative methods investigate the meanings of actions at the personal and collective levels; quantitative methods are neither designed nor suited to perform this task.

Human texts refer not only to written documents that are products of human action, for example, legislative transcripts and laws that originated as policy debates, they also refer to the actions themselves, whether or not they have been represented in a written form. Among various ways to demonstrate the importance of hermeneutic guidelines to the evaluation of policy arguments, a focus on ethical argumentation is most revealing. Consider alternative ethical arguments about a prisoner captured by soldiers from the opposing army:

- *Argument A.* The prisoner is not a member of a regular fighting force. He is a common criminal, a terrorist who lies when interrogated about terrorist plots and other military secrets. Because he does not qualify as a "prisoner of war," he should not be protected against what our opponents call "inhumane treatment."

- *Argument B.* The prisoner is a freedom fighter who is standing up against the terror and oppression inflicted by the enemy. He is a loyal soldier who has a moral duty to mislead interrogators about military secrets. He should be protected as a prisoner of war.

---

[48] Classic sources on formal logic include Irving M. Copi, *An Introduction to Logic* (New York: Macmillan, 1953).

[49] See Toulmin, Rieke, and Janik, *An Introduction to Reasoning,* Part V: *Fallacies: How Arguments Go Wrong,* pp. 129–97.

[50] The classic hermeneutics source, published originally in 1960, is Hans Georg Gadamer, *Truth and Method* (New York: Seabury, 1975).

[51] See Nicholas Rescher, *Induction* (Pittsburgh, PA: University of Pittsburgh Press, 1980).

[52] See, for example, a widely used text by Gary King, Robert Keohane, and Sidney Verba, *Designing Social Inquiry* (Princeton, NJ: Princeton University Press, 1994).

- *Argument C.* The prisoner is a member of a fighting force that perceives itself as a standing army. Presumably, he is a prisoner of war whose loyalty seems to demand that he mislead interrogators about military secrets. As such, it is perhaps reasonable that he receive the protections against inhumane treatment afforded any prisoner of war.

The evaluation of these arguments can benefit from guidelines for the interpretation of written or oral argumentation (Procedural Guide 8.3).

The main function of arguments A and B is rhetorical, not dialectical or logical-empirical. Although the use of A and B as rebuttals to one another would contribute to the dialectical function, this is not the purpose of A or B alone. A and B do present evidently factual statements, some of which appear to be empirically sound and even uncontroversial. A prisoner was captured, he was involved as a combatant, and he was not telling the truth. What is disputed are two main issues: Is it is morally and legally right to lie under the circumstances? Does the soldier qualify as a prisoner of war?

Other guidelines also apply. The quotation marks around some of the words ("prisoner of war" and "inhumane treatment") conceal or obscure meanings. The contexts of A and B are also important for understanding the arguments. Given the history of many conflicts, it is not surprising that both sides regard opponents as terrorists. The principle of hermeneutic charity encourages giving the benefit of the doubt to each party, for example, by trying to understand that both seek to be treated equally. The one side contests the moral and legal acceptability of attacks on their troops (and on civilians) by out-of-uniform combatants, arguing that such practices are unfair. The other side affirms the moral and legal acceptability of such acts, on grounds that such acts are fair under conditions where one side has a preponderance of modern weaponry ("asymmetric warfare"). Finally, both arguments make liberal use of pejoratives—"extremist," "criminal," "terrorist," "propagandists," "freedom fighter," "oppression"—that obscure rather than clarify moral and legal issues.

If we were to rephrase the arguments, introducing rebuttals and replacing absolute with qualified claims, it would look something like argument C. Argument C has the advantage of isolating the contested issue, which is one of *conflicting obligation*: In the ethics of war, there has been a widespread understanding that prisoners who mislead interrogators about military secrets are displaying courage, honor, patriotism, and other virtues. Here, the same understanding would presumably apply to both sides.

Guidelines from Informal and Formal Logic

Hermeneutic guidelines are designed to enhance the understanding of meanings that underlie arguments and argumentation. Questions concerning the soundness, credibility, or plausibility of arguments do not arise, because the principal aim is to achieve an accurate interpretation of what arguers mean. By contrast, the fields of informal and formal logic provide guidelines for recognizing and assessing the significance of informal fallacies.[53] Here as elsewhere the term "guideline" is used in place of "rule," because there is no way to determine absolutely whether an argument is fallacious. Hence, the analysis of informal fallacies does not permit all or none conclusions.

As we saw in the first part of this chapter, there are numerous modes of argumentation that are generally recognized as appropriate to policy discourse. Arguments of the following kinds are *formally* valid:

- *Hypothetical syllogism.* If *p* implies *q,* and *q* implies *r,* then *p* implies *r. Or: p ⊃ q, q ⊃; r, ∴ p ⊃ r* (⊃ = implies). Example: A transitive preference ordering is one form of the hypothetical syllogism. Given three projects, *A, B,* and *C,* if A *p* B, and B *p* C, then A *p* C (*p* = preferred to). This formally valid argument can be empirically unsound.

- *Modus ponens. Modus ponens* (method of affirming) asserts that if *p* implies *q,* and *p* occurs, then *q* will occur. If *p ⊃ q,* and *p,* then *q.* Example: If investment *I* in a project produces outcome *O,* and investment *I* is made, then outcome O will be the result. Although this argument is formally valid, the conclusion assumes that no causally relevant factor other than *I* is present, a situation that almost never exists. This formally valid argument can be empirically unsound.

- *Modus tollens. Modus tollens* (method of denying) asserts that if *p* implies *q,* and *q* does not occur, then *p* will not occur. If *p ⊃ q,* and *q* does not occur (~ *q*), then *p* will not occur (~ *p*). Example: If investment *I* in a program produces outcome O, and O does not occur, then *I* is not a cause. This formally valid argument can be empirically unsound.

We now turn to modes of argumentation that are generally recognized as formally invalid, inappropriate, or unsound—however persuasive they may appear on first glance. These modes of argumentation are called fallacies. A fallacy is an argument that is weakened or seriously flawed because it uses irrelevant or inadequate information, erroneous or unsound reasoning, or inappropriate and misleading language. Table 8.2 provides a listing of fallacies and guidelines that are helpful in recognizing them.

Systems of Argumentation

Another aspect of evaluating arguments is the examination of an argument as an entire system of reasoning. Among criteria that may be employed for this purpose are the following.[54]

---

[53] The terms "informal logic" and "informal fallacy" are used in the discipline of logic, where "formal logic" and "formal fallacy" are also distinguished.

[54] See Rescher, *Induction,* pp. 31–47. I have substituted the term criteria of plausibility assessment for what Rescher calls criteria of cognitive systematization.

Table 8.2   Guidelines for Identifying Invalid Arguments and Fallacies[1]

Fallacy	Guideline
Affirming the Consequent	A matter of formal (propositional) logic. A logically invalid argument is: If p then q, and q, then p (p ⊃ q, q, therefore p). An argument can be formally invalid, but practically useful. Example: "The paradigm of 'proof through prediction,'" says Merton, "is, of course, logically fallacious: If **A** (hypothesis), then **B** (prediction). **B** is observed. Therefore, **A** is true."[2] If the Senator calls for change in basic institutions, and socialists call for change in basic institutions, then the senator is a socialists. In scientific research, this form of argument, although formally invalid, can be useful because a hypothesis may be improved by testing conditions other than **B** that form rival hypotheses.
Denying the Antecedent	Again, a matter of formal logical validity. If p then q, and not-p, then not-q (p ⊃ q, ~ p, therefore ~ q) is fallacious. Example: Because market economies are democracies, and country **X** is not a market economy, it is not a democracy.
False Analogy	The comparison of two relationships believed to be similar disregards important differences that make the comparison relatively unsound. Example: Because drug addiction is like an infectious disease, quarantining addicts is the only policy that will work.
False Parallel	The comparison of two cases believed to be similar disregards important differences that make the comparison unsound. The acquiescence of the United States in World War II led to genocide and ethnic cleansing. The United States cannot acquiesce in ethnic cleansing in the Balkans.
Hasty Generalization	In making a generalization from particular instances of a case, a failure to recognize that there are too few instances of the case, or that the instances are exceptional rather than typical. In conducting opinion surveys, an inadequate sample size will yield too few instances, while a failure to use random sampling—where every element or instance has an equal chance of being selected—is likely to yield exceptional conclusions rather than those typical of the population. Example: "Focus group" interviews with fifteen typical voters conducted before the election show that there is greater support for candidate **A** than candidate **B**.
False Cause	In making a claim about cause and effect, arguing that a single cause is responsible for an effect, but without examining other plausible causes. False causes also stem from confusing statistical correlation or covariance with causality and inferring cause from temporal sequence alone (post hoc fallacy). Examples: Excessive government spending is responsible for the slow growth of GDP (single false cause). That economic conditions affect social well-being is evident from the statistically significant positive correlation ($r = 0.74$, $p = 0.05$) between suicide and unemployment (false cause based on correlation). After the Reagan (or Clinton) administration took office, we had the highest unemployment (or government spending) in twenty years (post hoc fallacy).
Fallacy of Composition	Concluding that something is true of the whole because it is true of its parts. The fallacy of composition (also called the aggregative or holistic fallacy) involves all parts, not just a sample, so it differs from the fallacy of hasty generalization (see above). Example: Vehicle safety studies of the severity of damage suffered by test robots riding at different speeds in automobiles show that speed and severity of damage are strongly and positively correlated. This is striking evidence that "speed kills!" But studies of fatal accidents show that approximately 20 percent of fatal accidents are related to speeding.
Fallacy of Division	Concluding that something is true of the parts because it is true of the whole (also called the individualistic fallacy). Example: Because the per capita income of a country has increased, everyone is better off. In many countries, however, this is false. Persons who are better off become even better off, while those worse off become even worse off. Another example is using the arithmetic mean and other averages to describe a group, without examining differences among the group's members (e.g., outliers in a scatter plot).

Table 8.2   Guidelines for Identifying Invalid Arguments and Fallacies[1] (*continued*)

Fallacy	Guideline
Fallacy of the Slippery Slope	Concluding on the basis of insufficient or inadequate evidence that if one event occurs, then others will follow in an inevitable or uncontrollable sequence. Example: If the legislature passes a new law requiring stricter registration of handguns, it will lead to government confiscation of all guns.
Begging the Question	A claim is assumed as a reason or evidence. Example: "With a force of 500,000 troops we will be able to invade Iraq and topple President Saddam Hussein. It will take this many troops to do the job."
Ad Hominem	An individual's personal characteristics are used as part of an argument, when such characteristics are irrelevant to an issue. Examples: "An eminent natural scientist concludes that welfare reform is unsound." "The argument of the environmentalists is deeply flawed. After all, these 'tree huggers' are just socialists in disguise." "Theories of economic development are products of Western thinking. Obviously, they are inapplicable to the non-Western world." Note that when personal characteristics are relevant, no ad hominem fallacy is involved. For example, "expert witnesses" in court cases should have appropriate expertise.
Ad Populum	The characteristics or beliefs of a group or community are used as part of an argument, when the characteristics or beliefs are irrelevant to the issue. "The majority of the community believes that fluoride causes cancer."
Appeal to Tradition	A claim is based on conformity to tradition, when tradition is largely or entirely irrelevant to the issue. Examples: "We have always done it this way." "The founding fathers would be appalled by the Senator's proposal." "The successful disciplines have succeeded because they have emulated physics. This should be the model the social sciences, if they want to succeed."
Accent	A misplaced emphasis on a word, phrase, or portion of an argument results in misunderstanding or misinterpretation. The use of italics, boldface print, variable fonts, photos, clip-art, and colors can accentuate the importance of relatively sound or plausible, as well as relatively unsound or implausible arguments, or parts of arguments. A leading example of the fallacy of accent is quoting or extracting information, reasons, or arguments out of context.

Notes:

[1]The first two are formally invalid argument (argument forms).

[2]Robert K. Merton *Social Theory and Social Structure,* rev.ed. (Glencoe, IL: Free Press, 1957), p. 99n. The same point is made by Donald T. Campbell, *Epistemology and Methodology for Social Science: Selected Eassys* (Chicago: University of Chicago Press, 1988), p. 168.

- *Completeness.* Elements of an argument should comprise a genuine whole that encompasses all appropriate considerations. For example, the plausibility of arguments about the effects of a policy depends on whether such arguments encompass a full range of plausible rival explanations similar in form and content to the classes of rival hypotheses (threats to validity) developed in the tradition of quasi-experimentation.[55]

---

[55] On threats to validity, see Donald T. Campbell and Julian C. Stanley, *Experimental and Quasi-experimental Designs for Research* (Chicago: Rand McNally, 1966); and Shadish, Cook, and Campbell, *Experimental and Quasi-Experimental Designs.* On a fifth class of validity threats (context validity), see William N. Dunn, "Pragmatic Eliminative Induction," *Philosophica* 60 (1997, 2): 75–112. Special issue dedicated to Donald T. Campbell.

Procedural Guide 8.3 Guidelines for Interpreting Arguments

- Policy argumentation has three major functions: to generate debate that improves the validity, soundness, and efficacy of policies (dialectical function); to present optimally valid and empirically sound conclusions (logical-empirical function); to persuade others to accept policy arguments (rhetorical function), apart from the validity, soundness, or usefulness of the arguments.

- Look for concealed meanings in words, sentences, and entire arguments. A word or sentence may not mean what it says on the surface. Example: "He is a good Liberal" does not mean that the person described performs well as a Liberal; it rather means that the person's identity as a Liberal is associated with some kind of weakness or limitation.

- Distinguish between the surface meaning of a word, sentence, or argument and its meaning in the context of the arguer. Try to identify any differences in your understanding from that of the arguer. Example: "The mayor should not have publicly acquiesced in the demonstrators' demands." Several potential misinterpretations are possible: someone except the mayor should have acquiesced; the mayor should not have acquiesced in public; the mayor should not have acquiesced at all.

- Observe the principle of hermeneutic charity, which requires that discrepancies in meaning be resolved by accepting, or trying to understand, what the arguer is trying to say. Example: Critics of arguments presented in quantitative language often label such arguments (and the arguers) as "logical positivists," notwithstanding the fact that quantification, per se, has nothing to do with logical positivism. A charitable effort to understand what the arguer actually believes can solve this problem.

- Look for terms that are used pejoratively to discredit a person or policy. On the surface, these terms can be neutral; but in context, they are often used pejoratively. Examples: "This is just another example of a new bureaucracy." "These are the arguments of typical 'tree-huggers.'" "The report, written by a bunch of logical-positivists, is unacceptable."

- *Consonance.* Elements of an argument should be internally consistent and compatible. For example, ethical arguments concerning the justice or fairness of a policy are plausible to the degree that they incorporate a system of internally and externally consistent ethical hypotheses.[56]

- *Cohesiveness.* lements of an argument should be operationally connected. For example, the plausibility of an ethical argument depends on whether responses to several levels of descriptive and valuative questions—levels ranging from verification and validation to vindication—are operationally linked.[57]

---

[56] Duncan MacRae Jr., *The Social Function of Social Science* (New Haven, CT: Yale University Press, 1976), pp. 92–93.

[57] Fischer, *Politics, Values, and Public Policy,* Table 10, pp. 207–8.

- *Functional regularity.* Elements of an argument should conform to an expected pattern. For example, statistical arguments that offer estimates of parameters of unobserved (and often unobservable) populations are plausible to the degree that patterns in the sample and the population from which it is drawn are functionally regular or uniform, not irregular, based on sample data and background knowledge.[58]

Criteria of plausibility assessment may be applied to modes of argument based on premises that are authoritative, intuitive, analogical, and ethical, as well as those that are causal, statistical, and classificational. The system of criteria is thus applicable to modes of argument typically employed by policy makers, policy analysts, and ordinary citizens. Finally, it should be noted that any claim about the plausibility of policy arguments based on these criteria is itself subject to argumentation and debate. Any *ex ante* claim about the success of arguments based on these criteria is itself plausible rather than certain.

CHAPTER SUMMARY

This chapter has provided an understanding of the structure and process of policy argumentation, focusing on contrasts among types of claims, the identification and arrangement of elements of policy arguments, and the effects of rebuttals on the dynamics of argumentation. The chapter proceeds to contrast different modes of policy reasoning and offer guidelines for the identification and assessment of common fallacies that weaken or seriously flaw policy arguments. Formal as well as informal fallacies are arguments that can appear to be plausible, although they involve unreliable or irrelevant information and unsound or unwarranted assumptions. Policy argumentation is central to policy analysis and the policy-making process.

LEARNING OBJECTIVES

- compare and contrast three types of policy claims
- identify and describe functions of the six elements of a policy argument
- explain how rebuttals affect the process of argumentation by changing the strength of qualifiers and (usually) diminishing the plausibility of policy claims
- distinguish modes of policy reasoning based on different kinds of warrants and backings
- evaluate the plausibility of elements of arguments and arguments as a whole
- apply guidelines for identifying formal and informal fallacies
- analyze and evaluate a complex policy argument

---

[58] Rescher, *Induction,* p. 41.

KEY TERMS AND CONCEPTS

advocative claim (383)
backing (378)
causality (402)
designative claim (383)
deductive-nomological (D-N)
   explanation (398)
evaluative claim (383)
formal fallacy (414)
hermeneutic guidelines (411)

hypothetico-deductive (H-D)
   explanation (399)
informal fallacy (414)
Mill's methods (402)
mode of argument (reasoning) (385)
practical syllogism (argument) (403)
qualifier (379)
rebuttal (383)
warrant (383)

REVIEW QUESTIONS

1. Use three (3) of the following problem situations to construct designative, evaluative, and advocative claims. There should be nine (9) claims in all.

crime	fiscal crisis
pollution	human rights
terrorism	ethnic cleansing
quality of life	unemployment
global warming	poverty

2. Take two (2) of the above problem situations and develop a policy argument.
   Provide *Q, C, W, B,* and *I.*

3. Construct a policy debate (or discourse) by providing rebuttals *R* for the above
   argument.

4. Describe how and why the qualifier *Q* changed (if it did) because of introducing
   the rebuttal *R*. If *Q* did not change, why?

5. What is a fallacy? Does the commission of a fallacy invalidate an argument?
   Explain and give examples.

DEMONSTRATION EXERCISES

1. Read a copy of a newspaper and find as many modes of reasoning (argument) as
   you can on the front page. List and describe them. In the same newspaper, read
   the letters to the editor. Find examples of fallacies discussed in the chapter. You
   should have twelve (12) fallacies in all. Be prepared to present the fallacies in
   class. A variation of the above is to break out into groups and complete the
   assignment.

2. Read Case 8, which is an editorial from the *Los Angeles Times* (January 24, 1993,
   p. A7). The article was obtained from the Internet.
   a. Take this statement as the *I* in a policy argument about Bosnia: "The agonizing
      conflict in Bosnia has been going on for several years." The *C* is "The Bosnia
      conflict is somebody else's trouble. The United States should not intervene mili-
      tarily." Display *I* and *C* with a drawing program such as Microsoft Word.

b. Each of the five bulleted paragraphs contains a **W** that answers the question: Why does this claim follow from the information given? The warrant (reason) supports, certifies, or justifies the movement from the data to the claim. In turn, there is a **B** that justifies or supports the **W.** Put the **W**s and **B**s in your drawing.

c. Each of the five bulleted paragraphs also contains one or more **R**s to the **I, W,** or **B.** (*Note:* The rebuttals follow the word "wrong"). When the rebuttal is more plausible than the **I, W,** or **B,** the **Q** changes the plausibility of the claim. Put the **R**s and the **Q**s in the drawing. Show how Q_1 changes (if it does) by entering Q_2.

d. Assess the overall plausibility of the claim **C** that "[t]he conflict in Bosnia is somebody else's trouble. The United States should not intervene militarily."

e. Hand in a printed copy of your diagram. Attach an explanation of your analysis.

REFERENCES

Alker, H. R. Jr. "The Dialectical Logic of Thucydides' Melian Dialogue." *American Political Science Review* 82, no. 3 (1988): 805–20.

Anderson, C. W. "Political Philosophy, Practical Reason, and Policy Analysis." In *Confronting Values in Policy Analysis.* Edited by F. Fischer and J. Forester. Newbury Park, CA: Sage Publications, 1987.

Apthorpe, R., and D. Gasper, eds. *Arguing Development Policy: Frames and Discourses.* London: Frank Cass, 1996.

Dunn, W. N. "Policy Reforms as Arguments." In *The Argumentative Turn in Policy Analysis and Planning.* Edited by F. Fischer and J. Forester. Durham, NC: Duke University Press, 1993.

Fischer, D. H. *Historians' Fallacies: Toward a Logic of Historical Thought.* New York: Random House, 1970.

Fischer, F. *Evaluating Public Policy.* Chicago: Nelson Hall, 1995.

Fischer, F., and J. Forester, eds. *The Argumentative Turn in Policy Analysis and Planning.* Durham, NC: Duke University Press, 1993.

Gasper, D., and R. V. George. "Analyzing Argumentation in Planning and Public Policy: Improving and Transcending the Toulmin-Dunn Model." *Environment and Planning B: Planning and Design* 25 (1998): 367–90.

Majone, G. *Evidence, Argument, and Persuasion in the Policy Process.* New Haven, CT: Yale University Press, 1989.

McCloskey, D. N. *The Rhetoric of Economics.* Madison: University of Wisconsin Press, 1988.

Mitroff, I. I., R. O. Mason, and V. Barabba. *The 1980 Census: Policy Making Amid Turbulence.* Lexington, MA: D. C. Heath, 1985.

Roe, E. *Narrative Policy Analysis.* Durham, NC: Duke University Press, 1994.

Scriven, M. *Reasoning.* New York: McGraw-Hill, 1976.

Stone, D. *Policy Paradox: The Art of Political Decision Making.* Rev ed. New York: W. W. Norton, 2002.

Toulmin, S., R. Rieke, and A. Janik. *An Introduction to Reasoning.* 2d ed. New York: Macmillan, 1984.

Case 8: Pros and Cons of Intervention in the Balkans[59]

Must the agony of Bosnia-Herzegovina be regarded, with whatever regrets, as somebody else's trouble? We don't think so, but the arguments on behalf of that view deserve an answer. Among them are the following:

- The Balkan conflict is a civil war and unlikely to spread beyond the borders of the former Yugoslavia. Wrong. Belgrade has missiles trained on Vienna. Tito's Yugoslavia claimed, by way of Macedonia, that northern Greece as far south as Thessaloniki belonged under its sovereignty. Those claims may return. "Civil" war pitting non-Slavic Albanians against Serbs could spread to Albania, Turkey, Bulgaria, and Greece.

- The United States has no strategic interest in the Balkans. Wrong. No peace, no peace dividend. Unless the West can impose the view that ethnic purity can no longer be the basis for national sovereignty, then endless national wars will replace the Cold War. This threat has appeared in genocidal form in Bosnia. If it cannot be contained here, it will erupt elsewhere, and the Clinton administration's domestic agenda will be an early casualty.

- If the West intervenes on behalf of the Bosnians, the Russians will do so on behalf of the Serbs, and the Cold War will be reborn. Wrong. The Russians have more to fear from "ethnic cleansing" than any people on Earth. Nothing would reassure them better than a new, post-Cold War Western policy of massive, early response against the persecution of national minorities, including the Russian minorities found in every post-Soviet republic. The Russian right may favor the Serbs, but Russian self-interest lies elsewhere.

- The Serbs also have their grievances. They do, but their way of responding to these grievances, according to the State Department's annual human rights report, issued this past week, "dwarfs anything seen in Europe since Nazi times." Via the Genocide Convention, armed intervention is legal as well as justified.

- The UN peace plan is the only alternative. Wrong. Incredibly, the plan proposes the reorganization of Bosnia-Herzegovina followed by a cease-fire. A better first step would be a UN declaration that any nation or ethnic group proceeding to statehood on the principle of ethnic purity is an outlaw state and will be treated as such. As now drafted, the UN peace plan, with a map of provinces that not one party to the conflict accepts, is really a plan for continued "ethnic cleansing."

---

[59] From the *Los Angeles Times,* January 24, 1993, p. A7.

9

Communicating Policy Analysis

Policy analysis is the beginning, not the end, of efforts to improve policies. This is why policy analysis was defined in the first part of this book as a process of creating, critically assessing, and communicating policy-relevant information. To be sure, the quality of policy analysis is important. But quality analysis is not necessarily used analysis. There is a large gap between the production of analysis and its use by policy makers (see Box 9.1).

THE PROCESS OF POLICY COMMUNICATION

The communication of policy-relevant knowledge may be viewed as a four-stage process involving policy analysis, materials development, interaction, and knowledge use. As Figure 9.1 shows, policy analysis is initiated on the basis of requests for information or advice from stakeholders situated in the various phases of the policy-making process discussed in Chapter 2. In responding to requests, policy

Box 9.1   Producing Policy Analysis Can Resemble a Poorly Managed Lumber Mill

"The social science researchers have gone into the forest of knowledge, felled a good and sturdy tree, and displayed the fruits of their good work to one another. A few enterprising, application-minded lumberjacks have dragged some logs to the river and shoved them off downstream ('diffusion' they call it). Somewhere down the river the practitioners are manning the construction companies. They manage somehow to piece together a few make-shift buildings with what they can find that has drifted down the stream, but on the whole they are sorely lacking lumber in the various sizes and forms they need to do their work properly. The problem is that someone has forgotten to build the mill to turn the logs into lumber in all its usable forms. The logs continue to pile up at one end of the system while the construction companies continue to make due at the other end. . . . There has been governmental and foundation support for the logging operation. There has also been some support for the construction companies. There has been almost nothing, however, for the planning and running of the mill."

Jack Rothman, *Social R&D: Research and Development in the Human Services* (Englewood Cliffs, NJ: Prentice Hall, 1980), p. 16.

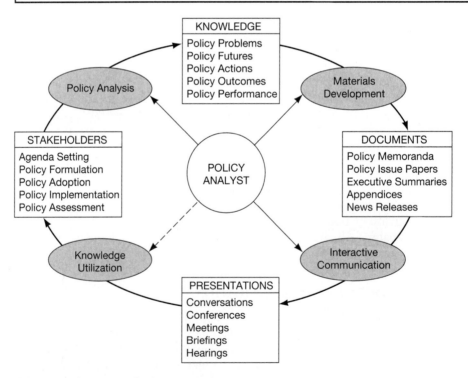

Figure 9.1   The process of policy communication.

analysts create and critically assess information about policy problems, policy futures, policy actions, policy outcomes, and policy performance. To communicate such information, however, analysts develop documents of different kinds: policy memoranda, policy issue papers, executive summaries, appendices containing qualitative and quantitative information, and news releases. In turn, the substance of these documents is communicated through oral presentations of different kinds: conversations, conferences, meetings, briefings, and hearings. The purpose of developing policy-relevant documents and making oral presentations is to enhance prospects for the use of knowledge.

The broken line in Figure 9.1 indicates that analysts influence the process of knowledge use only indirectly. By contrast, the solid lines indicate that policy analysts directly affect the reliability and validity of conclusions and recommendations reached through analysis. Analysts also directly affect the form, content, and appropriateness of policy-relevant documents and oral presentations.

Tasks in Policy Documentation

The knowledge and skills needed to conduct policy analysis are different from those needed to develop policy-relevant documents. The development of policy-relevant documents that convey usable knowledge requires knowledge and skills in synthesizing, organizing, translating, simplifying, displaying, and summarizing information.

Synthesis. Analysts typically work with hundreds of pages of previously published reports, newspaper and journal articles, summaries of interviews with stakeholders and other key informants, copies of existing and model legislation, tables of statistical series, and more. Information must be synthesized into documents ranging in length from one or two pages (policy memoranda) to more than twenty-five pages in length (policy issue papers and reports). Information also must be synthesized when summarizing policy issue papers in the form of executive summaries and news releases.

Organization. Analysts must be able to organize information in a coherent, logically consistent, and economical manner. Although documents vary in style, content, and length, they typically have certain common elements:

- Overview or summary of contents of paper
- Background of previous efforts to solve the problem
- Diagnosis of the scope, severity, and causes of the problem
- Identification and evaluation of alternative solutions
- Recommendations of actions that may solve the problem
- Policy issue papers, as contrasted with policy memos, usually including additional elements with tables and graphs, technical appendices that explain

results of data analysis, existing and proposed legislation, descriptions of formulas and equations, and other supporting material

Translation. The specialized terminology and techniques of policy analysis must be translated into the languages of policy stakeholders. In many cases this requires the conversion of abstract theoretical concepts and complex analytical and statistical routines into the ordinary language and arguments of nonexperts. When the audience includes experts on the problem (e.g., other analysts and staff specialists), a detailed exposition of theoretical concepts and analytical and statistical routines can be incorporated in appendices.

Simplification. Potential solutions to a problem are often complex. The combinations and permutations of policy alternatives and outcomes can easily exceed the hundreds. In such cases, a smaller set of options and outcomes can be displayed in the form of a matrix or "scorecard."[1] Another way to simplify complexity is to use a strategy table as part of a decision tree or to use a decision tree. Both scorecards and decision trees were presented in Chapter 1. The simplification of complex quantitative relationships also can be accomplished by presenting in ordinary language cases that typify quantitative profiles.[2]

Visual displays. The availability of advanced, user-friendly computer graphics has dramatically increased capabilities of effective visual communication. The visual display of quantitative information—bar charts, histograms, pie charts, line graphs, maps generated from geographic information systems (GIS)—is essential for effective policy communication.[3]

Summaries. Policy makers with crowded agendas operate under severe time constraints that limit their reading to no more than a few minutes a day. Members of the United States Congress spend approximately fifteen minutes per day reading, and most of this time is spent on local and national newspapers.[4] The same is true for higher-level policy makers in agencies such as the U.S. Department of State. Under these circumstances, staff analysts perform an essential role in briefing policy makers, who are far more likely to read an executive summary or condensed memorandum

---

[1] The scorecard or matrix displays developed by Bruce F. Goeller of the Rand Corporation are useful as means for simplifying a large set of interdependent alternatives. For an overview of the Goeller scorecard or matrix, see Bruce F. Goeller, "A Framework for Evaluating Success in Systems Analysis" (Santa Monica, CA: Rand Corporation, 1988).

[2] A good example is Ronald D. Brunner, "Case-Wise Policy Information Systems: Redefining Poverty," *Policy Sciences* 19 (1986): 201–23.

[3] The outstanding source on the methodology of graphic displays is Edward R. Tufte's trilogy, *The Visual Display of Quantitative Information* (Cheshire, CT: Graphics Press, 1983); *Envisioning Information* (Cheshire, CT: Graphics Press, 1990); and *Visual Explanations* (Cheshire, CT: Graphics Press, 1997).

[4] Personal communications with staff of the U.S. General Accounting Office.

than a full policy issue paper. Skills in preparing summaries are essential for effective policy communication. The most comprehensive and detailed document is the policy issue paper. A policy issue paper addresses questions such as the following:

- In what ways can the policy problem be formulated?
- What is the scope and severity of the problem?
- To what extent does it require public action?
- If no action is taken, how is the problem likely to change in coming months or years?
- Have other units of government addressed the problem, and if so, what were the consequences?
- What goals and objectives should be pursued in solving the problem?
- What major policy alternatives are available to achieve these goals and objectives?
- What criteria should be employed to evaluate the performance of these alternatives?
- What alternative(s) should be adopted and implemented?
- What agency should have the responsibility for policy implementation?
- How will the policy be monitored and evaluated?

Analysts are seldom requested to provide answers to all these questions. Instead, they are asked to address a smaller set of these questions that have arisen in one or several phases of the policy-making process—for example, in the agenda-setting phase, questions about the future costs, benefits, and availability of health care may arise. Policy issue papers, it should be noted, are less frequently requested than short policy memoranda or policy briefs ranging from one to several pages in length. Policy memoranda and briefs draw on and synthesize the substance, conclusions, and recommendations of policy issue papers, research reports, and other source documents. News releases, in turn, usually summarize the conclusions and recommendations of a major policy issue paper or report.

The multiplicity of policy documents draws attention to the fact that there are many ways to develop appropriate written materials on the basis of the same policy analysis. There are also multiple audiences for policy-relevant information. Immediate "clients" are often only one audience, and effective communication may demand that analysts develop different documents for different audiences, thus thinking strategically about opportunities for policy improvement. "Thinking strategically about the composition of the audience is essential for effective communication. The selection of the audience is not something to be left solely to the immediate client. . . . There are many clients to be reached; some may be peripheral, some remote, some in the future, yet all are part of a potential audience."[5] For example, when the preparation of news releases is permitted under standard operating

---

[5] See Arnold Meltsner, "Don't Slight Communication," *Policy Analysis* 2, no. 2 (1978): 221–31.

procedures, the news release is the most appropriate vehicle for reaching the general public through the mass media.[6] A policy issue paper is not. If the aim is to communicate with the immediate client, however, it is the executive summary or policy memorandum that is likely to be most effective.

Tasks in Oral Presentations and Briefings

Just as procedures for conducting analysis are different from procedures for developing policy-relevant documents, so are procedures for developing these documents different from procedures for their communication in the form of oral presentations and briefings. A common medium of communication is the mailed document, an impersonal means of reaching clients and other policy stakeholders by physically transmitting the document. The major limitation of this medium is the probability that a document will reach intended beneficiaries—but then sit on the shelf. The probability of utilization is enhanced when ideas are communicated through policy presentations. Policy presentations, which include conversations, conferences, briefings, meetings, and hearings, constitute an interactive mode of communication that is positively associated with the utilization of policy-relevant knowledge.[7]

Although there is no codified body of rules for making oral presentations, experience has shown that a number of general guidelines are important for effective policy communication. These guidelines offer multiple communications strategies appropriate for the various contingencies found in complex practice settings. Among these contingencies are:

- The size of the group that comprises the audience
- The number of specialists in the problem area addressed
- The familiarity of group members with methods of analysis
- The credibility of the analyst to the group
- The extent to which the presentation is critical to policies under active consideration

---

[6] On the role of the mass media in communicating social science knowledge, see Carol H. Weiss and Eleanor Singer, with the assistance of Phyllis Endreny, *Reporting of Social Science in the National Media* (New York: Russell Sage Foundation, 1987). A much-neglected area, the role of academic and commercial publishing in communicating ideas emanating from the sciences and humanities, is addressed in Irving Louis Horowitz, *Communicating Ideas: The Crisis of Publishing in a Post-Industrial Society* (New York: Oxford University Press, 1986).

[7] The efficacy of the "interactive" model of communicating and using information has been reported in literature for at least thirty years. See Ronald G. Havelock, *Planning for Innovation: Through Dissemination and Utilization of Knowledge* (Ann Arbor, MI: Institute for Social Research, Center for the Utilization of Scientific Knowledge, 1969); Carol H. Weiss, "Introduction," in *Using Social Research in Public Policy Making*, ed. Carol H. Weiss (Lexington, MA: D. C. Heath, 1977), pp. 1–22; Charles E. Lindblom and David Cohen, *Usable Knowledge: Social Science and Social Problem Solving* (New Haven, CT: Yale University Press, 1979); and Michael Huberman, "Steps toward an Integrated Model of Research Utilization," *Knowledge: Creation, Diffusion, Utilization* 8, no. 4 (June 1987): 586–611.

Box 9.2   Contingent Communication

Policy analyses are frequently presented to groups that have few experts in the problem area, minimum familiarity with analytic methods, limited confidence in analysts, and little time for meetings that take up precious time. What communications strategies are likely to be effective under these conditions?*

- Make sure that the presentation addresses the needs of key decision makers and recognizes audience diversity.
- Avoid giving too much background information.
- Focus on conclusions.
- Use simple graphics to display data.
- Discuss methods only if necessary to support conclusions.
- Pinpoint reasons for your lack of credibility, choosing a strategy to overcome the problem—for example, arrange to be introduced by a credible associate or present as part of a team.
- Be sensitive to time constraints and the possibility that the group is already committed to a course of action.
- Position your supporters next to people with anticipated negative reactions.
- Prioritize your points so that you present those that are most critical to the group's preferred decision.

*Adapted from Version 2.0 of *Presentation Planner*, a software package developed by Eastman Technology, Inc.

In such contexts, multiple communications strategies are essential: There is no "universal client" who uses the same standards to evaluate the plausibility, relevance, and usability of policy analysis. Effective policy presentations are contingent on matching communications strategies to characteristics of the audience for policy analysis (Box 9.2).

THE POLICY ISSUE PAPER

A policy issue paper should provide answers to a number of questions.

- What actual or potential courses of action are the objects of conflict or disagreement among stakeholders?
- In what different ways may the problem be defined?
- What is the scope and severity of the problem?
- How is the problem likely to change in future?
- What goals and objectives should be pursued to solve the problem?
- How can the degree of success in achieving objectives be measured?
- What activities are now under way to resolve the problem?

- What new or adapted policy alternatives should be considered as ways to resolve the problem?
- Which alternative(s) are preferable, given the goals and objectives?

In answering these questions, the analyst needs to acquire knowledge and skills in writing policy issue papers. Only recently have such knowledge and skills become integral parts of instructional programs in university departments and professional schools of public policy, public management, and public administration. Policy analysis, although it draws from and builds on social science disciplines, differs from those disciplines because it seeks to improve as well as understand policy-making processes. In this respect, policy analysis has characteristics that make it an "applied" rather than "basic" policy discipline.[8] Analysts need to acquire knowledge and skills provided in basic policy disciplines. But the purpose of policy analysis remains "applied" rather than "basic." Characteristics of basic and applied policy disciplines are displayed in Table 9.1.

Issues Addressed in the Policy Issue Paper

The policy issue paper may address issues in almost any area: health, education, welfare, crime, labor, energy, foreign aid, national security, human rights, and so on. Papers in any one of these issue areas may focus on problems at one or more levels of government. Air pollution, global warming, and terrorism, for example, are international, national, and local in scope. Issue papers may be presented as "staff reports," "briefing papers," "options papers," or so-called "white papers." An illustrative list of issues that may be the focus of a policy issue paper is presented below.

- Which of several contracts should a union bargaining team accept?
- Should the mayor increase expenditures on road maintenance?

Table 9.1 Two Kinds of Policy Disciplines

Characteristic	Basic	Applied
Origin of problems	University colleagues	Governmental clients and citizens
Typical methods	Quantitative modeling	Development of sound arguments
Type of research	Original data collection	Synthesis and evaluation of existing data
Primary aim	Improve theory	Improve practice
Communications media	Article or book	Policy memo or issue paper
Source of incentives	University departments	Government departments and citizen groups

[8] The terms "basic" and "applied" are used for convenience only. It is widely acknowledged that these two orientations toward science overlap in practice. Many of the most important advances in the "basic" social sciences originated in "applied" work on practical problems and conflicts. See, especially, Karl W. Deutsch, Andrei S. Markovits, and John Platt, *Advances in the Social Sciences, 1900–1980: What, Who, Where, How?* (Lanham, MD: University Press of America and Abt Books, 1986).

- Should the city manager install a computerized management information system?
- Which public transportation plan should the mayor submit for federal funding?
- Should a state agency establish a special office to recruit minorities and women for civil service positions?
- Should a citizens' group support environmental protection legislation now before Congress?
- Should the governor veto a tax bill passed by the state legislature?
- Should an agency director support a plan for flexible working hours (flex-time)?
- Should a legislator support a bill restricting the sale of handguns?
- Should the president withhold foreign aid from countries that violate human rights?
- Should the United Nations General Assembly condemn the violation of human rights in a particular country?
- Should the United States withdraw from the International Labor Organization?
- Should taxes on foreign investments of multinational corporations registered in the United States be increased?

Elements of the Policy Issue Paper

A policy issue paper should "explore the problem at a depth sufficient to give the reader a good idea of its dimensions and the possible scope of the solution, so that it might be possible for a decision maker to conclude either to do nothing further or to commission a definitive study looking toward some action recommendation."[9] In this author's experience, most issue papers deal primarily with the formulation of a problem and possible solutions. Rarely does the issue paper reach definitive conclusions or recommendations. While an issue paper may contain recommendations and outline plans for monitoring and evaluating policy outcomes, it is essentially the first phase of an in-depth policy analysis that may be undertaken at a later time.

In preparing an issue paper, the analyst should be reasonably sure that all major questions have been addressed. Although issue papers vary with the nature of the problem being investigated, most issue papers contain a number of standard elements.[10] These elements have been organized around the framework for policy analysis presented in the text.

---

[9] E. S. Quade, *Analysis for Public Decisions* (New York: American Elsevier Publishing, 1975), p. 69.

[10] Compare Eugene Bardach, *The Eight-Step Path to Policy Analysis: A Handbook for Practice* (Berkeley: University of California Press, 1996); Quade, *Analysis for Public Decisions*, pp. 68–82; and Harry Hatry and others, *Program Analysis for State and Local Governments* (Washington, DC: Urban Institute, 1976), appendix B, pp. 139–43.

Observe that each element of the issue paper requires different policy-analytic methods to produce and transform information. A policy issue paper, however, is essentially a prospective (*ex ante*) investigation. It is based on limited information about past actions, outcomes, and performance, and in this respect differs from program evaluations and other retrospective (*ex post*) studies. Appendix 1 provides checklist for preparing a policy issue paper.

The Policy Memorandum

It is widely but mistakenly believed that policy analysts spend most of their time developing policy issue papers, studies, and reports. In fact, the primary activity of most analysts is the preparation of policy memoranda. Whereas the issue paper is a long-term activity involving the conduct of policy research and analysis over many months, the policy memorandum is prepared over a short period of time—usually no more than one month, but often a matter of days. The differences between the issue paper, study, or report and the policy memorandum reflect some of the differences between basic and applied policy analysis summarized in Table 9.1.

The policy memorandum should be concise, focused, and well organized. It reports background information and presents conclusions or recommendations, usually in response to a request from a client. The policy memo often summarizes and evaluates one or more issue papers or reports, along with accompanying backup documents and statistical data.

The format for a memo, which varies from agency to agency, is designed for quick and efficient reading. Most memos display the name of the recipient, the name of the analyst submitting the memo, the date, and the subject on separate lines at the top of the page. Most agencies have preprinted forms for memos. Word processing programs have templates for memos and other standard documents. Writers of policy memo should take every opportunity to communicate clearly and effectively the main points of the analysis:

- The subject line should state in concise terms the main conclusion, recommendation, or purpose of the memo.
- The body of the memo (usually no more than two pages) should contain headings that describe major subdivisions.
- Bulleted lists should be used to highlight a small set (no more than five) of important items such as goals, objectives, or options.
- The introductory paragraph should review the request for information and analysis, restate the major question(s) asked by the client, and describe the objectives of the memo.

A sample policy memorandum is presented in Appendix 3.

Table 9.2 Elements of Issue Paper and Methods for Creating Information Relevant to Each Element

Element	Method
Letter of Transmittal	
Executive Summary	
I. Background of the problem	
A. Describe client's inquiry	Monitoring
B. Overview problem situation	
C. Describe prior efforts to solve problem	
II. Significance of the problem	
A. Evaluate past policy performance	Evaluation
B. Assess the scope and severity of problem	
C. Determine the need for analysis	
III. Problem statement	
A. Diagnose problem	Problem
B. Describe major stakeholders	Structuring
C. Define goals and objectives	
IV. Analysis of alternatives	
A. Describe alternatives	Forecasting
B. Forecast consequences of alternatives	
C. Describe any spillovers and externalities	
D. Assess constraints and political feasibility	
V. Conclusions and recommendations	
A. Select criteria or decision rules	Recommendation
B. State conclusions and recommendations	
C. Describe preferred alternative(s)	
D. Outline implementation strategy	
E. Summarize plan for monitoring and evaluation	
F. List limitations and unanticipated consequences	
References	
Appendices	

The Executive Summary

The executive summary is a synopsis of the major elements of a policy issue paper or report. The executive summary typically has the following elements:

- Purpose of the issue paper or study being summarized
- Background of the problem or question addressed
- Major findings or conclusions
- Approach to analysis and methodology (where appropriate)
- Conclusions and recommendations (when requested)

Appendix 2 provides a sample executive summary.

The Letter of Transmittal

A letter of transmittal will accompany a policy issue paper or study. Although the letter of transmittal has most of the elements of a policy memo, the purpose of the letter (or memo) is to introduce the recipient to a larger paper or study. Some common elements of a letter of transmittal are as follows:

- The letterhead or address of the person(s) transmitting the issue paper or study
- The name, formal title, and address of the person(s) or client(s) who requested the issue paper or study
- A short paragraph stating the question or problem that the person(s) or client(s) expect the analyst to address
- A brief summary of the most important conclusions or recommendations of the issue paper or study
- A review of arrangements for further communication or work with the client, for example, a scheduled briefing on the issue paper or study
- A concluding statement indicating where and how the analyst can be reached to answer any questions
- A signature with the name and title of the analyst or the analyst's supervisor.

THE ORAL BRIEFING AND VISUAL DISPLAYS

Written documents are only one means for communicating the results of policy analysis. The other is the oral briefing. Although the oral briefing or presentation has many of the same elements as the issue paper, the approach to planning and delivering an oral presentation is quite different. The elements of an oral briefing typically include the following:

- Opening and greeting to participants
- Background of the briefing
- Major findings of issue paper, study, or report
- Approach and methods
- Data used as basis for the analysis
- Recommendations
- Questions from participants
- Closing

Knowing the audience is one of the most important aspects of planning oral briefings. In this context, a series of important questions should be answered prior to the briefing.

- How large is the audience?
- How many members of the audience are experts on the problem you are addressing in the briefing?

- What percent of the audience understands your research methods?
- Are you credible to members of the audience?
- Does the audience prefer detailed or general information?
- Where does the briefing fall in the policy-making process?
- At the agenda-setting phase? The implementation phase?

Answers to these questions govern the strategy and tactics of communication appropriate for the particular audience. For example, if the audience is a medium-size group with twenty to twenty-five persons, the diversity of the audience calls for specific communications strategies and tactics:

- Circulate background materials before the meeting so that everyone will start from a common base.
- Tell the group that the strategy selected is designed to meet the objectives of the group as a whole but that it may not satisfy everyone's needs.
- Focus on the agendas of key policy makers, even if you lose the rest of the audience.

Another common problem in giving oral briefings is that policy makers may bring their own staff experts to the briefing. If a high percentage of the audience has expertise in the area you are addressing, the following strategies and tactics are appropriate.

- Avoid engaging in a "knowledge contest" with subject experts. Focus instead on the purpose of the presentation.
- Capitalize on the group's expertise by focusing on findings and recommendations.
- Avoid a lengthy presentation of background material and description of methods.
- Attempt to generate dialogue and a productive debate on policy options.

An equally important problem in oral briefings is knowing individual members of the group. For example, it is important to know if the immediate clients for policy analysis are:

- Experts in the problem area
- Familiar with your analytic methods
- Influential participants in the policy process
- Oriented toward detailed versus broad information
- Have a high, medium, or low stake in the outcome
- Politically important to the success of your recommendations

Finally, the effectiveness of oral briefings can be significantly enhanced by various graphic displays. The most common of these are transparencies used with overhead projectors, and slides created by computer graphics and presentation programs such as Microsoft PowerPoint. In using overhead transparencies and slides, it is important to recognize that they are not appropriate when you want an informal style of presentation—overheads tend to make briefings very formal and make open dialogue difficult. It is also important to observe the following guidelines:

- Keep transparencies and slides simple, with condensed and highlighted text.
- Use clear, bold, uncluttered letters and lines of text.
- Avoid complicated color schemes, pop art, and fancy templates.
- Highlight important points and use different colors. A dark background with superimposed white or yellow letters is effective.
- Limit the text on any page to a maximum of ten lines.
- Be sure the width of the screen is at least one-sixth of the distance between the screen and the farthest viewer.
- Make sure that the nearest viewer is a minimum of two screen widths from the screen.
- Remain on the same transparency or slide for a minimum of two minutes. This gives viewers time to read, plus an additional thirty seconds to study the content.
- Leave the room lights *on*—transparencies and slides are designed for lighted rooms. It is not a movie theater.
- Turn off the overhead projector, or blacken the computer screen, when you want to redirect attention back to you and reestablish eye contact.

These are but a few of the strategies and tactics that are appropriate for different audiences and communications media. Given the goal of selecting communications media and products that match the characteristics of the audience, there is today a rich array of techniques for the visual display of information. Appropriate computer graphics programs are widely available.

Many types of visual displays are available to the analyst who wishes to effectively communicate complex ideas. Examples of the following visual displays (created with *Harvard Graphics*) are provided in Appendix 4. The same graphics can be created with Microsoft Excel and PowerPoint.

- Options-impact matrices ("Goeller scorecards")
- Spreadsheets
- Bar charts
- Pie charts
- Frequency histograms
- Ogives (cumulative frequency curves)
- Scatter plots
- Interrupted time-series and control-series graphs
- Influence diagrams
- Decision trees
- Strategy tables

POLICY ANALYSIS IN THE POLICY-MAKING PROCESS

We began this book by defining policy analysis as *a process of multidisciplinary inquiry designed to create, critically assess, and communicate information that is useful in understanding and improving policies*. Throughout, we have emphasized that policy analysis is a series of *intellectual* activities embedded in a *social* process known as *policy making*. The distinction between these two dimensions—the intellectual and the social—is important for understanding the use, underuse, and nonuse of analysis by policy makers.

Recall the three interrelated dimensions of information use presented in Chapter 2:

- *Composition of users*. Analysis is used by individuals as well as collectives (e.g., agencies, bureaus, legislatures). When the use of analysis involves individual gains (or losses) in the perceived future value of information, the process of use is an aspect of individual decisions (*individual use*). By contrast, when the process of use involves public enlightenment or collective learning, the use of information is an aspect of collective decisions (*collective use*).

- *Effects of use*. The use of policy analysis has different kinds of effects. Policy analysis is used to think about problems and solutions (conceptual use). It is also used to legitimize preferred formulations of problems and solutions by invoking the authority of experts, religion, and methods (symbolic use). By contrast, behavioral effects involve the use of policy analysis as a means or instrument for carrying out observable policy-making activities (instrumental use). Conceptual, symbolic, and behavioral uses occur at individual and collective levels.

- *Scope of information used*. The scope of use ranges from the specific to the general. The use of "ideas in good currency" is general in scope (general use), whereas the use of a policy recommendation is specific (specific use). Information that varies in scope is used by individuals and collectives, with effects that are conceptual, symbolic, and behavioral.

With these distinctions in mind, the use of information in policy making is shaped by at least five types of factors.[11] These factors include differences in the characteristics of information, the modes of inquiry use to produce information, the structure of policy problems, political and bureaucratic structures, and the nature of interactions among policy analysts, policy makers, and other stakeholders.

---

[11] For case study research on these factors, see William N. Dunn, "The Two-Communities Metaphor and Models of Knowledge Use: An Exploratory Case Survey," *Knowledge: Creation, Diffusion, Utilization* no. 4 (June 1980): pp. 300–27.

Characteristics of Information

The characteristics of information produced by policy analyses influence information use by policy makers. Information that conforms to the product specifications of policy makers is more likely to be used than information that does not, because product specifications reflect policy maker needs, values, and perceived opportunities. Policy makers tend to value information that is communicated in personal verbal reports, rather than formal written documents, and expressed in a language that reflects concrete policy contexts rather than the more abstract vocabularies of the natural and social sciences.[12] Policy makers also attach greater value to information that is accurate, precise, and generalizable to similar settings.[13]

Modes of Inquiry

The use of information by policy makers is shaped by the process of inquiry used by analysts to produce and interpret that information. Information that conforms to standards of quality research and analysis is more likely to be used. Yet there are widely differing views about the meaning of "quality." For many analysts, quality is defined in terms of the use of social experimentation, random sampling, and quantitative measurement.[14] The assumption is that information use is a function of the degree to which policy research and analysis conforms to accepted scientific methods, provided that the resultant information is adapted to organizational constraints such as the need for timely information.

By contrast, other analysts define quality in different terms. Here, quality is defined in terms that emphasize nonquantitative procedures designed to uncover subjective understandings about problems and potential solutions held by policy makers and other stakeholders.[15]

Structure of Problems

The utilization of information by policy makers is also influenced by the goodness-of-fit between modes of inquiry and types of problems. Relatively well structured problems involving consensus on goals, objectives, alternatives, and their consequences require

---

[12] See Mark van de Vall, Cheryl Bolas, and Thomas Kang, "Applied Social Research in Industrial Organizations: An Evaluation of Functions, Theory, and Methods," *Journal of Applied Behavioral Science* 12, no. 2 (1976): 158–77.

[13] See Nathan Caplan, Andrea Morrison, and Roger J. Stambaugh, *The Use of Social Science Knowledge in Policy Decisions at the National Level* (Ann Arbor, MI: Institute for Social Research, 1975).

[14] See I. N. Bernstein and H. E. Freeman, *Academic and Entrepreneurial Research* (New York: Russell Sage Foundation, 1975).

[15] Martin Rein and Sheldon H. White, "Policy Research: Belief and Doubt," *Policy Analysis* 3, no. 2 (1977): 239–71; Michael Q. Patton, *Alternative Evaluation Research Paradigm* (Grand Forks: University of North Dakota, 1975); and H. Aeland, "Are Randomized Experiments the Cadillacs of Design?" *Policy Analysis* 5, no. 2 (1979): 223–42.

different methodologies than those required by relatively ill structured problems. Because the essential characteristic of ill-structured problems is conflict, not consensus, ill-structured problems require methodologies that are holistic and that bring to bear multiple perspectives of the same problem situation in defining the nature of the problem itself.[16]

The distinction between well-structured and ill-structured problems is associated with the distinction between lower-level (micro) and higher-level (meta) problems. Metalevel problems involve issues of how to structure a problem, how to assist policy makers in knowing what should be known, and how to decide which aspects of a problem should be resolved on the basis of "conceptual" knowledge.[17] Most policy research and analysis is oriented toward the production of "instrumental" knowledge, that is, knowledge about the most appropriate means for attaining taken for granted or agreed-upon ends. Instrumental knowledge, because it is appropriate for well-structured problems at the microlevel, is less likely to be used by policy makers who face ill-structured problems involving disagreements about the nature of problems and their potential solutions.

Political and Bureaucratic Structures

The use of information is also shaped by differences in the formal structures, procedures, and incentive systems of public organizations. The influence of policy-making elites, the bureaucratization of roles, the formalization of procedures, and the operation of incentive systems that reward conservatism and punish innovation contribute to the underuse and nonuse of information produced by analysts. These and other factors, although they are "external" to the methodology of policy analysis, create a political and bureaucratic context for information use.[18]

Interactions among Stakeholders

The nature and types of interaction among stakeholders in the various phases of policy making also influence the use of information by policy makers.[19] Policy analysis is not simply a scientific and technical process; it is also a social process where the structure, scope, and intensity of interaction among stakeholders govern the creation and use of information.

---

[16] Russell Ackoff, *Redesigning the Future: A Systems Approach to Societal Problems* (New York: Wiley, 1974); Ian I. Mitroff, *The Subjective Side of Science* (New York: American Elsevier Publishing, 1974); and Ian I. Mitroff and L. Vaughan Blankenship, "On the Methodology of the Holistic Experiment: An Approach to the Conceptualization of Large-Scale Social Experiments," *Technological Forecasting and Social Change* 4 (1973): 339–53.

[17] See Nathan Caplan, "The Two-Communities Theory and Knowledge Utilization," *American Behavioral Scientist* 22, no. 3 (1979): 459–70.

[18] Robert F. Rich, *The Power of Social Science Information and Public Policymaking: The Case of the Continuous National Survey* (San Francisco, CA: Jossey-Bass, 1981).

[19] See Weiss, "Introduction," *Using Social Research in Public Policy Making*, pp. 13–15.

The interactive nature of policy analysis makes questions of information use complex. Analysts rarely produce information that is or can be used merely for "problem solving," in the narrow sense of discovering through analysis the most appropriate means to ends that are well defined and about which there is substantial consensus. Many of the most important policy problems, as we have seen in this book, are sufficiently ill structured that the "problem-solving" model of policy analysis is inappropriate or inapplicable. For this reason, policy analysis has been described throughout this book as an integrated process of inquiry where multiple methods—problem structuring, forecasting, recommendation, monitoring, evaluation—are used continuously to create and transform information about policy problems, policy futures, policy actions, policy outcomes, and policy performance. Although the process of policy analysis is quintessentially methodological, it is also a process of communicative interaction. Policy analysis, because it aims at the creation, critical assessment, and communication of policy-relevant information, is vital to policy argumentation and public debate.

CHAPTER SUMMARY

This concluding chapter has provided an overview of the process of policy communication and its importance to the use of analysis by policy makers. Policy analysis is the beginning, not the end, of efforts to improve policy making. Knowledge and skills in conducting policy analysis are different from knowledge and skills in developing policy documents and giving oral briefings. To be effective, analysts need to master and apply a broad range of communications skills, thereby narrowing the great divide between intellectual and social dimensions of policy making.

LEARNING OBJECTIVES

- describe stages in the process of policy communication
- contrast policy analysis, materials development, interactive communication, and knowledge (information) use
- explain how the process of policy analysis is related to the process of policy making

- describe the main elements of policy issue papers and policy memos
- discuss factors that factors explain the use, abuse, and nonuse of policy analysis
- plan, present, and evaluate oral briefings that involve the communication of the same information to different audiences

KEY TERMS AND CONCEPTS

contingent communication (427)
executive summary (431)
interactive communication (422)
knowledge (information) use (435)

letter of transmittal (432)
materials development (422)
policy issue paper (427)
policy memo(randum) (430)

REVIEW QUESTIONS

1. Why are the communication and use of information central to the aims of policy analysis?
2. If policy analysis is an intellectual activity carried out within a social process, what are the implications for the use of analysis by policy makers?
3. "Policy analysis is the beginning, not the end, of efforts to improve the policy-making process." Comment.
4. Before intended beneficiaries can use policy-relevant information, it must be converted into policy-relevant documents and communicated in presentations of different kinds. Does this guarantee that intended beneficiaries will use information?
5. Describe stages of the process of policy communication.
6. Why are skills needed to develop policy documents and give oral presentations different from skills needed to conduct policy analysis?
7. Discuss factors that affect the use of policy analysis by policy makers and other stakeholders.
8. Why is the production of policy analysis described as a poorly managed lumber mill?

DEMONSTRATION EXERCISE

The purpose of this exercise is to sharpen knowledge and skills in planning and conducting effective oral briefings. This is a group exercise, although different individuals could also complete it. Divide the class into four groups. Each group should perform the following tasks.

1. Respond to one of the following requests (I, II, III, or IV) to give an oral briefing on the reduction of harmful levels of lead in gasoline. Assume that you are the authors of the analysis included as Case 9. It is an analysis prepared by David Weimer and Aidan Vining, two highly experienced policy analysts. Your group has been asked to make one of the four briefings below.
2. Each group will have fifteen minutes to give its briefing and respond to ten minutes of questioning. The main policy question you must answer is, should the government regulate lead additives in gasoline?
3. Other class members, who will be using the attached rating scale, will evaluate presentations. The evaluations will be used as a basis for a critique and discussion of the briefings.
   - *Group I.* Prepare an oral briefing for a community environmental group composed of sixty citizens who have little or no knowledge of statistical methods and biomedical research on lead. The audience does not appear to your group, which is composed of "outsiders" from Washington. Among members of the group is a potentially disruptive person who likes to get attention by engaging in a "knowledge contest." This person is running for public office in the next election. The environmental group wants to see new legislation on the public agenda. Your answer to the policy question stated above is supposed to help them.

- *Group II.* Prepare an oral briefing for a group of ten experts in biostatistics, econometrics, and environmental economists. All have extensive knowledge of the health effects of leaded gasoline. Most of them are colleagues with whom you have worked previously. One member of the working group, a respected biostatistician, is a paid consultant working for the International Lead and Zinc Union (ILZU), an organization that markets lead and zinc products. The ILZU takes the position that "statistical correlations do not prove causation." The working group is designing a research proposal to investigate the health effects of lead. Your answer to the policy question is supposed to help them.
- *Group III.* Prepare an oral briefing for a group of thirty business executives from the oil refining industry. They are opposed to government regulation of leaded gasoline. They believe that regulation will reduce profits and destroy the industry. Although they have been briefed by their staff experts, they are not familiar with statistics and biomedical research on lead. The executives are preparing to fight a Congressional bill which, if adopted next month, would regulate and eventually ban leaded gasoline. Your answer to the policy question is supposed to help them.
- *Group IV.* Prepare an oral briefing for a group of six experts from the Occupational Safety and Health Administration. They have done extensive research on the biomedical effects of lead exposure and are convinced that low levels of exposure to lead are extremely harmful, especially to inner city children who are exposed to unusually high amounts of automotive exhaust. The experts are evaluating your analysis in preparation for an annual conference. Your answer to the policy question is supposed to help them.

In preparing your briefing, use the structural model of argument (Chapter 8) as a framework for organizing your presentation, clearly stating your argument, and anticipating challenges. (*Note:* Do not present the model of argument as part of the briefing. It is an analytic tool.)

Your oral briefing should be based on a communications strategy appropriate to the characteristics of your audience. To develop an appropriate communications strategy, use the guidelines described in this chapter. The briefings will be evaluated on the basis of the attached checklist and rating scales. You or your instructor should make four (4) copies of the checklist—three to evaluate the other presentations and one for your records.

REFERENCES

Barber, Bernard. *Effective Social Science: Eight Cases in Economics, Political Science, and Sociology.* New York: Russell Sage Foundation, 1987.

Freidson, Elliot. *Professional Powers: A Study of the Institutionalization of Formal Knowledge.* Chicago: University of Chicago Press, 1986.

Hacker, Diana. *A Writer's Reference.* 4th ed. New York: St. Martin's Press, 1999.

Horowitz, Irving L., ed. *The Use and Abuse of Social Science: Behavioral Science and Policy Making.* 2d ed. New Brunswick, NJ: Transaction Books, 1985.

Evaluation of Oral Briefing

Group evaluated (circle): **I**   **II**   **III**   **IV**

Use the following rating scale for your evaluation. Provide a brief written justification in the space provided next to each item.

> 1 = Very good
> 2 = Good
> 3 = Adequate
> 4 = Poor
> 5 = Very poor

1. Rate the effectiveness of the following elements of the briefing:
   - (a) opening _____
   - (b) background _____
   - (c) findings _____
   - (d) methods _____
   - (e) evidence/data _____
   - (f) recommendations _____
   - (g) questions and answers _____
   - (h) closing _____

2. Appropriateness of briefing to:
   - (a) size of the audience _____
   - (b) expertise of audience _____
   - (c) familiarity of audience with methods _____
   - (d) audience information preferences _____
   - (e) phase of policy-making process _____
   - (f) perceptions of presenter's credibility _____

3. Logic, organization, and flow of briefing: _____

4. Use of visual displays: _____

5. Overall, this oral briefing was: _____

Jasanoff, Sheila. *The Fifth Branch: Science Advisors as Policymakers*. Cambridge, MA: Harvard University Press, 1990.

Lindblom, Charles E., and David K. Cohen. *Usable Knowledge: Social Science and Social Problem Solving*. New Haven, CT: Yale University Press, 1979.

Machlup, Fritz. *Knowledge: Its Creation, Distribution, and Economic Significance*, Vol. 1, *Knowledge and Knowledge Production*. Princeton, NJ: Princeton University Press, 1980.

Schmandt, Jurgen, and James E. Katz. "The Scientific State: A Theory with Hypotheses." *Science, Technology, and Human Values* 11 (1986): 40–50.

Tufte, Edward R. *The Visual Display of Quantitative Information*. Cheshire, CT: Graphics Press, 1983.

———. *Envisioning Information*. Cheshire, CT: Graphics Press, 1990.

———. *Visual Explanations*. Cheshire, CT: Graphics Press, 1997.

Weiss, Carol H. with Michael Bucuvalas. *Social Science Research and Decision Making*. New York: Columbia University Press, 1980.

Case 9. Adopting the EPA Lead Standard: Communicating Technical Analyses to Multiple Audiences

When Statistics Count: Revising the EPA Lead Standard[20]

David L. Weimer and Aidan L. Vining

Policy analysts must deal with many kinds of empirical evidence. Often the constraints of time and resources, as well as the nature of the policy problem under consideration, force analysts to rely on qualitative and fragmentary data. Sometimes, however, analysts can find data that enable them to estimate the magnitudes of the effects of policy interventions on the social, economic, or political conditions. The estimates may permit the analysts to calculate the likely net social benefits of proposed policies or even apply formal optimization techniques to find better alternatives.

The effective use of quantitative data requires an understanding of the basic issues of research design and a facility with the techniques of statistical inference. Even when analysts do not have the resources available to do primary data analysis, they often must confront quantitative evidence produced by other participants in the policy process or extracted from the academic literature. If they lack the requisite skills for critical evaluation, they risk losing their influence in the face of quantitative evidence that may appear more objective and scientific to decision makers. Well-trained analysts, therefore, need some facility with the basic concepts of statistical inference for reasons of self-defense, if for no others.

The basics of research design and statistical inference cannot be adequately covered in an introductory course in policy analysis. Similarly, we cannot provide

---

[20] From David Weimer and Aidan Vining, *Policy Analysis: Concepts and Practice*, 2d ed. (Englewood Cliffs, NJ: Prentice Hall Publishers, 1992), ch. 13, pp. 382–406.

adequate coverage in this book. Yet we can provide an example of a policy change where quantitative analysis was instrumental: the decision by the U.S. Environmental Protection Agency (EPA) in 1985 to reduce dramatically the amount of lead permitted in gasoline. The story of the new lead standard has a number of elements frequently encountered when doing quantitative analysis in organizational settings: replacement of an initial "quick and dirty" analysis with more sophisticated versions as more time and data become available; repeated reanalysis to rule out alternative explanations (hypotheses) offered by opponents of the proposed policy; and serendipitous events that influence the analytical strategy. Although our primary purpose is to tell what we believe to be an intrinsically interesting and instructive story about the practice of policy analysis, we hope to offer a few basic lessons on quantitative analysis along the way.

Background: The EPA Lead Standards

The Clean Air Amendments of 1970 give the administrator of the Environmental Protection Agency (EPA) authority to regulate any motor fuel component or additive that produces emission products dangerous to public health or welfare.[21] Before exercising this authority, however, the administrator must consider "all relevant medical and scientific evidence available to him" as well as alternative methods that set standards for emissions rather than for fuel components.[22]

In 1971 the EPA administrator announced that he was considering possible controls on lead additives in gasoline.[23] One reason given was the possible adverse health effects of emissions from engines that burned leaded gasoline, the standard fuel at the time. Available evidence suggested that lead is toxic in the human body, that lead can be absorbed into the body from ambient air, and that gasoline engines account for a large fraction of airborne lead. The other reason for controlling the lead content of gasoline was the incompatibility of leaded fuel with the catalytic converter, a device seen as having potential for reducing hydrocarbon emissions from automobiles. The first reason suggests considering whether reductions in the lead content of all gasoline might be desirable; the second argues for the total removal of lead from gasoline for use by new automobiles equipped with catalytic converters.

Without going any further one might ask: Why should the government be concerned with the level of lead in gasoline? And why had the federal government already decided to require the installation of catalytic converters? The following analysis does not explicitly deal with the desirability of catalytic converters. As we have argued, however, it is always important to make sure that there is a convincing rationale for public action. The interventions at hand, the catalytic converter and the related lead restrictions, deal with market failures—viewed as problems of either

---

[21] The Clean Air Act Amendments of 1970, Public Law 91–604, December 31, 1970.

[22] Section 211(c)(2)(A), 42 U.S.C. @ 1857f-6c(c)(2)(A).

[23] 36 *Fed. Reg.* 1468 (January 31, 1971).

negative externalities or public goods (ambient public goods). In addition, another market failure may come into play with respect to lead—imperfect consumer information about the impacts of lead on health and the maintenance cost of vehicles. Because the health and maintenance impacts may not manifest themselves for many years (leaded gasoline is a post-experience good), markets may be inefficient because of information asymmetry. These apparent market failures make a case for considering government intervention.

But intervention itself may be costly. It is quite conceivable that the costs of intervention could exceed the benefits. Several questions must be answered before the comparison of costs and benefits can be made: What are the impacts in the Economic Analysis Division that had worked on the 1982 regulations. Schwartz used his accumulated knowledge from previous analyses to complete in two or three days a quick and dirty benefit–cost analysis of a total ban on lead additives.

Because a total ban was one of the options considered in 1982, it was fairly easy for Schwartz to come up with a reasonable estimate of cost. As is often the case in evaluating health and safety regulations, the more difficult problem was estimating the benefits of a total ban. Schwartz looked at two benefit categories: increased IQ scores of children due to lower levels of blood lead and the avoided damage to catalytic converters.

Schwartz used estimates from a variety of sources to piece together a relationship between lead emissions and the present value of lifetime earnings of children. The first step involved using estimates from the 1982 analyses of the relationship between lead emissions and blood lead levels in children. He next turned to epidemiological studies that reported a relationship between blood lead levels and IQs. Finally, he found econometric studies that estimated the contribution of IQ points to the present value of future earnings.

As a first cut at quantifying the benefits resulting from the more effective control of other emissions, Schwartz estimated the cost of catalytic converters being contaminated under the current standards that would not be contaminated under a total ban. He used the number of converters saved multiplied by the price per converter as the benefit measure. Assuming that converters themselves have benefit–cost ratios greater than one, this benefit measure would be conservative.

These "back-of-the-envelope" calculations suggested that the benefits of a total ban on lead additives would be more than twice the costs. Schwartz discussed the results with his branch chief, G. Martin Wagner, who sent word to the office of the administrator that further analysis of a lead ban seemed worthwhile. A few weeks later, Schwartz and fellow analyst Jane Leggett began a two-month effort to move from the back of an envelope to a preliminary report.

Pulling the Pieces Together

The most urgent task facing Schwartz and Leggett was to develop better measures of the benefits of a lead ban. The key to improving the measure of benefits from avoided converter poisonings was a more sophisticated accounting of the future age composition of the U.S. vehicle fleet. The key to improving the measure of benefits from reduced lead emissions was a better quantitative estimate of the relationship between gasoline lead and blood lead. Modeling and statistical analysis would be an important part of their work.

The age composition of the vehicle fleet continually changes as old vehicles, some of which have contaminated or partially contaminated converters, are retired and new ones, with fresh converters, are added. A ban on lead would have different effects on different vintage vehicles. For instance, it would be irrelevant for vehicles that already have contaminated converters, but very important for vehicles that would otherwise be contaminated and remain in service for a long time.

The analysts developed an inventory model that tracked cohorts of vehicles over time. Each year a new cohort would enter the fleet. Each successive year a fraction of the vehicles would be retired because of accidents and mechanical failures. In addition, a fraction would suffer converter poisoning from misfueling. By following the various cohorts over time, it was possible to predict the total number of converters that would be saved in each future year from specified reductions in the lead content of leaded gasoline today and in the future. Avoided loss of the depreciated value of the catalytic converters (later avoided costs of the health and property damage from pollutants other than lead) could then be calculated for each future year. With appropriate discounting, the yearly benefits could then be summed to yield the present value of the lead reduction schedule being considered.

Two important considerations came to light during work on the vehicle fleet model. One was a body of literature suggesting that lead increases the routine maintenance costs of vehicles. Subsequently, a new benefit category, avoided maintenance costs, was estimated using the vehicle fleet model. The other consideration was the possibility that some engines might suffer premature valve-seat wear if fueled with totally lead-free gasoline. Although the problem was fairly limited (primarily automobile engines manufactured prior to 1971 and some newer trucks, motorcycles, and off-road vehicles), it suggested the need to consider alternatives to a total ban.

Efforts to quantify better the link between gasoline lead and blood lead focused on analysis of data from the second National Health and Nutrition Examination Survey (NHANES II). The NHANES II survey was designed by the National Center for Health Statistics to provide a representative national sample of the population between the ages of six months and seventy-four years. It included 27,801 persons sampled at sixty-four representative sites from 1976 to 1980. Of the 16,563 persons who were asked to provide blood samples, 61 percent complied. The lead concentrations in the blood samples were measured, providing data that could be used to track average blood levels over the four-year survey period. The amount of lead in gasoline sold over the period could then be correlated with the blood lead concentrations.

A positive relationship between blood lead concentrations from the NHANES II data and gasoline lead had already been found by researchers. The positive correlation is apparent in Figure 9.2, which was prepared by James Pirkle of the

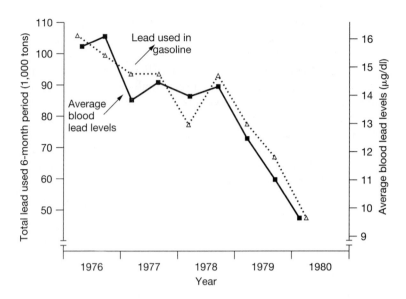

Figure 9.2 Lead use in gasoline production and average NHANES II blood lead levels.
Source: J. Schwartz et al., *Costs and Benefits of Reducing Lead in Gasoline: Final Regulatory Impact Analysis,* Publication No. EPA-230–05–85–006 (Washington, DC: EPA, 1985), p. E-5.

Centers for Disease Control to show the close tracking of blood lead concentrations and total gasoline lead. Much more than the apparent correlation, however, was needed for the benefit–cost analysis. Schwartz used multiple regression techniques, which we will discuss in detail later in our story, to estimate the increase in average micrograms of lead per deciliter of blood (µg/dl) due to each additional 100 metric tons per day of lead in consumed gasoline. He also employed models that allowed him to estimate the probabilities that children with specified characteristics will have toxic levels of blood lead (then defined by the Centers for Disease Control as greater than 30 µg/dl) and gasoline lead. These probabilities could then be used to predict the number of children in the population who would avoid lead toxicity if a ban on gasoline lead were imposed.

In early November of 1983, Schwartz and Leggett pulled together the components of their analyses and found a ratio of benefits to costs of a total ban to be greater than Schwartz's original back-of-the-envelope calculation. Together with their branch chief, they presented their results to Deputy Administrator Alm, who found them encouraging. He gave the green light for the preparation of a refined version that could be presented to the administrator as the basis for a new regulation. Alm also wanted the various components of the refined study to be subjected to peer review by experts outside the EPA. At the same time, he urged speed in order to reduce the chances that word would get out to refiners and manufacturers of lead additives, the primary opponents of a ban, before the EPA had an opportunity to review all the evidence.

The branch chief expanded the analytical team in order to hasten the preparation of the refined report that would be sent to the administrator. Joining Schwartz and Leggett were Ronnie Levin; Hugh Pitcher, an econometrician; and Bart Ostro, an expert on the benefits of ozone reduction. In little more than one month, the team was ready to send a draft report out for peer review.

The effort involved several changes in analytical approach. Because of the valve-head problem, the analysis focused on a major reduction in grams of lead per leaded gallon (from 1.1 gplg to 0.1 gplg) as well as a total ban. The available evidence suggested that the 0.1 gplg level would be adequate to avoid excessive valve-head wear in the small number of engines designed to be fueled only with leaded gasoline. At the same time, considerable effort was put into quantifying the maintenance costs that would be avoided by owners of other vehicles if the lead concentration were reduced. It soon appeared that the maintenance benefits consumers would enjoy would more than offset the higher prices they would have to pay for gasoline. Finally, the team decided that the benefits based on the blood lead (through IQ) to future earnings relationship would be too controversial. Instead, they turned their attention to the costs of compensatory education for children who suffered IQ losses from high blood lead levels.

In late December, sections of the report were sent to experts outside the EPA for comments. The list included automotive engineers, economists, biostatisticians, toxicologists, clinical researchers, transportation experts, and a psychologist. During January 1984, the team refined their analysis and incorporated, or at least responded to, the comments made by the external reviewers.

Finally, in early February, the team was ready to present its results to Administrator Ruckelshaus. He agreed that their analysis supported a new standard of 0.1 gplg. He told the team to finalize their report without a proposed rule and release it for public comment. Ruckelshaus also directed the Office of the Assistant Administrator for Air and Radiation to draft a proposed rule.

The team's *Draft Final Report* was printed and eventually released to the public on March 26, 1984.[24] The team continued to refine the analysis in the following months. It also had to devote considerable time to external relations. Executive Order 12291 requires regulatory agencies to submit proposed regulations that would have annual costs of more than $100 million to the Office of Management and Budget (OMB) for review. The team met with OMB analysts several times before securing their acceptance of the benefit–cost analysis of the tighter standard.

The political environment was taking shape pretty much as expected. Opposition would come from refiners and manufacturers of lead additives. The refiners, however, generally seemed resigned to the eventual elimination of lead from gasoline. Their primary concern was the speed of implementation. Some refiners seemed particularly concerned about the first few years of a tighter standard,

---

[24] Joel Schwartz, Jan Leggett, Bart Ostro, Hugh Pitcher, and Ronnie Levin, *Costs and Benefits of Reducing Lead in Gasoline: Draft Final Report* (Washington, DC: Office of Policy Analysis, EPA, March 26, 1984).

when they would have difficulty making the required reductions with their existing configurations of capital equipment. In response, the team began exploring the costs and benefits of less stringent compliance schedules.

The manufacturers of lead additives were ready to fight tighter standards. In May, Schwartz attended a conference at the Centers for Disease Control in Atlanta, Georgia, on the proposed revision of the blood lead toxicity standard for children from 30 µg/dl to 25 µg/dl. Representatives of the lead manufacturers were also there. They openly talked about their strategy for challenging tighter standards. They planned to argue that refiners would blend more benzene, a suspected carcinogen, into gasoline to boost octane if lead were restricted. Schwartz investigated this possibility following the conference. He found that, even if more benzene were added to gasoline, the total emissions of benzene would decline because of the reduction in the contamination of catalytic converters, which oxidize the benzene if not contaminated. The day that the proposed rule was published Schwartz put a memorandum on the docket covering the benzene issue, thus preempting the manufacturers' main attack.

The EPA published the proposed rule on August 2, 1984.[25] It would require that the permitted level of gasoline lead be reduced to 0.1 gplg on January 1, 1986. The proposal stated the EPA assumption that the new standard could be met with existing refining equipment, but indicated that alternative phase-in schedules involving more gradual reductions also were being considered in case this assumption proved false. Finally, the proposal raised the possibility of a complete ban on gasoline lead by 1995.

A Closer Look at the Link between Gasoline Lead and Blood Lead

Calculation of the direct health benefits of tightening the lead standard requires quantitative estimates of the contribution of gasoline lead to blood lead. The NHANES II data, combined with information on gasoline lead levels, enabled the study team to make the necessary estimates. Their efforts provide an excellent illustration of how statistical inference can be used effectively in policy analysis.

The Need for Multivariate Analysis

A casual inspection of Figure 9.2 suggests a strong positive relationship between gasoline lead and blood lead. Why is it necessary to go any further? One reason is the difficulty of answering, directly from Figure 9.2, the central empirical question: How much does the average blood lead level in the United States decline for each 1,000-ton reduction in the total gasoline lead used over the previous month? Figure 9.2 indicates a positive correlation between gasoline lead and blood lead—changes in blood lead track changes in gasoline lead quite closely. But for the same correlation in the data, we could have very different answers to our central question.

Figure 9.3 illustrates the difference between correlation and magnitude of effect with stylized data. If our data were represented by the diamonds, we might "fit" line one as our best guess at the relationship between blood lead and gasoline lead. The effect of reducing gasoline lead from 500 tons per day to 400 tons per day

---

[25] 49 *Fed. Reg.* 31031 (August 2, 1984).

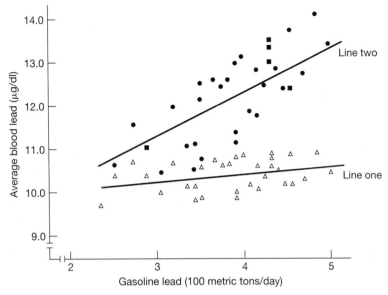

Figure 9.3 Data samples with identical correlations but different regression lines.

would be to reduce average blood lead from 10.1 µg/dl to 10.0 µg/dl, or 0.1 µg/dl per 100 tons per day. An alternative sample of data is represented by the dots, which are plotted to have approximately the same correlation between gasoline lead and blood lead as the data represented by triangles. The slope of line two, the best fit to the dots, is 1.0 µg/dl per 100 tons per day—ten times greater than the slope of line one. That is, although the two data sets have the same correlation, the second implies a much greater contribution of gasoline lead to blood lead than the first.

Even after we display the data in Figure 9.2 as a plot between blood lead and gasoline lead, our analysis is far from complete because the apparent relationship (the slopes of lines one and two in our example) may be spurious. Blood lead and gasoline lead may not be directly related to each other but to some third variable that causes them to change together. The classic illustration of this problem is the correlation sometimes found between the density of stork nests and the human birth rate. If one were to plot birth rates against the density of stork nests for districts in some region, one might very well find a positive relationship and perhaps conclude that there might be something to the myth about storks bringing babies.

Of course, there is a more plausible explanation. A variable measuring the degree to which a district is rural "intervenes" between birth rate and nest density—rural areas have farmers who want a lot of children to help with chores as well as lot of open land that provides nesting grounds for storks; more urbanized areas tend to have people who want smaller families as well as less hospitable nesting grounds. Looking across a sample that included both rural and urban districts could yield the positive correlation between birth rate and nest density. If we were to "control" statistically for the intervening variable by looking at either rural or urban districts separately rather than pooled together, we would expect the correlation between birth rate and nest density to become negligible.

Returning to our analysis of lead, we must be concerned that one or more intervening variables might explain the positive correlation between gasoline lead and blood lead. For example, there is some evidence that cigarette smokers have higher blood lead levels than nonsmokers. It may be that over the period that the NHANES II data were collected the proportion of smokers in the sample declined, so that much of the downward trend in average blood lead levels should be attributed to reductions in smoking rather than reductions in gasoline lead.

To determine whether smoking is an intervening, or confounding, variable, we might construct separate diagrams like Figure 9.3 for smokers and nonsmokers. In this way, we could control for the possibility that changes in the proportion of smokers in the sample over time were responsible for changes in blood lead levels. If we fit lines with similar positive slopes to each of the samples, we would conclude that smoking behavior was not an intervening variable for the relationship between gasoline lead and blood lead.[26]

With unlimited quantities of data, we could always control for possible intervening variables in this way. Unfortunately, with a fixed sample size, we usually stretch our data too thin if we try to form subsets of data that hold all variables constant (e.g., everyone is a nonsmoker) except the dependent variable (blood lead levels) we are trying to explain and the independent variable (gasoline lead) we are considering as a possible explanation. For example, occupational exposure, alcohol consumption, region, and age are only a few of the other variables that might be causing the relationship in our data between gasoline lead and blood lead. If we selected from our sample only adult males living in small cities in the South who are moderate drinkers and nonsmokers and have no occupational exposure to lead, we might have too few data to reliably fit a line as in Figure 9.3. Even if we had adequate data, we would end up with estimates of the relationship between gasoline lead and blood lead from all of our subsets. (The number of subsets would equal the product of the number of categories making up our control variables.) We might then have difficulty combining these subset estimates into an overall estimate.[27]

---

[26] If the two lines coincided, we would conclude that smoking did not contribute to blood lead. If the lines were parallel but not identical, the difference between their intercepts with the vertical axis would represent the average effect of smoking on blood lead. If the lines were not parallel, we might suspect that smoking interacted with exposure to gasoline lead so that their effects are not additive. That is, smokers were either more or less susceptible to exposure to gasoline lead than nonsmokers.

[27] If the relationship truly varies across our subsets, then it would generally not make sense to make an overall estimate. As we will explain later, however, we never really observe the true relationship—it always contains some unknown error. Therefore, we may not be sure if it is reasonable to combine our subsample data. Because the variance of the error will be larger, the smaller the size of our subsamples, the more we divide our data, the more difficult it is to determine whether observed differences reflect true differences.

The Basic Linear Regression Model

Linear regression provides a manageable way to control statistically for the effects of several independent variables.[28] Its use requires us to assume that the effects of the various independent variables are additive. That is, the marginal effect on the dependent variable of a unit change in any one of the independent variables remains the same no matter what the values of the other independent variables are.[29] We can express a linear regression model in mathematical form:

$$y = b_0 + b_1 x_1 + b_2 x_2 + b_3 x_3 + \cdots + b_k x_k + e$$

where y is the dependent variable, x_1, x_2, . . ., x_k are the k independent variables, b_0, b_1, . . ., b_k are parameters (coefficients) to be estimated, and e is an error term that incorporates the cumulative effect on y of all the factors not explicitly included in the model. If we were to increase x_1 by one unit while holding the values of the other independent variables constant, y would change by an amount b_1. Similarly, each of the coefficients measures the marginal effect of a unit change in its variable on the dependent variable.

Imagine that we set the values of all the independent variables except x_1 equal to zero. We could then plot y against x_1 in a graph like Figure 9.3. The equation $y = b_0 + b_1 x_1$ would represent the line fit to our sample of observations. The slope of the line is b_1, the magnitude of the change in y that will result from a unit change in x_1, other things equal. The actual observations do not lie exactly on the line, however. Their vertical distances from the line will be equal to the random error, represented in our model by e, incorporated in each of the observations of y. If the values of e are small, our line will fit the data well in the sense that the actual observations will lie close to it.

How should we go about fitting the line? The most commonly used procedure is the method of *ordinary least squares* (OLS). When we have only one independent variable, so we can plot our data on a two-dimensional graph like Figure 9.3, the OLS procedure picks the line for which the sum of squared vertical deviations from the observed data is smallest. When we have more than one independent

---

[28] For clear introductions, see Eric A. Hanushek and John E. Jackson, *Statistical Methods for the Social Sciences* (New York: Academic Press, 1977); and Christopher H. Achen, *Intrepreting and Using Regression* (Beverly Hills, CA: Sage Publications, 1982).

[29] This assumption is not as restrictive as it might at first seem. We can create new variables that are functions of the original independent variables to capture nonlinearities. For example, if we thought smokers were likely to absorb environmental lead faster than nonsmokers, we might include in our linear regression model a new variable that is the product of the number of cigarettes smoked per day and the level of gasoline lead. This new variable, capturing the interaction of smoking and gasoline lead, would have an effect that would be additive with the other independent variables in the model, including the smoking and gasoline lead variables. The marginal effect of gasoline lead on blood lead would consist of the contribution from the gasoline lead variable and the contribution from the variable representing its interaction with smoking, which will change depending on the particular level of smoking.

variable, OLS determines the values of the coefficients (b_0, b_1, . . ., b_k) that minimize the sum of squared prediction errors.[30] As long as the number of observations in our sample exceeds the number of coefficients we are trying to estimate, and none of our independent variables can be expressed as a linear combination of the other independent variables, the commonly available regression software packages will enable us to use computers to find the OLS fitted coefficients.[31]

The estimates of coefficients that we obtain from OLS will generally have a number of very desirable properties. If the independent variables are all uncorrelated with the error term (e), then our coefficient estimators will be *unbiased*.[32] (*Note:* An *estimator* is the formula we use to calculate a particular estimate from our data.) To understand what it means for an estimator to be unbiased, we must keep in mind that our particular estimate depends upon the errors actually realized in our sample of data. If we were to select a new sample, we would realize different errors and hence different coefficient estimates. When an estimator is unbiased, we expect that the average of our estimates across different samples will be very close to the true coefficient value. For example, if gasoline lead had no true effect on blood lead, we would almost certainly estimate its coefficient to be positive or negative, rather than exactly zero. Repeating OLS on a large number of samples and averaging our

---

[30] The *prediction error* is the observed value of the dependent variable minus the value we would predict for the dependent variables based on our parameter estimates and the values of our independent variables. For the ith observation, the prediction error is given by

$$y_i - (\hat{b}_0 + \hat{b}_1 x_{1i} + \ldots + \hat{b}_k x_{ki})$$

The prediction error is also referred to as the *residual of the observation*. OLS selects the parameter estimates to minimize the sum of the squares of the residuals.

[31] When one independent variable can be written as a linear combination of the others, we have a case of *perfect multicollinearity*. A related and more common problem, which we can rarely do anything about, occurs when the independent variables in our sample are highly correlated. This condition, called *multicollinearity*, is not a problem with the specification of our model but with the data we have available to estimate it. If two variables are highly correlated, positively or negatively, OLS has difficulty identifying their independent effects on the dependent variable. As a result, the estimates of the parameters associated with these variables will not be very reliable. That is, they will have large variances, increasing the chances that we will fail to recognize, statistically speaking, their effects on the dependent variable. One way to deal with multicollinearity is to add new observations to our sample that lower the correlation. For example, if we had a high positive correlation between smoking and drinking in our sample, we should try to add observations on individuals who smoke but do not drink and who drink but do not smoke. Unfortunately, we often have no choice but to work with the data that are already available.

[32] Strictly speaking, we must also assume that our independent variables are fixed in the sense that we could construct a new sample with exactly the same observations on the independent variables. Of course, even if the independent variables are fixed, we would observe different values of the dependent variable because of the random error term. In addition, for complete generality, we must assume that the expected value of the error term is constant for all observations.

estimates of the coefficient of gasoline lead, however, would generally yield a result very close to zero.[33] Indeed, by adding more and more samples, we could get the average as close to zero as we wanted.

Unfortunately, we usually only have a single sample for estimating coefficients. How do we decide if an estimate deviates enough from zero so that we would conclude that the true value of the parameter is not zero? Making the fairly reasonable assumption that the error term for each observation can be treated as a draw from a Normal distribution with constant variance, the OLS estimators will be distributed according to the Student-*t* distribution.[34] That is, we can interpret the particular numerical estimate of a coefficient as a draw from a random variable distributed as a Student-*t* distribution centered around the true value of the coefficient. (The OLS estimator is the random variable; the actual estimate based on our data is a realization of that random variable.)

Knowing the distribution of the OLS estimator enables us to interpret the *statistical significance* of our coefficient estimate. We determine statistical significance by asking the following question: How likely is it that we would observe a coefficient estimate as large as we did if the true value of the coefficient were zero? We answer this question by first assuming that the true value of the coefficient is zero (the null hypothesis) so that the distribution of our estimator is centered around zero. We then standardize our distribution to have a variance of one by dividing our coefficient estimate by an estimate of its standard error (a by-product of the OLS procedure). The resulting number, called the *t*-ratio, can then be compared to critical values in tabulations of the standardized Student-*t* distribution found in the appendix of almost any statistics text. For example, we might decide that we will reject the null hypothesis that the true value of the coefficient is zero if there is less than a 5 percent probability of observing a *t*-ratio (in absolute value sense) as large as we did if the null hypothesis is true.

---

[33] Our average will not be close to zero if gasoline lead is correlated with a variable excluded from our model that does have an effect on blood lead. In this case, gasoline lead stands as a proxy for the excluded variable. Other things equal, the stronger the true effect of the excluded variable on blood lead and the higher the absolute value of the correlation between gasoline lead and the excluded variable, the greater will be the bias of the coefficient of gasoline lead. We might not worry that much about the bias if we knew that it would approach zero as we increase sample size. (If the variance of the estimator also approached zero as we increased sample size, we would say that the estimator is *consistent*.) Although OLS estimators are consistent for correctly specified models, correlation with an important excluded variable makes an estimator inconsistent.

[34] The *Central Limit Theorem* tells us that the distribution of the sum of independent random variables approaches the Normal distribution as the number in the sum becomes large. The theorem applies for almost any starting distributions—the existence of a finite variance is sufficient. If we think of the error term as the sum of all the many factors excluded from our model, and further, we believe that they are not systematically related to each other or the included variables, then the Central Limit Theorem suggests that the distribution of the error terms will be at least approximately Normal.

(The probability we choose puts an upward bound on the probability of falsely rejecting the null hypothesis.)[35] To carry out the test, we look in the standardized tabulations of the Student-t distribution for the critical value corresponding to 5 percent.[36] If the absolute value of our estimated t-ratio exceeds the critical value, then we reject the null hypothesis and say that our estimated coefficient is statistically significantly different from zero.

Fortunately, most regression software saves us the trouble of looking up critical values in tables by directly calculating the probability under the null hypothesis of observing a t-ratio as large as that estimated. To do a classical test of hypothesis on the coefficient, we simply see if the reported probability is less than the maximum probability of falsely rejecting the null hypothesis that we are willing to accept. If it is smaller, then we reject the null hypothesis.

Consider the regression results presented in Table 9.3. They are based on data from 6,534 whites in the NHANES II survey for whom blood lead measurements were made.[37] The dependent variable is the individual's blood lead level measured in µg/dl. The independent variables are listed under the heading "Effect." The independent variable of primary interest is the national consumption of gasoline lead (in hundreds of metric tons per day) in the month prior to the individual's blood lead measurement. The other independent variables were included in an effort to control statistically for other factors that might be expected to affect the individual's blood lead level. With the exception of the number of cigarettes smoked per day and the dietary factors (vitamin C, riboflavin, and so on), these other statistical controls are indicator, or "dummy," variables that take on the value one if some condition is met and zero otherwise. So, for example, if the individual is male, the variable "male" will equal one; if the individual is female, it will equal zero. The variables "vitamin C," "phosphorus," "riboflavin," and "vitamin A," which are included as proxy measures for

---

[35] Falsely rejecting the null hypothesis is referred to as Type I error. Failing to reject the null hypothesis when in fact the alternative hypothesis is true is referred to as Type II error. We usually set the probability of Type I error at some low level like 5 percent. Holding sample size constant, the lower we set the probability of Type I error, the greater the probability of Type II error.

[36] The Student-t distribution is tabulated by degrees of freedom. In the basic OLS framework, the degrees of freedom is the total number of observations minus the number of coefficients being estimated. As the degrees of freedom becomes larger, the Student-t distribution looks more like a standardized Normal distribution.

You should also note the difference between a one-tailed and two-tailed test. Because the standardized Student-t is a symmetric distribution centered on zero, a 5 percent test usually involves setting critical values so that 2.5 percent of area lies under each of the tails (positive and negative). A one-tailed test, appropriate when the null hypothesis is that the true coefficient value is zero or less than zero, puts the entire 5 percent in the positive tail.

[37] The analysts estimated similar models for blacks and for blacks and whites together. Their estimates of the coefficient for gasoline lead never deviated by more than 10 percent across the different samples. To conserve space, they reported in detail only their regression results for whites. They chose whites because it was the largest subgroup and because it preempted the assertion that the relationship between blood lead and gasoline lead was due to changes in the racial composition of the sample over time.

Table 9.3   Basic Regression Model for Estimating the Effects of Gasoline Lead on Blood Lead[a]

Effect	Coefficient	Standard Error	P-value
Intercept	6.15		
Gasoline	2.14	.142	0.0000
Low income	0.79	.243	0.0025
Moderate income	0.32	.184	0.0897
Child (under 8)	3.47	.354	0.0000
Number of cigarettes	0.08	.012	0.0000
Occupationally exposed	1.74	.251	0.0000
Vitamin C	−0.04	.000	0.0010
Teenager	−0.30	.224	0.1841
Male	0.50	.436	0.2538
Male teenager	1.67	.510	0.0026
Male adult	3.40	.510	0.0000
Small city	−0.91	.292	0.0039
Rural	−1.29	.316	0.0003
Phosphorus	−0.001	.000	0.0009
Drinker	0.67	.173	0.0007
Heavy drinker	1.53	.316	0.0000
Northeast	−1.09	.332	0.0028
South	−1.44	.374	0.0005
Midwest	−1.35	.500	0.0115
Educational level	−0.60	.140	0.0000
Riboflavin	0.188	.071	0.0186
Vitamin A	0.018	.008	0.0355

[a]*Dependent variable:* Blood lead (μg/dl) of whites in NHANES II Survey.

Source: Joel Schwartz et al., *Costs and Benefits of Reducing Lead in Gasoline: Final Regulatory Impact Analysis* (Washington, DC: EPA, 1985), p. III-15. The original document reported incorrect standard errors. The standard errors reported here were provided by Joel Schwartz.

dietary intake of lead, each measure dietary intake in milligrams. Otherwise, the other variables are intended to capture demographic, income, occupational exposure, drinking habit, and locational effects. The reported R^2 indicates that, taken together, the independent variables explain about 33 percent of the total variation in blood lead levels.[38]

The estimated coefficient for gasoline lead is 2.14 μg/dl of blood per 100 metric tons per day of national gasoline lead consumption. Dividing the coefficient estimate by its estimated standard error of 0.192 yields a *t*-ratio of about 11. The probability of observing a *t*-ratio this large or larger if the true value of the

[38] R^2 is a measure of the *goodness of fit* of the model to the particular sample of data. It is the square of the correlation between the values of the dependent variable predicted by the model and the values actually observed. An R^2 of one would mean that the model perfectly predicted the independent variable for the sample; an R^2 of zero would mean that the model made no contribution to prediction.

coefficient were actually zero is less than one chance in 10,000 (the 0.0000 entry in Table 9.3 under "*P*-value"). We would thus reject the null hypothesis in favor of the alternative hypothesis that gasoline lead does contribute to blood lead. In other words, we would say that gasoline lead has a *statistically significant effect* on blood lead.

After finding a statistically significant effect, the next question to ask is whether the size of the coefficient is *substantively significant*. That is, does the variable in question have an effect that is worth considering?[39] One approach to answering this question is to multiply the estimated coefficient by the plausible change in the independent variable that might occur. For example, by the end of the NHANES II survey, gasoline lead was being consumed at a rate of about 250 metric tons per day nationally. A strict policy might reduce the level to, say, 25 metric tons per day. Using the estimated coefficient of gasoline lead, we would expect a reduction of this magnitude to reduce blood lead levels on average by about 4.8 µg/dl (the reduction of 225 metric tons per day times the estimated coefficient of 2.14 µg/dl per 100 metric tons per day).

To get a better sense of whether a 4.8 µg/dl reduction is substantively important, we can look at the blood lead levels for representative groups at the 250 and 25 metric ton levels. For example, at the 250 metric ton level a nonsmoking (number of cigarettes equals zero), moderate drinking (drinker equals one; heavy drinker equals zero), nonoccupationally exposed (occupationally exposed equals zero), adult female (child, teenager, male, male teenager, and male adult equal zero), living in a large Northeastern city (Northeast equals one; small city, rural, South, and Midwest equal zero), with moderate income, a college degree, and a high-nutrition diet (low income equals zero; moderate income, educational level, vitamin C, phosphorus, riboflavin, and vitamin A equal one) would be expected to have a blood lead level of 10.6 µg/dl. We would expect the same person to have a blood lead level of only 5.8 µg/dl if the gasoline lead level were cut to 25 metric tons per day—a reduction of about 45 percent. Thus, the effect of gasoline lead on blood lead appears substantively as well as statistically significant.

The study team was especially interested in estimating the contribution of gasoline lead to blood lead in children. As a first cut, they developed a logistic regression model[40] for predicting the probability that a child between the ages of six months and eight years will have blood levels in excess of 30 µg/dl, the definition of lead toxicity used by the Centers for Disease Control at the time. *Logistic regression*, which assumes a nonlinear relationship between the dependent and the

---

[39] The standard errors of the coefficient estimates decrease as sample size increases. Thus, very large samples may yield large *t*-ratios even when the estimated coefficient (and its true value) is small. We refer to the power of a statistical test as 1 minus the probability of failing to reject the null hypothesis in favor of the alternative hypothesis. Other things equal, larger sample sizes have greater power, increasing the chances that we will reject the null hypothesis in favor of alternatives very close to zero.

[40] For an introduction to logistic regression, see Hanushek and Jackson, *Statistical Methods*, pp. 179–216.

independent variables,[41] is usually more appropriate than linear regression when the dependent variable is dichotomous (Y equals one if the condition holds, Y equals zero if it does not).[42] The study team found a strong relationship in the NHANES II data between gasoline lead and the probability that a child has a toxic level of blood lead. In fact, they estimated that the elimination of gasoline lead would have reduced the number of cases of lead toxicity in the sample by 80 percent for children under eight years of age. The study team used logistic regression and other probability models to estimate how reductions in gasoline lead would change the number of children having various blood lead levels. These estimates were essential for their subsequent valuation of the effects of gasoline lead reductions on the health of children.

Reconsidering Causality

Finding that an independent variable in a regression model has a statistically significant coefficient does not by itself establish a causal relationship. That is, it does not guarantee that changes in the independent variable cause changes in the dependent variable. Even if the independent variable has no direct effect on the dependent variable, some other variable, not included in the model, may be correlated with both so as to produce an apparent relationship in the data sample (remember the apparent relationship between birth rates and the density of stork nests). Should the strong relationship between gasoline lead and blood lead be interpreted as causal?

The study team considered this question in detail. Although its demonstration was not legally necessary, they believed that adoption of the proposed rule would be more likely if a strong case for causality could be made. Their approach was to apply the criteria commonly used by epidemiologists to determine the likelihood of causality. Not all of the criteria are directly applicable outside of the health area. Nonetheless, the way the study team applied the criteria illustrates the sort of questioning that is valuable in empirical research. Therefore, we briefly review the six criteria that they considered.

Is the Model Biologically Plausible?

The study team noted that lead can be absorbed through the lung and gut. They pointed out that gasoline lead, the major source of environmental lead, is emitted predominantly as respirable particulates in

---

[41] The logistic regression model is written as

$$P(Y) = \frac{e^z}{(1 = e^z)}$$

where $P(Y)$ is the probability that condition Y holds, e is the natural base, and $Z = b_0 + b_1 x_1 + \ldots + b_k x_k$ is the weighted sum of the independent variables $x_1, x_2, \ldots, x_k$. The coefficients, $b_0, b_1, \ldots, b_k$, are selected to maximize the probability of observing the data in the sample. Note that the marginal contribution of x_i to the value of the dependent variable is not simply b_i, as would be the case in a linear regression model. Rather, it is $b_i[1 - P(Y)]P(Y)$, which has its greatest absolute value when $P(Y) = 0.5$.

[42] The logistic regression model, unlike the linear regression model, always predicts probabilities that lie between zero and one (as they should).

automobile exhaust. These particulates can be absorbed directly through the lungs. They also contaminate dust that can be inhaled through the lungs and absorbed through the gut. Therefore, they argued, it is biologically plausible that gasoline lead contributes to blood lead.

Biological plausibility is the epidemiological statement of a more general criterion: Is the model theoretically plausible? Prior to looking through data for empirical relationships, you should specify a model (your beliefs about how variables are related). If you find that your data are consistent with your model, then you can be more confident that the relationships you estimate are not simply due to chance.[43]

Is there Experimental Evidence to Support the Findings?   The study team found reports of several investigations specifically designed to measure the contribution of gasoline lead to blood lead. One was an experiment conducted in Turin, Italy, by researchers who monitored changes in the isotopic composition of blood lead as the isotopic composition of gasoline lead varied.[44] They found that at least 25 percent of the lead in the blood of Turin residents originated in gasoline. Thus, the experiment not only confirmed the biological plausibility of the contribution of gasoline lead to blood lead, but also suggested an effect on the order of magnitude of that estimated by the study team.

Being able to find such strong and directly relevant experimental support is quite rare in policy research, much of which deals with the behavioral responses of people. Controlled experiments in the social sciences are rare, not only because they are costly and difficult to implement, but also because they often involve tricky ethical issues concerning the assignment of people to "treatment" and "control" groups. Nevertheless, there have been a number of policy experiments in the United States over the last twenty years.[45] It is unlikely, however, that any of these experiments will be directly applicable to your policy problem. Therefore, you must typically broaden your search for confirmation beyond experiments to other empirical research.

----

[43] Imagine that you regress a variable on twenty other variables. Assume that none of the twenty independent variables has an effect on the dependent variable. (The coefficients in the true model are all zero.) Nevertheless, if you use a statistical test that limits the probability of falsely rejecting the null hypothesis to 5 percent, then you would still have a 0.64 probability $[1 - (.95)^{20}]$ of rejecting at least one null hypothesis. In other words, if you look through enough data, you are bound to find some statistically significant relationships, even when no true relationships exist. By forcing yourself to specify theoretical relationships before you look at the data, you reduce the chances that you will be fooled by the idiosyncrasy of your particular data sample. For a brief review of these issues, see David L. Weimer, "Collective Delusion in the Social Sciences: Publishing Incentives for Empirical Abuse," *Policy Studies Review* 5, no. 4 (May 1986): 705–8.

[44] S. Fachetti and F. Geiss, *Isotopic Lead Experiment Status Report*, Publication No. EUR8352ZEN (Luxembourg: Commission of the European Communities, 1982).

[45] For a review of the major policy experiments conducted in the United States, see David H. Greenberg and Philip K. Robins, "The Changing Role of Social Experiments in Policy Analysis," *Journal of Policy Analysis and Management* 5, no. 2 (Winter 1986): 340–62.

Do Other Studies Using Different Data Replicate the Results?   The study team reviewed several studies that also found relationships between gasoline lead and blood lead. These studies were based on data collected in conjunction with community-wide lead-screening programs funded by the Centers for Disease Control during the 1970s[46] and on data collected from the umbilical cord blood of over 11,000 babies born in Boston between April 1979 and April 1981.[47] These studies reported statistically significant relationships between gasoline lead and blood lead, and thus supported the study team's analysis based on the NHANES II data.

Does Cause Precede Effect?   The study team used information about the half-life of lead in blood to make predictions about the strengths of relationships between lagged levels of gasoline lead and blood lead that would be expected if gasoline lead contributes to blood lead. Lead has a half-life of about thirty days in blood. Noting that the average NHANES II blood test was done at mid-month, they predicted that the previous month's gasoline lead (which on average represents emissions occurring between fifteen and forty-five days before the test) should have a stronger impact on blood lead than that of either the current month (average exposure of zero to fifteen days) or the month occurring two months prior (average exposure of forty-five to seventy-five days). They tested their predictions by regressing blood lead levels on current, one-month lagged, and two-month lagged gasoline lead levels. As predicted, one-month lagged gasoline lead was the most significant of the three. Also, consistent with the thirty-day half-life, two-month lagged gasoline lead had a coefficient approximately one-half that of one-month lagged gasoline lead. Thus, cause did appear to precede effect in the expected way.

Does a Stable Dose–Response Relationship Exist?   The regression model used by the study team assumed a linear relationship between gasoline lead and blood lead. Did this relationship remain stable as the level of gasoline lead changed? To answer this question, the study team took advantage of the fact that, on average, gasoline lead levels were about 50 percent lower in the second half of the NHANES II survey than in the first half. If the relationship between gasoline lead and blood lead is stable and linear, then reestimating the regression model using only data from the second half of the survey should yield a coefficient for gasoline lead comparable with that for the entire sample. They found that the coefficients were indeed essentially the same. In addition, estimation of regression models that directly allowed for the possibility of nonlinear effects supported the initial findings of a linear relationship between gasoline lead and blood lead.

---

[46] Irwin H. Billick et al., *Predictions of Pediatric Blood Lead Levels from Gasoline Consumption* (Washington, DC: U.S. Department of Housing and Urban Development, 1982).

[47] Michael Rabinowitz and Herbert L. Needleman, "Petrol Lead Sales and Umbilical Cord Blood Lead Levels in Boston, Massachusetts," *Lancet*, January 1/8, 1983, p. 63.

Is it Likely That Factors Not Included in the Analysis Could Account for the Observed Relationship? The study team considered several factors that might confound the apparent relationship between gasoline lead and blood lead: dietary lead intake, exposure to lead paint, seasonality, and sampling patterns.

The basic regression model included nutrient and demographic variables as proxy measures for the intake of lead in the diet. Yet these variables may not adequately control for a possible downward trend in dietary lead that could be causing the estimated relationship between gasoline lead and blood lead. Market basket studies conducted by the Food and Drug Administration over the survey period, however, showed no downward trend in dietary lead intake. Also, lead intake from drinking water is largely a function of acidity, which did not change systematically over the survey period. Evidence did suggest that changes in solder reduced the content of lead in canned foods over the period. But the study team was able to rule out the lead content in canned foods as a confounding factor when they added the lead content in solder as an independent variable, reestimated the basic regression model, and found that the coefficient of gasoline lead remained essentially unchanged.

The study team recognized changing exposure to lead paint as another potential confounding factor. They dismissed the possibility on three grounds.

First, paint lead is a major source in blood lead for children (who eat paint chips) but not for adults. If declining exposure to lead paint were responsible for the estimated relationship between gasoline lead and blood lead, we would expect the reduction in blood lead to be much greater for children than for adults. In fact, the average reduction over the survey period for adults was only slightly smaller than that for children (37% versus 42%).

Second, the ingestion of paint lead usually results in large increases in blood lead levels. If reduced exposure to paint lead were responsible for declining blood lead levels, then we would expect to observe the improvement primarily in terms of a reduction in the number of people with very high blood lead levels. In fact, blood lead levels declined over the survey period even for groups with low initial levels.[48]

Third, declining exposure to paint lead should be a more important factor in central cities than in suburbs because the latter tend to have newer housing stocks with lower frequencies of peeling lead paint. Yet the gasoline lead coefficient was essentially the same for separate estimations based on central city and suburban subsamples.

Blood lead levels in the United States are on average higher in the summer than in the winter. To rule out the possibility that seasonal variation confounds the relationship between gasoline lead and blood lead, the study team reestimated the basic model with indicator variables included to allow for the possibility of independent seasonal effects. The coefficients of the seasonal variables were not

---

[48] The study team also used data from the lead-screening program in Chicago to estimate the probability of toxicity as a function of gasoline lead for children exposed and not exposed to lead paint. They found that gasoline lead had statistically significant positive coefficients for both groups.

statistically significant when gasoline lead was kept in the model. Thus, it appeared that changes in gasoline lead could adequately explain seasonal as well as long-term changes in blood lead levels.

As already mentioned, the study team estimated the basic model on a variety of demographic subsamples and found no more than a 10 percent difference across any two estimates of the gasoline lead coefficient. They were also concerned, however, that changes in NHANES II sampling locations over the survey period might have confounded the estimation of the gasoline lead coefficient. Therefore, they reestimated the basic model with indicator variables for forty-nine locations and found that the gasoline lead coefficient changed by only about 5 percent. Further, they found that, even when including variables to allow for different gasoline lead coefficients across locations, the coefficient representing the nationwide effect of gasoline lead was statistically and substantively significant. Together, these tests led the study team to dismiss the possibility of serious sampling bias.

The Weight of the Evidence

The study team produced a very strong case in support of an important causal relationship between gasoline lead and blood lead. In many ways their efforts were exemplary. They drew relevant evidence from a wide variety of sources to supplement their primary data analysis. They gave serious attention to possible confounding factors, considering both internal tests (such as subsample analyses and model respecifications) and external evidence to see if they could be ruled out. As a consequence, opponents of the proposed policy were left with few openings for attacking its empirical underpinnings.

Finalizing the Rule

The primary task facing the analytical team after publication of the proposed rule was to respond to comments made by interested parties. Team members participated in public hearings held in August and spent much of the fall of 1984 responding to comments placed in the public docket, which closed on October 1. During this process, they became more confident that the proposed rule would produce the large net benefits they predicated. At the same time, they discovered another benefit category—reductions in adult blood pressure levels—that could potentially swamp their earlier estimates of benefits.

In 1983 Schwartz chanced upon a research article reporting a correlation between blood lead and hypertension.[49] He began work with researchers at the Centers for Disease Control and the University of Michigan to determine whether a relationship existed between blood lead and blood pressure levels. By the summer of 1984, their analysis of the NHANES II data suggested a strong link.[50] Because

---

[49] V. Batuman, E. Landy, J. K. Maesaka, and R. P. Wedeen, "Contribution of Lead to Hypertension with Renal Impairment," *New England Journal of Medicine* 309 (1983): 17–21.

[50] The results of their research were later published in J. L. Pirkle, J. Schwartz, J. R. Landes, and W. R. Harlan, "The Relationship between Blood Lead Levels and Blood Pressure and Its Cardiovascular Risk Implications," *American Journal of Epidemiology* 121, no. 2 (1985): 246–58.

high blood pressure contributes to hypertension, myocardial infarctions, and strokes, the potential benefits from blood lead reductions were enormous. Although the final rule was ultimately issued without reference to quantitative estimates of the benefits of lower adult blood lead levels, the team provided estimates in the supporting documents.

The one remaining issue was the compliance schedule. The costs of various lead standards were estimated, using a model of the U.S. refining sector originally developed for the Department of Energy. The model represents the various types of refining capabilities that are available to convert crude oils to final petroleum products. It employs an optimization procedure for finding the allocations of crude oils and intermediate petroleum products among refining units that maximizes social surplus, the sum of consumer and producer surpluses. This allocation corresponds to that which would result from a perfectly competitive market operating without constraints on the utilization of available units. Cost was estimated by looking at the decline in social surplus resulting when the lead constraint was tightened—for instance, from 1.1 gplg to 0.1 gplg. The manufacturers of lead additives challenged these results on the grounds that the model assumed more flexibility in capacity utilization across different refineries than was realistic.

The analytical team held meetings with staffers from other EPA offices to consider alternative compliance schedules. Although a tentative decision was reached to set an interim standard of 0.5 gplg, to be effective July 1, 1985, and a final standard of 0.1 gplg, to be effective January 1, 1986, several staffers feared that some refiners would be unable to comply with their existing equipment. If these fears were realized, the economic costs of the new rule would be higher than estimated and perhaps raise political problems.

A consultant to the project, William Johnson of Sobotka and Company, suggested a solution. If the physical distribution of equipment among refineries interfered with the flexibility in petroleum transfers assumed in the model, he reasoned, perhaps a secondary market in lead rights could be created to facilitate trading to get around specific bottlenecks. Taking the total permitted lead content from July 1, 1985 to January 1, 1988 as a constraint, he found that the key was to create an incentive for refiners who could make the least costly reductions in lead additives below the interim 0.5 gplg standard to do so. Their additional reductions could then be used to offset excess lead in gasoline produced by refiners who could not easily meet the basic standards with the equipment they had in place. Because current reductions below the standard create a right to produce above the standard some time in the future, the trading process was called "banking of lead rights." Refiners would be free to buy and sell lead rights at prices that were mutually beneficial. As a result, the aggregate cost of meeting the new standard would be reduced.

Representatives from the various EPA offices involved with the lead rule agreed that banking seemed to be a good way to deal with concerns about the compliance schedule. Because it had not been discussed in the proposed rule published in August, banking could not be part of the final rule. Nevertheless, by moving quickly to propose banking in a supplemental notice, it would be available shortly after the new standard became final.[51]

The remaining task for the team was to prepare the *Final Regulatory Impact Analysis*, which would be published in support of the final rule.[52] The resulting document began by discussing the misfueling and health problems associated with lead additives along with alternatives (public education and stepped-up local enforcement to deal specifically with misfueling, pollution charges to deal generally with lead as a negative externality, and other regulatory standards) to the final rule. It then detailed the methods used to estimate the costs of tighter lead standards, the link between gasoline lead and blood lead, the health benefits of reducing the exposure of children and adults to lead, the benefits of reducing pollutants other than lead, and the benefits from reduced vehicle maintenance costs and increased fuel economy.

The present value of the net benefits of the final rule was presented with various assumptions about misfueling (the use of leaded gasoline in vehicles with catalytic converters). The lower level of permitted lead would reduce the price differential between leaded and unleaded gasoline, thereby reducing the economic incentive for misfueling. It was not possible to predict with confidence, however, how much misfueling would actually decline. Therefore, the reasonable approach was to consider net benefits over the range of possibilities. Table 9.4 presents the

Table 9.4 Present Values of Costs and Benefits of Final Rule, 1985–92
          (Millions of 1983 Dollars)

	No Misfueling	Full Misfueling	Partial Misfueling
Monetized benefits			
Children's health effects	2,582	2,506	2,546
Adult blood pressure	27,936	26,743	27,462
Conventional pollutants	1,525	0	1,114
Maintenance	4,331	3,634	4,077
Fuel economy	856	643	788
Total monetized benefits	37,231	33,526	35,987
Total refining costs	2,637	2,678	2,619
Net benefits	34,594	30,847	33,368
Net benefits excluding blood pressure	6,658	4,105	5,906

Source: Joel Schwartz et al., *Costs and Benefits of Reducing Lead in Gasoline* (Washington, DC: EPA, 1985), Table VIII-8, p. VIII-26.

---

[51] *Fed. Reg.* 718 (January 4, 1985); and 50 *Fed. Reg.* 13116 (April 2, 1985).

[52] Joel Schwartz, Hugh Pitcher, Ronnie Levin, Bart Ostro, and Albert L. Nichols, *Costs and Benefits of Reducing Lead in Gasoline: Final Regulatory Impact Analysis*, Publication No. EPA-230–05–85–006 (Washington, DC: Office of Policy Analysis, EPA, February, 1985). By the time the final report was prepared, Jane Leggett left the project team. In the meantime, Albert Nichols, a Harvard University professor who was visiting the EPA as the acting director of the Economic Analysis Division, began working closely with the team to produce the final document.

results of this sensitivity analysis. Note that net benefits were given both including and excluding the adult blood pressure benefits. Although the blood pressure benefits appeared huge, they were the last of the benefit measures considered and hence had the least-developed supporting evidence. Nevertheless, even assuming that the standard would produce no reduction in misfueling and no health benefits for adults, the present value of benefits appeared to be more than double the present value of costs. Indeed, it appeared that maintenance benefits alone would more than cover higher refining costs.

The *Final Regulatory Impact Analysis* was released in February 1985. On March 7, 1985, the final rule was published in the *Federal Register*.[53] The 0.1 gplg standard would take effect on January 1, 1986, almost three years after work on the supporting analysis began.

Conclusion

We have described a case where statistical analysis made an important contribution to changing policy. Is this case typical? Yes and No. You should not expect that such a confluence of skill, time, data, resources, and interest will often arise to produce such definitive empirical findings. At the same time, you should expect to encounter empirical questions that at least can be approached, if not confidently answered, with the sort of statistical methods used by the EPA analysts. Consider a few prominent examples from recent years: Does the death penalty deter homicide?[54] Do higher minimum legal drinking ages and the 55-mile-per-hour speed limit reduce traffic fatalities?[55] Do smaller class sizes improve student performance?[56] Although widely accepted answers to these empirical questions would not necessarily be decisive in resolving policy debates, they would at least move the debates beyond disputes over predictions to explicit considerations of values. Such highly controversial issues aside, you are likely to find that making empirical inferences and critically consuming those of others often contribute in important ways to the quality of your policy analyses.

---

[53] 50 *Fed. Reg.* 9386 (March 7, 1985).

[54] See Isaac Ehrlich, "The Deterrent Effect of Capital Punishment: A Question of Life and Death," *American Economic Review* 65, no. 3 (June 1975): 397–417; and Alfred Blumstein, Jacqueline Cohen, and Daniel Nagin, eds, *Deterrence and Incapacitation: Estimating the Effects of Criminal Sanctions on Crime Rates* (Washington, DC: National Academy of Sciences, 1978).

[55] See Charles A. Lave, "Speeding, Coordination, and the 55 MPH Limit," *American Economic Review* 75, no. 5 (December 1985): 1159–64; and Peter Asch and David T. Levy, "Does the Minimum Drinking Age Affect Traffic Fatalities?" *Journal of Policy Analysis and Management* 6, no. 2 (Winter 1987): 180–92.

[56] See Eric A. Hanushek, "Throwing Money at Schools," *Journal of Policy Analysis and Management* 1, no. 1 (Fall 1981): 19–41.

Appendix 1

The Policy Issue Paper

The policy issue paper is a report that presents an analysis of a policy issue. The kinds of questions addressed in policy issue are these: What actual or potential courses of action are the objects of disagreement among policy makers and other stakeholders? In what different ways may the problem be defined? What is the scope and severity of the problem? If nothing is done, is the problem likely to get worse in future months or years? What goals and objectives should be pursued to solve the problem? How can the degree of success in achieving objectives be measured? What activities are now under way to resolve the problem? What new policy alternatives should be considered? Which are preferable and why?

In answering these questions, the analyst needs to acquire knowledge and skills in developing written materials and communicating them in policy presentations and other briefings. Only recently have such knowledge and skills been included in instructional programs in public policy analysis. Policy analysis is an "applied" rather than "basic" policy discipline.[1] Analysts must acquire much of the knowledge and many of the skills provided in basic policy disciplines. But the mission of policy analysis is mainly "applied" (see the following table and Chapter 9, Table 9.1).

---

[1] The terms "basic" and "applied" are used for convenience only. It is widely acknowledged that these two orientations toward science overlap in practice. Indeed, there is much evidence to support the conclusion that many of the most important theoretical, methodological, and substantive advances in the "basic" social sciences originated in "applied" work on practical problems and conflicts. See, especially, Karl W. Deutsch, Andrea S. Markovits, and John Platt, *Advances in the Social Sciences, 1900–1980: What, Who, Where, How?* (Lanham, MD: University Press of America and Abt Books, 1986).

Two Kinds of Policy Disciplines

Characteristic	Basic	Applied
Origin of problems	• University colleagues	• Governmental clients and citizens
Typical methods	• Quantitative modeling	• Development of sound arguments
Type of research	• Original data collection	• Synthesis and evaluation of existing data
Primary aim	• Improve theory	• Improve practice
Communications media	• Article or book	• Policy memo or issue paper
Source of incentives	• University departments	• Government departments and citizen groups

FOCUS AND FORMS OF THE POLICY ISSUE PAPER

The policy issue paper may focus on problems at one or more levels of government. Global warming and air pollution, for example, are international, national, and local in scope. The issue paper may take a number of specific forms, depending on the audience and the particular issue at hand. Thus, issue papers may be presented in the form of "staff reports," "briefing papers," "options papers," or so-called "white papers." An illustrative list of issues that may serve as the focus of a policy issue paper is presented below.

- Which of several alternative contracts should be accepted by a union bargaining team?
- Should the mayor increase expenditures on road maintenance?
- Should the city manager install a computerized management information system?
- Which public transportation plan should the mayor submit for federal funding?
- Should a state agency establish a special office to recruit minorities and women for civil service positions?
- Should a citizens' group support environmental protection legislation now before Congress?
- Should the governor veto a tax bill passed by the state legislature?
- Should an agency director support a plan for flexible working hours (flextime)?
- Should a legislator support a bill restricting the sale of hand guns?
- Should the president withhold foreign aid from countries that violate human rights?
- Should the United Nations General Assembly condemn the violation of human rights in a particular country?
- Should the United States withdraw from Iraq?

ELEMENTS OF THE POLICY ISSUE PAPER

A policy issue paper should be as complete as time and available information permit. An issue paper should "explore the problem at a depth sufficient to give the reader a good idea of its dimensions and the possible scope of the solution, so that it might be possible for a decision maker to conclude either to do nothing further or to commission a definitive study looking toward some action recommendation."[2] In this author's experience, most issue papers deal primarily with the formulation of a problem and possible solutions. Only rarely does the issue paper reach definitive conclusions or recommendations. Although an issue paper may contain recommendations and outline plans for monitoring and evaluating policy outcomes, it is essentially the first phase of an in-depth policy analysis that may be undertaken at a later time.

In preparing an issue paper, the analyst should be reasonably sure that all major questions have been addressed. Although issue papers will vary with the nature of the problem being investigated, most issue papers contain a number of standard elements.[3] These elements, already presented in Figure 9.2, have been organized around the framework for policy analysis presented in the text.

Element	Method
Letter of Transmittal	
Executive Summary	
I. Background of the problem	
A. Describe client's inquiry	Monitoring
B. Overview problem situation	
C. Describe prior efforts to solve problem	
II. Significance of the problem	
A. Evaluate past policy performance	Evaluation
B. Assess the scope and severity of problem	
D. Determine the need for analysis	
III. Problem statement	
A. Diagnose problem	Problem structuring
B. Describe major stakeholders	
C. Define goals and objectives	
IV. Analysis of alternatives	
A. Describe alternatives	Forecasting
B. Forecast consequences of alternatives	
C. Describe any spillovers and externalities	
D. Assess constraints and political feasibility	
IV. Conclusions and recommendations	
A. Select criteria or decision rules	Recommendation
B. State conclusions and recommendations	
C. Describe preferred alternative(s)	
D. Outline implementation strategy	
E. Summarize plan for monitoring and evaluation	
F. List limitations and unanticipated consequences	
References	
Appendices	

[2] Edgar S. Quade, *Analysis for Public Decisions* (New York: American Elsevier Publishing, 1975), p. 69.

[3] Compare Quade, *Analysis for Public Decisions*, pp. 68–82; and Harry Hatry and others, *Program Analysis for State and Local Governments* (Washington, DC: The Urban Institute, 1976), Appendix B, pp. 139–43.

Observe that each element of the issue paper requires different policy-analytic methods to produce and transform information. A policy issue paper, however, has one major characteristic not shared by integrated policy analysis. The issue paper is essentially a prospective (*ex ante*) investigation that begins with limited information about past policy outcomes and performance and ends with as much information as possible about the nature of policy problems, expected policy outcomes, and preferred policies.

A CHECKLIST

This checklist is designed as a practical guide to the preparation and self-evaluation of policy issue papers. Items in the checklist are based on guidelines for preparing policy issue papers presented earlier in this appendix. The checklist operationalizes these guidelines, provides brief examples, and contains a rating scale that may be used to evaluate the adequacy of specific elements of the paper. Remember, however, that some elements in the checklist may not be appropriate for each and every paper. The checklist should therefore be used in a flexible and creative manner.

Rating Scale
1 = totally adequate
2 = adequate
3 = inadequate
4 = totally inadequate
0 = not applicable

Element of Policy Issue Paper	Example/Note	Rating
Letter of transmittal		
1. Are all relevant stakeholders expected to act on the paper addressed?	A paper on local law enforcement might be addressed to the chief of police, the mayor, and the director of public safety.	[ ]
2. Does the letter describe all attached materials?	"Enclosed please find a policy issue paper on options to increase the productivity of municipal employees. An executive summary of this paper is also included, along with relevant statistical materials appended to the text."	[ ]
3. Does the letter specify who is expected to take action, how, and when?	"We look forward to your reply well in advance of the meeting scheduled for June 15."	[ ]
Executive summary		
4. Are all elements of the issue paper described in the executive summary?	Every element of the issue paper (Source and Background of the Problem, the Policy Problem, and so on) should be included in the summary.	[ ]
5. Is the summary clear, concise, and specific?	"This paper reviews problems of air pollution over the past ten years, showing that the level of industrial pollutants has increased by more than 200 percent in the 1968–1978 period."	[ ]
6. Is the summary understandable to all who will read it?	The point here is to avoid unnecessary jargon, long sentences, and complex arguments as much as possible.	[ ]
7. Are recommendations appropriately highlighted in the summary?	"In conclusion, we recommend that funds in the range of $15,000–20,000 be allocated to conduct an assessment of recreational needs in the Oakland area."	[ ]

(*continued*)

Element of Policy Issue Paper	Example/Note	Rating
I. Background of the problem		
8. Are all dimensions of the problem situation described?	Increasing crime rates may be analyzed in conjunction with data on unemployment, police recruitment, citizen surveys, migration, and so on.	[ ]
9. Have outcomes of prior efforts to resolve problems in the area been described?	"Similar training programs have been implemented in New York, Florida, and California, at a cost of $4,000–5,000 per trainee."	[ ]
10. Is there a clear assessment of past policy performance?	"Training programs in New York and California resulted in a 1 percent reduction in hard-core unemployment and were judged to be highly successful."	[ ]
II. Scope and severity of problem		
11. Is the scope and severity of the problem situation clearly described?	"Problems of industrial pollution are more severe today than at any time in our history and affect the physical well-being of 60 percent of the population. The resolution of these problems is an urgent matter that calls for timely and decisive action."	[ ]
III. Problem statement		
12. Is the problem clearly stated?	"The problem addressed in this paper is how best to satisfy the need for increased fiscal accountability among local governments in the region."	[ ]
13. Is the issue clearly stated?	"The issue addressed in this paper is whether the state's Department of Community Affairs should increase its technical assistance to local governments in the area of financial management."	[ ]
14. Is the approach to analysis clearly specified?	"In addressing this issue we have employed cost-effectiveness analysis as a way to determine the levels of investment necessary to train 10,000 local officials in cash management techniques."	[ ]
15. Are all major stakeholders identified and prioritized?	The task here is to identify all persons and groups who significantly affect and are significantly affected by the formulation and implementation of policies. Stakeholders who are only marginally influential (or affected) may be dropped from the analysis, but this requires prioritization.	[ ]
16. Are goals and objectives clearly specified?	"The goal of this policy is to improve the physical security of the community. The objective is to reduce reported crimes by 10 percent or more in the 1979–80 period."	[ ]
17. Are measures of effectiveness clearly specified?	Here there are many choices: benefit-cost ratios, net benefits, distributional benefits, and so on.	[ ]
18. Are all sets of potential solutions outlined?	"Any effort to reduce crime in the area should take into account the effectiveness of law enforcement programs, the unemployment rate, population density, and urbanization."	[ ]
IV. Policy alternatives		
19. Are alternative solutions specified?	"Three policy alternatives are analyzed in the course of this paper: educational programs to alert citizens to the role they can play in crime control; policy training programs; and advanced crime control technology."	[ ]

(*continued*)

(continued)

Element of Policy Issue Paper	Example/Note	Rating
20. Are alternatives systematically compared in terms of their probable costs and effectiveness?	"Program A has a benefit-cost ratio which is twice that of program B."	[ ]
21. Are relevant spillovers and externalities included in the analysis of alternatives?	"The early childhood educational program is not only cost-effective. It will also produce spill overs in the form of increased participation of family members in the school. At the same time there are important externalities in the form of increased costs for transportation to and from school."	[ ]
22. Are all relevant constraints taken into account?	These may be financial (e.g., fixed costs), legal (e.g., laws proscribing certain actions), or political (e.g., lack of political support).	[ ]
23. Have alternatives been systematically compared in terms of political feasibility?	The point here is to make informed judgments about the probable support, relevance, and influence of key stakeholders in gaining acceptance for and implementing each alternative.	[ ]
V. Policy recommendations		
24. Are all relevant criteria for recommending alternatives clearly specified?	Criteria may include: net welfare improvement; distributional improvement; cost effectiveness; and so on.	[ ]
25. Has the preferred alternative been clearly described?	"We therefore recommend that the second alternative be adopted and implemented, since it is likely to be more cost-effective and is politically feasible under present conditions."	[ ]
26. Is a strategy for implementation clearly outlined?	"The proposed policy should be implemented by the Department of Labor and state employment offices. Implementation should be phased over a period of three years and focus on cities with more than 50,000 persons."	[ ]
27. Are provisions made for monitoring and evaluating policies?	"The state employment offices should establish special units to engage in process and outcome evaluations, at intervals of 30 days. Results of monitoring and evaluation should be stored in a management information system and reports should be filed quarterly."	[ ]
28. Are limitations and possible unintended consequences taken into account?	Here the point is to specify how limitations of the analysis affect the confidence one has in the conclusions. Possible unintended consequences (e.g., abuses of social welfare programs, nuclear meltdowns, and so on) should also be thought through.	[ ]
References		
29. Are references cited in the text included in the appropriate form?	It is preferable to use the "name–date" bibliographic form in a policy issue paper. Only the name of the author, the date of publication, and page numbers will be included in the text, with no footnotes at the bottom of the page. For example: (Jones, 1975: 20–23). The citation in the references will read: Jones, John (1975), *A Report on the Fiscal Crisis*. Washington, DC: Fiscal Institute.	[ ]

(*continued*)

Element of Policy Issue Paper	Example/Note	Rating
Appendices		
30. Is relevant supporting information (statistics, legislation, documents, correspondence) included?	All statistical tables should be properly numbered and headed and the source of data specified at the bottom of the table. Legislation, documents, and correspondence should be identified as to its source, date, author(s), and so on.	[ ]

Appendix 2

The Executive Summary

The executive summary is a synopsis of the major elements of the policy issue paper. The executive summary usually has these elements:

- Purpose of the issue paper or study being summarized
- Background of the problem or question addressed
- Major findings or conclusions
- Approach to analysis or methodology
- Recommendations (Optional: depends on expectations of the client.)

The following executive summary provides a synopsis of a ninety-page study titled *Freight Trucking: Promising Approach for Predicting Carriers' Safety Risks* (Washington, DC: U.S. General Accounting Office, Program Evaluation and Methodology Division, April 1991).

Executive Summary

Purpose	Freight trucks pose special safety risks. Over 4,000 people are killed annually in accidents related to heavy trucks. Fatalities are about twice as likely in accidents involving tractor-trailer trucks as in those involving automobiles only.
	In recent years, the Congress has approved legislation to prevent situations that give rise to unsafe trucking operations. As a means toward this end, the House Committee on Public Works and Transportation and its Surface Transportation Subcommittee requested that United States General Accounting Office (GAO) determine whether certain economic and other conditions could be used as predictors of safety outcomes. GAO's study had the following three objectives: (1) to formulate a predictive model specifying hypothetical relationships between safety and a set of conditions in the trucking industry; (2) to assess the availability and quality of federal data required to test the model; and (3) to use available data, to the extent possible, to develop a set of indicators that would predict safety problems in the freight-trucking industry.
	The value of a workable model is that the Department of Transportation (DOT) could use it as an early warning system for predicting safety problems.

(continued)	Executive Summary

Background

Although the Motor Carrier Act of 1980 codified the relaxation of federal economic control over the trucking industry, the Congress approved legislation in the 1980s designed to monitor and prevent situations that result in unsafe trucking operations.

GAO developed a model that hypothetically links changes in economic conditions to declining safety performance in the freight-trucking industry (see pages 18 through 23). The hypothesis is that a decline in economic performance among motor carriers will lead to declining safety performance in one or more ways, described by five submodels: (1) a lowering of the average quality of driver performance, (2) downward wage pressures encouraging noncompliance by drivers with safety regulations, (3) less management emphasis on safety practices, (4) deferred truck maintenance and replacement, and/or (5) introduction of larger, heavier, multitrailer trucks.

Results in brief

GAO's preliminary findings, using data on 537 carriers drawn from both DOT and the Interstate Commerce Commission (ICC), are that seven financial ratios show promise as predictors of safety problems in the interstate trucking industry. For example, three measures of profitability—return on equity, operating ratio, and net profit margin—were associated with subsequent safety problems as measured by accident rates. The data agreed with GAO's model for five of seven financial ratios: Firms in the weakest financial position had the highest subsequent accident rates. GAO also used a number of other factors to predict safety outcomes, including the following. First, the smallest carriers, as a group, had an accident rate that exceeded the total group's rate by 20 percent. Second, firms operating closer to a broker model—that is, those that rely on leased equipment and/or drivers to move freight—had a group accident rate 15–21 percent above the total group's rate.

With regard to two of the submodels (driver quality and compliance), driver's age, years of experience, and compensation were all good predictors of safety problems. GAO's evidence is generally consistent with the model's hypotheses because younger, less experienced drivers and lower paid company drivers posed greater-than-average accident risks.

GAO's study thus demonstrates the potential for developing preventive strategies geared to differences among carriers and drivers, and it also suggests the importance of monitoring by DOT of the variations in carrier accident rates in order to have a sound basis for developing those preventive strategies.

GAO's Analysis
Available Federal Data

To identify and evaluate data to test a carrier-safety model, GAO reviewed the literature, talked with industry experts, and conducted interviews with federal officials responsible for maintaining data sets. GAO then combined data provided by DOT and ICC to conduct analyses. GAO found that existing federal data sets did not bring together the necessary data to fully test this model. The federal collection of truck accident data was essentially independent of the gathering of economic data, and combining the two types of data from separate federal sources was generally impractical. Most importantly, the federal data allowing calculation of accident rates for individual motor carriers did not provide for a generalizable picture of a definable segment of the industry or an analysis of safety trends over time. The needed information about truck drivers and their accident rates was also lacking. As a result, GAO could test only two of the submodels (by obtaining data from two private surveys). One unfortunate implication of this is that even if all of the submodels do prove to have predictive validity, existing federal databases still do not contain sufficient information to convert the model to an effective monitoring system.

(continued)

(continued)	**Executive Summary**

Economic Predictors   GAO judged that the best available accident rate data to combine with ICC's extensive financial data are those obtained from DOT's safety audits. Since the safety audits were discontinued after October 1986, GAO's analysis was limited to the larger, for-hire ICC carriers with financial reporting requirements that were also audited by DOT during the years 1984–86.

     GAO found evidence among these interstate carriers that carriers in different markets or different financial situations pose different safety risks. For example, carriers with losses of 0.3 percent or more on equity had a group accident rate (rates are defined as accidents per million miles) two years later that was 27 percent above the overall group's rate.

Predictors from the Driver Quality Submodel   One of the private surveys GAO used supplied data on approximately 1,300 interstate drivers serving Florida in 1989. As was predicted by the driver quality submodel, GAO found that younger and less experienced truck drivers were more likely to be in accidents. For example, the odds for drivers aged twenty-one to thirty-nine having been involved in an accident in the prior twelve months were higher than the odds for drivers over age forty-nine by a factor of 1.6.

Predictors from the Driver Compliance Submodel   The other private survey GAO used yielded pertinent data from a national sample of drivers in rail-competitive trucking. GAO found that lower paid drivers were more likely than their higher paid counterparts to violate safety regulations, but only in the case of company drivers and excluding owner-operators (those drivers owning their own trucks). Among company drivers, those earning less than 18.5 cents per mile had about twice the odds of having received either speeding or hours-of-service citations (or warnings) in the past ninety days.

Recommendation to the secretary of transportation   The monitoring, enforcement, and policy-making value of much of the truck accident information gathered by DOT is lessened by the inability to construct accident rates. Although DOT already collects accident *data*, the mileage data required to calculate accident *rates* are not routinely collected from carriers. As a first step toward reducing the accidents of motor carriers, GAO therefore recommends that the Secretary of Transportation direct the Administrator of the Federal Highway Administration (FHWA) to require that mileage data on motor carriers falling under FHWA regulations be obtained annually to improve accident analysis. How such data are obtained may depend on a number of considerations, such as costs and respondent burden, but the foremost consideration should be that data obtained allow for the calculation of accident rates for carriers falling under FHWA safety regulations in order to support monitoring and enforcement efforts and to permit analysis of safety trends.

     In implementing GAO's recommendation, DOT should consider further development of predictors of safety problems. For example, GAO's analysis suggests that indicators of financial health, market segment, and driver information may be useful to DOT in identifying higher risk groups of carriers for closer monitoring or enforcement efforts. More work needs to be done in validating these preventive indicators and identifying other predictors of safety outcomes. DOT should consider advancing this work on preventive indicators because, if successful, it would signal the policy changes needed to avoid or abate the predicted unsafe conditions. GAO's demonstration illustrates the kind of work that DOT will be able to do in prevention, particularly if better information on accident rates and economic and other intermediate factors is developed.

Appendix 3
The Policy Memorandum

The primary activity of many analysts is writing policy memoranda. Whereas the policy issue paper, study, or report is the product of a lengthy process requiring many months of research and analysis, the policy memorandum is prepared over a short period of time—usually no more than one month, but often a matter of weeks or days. In fact, policy memoranda are often based on syntheses of one or many issue papers, studies, or reports. The differences between the issue paper, study, or report, on one hand, and the policy memorandum on the other are nicely illustrated by contrasts between "basic" and "applied" styles of policy analysis (see Appendix 1).

The policy memo (short for *memorandum*) is a form of written communication used in public, nonprofit, and business organizations. Policy memos are brief, well organized, and understandable to nonspecialists. Policy memos usually summarize the conclusions of an analysis requested by a client. In some cases, they include policy recommendations (but only if requested). The clients for policy memos may be appointed officials, elected officials, citizens groups, or representatives of nonprofit organizations (NPOs), nongovernmental organizations (NGOs), and private business organizations.

Policy memos take different forms, depending on the agency or organization. For example, different agencies, departments, or ministries have their own letterhead stationery that is preformatted, while others use word-processing templates. Despite these differences, there are several common elements. Most memos display the date, the name of the recipient, the name of the analyst, and the subject of the memo on separate lines at the top of the page. Because memos are designed to communicate with the busy policy maker or manager, do not expect memos to be read thoroughly and carefully. For this and other reasons, memos should be brief (most are no more than three to five pages in length), clearly organized with appropriate headings, and understandably written with as little technical jargon as possible. The content of the memo should be concisely communicated on the subject line. Technical and analytic material (tables, graphs, charts, legal documents, etc.)

that supports the conclusions and recommendations in the memo should be appended to the memo as an attachment, or kept on hand to respond to questions that may be (and often are) raised later.

- The introductory paragraph should state the purpose of the memo and the question or issue to which the memo is a response.
- There may be a brief description of the methods used in doing the analysis. But remember that busy readers usually do not care very much about your methods (this does *not* mean that you will not have to justify your methods to someone else later).
- As appropriate, the memo should use headers, bullets, underlining, italics, and other stylistic devices to highlight material that is especially important.
- The memo should use "TO," "FROM," "DATE," "SUBJECT" (or "RE") lines at the beginning.
- The memo should end with information about where you can be reached for further questions (e.g., telephone, fax, e-mail).

The policy memo beginning on the next page is a concise summary of a report titled *Budget Issues: Immigration to the United States—Federal Budget Impacts, 1984–1995* (Washington, DC: U.S. General Accounting Office, August 1986).

B-223169

August 28, 1986

The Honorable Butler Derrick
Chairman, Task Force on the Budget Process
Committee on the Budget
House of Representatives

Dear Mr. Chairman:

In response to your letter of May 8, 1985, we have examined the potential impacts of immigration on the federal budget over the next 10 years. This effort was undertaken with dual objectives: obtaining the best possible estimate of budgetary impacts despite known data inadequacies and beginning the development of a methodology for dealing with long-term, crosscutting issues of budgetary significance, of which immigration is a prime example. On May 1, 1986, we presented a briefing to you and other task force members and staff on the results of our study. This report is a written version of that briefing. We have also included additional detail on the budgetary impact of immigration on state and local governments.

Our study established fiscal year 1984 as a baseline. We identified, and where necessary estimated, major federal immigrant-related outlays and revenues for that period. We then projected these data to yield 1990 and 1995 estimates under three different sets of assumptions (scenarios) as to the future social, economic, and political environment. These projections are not intended as forecasts but were developed to provide illustrative ranges. We also sought similar data for selected programs and localities in the five most impacted states, for illustrative purposes, but we made no projections at this level.

Although there are constraints and limitations to our analysis, it demonstrates that significant budgetary impacts of immigration exist at the federal level, in terms of both outlays and revenues. Dollar amounts can be assigned to such impacts only if major assumptions are made concerning immigrant participation in major social and income security programs. This is due to the uncertainties of population size and characteristics in 1984, as well as to the lack of direct information regarding immigrant-related outlays and revenues, data gaps which are even more apparent in the out year projections. We assumed, therefore, that these participation rates would be comparable, on the average, to those of U.S. citizens. We could not test this hypothesis, and expert opinion varies.

Using these assumptions, we found that for fiscal year 1984 in the programs we examined

—per capita federal outlays for immigrants were roughly comparable to those for average U.S. residents;

—per capita, immigrants contributed fewer revenues to the federal government than average U.S. residents; and

—total immigrant-related outlays differed only slightly from total immigrant-related revenues.

Under all three scenarios examined, these observations remain valid for 1990 and 1995, although uncertainty increases.

Regarding the broader methodological interests which it was designed to explore, this study of a crosscutting issue has both value and limitations. While specific total dollar amounts cannot be assigned on any supportable basis, minimum outlays and revenues can be identified, ranges can be estimated, and comparisons can be drawn based on explicit assumptions. Because both federal outlays and revenues are significantly affected by immigration and remain roughly in balance, the committee may wish to monitor the key conditions and trends to determine whether this balance is being maintained. Thus, we believe we have demonstrated the feasibility of this approach, but its usefulness will vary with the circumstances.

I would be pleased to discuss this information with you further at your convenience. As agreed with your office, we have not obtained agency comments on this report. We are sending copies of this report to interested parties, and copies will be made available to others upon request.

If you or your staff have any questions on this report, please call me at 275-9455.

Sincerely yours,

Kenneth W. Hunter
Assistant to the Director

Appendix 4

Planning Oral Briefings

Written documents are only one means for communicating the results of policy analysis. The other is the oral briefing. Although the oral briefing or presentation has most of the same elements as the issue paper, the approach to planning and delivering an oral presentation is quite different.

The elements of an oral briefing typically include the following:

- Opening and greeting to participants
- Background of the briefing
- Major findings of the analysis
- Approach and methods
- Data used as basis for the analysis
- Recommendations
- Questions from participants
- Closing

As we saw in Chapter 9, an essential aspect of oral communications is knowing the audience. Here a series of important questions should be asked prior to the briefing. How large is the audience? How many members of the audience are experts on the problem you are addressing in the briefing? What percent of the audience understands your research methods? Are you credible to members of the audience? Does the audience prefer detailed or general information? Where does the briefing fall in the policy-making process? At the agenda setting or formulation and adoption phases? Or the implementation and evaluation phases?

Answers to these questions govern the choice of a communications strategy appropriate for a particular audience. For example, if the audience is a medium-sized group with twenty to twenty-five persons, the diversity of the audience calls for these specific communications strategies.[1]

- Circulate background materials before the meeting so that everyone will start from a common base.
- Tell the group that the strategy selected is designed to meet the objectives of the group as a whole but that it may not satisfy everyone's needs.
- Focus on the agendas of key policy makers, even if you lose the rest of the audience.

Another common problem in giving oral briefings is that policy makers may bring their own staff experts to the briefing. In this case, a high percentage of the audience has expertise in the area you are addressing. Here, the following strategies are appropriate:

- Avoid engaging in a "knowledge contest" with experts by focusing on the purpose of your own presentation.
- Capitalize on the group's expertise by focusing on evidence bearing on findings and recommendations.
- Avoid a long presentation of background material and lengthy description of methods.
- Attempt to generate dialogue and a productive debate on potential solutions for the problem.

An equally important problem in oral briefings is understanding individual members of the group.[2] For example, it is important to know if the immediate clients for policy analysis are

- Experts in the problem area.
- Familiar with your analytic methods.
- Influential participants in the policy-making process.
- Oriented toward detailed or broad information.
- Faced with high, medium, or low stakes in the problem.
- Politically important to the success of your recommendations.

Finally, oral briefings employ various kinds of graphic displays.[3] One of these is the transparency sheet used with an overhead projector (also known as a "beamer"). In using overhead transparencies, it is important to recognize that they are not appropriate if you want an informal style of presentation—overheads tend to make

---

[1] The foregoing guidelines are based on *Presentation Planner* (Pitsford, NY: Discus Electronic Training, Eastman Technology, 1991).

[2] *Presentation Planner*, Individual Questions Menu.

[3] *Presentation Planner*, Graphics Submenu.

briefings formal, making open dialogue difficult. Alternatively, you may want to limit discussion, and strict adherence to transparencies helps.

It is also important to observe the following guidelines in using transparencies:

- Keep transparencies simple, with condensed and highlighted text.
- Use clear, bold, uncluttered letters and lines of text.
- Highlight important points and use a few different colors (but no more than three).
- Limit the text on any page to a maximum of ten lines.
- Be sure the width of the screen is at least one-sixth of the distance between the screen and the farthest viewer.
- Make sure that the nearest viewer is a minimum of two screen widths from the screen.
- Remain on the same overhead for a minimum of two minutes to give viewers time to read plus an additional thirty seconds to study the content.
- Leave the room lights *on*—overheads are not films.
- Turn off the overhead projector when you want to redirect attention back to you and reestablish eye contact.

These are but a few of the strategies and tactics that are appropriate for different audiences and communications media. Given the goal of selecting communications media and products that match the characteristics of the audience, there is today a rich body of theory and techniques to guide the visual display of information.[4] Appropriate computer graphics, presentation packages and statistical programs are now widely available. These include the *Statistical Package for the Social Sciences (SPSS), Microsoft Excel, and Microsoft Power Point.*

Many types of visual displays are available to the analyst who wishes to effectively communicate complex ideas. Examples of the following visual displays are provided below:

- Bar charts
- Pie charts
- Frequency histograms
- Relative frequency histograms
- Ogives
- Scatter plots
- Time-series graphs

---

[4] Anyone who wishes to achieve competency in addressing these questions should read Edward R. Tufte's award-winning trilogy: *The Visual Display of Quantitative Information* (Cheshire, CT: Graphics Press, 1983); *Envisioning Information* (Cheshire, CT: Graphics Press, 1990); and *Visual Explanations: Images and Quantities, Evidence and Narrative* (Cheshire, CT: Graphics Press, 1997).

- Graphs with data tables
- Decision trees and other diagrams

These displays are useful for effectively communicating simple as well as complex aspects of policies. In most policy presentations, however, a key visual display is one that summarizes relationships between two or more alternatives and their respective impacts. The options–impacts matrix (see below), which is a rectangular array of policy alternatives and their anticipated impacts, is well suited for this purpose. The matrix provides a concise visual map of the range of impacts associated with alternatives. The preferred impacts may be shaded, as below, so that participants in a presentation can easily examine the pattern of trade-offs between impacts before they have been represented quantitatively in the form of coefficients, indexes, or ratios (e.g., a benefit–cost ratio), which can obscure issues and prevent informed discussion.

Options–Impacts Matrix		
POLICY IMPACT	_POLICY ALTERNATIVES_	
	55 MPH	85 MPH
TRAVEL TIME IN HOURS	22.6 Billion	20.2 Billion
GALLONS GASOLINE CONSUMED	81.6 Billion	87.1 Billion
CHANGE IN AIR POLLUTION	1 % Decrease	3 % Increase
TRAFFIC FATALITIES	45,200	54,100
INJURIES	1,800,000	2,000,000
PUBLIC SUPPORT	70 %	30 %

NOTE: Shaded boxes are preferred impacts.

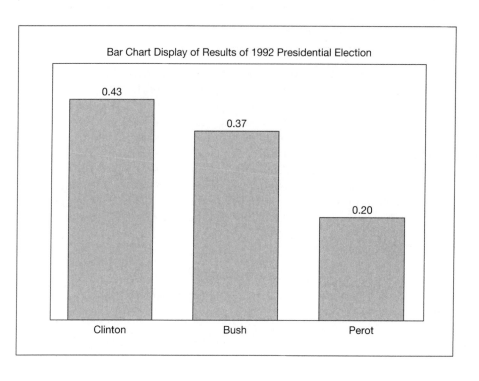

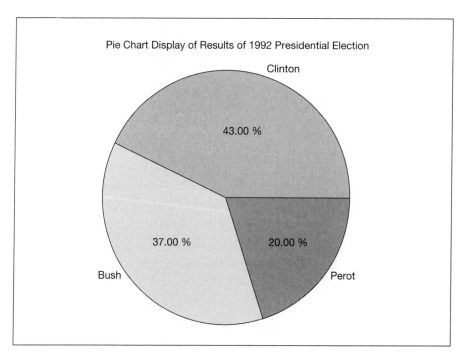

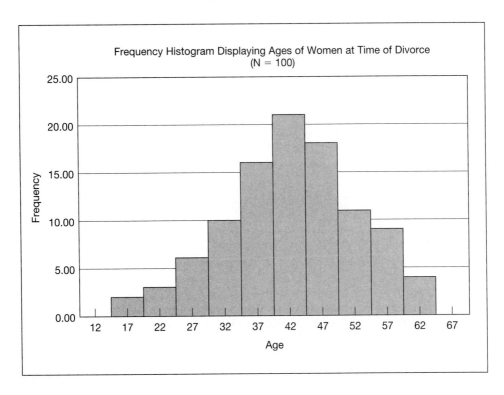

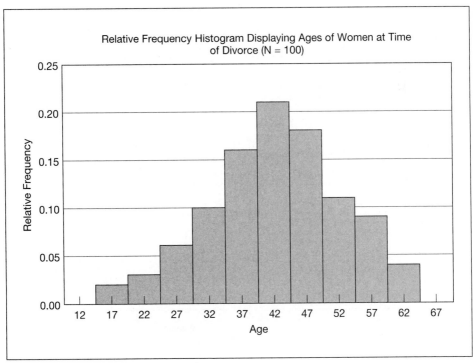

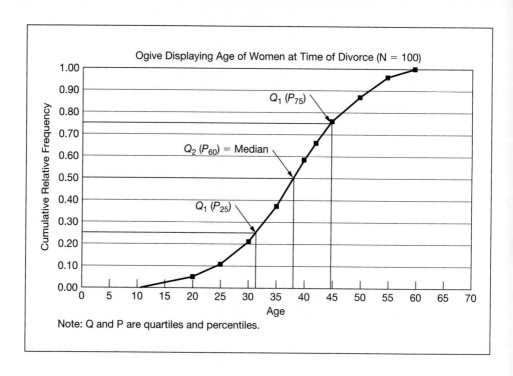

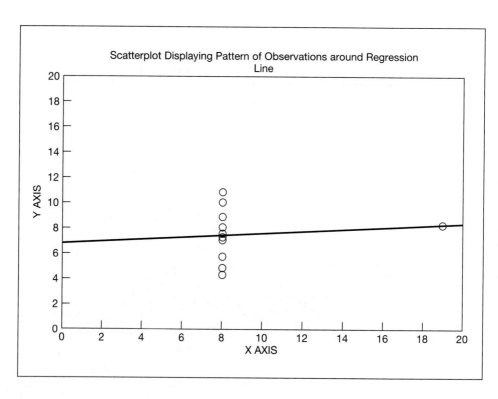

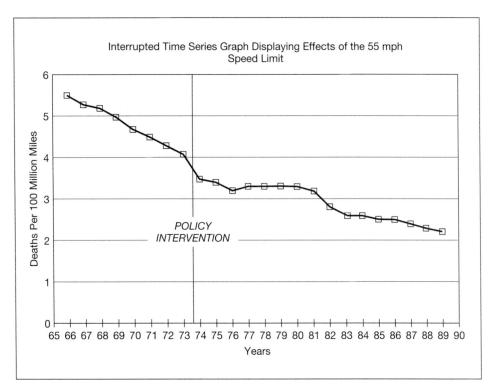

Interrupted Time Series Graph Displaying Effects of the 55 mph Speed Limit

POLICY INTERVENTION

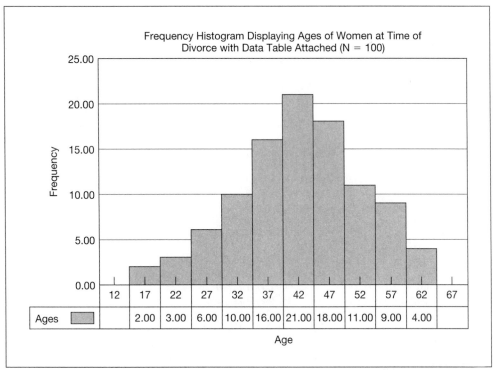

Frequency Histogram Displaying Ages of Women at Time of Divorce with Data Table Attached (N = 100)

| Ages | | 2.00 | 3.00 | 6.00 | 10.00 | 16.00 | 21.00 | 18.00 | 11.00 | 9.00 | 4.00 | |

Author Index

Subject Index